"This is the most authoritative volume available today covering the wide-ranging impacts of sentencing on individual, community, and societal outcomes about which we care deeply. With detailed reviews by top scholars, those who want to understand what we know about sentencing policy need go no further than this superb collection."

—Todd R. Clear, Distinguished Professor of Criminal Justice, Rutgers University

"This volume is a tremendously thorough and nuanced analysis of the visible and hidden consequences of punishment and sentencing decisions. The articles explore not only the multi-faceted and wide ranging impacts from imprisonment but importantly and uniquely also include those that result from pre-trial detention, increasing privatization, and even restrictive housing policies. The impressive breadth of topics, all broadly falling under the rubric of mass criminal justice contact, in addition to specific policy proposals, make this essential reading for academics and practitioners alike."

—Michael Jacobson, Executive Director, CUNY Institute for State and Local Governance

HANDBOOK ON THE CONSEQUENCES OF SENTENCING AND PUNISHMENT DECISIONS

Handbook on the Consequences of Sentencing and Punishment Decisions, the third volume in the Routledge ASC Division on Corrections & Sentencing Series, includes contemporary essays on the consequences of punishment during an era of mass incarceration. The Handbook Series offers state-of-the-art volumes on seminal and topical issues that span the fields of sentencing and corrections. In that spirit, the editors gathered contributions that summarize what is known in each topical area and also identify emerging theoretical, empirical, and policy work. The book is grounded in the current knowledge about the specific topics, but also includes new, synthesizing material that reflects the knowledge of the leading minds in the field.

Following an editors' introduction, the volume is divided into four sections. First, two contributions situate and contextualize the volume by providing insight into the growth of mass punishment over the past three decades and an overview of the broad consequences of punishment decisions. The overviews are then followed by a section exploring the broader societal impacts of punishment on housing, employment, family relationships, and health and well-being. The third section centers on special populations and examines the unique effects of punishment for juveniles, immigrants, and individuals convicted of sexual or drug-related offenses. The fourth section focuses on institutional implications with contributions on jails, community corrections, and institutional corrections.

Beth M. Huebner is a professor in the Department of Criminology and Criminal Justice at the University of Missouri–St. Louis. Her principal research interests include the collateral consequences of incarceration, racial and gender disparities in the criminal justice system, and public policy. She is currently serving as co-principal investigator for the St. Louis County MacArthur Safety + Justice Challenge and collaborating on a study of monetary sanctions in Missouri with funding from the Arnold Foundation. She is the current chair of the Division on Corrections and Sentencing for the American Society of Criminology. She earned her PhD in Criminal Justice from Michigan State University in 2003.

Natasha A. Frost is a professor in the School of Criminology and Criminal Justice at Northeastern University in Boston, Massachusetts. She also currently serves as associate dean for graduate studies in the College of Social Sciences and Humanities at Northeastern. Professor Frost's primary scholarly interests are in the area of punishment and social control, with a focus on mass incarceration and its consequences. Professor Frost was recently awarded NIJ funding to study the many impacts of correctional officer suicide, with a specific focus on its impacts on the officer's families, friends, co-workers, and supervisors, and on the well-being of those who continue to work in correctional settings where suicides have concentrated. Professor Frost holds a PhD in criminal justice from the City University of New York's Graduate School and University Center (2004).

THE ASC DIVISION ON CORRECTIONS & SENTENCING HANDBOOK SERIES

Edited by Pamela K. Lattimore and John R. Hepburn.

The American Society of Criminology's Division on Corrections & Sentencing sponsors a series of volumes published by Routledge on seminal and topical issues that span the fields of sentencing and corrections. The critical essays, reviews, and original research in each volume provide a comprehensive assessment of the current state of knowledge, contribute to public policy discussions, and identify future research directions. Each thematic volume focuses on a single topical issue that intersects with corrections and sentencing research. The contents are eclectic in regard to disciplinary foci, theoretical frameworks and perspectives, and research methodologies.

EDITORIAL BOARD

Gaylene Armstrong, University of Nebraska, Omaha

Todd Clear, Rutgers University

Francis T. Cullen, University of Cincinnati

Natasha Frost, Northeastern University

Beth Huebner, University of Missouri-St. Louis

Brian Johnson, University of Maryland

Jodi Lane, University of Florida

Dan Mears, Florida State University

Michael Osterman, Rutgers University

Cassia Spohn, Arizona State University

Jeffery Ulmer, Pennsylvania State University

Christy Visher, University of Delaware

HANDBOOK ON PUNISHMENT DECISIONS
Locations of Disparity
Ulmer and Bradley

HANDBOOK ON THE CONSEQUENCES OF SENTENCING AND PUNISHMENT DECISIONS
Huebner and Frost

HANDBOOK ON THE CONSEQUENCES OF SENTENCING AND PUNISHMENT DECISIONS

Edited by Beth M. Huebner and Natasha A. Frost

NEW YORK AND LONDON

First published 2019
by Routledge
52 Vanderbilt Avenue, New York, NY 10017

and by Routledge
2 Park Square, Milton Park, Abingdon, Oxon, OX14 4RN

First issued in paperback 2020

Routledge is an imprint of the Taylor & Francis Group, an informa business

© 2019 Taylor & Francis

The right of Beth M. Huebner and Natasha A. Frost to be identified as the authors of the editorial material, and of the authors for their individual chapters, has been asserted in accordance with sections 77 and 78 of the Copyright, Designs and Patents Act 1988.

All rights reserved. No part of this book may be reprinted or reproduced or utilised in any form or by any electronic, mechanical, or other means, now known or hereafter invented, including photocopying and recording, or in any information storage or retrieval system, without permission in writing from the publishers.

Trademark notice: Product or corporate names may be trademarks or registered trademarks, and are used only for identification and explanation without intent to infringe.

Library of Congress Cataloging-in-Publication Data
A catalog record for this book has been requested

ISBN 13: 978−0−367−58056−8 (pbk)
ISBN 13: 978−1−138−60893−1 (hbk)

Typeset in Bembo
by Apex CoVantage, LLC

In memory of Marie L. Griffin and Chester L. Britt, III

CONTENTS

List of Contributors	*xii*
Acknowledgments	*xix*

Introduction	**1**

The Consequences of Sentencing and Punishment Decisions *Beth M. Huebner and Natasha A. Frost*	3

PART I **Consequences of Punishment Decisions**	**11**

1 Historical Trends in Punishment and the Lens of American Federalism *Michael C. Campbell and Paige E. Vaughn*	13
2 Collateral Sanctions: The Intended Collateral Consequences of Felony Convictions *Tanya N. Whittle*	32

PART II **Broad Impacts**	**51**

3 The Collateral Consequences of Incarceration for Housing *David S. Kirk*	53
4 Residential Insecurities and Neighborhood Quality Following Incarceration *Brianna Remster and Cody Warner*	69

Contents

5 Impact of Incarceration on Employment Prospects 85
Robert Apel and Anke Ramakers

6 Incarceration, Reentry, and Health 105
Chantal Fahmy and Danielle Wallace

7 The Psychological Effects of Contact With the Criminal Justice System 122
Thomas P. LeBel and Matt Richie

8 Impacts of Incarceration on Children and Families 143
Miriam Northcutt Bohmert and Sara Wakefield

9 Impacts of Conviction and Imprisonment for Women 161
Miriam Northcutt Bohmert, Matthew Galasso, and Jennifer Cobbina

PART III
Consequences of Sentencing Decisions 173

10 Punished for Being Punished: Collateral Consequences of a
Drug Offense Conviction 175
Ashley Nellis

11 Compounded Stigmatization: Collateral Consequences of a
Sex Offense Conviction 188
Kimberly R. Kras, Morgan McGuirk, Breanne Pleggenkuhle, and Beth M. Huebner

12 The Hidden Consequences of Visible Juvenile Records 204
Megan C. Kurlychek and Riya Saha Shah

13 Deportation as a Collateral Consequence 221
Carlos E. Monteiro

PART IV
Institutional Contexts 243

14 Mass Jail Incarceration and Its Consequences 245
Joshua C. Cochran and Elisa L. Toman

15 Collateral Consequences of Pretrial Detention 271
Natalie Goulette and John Wooldredge

Contents

16 The Impact of Restrictive Housing on Inmate Behavior: A Systematic
    Review of the Evidence   290
    Ryan M. Labrecque and Paula Smith

17 The Impacts of Privatization in Corrections: The State of Evidence and
    Recommendations for Moving Forward   311
    Andrea Montes Lindsey and Daniel P. Mears

PART V
Broad Implications   **331**

18 "Raise the Age" Legislation as a Prevention Approach to Address Mass
    Incarceration   333
    Danielle Tolson Cooper and Jennifer L. Klein

19 Mass Incarceration in Jail and Family Visitation   346
    Emma Conner

20 The Hardest Time: Gang Members in Total Institutions   361
    David C. Pyrooz and Meghan M. Mitchell

21 Exportation Hypothesis: Bringing Prison Violence Home to the Community 379
    Don Hummer and Eileen M. Ahlin

Index   *400*

CONTRIBUTORS

Eileen M. Ahlin is an assistant professor in the School of Public Affairs at Penn State Harrisburg. She is the co-author of *Rethinking America's Correctional Policies: Commonsense Choices from Uncommon Voices* (2017, Lexington Books), and her research interests include violence, neighborhood effects, and corrections.

Robert Apel is a professor of Criminal Justice at Rutgers University, Newark. His areas of specialization include labor markets, the life course, criminal justice policy, and applied econometrics.

Michael C. Campbell is an assistant professor in the Department of Criminology and Criminal Justice at the University of Denver, and he earned his PhD from the University of California, Irvine. His research employs mixed research methods to examine the social, historical, and political forces that shape law and policy, especially those associated with mass incarceration. His work has been published in the *American Journal of Sociology, Law and Society Review, Criminology, Punishment and Society*, and other sociological and criminological journals. His current research is supported by the National Science Foundation and involves the study of state-level criminal justice reforms that affect correctional populations. The goal is to compare and contrast reforms across state contexts since 2000 to better understand how state and national forces have shaped policy reform efforts in the United States.

Jennifer Cobbina is an associate professor in the School of Criminal Justice at Michigan State University. Her research interests focus on gender and prisoner reentry, desistance, and recidivism. Her work also examines the intersection of gender, race, class, and crime.

Joshua C. Cochran is an assistant professor at the University of Cincinnati, School of Criminal Justice. His research interests include theory, imprisonment, prisoner reentry, and sentencing. His work has appeared in *Criminology*, the *Journal of Quantitative Criminology, Justice Quarterly*, the *Journal of Research in Crime and Delinquency* and in a recent book, with Daniel P. Mears, *Prisoner Reentry in the Era of Mass Incarceration* (Sage).

Emma Conner is a doctoral student in the Department of Criminology, Law, and Society at the University of California, Irvine. She is interested in punishment and society, with a focus on the collateral consequences of incarceration; race and inequality; and imprisonment. She has published work on methodological issues related to researching children and parental substance abuse.

Contributors

Danielle Tolson Cooper is an assistant professor of Criminal Justice at the University of New Haven and completed her doctoral work at the University of Florida (2015). Her research interests are juvenile delinquency/ justice, resistance to authority, and other psychology, law, and society issues.

Chantal Fahmy is a doctoral candidate in the School of Criminology and Criminal Justice at Arizona State University. She received her bachelor's degree in Criminology, Law, and Society from University of California, Irvine and her master's degree in Criminal Justice from California State University, Long Beach. Her primary research interests include prisoner reentry and reintegration, social support and health, and institutional corrections more broadly. She recently received the Bureau of Justice Statistics Graduate Research Fellowship to complete her dissertation project. Her work has been published in the *Journal of Criminal Justice Education, International Journal of Offender Therapy and Comparative Criminology*, and *Deviant Behavior*. Currently, she manages a longitudinal National Institute of Justice grant assessing the implications of prison and street gang membership for recidivism and reentry.

Natasha A. Frost is a professor in the School of Criminology and Criminal Justice at Northeastern University in Boston, Massachusetts. She also currently serves as associate dean for graduate studies in the College of Social Sciences and Humanities at Northeastern. Professor Frost's primary scholarly interests are in the area of punishment and social control, with a focus on mass incarceration and its consequences.

Matthew Galasso is a doctoral student in the School of Criminal Justice at Michigan State University. He received his master's degree from the Indiana University School of Public and Environmental Affairs in 2016, his juris doctorate from the Indiana University Robert H. McKinley School of Law in 2009, and his bachelor's degree from DePauw University in 2006. His research interests include sentencing and correctional policy, as well as the intersection of the criminal justice system, politics, and public policy.

Natalie Goulette is an assistant professor in the Department of Criminal Justice at the University of West Florida. She received her PhD from the School of Criminal Justice at the University of Cincinnati. Her research interests include extralegal disparities in case processing and the use of collateral consequences in criminal convictions. Her other research interests include influences of juvenile delinquency and the use of evidence-based practices in correctional programming.

Beth M. Huebner is a professor in the Department of Criminology and Criminal Justice at the University of Missouri-St. Louis. Her principal research interests include the collateral consequences of incarceration, racial and gender disparities in the criminal justice system, and public policy. She is currently serving as co-principal investigator for the MacArthur Safety + Justice Challenge.

Don Hummer is a faculty member in the School of Public Affairs at Penn State Harrisburg. His research interests are broadly focused on policy analysis, violence, and the implications of technological advances for justice system actors.

David S. Kirk is a professor in the Department of Sociology and a Professorial Fellow of Nuffield College at the University of Oxford. For more than a decade he has been examining the consequences of the forced migration from Hurricane Katrina on the lives of former Louisiana prisoners, with a book manuscript in process with *Oxford University Press*. Kirk's recent research has appeared in the *Proceedings of the National Academy of Sciences, Journal of Experimental Criminology*, and *American Sociological Review*.

Contributors

Jennifer L. Klein is an assistant professor of Criminal Justice at the University of Texas at Tyler and completed her doctoral work at the University of Florida (2014). Her primary research interests include sexual offenders and the effects the registry has on those registered, deviant behaviors of college students, and the Jerry Sandusky scandal.

Kimberly R. Kras is an assistant professor in the School of Criminology and Justice Studies at the University of Massachusetts Lowell. She earned her PhD in Criminology and Criminal Justice from the University of Missouri-St. Louis in 2014, following a career with the Missouri Department of Corrections. Her work centers on the study of community corrections, reentry, and desistance from offending behavior, and utilizes both quantitative and qualitative methodologies. Her research considers how offender behavior change occurs from both the offenders' and community corrections agents' perspectives by examining reentry-related experiences, collateral consequences of convictions, and evidence-based practices. Her work has been published in *Criminology and Public Policy*, the *Journal of Criminal Justice*, and the *Journal of Drug Issues*. Her work is also focused on translating research findings into practice through practitioner publications and on-site and web-based trainings.

Megan C. Kurlychek is an associate professor in the School of Criminal Justice at the University at Albany, SUNY, Executive Director of the Hindelang Criminal Justice Research Center, and currently serves as Editor of *Justice Quarterly*. Her primary research interests are juvenile justice and delinquency, sentencing and corrections, and the life-long collateral consequences of obtaining a criminal record. Her research has been published in top journals in the field including *Criminology*, *Criminology and Public Policy*, *Justice Quarterly*, and *Crime and Delinquency*. She is co-author of *The Cycle of Juvenile Justice 2nd Edition*, the 2012 recipient of the Academy of Criminal Justice Sciences 2012 Tory J. Caeti award for Outstanding Young Scholar in Juvenile Justice, and was recognized for 2012 Best Article of the Year by Sage for her publication in *Youth Violence and Juvenile Justice*.

Ryan M. Labrecque is an assistant professor in the Department of Criminology and Criminal Justice at Portland State University. He earned his PhD in Criminal Justice from the University of Cincinnati in 2015 and was the recipient of a 2014 Graduate Research Fellowship Award from NIJ for his dissertation on the effect of solitary confinement on institutional misconduct. His research interests focus on offender classification and assessment, correctional rehabilitation, restrictive housing, program implementation and evaluation, and the transfer of knowledge to practitioners and policy makers. He has a number of published articles, book chapters, and conference presentations on these topics. Ryan is a recipient of a 2017 New Investigator Award from NIJ for a study on interpersonal violence and institutional misconduct in the Los Angeles County Jail system. He is also a Co-Principal Investigator on an Encouraging Innovation Grant from BJA to develop and evaluate a treatment program in restrictive housing.

Thomas P. LeBel is an associate professor in the Department of Criminal Justice in the University of Wisconsin–Milwaukee's Helen Bader School of Social Welfare. His research focuses on prisoner reintegration, desistance from crime, the stigma of incarceration, drug treatment courts, and interventions for criminal justice involving women with drug and alcohol problems.

Andrea Montes Lindsey is a doctoral candidate at Florida State University's College of Criminology and Criminal Justice. Her work has appeared in *Criminology and Public Policy, Crime and Delinquency, Criminal Justice and Behavior*, and the *Journal of Criminal Justice Education*. Her research interests include theories of crime and punishment, crime prevention and school safety, and privatization.

Contributors

Morgan McGuirk is a Criminology and Criminal Justice PhD student at the University of Missouri–St. Louis (UMSL). Her research interests include prisoner reentry and the collateral consequences of punishment. Additionally, she is interested in procedural justice within the criminal court system. She is currently working with Beth Huebner (UMSL) on a research project looking at the needs of pre-trial detainees and probation violators, and on a project exploring defendant court debt.

Daniel P. Mears is the Mark C. Stafford Professor of Criminology at Florida State University's College of Criminology and Criminal Justice. His work has appeared in leading crime and policy journals and in *American Criminal Justice Policy* (Cambridge University Press), *Prisoner Reentry in the Era of Mass Incarceration*, with Joshua C. Cochran (Sage), and *Out-of-Control Criminal Justice* (Cambridge University Press).

Meghan M. Mitchell is a doctoral candidate in the Department of Criminal Justice and Criminology at Sam Houston State University. Her research includes the areas of corrections, subculture, inequality, and communities and crime. She has published in the *Journal of Criminal Justice and Deviant Behavior*, and is a co-author of an edited book chapter in *The Handbook of Gangs*. The Bureau of Justice Statistics and the Charles Koch Foundation are funding her dissertation research, which evaluates the psychometric properties of the convict code and determines implications of the code on misconduct and victimization while incarcerated. Her current role is managing a National Institute of Justice grant that evaluates the importation and exportation of prison gang subcultures longitudinally, with an emphasis on reentry.

Carlos E. Monteiro is an assistant professor in the Sociology Department at Suffolk University. Before joining Suffolk in 2017, Carlos was a senior research associate at the Institute of Race and Justice at Northeastern University. He earned a Master of Education degree from the University of Connecticut and his PhD in criminology and justice policy from Northeastern University. With combined expertise in education and criminal justice policy, Carlos's research interests have long centered on the factors affecting access to, and quality of, education for young adults of color. His scholarly interests are tied to race, ethnicity, and educational access but, in particular, as those interact to produce disparate outcomes across the criminal justice system and within corrections specifically.

Ashley Nellis has an academic and professional background in analyzing criminal justice policies and practices, and has extensive experience in studying racial and ethnic disparities in the justice system. She regularly delivers testimony, publishes articles and reports, and conducts research in the areas of juvenile and criminal justice. Her work is particularly concerned with elevating awareness about the growing number of individuals serving lengthy sentences in prison such as life sentences and sentences of life without parole (LWOP). She is also the author of *A Return to Justice: Rethinking our Approach to Juveniles in the System*, a book that chronicles America's historical treatment of youth in the justice system and discusses the work that remains in order to reorient juvenile justice practices toward the original vision.

Miriam Northcutt Bohmert is an assistant professor of Criminal Justice at Indiana University Bloomington. Her research focuses on gender and crime, community supervision, sexual offenses, and restorative justice. Her work has appeared in *British Journal of Criminology, Crime & Delinquency, Criminal Justice & Behavior*, and *Social Forces*.

Breanne Pleggenkuhle is an assistant professor in the Department of Criminology and Criminal Justice at Southern Illinois University Carbondale. Her recent research has been published in *Justice*

Contributors

Quarterly and *Criminal Justice and Behavior*. Her primary interests focus on prisoner reentry, looking at recidivism, collateral consequences of a felony conviction, and contextual characteristics of residence post-release.

David C. Pyrooz is an assistant professor of Sociology and faculty associate of the Institute of Behavioral Science at the University of Colorado Boulder. His research interests are in the areas of gangs and criminal networks, incarceration and reentry, and developmental and life course criminology. He received the Ruth Shonle Cavan Young Scholar Award from the American Society of Criminology and New Scholar Award from the Academy of Criminal Justice Sciences. His recent research has appeared in *Criminology*, *Journal of Quantitative Criminology*, *Journal of Research in Crime and Delinquency*, and *Justice Quarterly*. He the co-author of *Confronting Gangs: Crime and Community* (Oxford) and *The Handbook of Gangs* (Wiley-Blackwell).

Anke Ramakers is assistant professor of criminology at Leiden University, the Netherlands. Her research interests include offender employment, consequences of imprisonment, and consequences of criminal justice and social policies.

Brianna Remster is an assistant professor of sociology and criminology at Villanova University. She studies inequality, formal social control, and crime over the life course. Her work appears in *Social Forces*, *Justice Quarterly*, *Socius*, and *Du Bois Review*, among other outlets.

Matt Richie is a doctoral student in the Helen Bader School of Social Welfare, Department of Criminal Justice at the University of Wisconsin–Milwaukee. His current research focuses on the process of desistance, risk assessment validation, police officer use of force, as well as jail reentry in non-metropolitan areas.

Riya Saha Shah is a senior supervising attorney at Juvenile Law Center. Riya has represented youth in dependency court, written amicus briefs, and conducted trainings for child-serving professionals and youth. Riya also leads Juvenile Law Center's Second Chances initiative, focusing her efforts on juvenile record confidentiality and expungement. She has written extensively on collateral consequences, expungement, and the right to counsel. Riya was instrumental in Pennsylvania's successful challenge to the imposition of harsh registration laws for youth charged with sexual offenses. Riya graduated cum laude from Loyola University Chicago School of Law where she was a Civitas ChildLaw Fellow and Editor-in-Chief of *The Children's Legal Rights Journal*. Riya is a graduate of University of Michigan Ann Arbor where she earned her B.A. in Psychology and American Culture. Before going to law school, Riya taught second grade in Jersey City, New Jersey, through Teach for America, and third grade to bilingual students in Detroit, Michigan.

Paula Smith is an associate professor in the School of Criminal Justice at the University of Cincinnati. She received her PhD in Psychology from the University of New Brunswick, Saint John in 2006. Her research interests include offender classification and assessment, correctional rehabilitation, the psychological effects of incarceration, program implementation and evaluation, the transfer of knowledge to practitioners and policymakers, and meta-analysis. She is co-author of *Corrections in the Community*, and has also authored more than thirty journal articles and book chapters. She has directed numerous federal and state funded research projects, including studies of prisons, community-based correctional programs, juvenile drug courts, probation and parole departments, and mental health services. Furthermore, she has been involved in evaluations of more than 280 correctional programs throughout the United States.

Contributors

Elisa L. Toman is an assistant professor at Sam Houston State University's Department of Criminal Justice and Criminology in Huntsville TX. Her research interests include theories of punishment, trends in criminal sentencing, and the implications of individuals' experiences with the corrections system. She has published recently in *Journal of Quantitative Criminology*, *Justice Quarterly*, and *Journal of Criminal Justice*.

Paige E. Vaughn is a Criminology and Criminal Justice PhD student at the University of Missouri–St. Louis. Her research interests include law and society, race and inequality, and crime control policy. Her present research involves examining policing strategies in disadvantaged African American communities characterized by high levels of violence and how interest groups and organizations associated with historically disadvantaged groups are mobilized to engage in criminal justice reforms. She is currently collaborating with Michael C. Campbell (UMSL) and Heather Schoenfeld (Northwestern) on a comparative case study that tracks state-level legislative changes, political actors and organizations, and resource deployments, which have interacted to alter state prison populations and criminal justice system processes.

Sara Wakefield is an associate professor at Rutgers School of Criminal Justice. Her research interests focus on the consequences of mass imprisonment for the family, with an emphasis on childhood well-being and racial inequality, culminating in a series of articles and a book, *Children of the Prison Boom: Mass Incarceration and the Future of American Inequality*. Related work examines the social networks and conditions of confinement of inmates as well as the influence of DNA databases on crime rates and racial inequality. Her work has appeared in such journals as *Justice Quarterly*, *American Journal of Sociology*, *Criminology & Public Policy*, *Journal of Adolescent Health*, and *Journal of Marriage and Family*.

Danielle Wallace is an associate professor in the School of Criminology and Criminal Justice at Arizona State University and received her PhD in Sociology from the University of Chicago in 2009. Her research interests focus on policing, recidivism, crime and health, as well as neighborhoods and crime. Currently, she is working with local agencies assisting them with identifying racially biased policing and in technical and training assistance for law enforcement agencies adopting body worn cameras. Danielle has published in well-known crime journals, like the *Journal of Quantitative Criminology* and *Journal of Crime and Delinquency Research*, as well as top health studies outlets, such as *Social Science and Medicine* and *American Sociological Review*.

Cody Warner is an assistant professor of Sociology in the Department of Sociology and Anthropology at Montana State University. Through the lens of the life course perspective, he studies the impact of the American criminal justice system on housing and residential outcomes. In particular, published and ongoing research examines how life events such as residential independence, returning to the parental home, and residential mobility are impacted by criminal justice contact. Related work examines larger patterns of neighborhood quality before and after spells of incarceration. Cody's work appears in journals such as the *American Sociological Review*, *Social Science Research*, and *City & Community*.

Tanya N. Whittle completed her doctorate in Sociology at the University of Delaware and researches corrections and legal consciousness. Her recent research examines prisoner reentry policies and programs, collateral sanctions, and service providers' roles in constructing prisoner reentry policy and practice.

John Wooldredge is a professor in the School of Criminal Justice at the University of Cincinnati. His research and publications focus on institutional corrections (crowding, inmate crimes and victimizations) and criminal case processing (sentencing and recidivism, and micro- versus macro-level extralegal disparities in case processing and outcomes). Some publications have recently appeared in

Contributors

Crime and Delinquency, Criminology and Public Policy, Journal of Criminal Law and Criminology, Journal of Quantitative Criminology, and *Justice Quarterly.* He is currently involved in an NIJ funded study of the use and impacts of restrictive housing in Ohio prisons (with Joshua C. Cochran), and in projects focusing on prison program effects on subsequent misconduct during incarceration and post-release recidivism, and extralegal disparities in prison sanctions imposed for rule violations.

ACKNOWLEDGMENTS

Thank you to Morgan McGuirk and Jessica Trapassi for their assistance in compiling the book materials, and to Jean Merrell for her unwavering support for the Division on Corrections and Sentencing.

Introduction

THE CONSEQUENCES OF SENTENCING AND PUNISHMENT DECISIONS

Beth M. Huebner and Natasha A. Frost

The ASC Division on Corrections & Sentencing Handbook Series was designed with the goal of disseminating emerging research to the field. Each volume offers state-of-the-art work on seminal and topical issues that span the fields of sentencing and corrections. Handbook contributions summarize what is known in each topical area, but as important, identify emerging theoretical, empirical, and policy work. This is the third volume in the series. Volume 1, edited by Faye Taxman, centered on risk assessment for correctional populations. The volume contains timely work on new research on evidence-based correctional policy and is broadly applicable to scholars and practitioners alike. Volume 2, edited by Jeffrey Ulmer and Mindy Bradley, extends this important work by considering punishment disparity. Volume 2 includes cutting edge research on both the locations of disparity in the criminal justice system, as well as the definitions and measurement of this phenomenon.

The current volume, Volume 3, includes contemporary essays on the consequences of punishment during an era of mass incarceration. This volume opens with work by Campbell and Vaughn (Chapter 1) highlighting the trends in mass incarceration over the past three decades and setting the context for what follows. The volume builds upon existing work in this area in several ways. Early work in this area focused primarily on the consequences of a stay in prison for the incarcerated person. These sanctions have often been deemed invisible punishments because they are not formally imposed during sentencing and instead are enacted largely by legislators. Scholars then extended the work in this area on the effect of incarceration on families, communities, and social order. Whittle (Chapter 2) describes the work that has been done in this area to date. While increasingly scholars are considering the ways in which there may be intended and unintended consequences of punishment and sentencing decisions that extend far beyond the confines of the justice system, no volume has brought all of the latest work across the area together.

The current volume extends extant work in several ways. First, we move beyond imprisonment to consider mass contact with the criminal justice system. For example, LeBel and Richie (Chapter 7) conceive of contact very broadly and it includes behaviors that range from,

> a dip of the toe in the shallow end (arrest, probation) of the criminal justice system, to incarceration in prison and release to the community from the darkest depths (supermax prison, after serving a life sentence, or after exoneration from death row) of the proverbial ocean of the carceral state.

By defining criminal contact quite broadly, we solicited chapters that capture a wide variation of contacts with the criminal justice system.

We move past describing contact with the criminal justice as a singular event and denote how repeated contact with the criminal justice system can influence long-term trajectories not only of those most directly affected but also of their families, friends, and neighbors. For example, familial relationships can be permanently altered (Chapters 8 and 19), housing options constrained (Chapters 3 and 4), and access to public housing and public assistance permanently denied (Chapter 10). Contact with the criminal justice system and the stigma of the criminal record limit job opportunities and future employment prospects in ways that impact not only immediate financial security but also lifetime earning potential (Chapter 5). In other words, the many consequences of system contact compound to permanently alter life prospects. We also consider how the rise in mass contact with the criminal justice system has had differential consequences for certain populations and for society as a whole. While the collateral consequences of criminal convictions are far reaching and have broad implications for life outcomes, they—like justice system contact itself—do not distribute evenly. Individuals convicted of drug offenses (Chapter 10) or sexual offenses (Chapter 11) are subjected to more and further reaching consequences than those convicted of most other classes of offense. Many of the housing and public assistance restrictions apply only to those convicted of drug offenses, while those convicted of sex offenses face additional consequences in the form of enhanced community surveillance, additional residency restrictions, and registration requirements. Those who are convicted of juvenile offenses, once shielded from the long reach of the criminal justice system, increasingly face adult consequences for delinquency in adolescence (Chapters 18 and 12). Immigrants and non-citizens face potential deportation following criminal convictions, and the separation that follows impacts loved ones both here and abroad (Chapter 13).

Finally, we consider the consequences and effects of system-wide institutional segregation of gang members (Chapter 20), how prison violence influences the long-term behavior of incarcerated persons and employees, and efforts to privatize more and more criminal justice functions (Chapter 21). The structure of the book reflects the variety of contributions.

Chapter Summaries

The first section of the book is designed to situate and contextualize the volume by providing insight into the growth of mass punishment over the past three decades and an overview of the broad consequences of punishment decisions. In Chapter 1, Michael Campbell and Paige Vaughn outline some of the most important trends in criminalization and punishment over the past three decades with a key emphasis on macro state-level trends. They describe how the growth in legal sanctions contributed to the rise of mass incarceration by criminalizing more behaviors and imposing new laws and policies that required longer prison stays. The chapter also includes a nuanced historical introduction to the rise of mass incarceration, a critical read for those new to this area of research. The authors conclude with a nuanced discussion on how the changes in legislation and policy have reinforced inequalities in the criminal justice system.

In Chapter 2, Tanya Whittle provides an introduction to the broad scope of collateral consequences. She providers a detailed description of the numerous forms of collateral sanctions that exist, and she includes online resources where individuals can go to find data on the sanctions implemented in each state. Her work is an excellent primer for those readers new to the topic. As important, she contrasts the legal and administrative sanctions of a criminal conviction and the hidden costs of contact with the criminal justice. Important to policy, she reviews the extant literature on the role of collateral consequences on crime and recidivism. She also highlights the disproportionate impact consequences have on racial and ethnic minorities and explores how the disparity in sanctions can compound existing concentrated disadvantage.

Punishment and Sentencing Decisions

The second section of the book is dedicated to works that explore the broader societal impacts of punishment on housing, employment, family relationships, and health and well-being. Recognizing the centrality of access to housing for successful reentry, David Kirk (Chapter 3) offers a comprehensive explication of the many ways in which that access is compromised for formerly incarcerated persons and those with criminal records. Although Kirk recognizes that some of the issues in accessing housing are the result of deliberate policy choices, he argues that the problem of access is exacerbated by broader changes in housing markets. Given the dearth of affordable housing options in the United States, access to affordable and stable housing can be a challenge for even the person unburdened by the stigma of a criminal record. Kirk argues that when compounded by that stigma of a criminal record, made increasingly available to potential landlords, and the challenges of securing steady employment, stable housing—widely recognized as essential to reentry—is a rare commodity for a person with a criminal history. Kirk then provides a comparative lens through reviewing the decidedly less exclusionary housing policies in the United Kingdom. He concludes with a discussion of the reasons why there is so little research on housing barriers for those convicted of criminal offenses arguing that selection bias plagues this research and a lack of longitudinal data makes it difficult to track housing outcomes over time. He argues that increased access to affordable and stable housing will require fundamental shifts not only in sentencing and incarceration policies, but also in housing policy.

Taking a broad scope of reentry, Brianna Remster and Cody Warner, in Chapter 4, describe how terms of incarceration affect housing insecurities, which they conceptualize as a continuum ranging from frequent residential movement to homelessness. They provide an important discussion of the mechanisms by which incarceration perpetuates inequality. They conclude their chapter with a call for housing first approaches to public policy that prioritize a stable residence over other services. They provide examples of recent policy developments in Washington State that could be used as models for future research, and echo the structural needs for housing services also presented by Kirk (Chapter 3).

The mark of a criminal record on employment outcomes has been well documented. Robert Apel and Anke Ramakers, in Chapter 5, consider the topic from both the employee and employer perspective. They provide a detailed summary of the following types of research: non-representative research, administrative research, survey research, reentry research, and cross-national research. Doing so allows the authors to unpack the mechanisms behind the punishment and labor outcome relationship. Considering the mechanisms and nature of the broad body of research allows practitioners and scholars alike to move beyond "nothing works" to better understand the areas of intervention most ripe to change. Unique to this work, they also explore the broad body of work on criminal convictions outside of the U.S. They find that punishment is highly disruptive for individuals, even in countries often considered to have more liberal criminal justice systems. They conclude the chapter with a discussion of possible legislative and policy changes to mitigate the stigma of a criminal record. They explore the recent movement to ban the box and legislation outside the U.S. that reduces the length of time that criminal history data are available. Although they find promise in both strategies, they caution that policy makers should be careful that people do not use other types of data to signal criminality if race is not available.

Recognizing the limits of reentry literature focused almost exclusively on post-release reoffending, Chantal Fahmy and Danielle Wallace, in Chapter 6, turn to the many impacts of incarceration on individual and public health. Because physical health of incarcerated persons has been particularly overlooked, they describe the troubling health outcomes that have been reported among incarcerated populations. While some of these outcomes stem from the more rapid spread of communicable diseases in the institutional context, Fahmy and Wallace are keen to point out that many of the health effects of incarceration, like hypertension and diabetes, might be explained by the chronic stress associated with the experience of incarceration. After focusing on the health effects, as measured by outcomes, Fahmy and Wallace offer a number of theoretical mechanisms by which the health effects of incarceration might be linked to health effects in the community. Given the relative paucity of research in this area, Fahmy and Wallace conclude by describing some of the many publicly available datasets that might help future scholars interested in health outcomes pursue their research agendas.

Work on the consequences of incarceration has traditionally been centered on discrete outcomes, like housing and employment. The work presented in Thomas LeBel and Matt Richie's chapter broadens the perspective by examining the potential long-term psychological effects of varying levels of contact with the criminal justice system (Chapter 7). This review considers psychological effects related to the pains of imprisonment and post-imprisonment supervision, post-traumatic stress disorder influenced by negative incarceration experiences (trauma and victimization, solitary confinement), and perceptions of and responses to "ex-con" stigma in the community. They draw heavily on the psychological literature that may be of particular import to a new scholar to this area. As important, they describe how individuals internalize and manage the stigma of a conviction using the voices of formerly incarcerated persons. They conclude with several potential changes for policy. They describe recent legislative work that serves to mitigate the long-term impact of the criminal record. Similar to the suggestions provided by Apel and Ramakers (Chapter 5) they describe recent certificate of rehabilitation legislation that allows individuals relief from the forfeitures associated with a criminal conviction, if a certain amount of time has passed and qualifications met. They also encourage that we give voice to those in the criminal justice system and hold up organizations like Just Leadership as good models.

In Chapter 8, Miriam Northcutt Bohmert and Sara Wakefield provide a comprehensive review of the ways in which incarceration can impact children and families. They document the many collateral consequences for the growing number of families who are experiencing the incarceration of a loved one. These impacts span such diverse areas as family relationships, health, economic security, and delinquency. After presenting the troubling statistics on the probability of being directly or indirectly impacted by incarceration, they describe whole families "bound up in the criminal justice system" and suffering many of the same consequences as their loved ones who are subject to the system. Northcutt Bohmert and Wakefield describe what we know, outline what we don't know, and help us think about how to learn more about the collateral consequences that impact children and families. Most importantly they lament that the growing body of empirical research documenting deleterious effects has led to little by way of actual policy prescriptions for ameliorating those effects. They therefore end their chapter with a call for the development of a better understanding of potential sites of intervention (schools, for example), with the important caveat that we not inadvertently pursue policies or interventions that would further stigmatize the children and families impacted by the incarceration of a loved one.

The second section of the book concludes with Chapter 9, which considers the unique effects of a criminal conviction for women. Miriam Northcutt Bohmert, Matthew Galasso, and Jennifer Cobbina describe the pathways that women take to criminal involvement and the subsequent implications for recidivism and reentry. They put particular emphasis on the effect of a conviction on employment, social services, and housing, and their review provides an important primer to this line of research. Emphasis is also placed on the centrality of child and family relationships in understanding the consequences of a criminal conviction. In terms of policy, they argue for the need for gender responsive programming and contend that specialty courts may attend to the needs of women.

The third section of the handbook is centered on special populations including the unique effects of punishment for juveniles, immigrants, and individuals convicted of sexual or drug related offenses. In her chapter, Ashley Nellis (Chapter 10) focuses specifically on the consequences of housing and public assistance restrictions, which typically apply only to those convicted of drug offenses. She contextualizes the development of these particularly deleterious consequences through tracing the history of the war on drugs from the importance of the late-1980s disparities in crack cocaine sentencing to the more promising developments as we contend with the current opioid epidemic. As Nellis argues it has been difficult to assess the actual impact of these policies because of how diffuse the enforcement tends to be. Although driven by federal policy, enforcement of the housing provisions, for example, varies by state and even locality as it relies on the judgments of local public housing officials. Nellis describes the ways in which communities, and particularly communities of color, have been impacted by collateral consequences driven by decades of federal policy designed to prevent those who have been convicted of drug offenses from accessing the safety nets of public housing and assistance that are often so crucial to a successful reentry experience.

Just as Nellis (Chapter 10) documents the policies that have differentially impacted those convicted of drug offenses, Kimberly Kras and colleagues remind us of the compounded stigmatization of a conviction for a sex offense specifically (Chapter 11). Despite evidence of better than average post-release outcomes among those convicted of sex offenses, these individuals tend to face many more collateral consequences than those convicted of other offenses, including in some cases forced treatment, ongoing surveillance and monitoring, and enhanced restrictions that further restrict housing and freedom of movement. After describing the ways in which those convicted of sexual offenses have been singled out for exceptional treatment, Kras et al. discuss the potential impacts of these policies for populations of increasing interest in the field (women, juveniles, and tribal groups). Troubled by the universal application of laws targeting those convicted of sex offenses, they lament the male-centric lens of most existing research, advocate for a more gender-responsive approach, and laud the removal of juveniles from public registries. They also document the development of registries in at least 18 other countries and contrast those registries with those typically used in the United States.

The stigma of a criminal record can impact outcomes for adults well into the future, but Megan Kurlychek and Riya Saha Shah (Chapter 12) remind us of the troubling ways in which changes in policy around access to juvenile records can mean that young adolescents can face a near certain path to a criminal history. Kurlychek and Shah trace the development of the separate body of juvenile law that was designed to ensure that transgressions in adolescence would not follow youth into their adulthood. Over time, though, those laws have been eroded and the line between the juvenile and adult systems has become increasingly blurred. Kurlychek and Shah offer a concise history of that erosion and its deleterious effects. While they argue for a return to confidentiality in juvenile proceedings and to the sealing of juvenile records, they recognize the limits of sealing and expungement and so also highlight the need to restrict access to and use of criminal records across a host of contexts.

Unlike other sanctions described in this handbook, Carlos Monteiro, in Chapter 13, documents the transformative and permanent outcome of deportation as a collateral consequence. He begins his chapter with a nuanced presentation of the history of deportation in U.S. correctional policy and links the concomitant increase in drug enforcement with heightened deportation. Research in this area is scant, but Monteiro provides timely statistics on the increase in deportation cases. He also draws from research outside of criminology to describe the effect that threats of deportation have on individuals, families, and whole communities. The threat of deportation often causes individuals to avoid help seeking behaviors; individuals are reluctant to seek TANF benefits or other social services in fear of being reported. Given the lack of data on deportation, Monteiro concludes his chapter with guidance to future researchers and practitioners who wish to advance the literature in this area.

The last section focuses on institutional implications with contributions on jails, community corrections, and institutional corrections. The section opens with Joshua C. Cochran and Elisa Toman's chapter on jails. In Chapter 14, they contend that the existing work on mass incarceration has ignored the role of jail incarceration, which is problematic as experiences in jails may be especially adverse. They provide a rationale for studying mass jail incarceration and denote the implications of jails for individuals, families, and communities. Responding to the lack of systematic research attention to jail experiences, they outline a conceptual framework for advancing research on jails. Like most research presented in this volume, they contend that jail incarceration can deepen inequalities. In conclusion, they denote some of the potential barriers to this line of research and describe possible solutions, including avenues for future data collection.

While so much of the literature on collateral consequences focuses on criminal convictions and post-sentencing incarceration, Natalie Goulette and John Wooldredge (Chapter 15) remind us all of the very real impacts of pre-trial detention on outcomes for those exposed to the system. They demonstrate the ways in which pre-trial detention can influence outcomes at every subsequent stage of criminal justice processing, creating a cumulative disadvantage for those who are detained before trial. Goulette and Wooldredge simultaneously argue that even without the cumulative disadvantage, pre-trial detention would have adverse effects on the individual and their families that are important to consider in any assessment of the consequences of the American system of punishment and sentencing. Pre-trial detention can be critiqued on a number of grounds so Goulette and Wooldredge walk the reader through the many different points at which this early decision can impact outcomes. Crucially the pre-trial detention experience affects some groups far more than others, creating disparities from one of the earliest junctures of the process. They use examples from the limited research to demonstrate the potential impact of pre-trial detention on not only the individual subject to it, but also their families as a way of emphasizing the reach of some of these collateral consequences. They conclude by arguing for an expansion of research on the effects of the pre-trail detention decision and offer some suggestions for potential directions that research could take.

Many of the chapters in this volume have focused on the ways in which sentencing and punishment decisions have direct or indirect consequences for individuals and communities. In Chapter 16, Ryan Labrecque and Paula Smith focus more specifically on the ways in which institutional policy decisions—such as decisions around the use of restrictive housing in the prison context—can similarly have implications for individuals (in terms of behavior while incarcerated and post-release outcomes) and for the institutions themselves (in terms of both the conditions of confinement and overall levels of violence). Labrecque and Smith review the extant literature on the effects of restrictive housing and conclude that the research overall suggests limited efficacy of restrictive housing, particularly in terms of its ability to affect the behavior of incarcerated persons either while incarcerated or post-release. Given the potential for negative effects on health and well-being associated with restrictive housing use, Labrecque and Smith argue for reformation of this institutional practice.

Andrea Montes Lindsey and Daniel Mears (Chapter 17) offer a sweeping overview of the many ways in which privatization has spread across the entire punishment system—from the privatization of probation and parole through courts and community supervision to the more commonly recognized privatization of institutions such as prisons. They argue that the privatization movement relies on exceptionally weak (often non-existent) empirical evidence concluding that "there exists no systematic, credible empirical evidence to suggest that private corrections or public corrections, as compared to each other, operate more effectively and at less cost or does so in a comparable or more ethical manner." Crucially, though, they do not simply decry the lack of an evidence base, but instead offer a path forward through outlining the contours of a research agenda for building that evidence base. While they explain the ways in which privatization across the system may lead to collateral consequence of net-widening and fiscal waste, they also emphasize that there may be instances in which it makes sense to privatize and instances in which it does not—unfortunately, at the moment, we lack the evidence base to make either determination.

While Kurlychek and Shah (Chapter 12) focus specifically on the need to restrict access to juvenile records to ensure that those adjudicated for offenses in their youth are not negatively impacted by those transgressions well into the future, Danielle Tolson Cooper and Jennifer Klein (Chapter 18) provide a nice summary of efforts to "raise the age" (RTA) at which youth are considered "adults" and subject to criminal justice instead of juvenile justice processing. Like Kurlychek and Shah, Cooper and Klein trace the history of juvenile justice, but they focus more explicitly on the age at which youth can or must be processed as adults. Raise the age laws can focus on the upper age at which youth can be excluded from the juvenile system (and processed as adults), the age at which youth must be excluded from the juvenile system, and the lowest age at which youth can be processed at all (e.g., when the defense of infancy no longer applies). Cooper and Klein provide some empirical justification for raising the age and review some of the legislative activity on this front. Because RTA laws result in a time-stamped change in the ways in which youth are (or are not) processed through juvenile justice systems, interrupted time series designs offer a particularly promising method for assessing the effects of shifting policy around the age of first exclusion and of last inclusion.

The rise in incarceration rates has been cause for reform in many states, but some of the most sweeping changes have been made in California. Emma Conner, in Chapter 19, merges the literature on mass jail incarceration with the work on parental incarceration to provide a unique perspective on California's reunification experiment. She begins by describing how the unique characteristics of jail have the potential to impact familial connectedness and visitation. Her work calls into question the long-term effects of the decarceration movement, if punishment is merely shifted to jails. Similar to the work presented by Cochran and Toman in Chapter 14, she details a proposed agenda for research in this area. She concludes with a detailed discussion of policy. Her ideas for reform range from institutional changes like improved waiting areas to recent controversies over the use of video visitation.

In Chapter 20, David Pyrooz and Meghan Mitchell focus specifically on the potential consequences of incarceration policies for those individuals thought to be gang members. Those who are identified as gang members (or members of security threat groups) face many restrictions on access to programming and housing while incarcerated that could impact their outcomes post-release. Pyrooz and Mitchell offer a concise history of the relationship between street and prison gangs before describing the evolution of differential policies for those who are identified as gang members while incarcerated. They argue that this identification and labeling can have a host of consequences for the individual while incarcerated—most prominent among them, severely limited access to programming, often as a result of institutional housing decisions (particularly the use of restrictive housing for this population—see Labrecque and Smith, Chapter 15). Pyrooz and Mitchell include findings from their 2016 survey of 38 states, which updates our understanding of state-level policies around the treatment of those identified as gang-involved in their correctional systems.

The book ends with the work of Don Hummer and Eileen Ahlin (Chapter 21) who describe how a criminal conviction that results in imprisonment can have long-term effects on the outside of the institution. The focus of the chapter is on the culture of violence and the manner in which exposure to misconduct and other incivilities in prison can influence post-release transitions. They first guide the reader through the empirical and theoretical work on the culture of prison violence and the interconnected nature of prison and street violence. Next, they introduce exportation theory that describes the mechanisms by which violence begets violence, in the community and the institution. Unique to this type of research, they explore how violence influences prison staff, as well as the formerly incarcerated person. They conclude with a call for greater attention to be paid to the institutional environment in understanding and studying the consequences of imprisonment.

Conclusions

The range of contributions in this volume reflects our effort to encourage fellow scholars to think broadly about the implications of punishment and sentencing decisions and their differential impacts. Each of our authors has offered comprehensive overviews of an important body of scholarly research related to the consequences of criminal justice system contact. Each was encouraged to not only synthesize what is known and identify gaps in the knowledge base, but to also wrestle with the policy implications of such far-ranging consequences. Where relevant, authors situated U.S.-based work in international context through offering comparative examples and best practices from other places. What has resulted is, we think, a truly comprehensive volume on the collateral consequences of punishment. We hope you will agree.

PART I

Consequences of Punishment Decisions

1

HISTORICAL TRENDS IN PUNISHMENT AND THE LENS OF AMERICAN FEDERALISM

Michael C. Campbell and Paige E. Vaughn

The well-chronicled increases in imprisonment in the United States (U.S.) in the latter third of the twentieth century have had broad repercussions that have recently triggered a period of reflection. Reformers have begun to ask whether the fiscal costs of mass incarceration are too high and whether gross racial disparities in imprisonment rates exacerbate and perpetuate inequality (Travis, Western, & Redburn, 2014; Aviram, 2015). Certainly, the emerging dominance of a "law and order" ethos that prioritized aggressive law enforcement tactics and harsh punishments for all types of crimes has reshaped fundamental notions of justice and helped transform how Americans have thought about crime and punishment in the last half-century (Clear & Frost, 2014). Among other things, the long-term trend toward greater criminalization and the broadening of legal sanctions has reshaped the political context of crime control in ways that now limit policy options and pervade other key social institutions (Simon, 2007). The legal and policy choices that drove this fundamental shift have had broad and lasting consequences that pervade all levels of American government, have fundamentally altered power structures in the nation's courtrooms, and have created lawmaking contexts that stymie reform (Clear & Frost, 2014).

Research on changes in punishment in the U.S. since the latter twentieth century, and the broad impact that this has had on America's institutions, has now extended to provide new and exciting insights into how these processes unfolded at the federal, state and local levels. What might be called the rise of mass incarceration, the "transformation of America's penal order," or the growth of the carceral state requires careful attention to how changes in law, policy, and practice unfolded across different levels of American federalism (Campbell & Schoenfeld, 2013; Gottschalk, 2014; Miller, 2008, 2010). Indeed, the nation embarked on an ambitious social program that was unlike others of the twentieth century, and this commitment endured through economic booms and busts and thrived within changing political contexts (Clear & Frost, 2014; Gottschalk, 2014). Federal officials enacted laws that created new incentives for lawmakers and practitioners to expand criminal justice infrastructure and to extend the ways that correctional systems responded to offenders through heightened surveillance and harsher punishments (Murakawa, 2014). State lawmakers continuously rewrote criminal laws in ways certain to increase prison populations, and those lawmakers provided billions of dollars in funding to expand state correctional systems to accommodate the growing tide of inmates, parolees, and probationers. These changes empowered local prosecutors to pursue aggressive penalties for offenders of all stripes, and those actors who might have mitigated the harshest punishments—judges and defense attorneys—saw their power eroded (Simon, 2007; Stuntz, 2011). These changes helped create an adversarial legal system largely unchecked in its punitive response to lawbreaking and helped fuel the creation of an increasingly punitive political context where alternative responses to crime stood little chance of limiting the carceral tide.

The social and political costs of mass incarceration are difficult to assess, but most scholars agree that it has exacerbated racial and class inequalities and weakened political institutions (i.e., Beckett & Sasson, 2004; Clear & Frost, 2014; Gottschalk, 2014; Uggen & Manza, 2005; Western, 2006). The costs of mass imprisonment have not been evenly distributed and have disproportionately affected the urban poor (Mauer, 2004). Mass imprisonment has had profound fiscal consequences that are somewhat easier to measure, as state governments were forced to expand prison facilities to incarcerate offenders within constitutional limits imposed by federal courts (Feeley & Rubin, 1998; Guetzkow & Schoon, 2015). By the millennium, correctional costs were consuming a far greater share of state resources that might have supported other state institutions such as education and mental health facilities (Aviram, 2015). Indeed, mass incarceration now reflects and reinforces deep structural inequalities rooted in an economy lacking sustainable employment opportunities for lower-skilled workers (Apel and Ramakers, Chapter 5; Gottschalk, 2014).

This chapter outlines some of the most important trends in criminalization and punishment, and outlines key findings in the scholarship that works to explain them. We emphasize how explanations of these legal and policy changes require careful attention to American federalism, political arrangements, and institutions that are deeply interrelated and connected to criminal justice systems. We examine how the nation's adversarial legal system has both been affected by and has helped drive the nation's incarceration binge by empowering prosecutors with more tools and resources to put more offenders away for longer sentences. These changes eroded judicial discretion and allowed prosecutors to leverage aggressive plea bargains and increase prison commitments for a whole range of offenders, especially drug, violent, and repeat offenders. We show how this operated in local settings, drawing on recent research that highlights how even misdemeanor offenders are punished through court processes. The last section addresses current criminal justice policy developments that seem to favor reform and outlines potential avenues for future research.

Federal Law and Policy

Legal and Policy Developments

The increasingly harsh laws and policies that contributed to the growth of the carceral state in the latter twentieth century were not an abrupt departure from the nation's longer history. Fear over crime and disorder fueled strong political responses to crime long before mass incarceration took hold, most notably through Prohibition. And several features of American government (i.e., election of prosecutors, underdeveloped welfare state) and social structure (e.g., structural racism) created conditions favorable for a heightened political focus on crime (Gottschalk, 2006). But around the 1960s several powerful socioeconomic and political forces converged to stimulate a historically unprecedented expansion of criminal justice systems and their underpinning logics. Urban unrest, concerns about law enforcement professionalism, rising crime and violence, and the realities of post-Civil Rights era politics all contributed to an energized focus on the nation's criminal justice systems, especially at the federal level (Flamm, 2005; Schoenfeld, 2018). These events helped stimulate Congressional action that culminated in the passage of the Omnibus Crime Bill and Safe Streets Act of 1968, which created the Law Enforcement Assistance Administration (LEAA). Among other things, LEAA programs provided new funding streams through block grants designed to modernize state and local criminal justice agencies by supporting greater centralization and professionalization (Berk, Brackman, & Lesser, 1977; Feeley & Sarat, 1980). The passage of the Omnibus Crime Bill and Safe Streets Act marked an important escalation in federal engagement with criminal justice systems that had historically been funded and managed by state and local officials.

Federal activity continued to expand during President Richard Nixon's administration that emphasized the need to aggressively combat drugs and crime and provided more resources for federal agencies and continued to support LEAA activities (Hinton, 2016). Federal courts also played an important role in unsettling criminal justice policies and institutions, especially in corrections, where federal courts issued sweeping rulings that forced states to reform prison systems that were ruled unconstitutional, especially in most Southern states (Feeley & Rubin, 1998). These federal activities did not directly rewrite the state laws that were responsible for the vast majority of prisoners that contributed to the rapid expansion in prison populations in the 1970s, but these developments had significant long-term implications for state law and policy (Campbell & Schoenfeld, 2013). Federal courts unsettled correctional regimes, and new LEAA funding streams stimulated organizational expansion and centralization within state and local criminal justice systems (Feeley & Sarat, 1980; Schoenfeld, 2018). As state lawmakers determined how to distribute large sums of federal funds, local criminal justice actors (i.e., prosecutors, sheriffs, prison guards) became more organized and far more politically engaged in lobbying for their share of resources, and directly shaped criminal law and policy in state politics (Berk et al., 1977; Campbell, 2011; Campbell, 2012).

The 1980s reflected an entirely new level of federal activism in law enforcement as President Ronald Reagan backed up campaign promises to wage a war on crime and drugs by expanding law enforcement and calling for harsher punishments. The Democratic-controlled Congress obliged executive calls to rewrite federal sentencing laws, fund a drastic expansion in the size and reach of federal law enforcement agencies, eliminate federal parole, and expand correctional facilities (Beckett, 1997; Clear & Frost, 2014). These laws not only extended prison sentences but also established mandatory minimum sentences for low-level drug dealing and the possession of crack cocaine and included new requirements and penalties, including those that mandated strict lease enforcement for convicted offenders that encouraged the eviction of public housing tenants (Alexander, 2010; Clear & Frost, 2014). These ancillary penalties ensured that those released from federal facilities or living in public housing would face harsher conditions after prison. The federal incarceration rate doubled during Reagan's presidency, and sharp growth in the federal prison population persisted throughout the 1990s, cumulating in a 500% increase by the millennium (Bureau of Justice Statistics, 2015). At the same time, federal agencies continued to provide resources to state and local governments to facilitate arrests, prosecutions, and incarceration, indirectly fueling state-level incarceration growth (Campbell & Schoenfeld, 2013).

Aggressive federal legislation expanded with the passage of the 1994 Omnibus Crime Bill, which provided states with billions of dollars to support prison expansion (as long as they passed so-called "truth-in-sentencing" statutes), required states to create sex offender registries, and expanded federal criminal law into several new types of crimes (Clear & Frost, 2014). Then, in 1996, President Clinton proposed "One Strike and You're Out" legislation that strengthened eviction rules and barred ex-offenders from public housing. This was important because it

> not only authorized public housing agencies to exclude automatically (and evict) drug offenders and other felons; it also allowed agencies to bar applicants *believed* to be using illegal drugs or abusing alcohol—whether or not they had been convicted of a crime.
>
> (Alexander, 2010, p. 145)

On job applications, inmates were forced to check boxes that demonstrated they had been charged with minor or serious offenses (Pager, 2003). Congress then passed and President Clinton signed a law restricting inmate access to federal courts, drastically reducing the already declining federal court activism in regulating the conditions of confinement (Calavita & Jenness, 2014; Feeley & Rubin, 1998).

Some changes in federal responses to drug offenders during the Obama Administration seemed to suggest that the grip of the carceral state might be weakening. Federal sentencing reforms were implemented that reduced the most punitive sentences for low-level drug offenders and attempted to address the racial disparities generated by the crack versus powder cocaine distinctions (Holder, 2016). Federal agencies have supported some community-based programs and have provided support for the implementation of "evidence-based practices" that claim to reduce the severity of sanctions for lower level offenders and improve public safety by targeting more serious offenders with supervision and programming (Clear & Frost, 2014). These changes seemed to mark an important rethinking of the wars on crime and drugs that gained considerable bipartisan momentum as questions about effectiveness and concerns about cost grew (Aviram, 2015). However, the 2016 election and policy changes implemented in the early stages of the Trump Administration that echo the war-on-drug era reinforce how changes in political context can threaten momentum for reform (Horwitz, 2017).

Explanations

Scholars have identified a number of forces that likely abetted the national-level shift toward a more active and aggressive federal role in law enforcement and the formation of the carceral state. David Garland's (1990, 1996, 2001) work has pointed to greater demands for social control and growing skepticism of the state's effectiveness in responding to crime. Garland suggests that rehabilitative values and ideologies characterized punishment in early twentieth century America, but that punishment practices were plagued by doubt, dissatisfaction, and confusion that fostered a new era where many policy makers and practitioners shifted to a "nothing works" mentality (Garland, 2001). Fundamental changes in social and economic institutions eroded public faith in the state's ability to effectively respond to social problems, eroding public confidence in criminal justice practitioners and criminological scholars.

Others have situated the heightened focus on crime within broader shifts in politics. Katherine Beckett (1997) points to racialized political strategies that exploit crime and skewed media portrayals of its seriousness (2004 with Theodore Sasson). For example, news media portrayals of violent crime disproportionately focused on crimes involving black offenders and white victims (Beckett, 1997; Beckett & Sasson, 2004). Politicians deployed highly racialized rhetoric that linked urban unrest and black protests to street crime and called for a return to "law and order," which operated as code for using the state to control African Americans who were no longer bound by the laws upholding segregation (Alexander, 2010; Beckett & Sasson, 2004; Weaver, 2007). Rather than rising crime rates driving public punitive opinion shifts and attendant political responses, this line of scholarship points to crime's utility as a political wedge issue. Jonathan Simon extends a similarly political take, linking fear mongering politics to a broader shift toward "governing through crime" in which the same technologies and mentalities from crime control penetrated various institutions with problematic consequences (Simon, 2007). Political executives, especially presidents and governors, strategically deployed crime to expand their powers and their ability to alter the lives of law-abiding citizens as well as inmates and formerly incarcerated persons (Simon, 2007). Whereas in the past, presidents and governors adhered to regulatory and protective roles, such actors were provided the authority to control and "fight crime" to satisfy the fearful and angry public, becoming "prosecutors in chief" (Simon, 2007). Not only is governing through crime "making America less democratic and more racially polarized," but through the promotion of fear and paranoia, America's ways of governing have actually lowered security (Simon, 2007, p. 6).

While these explanations emphasize racialized post-Civil Rights political processes as the central ingredient triggering support for incarceration, other scholars emphasize the enduring centrality of race in the nation's socioeconomic order. Loic Wacquant (2001, 2006) links support for imprisonment to the changing conditions of America's neoliberal economic system, citing links between changing labor structures and systemic oppression of African Americans through slavery, black ghettos, and mass incarceration. Michelle Alexander's (2010) work identifies similarities between the caste system that sustained the nation's pre–Civil Rights order and the legal and policy dynamics associated with the wars on drugs and crime. America's racial order is reinforced by new "colorblind" legal structures that perpetuate historical racism.

Other scholars have taken a longer view of the historical forces that gave rise in the "law and order" movement, noting that the changes in the latter 1960s and '70s were not without precedent and that federal efforts to criminalize more behavior and expand federal law enforcement have deep political and institutional roots (Gottschalk, 2006; Murakawa, 2014). Recent scholarship has helped trigger a rethinking of the role that liberalism played in shaping federal responses to crime. Naomi Murakawa (2014) argues that liberal lawmakers and policy experts as early as the 1940s framed crime in racialized ways that made punitive responses more likely. Elizabeth Hinton's (2016) work also digs into LEAA activities that, while on their surface purported a progressive response to crime, actually helped militarize police agencies and expanded surveillance and control of black communities.

Recent scholarship has problematized the idea that the rise of mass incarceration reflects a total rupture with the nation's longer criminal justice history. Michael Campbell and Heather Schoenfeld (2013) have noted that mass incarceration shares important continuities with harsh approaches to crime that were common in Sunbelt states and were essentially federalized through interactions between state and federal governing and political institutions. They contend that the carceral order that became entrenched by the 1990s reflected the outcomes of successive responses to new legal and policy problems that unfolded against long-term shifts in political power that favored states with histories of aggressive and highly racialized law enforcement regimes.

Other accounts have highlighted how the changes in law and policy that helped drive the carceral state were not the product of inevitable policy or opinion swings, but instead reflect ongoing conflicts between actors and organizations struggling to shape change. Phillip Goodman, Joshua Page, and Michelle Phelps' (2017) recent work notes that changing criminal justice policies were characterized by variation, conflict, and uncertainty. They propose an "agonistic" view of penal change that accounts for struggles "between actors with different types and amounts of power," and they argue that any notion of consensus overlooks the enduring conflicts that created a more braided approach to punishment (Goodman et al., 2017, p. 8). They challenge the tendency to think of correctional eras or regimes as distinct and dominated by any singular ideology or philosophy and instead highlight points of resistance where new conflicts emerge within specific historical contexts. For example, they note that while some people describe the post–World War II correctional era as one dominated by rehabilitation, in reality most penal institutions embraced a custodial approach that emphasized discipline, control, and staff security far more than treatment (Goodman et al., 2017). Similarly, they note that even as mass incarceration became entrenched in many state penal systems, seemingly less punitive practices such as probation endured and even thrived (Goodman et al., 2017).

Lastly, explanations of the recent trends away from mass incarceration point to a variety of factors that seems to be generating a rethinking of the carceral state. Hadar Aviram (2015) argues that these shifts reflect an inevitable reckoning with the ever-escalating costs of expanding sanctions and correctional institutions. While a general state of reflection might be mounting, Aviram warns that laws and policies aimed at reducing costs often create even more unequal systems for those with and without resources, and that these reductions might do more harm than good for many offenders. Todd Clear and Natasha Frost (2014) view the era as a new opening in which the national commitment to a "punishment imperative" has started to wane and point to the potential that community-based policies have for improving both efficiency and public safety.

State Law and Policy

Legal and Policy Developments

State governments have a remarkable degree of latitude in establishing criminal laws and operating correctional departments that have been responsible for punishing the vast majority of offenders in the United States (Zimring & Hawkins, 1991). Lawmakers in state capitols across the country engaged in a frenetic period of legislative activity that intensified throughout the 1980s and 1990s, criminalizing more acts, extending penalties, and creating new legal and policy mechanisms that extended the reach and power of the nation's criminal justice systems. Some states disassembled indeterminate sentencing regimes that had existed for decades, replacing these systems that granted judges and parole boards considerable discretion with determinate sentencing systems that allowed legislatures to establish sentence ranges (Stemen, Rengifo, & Wilson, 2005). Lawmakers crafted innovative new ways to punish and surveil offenders, stripping them from access to state services, making criminal records easily accessible, and adding mandatory periods of post-prison surveillance (Alexander, 2010; Clear & Frost, 2014). For example, all 50 states created sex offender registries that are publicly accessible and list varying degrees of information about offenders for life, even those who did not commit sexual assault (Lowe, 2016). In addition, state- and community-level restrictions have been introduced to control sex offender populations, but they have been costly to implement, inconsistently applied within and across locales, are ineffective in lowering recidivism, and have important collateral consequences, including residential restrictions that leave registered sex offenders with few residential options (Huebner et al., 2014; Rydberg, Grommon, Huebner, & Bynum, 2014; Kirk Chapter 3; Whittle Chapter 2).

Lawmakers also committed an enormous proportion of state resources to expanding carceral capacity, building and operating expensive facilities, and expanding the size and reach of probation and parole. As Michelle Phelps (2017) has shown in her analysis of "mass probation," median state probation and imprisonment rates increased dramatically between 1980 and 2010, with median state probation rates increasing from 284 to 995 probationers per 100,000 residents and median imprisonment rates increasing from 105 to 386 prisoners per 100,000 residents. Rather than operating as a moderating mechanisms that might reduce prison populations, mass probation emerged alongside mass incarceration, further extending the size and reach of the carceral state (Phelps, 2013, 2017).

It is essential to consider the enduring regional differences in criminal justice practices that have always characterized punishment in the U.S. Incarceration rates and the conditions of confinement have differed markedly, and the turn to mass incarceration in the latter twentieth century reflected these differences. Table 1.1 provides data on changes in incarceration rates and other variables for some of the nation's most populous states from 1960–1976, the period just before the national incarceration rate began increasingly sharply and consistently.[1] As the table shows, state correctional trends varied widely and had a clear regional pattern. While scholars often point to the mid-1970s as the point when the U.S. began incarcerating far more people, the trend had clearly started far sooner in many Southern states that already had higher incarceration rates than other regions. At the same time many other states across the nation exhibited large declines in incarceration.[2] By the middle of the 1980s this variation transformed into broad state-level increases in incarceration rates across all states, though the magnitude of change still varied and regional differences in overall rates persisted.

State-level political actors ramped up anti-crime rhetoric, and many statewide politicians, especially governors, grounded their campaigns in promises to aggressively fight crime, a trend amplified by Ronald Reagan's successful presidential campaign in 1980. By the early 1980s, Republican politicians were making inroads in traditionally Democratic Southern states by calling for "law and order" (Campbell, 2011). Tough-on-crime laws certainly were not new to state politics. Ronald Reagan's successful gubernatorial campaigns in California in the 1960s and New York's notoriously punitive

1 Trends in Punishment and Lens of Federalism

Table 1.1 Incarceration Rates and Percentage Changes in Select Variables, 1960–1976★

Ten Highest Percent Growth	Incarceration Rate (1960)	Incarceration Rate (1976)	Incarceration Rate Change	Homicide Rate Change	Violent Crime Rate Change
South Carolina	87	219	151.40%	−12.10%	317.00%
North Carolina	131	207	57.90%	4.70%	80.50%
Florida	143	205	43.10%	0.90%	190.20%
Texas	118	161	36.10%	41.90%	120.90%
Tennessee	88	111	26.40%	29.40%	331.70%
Massachusetts	37	46	24.60%	135.70%	718.00%
Oregon	97	119	22.60%	75.00%	556.20%
Georgia	177	215	21.50%	16.80%	166.40%
Missouri	86	104	20.50%	111.40%	159.90%
Washington	86	102	18.80%	104.80%	586.60%
Ten Highest Percent Decline					
Alabama	164	81	−50.50%	21.80%	108.40%
California	138	83	−40.20%	164.10%	180.00%
Indiana	116	78	−32.50%	61.40%	272.80%
Minnesota	60	41	−31.60%	91.70%	350.00%
Colorado	118	85	−27.90%	61.90%	203.70%
Pennsylvania	69	56	−18.90%	134.60%	197.90%
Iowa	80	65	−18.60%	283.30%	458.40%
Kansas	106	90	−14.70%	55.20%	383.90%
Kentucky	119	104	−13.00%	58.20%	169.50%
Mississippi	91	80	−12.50%	25.00%	187.60%

★ Data excludes states with populations < 1% of U.S. total in 1970.

Rockefeller Drug Laws are some of the most obvious examples (Barker, 2009). And as Table 1.1 shows, many states started cramming more prisoners into carceral facilities long before the 1980s. But crime's politicization took on a new charge in the 1980s generating waves of legislation targeting repeat offenders, drug crimes, restricting parole, and expanding victims' rights (Barker, 2009; Campbell, 2014; Campbell & Schoenfeld, 2013; Lynch, 2010).

Table 1.2 shows changes in incarceration rates and other select variables for the more populous states (those with at least 1% of the total U.S. population in 2000) for 2001 and 2013 including percent changes. This table shows how state incarceral trajectories again diverged markedly, with many Northeastern states making considerable reductions in their rates, while Midwestern states and several Southern state incarceration rates grew sharply. As Table 1.2 shows, violent crime rates do not correspond closely to changes in incarceration rates and the magnitude of variation in state incarceration persisted, with some states as high as 647 per 100,000 (Alabama) and others as low as 189 (Minnesota). U.S. states exhibit an enduring and remarkable degree of variation that reflects different state institutional structures and regional cultures.

By the 1990s the political focus on crime in the states generated remarkable momentum that produced draconian laws, especially in states with institutional structures that allowed popular anti-crime angst to easily penetrate political and law making institutions (Campbell & Schoenfeld, 2013). In California, for example, the state's readily accessible proposition process allowed "law and order" politicians and interest groups to propose and pass sweeping legal changes that funded prison expansion, drastically limited the rights of the accused, and increased mandatory minimums (Barker, 2009;

Table 1.2 Incarceration Rates and Percentage Changes in Select Variables 2001–2013*

Ten Highest Percent Growth	Incarceration Rate (2001)	Incarceration Rate (2013)	Incarceration Rate Change	Homicide Rate	Violent Crime Rate
Minnesota	132	189	43.30%	−25.00%	−12.40%
Indiana	341	454	33.10%	−29.90%	−6.80%
Pennsylvania	310	391	26.30%	1.90%	−14.90%
Kentucky	371	462	24.40%	2.30%	−13.80%
Florida	437	524	19.90%	−1.90%	−39.00%
Arizona	492	586	19.20%	−26.70%	−20.60%
Oregon	327	385	17.70%	0.00%	−19.20%
Ohio	398	446	12.20%	7.50%	−14.70%
Alabama	584	647	10.80%	−16.50%	2.70%
Illinois	355	377	6.30%	−25.60%	−34.50%
Ten Highest Percent Decline					
New Jersey	331	252	−24.00%	12.80%	−25.40%
New York	355	271	−23.60%	−30.00%	−20.80%
California	453	353	−22.00%	−21.90%	−31.20%
Massachusetts	243	192	−20.90%	−18.20%	−15.10%
Maryland	422	353	−16.40%	−24.10%	−39.00%
South Carolina	529	447	−15.50%	−14.80%	−31.50%
Texas	711	602	−15.30%	−29.00%	−28.50%
Connecticut	387	338	−12.80%	32.30%	−15.40%
Michigan	488	441	−9.60%	4.50%	−17.90%
Wisconsin	383	370	−3.40%	−16.70%	21.40%

* Data excludes states with populations < 1% of U.S. total in 2000.

Campbell, 2014; Gilmore, 2007; Zimring, Hawkins, & Kamin, 2001). California's draconian "Three Strikes" law that imposed 25-year to lifelong sentences for nonviolent, qualifying third offenses stands as one of the most extreme examples (Zimring et al., 2001). State governments across the nation passed asset forfeiture laws that empowered local criminal justice agencies to seize the assets of people suspected (not convicted) of engaging in drug dealing (Alexander, 2010). Layers of new criminal punishments flowed through state legislatures, creating complicated and increasingly punitive restrictions and mandates that reflected crime's position as the most important issue in state politics in the 1980s and much of the 1990s (Clear & Frost, 2014).

State lawmakers also deployed the necessary state resources to give punitive legislation the institutional backing to impose real costs on offenders, pumping billions of dollars into prison expansion. From 1980–1999 state spending on corrections increased sharply as a proportion of state budgets from 1.6% to 3% (Stucky, Heimer, & Lang, 2007, p. 92), and by the end of the 1990s the fiscal costs of the American way of punishment started to stimulate reforms in states that viewed the costs as too high (Aviram, 2015). Some state prison populations began to stabilize and even decline starting in the late 1990s, reflecting concerns about cost, effectiveness, and shifting political currents (Aviram, 2015). Reforms that scaled back state prison populations included changes in parole that reduced the number of technical parole violators that would be returned to prison (Aviram, 2015) and programs and policies that diverted low-level drug offenders from prison. For example, New York revised the punitive Rockefeller Drug Laws and implemented new policies that allowed judges to divert people convicted of low-level drug offenses into treatment programs and away from prisons (Lippman, 2010). By 2014, even many Southern states with high incarceration rates and comparatively punitive penal regimes had begun to implement reforms, supported by conservative political concerns that mass incarceration was inefficient and too costly (Dagan & Teles, 2014). By 2010, overall state incarceration rates declined for the first time in decades but the trend was again uneven, as many state incarceration rates continued to grow, including states like Pennsylvania, Indiana, and Minnesota where rates increased by more than 25% (see Table 1.2; Sentencing Project, 2013). As Marie Gottschalk (2014) has noted, recent reforms might make marginal reductions in incarceration rates, but the underpinning depths of social inequality and the neoliberal faith in individual solutions to social and economic problems render a deep reckoning with mass incarceration highly unlikely.

Explanations

Scholarship explaining state-level developments has identified the important role that state political cultures, penal histories, and institutional structures have played in shaping law and policy over the last several decades. Explanations of state-level developments have provided especially valuable insights because they can leverage variation in timing and magnitude to explore when and where certain factors matter most. This line of scholarship digs into state-specific developments, including the activities of actors and organizations that were engaged in policy-making processes, to explain the specific changes in law and policy that helped drive carceral expansion. These works have helped build explanations of penal change that embed state-specific developments within the broader national trends that affected all states.

Several scholars argue that state political and penal developments demonstrate important consistencies over time that are rooted in their histories. Mona Lynch (2010) argues that to understand the changes in law and policy that helped make Arizona one of the nation's most punitive states, it is essential to understand the state's political culture that has always emphasized a rugged, aggressive approach to criminal justice. Arizona was one of the last states to join the U.S., and state lawmakers have resisted efforts by outsiders to force the state to adopt laws and policies that contradict its "cheap and mean" penal culture that demeans inmates and emphasizes brutal policies to pinch pennies (Lynch, 2010). Similar dynamics shaped developments in Texas, where the state's prison was literally built by former slaves who were returned to their demeaning status in the wake of Reconstruction as Texas lawmakers imposed a new form of the state's racial order (Perkinson, 2010). Political debates over law and policy that intensified in the 1980s and 1990s, helping to propel Texas to the highest ranks of punitiveness, reflected this racialized view of criminal justice that emphasized "order" through the imposition of state power (Campbell, 2011). Thus, the "emergence" of mass incarceration or punitive regimes in the latter twentieth century, in fact, reflected new iterations of enduring penal logics within state contexts.

Other accounts of state-level changes have worked to untangle how various actors and organizations have affected the politics of crime and punishment. Josh Page (2011) examined how California's prison guards union emerged as one of the most powerful political interest groups in the state, and suggests that using the concept of field theory helps make sense of penal change. Page builds on Pierre Bourdieu and Loic Wacquant's (1992) conceptualization of fields as useful frameworks for linking macro-level developments to individual or group-level behavior within specific institutional contexts. Penal fields include the actors and groups engaged within a specific realm of activity (i.e., those seeking to shape penal policy and practice), their relative positions, their resources, strategies, assumptions and values, and the rules that shape how variously situated actors work to pursue their goals (Page, 2011). Page argues that thinking in terms of developments within the penal field helps explain how actors engage with each other across shifting terrains and why those pressing for a more aggressive, prison-focused response to crime were increasingly successful in the latter twentieth century (Page, 2011). His contributions highlight the importance of state-level interest groups that have been key players in driving more punitive laws and in preventing reforms that might divert offenders from prison (Page, 2011). Prosecutors associations, sheriffs associations, and other interest groups representing law enforcement agents played important roles in shaping law and policy in many states (Campbell, 2012; Cate, 2010; Lynch, 2010; Schoenfeld, 2018). For example, the Texas prosecutors' association is a well-organized group that actively engages in lobbying activities and political capital rooted in their key role as local political actors to shape criminal law in the Lone Star State (Campbell, 2012).

The complexity of the nation's federal structure also provides useful insights into legal and policy changes because state institutional structures have important differences. For example, Vanessa Barker's (2009) work highlights how the state of New York thwarts some populist impulses because the policy-making process limits inputs from the public and empowers specialists and experts to shape penal policy and practice, while California's proposition process allows for rapid change while failing to generate constructive discussions and compromises on complex social issues like crime and race. Legal and policy changes associated with mass incarceration have actually transformed state structures at both the state and local levels. When California rewrote the state criminal code in 1976 and switched from indeterminate to determinate sentencing, lawmakers transferred considerable power over how long inmates would be in prison from judges and parole boards to the legislature and local prosecutors (Campbell, 2014). This was important because judges and parole boards were not directly subjected to political pressure to increase time served. This change meant that legislators would have the power to determine sentencing lengths and that interest groups and political opponents could politicize their resistance to harsher punishments as "soft on crime." As Michael Campbell (2014) argues, this fundamentally restructured the institutional logics structuring punishment and opened crime policy up to relentless political attacks that were key to driving up calls for prison expansion and harsher punishment.

Local Law and Policy

Legal and Policy Developments

The U.S. Constitution allows states to legislate their own criminal laws and to establish criminal court systems whose jurisdictions are usually organized around county and municipal levels of government. This structure is largely decentralized and leaves remarkable degrees of control and discretion over the enforcement of criminal law to local officials, especially to the prosecutors and judges who are permanent fixtures in local courts (Lynch, 2011; Tonry, 2012; Stuntz, 2011). Prosecutors are especially powerful figures because they have nearly unsupervised authority to decide whether to charge individuals with a crime and what charges that offender will face (Pfaff, 2017; Tonry, 2012). As publicly elected political figures whose campaigns often feature explicit statements that they will be harsher than their political opponents (Gordon & Huber, 2002; Tonry, 2012), prosecutors are especially attuned to the political currents shaping criminal justice and their practices seemed to reflect an increasingly punitive public opinion (Enns, 2014).

As state and federal politicians made increasingly aggressive calls for punishing offenders and passed legislation reflecting the warlike anti-crime rhetoric, local criminal justice system dynamics changed as well (Pfaff, 2017; Stuntz, 2011). Federal funding streams linked to the Law Enforcement Assistance Agency (LEAA) fueled the steady expansion of increasingly militarized local police forces capable of arresting and detaining far more offenders (Berk et al., 1977; Feeley & Sarat, 1980; Hinton, 2016; Schoenfeld, 2018). For each fiscal year that it was in operation, the Omnibus Crime Control Act provided hundreds of millions of federal dollars to the LEAA and its operations, beginning with a $100 million provision during the 1969 fiscal year and reaching a high of $1.75 billion in 1973 (Feeley & Sarat, 1980). Local criminal justice agencies could apply for federal resources that were then used to expand criminal justice system infrastructure. At the same time, state and federal lawmakers passed mandatory sentencing and "truth-in-sentencing" laws that required judges to sentence people convicted of certain crimes to longer terms of incarceration and mandated that they serve a longer proportion of it behind bars (Mauer, 1999).

The passage of mandatory sentencing and "truth-in-sentencing" laws shifted considerable power to prosecutors who could use the threat of long and certain prison terms to leverage people accused of crimes into punitive plea bargains (Alexander, 2010; Lynch, 2011; Natapoff, 2009; Pfaff, 2017; Stuntz, 2011; Tonry, 2012). As elected officials, prosecutors controlled case outcomes across large jurisdictions where electoral power was dominated by suburban and affluent neighborhoods that were often insulated from higher-crime, mixed-race neighborhoods plagued by violence (Alexander, 2010; Miller, 2015; Tonry, 2012). As Michael Tonry (2012) has noted, American prosecutors enjoy a remarkable degree of discretion in deciding whether to charge people and how serious of an offense to charge them with. This shift in power away from judicial discretion (to potentially limit the most punitive sentences) to prosecutors in charging decisions meant that individuals who, prior to the 1980s, might have been granted more lenient plea bargains were now more likely to go to prison (Pfaff, 2017).

Crime's politicization and the warlike mentality that increasingly dominated criminal justice policy also had important implications for judges, defense attorneys, and other justice officials whose positions might have mitigated relentless pressure to increase punishment (Simon, 2007). Prosecutors came to be viewed as better equipped to prioritize the rights of victims, ensure public safety, and isolate troublesome offenders from their communities in ways that judges had failed to do (Pfaff, 2017; Simon, 2007; Stuntz, 2011). Determinate and mandatory sentencing laws reduced judicial discretion and resources for public defenders remained meager as lawmakers expanded law enforcement budgets while failing to provide adequate resources for indigent defendants (Simon, 2008; Stuntz, 2008). David A. Simon (2008) provides examples of such problems in his examination of Minnesota and Mississippi public defender systems, noting that although the Minnesota Board of Public Defense requested 100 new attorney positions in the early 2000s, funds for public defense offices were reduced and 20 attorney positions were actually eliminated.

As prosecutorial power expanded, local courts were strained by surging caseloads. Increases in arrests, criminalization of more activities, especially drug offenses (Alexander, 2010), and expanding police capacity (Weidner & Frase, 2003) increased the volume of citizens charged and sentenced in local courts. Increased policing and court volume was especially acute in poor urban communities where the war on drugs flooded the courts with individuals charged with a drug crime who were disproportionately African American (Alexander, 2010; Miller, 2015). Increased case volumes undermined whatever capacity local courts might have had to provide individualized treatment for offenders, as courts worked to manage overwhelming backlogs (Miller, 2015). These developments and attendant punishments for drug offenses were especially acute for people living in low-income minority communities and had long-term deleterious consequences for those most seriously affected by crime and violence (Alexander, 2010; Miller, 2015; Nellis Chapter 10; Wakefield & Uggen, 2010).

The rising flood of people charged with criminal offenses caused problems for local correctional institutions, including locally managed jails, and departments of probation and parole. Correctional strategies emphasized increasing surveillance and control but recidivism rates remained high, especially in urban neighborhoods with the highest rates of prosecution and incarceration (Phelps, 2017; Wakefield & Uggen, 2010). In states like Minnesota and Washington where incarceration rates increased modestly compared to the nation, lawmakers and local criminal justice officials turned to large-scale probation (Phelps, 2017). Systems and penalties associated with probation, parole, and community-based sanctions grew rapidly, and correctional officers increasingly labeled and tracked formerly incarcerated persons through the use of electronic monitoring and frequent drug tests (Lynch, 1998, 2000; Nellis, 2010; Petersilia, 2003; Robinson, McNeill, & Maruna, 2013). From 1980 to 1998 the number of parolees who were reincarcerated for technical parole violations increased more than 700% (Petersilia, 2003, p. 148), lending support to what has been termed the "revolving door at the prison gate" (Bureau of Justice Statistics [BJS], 2009; Padfield & Maruna, 2006). A high proportion of parolees were also rearrested within three years of release. Langan and Levin (2002) found that nearly two-thirds of all inmates released in their sample were rearrested for a serious crime within three years of their release.

Some local courts aggressively enforced punishments and fines for low-level offenses, as the "law and order" approaches often associated with "broken windows" policing were incorporated into legal systems, even privatizing probation enforcement and collection of debt from indigent offenders (Aviram, 2015). One prominent example is the Department of Justice's Civil Rights Division ruling in 2015 that the Ferguson, Missouri, courts and police department were systematically engaging in unconstitutional practices (DOJ, 2015). The report demonstrated that police officers in Ferguson had been aggressively policing minorities in an attempt to generate revenue and that arrest warrants often resulted from missed court dates, failure to pay fines, parking infractions, traffic tickets, and minor housing violations (DOJ, 2015). Sociologist Alexes Harris (2016) has chronicled how the use of monetary punishments on the poor expanded in the "tough on crime" era and how these penalties often inflict lifelong damage on people who already face extreme financial hardship. Her work highlights how these policies undermine the likelihood that people convicted of crimes and forced to pay fines can successfully avoid further contact with the criminal justice system (Harris, 2016). Some jurisdictions have even privatized probation firms, allowing for-profit companies to doggedly pursue the payment of public debts. These firms came under scrutiny when the Human Rights Watch demonstrated that offender-funded models of probation discriminate against low-income minorities while failing to adequately reintegrate them into society (Albin-Lackey, 2014). Examples abound of the ways courts imposed burdensome sanctions that undermined reentry, stressed whole communities, and destabilized public safety (Clear & Frost, 2014; Harris, 2016; Hinton, 2016).

Litigation, high profile events, and concerns that these policies exacerbated class and racial inequalities helped stimulate reforms to local courts. Municipal courts in New York began diverting low-level drug offenders from prison (Lippman, 2010), and in 2014 New Jersey voters approved a constitutional amendment that drastically reformed bail practices, essentially eliminating bail requirements for poor, low-level offenders (Foderaro, 2017). Many jurisdictions have implemented alternatives to jails and prisons, such as drug court programming, in an attempt to divert defendants from overcrowded facilities and to lower the costs associated with corrections (Aviram, 2015; Clear & Frost, 2014). These recent reforms seem to suggest that a broader rethinking of the warlike anti-crime mentality that dominated much of the latter twentieth century might be emerging. But, as Table 1.2 illustrates, those changes have been uneven across the states.

Explanations

Understanding how crime and punishment operate in local settings is especially challenging in America's decentralized criminal justice systems, where enforcement of the law varies markedly across jurisdictions, making generalizations difficult (Walker, 1998). But scholars have generated a growing and insightful body of research that has identified crucial questions about how local criminal justice settings operate and how they have affected and been affected by broader shifts in state and federal law and policy. Some scholars have attributed greater criminalization and higher incarceration rates to the power that local prosecutors wield in their choices to charge, convict, and commit offenders (Stuntz, 2011; Pfaff, 2017; Tonry, 2012). Others argue that federal- and state-level activities largely usurped the power local officials once enjoyed to moderate and regulate the state's response to offending (Miller, 2015). Still others have illuminated how local court operations impose burdensome costs on offenders who have not yet been convicted of a crime, even those charged with low-level misdemeanor offenses (Kohler-Hausmann, 2013; Natapoff, 2009). Below, we provide an overview of some of the key research focused on developments in local courts and highlight some of the important differences between their positions.

Scholars have highlighted the problematic institutional and political nature of American prosecutors, noting the remarkable degree of discretion that prosecutors have in charging offenders and committing them to prison. As these researchers note, prosecutors have almost unfettered power over deciding whether to charge people with crimes and in determining the severity of the charge (Tonry, 2012; Pfaff, 2017). The vast majority of all criminal cases are decided by plea bargains, and prosecutors have remarkable power in negotiating with defense attorneys (Tonry, 2012). Michael Tonry (1995, 2011, 2012) argues that prosecutors are the most powerful actors in local criminal courts. Tonry (2012) suggests that prosecutors' roles are more akin to judges in European style inquisitorial justice systems, but unlike those systems where judges are neutral arbiters, prosecutors are instead highly motivated to compel guilty pleas because of the political nature of their position. Many scholars acknowledge that the rising criminalization and punitive ethos that became entrenched in the latter twentieth century eroded judicial discretion and shifted more power to prosecutors, and that this has contributed to mass imprisonment and racial disparities in imprisonment (Alexander, 2010; Natapoff, 2004, 2009; Pfaff, 2017; Simon, 2007; Tonry, 2012).

Others have pointed to the informal nature of prosecutorial power and how local jurisdictions can adjust changes in higher order law (state or federal) to suit local cultures. Mona Lynch and Marisa Omori's (2014) study of federal courts found that jurisdictions displayed remarkably stable outcomes over time despite U.S. Supreme Court rulings that seemed to open charging decisions up to greater degrees of judicial discretion. Anjuli Verma's (2015) work has extended this line of inquiry into local courts in California counties, finding that "the law before," or preexisting local sentencing norms, persisted despite dramatic changes in state laws and policies aimed at reducing prison commitments and decriminalizing low-level offenses. These local trends in county-level prison commitments cannot be explained by crime trends in local jurisdictions (Ball, 2011), but instead reflect the remarkable latitude and scant legal and administrative mechanisms in place to regulate how law operates on the ground (Verma, 2015). These exciting findings highlight how much is left to be learned about how local court cultures affect trends in charging and committing offenders to prison and its contribution to higher incarceration.

Scholars have also argued that other trends, such as the decline in electoral power in poor city neighborhoods, the criminalization of more behaviors, the professionalization and detachment of criminal justice organizations, and the incorporation of crime issues into politics empowered suburban and rural residents at the expense of the urban poor (Stuntz, 2008, 2011). William Stuntz (2008) argues that local criminal justice actors, such as locally elected trial judges, were once more likely to moderate harsher punishments because they were more tightly bound to their neighborhoods and residents. He argues that as the war on crime gained steam punishment decisions were made by prosecutors who were increasingly detached from those constituents most directly affected by crime and punishment. According to this argument, areas that are well policed and in which jury trials and acquittals are common, where laws are more ambiguous and less clearly defined, and where political and criminal justice powers lie within communities will have more stable and lenient punishment across groups (Stuntz, 2008).

These arguments point to the political and institutional structures that shape how legal power is wielded in local settings and they see the disenfranchisement of local communities that are most in need of law and order as a key factor in explaining both incarceration and the state's failure to reduce violence. Lisa Miller's (2015) work suggests that persistent high levels of violence in certain (primarily minority) neighborhoods reflect the weaknesses of a political system that fails to effectively address even the most basic needs of the disadvantaged. These scholars argue that power must be concentrated in the hands of those most affected by crime and must be more locally democratic (Stuntz, 2008; Miller, 2015). Thus,

> The need is for more politics: not the kind in which images of furloughed prisoners swing national elections, but the kind that happens locally, where crime and punishment alike cut

deepest[, for] when police chiefs and (especially) prosecutors listen to those who live in the places we call 'war zones' and heed their wishes, American criminal justice may, at long last, grow more equal.

(Stuntz, 2008, p. 2040)

Yet another strand of research into the role local courts and the adversarial legal system play in rising incarceration rates has unearthed sometimes overlooked ways that criminal courts exert control over and punish offenders. Issa Kohler-Hausmann's (2013) work demonstrates how the high costs of adjudication have coupled with conflicting courtroom processes and prosecutor and judicial roles to promote ineffective and punitive forms of social control. She demonstrates that rules that were initially developed to promote fairness and equality can be used in ways that actually allow prosecutors to punish and surveil even low-level offenders who have not been convicted of a crime (Kohler-Hausmann, 2013). Though New York reduced prison commitments, mass misdemeanor arrests, processes of marking, procedural hassle, and performance underlie social control mechanisms that are psychologically and economically taxing and well aligned with the punitive ethos of mass incarceration (Kohler-Hausmann, 2013). These misdemeanor charges disproportionately affect low-income minority populations and add to layers of disadvantage in poor communities.

The expansion of prosecutorial power has generated problematic—and in some cases dangerous—policies. Natapoff (2004, 2009) and others argue that law enforcement's use of "snitching," for example, has promoted inequalities in punishment and increases in retaliatory violence and has weakened relations between community members and criminal justice actors (Leovy, 2015; Natapoff, 2004, 2009; Rios, 2011). Studies examining the use of informants in criminal cases demonstrate how seemingly democratic processes have in fact perpetuated inequality in the criminal justice system and in society writ large (Leovy, 2015; Natapoff, 2004, 2009; Rios, 2011). In her analysis of snitching, Natapoff (2004, 2009) shows how the use of informants by criminal justice actors such as prosecutors and police officers not only exacerbates tensions between law enforcement officials and community residents, but can also reward criminals with lenience and places innocent individuals in highly dangerous situations. Importantly, "When a government permits criminals to continue offending in exchange for information and cooperation, the community in which those crimes are committed suffers in a number of ways" (Natapoff, 2009, p. 207). This disconnect between community residents and criminal justice actors in minority communities has had problematic consequences, such as the development of a "stop snitching" campaign, decreased witness cooperation, and increasing retaliatory violence, all of which might increase crime and lower criminal justice actors' crime-solving abilities (Leovy, 2015; Rios, 2011).

Lastly, other scholars have examined how laws relating to banishment and civil statute violations have come to manage space and have allowed police, prosecutors, and other criminal justice actors to use their discretion in ways that disproportionately punish minorities living in disadvantaged areas (Beckett & Herbert, 2009). Park exclusion orders, trespassing laws, and off-limits orders have shaped the lives of individuals in particularly devastating ways (Beckett & Herbert, 2009). Though advocates of banishment techniques argue that these practices decrease community disorder, improve quality of life, and provide fair alternatives to incarceration, in reality banishment orders cause individuals to feel psychologically damaged and as though they have been deprived of liberty, autonomy, security, and goods and services (Beckett & Herbert, 2009; Lebel & Richie Chapter 7).

Ultimately, the "anti-crime," law and order ethos has penetrated American culture and institutions in innumerable and unpredictable ways. As Jonathan Simon (2007) argues, ideas that were driven by fear of crime and the systems of thought and process that it stimulated have come to affect family issues, approaches to education, workplace norms, and a number of other matters once handled privately. Criminal justice agencies are now involved in what used to be family matters, such as custody battles and other marital conflicts, public schools are patrolled by police and security officers (rather

Future Research

Researchers have dramatically expanded our understanding of the complex historical forces that have shaped criminal justice law and policy over the last several decades, illuminating the complexity that American federalism creates in criminal justice and unearthing new and exciting avenues for future research. This work also demonstrates the continued need for complex and mixed research methodologies that can link local processes to the state and federal level forces that structure them. Recent declines in both the national rate and many state incarceration rates open up new avenues for comparative and historical analyses. Below, we outline several potential avenues for future research and propose potential research questions that might drive the field forward.

Few areas have more promise than those seeking to illuminate how local criminal justice actors' actions are shaped by the broader legal and political structures that are supposed to regulate them. Recent legal scholarship highlighting how prosecutorial activity played a central role in driving up charges and more severe sanctions (Pfaff, 2017; Stuntz, 2011; Tonry, 2012) seems to challenge theories that are more aligned with political and legal accounts of changes in state law and policy (Campbell & Schoenfeld, 2013; Goodman et al., 2017). Work highlighting the resilience of local court outcomes despite significant changes in the legislative and appeals court rulings that are meant to regulate those outcomes reminds us that America's decentralized legal system leaves plenty of flexibility for local jurisdictions to adhere to norms despite changes at the federal and state levels (Lynch & Omori, 2014; Verma, 2015).

These arguments raise important questions: Are law enforcers on the ground really equipped with such sweeping discretion that they can adjust state and federal laws to simply persist with local preferences? And if so, is this power consistent across different types of jurisdictions and within particular state contexts depending on state legal and political structures? Some research on elected versus appointed judges suggests that their decisions are influenced by politics and election cycles (Gordon & Huber, 2007), but how do shifts in legal and political context affect prosecutors? It will be important to discern whether and how the passage of more stringent sentencing laws affects prosecutorial decision-making on the ground. State and federal legislation might send rhetorical signals that enable or induce prosecutors to pursue more or less severe sentences that they might not otherwise seek. Much work remains to be done in building stronger theoretical accounts of the links between local criminal justice actors, state legislators and administrators, and federal actors.

Though scholarship on changes in punishment and corrections has understandably amassed thorough accounts of the historical forces that combined to increase the use of imprisonment, much work remains to be done to explain other elements of the carceral state that have sometimes been underappreciated. For example, Michelle Phelps's (2017) work on probation shows that while some states retained low levels of incarceration, they used probation on a massive scale. Similarly, Issa Kohler-Hausmann's (2013) work highlights how some pointed to New York City's "successes" in reducing prison commitments as progressive reform without realizing how local courts were still imposing severe costs on the lowest level defendants who had not even been convicted. Similar issues remain in studying whether the same historical shifts that have shaped incarceration also affect probation, parole, services for former inmates, and so on. Though scholars have been examining the ancillary consequences and disadvantages that are so often incorporated into state sanctions for some time (Mauer, 2002), we know little, for example, about how budget strains linked to the 2008 recession might exacerbate oppressive conditions as states seek to reduce costs.

Lastly, comparative research exploring why states have or have not implemented reforms that have reduced incarceration or decriminalized drugs and other low-level offenses promises to provide valuable insights into the forces that drive and inhibit reform. As was the case in the years before incarceration's sharp upward national trajectory (see Table 1.1), states in the U.S. are entering a period of stark variation. This is promising for reformers and an opportunity for scholars whose work should dig into state-level developments and explore the forces operating within particular state penal and political fields to shape penal change. For the first time since the nation embarked on its great incarceral experiment, researchers have some sustained examples of decarceration that are ripe for explanation and comparison.

Notes

1 States with small populations often exhibit sharp percent changes that might reflect the opening of a single mid-sized facility, and smaller states played a limited role in driving carceral expansion on a national scale. To better understand trends in more populous states we created a pool of states that excluded those with a population under 1% of the national total for Tables 1.1 and 1.2. For Table 1.1 we used 1970 U.S. Census figures to establish a threshold for inclusion that was 2,030,436 residents; for Table 1.2 we used 2000 U.S. Census figures to establish a 1% threshold of 3,087,253. Our new pool of larger states included 92% of the total U.S. population in 1970 and 89% of the total U.S. population in 2000, which included 31 states for Table 1.1 and 29 for Table 1.2. Both tables reflect the states with the highest and lowest percent changes for the specified time periods for states whose populations exceeded the 1% threshold (for example, in 1970 Alaska, Wyoming, Vermont, and Nevada had populations under 500,000 residents and were excluded; in 2000, Wyoming, Alaska, and Vermont had populations under 600,000 and were excluded).
2 Alabama's decline was an anomaly and was imposed by federal control of its prison system (Feeley & Rubin, 1998).

References

Albin-Lackey, C. (2014). *Profiting from probation: America's "offender-funded" probation industry*. Washington, DC: Human Rights Watch.

Alexander, M. (2010). *The new Jim Crow: Mass incarceration in the age of colorblindness*. New York, NY: The New Press.

Aviram, H. (2015). *Cheap on crime: Recession-era politics and the transformation of American punishment*. Oakland, CA: University of California Press.

Ball, W. D. (2011). Tough on crime (on the state's dime): How violent crime does not drive California counties' incarceration rates – and why it should. *Georgia State University Law Review, 28*, 987–1084.

Barker, V. (2009). *The politics of imprisonment: How the democratic process shapes the way America punishes offenders*. Oxford: Oxford University Press.

Beckett, K. (1997). *Making crime pay: Law and order in contemporary American politics*. Oxford: Oxford University Press.

Beckett, K., & Herbert, S. (2009). *Banished: The new social control in urban America*. Oxford: Oxford University Press.

Beckett, K., & Sasson, T. (2004). *Politics of injustice: Crime and punishment in America* (2nd ed.). Thousand Oaks, CA: SAGE Publications.

Berk, R. A., Brackman, H., & Lesser, S. (1977). *A measure of justice: An empirical study of changes in the California Penal Code, 1955–1971*. New York, NY: Academic Press.

Bourdieu, P., & Wacquant, L. J. (1992). *An invitation to reflexive sociology*. Chicago, IL: University of Chicago Press.

Bureau of Justice Statistics. (2009). *Probation and parole in the United States, 2008* (NCJ 228230). Washington, DC: U.S. Government Printing Office.

Bureau of Justice Statistics. (2015). *Incarceration rates for prisoners under state or federal jurisdiction, per 100,000 residents*. Washington, DC: U.S. Government Printing Office.

Calavita, K., & Jenness, V. (2014). *Appealing to justice: Prisoner grievance, rights, and carceral logic*. Oakland, CA: University of California Press.

Campbell, M. C. (2011). Politics, prisons, and law enforcement: An examination of the emergence of "law and order" politics in Texas. *Law & Society Review, 45*(3), 631–665.

Campbell, M. C. (2012). Ornery alligators and soap on a rope: Texas prosecutors and punishment reform in the Lone Star State. *Theoretical Criminology, 16*(3), 1–23.

Campbell, M. C. (2014). The emergence of penal extremism in California: A dynamic view of institutional structures and political processes. *Law & Society Review, 48*(2), 377–409.

Campbell, M. C., & Schoenfeld, H. (2013). The transformation of America's penal order: A historicized political sociology of punishment. *American Journal of Sociology, 118*(5), 1375–1423.

Cate, S. D. (2010). *Untangling prison expansion in Oregon: Political narratives and policy outcomes* (Doctoral dissertation). University of Oregon, Eugene.

Clear, T., & Frost, N. (2014). *The punishment imperative: The rise and fall of the grand social experiment in mass incarceration*. New York, NY: New York University Press.

Dagan, D., & Teles, S. M. (2014). Locked in? Conservative reform and the future of mass incarceration. *Annals of the American Academy of Political and Social Science, 651*(1), 266–276.

Enns, P. K. (2014). The public's increasing punitiveness and its influence on mass incarceration in the United States. *American Journal of Political Science, 58*(4), 857–872.

Feeley, M. M., & Rubin, E. L. (1998). *Judicial policy making and the modern state: How the courts reformed America's prisons*. Cambridge: Cambridge University Press.

Feeley, M. M., & Sarat, A. D. (1980). *The policy dilemma: Federal crime policy and the Law Enforcement Assistance Administration, 1968–1978*. Minneapolis, MN: University of Minnesota Press.

Flamm, M. W. (2005). *Law and order: Street crime, civil unrest, and the crisis of liberalism in the 1960s*. New York, NY: Columbia University Press.

Foderaro, L. W. (2017, February 8). New Jersey alters its bail system and upends legal landscape. *The New York Times*. Retrieved from www.nytimes.com/2017/02/06/nyregion/new-jersey-bail-system.html?mcubz=3

Garland, D. (1990). *Punishment and modern society: A study in social theory*. Chicago, IL: University of Chicago Press.

Garland, D. (1996). The limits of the sovereign state: Strategies of crime control in contemporary society. *The British Journal of Criminology, 36*(4), 445–471.

Garland, D. (2001). *The culture of control: Crime and social order in contemporary society*. Oxford: Oxford University Press.

Gilmore, R. W. (2007). *Golden gulag: Prisons, surplus, crisis, and opposition in globalizing California*. Berkeley, CA: Unversity of California Press.

Goodman, P., Page, J., & Phelps, M. (2017). *Breaking the pendulum: The long struggle over criminal justice*. Oxford: Oxford University Press.

Gordon, S. C., & Huber, G. A. (2002). Citizen oversight and the electoral incentives of criminal prosecutors. *American Journal of Political Science, 46*(2), 334–351.

Gordon, S. C., & Huber, G. A. (2007). The effect of electoral competitiveness on incumbent behavior. *Quarterly Journal of Political Science, 2*(2), 107–138.

Gottschalk, M. (2006). *The prison and the gallows: The politics of mass incarceration in America*. Cambridge: Cambridge University Press.

Gottschalk, M. (2014). *Caught: The prison state and the lockdown of American politics*. Princeton, NJ: Princeton University Press.

Guetzkow, J., & Schoon, E. (2015). If you build it, they will fill it: The consequences of prison overcrowding litigation. *Law & Society Review, 49*(2), 401–432.

Harris, A. (2016). *A pound of flesh: Monetary sanctions as punishment for the poor*. New York, NY: Russell Sage Foundation.

Hinton, E. (2016). *From the war on poverty to the war on crime: The making of mass incarceration in America*. Cambridge, MA: Harvard University Press.

Holder, E. (2016, August 11). Eric Holder: We can have shorter sentences and less crime. *The New York Times*. Retrieved from www.nytimes.com/2016/08/14/opinion/sunday/eric-h-holder-mandatory-minimum-sentences-full-of-errors.html?mcubz=3

Horwitz, S. (2017, April 8). How Jeff Sessions wants to bring back the war on drugs. *The Washington Post*. Retrieved from www.washingtonpost.com/world/national-security/how-jeff-sessions-wants-to-bring-back-the-war-on-drugs/2017/04/08/414ce6be-132b-11e7-ada0-1489b735b3a3_story.html?utm_term=.9d6c84f8ad36

Huebner, B. M., Kras, K. R., Rydberg, J., Bynum, T. S., Grommon, E., & Pleggenkuhle, B. (2014). The effect and implications of sex offender residence restrictions. *Criminology & Public Policy, 13*(1), 139–168.

Kohler–Hausmann, I. (2013). Misdemeanor justice: Control without conviction. *American Journal of Sociology, 119*(2), 351–393.

Langan, P., & Levin, D. (2002). *Recidivism of prisoners released in 1994* (NCJ 193427). Washington, DC: Bureau of Justice Statistics.

Leovy, J. (2015). *Ghettoside*. New York, NY: Spiegel & Grau.

Lippman, J. (2010). How one state reduced both crime and incarceration. *Hofstra Law Review*, *38*(1035), 1045–1057.

Lowe, W. C. (2016). Sex offender registries. In P. Dixon (Ed.), *Surveillance in America: An encyclopedia of history, politics, and the law* (p. 301). Santa Barbara, CA: ABC-CLIO.

Lynch, M. (1998). Waste managers? The new penology, crime fighting, and parole agent identity. *Law & Society Review*, *32*(4), 839–870.

Lynch, M. (2000). Rehabilitation as rhetoric: The ideal of reformation in contemporary parole discourse and practices. *Punishment & Society*, *2*(1), 40–65.

Lynch, M. (2010). *Sunbelt justice: Arizona and the transformation of American punishment*. Stanford, CA: Stanford University Press.

Lynch, M. (2011). Mass incarceration, legal change, and locale. *Criminology & Public Policy*, *10*(3), 673–698.

Lynch, M., & Omori, M. (2014). Legal change and sentencing norms in the wake of Booker: The impact of time and place on drug trafficking cases in federal court. *Law & Society Review*, *48*(2), 411–445.

Mauer, M. (1999). *Race to incarcerate*. New York, NY: The New Press.

Mauer, M. (2002). Analyzing and responding to the driving forces of prison population growth. *Criminology & Public Policy*, *1*(3), 389–392.

Mauer, M. (2004). Race, class, and the development of criminal justice policy. *Review of Policy Research*, *21*(1), 79–92.

Miller, L. L. (2008). *The perils of federalism: Race, poverty, and the politics of crime control*. Oxford: Oxford University Press.

Miller, L. L. (2010). The invisible black victim: How American federalism perpetuates racial inequality in criminal justice. *Law & Society Review*, *44*(3–4), 805–842.

Miller, L. L. (2015). What's violence got to do with it? Inequality, punishment, and state failure in US politics. *Punishment & Society*, *17*(2), 184–2010.

Murakawa, N. (2014). *The first civil right: How liberals built prison America*. Oxford: Oxford University Press.

Natapoff, A. (2004). Snitching: The institutional and communal consequences. *University of Cincinnati Law Review*, *73*, 645–703.

Natapoff, A. (2009). *Snitching: Criminal informants and the erosion of American justice*. New York, NY: New York University Press.

Nellis, A. (2010). Throwing away the key: The expansion of life without parole sentences in the United States. *Federal Sentencing Reporter*, *23*(1), 27–32.

Padfield, N., & Maruna, S. (2006). The revolving door at the prison gate: Exploring the dramatic increase in recalls to prison. *Criminology & Criminal Justice*, *6*(3), 329–352.

Page, J. (2011). *The toughest beat: Politics, punishment, and the prison officers union in California*. Oxford: Oxford University Press.

Pager, D. (2003). The mark of a criminal record. *American Journal of Sociology*, *108*(5), 937–975.

Perkinson, R. (2010). *Texas tough: The rise of America's prison empire*. New York, NY: Metropolitan Books.

Petersilia, J. (2003). *When prisoners come home: Parole and prisoner reentry*. Oxford: Oxford University Press.

Pfaff, J. F. (2017). *Locked in: The true causes of mass incarceration and how to achieve real reform*. New York, NY: Basic Books.

Phelps, M. (2013). The paradox of probation: Community supervision in the age of mass incarceration. *Law & Policy*, *35*(1–2), 51–80.

Phelps, M. (2017). Mass probation: Toward a more robust theory of state variation in punishment. *Punishment & Society*, *19*(1), 53–73.

Robinson, G., McNeill, F., & Maruna, S. (2013). Punishment in society: The improbable persistence of probation and other community sanctions and measures. In J. Simon & R. Sparks (Eds.), *The SAGE handbook of punishment and society* (pp. 321–340). Thousand Oaks, CA: SAGE Publishing.

Rios, V. M. (2011). *Punished: Policing the lives of black and Latino boys*. New York, NY: New York University Press.

Rydberg, J., Grommon, E., Huebner, B. M., & Bynum, T. (2014). The effect of statewide residency restrictions on sex offender post-release housing mobility. *Justice Quarterly*, *31*(2), 421–444.

Schoenfeld, H. (2018). *Building the prison state: Race and the politics of mass incarceration*. Chicago, IL: University of Chicago Press.

Simon, D. A. (2008). Equal before the law: Toward a restoration of Gideon's promise. *Harvard Civil Rights-Civil Liberties Law Review*, *43*, 581–594.

Simon, J. (2007). *Governing through crime: How the war on crime transformed American democracy and created a culture of fear*. Oxford: Oxford University Press.

Stemen, D., Rengifo, A., & Wilson, J. (2005). *Of fragmentation and ferment: The impact of state sentencing policies on incarceration rates, 1975–2002*. New York, NY: Vera Institute of Justice.

Stucky, T. D., Heimer, K., & Lang, J. (2007). A bigger piece of the pie? State corrections spending and the politics of social disorder. *Journal of Research in Crime and Delinquency, 44*(1), 91–123.

Stuntz, W. J. (2008). Unequal justice. *Harvard Law Review, 121*, 1969–2040.

Stuntz, W. J. (2011). *The collapse of American criminal justice.* Cambridge, MA: Harvard University Press.

Tonry, M. (1995). *Malign neglect: Race, crime, and punishment in America.* Oxford: Oxford University Press.

Tonry, M. (2011). *Punishing race: A continuing American dilemma.* Oxford: Oxford University Press.

Tonry, M. (2012). *Punishment and politics: Evidence and emulation in the making of English crime control policy.* Portland, OR: Willan Publishing.

Travis, J., Western, B., & Redburn, S. (2014). *The growth of incarceration in the United States: Exploring causes and consequences of high incarceration.* Washington, DC: The National Academies Press.

Uggen, C., & Manza, J. (2005). Disenfranchisement and the civil reintegration of convicted felons. In C. Mele & T. A. Miller (Eds.), *Civil penalties, social consequences* (pp. 65–83). New York, NY: Routledge.

United States Department of Justice. (2015). *Investigation of the Ferguson Police Department.* Washington, DC: Government Printing Office.

Verma, A. (2015). The law-before: Legacies and gaps in penal reform. *Law & Society Review, 49*(4), 847–882.

Wacquant, L. (2001). Deadly symbiosis: When ghetto and prison meet and mesh. *Punishment & Society, 3*(1), 95–134.

Wacquant, L. (2006). Penalization, depoliticization, and racialization: On the overincarceration of immigrants in the European Union. In S. Armstrong & L. McAra (Eds.), *Contexts of control: New perspectives on punishment and society* (pp. 83–100). Oxford: Clarendon Press.

Wakefield, S., & Uggen, C. (2010). Incarceration and stratification. *Annual Review of Sociology, 36*, 387–406.

Walker, S. (1998). *Popular justice: A history of American criminal justice* (2nd ed.). Oxford: Oxford University Press.

Weaver, V. (2007). Frontlash: Race and the development of punitive crime policy. *Studies in American Political Development, 21*(2), 230–265.

Weidner, R., & Frase, R. (2003). Legal and extralegal determinants of intercounty differences in prison use. *Criminal Justice Policy Review, 14*(3), 377–400.

Western, B. (2006). *Punishment and inequality in America.* New York, NY: Russell Sage Foundation.

Zimring, F. E., & Hawkins, G. (1991). What kind of drug war? *Social Justice, 18*(4), 104–121.

Zimring, F. E., Hawkins, G., & Kamin, S. (2001). *Punishment and democracy: Three strikes and you're out in California.* Oxford: Oxford University Press.

2
COLLATERAL SANCTIONS
The Intended Collateral Consequences of Felony Convictions

Tanya N. Whittle

Collateral Consequences of Punishment

The term "collateral consequences" is generally used to describe the unintended results of social policy and action. A growing body of literature documents the many collateral consequences of informal and formal punishments, particularly via the criminal justice system and felony convictions (Travis, 2002; Mauer & Chesney-Lind, 2002; Pager, 2003; Clear, 2007; Alexander, 2010; Arditti, 2012; Whittle, 2016). Collateral consequences of punishment include informal person-to-person and structural discrimination as well as formalized collateral sanctions. The collateral effects of punishment include stigma, strain, diminished social bonds, and emotional distress—to name a few. Collateral consequences of punishment can contribute to deviant labels and identities, antisocial behavior, substance abuse, and crime.

Punishment—especially through the criminal justice system—can have serious collateral consequences that negatively impact individuals and communities. Informal punishments can contribute to future formal punishment, and punishments in one social institution can impact treatment and punishment in others. For example, punishment in schools contributes to adverse experiences later in life, including involvement in the criminal justice system via the "school-to-prison pipeline" (Wolf & Kupchik, 2017; Mallett, 2016). The school-to-prison pipeline is a metaphor used to describe the pattern researchers have identified where youth who get into trouble at school are at higher likelihood of future involvement in the criminal justice system. Zero tolerance policies and increased securitization of schools contribute to the school-to-prison pipeline. Minorities are disproportionately punished in school and placed on a trajectory for involvement with the criminal justice system.

Arrest, prosecution, conviction, and punishment all have collateral consequences. For example, arrest can result in lost income due to incapacitation, which could result in the inability to buy essentials or pay household bills. This can in turn result in eviction or foreclosure,[1] repossession of one's property, incarceration for failing to pay child support, legal fees, and so on (Mauer & Chesney-Lind, 2002; Arditti, 2012; Harris, 2016). The arrest also results in an arrest record that can have long-term ramifications on employability,[2] even if the arrest does not result in prosecution or conviction. Hiring managers may have subtle fears and distrust of an applicant upon learning of his/her arrest history. Collateral consequences of punishment can also impact health[3] and family[4] (Mauer & Chesney-Lind, 2002; Travis, 2002).

The collateral consequences of punishment vary case by case, depending on an individual's life circumstances. Collateral consequences tend to snowball, especially for those who start with greater disadvantage. Punishments that are equal at time of application can have disparate impacts on those being punished. For example, fining a millionaire and homeless person $500 for panhandling is technically equal, but it is not equitable. The millionaire in this scenario would likely be able to pay the fine without significant immediate or long-term consequences. The homeless person on the other hand would likely not be able to pay the fine, which could result in additional fines and criminal charges. Additionally, the homeless person in this scenario could be detained throughout the course of the trial and would likely not be able to afford private counsel. The person therefore would be at greater likelihood of conviction and an unfavorable sentence. At greater risk of incarceration, the homeless person would be more likely to experience the collateral consequences of conviction and incarceration.

Collateral consequences of incarceration include severed social bonds (discussed in the "Social Bonds" section below), significant gaps in work history, exposure to environments and peers that can contribute to crime, psychological distress, PTSD, substance abuse disorders, and so on (Travis, 2002; Mauer & Chesney-Lind, 2002; Pager, 2003; Arditti, 2012). Many incarcerated people suffer from mental health and substance abuse issues, and those issues often go untreated and/or are aggravated during incarceration (James & Glaze, 2006; Visher & Travis, 2003). As a result, many people return from prison to the community in a worse condition than before their incarceration and at a high risk of reoffending. Collateral consequences such as these are generally considered unintended. However, given the theoretical and empirical literature documenting the negative collateral consequences of incarceration, some argue that the cumulative effect of punishment and particularly the criminal justice system are at least in part intentional (Alexander, 2010; Wacquant, 2009; Parenti, 2001). To reduce the collateral consequences of incarceration, many advocate for an end to mass incarceration (Alexander, 2010; Wacquant, 2009; Parenti, 2001).

Even without incarceration, formal conviction via the criminal justice system has significantly greater collateral consequences compared to the unintended consequences of informal punishments.[5] Convictions result in formal sentences and extrajudicial punishments (i.e., punishments not put in place by a judge) in the form of collateral consequences (Travis, 2002; Mauer & Chesney-Lind, 2002). Extrajudicial punishments in the form of collateral consequences are formalized as codified laws and policies. Examples include voter disenfranchisement, public assistance bans, and firearm restrictions. These formal, codified collateral consequences of criminal conviction are called collateral consequence policies, collateral restrictions, or collateral sanctions of conviction (Travis, 2002; Wheelock, 2005; Whittle, 2016).

Collateral Sanctions of Felony Convictions

Collateral sanctions are laws, rules, and regulations that automatically apply to people convicted of a felony. Examples of collateral sanctions include voter disenfranchisement, elimination from jury pools, firearm restrictions, employment restrictions, reduction or removal of driving privileges, lost or amended parental rights, and public assistance bans. In the U.S.,[6] public assistance collateral sanctions include restrictions to higher education, housing, Temporary Assistance for Needy Families (TANF), and Supplemental Nutrition Assistance Program (SNAP) (Travis, 2002; Mauer & Chesney-Lind, 2002).

Codified in federal, state, and local law and policies, persons convicted of felony crimes face collateral sanctions that limit convicted felons' access to public assistance, civil rights typically protected by the Fourteenth Amendment, and life opportunities. People convicted of felony crimes are subject to a myriad of collateral sanctions in the form of "laws, rules, and regulations [that] operate to discriminate against ex-offenders and effectively prevent their reintegration into the mainstream society and economy" (Alexander, 2010, p. 142).

Collateral sanctions are sometimes called invisible punishments because they are not a part of the formal punishments imposed by judges during sentencing. Instead, they automatically apply to persons convicted of a felony, and many people—including defendants and legal professionals—are not aware of the sanctions. Additionally, because they are typically civil in nature, collateral sanctions are often grouped in with *unintended* consequences of conviction. However, this is a misnomer as collateral sanction laws and policies are *intentionally* established by legislators and bureaucrats who enact the laws and policies (Travis, 2002).

Common Types of Collateral Sanctions

The number and types of collateral sanctions are difficult to assess because they exist at all levels of law, and many are riders (i.e., loosely connected or unrelated provisions) on non-criminal justice policy. For instance, restrictions barring people with drug felonies from receiving public assistance are a part of the 1996 Personal Responsibility and Work Opportunity Reconciliation Act, not the Crime and Criminal Procedure Codes. Additionally, the number and types of sanctions that apply to individual felons vary considerably depending on the jurisdiction of conviction, offense type, and a felon's location post-conviction. Although collateral sanctions apply to felons immediately upon conviction, they may not impact the individual until years after conviction once he/she is released from incarceration, begins job and house seeking, and/or applies for public assistance (Travis, 2002; Mauer & Chesney-Lind, 2002).

The National American Bar Association's Inventory of Collateral Consequences of Conviction (www.abacollateralconsequences.org) catalogues thousands of collateral sanction statues in each state. Similarly, the Legal Action Center's website (http://lac.org/roadblocks-to-reentry) provides data on seven general types of collateral sanctions as well as state-level Roadblock to Reentry Report Cards. Below is a summary of the general types of collateral sanctions most commonly associated with felony convictions.[7]

Financial Legal Obligations

Persons convicted of felony crimes, whether resulting in incarceration or not, likely begin the reintegration process owing considerable financial legal obligations such as fines, court fees, victim compensation, child support, subsistence fees, and so on. (Levingston & Turetsky, 2007; Brown & Bloom, 2009). Formally incarcerated parents are also held accountable by the state "to reimburse the state for welfare payments made to their children while the [parents] were incarcerated" (Brown & Bloom, 2009, p. 320).

Legal financial obligations often continue to accrue for ex-offenders after conviction: Ex-offenders "are required to make payments to a host of agencies ... [and] ex-offenders are billed for drug testing and even for the drug treatment they are supposed to receive as a condition of parole" (Alexander, 2010, p. 154). They are also frequently charged fees for being on probation and GPS monitoring. Legal debt that results from conviction accrues interest and is subject to late and minimum payment charges. Those who cannot or do not pay financial legal obligations risk having their wages garnished and/or (re)incarceration (Beckett & Harris, 2011; Harris, 2016).

Criminal Records and Background Checks

Criminal conviction records are generally available to the public, depending on state law, even if the conviction did not result in incarceration. In some states, arrests that do not result in conviction are also publicly available. The intersection of mass criminalization and incarceration with modern open criminal records databases results in an ever-growing number of citizens who have criminal records that are easily accessible to the public. Criminal records open to the public can negatively impact housing and employment opportunities, which in turn impacts their financial situation. Additionally, since criminal databases in many states are available online to the public, private and commercial background checks of potential employees, tenants, and even suitors are prolific (Mauer & Chesney-Lind, 2002; Petersilia, 2003; Alexander, 2010).

Due to the public and permanent nature of online criminal background records, "Today's criminal records create a lifetime of stigmatization for a person" (Murphy, Flehhan, Richards, & Jones, 2011, p. 101). Criminal records and databases mark convicted felons as "others" warranting disparate treatment; as such, modern criminal records serve as "an electronic scarlet letter" (Murphy et al., 2011, p. 112).

Public Assistance

A felony record can result in loss or denial of public assistance in the forms of SNAP food stamps, TANF, social security insurance, Medicaid, and public housing (Rubinstein & Mukamal, 2002; Travis, 2005; Harding, Wyse, Dobson, & Morenoff, 2014). According to Wacquant (2009), America's "War on Poverty" has given way to a war against the poor: During the 1970s–1990s spending on welfare decreased while spending on military, the criminal justice system, and catching people who commit welfare fraud increased. A variety of policies reduced public assistance eligibility, particularly convicted criminals from state-funded housing, medical, food, and education assistance programs. For example, during this time period, "Despite no federal law mandating Medicaid termination for prisoners, 90 percent of states have implemented policies that withdraw inmates' enrollment upon incarceration" (Wakeman, McKinney, & Rich, 2009, p. 860).

Drug offenders[8] are particularly targeted by public assistance collateral sanctions. For example, federal law "requires that states permanently bar individuals with drug-related felony convictions from receiving federally funded public assistance," particularly TANF and SNAP benefits (Alexander, 2010, p. 157). While drug offenders are banned—often permanently—from receiving such public assistance benefits, those who have been convicted of murder, kidnapping, and fraud remain eligible. Although there is a provision allowing states to opt out of the ban against ex-drug felons receiving public benefits, few states fully do so:

> Most states have partially opted out, affording exceptions for people in drug treatment. . . . It remains the case, however, that thousands of people with felony drug convictions in the United States are deemed ineligible for food stamps for the rest of their lives.
> (Alexander, 2010, p. 158)

Ex-drug offenders also face collateral sanctions that limit their access to public housing:

> The Anti-Drug Abuse Act of 1988, passed by Congress as part of the War on Drugs, called for strict lease enforcement and eviction of public housing tenants who engage in criminal activity. . . . In 1996, President Clinton, in an effort to bolster his 'tough on crime' credentials, declared that public housing agencies should exercise no discretion when a tenant or guest engages in criminal activity, particularly if it is drug-related.
> (Alexander, 2010, p. 145)

The U.S. Department of Housing and Urban Development's "one strike and you're out" policy authorizes Public Housing Authorities (PHAs) to "evict all members of the household for criminal activities committed by any one member of a household" (Petersilia, 2003, p. 122). PHA decisions can be appealed, but "appeals are rarely successful without an attorney—a luxury most public housing applicants cannot afford" (Alexander, 2010, p. 145). Because of the wide net of reasons a family can be evicted from public housing "many families are reluctant to allow their relatives—particularly those who are recently released from prison—to stay with them, even temporarily" (Alexander, 2010, p. 147). In short, people with felony records are often not welcome to return to their families who live in public housing (Petersilia, 2003), and housing options for people with felony records are substantially limited, increasing the chance of homelessness for ex-offenders and their families (Travis, 2005). Persons with felony records are effectively "banished" or excluded from some public spaces, including public housing complexes via trespassing policies and strict residence rules (e.g., no ex-offender policies) (Beckett & Herbert, 2010).

Employment

It is commonly accepted that employment is considerably important during reintegration to reduce recidivism[9] (Sampson & Laub, 1993; Uggen, 2000; Uggen, Wakefield, & Western, 2005), and employment is frequently a condition for supervised release. However, people with felony criminal records face many barriers to obtaining and keeping gainful, legal employment. Difficulty obtaining legal employment can contribute to violation of probation and commission of new crimes that can result in incarceration.

In addition to the collateral consequences of conviction that negatively impact employment (e.g., distrust among hiring managers, gaps in work history) (Stoll & Bushway, 2008), federal and state collateral sanction laws deny licensure for many professions: "A number of occupations are closed to some or most categories of ex-felons—for example, jobs requiring contact with children, certain health service occupations, and security services" (Uggen, Manza, Thompson, 2006, p. 298). Although the 14th Amendment protects many people from legal discrimination, and employers are not allowed to enforce blanket ex-felon bans unless the crime is associated with employment activities (e.g., drug convictions and working in a pharmacy), in practice, ex-offenders are formally barred from occupations unassociated with criminal convictions (e.g., drug conviction and working as a barber). Further, employers are generally allowed to ask about convictions (and even arrests) on applications early in the applicant review process. As a result, ex-offenders experience diminished employability and earnings in the immediate future and their long-term trajectories.

Firearm Restrictions

Depending on the jurisdiction and conviction type, convicted felons, especially those with violent offenses on their records, are frequently denied access to owning or even possessing firearms. Although such policies are usually rationalized by arguments that this prevents dangerous people from accessing weapons, not all persons banned from possessing firearms have a prior firearm-related charge or even a violent criminal conviction. Additionally, it does not completely eliminate firearm access by felons because some sales are exempt from required background checks (e.g., personal sales, sales at flea markets, gun shows), and firearms are available on the black market.

Voter Disenfranchisement

One of the more commonly known collateral sanctions of a felony conviction is legal voter disenfranchisement.[10] Only two of 50 states in the U.S. (Maine and Vermont) do not disenfranchise people based on their criminal records, including those who are currently incarcerated. Of the remaining 48 states, 35 disenfranchise people on parole, and 31 disenfranchise people on probation (The Sentencing Project, 2014). Twelve states have measures in place that disenfranchise people for life: Eight disenfranchise certain categories of felons for life and/or permit application for restoration of rights after a fixed period of time, and four states impose lifetime disenfranchisement on all felons in the state (The Sentencing Project, 2014). As a result, approximately 5.85 million Americans (one in 40 adults) are disenfranchised due to felony conviction (The Sentencing Project, 2014). Of those 5.85 million people, an estimated 45% have completed their formal sentences and "paid their debt to society" (The Sentencing Project, 2014).

Sex Offender Laws[11]

Sex offenders have received considerable attention in the past two decades, particularly in the mid-1990s with high profile cases and passage of the Jacob Wetterling Act and Megan's Law in 1994, which required states to register sex offenders in statewide databases available to the public (Barnes, Dukes, Tewksbury, & Troye, 2009). Proponents of the laws argue registries promote community awareness of sex offenders who reside in the community, reducing offender opportunities to recidivate (Tewksbury & Lees, 2006). As a result, sex offender registry and notification (SORN) policies have been implemented nationwide. In addition to federally mandated SORN policies, state and local policies result in great variation in the collateral sanctions sex offenders may face, including civil commitment, chemical castration, GPS monitoring, lifetime supervision, and residency restrictions.

Collateral Sanctions and Recidivism

Collateral sanctions are enacted in order to punish criminals and to prevent crime. However, according to theoretical predictions and empirical findings, collateral sanctions in general do not reduce crime. In fact, collateral sanctions may increase crime, especially recidivism[12] among convicted criminals directly impacted by collateral sanctions. This section reviews the major criminological theories' predictions of collateral sanctions' effects on recidivism as well as the empirical evidence.

Theoretical Predictions

Because there are many different types of collateral sanctions aimed at various offender types and each sanction type can manifest in a myriad of different policy forms, there is no one theoretical perspective driving the field. Instead, authors who write on collateral sanctions draw from a large variety of theories including rational choice, routine activities, strain, social bonds, labeling/shaming/identity, and social disorganization. Many of these are combined with a life course perspective (see below), either explicitly or implicitly. When looking specifically at the relationship between collateral sanctions and recidivism, routine activities, strain, social bonds, and labeling/shaming/identity theories are heavily utilized. This section reviews the theoretical perspectives most often invoked by collateral sanction scholars and what each perspective predicts for collateral sanctions' effect on recidivism (see Table 2.1).

Table 2.1 Collateral Sanctions' Predicted Effects on Recidivism by Theoretical Perspectives

Theoretical Perspectives	Predicted Effect of Collateral Sanction Policies Discussed in the Literature
Rational Choice/Deterrence	N/A
Opportunity/Routine Activities	+/−
Labeling/Shaming/Identity	+/−
Strain	+
Social Disorganization	+
Social Bonds	+
Life Course	+

Note: +/− indicates mixed or contextual effects.

Rational Choice/Deterrence

Rational choice and deterrence theories are often invoked to justify collateral sanctions policies, particularly among politicians and laymen. Through this perspective people are viewed as rational actors who intentionally act in order to minimize pain and maximize pleasure (Beccaria, 1764). To deter crime, the costs of a crime must outweigh the rewards. This can be accomplished by implementing certain, swift, and proportionality severe punishments to those who commit crime. Such punishment can result in specific and general deterrence (Bentham, 1789). Such deterrence, however, is only possible if potential offenders' perceptions of punishment result in him/her perceiving the costs to outweigh the benefits. In other words, the subjective perceptions of punishment are more important in influencing behavior than objective perceptions (Paternoster, 2010).

Policy makers frequently justify collateral sanctions with "Tough on Crime" rhetoric influenced by deterrence/rational choice theories. For instance, during open debate over the TANF ban in 1996, Senator Phil Gramm (R–TX) argued, "If we are serious about our drug laws, we ought not to give people welfare benefits who are violating the nation's drug laws" (Rubinstein & Mukamal, 2002, p. 42). However, this is a poor theoretical framework for studying collateral sanctions and pursuing decreases in recidivism because collateral sanctions are usually not known about by the general public, offenders, or even those who work within the criminal justice system. If such sanctions are unknown, they will not effectively deter crime (Demleitner, 1999; Pinard, 2006). Additionally, such sanctions are generally not applied swiftly. Instead, they often do not impact a convicted felon until months if not years after committing a crime. Finally, collateral sanctions are not applied proportionately. The severity of crime is generally not related to the severity of collateral sanctions or tailored to fit specific crimes (Demleitner, 1999). In most jurisdictions, all felons are subject to the same felon disenfranchisement laws, and only drug and sex offenders (no matter the type or severity of crime within that category) face public assistance bans. Therefore, collateral sanctions are unlikely to deter crime in general or reoffending (Whittle, 2016; Pinard, 2010). (See Empirical Findings below.)

Opportunity/Routine Activities

Opportunity/routine activities perspectives are commonly invoked in support of collateral sanctions, especially those relating to sex offenders and firearm restrictions. Rooted in rational choice (Beccaria, 1764) and human ecology literature (see Shaw, McKay, Zorbaugh, & Cottrell, 1929; Reiss, 1976), opportunity theories posit that crime can only occur when a likely offender, a suitable target, and the absence of a capable guardian converge in time and space. Target-hardening and changes in routine activities can prevent crime (Cohen & Felson, 1979; Wilcox, Madensen, & Tillyer, 2007).

Some collateral sanctions (e.g., residency, firearm, and driving restrictions) attempt to prevent crime by preventing the convergence of previously convicted individuals and suitable, unguarded targets. For example, SORN laws are intended to deter sex offense recidivism by making the general public aware of convicted sex offenders so the public will take preventative measures to reduce opportunities for crime (e.g., target hardening, not trusting known offenders as guardians). Public housing policies that deny residency to people with convictions may reduce crime in housing developments by displacing drug markets, but they can also contribute to crime by increasing strain. Opportunity/routine activities theories predict both positive and negative relationships between collateral sanctions and recidivism due to the wide variety of sanctions and contexts through which sanctions are implemented. Collateral sanctions have the capacity of increasing or decreasing opportunities for crime and recidivism depending on the nature of the person, policy specifics, and environment.

Labeling/Shaming/Identity

Labeling, shaming, and identity theories are frequently invoked in collateral sanctions literature. Unlike most other criminological theories, labeling theorists focus on the effects societal reactions can have on future identity and behavior. It is possible that societal reaction may scare or shame a person into conformity; however, social reactions to deviance (e.g., arrest and conviction) can have negative, unanticipated consequences that deepen criminal identity and behavior. Labeling and differential treatment can reinforce a deviant status and criminal behavior (Tannenbaum, 1938; Lemert, 1951). Labeling thus becomes a confirming, self-fulfilling prophecy, and the label of criminal can become one's master status (i.e., most salient status), overshadowing all others (Becker, 1963). The labeled individual may also start seeing him/herself as deviant, acting in ways to live up to that new identity. Labeling also indirectly impacts social networks and opportunities potentially increasing criminal involvement (Sampson & Laub, 1997).

Contemporary labeling theory explores why a criminal label sometimes results in a criminal self-concept and future criminal activity while other times it seems to have the opposite effect. Braithwaite (1989) argues the drastically different outcomes are the result of the nature of shaming by societal reactors. Shaming is used to invoke remorse in a person who has violated social norms, but shaming can be re-integrative or dis-integrative. Re-integrative shaming focuses on labeling acts as undesirable; violators of social norms are shamed, but they are not shunned. Bonds between shame-ers and those being shamed are maintained, and the offender is eventually expected to fully rejoin society as a conforming individual. Dis-integrative shaming focuses on shunning offenders who are themselves considered deviant (opposed to the act) and blocks offenders from fully rejoining conforming society. As a result, shamed offenders are permanently stigmatized and are more likely to take on a deviant self-image.

Most modern criminal justice system policies are dis-integrative, resulting in a spoiled identity of 'criminal' (Murphy et al., 2011; Goffman, 1963). Modern collateral sanctions are frequently dis-integrative, particularly those associated with lifetime records and sanctions. With modern open criminal record databases available online, labeling by the criminal justice system via arrest and conviction serves as status degradation ceremonies that can reduce future life chances (Murphy et al., 2011; Garfinkel, 1956). Lifetime criminal records and sex offender registries and lifetime bans on voting, professional licensure, and public assistance do not provide mechanisms for redemption. They label *people* instead of *acts* as deviant, and they likely deepen criminal identities among convicts.

This is not to say that someone who is labeled a criminal and subject to dis-integrative shaming cannot desist from crime and take on pro-social identities. Positive turning points (see Life Course Perspective below) that create changes in social roles and relationships may encourage adoption of new identities and self-concepts (Maruna, 2001). However, "People are likely to remain in roles if they do not perceive the opportunity to change, even if opportunity exists objectively" (Matsueda & Heimer, 1997, p. 177).

Redemption rituals provide a mechanism to alter criminal images and combat societal stigmatization and marginalization. Redemption rituals counter CJS degradation ceremonies and certify rehabilitation, replacing the criminal label with a non-criminal label. Redemption rituals can make pro-social identities more salient or prominent, increasing the cognitive commitment and socioemotional attachment to them, and increasing the costs of jeopardizing newly achieved pro-social roles until such pro-social behavior is habitualized in a broad range of contexts (Matsueda & Heimer, 1997). Redemption ceremonies also signal to others (e.g., potential employers, family, friends, neighbors) that the convicted person has paid their debt to society and should be reintegrated into society.

Through a labeling/shaming/identity lens, collateral sanctions are theoretically positively and negatively associated with recidivism. Variation is determined by state and local implementation of sanctions (i.e., if they are re-integrative or dis-integrative). States that impose fewer collateral sanctions, particularly fewer lifetime collateral sanctions, have greater potential for shaming deviant actions and returning convicted felons to mainstream society as pro-social conformists. This is also true for states that impose collateral sanctions, even lifetime sanctions, but build in redemption mechanisms. These mechanisms may include re-enfranchisement of voting rights or access to public assistance for those who complete treatment, pay off financial legal obligations, and/or live arrest-free for a set period of time.

Strain

Strain theories hold that people are naturally social and compliant under normal or healthy social conditions, but people deviate from their natural state of compliancy when faced with pressure, lack of basic needs, and/or negative life experiences. Durkheim (1897 [1951]) stated that individuals experiencing crisis (either at the individual or societal level) experience a state of anomie or normlessness and are more prone to deviance such as crime or suicide. Merton (1938) argued that people in society experience anomie when they experience a disjunction between societal goals (particularly economic success) and access to goals through socially accepted means. When a society places more emphasis on goal attainment over legitimate means of attainment, people are more likely to react to lack of legitimate means through innovation (i.e., crime).

Agnew's (1992) General Strain Theory (GST) focuses on negative relationships with others that can increase the likelihood of a person experiencing negative affect and adapting via innovation/crime. According to Agnew, in addition to economic strain, strain can result from any social relationships or interactions of various recency, duration, and magnitude that: (a) prevent or threaten to prevent an individual from obtaining positively valued goals, (b) remove or threaten to remove positively valued things, and/or (c) present or threaten negative stimuli. Objective and subjective strain lead to adaptions via coping mechanisms. When strain results in negative emotions such as depression and especially anger, people are more likely to utilize criminal adaptions (Agnew, 1992, 2001). Negative life events and life hassles have a great impact on negative affect and criminal adaption (Agnew & White, 1992).

From a strain perspective, collateral sanctions likely increase recidivism. Many collateral sanctions prevent attainment of positively valued goals (e.g., occupational or status attainment, attainment of monetary and basic needs). They also remove positively valued things from convicted offenders (e.g., driving privileges, gun rights, participation in democracy, parental rights, housing, employment). Collateral sanctions can also present negative stimuli (e.g., SORN). Those who view such sanctions as unfair or unjust are even more likely to experience negative affect when faced with such strains and adapt via criminal innovation, increasing recidivism.

Social Disorganization

Social disorganization theory is often invoked in discussions of sex offender policy, especially evaluations of SORN and residency restrictions. According to social disorganization theorists, neighborhood cohesiveness and the ability of a community to organize and realize common goals (i.e., reducing crime) greatly influence crime rates in that area (Park, 1915; Shaw & McKay, 1942). Individuals within disorganized communities are less likely to experience effective social control and therefore are more likely to act in self-interested ways and commit crime (Shaw & McKay, 1942; Bursik & Grasmick, 1993).

Social disorganization theorists generally consider social control to be a positive force. However, formal social control in disorganized neighborhoods can weaken informal social control and unintentionally increase crime because high rates of incarceration of residents contributes to residential instability,[13] low economic status, and family disruption (Rose & Clear, 1998). Similarly, residency restrictions, public assistance bans, and employment blockages increase residential instability, low economic status, and family disruption. They may also decrease informal social control within neighborhoods. Concerns have also been raised in the collateral sanctions literature that residency restrictions, depending on how they are constructed and implemented, may result in convicted offenders being relegated to socially disorganized neighborhoods. This means they would have less access to needed services and informal social control and would be at a greater chance of recidivism.

Social Bonds

Hirschi's social bond theory (1969) argues that people are inherently deviant and prone to committing crime, but social bonds restrain nonconformity. Social bonds include attachment, commitment, involvement, and beliefs. Attachment refers to a connection to parents initially and one's spouse and children in adulthood. Commitment involves the investment to mainstream society. Involvement means participation in prosocial activities (e.g., school and employment). Belief refers to level of belief in law's legitimacy—result in constraining nonconformity. Social control from bonds is an external influence and subject to variability across time and space. Anything that weakens one's social bonds increases nonconformity and the likelihood that he/she will commit a crime (Hirschi, 1969).

Collateral sanctions that negatively impact social bonds can contribute to crime and recidivism. Loss of parental rights and driving privileges can seriously diminish family attachment bonds. Public assistance bans also threaten convicted felons' attachment to family. For instance, convicted felons may not be allowed to live in the same residence as their family due to housing restrictions. Similarly, they may not be welcomed as a contributing member of the household if they are not employed or able to bring in public assistance funds. Employment barriers due to criminal records limit involvement and commitment to pro-social bonds. Legal financial obligations (LFOs) may encourage involvement in licit employment by placing financial expectations on a convicted felon that could result in incarceration if not paid, but they may discourage employment if substantial portions of the earnings go toward paying LFOs and the person feels that they cannot get ahead. These sanctions that can limit one's sense of inclusion in society may reduce his/her stake in conformity, involvement/commitment to pro-social activities, and belief in law's legitimacy, especially if punishments are viewed as unfair, increasing the likelihood of recidivism.

Life Course Perspective

Most prisoner reentry and desistance literature (but not policy) is guided by social control theory and labeling theory via the life course perspective, which is developmental in nature (Laub & Sampson, 2001; Sampson & Laub, 1993, 1992). Early life conditions and life experiences set and reset crime trajectories. Transition points such as marriage or the start of a new career can result in greater social bonds, social control, and conformity. When such life events or transition points result in changed trajectories, they are referred to as "turning points." In addition to providing new opportunities for establishing quality pro-social bonds and informal social control, turning points can provide for different routine activities, reduced strain, and changes in social roles and identity (Sampson & Laub, 1993; Sampson & Laub, 1997; Warr, 1998; Maruna, 2001). As a result, turning points can alter or solidify one's criminal trajectory.

Labeling someone as criminal followed by possible incarceration contributes to cumulative disadvantage over the life course:

> [I]ncarceration appears to cut off opportunities and prospects for stable employment later in life. This 'knifing off' has important developmental implications—job stability and also

marital attachment in adulthood are significantly related to change in adult crime. . . . Therefore, even if the direct effect of incarceration is zero or possibly even negative (i.e., a deterrent), its indirect effects may well be criminogenic (positive) as structural labeling theorists have long argued.

(Sampson & Laub, 1997, p. 150)

Similarly, being subject to numerous collateral sanctions as the result of felony conviction can also 'knife' off positive social bonds, pro-social opportunities that can reduce strain, and pro-social identities. More specifically, labeling someone as a felon at one stage in his/her life and subjecting them to long lasting punishments that limit family bonds, work opportunity, safe and stable residency, and inclusion in greater society may lead to greater rates of recidivism by denying the person access to mechanisms for desistance. Disadvantage accumulates, and for those who are most disadvantaged in our society, "Deficits and disadvantages pile up faster, and this has continuing negative consequences for later development in the form of 'environmental traps.'" (Sampson & Laub, 1997, p. 153).

Empirical Findings

Since 2000, there has been a substantial increase in research looking at collateral consequences of punishment and collateral sanctions in particular (Morenoff & Harding, 2014; Mauer & Chesney-Lind, 2002; Travis, 2005; Whittle, 2016). However, the empirical literature on collateral consequences is still incomplete, especially when looking at the relationship between collateral sanctions and recidivism. Research on collateral sanctions and recidivism is limited in part due to the significant difficulty in conducting such research. The "invisible" nature of collateral sanctions makes it difficult to identify if and how policies impact individual or community crime and recidivism rates, and recidivism research itself is complicated as recidivism is difficult to effectively study or even define. Research rarely looks directly at collateral sanctions and recidivism, leaving policy makers and social scientists making inferences based on findings from related research.

As predicted by the major theories of crime, the growing body of literature on collateral sanction policies and recidivism indicates that such collateral sanctions typically contribute to recidivism or have a null effect. Much of the literature indicates mixed findings. (For a review of the empirical literature on collateral sanctions' effects on recidivism, see Whittle, 2016).

The literature indicates that collateral sanctions in the forms of legal financial obligations are positively related with recidivism (Becket & Harris, 2011; Harris, 2016). Open access to criminal records prevents reintegration, which contributes to recidivism (Sampson & Laub, 1993; Uggen, 2000; Chiricos, Barrick, Bales, & Bontrager, 2007). Criminal records result in lower callback and employment rates (Pager, 2003, 2007). States with greater access to criminal record information online have higher recidivism rates (Sohoni, 2014).

Overall, research on collateral sanctions in the forms of public assistance bans (TANF, SNAP, and public housing assistance) finds them to be positively associated with recidivism. Access to welfare benefits among ex-offenders with serious medical needs was found to reduce recidivism (Sung, 2011). Stable, quality housing contributes to desistance from crime and reduces recidivism rates (Bruce, Crowley, Jeffcote, & Coulston, 2014; Metraux & Culhane, 2004; Wright, Zhang, Farabee, & Braatz, 2014). State-based financial support for housing assistance and life skills programs can reduce recidivism (Holtfreter, Reisig, & Morash, 2004), but "welfare laws restricting offenders with drug convictions from obtaining public assistance (e.g., food stamps) create additional hurdles" to moving out of poverty. However, according to state-level research, states that restrict convicted felons' access to public assistance have lower recidivism rates (Sohoni, 2014).

Research on voter disenfranchisement laws indicates that such collateral sanctions may also contribute to recidivism but findings to date are mixed. Voters have lower arrest rates than nonvoters

(Manza & Uggen, 2004); however, it is difficult to establish a causal relationship between voter disenfranchisement laws or voting and recidivism. As stated by Manza and Uggen (2006), doing so "would require a large-scale longitudinal survey that tracked released felons in their communities and closely monitored changes in their political and criminal activity." It is unclear how many people who are disenfranchised would vote if allowed by law, and it is difficult to assess how disenfranchisement impacts identity, bonds, opportunities, strain, social disorganization, and so on. Interviews with convicted felons indicate that 78% of convicted felons want to vote and/or feel voting is related to reintegration (Miller & Spillane, 2012); for individuals in this population, disenfranchisement may contribute to feelings of alienation and marginalization, indirectly contributing to crime and recidivism. State-level analysis however indicates that felon disenfranchisement laws are associated with lower recidivism.

Research on sex offender-specific collateral sanctions including registration, notification, and residency restrictions laws generally finds mixed or null effects on recidivism (Huebner et al., 2014; Nobles, Levenson, & Youstin, 2012; Socia, 2012). Qualitative research on convicted sex offenders indicates collateral sanctions can contribute to recidivism (Tewksbury & Lees, 2006; Kilmer & Leon, 2017). Sex offender-specific collateral sanctions have been found to interact with extralegal restrictions, contributing to social rejection and isolation, which in turn diminish reintegration and desistance from crime (Kilmer & Leon, 2017).

Firearm restrictions for persons convicted of felony crimes are the only collateral sanctions research indicates may reduce recidivism. Waiting periods for gun purchases are associated with lower homicide rates (McDowall, Loftin, & Wiersema, 1995), and convicted felons prevented from buying guns due to background checks were 18% less likely to be charged with a gun offense at three-year follow-up compared to people arrested for but not convicted of a felony (and therefore permitted to purchase a gun) (Wright, Wintemute, & Rivara, 1999).

Other than firearm restrictions, research indicates that collateral sanctions in general do not reduce recidivism and may in fact contribute to recidivism. Despite the growing body of literature on collateral sanctions, much is unknown about the impacts of these policies on recidivism and other social issues: "Further research should attempt to understand how collateral restrictions fit into a broader system of disadvantage for already marginalized social groups" (Wheelock, 2005, p. 87).

Collateral sanction policies remain pervasive in the United States despite theoretical predictions and empirical evidence indicating they and other forms of punishment significantly contribute to crime, recidivism, and other social ills. Many states, however, have made policy changes to reduce felon disenfranchisement and other forms of collateral sanctions (The Sentencing Project, 2014).

Collateral Sanctions and Concentrated Disadvantage

Although written in race- and class-neutral terms, collateral sanctions disproportionately impact convicted felons who are impoverished, are racial/ethnic minorities, or who have mental or physical health problems. Felony collateral sanctions contribute to "the disadvantages that characterize this population, including low levels of human capital and a high prevalence of mental health problems and substance use (Visher & Travis, 2003) . . . [and] make economic stability and security a significant challenge" (Harding et al., 2014, p. 441).

People from marginalized groups and disadvantaged backgrounds are more likely to be financially strained, have weak social networks, come from disorganized or disenfranchised communities, have greater health problems, and need public assistance. They are at higher risk of experiencing victimization and discrimination. They are also more likely to come into contact with the criminal justice system, be convicted of a felony, and therefore be susceptible to felony collateral sanction policies. Once labeled a felon, most are left more disadvantaged than they were before conviction.

People who are financially disadvantaged before conviction often struggle to pay post-conviction legal financial obligations. Convicted felons in some jurisdictions must pay monitoring fees and minimum payment penalties. Unpaid LFOs can accrue interest and result in wage garnishment, criminal charges, and additional punishments (Harris, 2016). People who cannot afford to pay off LFOs may remain under formal supervision for longer and may have their voting rights reinstatement delayed.

Housing and employment limitations caused by collateral sanctions disproportionately impact people from disadvantaged backgrounds. Take housing sanctions for example: If an individual cannot afford his/her own residence after conviction, he/she may try to live with family or friends. However, people from impoverished families are more likely to be unable to live with their family or friends if they reside in public housing since convicted felons are generally barred for a set period of time after conviction or release from prison. This prevents many people from returning to live with their families in public housing and can diminish social bonds and reintegration. Felony conviction can also result in banishment from homeless shelters and community centers (Beckett & Herbert, 2010). Additionally, people on probation or parole are often not allowed to live with family and friends if they have criminal record. Although written in race- and class-neutral terms, policies that prohibit convicted felons from accessing public assistance and other forms of social service disproportionately impact people who have greater need for assistance and face greater barriers. Collateral sanctions are a way society punishes the poor in particular (Wacquant, 2009).

Employment sanctions also disproportionately impact minorities. Employment is difficult to obtain for convicted felons in general. However, it is particularly difficult for people with sparse legal work histories, low educational attainment, poor life and social skills, and mental and physical health conditions. Undocumented persons, whether in the U.S. legally or not, also struggle obtaining legal identification and employment. Racial minorities with felony convictions face particular difficulty finding gainful employment. Pager (2003, 2007) found that persons identified as convicted felons were less likely to receive a callback from a potential employer than applicants without a criminal record, no matter the applicant's race. However, there are significant racial disparities between job applicants: Among African-American applicants, those *without* a criminal record were called back 14% of the time compared to 5% of applicants *with* a criminal record. Among white applicants, those *without* a criminal record received a callback 34% of the time compared to 17% of applicants *with* a criminal record (Pager, 2007). In other words,

> A white applicant *with* a *criminal record* was just as likely to receive a callback as a black applicant *without* any criminal record (17 vs. 14 percent). . . . [B]eing black in America today is just about the same as having a felony conviction in terms of one's chances of finding a job.
>
> (Pager, 2007, pp. 90–91)

Racism and collateral sanctions (e.g., open criminal records, legally allowing questions about criminal history on job applications) make reintegration more difficult. Research like Pagers's (2003, 2007) helps illustrate how collateral sanctions "fit into a broader system of disadvantage for already marginalized social groups" (Wheelock, 2005, p. 87). Michelle Alexander describes the web of formally race- and class-neutral collateral sanction laws that disproportionately impact minorities as a modern-day reincarnation of Jim Crow in which individuals convicted of a felony are stigmatized and made permanent second-class citizens (Alexander, 2010).

Although collateral sanctions apply to individuals convicted of a felony, collateral sanctions have macro-level effects. Convicted felons typically return to disadvantaged communities that suffer from resource deprivation and racial segregation, which are positively associated with recidivism. Cycling of convicted felons in and out of disadvantaged neighborhoods contributes to disadvantage for individuals and communities by further concentrating marginalized individuals in highly policed communities (Clear, 2002; Clear, 2007; Burch, 2013).

Concentrations of convicted individuals in impoverished communities can contribute to social disorganization and compounded community-level disadvantage. For instance, felon disenfranchisement has disproportionately impacted non-white communities. African Americans in particular are disproportionately barred from serving on juries and voting; one in 13 potential black voters are disenfranchised compared to one in 56 potential non-black voters (Manza & Uggen, 2006; Alexander, 2010; The Sentencing Project, 2014). In other words, African Americans are disproportionately not included in the democratic process; they are denied political voice as an individual and arguably the right to be tried by a jury of peers (Manza & Uggen, 2006; Alexander, 2010). At the community level, felon disenfranchisement has been found to have contributed to Republican victories between 1972 and 2000 (Manza & Uggen, 2006). Conservative climate, racial threat, and religiosity are significantly related to state-level collateral sanctions (Whittle & Parker, 2014). Not only do collateral sanctions compound already existing disadvantage for individuals and communities, collateral sanction policies can also contribute to perpetuation and expansion of collateral sanctions. Collateral sanctions stigmatize already disadvantaged groups as second-class communities, which maintains inequality and reifies the New Jim Crow and the United States' modern caste system (Alexander, 2010):

> Given the imprint that the criminal justice system has stamped on racial minorities throughout U.S. history, it was foreseeable that the expansion of collateral consequences would impact African Americans and Latinos disproportionately. Thus, the dramatic growth of collateral consequences, particularly those that attach to drug offenses, can be understood as extensions of criminal justice policies that unfairly target people of color.
>
> (Pinard, 2010, p. 517)

Conclusion

Collateral sanctions are laws, rules, and regulations that limit convicted felons' civil rights, access to public assistance, and life opportunities in addition to formal sentences imposed by a judge. These "invisible punishments" can greatly diminish ex-felons' ability to reintegrate into society and may contribute to recidivism. Despite harms associated with collateral sanction policies, collateral sanctions are prevalent at the federal, state, and local levels and impact almost every realm of life among convicted felons. To better understand collateral sanctions' relationship to recidivism and the pervasiveness of such policies, a review of collateral sanction literature was conducted. This article reviewed the theories most commonly invoked in collateral sanctions literature, including theoretical predictions regarding how various collateral sanctions and recidivism relate. This concluding section discusses why collateral sanction policies persist despite lack of empirical support or theoretical grounding.

Due to the many forms of collateral sanctions and various criminological theories, the field of collateral sanctions invokes many theoretical frames. Labeling/shaming/identity, social bonds, and strain theories in the life course perspective are most commonly invoked. Deterrence, opportunity/ routine activities, strain, and social disorganization are also used to discuss collateral sanctions' potential effects and guide empirical research; however, these are used less commonly—except in regard to policies and studies that commonly rely on routine activities/opportunity theory when evaluating the effects of sex offender residency restrictions and SORN policies.

Rational choice/deterrence theories are frequently used to discuss and even justify collateral sanctions related to public criminal records, voter disenfranchisement, employment and public assistance restrictions, financial legal opportunities, and sex offender-specific sanctions despite theoretical predictions that such sanctions will have no effect on recidivism, especially given that most people are not fully aware of collateral sanctions and therefore do not factor such sanctions into decisions to commit crime. Opportunity/Routine activities theories are commonly invoked when discussing public criminal records, voter disenfranchisement (in the case of voter fraud only), employment and public assistance restrictions, sex offender-specific sanctions, and firearm restriction collateral sanctions; however, theoretical predictions and empirical findings regarding sanctions and recidivism are mixed. Labeling/shaming/identity theories' predictions are mixed depending on the nature of sanctions connected to public criminal records, voter disenfranchisement, employment restrictions, sex offender-specific, and legal financial obligation sanctions although empirical research indicates a positive association between sanctions and recidivism. Strain, social disorganization, and social bonds theories and life course perspective are frequently included in public criminal records, voter disenfranchisement, employment and public assistance restrictions, sex offender-specific sanctions, and legal financial obligation sanctions; these theories predict a positive association between collateral sanctions and recidivism.

To reduce crime and lower recidivism, policies should be theoretically and empirically informed. Collateral sanction policies however are not theoretically informed. This review of the literature finds the major theories of crime invoked in the collateral sanction discourse typically predict a positive relationship between many collateral sanction policies and recidivism (see Table 2.1). Strain, social disorganization, social bonds, and life course perspectives all predict a positive relationship between recidivism and most collateral sanction policies, especially permanent and/or harsh sanctions. Opportunity/routine activities and labeling/shaming/identity theories' predictions are mixed and often contextual, with labeling/shaming/identity theories predicting positive associations between recidivism and harsh or dis-integrative policies.

These theoretical predictions hold true in the empirical literature. Except in the category of firearm restrictions, findings from empirical studies looking at the relationship between felony collateral sanctions and recidivism do not support such policies; 39 studies found a positive relationship between collateral sanctions and recidivism compared to only nine that found a negative association (Whittle, 2016).[14] This should come as no surprise to those familiar with criminological theories and prisoner reentry issues. Collateral sanctions serve as barriers to prisoner reentry, promote recidivism among people convicted of a felony, and contribute to crime and recidivism.

Although formally race- and class-neutral, collateral sanctions disproportionately impact racial minorities and people struggling financially. Collateral sanction policies interact with one another as well as extralegal factors (e.g., race, ethnicity, appearance, work history) to create additional barriers to reentry, which compound existing disadvantage. Compound disadvantage resulting from collateral sanctions occur at the individual level and have community-level effects, including influencing political representation and policy.

Collateral sanctions are typically considered a part of or a type of collateral consequences of felony conviction and therefore are argued to be "unintended consequences." However, keystone criminological theories invoked in collateral sanction discourse and literature as reviewed in this article predict positive relationships between such sanctions and recidivism. Additionally, empirical research on the effects of collateral sanctions over the last two decades indicates such sanctions typically increase recidivism. Given the growing body of literature including consensus between theoretical predictions and empirical findings, collateral sanction policies should cease to be considered "unintended consequences" of felony convictions. If theory predicts increases in recidivism and empirical evidence supports those predictions, collateral sanctions and associated increases in recidivism should not be categorized as *unintended* consequences; they should instead be understood as *intended* consequences of collateral sanction policies.

The question remains then, why do such sanctions persist despite theoretical predictions and empirical evidence? Why would political leaders intentionally design and implement collateral sanction policies that predictably increase recidivism?

It is possible that political leaders perpetuate collateral sanction policies because they are unaware of criminological theory and empirical evidence that collateral sanctions often contribute to recidivism, and often times this is the case as many legal actors are not aware of collateral sanction policies and their ramifications. Or it may be that political leaders are informed and at least partially aware of collateral sanction policies' impacts on recidivism and continue implementing and sustaining criminogenic policies anyways. Political leaders and street-level bureaucrats may knowingly implement and carry out criminogenic collateral sanction policies because of financial constraints, legal considerations, and political demands from constituents or special interest groups (see Alexander, 2010). Collateral sanctions are intended extensions of punishment for criminal actions and a mechanism for extending social control beyond formal periods of punishment to perpetuate inequality.

Notes

1 See Chapter 3 "The Collateral Consequences of Incarceration for Housing" by Kirk.
2 See Chapter 5 "Impact of Incarceration on Employment Prospects" by Apel & Ramakers.
3 See Chapter 6 "Incarceration, Reentry, and Health" by Fahmy & Wallace and Chapter 7 "The Psychological Effects of Contact With the Criminal Justice System" by LeBel & Richie.
4 See Chapter 8 "Impacts of Incarceration on Children and Families" by Northcutt Bohmert & Wakefield. Criminal records are frequently used as justification to deny parents custody of their children. The Adoption and Safe Families Act of 1997 "accelerates the termination of parental rights for children who have been in foster care for fifteen of the most recent twenty-two months" (Travis, 2002, p. 24). Additionally, the Adoption and Safe Families Act of 1997 prohibits people with felony records from being foster or adoptive parents.
5 Although collateral consequences of interactions with formal punishment systems are generally greater than informal punishments, informal punishments can contribute to formal involvement in the criminal justice system. As such, a collateral consequence of non-criminal punishments can be formal involvement with the criminal justice system (e.g., school-to-prison pipeline).
6 See Pinard (2010) for a comparative analysis of collateral sanctions in the U.S., England, Canada, and South Africa.
7 This overview does not include all types of collateral sanctions, in part due to the impractical nature of identifying all of the policies given the nature of these "invisible punishments." Also, some categories of collateral sanctions were excluded from the current review due to insufficient literature for synthesis.
8 See Chapter 10 "Punished for Being Punished: Collateral Consequences of a Drug Offense Conviction" by Nellis.
9 Definitions of recidivism include committing a new crime or technical violation of the conditions of one's release, being charged with a new crime or technical violation of the conditions of one's release, re-arrest, and/or re-incarceration. Being charged with a new crime/technical violation, re-arrest, and re-incarceration definitions are typically used in recidivism research as they are easier to measure than committing new crimes and technical violations that frequently go undetected or unrecorded.
10 Voter disenfranchisement often goes hand-in-hand with elimination from jury pools; however, research and discussion of collateral sanctions' impacts on jury pools is not robust.
11 See Chapter 11 "Compounded Stigmatization: Collateral Consequences of a Sex Offense Conviction" by Kras, McGuirk, Pleggenkuhle & Huebner.
12 Recidivism includes committing a new crime or technical violation of the conditions of one's release, being charged with a new crime or technical violation, re-arrest, and/or re-incarceration. Measuring new crimes and technical violations is difficult as they frequently go undetected or unrecorded. Therefore, most research on recidivism and collateral sanctions uses new charges, re-arrest, and re-incarceration definitions of recidivism.
13 See Chapter 4 "Residential Insecurities and Neighborhood Quality Following Incarceration" by Remster & Warner.
14 Null or mixed findings were found in 26 studies, particularly among those looking at sex offender residency restrictions and SORN policies.

References

Agnew, R. (1992). Foundation for a general strain theory of crime and delinquency. *Criminology, 30*(1), 47–88.
Agnew, R. (2001). Building on the foundation of general strain theory: Specifying the types of strain most likely to lead to crime and delinquency. *Journal of Research in Crime and Delinquency, 38*(4), 319–361.
Agnew, R., & White, H. R. (1992). An empirical test of general strain theory. *Criminology, 30*(4), 475–500.
Alexander, M. (2010). *The new Jim Crow: Mass incarceration in the age of colorblindness.* New York, NY: New Press.
Arditti, J. A. (2012). *Parental incarceration and the family: Psychological and social effects of imprisonment on children, parents, and caregivers.* New York, NY: New York University Press.

Barnes, J. C., Dukes T., Tewksbury R., & De Troye T. M. (2009). Analyzing the impact of a statewide residence restriction law on South Carolina sex offenders. *Criminal Justice Policy Review, 20*(1), 21–43.

Beccaria, C. (1764, 1986). *On crimes and punishment.* Indianapolis: Hackett Pub. Co.

Becker, H. S. (1963). *Outsiders: Studies in the sociology of deviance.* London: Free Press of Glencoe.

Beckett, K., & Harris, A. (2011). On cash and conviction: Monetary sanctions as misguided policy. *Criminology and Public Policy, 10*(3), 509–537.

Beckett, K., & Herbert, S. (2010). *Banished: The new social control in urban America.* New York, NY: Oxford University Press.

Bentham, J. (1789). *An introduction to the principles of morals and legislation.* London, UK: Pickering.

Braithwaite, J. (1989). *Crime, shame, and reintegration.* New York, NY: Cambridge University Press.

Brown, M., & Bloom, B. (2009). Reentry and renegotiating motherhood: Maternal identity and success on parole. *Crime and Delinquency, 55*(2), 313–336.

Bruce, M., Crowley, S., Jeffcote, N., & Coulston, B. (2014). Community DSPD pilot services in South London: Rates of reconviction and impact of supported housing on reducing recidivism. *Criminal Behavior and Mental Health, 24*(2), 129–140.

Burch, T. R. (2013). *Trading democracy for justice: Criminal convictions and the decline of neighborhood political participation.* Chicago, IL: University of Chicago Press.

Bursik, R. J., & Grasmick, H. G. (1993). Longitudinal neighborhood profiles in delinquency: The decomposition of change. *Journal of Quantitative Criminology, 8*(3), 247–263.

Chiricos, T., Barrick, K. Bales, W., & Bontrager, S. (2007). The labeling of convicted felons and its consequences for recidivism. *Criminology, 45*(3), 547–581.

Clear, T. R. (2002). The problem with 'addition by subtraction': The prison-crime relationship in low-income communities. In M. Mauer & M. Chesney-Lind (Eds.), *Invisible punishment: The collateral consequences of mass incarceration* (pp. 181–193). New York, NY: New Press.

Clear, T. R. (2007). *Imprisoning communities: How mass incarceration makes disadvantaged neighborhoods worse.* Oxford: Oxford University Press.

Cohen, L. E., & Felson, M. (1979). Social change and crime rate trends: A routine activities approach. *American Sociological Review, 8*(4), 389–406.

Demleitner, N. (1999). Preventing internal exile: The need for restrictions on collateral sentencing consequences. *Stanford Law and Policy Review, 11*, 153–162.

Durkheim, E. (1897, 1951). *Suicide: A study of sociology.* New York, NY: Free Press.

Garfinkel, H. (1956). Conditions of successful degradation ceremonies. *American Journal of Sociology, 61*(5), 420–424.

Goffman, E. (1963). *Stigma: Notes on the management of spoiled identity.* Englewood Cliffs, NJ: Prentice-Hall.

Harding, D. J., Wyse, J. J. B., Dobson, C., & Morenoff, J. D. (2014). Making ends meet after prison. *Journal of Policy Analysis and Management, 33*(2), 440–470.

Harris, A. (2016). *A pound of flesh: Monetary sanctions as a permanent punishment for poor.* New York, NY: Russell Sage Foundation.

Hirschi, T. (1969). *Causes of delinquency.* Berkeley, CA: University of California Press.

Holtfreter, K., Reisig, M. D., & Morash, M. (2004). Poverty, state capital, and recidivism among women offenders. *Criminology and Public Policy, 3*(2), 185–208.

Huebner, B. M., Kras, K. R., Rydberg, J., Bynum, T. S., Grommon, E., & Pleggenkuhle, B. (2014). The effect and implications of sex offender residence restrictions. *Criminology and Public Policy, 13*(1), 139–168.

James, D. J., & Glaze, L. E. (2006). Mental health problems of prison and jail inmates. Retrieved from www.bjs.gov/content/pub/pdf/mhppji.pdf

Kilmer, A., & Leon, C. (2017). 'Nobody worries about our children': Unseen impacts of sex offender registration on families with school-age children and implications for desistance. *Criminal Justice Studies, 30*(2), 181–201.

Laub, J. H., & Sampson, R. J. (2001). Understanding desistance from crime. *Crime and Justice, 28*, 1–69.

Legal Action Center. (2009). After prison: Roadblocks to reentry: A report on state legal barriers facing people with criminal records. Retrieved from www.lac.org/roadblocks-to-reentry/upload/lacreport/Roadblocks-to-Reentry—2009.pdf

Lemert, E. M. (1951). *Social pathology: A systematic approach to the theory of sociopathic behavior.* New York, NY: McGraw-Hill.

Levingston, K. D., & Turetsky, V. (2007). Debtors' prison: Prisoners' accumulation of debt as a barrier to reentry. *Clearinghouse Review, Journal of Poverty Law and Policy, 41*, 187–197.

Mallett, C. A. (2016). The School-to-prison pipeline: From school punishment to rehabilitative inclusion. *Preventing School Failure, 60*(4), 296–304.

Manza, J., & Uggen, C. (2004). Punishment and democracy: Disenfranchisement of nonincarcerated felons in the United States. *Perspectives on Politics, 2*(3), 491–505.

Manza, J., & Uggen, C. (2006). *Locked out: Felon disenfranchisement and American democracy.* New York, NY: Oxford University Press.

Maruna, S. (2001). *Making good: How ex-convicts reform and rebuild their lives.* Washington, DC: American Psychological Association.

Matsueda, R. L., & Heimer, K. (1997). A symbolic interactionist theory of role-transitions, role-commitments, and delinquency. In T. P. Thornberry (Ed.), *Developmental Theories of Crime and Delinquency* (pp. 163–213). New Brunswick, NJ: Transaction Publishers.

Mauer, M., & Chesney-Lind, M. (2002). *Invisible Punishment: The Collateral Consequences of Mass Imprisonment.* New York, NY: New Press.

McDowall, D., Loftin, C., & Wiersema, B. (1995). Easing concealed firearms laws: Effects on homicides in three states. *Journal of Criminal Law and Criminology, 86,* 193–206.

Merton, R. K. (1938). Social structure and anomie. *American Sociological Review, 3,* 672–682.

Metraux, S., & Culhane, D. P. (2004). Homeless shelter use and reincarceration following prison release. *Criminology and Public Policy, 3*(2), 139–160.

Miller, B. L., & Spillane, J. (2012). Civil death: An examination of ex-felon disenfranchisement and reintegration. *Punishment & Society, 14*(4), 402–428.

Morenoff, J. D., & Harding, D. J. (2014). Incarceration, prisoner reentry, and communities. *Annual Review of Sociology, 40,* 411–429.

Murphy, D. S., Flehhan, B., Richards, S. C., & Jones, R. S. (2011). The electronic "Scarlet Letter": Criminal backgrounding and a perpetual spoiled identity. *Journal of Offender Rehabilitation, 50*(3), 101–118.

National American Bar Association. *National inventory of the collateral consequences of conviction.* Retrieved from https://niccc.csgjusticecenter.org

Nobles, M. R., Levenson, J. S., & Youstin, T. J. (2012). Effectiveness of residence restrictions in preventing sex offense recidivism. *Crime and Delinquency, 58,* 491–513.

Pager, D. (2003). The mark of a criminal record. *American Journal of Sociology, 108*(5), 937–975.

Pager, D. (2007). *Marked: Race, crime, and finding work in an era of mass incarceration.* Chicago, IL: University of Chicago Press.

Parenti, C. (2001). *Lockdown America: Police and prisons in the age of crisis.* New York, NY: Versa.

Park, R. E. (1915). The city: Suggestions for the investigation of human behavior in the city environment. *American Journal of Sociology, 20,* 577–612.

Paternoster, R. (2010). How much do we really know about criminal deterrence? *Journal of Criminal Law and Criminology, 100*(3), 765–824.

Petersilia, J. (2003). *When prisoners come home: Parole and prisoner reentry.* New York, NY: Oxford University Press.

Pinard, M. (2006). An integrated perspective of the collateral consequences of criminal convictions and the reentry of formerly incarcerated individuals. *Boston Law Review, 86,* 623–690.

Pinard, M. (2010). Collateral consequences of criminal conviction: Confronting issues of race and dignity. *New York University Law Review, 85*(2), 457–534.

Reiss, A. J., Jr. (1976). Delinquency as the failure of personal and social controls. *American Sociological Review, 16,* 196–207.

Rose, D., & Clear, T. (1998). Incarceration, social capital and crime: Implications for social disorganization theory. *Criminology, 36,* 441–479.

Rubinstein, G., & Mukamal, D. (2002). Welfare and housing: Denial of benefits to drug offenders. In M. Mauer and M. Chesney-Lind (Eds.), *Invisible punishment: The collateral consequences of mass imprisonment* (pp. 37–49). New York, NY: New York Press.

Sampson, R. J., & Laub, J. H. (1992). Crime and deviance in the life-course. *Annual Review of Sociology, 18,* 63–84.

Sampson, R. J., & Laub, J. H. (1993). *Crime in the making: Pathways and turning points through life.* Cambridge, MA: Harvard University Press.

Sampson, R. J., & Laub, J. H. (1997). A life-course theory of cumulative disadvantage and the stability of delinquency. In T. P. Thornberry (Ed.), *Developmental theories of crime and delinquency.* New Brunswick, NJ: Transaction Publishers.

The Sentencing Project. (2014). *Felony disenfranchisement laws in the United States.* Retrieved from www.sentencingproject.org/publications/felony-disenfranchisement-laws-in-the-united-states/

Shaw, C. R., & McKay, H. S. (1942). *Juvenile delinquency in urban areas.* Chicago, IL: University of Chicago Press.

Shaw, C. R., McKay, H. D., Zorbaugh, F., & Cottrell, L. S. (1929). *Delinquency areas.* Chicago, IL: University of Chicago Press.

Socia, K. M. (2012). The efficacy of county-level sex offender residence restrictions in New York. *Crime and Delinquency, 58*, 612–642.

Sohoni, T. W. P. (2014). *The effects of collateral consequence laws on state rates of returns to prison.* Washington, DC: National Institute of Justice.

Stoll, M. A., & S. D. Bushway. (2008). The effect of criminal background checks on hiring ex-offenders. *Criminology and Public Policy, 7*(3), 371–404.

Sung, H. E. (2011). From diversion to reentry: Recidivism risks among graduates of an alternative to incarceration program. *Criminal Justice Policy Review, 22*(2), 219–234.

Tannenbaum, F. (1938). *Crime and the community.* New York, NY: Ginn & Company.

Tewksbury, R., & Lees, M. (2006). Perceptions of sex offender registration: Collateral consequences and community experiences. *Sociological Spectrum, 26*(3), 309–334.

Travis, J. (2002). Invisible punishment: An instrument of social exclusion. In M. Mauer & M. Chesney-Lind (Eds.), *Invisible punishment: The collateral consequences of mass imprisonment* (pp. 15–36). New York, NY: New Press.

Travis, J. (2005). *But they all come back: Facing the challenges of prisoner reentry.* Washington, DC: U.S. Department of Justice, Urban Institute Press.

Uggen, C. (2000). Work as a turning point in the life course of criminals: A duration model of age, employment and recidivism. *American Sociological Review, 65*, 529–546.

Uggen, C., Manza, J., & Thompson, M. (2006). Citizenship, democracy, and the civic reintegration of criminal offenders. *Annals of the American Academy of Political and Social Science, 605*, 281–310.

Uggen, C., Wakefield, S., & Western, B. (2005). Work and family perspectives on reentry. In J. Travis & C. Visher (Eds.), *Prisoner reentry in America.* New York, NY: Cambridge University Press.

Visher, C., & Travis, J. (2003). Transitions from prison to community: Understanding individual pathways. *Annual Review of Sociology, 19*, 89–113.

Wakeman, S. E., McKinney, M. E., & Rich, J. D. (2009). Filling the gap: The importance of Medicaid continuity for former inmates. *Journal of General Internal Medicine, 24*(7), 860–862.

Wacquant, L. (2009). *Punishing the poor: The neoliberal government of social insecurity.* Durham, NC: Duke University Press.

Warr, M. (1998). Life-course transitions, self-control and desistance from crime. *Criminology, 36*(2), 183–216.

Wheelock, D. (2005). Collateral consequences and racial inequality: Felon status restrictions as a system of disadvantage. *Journal of Contemporary Criminal Justice, 21*(1), 82–90.

Whittle, T. N. (2016). Felony collateral sanctions effects on recidivism: A literature review. *Criminal Justice Policy Review.* doi:10.1177/0887403415623328

Whittle, T. N., & Parker, K. F. (2014). Public ideology, racial threat, and felony collateral sanctions: A state-level analysis. *Criminal Justice Review, 39*(4), 432–454.

Wilcox, P., Madensen, T. D., & Tillyer, M. S. (2007). Guardianship in context: Implications for burglary victimization risk and prevention. *Criminology, 45*(4), 771–803.

Wolf, K. C., & Kupchik, A. (2017). School suspensions and adverse experiences in adulthood. *Justice Quarterly, 34*(3), 407–430.

Wright, B. J., Zhang, S. X., Farabee, D., & Braatz, R. (2014). Prisoner reentry research from 2000 to 2010: Results of a narrative review. *Criminal Justice Review, 39*(1), 37–57.

Wright, M. A., Wintemute, G. J., & Rivara, F. A. (1999). Effectiveness of denial of handgun purchase to persons believed to be at high risk for firearm violence. *American Journal of Public Health, 89*(1), 88–90.

PART II

Broad Impacts

3

THE COLLATERAL CONSEQUENCES OF INCARCERATION FOR HOUSING

David S. Kirk

Introduction

At this very moment, about one in every 37 U.S. adults—almost 7 million individuals—is in prison, jail, or under some form of community supervision (Kaebel & Glaze, 2016). An additional 5 million people previously served time in prison and 20 million people in the U.S. have a felony conviction (Shannon et al., 2017; see also Muller & Wildeman, 2016). For a variety of reasons related to not only the stigma of a criminal record, but also the loss of human and social capital, formerly incarcerated persons and, more broadly, individuals with a criminal record face daunting challenges to securing stable housing. This is problematic because stable housing is the foundation of rehabilitation and reintegration.

In this chapter, I take stock of what is known about the collateral consequences of contact with the criminal justice system with respect to housing barriers. The American Bar Association (ABA) defines "collateral consequences of conviction" as "legal and regulatory sanctions and restrictions that limit or prohibit people with criminal records from accessing employment, occupational licensing, housing, voting, education, and other opportunities" (ABA, 2013). To this definition it is important to add that the consequences of punishment do not just accrue to the convicted individual, but also to families and communities.

To proceed, I first provide an overview of the common barriers to housing for persons with criminal records. As part of this overview, I provide a contrast between the United States and the United Kingdom in terms of approaches to the privacy of criminal records as well as differences in the provision of government-funded housing assistance. I then describe what is known empirically about the collateral consequences of contact with the criminal justice system for housing opportunities and housing instability. Thereafter I highlight enduring challenges to advancing the collateral consequences literature, particularly data challenges and selection bias.

Barriers to Housing

Formerly imprisoned and convicted individuals face many barriers to securing safe and stable housing, including a lack of income, reluctance or discrimination by private landlords, and a lack of access to public housing and housing vouchers.

Lack of Income and Employment

Perhaps the most basic hurdle to finding secure housing is a lack of income, which is obviously related to the generally dismal employment prospects of formerly imprisoned individuals, but also to restrictions on benefits to convicted individuals including food stamps, Temporary Assistance for Needy Families (TANF), and Supplemental Security Income (SSI) (Geller & Curtis, 2011; Harding, Wyse, Dobson, & Morenoff, 2014; Herbert, Morenoff, & Harding, 2015). It has been well documented that the employment histories of convicted individuals before even entering prison tend to be low paying and unstable (see Western, 2006). In turn, a criminal record and a stint of incarceration have a negative impact on the likelihood of employment and reduces wages and wage-growth among those individuals who do manage to find employment post-release (Apel & Ramakers, 2018; Apel & Sweeten, 2010; Pager, 2003; Western & Pettit, 2005). Some research finds that income and employment are more important considerations in landlords' housing decisions than criminal records (Clark, 2007; Evans, 2016; Roman & Travis, 2004), although certainly there is at least an indirect link between criminal records and housing decisions through income and employment.

Housing Market Dynamics

In combination with the lack of income and unstable employment, access to housing for persons with criminal records is hindered by the dearth of affordable housing in the U.S. Households are regarded as "cost-burdened" if they spend 30 percent or more of their income on housing, and "severely" cost-burdened if housing costs exceed 50 percent of income. The Joint Center for Housing Studies of Harvard University (2016) reports that the number of cost-burdened households in the U.S. increased from 17.7 million in 2008 to 21.3 million in 2014. Moreover, there are 11.4 million households in the U.S. paying more than 50 percent of income for housing.

This increase in the number of cost-burdened households is influenced by a variety of factors, including the fact that wages have not kept pace with the growth in housing costs over the last several decades (Herbert et al., 2015). Rental vacancy rates plunged to a three-decade low in 2015, down from double-digits to 7.1 percent (Joint Center for Housing Studies, 2016). In turn, low vacancy rates have contributed to an increase in median rents, with rents increasing by 3.6 percent just between 2015 and 2016. When vacancy rates are low, landlords and property owners may have the luxury of being very selective when considering stigmatizing characteristics of prospective renters such as a criminal record. When vacancies are abundant, then landlords and property owners may be more inclined to accept individuals with criminal backgrounds as well as questionable employment, credit, and rental histories.

Stigma and Discrimination

Discrimination against individuals with a criminal record likely renders many housing units off-limits even if a formerly imprisoned individual could afford it. A traditional method used to test such assertions about housing discrimination is called a paired-tester study. With this method, otherwise equal individuals apply for the same housing, with the individuals differing only on the characteristics of suspected discrimination. Whereas numerous studies have used this method to examine discrimination by applicant race and ethnicity, few researchers have applied the method to examine the stigmatizing effect of a criminal record on housing. One exception is a recent study by Evans and Porter (2015), who find that prospective tenants admitting to having a criminal record were only invited to see the rental property 43 percent of the time. In contrast, paired individuals without a criminal record were invited to see the dwellings in almost every instance (see also Evans, 2016). Evans and Porter (2015) also find substantial variation across offense type as to whether self-disclosed offenders were able to get an appointment to view a dwelling: Almost half of the time, drug traffickers and individuals convicted of statutory rape were able to schedule a showing, whereas individuals disclosing they had been convicted of child molestation only received an appointment to view the dwelling one-third of the time. Prospective male tenants appeared to be penalized to a greater extent by a criminal record than females.

It is important to note that the Fair Housing Act prohibits discrimination in the sale, rental, or financing of housing on the basis of race, color, religion, sex, disability, familial status, or national origin. Criminal background information may still be used when making housing decisions, but it depends upon how it is used. Specifically, a set of U.S. Department of Housing and Urban Development (2016, p. 2) guidelines for public and private housing providers explains, "A housing provider violates the Fair Housing Act when the provider's policy or practice has an unjustified discriminatory effect, even when the provider had no intent to discriminate. Under this standard, a facially-neutral policy or practice that has a discriminatory effect violates the Act if it is not supported by a legally sufficient justification" (see also HUD, 2015). The guidance goes on to clarify the definition of "legally sufficient justification," explaining "A housing provider must, however, be able to prove through reliable evidence that its policy or practice of making housing decisions based on criminal history actually assists in protecting resident safety and/or property" (HUD, 2016, p. 5). A recent U.S. Supreme Court ruling in *Texas Department of Housing & Community Affairs v. The Inclusive Communities Project, Inc.* upheld the use of disparate impact claims under the Fair Housing Act. Yet, whereas there may be legal bases to bring lawsuits against housing providers engaging in discriminatory practices against the formerly incarcerated, threat of lawsuits over the improper use of criminal records in tenant screening will not resolve the shortage of housing for persons with criminal records because of the aforementioned challenges related to income, under-employment, and low vacancy rates.

Public Housing and Housing Vouchers

Because of the combination of lack of income, high rents, and lack of affordable housing in the private market, it seems that much of the discussion of housing for formerly imprisoned individuals centers on the issue of public and government-assisted housing. Yet it is important to understand that the vast majority of low-income residents in the U.S. do not live in public housing or receive any kind of housing assistance (Desmond, 2016; Schwartz, 2015). Based on analysis of the 2013 American Housing Survey, the Center on Budget and Policy Priorities (Fischer & Sard, 2017; see also Joint Center for Housing Studies, 2016) reports that only one-quarter of families eligible for federal rental assistance actually receive it. Government data reveal that the availability of subsidized housing (including public housing, housing vouchers, and private, project-based housing programs) has remained flat over the past two decades, at roughly 5 million subsidized units, despite the fact that the population size of the U.S. has increased 20 percent during this time period from 270 million to 325 million (U.S. Department of Housing and Urban Development, n.d.). Nevertheless, a discussion of opportunities for, and barriers to, assisted housing is pertinent to the theme of collateral consequences of incarceration.

In the U.S, there are three main rental assistance programs for low-income residents: public housing, "Section 8" vouchers, and project-based rental assistance. However, there is much misunderstanding among convicted individuals, their families, and even public housing authorities (PHAs) about the extent to which people with criminal records are legally barred from public housing and other assistance programs (versus denied admission via discretionary mechanisms). In fact, the Obama Administration took considerable steps to dispel the myth that convicted criminals are necessarily banned from public housing. As of this writing, there are only two circumstances under federal law that legally preclude eligibility for public housing assistance: (1) if an individual is a lifetime registered sex offender and (2) if an individual has been convicted of manufacturing methamphetamine on the premises of federally assisted housing (Federal Interagency Reentry Council, 2011).

The myths about blanket housing bans by HUD and PHAs are surely the product of housing policies enacted during the height of the War on Drugs to deter and punish individuals convicted of drug offenses and their associates. In 1988, Congress enacted the Anti-Drug Abuse Act, which enabled PHAs to evict tenants for drug activity on the premises (Carey, 2005). In 1996, President Clinton enacted the infamous "one strike and you're out" public housing policy; families could be denied admission or evicted from public housing for the alleged criminal behavior of an occupant or a guest, even if the criminal behavior had not been prosecuted (U.S. Department of Housing and Urban Development, 1997).

Under the Obama presidency, HUD reversed course and took considerable steps toward removing barriers to assisted housing for individuals with criminal records. For instance, then-HUD secretary Shaun Donovan, in a letter to PHAs in June of 2011, reminded them that except for the two aforementioned lifetime bans, they have much discretion when considering whether to provide housing for individuals with criminal records. He went on to encourage PHAs to allow formerly imprisoned individuals to reunite with their family members residing in public housing or making use of housing vouchers.

Some PHAs have been experimenting with family reunification programs that allow formerly imprisoned individuals the opportunity to move back in with family members. It is unknown how many formerly imprisoned individuals are unofficially living in public housing without the PHA's knowledge of it, but it does occur and puts the actual leaseholder at risk of losing her or his dwelling (Venkatesh, 2002). Family reunification programs provide a legal, authorized mechanism for the formerly imprisoned to move back in with families in public housing. A recent Vera Institute evaluation of a family reunification pilot program in New York revealed some reluctance among formerly imprisoned individuals about moving into cramped public housing spaces with their families as well as much suspicion about the intentions of the New York City Housing Authority (Bae, diZerega, Kang-Brown, Shanahan, & Subramanian, 2016). Hence, even programs designed with good intentions to lower the barriers to housing for people with criminal records are not without challenges.

While HUD showed considerable leadership during the Obama presidency in regards to fostering second chances for individuals with criminal records, necessarily this emphasis and motivation must trickle down to the local PHAs, many of which still have admissions policies (as documented in their admissions and continued occupancy policies [ACOPs]) reflective of the punitiveness of Clinton's one-strike policy and earlier eras. In fact, in a review of more than 300 criminal background screening policies used by federally subsidized housing developments in the U.S., the Sargent Shriver National Center on Poverty Law (Tran-Leung, 2015) identified four major barriers to admission to federal housing assistance for people with criminal records: (1) unreasonably lengthy criminal history lookback periods, (2) failure to consider mitigating circumstances surrounding criminal activity, (3) use of arrest records in admissions decisions, and (4) overly broad categories of criminal activity. Hence, despite the push by the Obama Administration to provide second chances to formerly incarcerated individuals, barriers to obtaining federally assisted housing are entrenched in many locations, and those PHAs experimenting with innovative solutions to lower barriers to housing for convicted individuals are confronted with the challenge of overcoming public suspicion about their practices. Moreover, a skeptic may conclude that progress by HUD and PHAs toward providing second chances for convicted individuals will stagnate under the renewed punitive rhetoric of the current presidential administration.

Criminal Justice Barriers

Beyond the personal circumstances influencing housing barriers as well as the housing market-related reasons, there are also barriers to housing put in place by the criminal justice system. One issue is a lack of reentry preparation for formerly incarcerated individuals, which is a problem examined extensively elsewhere (see, e.g., Petersilia, 2003; Roman & Travis, 2004).

A second barrier related to housing is the requirement by some state prison systems that individuals released onto parole must have housing lined up prior to release. In Washington State, a consequence of this practice was that prisoners were sometimes held past their earned release date because they did not have a place to reside if released. In response, the Washington State Department of Corrections developed a particularly innovative housing voucher program that paid for three months of rental housing for former prisoners following release (Hamilton, Kigerl, & Hays, 2015). The rationale underlying the program is that paying for housing for the formerly incarcerated is cheaper than incarcerating an individual in prison. Moreover, assistance with housing helps the formerly incarcerated reintegrate back into society.

A third barrier concerns legal restrictions on where individuals can reside (Beckett & Herbert, 2010). Conditions of parole may stipulate who an individual can reside with and even where she or he can reside (Steiner, Makarios, & Travis, 2015). Similarly, stay away orders and off-limits orders stipulate areas where convicted individuals are prohibited from going. Beckett and Herbert (2010) provide a penetrating analysis of the deleterious consequences and limited effectiveness of such compulsory laws and practices. That being said, in prior work I found substantial reductions in rates of reincarceration among formerly imprisoned individuals who moved away from their prior city of residence (Kirk, 2009, 2012, Forthcoming). In this work, I used the neighborhood destruction in New Orleans, Louisiana, following Hurricane Katrina in 2005 as a natural experiment to investigate the effects of residential change on recidivism. Compared to an otherwise similar cohort of individuals released from prison prior to Hurricane Katrina and who returned to their home cities, individuals released from prison post-Katrina who moved to different cities were 15 percentage points less likely to be reincarcerated. Hence, in some cases legal restrictions barring individuals from returning to former neighborhoods may lower the likelihood of recidivism. That being said, providing opportunities and incentives for staying away from certain criminogenic locations may be a more just and humane approach than making it illegal for individuals to visit or reside in certain locations.

Housing Barriers and Opportunities in the UK

For the sake of comparison and for understanding American exceptionalism in the barriers to housing, I'll briefly touch upon policies and practices surrounding the use of criminal records in the UK as well as the provision of housing benefits for low-income residents. The criminal background check industry is a $4 billion industry in the U.S. (see Jacobs, 2015 for an extensive review of policies, practices, and their implications). In continental Europe, in contrast, criminal records are largely considered private and are not disclosed widely. A basic premise underlying policies on dissemination of criminal records in Europe is the recognition that the public disclosure of criminal records undermines a person's ability and right to rehabilitation (Jacobs, 2015), whereas a similar right to rehabilitation is not a prime consideration in the approach to criminal records in the U.S. Indeed, U.S. policies and practices such as sex offender registration and notification severely stigmatize individuals convicted of sex offenses, reduce housing opportunities, and arguably undermine the prospects of desistance in the process, yet a purported reason for the disclosure of such records is so the general public has information on the whereabouts of would-be predators.

Policies about sealing and expungement of criminal records vary considerably across U.S. jurisdictions, but very rarely is sealing or expungement of records automatic even in those instances when cases are eligible. The costly and confusing legal process to seal or expunge a record means that most eligible individuals will not bother, especially given that their criminal records are just one Google search away even if their official records are sealed or expunged. In contrast, the UK Rehabilitation of Offenders Act of 1974 was enacted for the purposes of lowering the barriers to reintegration back into society among rehabilitated individuals. Under the Act, if a formerly incarcerated individual has avoided reconviction, then after a reasonable look-back period—from two to seven years depending upon the criminal sentence—the individual is deemed rehabilitated and the prior conviction is considered "spent." In this case, the conviction no longer needs to be disclosed by the individual on employment applications or housing applicatio.ir.

Another important distinction between the UK and the U.S. is the former's relatively greater provision of housing assistance to low-income populations, including those with criminal records.[1] Private market tenants in the UK can receive a local housing allowance to be put towards their rent, with the allowance equivalent to the 30th percentile level for rents in the market rental area. For instance, the local housing allowance in central Manchester for a one-bedroom apartment is £443/month and in central London it is £1,133/month (UK Valuation Office Agency, 2017). Importantly, a criminal record does not disqualify individuals from obtaining housing funds.

To qualify for the housing benefit, individuals must be low-income with minimal savings, and actively paying rent. A suspected offender in custody while on trial in the UK can keep her or his housing benefit for up to 52 weeks. Sentenced prisoners can keep their housing benefit, as long as their sentence is fewer than 13 weeks in duration. For those individuals with longer sentences, upon release from prison they are immediately eligible to re-establish their housing benefit.

For released individuals who are sent back to prison on a parole or probation revocation, they can still keep their housing benefit as long as they are not reincarcerated for longer than 13 weeks. This practice enables individuals to retain their housing. In contrast, a series of recent studies by David Harding, Claire Herbert, and Jeff Morenoff (Harding, Morenoff, & Herbert, 2013; Herbert et al., 2015) drawing upon a U.S. sample of formerly imprisoned individuals in Michigan reveals that revocations and intermediate sanctions that temporarily remove individuals from their homes significantly elevate the likelihood of housing loss and residential instability, which is then predictive of recidivism. In the U.S., when individuals have their parole or probation revoked, they risk losing their dwellings since they are unlikely to have any kind of housing assistance in the first place and would not likely keep that benefit once incarcerated even if they did have such a benefit.

In summary, formerly incarcerated individuals in the UK arguably have fewer barriers to housing than former prisoners in the U.S. because: (1) criminal records are generally regarded as more private in the UK than in the U.S., and a conviction does not need to be disclosed if sufficient time has passed since the last conviction, and (2) the provision of housing assistance is in many regards more supportive than in the U.S. In practice, though, there are still many challenges to finding housing in the UK. For instance, because the local housing allowance is equivalent to just the 30th percentile of the area rent, most dwellings are out of reach financially. Moreover, the benefit is generally distributed at the end of a given month, but most landlords want payment of rent for the month in advance. This is hard to do when exiting prisoners may only have the £46 in gate/discharge money to their name.

Extant Research

Having reviewed and described the most common barriers to securing stable housing among formerly convicted and imprisoned individuals, in this section I assess the empirical literature on collateral consequences of conviction and incarceration for housing.

Assessing Risk to Property and Other Residents

I earlier described the implications of the Fair Housing Act for criminal record screening in housing decisions, noting that background screening is potentially allowable if there is "legally sufficient justification" for excluding certain convicted individuals from a given housing situation.

A common justification offered by landlords is the pursuit of safety for residents and protection of property. An implicit assumption then is that people with criminal records are more dangerous than other tenants and are more likely to damage the property. However, there is virtually no rigorous research examining whether, for example, apartment residents who have a criminal record are any more dangerous or abusive to the property compared to otherwise similar tenants without a criminal record.

Of the limited research that attempts to answer related questions, Malone (2009) sampled homeless adults with behavioral health disorders who participated in a supportive housing intervention to determine if those participants with a criminal record were any more or less likely to successfully complete the program and remain in the housing than individuals without a criminal record. Ultimately Malone found that a criminal background did not predict housing failure. Clifasefi, Malone, and Collins (2012) and Tsai and Rosenheck (2012) similarly find in samples of homeless individuals that a criminal record does not bear upon whether an individual successfully completes a homeless housing intervention or not.

Even if there is little existing evidence about the would-be threat of individuals with criminal records to the safety of property and other residents, governments can take steps to alleviate landlord concern about the safety of residents and property, and the potential liability for renting to individuals with criminals records. For instance, during the 2015 Texas Legislature, House Bill 1510 was passed providing some liability protection to landlords for renting dwellings to individuals with criminal records (Smith, 2015).[2]

The limited research to date suggests little predictive value of criminal history information in judging housing success and failure, at least among samples of homeless individuals. There has been no rigorous research on whether individuals with criminal records are more likely to victimize fellow residents or damage property than non-offenders. Yet, it is important to consider the downside of not asking about criminal history. Here I draw upon lessons from research on employment and "ban-the-box" initiatives.

Holzer and colleagues (2006) have argued that criminal background screening of job applicants may actually be beneficial to the employment prospects of black individuals, at least those without a criminal record. Absent information about criminal history, prospective employers may statistically discriminate against blacks, assuming that they have a criminal record and should not be hired in the absence of information to counter that assumption. The same form of implicit bias may surface in housing decisions in the absence of criminal history information.

On many employment applications, there is a check-box asking applicants whether they have been arrested or convicted of a crime. "Ban the box" refers to the practice of removing those questions about a criminal record from job applications, thereby eliminating or at least delaying any criminal background check until after the applicant's qualifications for the job in question have actually been assessed. In a field experiment of the efficacy of ban-the-box policies, Agan and Starr (2018) submitted roughly 15,000 fictitious online job applications to employers in New Jersey and New York City, both before and after these jurisdictions enacted ban-the-box policies. They find that before the policy went into effect, there was a 7 percent race gap in favor of whites in the likelihood of an applicant receiving a call-back about a job. After ban-the-box went into effect, the gap grew to 43 percent. These results suggest that absent criminal history information, statistical discrimination is likely to take place. While their research focused on the employment context, it is not a stretch to assume that the same scenario would follow in housing decisions. In sum, criminal background checks as a method for assessing risk may ultimately reduce the likelihood of statistical discrimination against racial and ethnic minorities. Yet in the discussion of risk and background checks, it is important to understand that the risk of recidivism is not the same as the risk of being a bad tenant, but oftentimes criminal records are used as a proxy for assessing the risk of being a problematic renter.

Residential Instability and Housing Insecurity

Numerous studies have found that housing and residential instability are common among formerly imprisoned individuals, with some research also implicating a history of incarceration as a prime reason for the instability. In the initial period out of prison, it is typical for individuals to stay with family members. For instance, in a sample of formerly imprisoned individuals living in Chicago, La Vigne and colleagues (2004) found that 62 percent stayed with a family member their first night out of prison. In a Boston sample, Western and colleagues (2015) found that 40 to 50 percent of newly released individuals resided with family in the first week out of prison, yet the proportion living with family members quickly declined with time, with formerly incarcerated individuals increasingly turning to peers for a place to live.

In terms of the frequency of moves, Makarios, Steiner, and Travis (2010) find that, on average, sampled Ohio parolees lived in two different residences in the first year post-release and 30 percent lived in three or more places. In a sample of individuals imprisoned prior to the modern era of mass incarceration, Rossi and colleagues (1980) found that formerly imprisoned individuals in Georgia and Texas resided, on average, in 1.5 residences in the first three months after release and approximately 16 percent of releasees resided in three or more places.

Geller and Curtis (2011), using data from the Fragile Families study, found that 31 percent of sampled urban fathers with incarceration histories experienced housing instability of some form (e.g., eviction, skipping a mortgage payment, or moving into a shelter) versus 14 percent of otherwise similar fathers without an incarceration record. They find that the effect of incarceration on subsequent eviction is present only for men who were living in, or who had partners living in, public housing prior to their incarceration. They take these findings as evidence of the impact of the one-strike policies enacted during the Clinton presidency to exclude individuals with a recent conviction from residence in public housing.

Harding et al. (2013) find that parolees in Michigan move frequently—an estimated 2.6 times per year for the median parolee. Herbert et al. (2015) prospectively tracked the residential circumstances of Michigan parolees, finding that most periods of residence for the parolees lasted just a few months, with 50 percent of the residential periods lasting eight weeks or less. Moreover, they find that one-third of residential episodes—i.e., continuous periods of time living in the same place, excluding correctional settings—were interrupted by some form of intermediate sanction by the criminal justice system (e.g., for a parole violation).

In terms of racial-ethnic variation, Warner (2015) finds that blacks tend to have more residential instability post-prison relative to their pre-prison experience, but incarceration does not appear to increase residential mobility among whites and Latinos. He also finds that the effect of incarceration on residential instability decays with time, once again reaffirming that the period right after release from prison is marked by extreme challenges for formerly incarcerated individuals and an elevated risk of recidivism. Finally, Warner's findings suggest that residential instability is more likely the result of the stigma of a criminal record than the detachment induced by a lengthy prison sentence.

A growing body of research has found that residential instability increases the likelihood of recidivism (Makarios et al., 2010; Meredith, Speir, & Johnson, 2007; Steiner et al., 2015), as do periods of homelessness (Metraux & Culhane, 2004; Steiner et al., 2015). There is also evidence that providing housing assistance, particularly soon after release from prison for individuals at high risk of re-offending, can lower the likelihood of recidivism (Hamilton et al., 2015; Kirk, Forthcoming; Kirk, Barnes, Hyatt, & Kearley, Forthcoming; Lutze, Rosky, & Hamilton, 2013). As noted, Herbert and colleagues (2015) found that by increasing residential instability, the use of intermediate sanctions at least indirectly increases the likelihood of future recidivism. In other words, by attempting to curb misbehavior through intermediate sanctions, the criminal justice system may be contributing to a self-fulfilling prophesy by inducing residential instability and therefore a heightened risk of recidivism.

Neighborhood Attainment

While it is clear that residential instability is common among the newly released, it is also important to consider if a record of incarceration penalizes individuals in terms of post-prison neighborhood quality. The Returning Home studies produced by the Urban Institute yielded some of the earliest findings about the characteristics of neighborhoods in which formerly imprisoned individuals return. La Vigne, Mamalian, and colleagues (2003) found that the geographic distribution of formerly imprisoned individuals is highly concentrated in a relatively small number of neighborhoods within metropolitan areas. For instance, more than one-half of individuals released from Illinois prisons in 2001 returned to the City of Chicago; among these, one-third were concentrated in just six of 77 community areas. These six communities are among the most economically and socially disadvantaged in the city. La Vigne, Kachnowski, and colleagues (2003) found a similar pattern in Baltimore.

There are also important racial dimensions to the patterns of neighborhood attainment. Hipp and colleagues (2010; see also Lee, Harding, & Morenoff, 2017) observe that African American parolees tend to move to neighborhoods with more concentrated disadvantage, residential instability, and racial/ethnic heterogeneity than white parolees. While that may be the case, it is a separate question to examine whether or not the same person moved to a more disadvantaged and disorganized neighborhood post-release relative to her or his pre-prison neighborhood. That is the question that Massoglia, Firebaugh, and Warner (2013) sought to answer. They find that whites tend to live in more socioeconomically disadvantaged neighborhoods upon release from prison relative to where they lived pre-prison, but blacks and Latinos do not face such a penalty. In other words, there appears to be a collateral consequence of incarceration on neighborhood attainment for whites but not for blacks and Latinos (but see Simes, 2017 for contrary evidence).

Lee et al. (2017) observe that whereas there is considerable residential mobility among their sample of Michigan parolees, parolees tend to move to similar types of neighborhoods relative to the neighborhoods they left, as measured by socioeconomic disadvantage and other sociodemographic characteristics. In other words, when parolees have unstable residential patterns, it does not mean they are moving to worse neighborhoods, or moving out of bad neighborhoods to reside in more advantaged neighborhoods. They are often just moving from one disadvantaged neighborhood to another.

Homelessness

Another key collateral consequence to examine is the effect of incarceration on the risk of homelessness. Metraux and Culhane (2004) found that 11.4 percent of a sample of formerly incarcerated individuals returning to New York City entered a homeless shelter within two years of prison release, with most of these admissions occurring within the first month of release. They also found that the likelihood of shelter use among the formerly incarcerated was inversely related to the severity of the offense that led to the incarceration.

Geller and Curtis (2011), based on data from the Fragile Families study, find that recently incarcerated men face odds of homelessness that are more than double that of otherwise similar men without a recent incarceration. They also compared individuals with an incarceration at some point in their lives to otherwise similar individuals who had never been incarcerated, finding that the formerly incarcerated face odds of homelessness that are almost 4 times greater than the never incarcerated.

In contrast, Herbert, Morenoff, and Harding (2015) find that periods of homelessness were infrequent in their sample of Michigan parolees, and that just 9 percent of the sample had any period of homelessness from 2003 to 2009.

Sex Offender Registration and Notification

Perhaps the most obvious and severe form of collateral consequence in the realm of housing comes in the form of sex offender registration, notification, and residency laws. The empirical literature described thus far was not generally specific to a certain type of offender, but I conclude the discussion of empirical findings by specifically examining work on the collateral consequences associated with sex offender policies.

Briefly, registration provides information on the whereabouts of individuals convicted of sex offenses, and notification ensures that this information is made available to not only criminal justice officials but also the public. Registration and notification produce collateral consequences by further stigmatizing and ostracizing individuals convicted of sex offenses. Residency laws go a step further and restrict where such individuals can reside, typically mandating a buffer around locations with vulnerable populations such as schools, day care centers, and playgrounds. A common argument is that these restrictions increase the likelihood of housing insecurity and homelessness among targeted individuals, decrease access to jobs and the possibility of employment, undermine familial relations and social capital, and thereby increase the likelihood of recidivism (Zgoba, Levenson, & McKee, 2009).

Zgoba et al. (2009) investigate a vital question: What proportion of individuals convicted of sex offenses would be affected by the implementation of residency restrictions? The context was Camden County, New Jersey, a jurisdiction attempting to enact residency restrictions on sex offenders, but which ran into legal challenges in the process. Using data on the 211 county residents registered in the state sex offender registry as of March 2007, Zgoba and colleagues found that the proportion of individuals convicted of a sex offense residing within 2,500 feet of a school, day care center, church, or park equaled 88 percent. Seventy-one percent of registered individuals lived within 2,500 feet of a school specifically, and 80 percent lived within the same distance from a day care center. In this sense, the residential situation for the vast majority of registered individuals would be affected by implementation of residency restrictions against sex offenders. Accordingly, when such laws are put into place, individuals convicted of sex offenses may be severely constrained in finding legal places to reside, with some pushed to the shadows because they cannot find a place to live.

Hipp, Turner, and Jannetta (2010) examine the consequences of sex offender residency restrictions in California, which stipulated that registered sex offenders could not reside within 2,000 feet of a school, day care center, or other place where children congregate. They find that relative to other types of parolees, individuals convicted of sex offenses are more likely to move to socially disorganized neighborhoods, as measured by higher levels of concentrated disadvantage and residential instability (see also Mustaine & Tewksbury, 2011; Mustaine, Tewksbury, & Stengel, 2006; Tewksbury, Mustaine, & Rolfe, 2016). The effect is particularly pronounced among whites and Latinos. Moreover, with each subsequent move, on average individuals convicted of sex offenses find themselves moving to areas with even more disadvantage and residential instability.

Prescott and Rockoff (2011) find both an upside and downside to sex offender notification laws. On the upside, there appears to be a general deterrent effect of such laws, reducing the incidence of sex offenses against known victims (i.e., offenses where the victim is known to the perpetrator). However, in terms of the downside, notification laws appear to increase the likelihood of recidivism among individuals convicted of prior sex offenses, which is consistent with the idea that notification yields collateral consequences such as stigmatization.

Conversely, Huebner and colleagues (2014) examine residential patterns and recidivism among individuals convicted of sex offenses in Michigan and Missouri, both before and after registration laws went into effect. After geocoding the first post-release addresses of a sample of formerly incarcerated individuals in each state, they find that in both states, individuals imprisoned for sex offenses in the period after residency restrictions were enacted were no more or less likely to be living in a restricted area when compared with prerestriction sex offender addresses. They also find that residency restrictions had little influence on recidivism rates among individuals convicted of sex offenses, although with some variation across the two states.

In summary, sex offender registration, notification, and residency laws appear to have a detrimental influence on the housing opportunities of registered sex offenders and increase the likelihood of residing in a socioeconomically disadvantaged area. Findings about whether residency restrictions and other similar laws influence recidivism are mixed.

Enduring Challenges to the Literature

Described so far have been the various barriers to housing for individuals with criminal records, and the consequences for residential instability, homelessness, and neighborhood attainment. In the remainder of the chapter, I highlight major challenges to advancing research on the collateral consequences of convictions and incarceration.

Selection Bias

Does incarceration causally increase the likelihood of homelessness, housing instability, and residence in disadvantaged neighborhoods, or is incarceration merely one of many deleterious outcomes associated with antecedent factors such as low self-control, drug addiction, and mental health problems? To examine the consequences of incarceration for housing outcomes, it is imperative to account for how people "select" into prison—i.e., researchers must account for very large differences between people who select into prison versus those individuals who have not been incarcerated. Failing to do so may lead to erroneous conclusions about whether incarceration has collateral consequences.

One strategy besides using the non-incarcerated as a counterfactual comparison is to use convicted individuals, but ones who were not sentenced to prison (e.g., probation). Yet comparing ex-prisoners to ex-probationers in order to assess the collateral consequences of incarceration is not without challenges. Pre-trial detention is extremely common in the U.S., in part because of bail systems in many jurisdictions that arguably infringe upon individuals' Eighth Amendment protections against excessive bail. Sixty percent of the jail population in the U.S. consists of individuals waiting for trial (i.e., not even convicted) (Minton & Zeng, 2016), and more than 40 percent of defendants are detained in jail from arrest until their cases are disposed, most often because the defendant could not afford bail (Cohen & Reaves, 2007).

Because of the lengthy amount of pre-trial detention by many defendants, the proportion of probationers who serve significant time in jail prior to sentencing (or others measured as "never incarcerated") is non-trivial (Dobbie, Goldin, & Yang, 2016). Accordingly, probationers are not necessarily a clear-cut counterfactual for examining the collateral consequences of incarceration because even probationers spend a lot of time incarcerated (in this case, pre-trial). That is all to say that it seems generally better to compare the incarcerated against some other convicted individual in order to assess the specific consequences of being incarcerated (rather than comparing the incarcerated to a non-sanctioned individual), but even these comparisons have complexities that make unbiased estimates of collateral consequences hard to achieve.

There are several other common strategies besides incarcerated vs. probationer comparisons used in the incarceration effects literature to try to minimize selection bias. These strategies include comparisons between the incarcerated and individuals who will later be incarcerated (Porter & King, 2015), sample restrictions to compare recent and multiple incarcerations (Wakefield & Wildeman, 2013), placebo regressions (Wakefield & Wildeman, 2013), random assignment of judges to criminal cases (Kling, 2006; Loeffler, 2013), and research using policy shocks such as the California Public Safety Realignment Act (Petersilia, 2014). While rare in this domain, experimental research employing random assignment is the most rigorous design for making causal inferences about the effects of incarceration (see, e.g., Gaes & Camp, 2009; Pager, 2003; Schwartz & Skolnick, 1962).

While there are many good strategies for attempting to minimize selection bias, often they are data intensive and the study of crime and punishment is routinely challenged by data inadequacies. Yet careful attention to the issue of selection is necessary in order to advance work on collateral consequences. Care must be taken when evaluating extant research on collateral consequences to consider whether the research is actually comparing "apples to apples" or "apples to oranges."

Data Infrastructure

As noted, the data challenges for advancing research on collateral consequences are many. These challenges have been discussed in length elsewhere, including my own review of the wider collateral consequences literature (Kirk & Wakefield, 2018) and the landmark *National Research Council* (2014) report on the causes and consequences of mass incarceration. Both of these reviews call for collection of data on the conditions of confinement, thereby allowing for research on how and why the actual experience of incarceration may have collateral consequences post-release. These reviews also call for greater attention in longitudinal surveys to data collection about the various stages of criminal case processing. Surveys often used in the collateral consequences literature, such as *the National Longitudinal Study of Adolescent to Adult Health (Add Health), the National Longitudinal Survey of Youth*, and *Fragile Families*, generally lack information about whether incarcerations occurred in a local jail, state prison, or federal facility. They also tend to lack precise information about non-custodial sentences, time served, the number of spells of incarceration, and whether a suspected individual was detained pre-trial.

As for research specific to the collateral consequences for housing, the most extensive data collections on this subject over the past two decades are arguably the Urban Institute's Returning Home study[3] and The Michigan Study of Life After Prison.[4] Throughout this chapter, I have drawn extensively upon the research from both efforts. Both studies collected vast amounts of information about the locations of residence post-release, employing data collection strategies such as repeated surveys and systematic review of paper parole files. These are extremely costly and time-consuming methods of data collection, but these studies have certainly enriched our understanding of the housing situations of formerly imprisoned individuals.

There are other possibilities for collecting longitudinal information about place of residence among the formerly incarcerated. For instance, the population register data in some Western European and Nordic countries provide considerable opportunities for examining the collateral consequences of conviction and incarceration (see Lyngstad & Skardhamar, 2011 for a thorough review about Nordic register data). Residents are assigned a personal identification number like a social security number in the U.S., and this number provides a link between an individual's records across a variety of government databases. As former U.S. Census Director Kenneth Prewitt notes (2010, p. 12),

> European populations understand and cooperate with national registration systems that track such key variables as birth, schooling, changes in residence, employment, marriage and divorce, parenting, retirement, and death. The U.S. has administrative data on all of these population variables . . . But of course this is fragmented and decentralized record keeping. There is no national registration system to integrate it.

Related to housing, for example, one could use the personal identifier common across government databases to link data from the Prison and Probation Service on all people who were formerly incarcerated with housing register data that provide information on places where someone has lived as well as the timing of residential moves. Rather than having to scour parole files, as Harding and colleagues

(2013) have so meticulously done, one could assess residential mobility and housing insecurity with the register data. These register data could also be used to determine who else is residing in the same dwelling. Moreover, register data are not just a snapshot in time; rather, it is an ongoing record of events in one's life (residential moves, arrests, birth of a child) and interactions with government data systems.

In sum, empirical criminology is challenged by a lack of adequate and complete data. To advance research on the collateral consequences of incarceration, investment in data infrastructure is crucial. Merging administrative records with longitudinal surveys is one good idea, as is the inclusion of more detailed questions about criminal case processing and conditions of confinement in surveys used in the collateral consequences literature. I drew attention to European register data to illustrate data resources perhaps not widely known or accessed outside of the European research community. These data are a valuable resource for furthering research on the collateral consequences of conviction and incarceration.

Conclusion

The academic research literature has coalesced around a general agreement that the era of mass incarceration has produced dramatic social costs, in terms of not only housing barriers, but also unemployment, ill health, disintegration of families, civic death, and more. The collateral consequences of mass incarceration have come with limited crime control benefit. Estimates suggest that mass incarceration contributed to a decrease in the violent crime rate of roughly 10 to 25 percent, but with diminishing returns over time (Johnson & Raphael, 2012; Sampson, 2011; Western, 2006). There are more cost-beneficial and effective ways to reduce crime.

In this chapter I have reviewed the specific collateral consequences of conviction and incarceration in the realm of housing. The breadth of mass incarceration in combination with declining investment by the federal government in assisted housing as well as the disturbing lack of progress in the development of affordable housing in the U.S. has created and perpetuated a massive housing crisis for individuals with criminal records. Dismantling that crisis will require far more than just altering sentencing practices for low-level drug offenses. It will require a fundamental rethinking of incarceration, sentencing, and housing policy.

Acknowledgments

This research draws influence from collaborative work with Sara Wakefield on the collateral consequences of punishment, as well as work with the Austin/Travis County Reentry Roundtable on removing the barriers to stable housing for the formerly incarcerated.

Notes

1 Some U.S. cities do provide "shelter allowances" to individuals receiving public assistance (Cortes & Rogers, 2010).
2 www.capitol.state.tx.us/BillLookup/History.aspx?LegSess=84R&Bill=HB1510
3 www.urban.org/policy-centers/justice-policy-center/projects/returning-home-study-understanding-challenges-prisoner-reentry
4 https://prisonerreentryresearch.org/

References

Agan, A.Y., & Starr, S. B. (2018). Ban the box, criminal records, and racial discrimination: A field experiment. *Quarterly Journal of Economics*, *133*, 191–235.
American Bar Association. (2013). *National inventory of the collateral consequences of conviction*. Chicago, IL: American Bar Association. Retrieved from https://niccc.csgjusticecenter.org/

Apel R., & Ramakers, A. (2018). Impact of criminal punishment on employment. In B. M. Huebner & N. Frost (Eds.), *Handbook on the consequences of sentencing and punishment decisions*. New York, NY: Routledge.

Apel R., & Sweeten, G. (2010). The impact of incarceration on employment during the transition to adulthood. *Social Problems, 57*, 448–479.

Bae, J., diZerega, M., Kang-Brown, J., Shanahan, R., & Subramanian, R. (2016). *Coming home: An evaluation of the New York City Housing Authority's Family Reentry Pilot Program*. New York, NY: Vera Institute of Justice.

Beckett, K., & Herbert, S. (2010). *Banished: The new social control in urban America*. New York, NY: Oxford University Press.

Carey, C. (2005). No second chance: People with criminal records denied access to public housing. *Toledo Law Review, 36*, 1–58.

Clark, L. M. (2007). Landlord attitudes toward renting to release offenders. *Federal Probation, 71*, 20–60.

Clifasefi, S. L., Malone, D. K., & Collins, S. E. (2012). Exposure to project-based housing first is associated with reduced jail time and bookings. *International Journal of Drug Policy, 24*, 291–296.

Cohen, T. H., & Reaves, B. A. (2007). *Pretrial Release of felony defendants in state courts*. Washington, DC: Bureau of Justice Statistics.

Cortes, K., & Rogers, S. (2010). *Reentry housing options: The policymakers' guide*. New York, NY: Council of State Governments Justice Center.

Desmond, M. (2016). *Evicted: Poverty and profit in the America city*. New York, NY: Crown.

Dobbie, W., Goldin, J., & Yang, C. (2016). *The effects of pre-trial detention on conviction, future crime, and employment: Evidence from randomly assigned judges*. Cambridge, MA: National Bureau of Economic Research Working Paper No. 22511.

Evans, D. N. (2016). The effect of criminal convictions on real estate agent decisions in New York City. *Journal of Crime and Justice, 39*, 363–379.

Evans, D. N., & Porter, J. R. (2015). Criminal history and landlord rental decisions: A New York quasi-experimental study. *Journal of Experimental Criminology, 11*, 21–42.

Federal Interagency Reentry Council. (2011). *Reentry mythbusters*. New York, NY: The National Reentry Resource Center, Council of State Governments Justice Center. Retrieved from https://csgjusticecenter.org/wp-content/uploads/2012/12/Reentry_Council_Mythbuster_Housing.pdf

Fischer, W., & Sard, B. (2017). *Chart book: Federal housing spending is poorly matched to need*. Washington, DC: Center on Budget and Policy Priorities.

Gaes, G. G., & Camp, S. D. (2009). Unintended consequences: Experimental evidence for the criminogenic effect of prison security level placement on post-release recidivism. *Journal of Experimental Criminology, 5*, 139–162.

Geller, A., & Curtis, M. A. (2011). A sort of homecoming: Incarceration and the housing security of urban men. *Social Science Research, 40*, 1196–1213.

Hamilton, Z., Kigerl, A., & Hays, Z. (2015). Removing release impediments and reducing correctional costs: Evaluation of Washington state's housing voucher program. *Justice Quarterly, 32*, 255–287.

Harding, D. J., Morenoff, J. D., & Herbert, C. (2013). Home is hard to find: Neighborhoods, institutions, and the residential trajectories of returning prisoners. *The Annals of the American Academy of Political and Social Science, 647*, 214–236.

Harding, D. J., Wyse, J., Dobson, C., & Morenoff, J. D. (2014). Making ends meet after prison. *Journal of Policy Analysis and Management, 33*, 440–470.

Herbert, C. W., Morenoff, J. D, & Harding, D. J. (2015). Homelessness and housing insecurity among former prisoners. *The Russell Sage Foundation Journal, 1*, 44–79.

Hipp, J. R., Turner, S., & Jannetta, J. (2010). Are sex offenders moving into social disorganization? Analyzing the residential mobility of California parolees. *Journal of Research in Crime and Delinquency, 47*, 558–590.

Holzer, H. J., Raphael, S., & Stoll, M. A. (2006). Perceived criminality, criminal background checks, and racial hiring practices of employers. *Journal of Law and Economics, 49*, 451–480.

Huebner, B., Kras, K. R., Rydberg, J., Bynum, T. S., Grommon, E., & Pleggenkuhle, B. (2014). The effect and implications of sex offender residence restrictions: Evidence from a two-state evaluation. *Criminology and Public Policy, 13*, 139–168.

Jacobs, J. B. (2015). *The eternal criminal record*. Cambridge, MA: Harvard University Press.

Johnson, R., & Raphael, S. (2012). How much crime reduction does the marginal prisoner buy? *Journal of Law and Economics, 55*, 275–310.

Joint Center for Housing Studies of Harvard University. (2016). *The state of the nation's housing: 2016*. Cambridge, MA: Harvard University.

Kaebel D., & Glaze, L. E. (2016). *Correctional populations in the United States, 2015*. Washington, DC: Bureau of Justice Statistics.

Kirk, D. S. (2009). A natural experiment on residential change and recidivism: Lessons from Hurricane Katrina. *American Sociological Review, 74*, 484–505.

Kirk, D. S. (2012). Residential change as a turning point in the life course of crime: Desistance or temporary cessation? *Criminology, 50*, 329–358.

Kirk, D. S. (Forthcoming). *Home free: Residential change and redemption after Hurricane Katrina*. New York, NY: Oxford University Press.

Kirk, D. S., Barnes, G., Hyatt, J., & Kearley, B. (Forthcoming). The impact of residential change and housing stability on recidivism: Pilot results from the Maryland Opportunities through Vouchers Experiment (MOVE). *Journal of Experimental Criminology.*

Kirk, D. S., & Wakefield, S. (2018). Collateral consequences of punishment: A critical review and path forward. *Annual Review of Criminology, 1*, 171–194.

Kling, J. (2006). Incarceration length, employment and earnings. *American Economic Review, 96*, 863–876.

La Vigne, N. G., Kachnowski, V., Travis, J., Naser, R., & Visher, C. (2003). *A portrait of prisoner reentry in Maryland.* Washington, DC: Urban Institute.

La Vigne, N. G., Mamalian, C. A., Travis, J., & Visher, C. (2003). *A portrait of prisoner reentry in Illinois.* Washington, DC: Urban Institute.

La Vigne, N. G., Visher, C., & Castro, J. (2004). *Chicago prisoners' experiences returning home.* Washington, DC: Urban Institute.

Lee, K., Harding, D. J., & Morenoff, J. D. (2017). Trajectories of neighborhood attainment after prison. *Social Science Research, 66*, 211–233. Retrieved from https://doi.org/10.1016/j.ssresearch.2016.12.004.

Loeffler, C. (2013). Does imprisonment alter the life course? Evidence on crime and employment from a natural experiment. *Criminology, 51*, 137–166.

Lutze, F. E., Rosky, J. W., & Hamilton, Z. K. (2013). Homelessness and reentry: A multisite outcome evaluation of Washington State's Reentry Housing Program for high risk offenders. *Criminal Justice and Behavior, 41*, 471–491.

Lyngstad, T. H., & Skardhamar, T. (2011). Nordic register data and their untapped potential for criminological research. *Crime & Justice, 40*, 613–645.

Makarios, M., Steiner, B., & Travis III, L. F. (2010). Examining the predictors of recidivism among men and women released from prison in Ohio. *Criminal Justice and Behavior, 37*, 1377–1391.

Malone, D. K. (2009). Assessing criminal history as a predictor of future housing success for homeless adults with behavioral health disorders. *Psychiatric Services, 60*, 224–230.

Massoglia, M., Firebaugh, G., & Warner, C. (2013). Racial variation in the effect of incarceration on neighborhood attainment. *American Sociological Review, 78*, 142–165.

Meredith, T., Speir, J. C., & Johnson, S. (2007). Developing and implementing automated risk assessments in parole. *Justice Research and Policy, 9*, 1–24.

Metraux, S., & Culhane, D. P. (2004). Homeless shelter use and reincarceration following prison release: Assessing the risk. *Criminology & Public Policy, 3*, 201–222.

Minton T. D., & Zeng Z. (2016). *Jail inmates in 2015.* Washington, DC: Bureau of Justice Statistics.

Muller, C., & Wildeman, C. (2016). Geographic variation in the cumulative risk of imprisonment and parental incarceration in the United States. *Demography, 53*, 1499–1509.

Mustaine, E. E., & Tewksbury, R. (2011). Residential relegation of registered sex offenders. *American Journal of Criminal Justice, 36*, 44–57.

Mustaine, E. E., Tewksbury, R., & Stengel, K. M. (2006). Residential location and mobility of registered sex offenders. *American Journal of Criminal Justice, 30*, 177–192.

National Research Council. (2014). *The growth of incarceration in the United States: Exploring causes and consequences.* Committee on Law and Justice, Division of Behavioral and Social Sciences and Education. Washington, DC: National Academies Press.

Pager D. (2003). The mark of a criminal record. *American Journal of Sociology, 108*, 937–975.

Petersilia, J. (2003). *When prisoners come home: Parole and prisoner reentry.* New York, NY: Oxford University Press.

Petersilia, J. (2014). California prison downsizing and its impact on local criminal justice systems. *Harvard Law & Policy Review, 8*, 327–358.

Porter, L. C., & King, R. (2015). Absent fathers or absent variables? A new look at paternal incarceration and delinquency. *Journal of Crime and Delinquency, 52*, 414–443.

Prescott, J. J., & Rockoff, J. E. (2011). Do sex offender registration and notification laws affect criminal behavior? *The Journal of Law & Economics, 54*, 161–206.

Prewitt, K. (2010). Science starts not after measurement, but with measurement. *The Annals of the American Academy of Political and Social Science, 631*, 7–16.

Roman, C. G., & Travis, J. (2004). *Taking stock: Housing, homelessness, and prisoner reentry*. Final Report to the Fannie Mae Foundation. Washington, DC: Urban Institute.

Rossi, P. H., Berk, R. A., & Lenihan, K. J. (1980). *Money, work, and crime: Experimental evidence*. New York, NY: Academic Press.

Sampson, R. J. (2011). The incarceration ledger: Toward a new era in assessing societal consequences. *Criminology & Public Policy, 10*, 819–828.

Schwartz, A. F. (2015). *Housing policy in the United States* (3rd ed.). New York, NY: Routledge.

Schwartz, R. D., & Skolnick, J. (1962). Two studies of legal stigma. *Social Problems, 10*, 133–142.

Shannon, S. K. S., Uggen, C., Schnittker, J., Thompson, M., Wakefield, S., & Massoglia, M. (2017). The growth, scope, and spatial distribution of people with felony records in the United States, 1948–2010. *Demography, 54*, 1795–1818.

Simes, J. (2017). *Neighborhood attainment after prison*. Working paper. Boston, MA: Boston University.

Smith, D. (2015). *Fact sheet 2015: HB 1510*. Austin, TX: Texas Criminal Justice Coalition. Retrieved from www.texascjc.org/system/files/publications/TCJC%20Fact%20Sheet%20HB%201510%20%28Landlord%20Protection%29.pdf

Steiner, B., Makarios, M. D., & Travis III, L. F. (2015). Examining the effects of residential situations and residential mobility on offender recidivism. *Crime and Delinquency, 61*, 375–401.

Tewksbury, R., Mustaine, E. E., Rolfe, S. (2016). Sex Offender Residential Mobility and Relegation: The Collateral Consequences Continue. *American Journal of Criminal Justice, 41*, 852–866.

Tran-Leung, M. (2015). *When discretion means denial. A national perspective on criminal records barriers to federally subsidized housing*. Chicago, IL: Sargent Shriver National Center on Poverty Law.

Tsai, J., & Rosenheck, R. A. (2012). Incarceration among chronically homeless adults: Clinical correlates and outcomes. *Journal of Forensic Psychology Practice, 12*, 307–324.

UK Valuation Office Agency. (2017). *Local housing allowance (LHA) rates applicable from April 2017—March 2018*. London: Valuation Office Agency. Retrieved from www.gov.uk/government/publications/local-housing-allowance-lha-rates-applicable-from-april-2017-march-2018

U.S. Department of Housing and Urban Development (HUD). (1997). *Meeting the challenge: Public housing authorities respond to the "One Strike and You're Out" initiative*. Washington, DC: HUD.

U.S. Department of Housing and Urban Development (HUD). (2015). *Guidance for public housing agencies (PHAs) and owners of federally-assisted housing on excluding the use of arrest records in housing decisions*. Washington, DC: HUD.

U.S. Department of Housing and Urban Development (HUD). (2016). *Application of Fair Housing Act standards to the use of criminal records by providers of housing and real estate-related transactions*. Washington, DC: HUD.

U.S. Department of Housing and Urban Development (HUD). (n.d.). *Assisting housing: National and local* [Data file]. Retrieved from www.huduser.gov/portal/datasets/assthsg.html

Venkatesh, S. A. (2002). *The Robert Taylor homes relocation study*. New York, NY: Columbia University Center for Urban Research and Policy.

Wakefield S., & Wildeman, C. (2013). *Children of the prison boom: Mass incarceration and the future of American inequality*. New York, NY: Oxford University Press.

Warner, C. (2015). On the move: Incarceration, race, and residential mobility. *Social Science Research, 52*, 451–464.

Western, B. (2006). *Punishment and inequality in America*. New York, NY: Russell Sage Foundation.

Western, B., Braga, A. A., Davis, J., & Sirois, C. (2015). Stress and hardship after prison. *American Journal of Sociology, 120*, 1512–1547.

Western, B., & Pettit, B. (2005). Black–white wage inequality, employment rates, and incarceration. *American Journal of Sociology, 111*, 553–578.

Zgoba, K. M., Levenson, J., & McKee, T. (2009). Examining the impact of sex offender residence restrictions on housing availability. *Criminal Justice Policy Review, 20*, 91–110.

4

RESIDENTIAL INSECURITIES AND NEIGHBORHOOD QUALITY FOLLOWING INCARCERATION

Brianna Remster and Cody Warner

Introduction

As a result of the prison boom, scholars have dedicated considerable attention to documenting the consequences of having a criminal justice system whose size is unparalleled in time and place (Garland, 2001). Perhaps not surprisingly, incarceration is linked with residential hardship, ranging from increased mobility and insecurity to homelessness. Although intuitive, this line of work has lagged behind other key life domains such as family or work, in part due to data limitations. Because of these challenges, past review chapters are primarily conceptual in nature (Metraux, Roman, & Cho, 2008; Roman & Travis, 2006; Travis, 2005). Indeed, in one of the more comprehensive examinations of reentry, Petersilia (2003) noted that "we know almost nothing about the exact housing arrangements of former prisoners" (p. 121). Now more than a decade since the surge in research, we review research to date in detail.

While the empirical evidence lagged until recently, researchers have long recognized the importance of stable housing in the reintegration process. For instance, Bradley and colleagues characterize housing as the "lynchpin" that holds the reentry process together (2001, p. 1). Similarly, Lutze, Rosky, and Hamilton declare it "one of the greatest challenges confronting ex-offenders and their chance to achieve successful reintegration" (2014, p. 472). Although stable housing is itself an indicator of reintegration, it is also a precursor or correlate of other key forms of reintegration. For example, in order to obtain a job, an address is typically needed. Accessing healthcare and drug or mental health treatment are also—at least partially—dependent on stable housing. And more generally, housing fosters a sense of security and consistency that enhances overall well-being (B. A. Lee, Tyler, & Wright, 2010; Lutze, Rosky, & Hamilton, 2014). It comes as no surprise, then, that residential insecurities are associated with elevated recidivism (Lutze et al., 2014; Metraux & Culhane, 2004; Steiner, Makarios, & Travis, 2015). Moreover, the sheer number of those at risk of housing insecurities is cause for concern; approximately 641,000 individuals are released annually from prison while more than 5 million Americans have ever been incarcerated (Carson & Anderson, 2016; Shannon et al., 2017). Given the spatial concentration of incarceration and reentry in certain neighborhoods (Sampson & Loeffler, 2010), it is easy to see how incarceration can subsequently affect the functioning and well-being of entire communities.

Following prior work, we conceptualize housing insecurity on a continuum (B. A. Lee et al., 2010). On one end of this continuum are individuals who move frequently, often not by choice. At the other end of the continuum is literal homelessness. As a person's circumstances worsen, s/he slides further, often slowly, toward more acute insecurity. Difficulty paying rent, for instance, can be a precursor to residential mobility and homelessness. This approach illuminates the varied forms of residential hardships individuals exiting prison face, providing us with a more nuanced understanding of residential context among the formerly incarcerated.

Before describing the organization of our chapter, we first clarify the scope. We focus on the residential context following felony convictions, which are typically associated with an incarceration spell of one year or more. Little work assesses the impact of misdemeanor convictions or pretrial detention, which we note is an overlooked gap in our recommendations for future research. Additionally, rather than provide an exhaustive review, we highlight general themes in research to date.

We begin by reviewing research on residential mobility and neighborhood quality following prison. Here, and where applicable, we highlight racial variation in the consequences of incarceration, as this aspect is central to understanding the housing difficulties formerly incarcerated persons face, and, more broadly, how incarceration perpetuates inequality via the residential context. We also cover here the effect of concentrated incarceration and reentry on neighborhood quality and safety. After discussing mobility and neighborhood context, we summarize research on other forms of housing insecurity often overlooked in the literature including doubling up, difficulty paying rent, and eviction. We then review research on patterns of homelessness after release. In both of these sections, we also highlight research documenting residential consequences of incarceration for partners and children of the incarcerated. Next, we review some of the key mechanisms that may be driving the associations of interest. We close with a series of recommendations for housing-related policies during reentry as well as areas for future research.

But before moving to our substantive discussion, we first note the methodological challenges of this literature. Like other consequences of incarceration, assessing the causal effect of a felony conviction on residential outcomes is difficult, particularly because incarcerated persons are disproportionately disadvantaged prior to going to prison (Wakefield & Uggen, 2010). Thus, ascertaining whether incarceration causes residential hardship or whether such hardship would have occurred if the person had never been incarcerated is a key challenge. In addition, research in this area faces large constraints on data availability and quality. Simply put, identifying where someone lives—and who they live with—before and after prison is often quite difficult—if not impossible—with commonly used data sources. We discuss some of these data difficulties, and responses by researchers, in the sections that follow. We also call on future research to gather more nuanced forms of data to answer lingering questions. That said, however, researchers have been able to leverage advanced statistical methods and multiple forms of data to shed light on housing and residential outcomes after prison.

Residential Mobility

In the general population, residential mobility is cast as a rational choice process, driven by life events and housing preferences (Rossi, 1980). Moves often follow common life course transitions such as homeownership, parenthood, relationship formation and dissolution, educational attainment, and employment (B. A. Lee & Hall, 2009). Adding to this literature, Pettit and Western (2004) made a convincing case that incarceration should be placed among these standard life transitions, especially for low skill men of color. However, little was known about the relationship between incarceration and mobility until recently, in part due to conventional wisdom that people return to the same household or neighborhood where they lived prior to incarceration (Harding, Morenoff, & Herbert, 2013). Now a growing body of work is pushing back against this conventional wisdom, showing that many individuals move to new neighborhoods upon release from prison and experience elevated rates of mobility across time.

Much of the initial work on the residential context following incarceration came from the Urban Institute's Returning Home Study. This study drew on pre- and post-release interviews, interviews with family members, and community focus groups in four major cities and touched on a variety of issues related to reentry, including where returning citizens went and who they lived with in the days and months following release from prison. Not surprisingly, participants were likely to lean heavily on family members during the initial stages of reentry (La Vigne, Visher, & Castro, 2004; Solomon, Visher, Vigne, & Osborne, 2006). However, this did not necessarily mean that respondents were returning to their pre-prison neighborhood. For instance, approximately half of all Chicago respondents moved to a new residence upon release (La Vigne et al., 2004), and similar patterns were documented in Cleveland and Houston (La Vigne, Shollenberger, & Debus-Sherrill, 2009; Visher & Courtney, 2007).

These Returning Home findings have been generally validated by more recent and sophisticated work using larger and more representative samples. Analyzing data on individuals released on parole in Michigan, Harding and colleagues (2013) found that only 41% returned to their pre-prison neighborhood. Indeed, across their two-year observation period, the authors noted that 56% of the sample lived more than 2 miles from their pre-prison home at any given time, and over one-third lived at least 5 miles away. Similarly, and drawing on nationally representative longitudinal data from the National Longitudinal Survey of Youth, 1979 cohort (NLSY79), Warner (2015) found that about 60% of respondents lived in a different census tract after prison than before prison. Importantly, this high mobility at the moment of release cannot be explained by known correlates of mobility such as relationship or employment transitions (Warner & Sharp, 2016).

Rates of mobility stay elevated in the months and years following release from prison. More than half of the Returning Home participants in Cleveland moved two or three times during their first year out of prison (Visher & Courtney, 2007). Correspondingly, with their Michigan data, Harding and colleagues (2013) found that the average person moved every four and a half months and the median number of moves over the two year follow-up was 2.6. In comparison, only about 12% of the general population moves every year (Ihrke & Faber, 2012). Additionally, moves among the recently released were primarily short term; over half of all residential episodes lasted eight weeks or less before a person moved again (Herbert et al., 2015). However, mobility rates were lower for Michigan individuals who returned to their pre-prison neighborhood (Herbert et al., 2015). There is also evidence that the likelihood of mobility after prison declines with time (Warner, 2015), but many individuals likely find themselves reincarcerated before their rates of mobility decline to pre-prison averages. Approximately, 55% of individuals are reincarcerated within five years of release; the likelihood of mobility, on the other hand, remains elevated for at least eight years following release from prison (calculations based on Durose, Cooper, & Snyder, 2014; Warner, 2015, Table 2, p. 458).

In addition to extended rates of elevated mobility, some research finds racial variation in mobility. African Americans are more likely to move post-release—compared to their own mobility in the years leading up to prison. This is perhaps expected, as African Americans are more susceptible than whites to push factors associated with involuntary mobility (South & Deane, 1993). Moreover, the likelihood of mobility declined with time for formerly incarcerated whites and Hispanics, but not for blacks (Warner, 2015). Although not all research has found racial variation in post-prison mobility (Harding et al., 2013), the quality of the neighborhood a person moves to after prison, which we turn to next, is strongly shaped by race and ethnicity.

In sum, then, recent evidence shows that—contrary to conventional wisdom—many individuals move to new neighborhoods following release from prison. In addition, these landing spots are often only temporary, with the reentry period largely characterized by residential instability. In fact, elevated rates of mobility extend long after the typical six month–two year period used to characterize reentry. Beyond the hardships associated with these high and extended rates of mobility, frequent moves place formerly incarcerated persons at risk for sliding further down the housing continuum, toward increasingly unstable housing.

Neighborhood Context

Residential mobility does not, of course, take place in a vacuum, and of equal relevance is the quality of neighborhoods that people reside in following prison. To understand the residential attainment process, that is, how individuals use social and human capital to achieve residence in desirable neighborhoods, researchers draw on traditional concepts of concentrated disadvantage and social disorganization. As a whole, findings from recent studies indicate that (1) returning citizens tend to cluster in poor and disadvantaged neighborhoods after release, (2) that there is some movement between neighborhoods of varying quality, and (3) that neighborhood quality after prison is largely determined by race/ethnicity.

Lacking data on pre-prison neighborhoods, some of the first examinations of post-prison neighborhood quality focused on differences by offense and race/ethnicity. Using a sample of individuals released on parole in California, Hipp, Turner, and Janetta (2010) found that blacks entered more disadvantaged neighborhoods than whites. Additionally, when they moved, blacks moved into more disadvantaged and residentially unstable neighborhoods than whites over time. Sex offenders also lived in neighborhoods that were more disadvantaged and less stable than individuals convicted of other offenses. Somewhat surprisingly, the authors did not find any evidence that individuals convicted of more serious property or violent offenses or those with longer criminal histories lived in worse neighborhoods after prison compared to other offenders.

More recently, researchers have overcome data limitations to consider how post-prison neighborhoods compare to pre-prison neighborhoods. Findings indicate a fair amount of stability in neighborhood quality before and after prison, but that neighborhood environment can shift following incarceration in important ways. Most individuals tracked in Michigan, for example, lived in a neighborhood after prison that had a similar poverty rate to the neighborhood they lived in before prison (Harding et al., 2013). Furthermore, the first neighborhood after prison largely set the stage for neighborhood quality during reentry among this sample; Lee and colleagues (2017) found that individuals who first lived in poor neighborhoods after prison were likely to remain in such neighborhoods over time.

High levels of racial residential inequality in the United States also mean that initial neighborhood quality is largely shaped by race/ethnicity. Across U.S. metropolitan areas, for example, blacks are about 4 times more likely than other individuals to live in a neighborhood where at least 40% of the residents are poor (Reardon, Fox, & Townsend, 2015). It comes as little surprise, then, that crime-involved African Americans are consistently found to live in poorer and more disadvantaged neighborhoods than formerly incarcerated whites (K. Lee et al., 2017; Massoglia, Firebaugh, & Warner, 2013). In Michigan, for instance, more than 60% of blacks lived in high-poverty (poverty rate greater than 20%) neighborhoods before prison, compared to less than 20% of whites (Harding et al., 2013).

There is also evidence that a non-negligible proportion of individuals released from prison experience upward or downward neighborhood mobility, and this is also largely structured by race. While formerly incarcerated African Americans moved to poorer, more disadvantaged, and less residentially stable neighborhoods than their white counterparts (Hipp, Turner, et al., 2010), formerly incarcerated whites experienced the greatest pre- to post-prison shifts in neighborhood quality, at least in the short term. Massoglia and colleagues (2013) referred to this as a "more to lose" phenomenon, as African Americans who go to prison are already largely living in poor and disadvantaged neighborhoods. Whites, thanks to a pre-prison neighborhood advantage, have the most to lose in terms of post-prison neighborhood quality. An analysis of neighborhood attainment before and after prison using nationally representative longitudinal data found that only formerly incarcerated whites were living in worse neighborhoods after prison than before prison (Massoglia et al., 2013). Furthermore, only whites with a history of incarceration were more likely than their never-incarcerated counterparts to move from a non-poor to a poor neighborhood after prison (Warner, 2016). This is partly due to the role of institutional sanctions, such as being sent to drug treatment facilities or short-term correctional institutions. Such facilities tend to be located in more disadvantaged neighborhoods than formerly incarcerated whites typically live in during reentry (K. Lee et al., 2017). Over time, however, formerly incarcerated blacks become increasingly more likely to exit non-poor neighborhoods than their never-incarcerated counterparts. For whites, on the other hand, there is increasing convergence in the likelihood of downward mobility between those with and without a history of incarceration (Warner, 2016).

In addition to incarceration affecting individual neighborhood quality, concentrated incarceration and reentry affect larger neighborhood structure and functioning. Rose and Clear (1998) were among the first to argue that the spatial concentration of incarceration and, consequently, reentry may damage communities, in particular, the capacity for the neighborhood to self-regulate. A handful of studies have since found that incarceration is generally linked to neighborhood-level crime rates, especially in neighborhoods with high levels of admissions and releases (Dhondt, 2012; Drakulich, Crutchfield, Matsueda, & Rose, 2012; Hipp & Yates, 2009; Renauer, Cunningham, Feyerherm, O'Connor, & Bellatty, 2006). The exact mechanisms, though, remain unclear. Some work finds evidence that individuals released from prison increase crime directly because of the crime they commit once back in the community (Hipp & Yates, 2009). Other work shows evidence of indirect pathways because concentrated incarceration damages key institutions of crime control. Chamberlain (2016), for instance, found that higher numbers of individuals returning from prison trigger increases in residential vacancies and property sales. Using a combination of survey, Census, and reentry data, Drakulich and colleagues (2012) found that incarceration reduces neighborhood collective efficacy, which is essential for formal and informal crime control, largely because of the effects of incarceration on local labor and housing markets. Indeed, the likelihood of successful reentry declines as the concentration of formerly incarcerated persons in one's neighborhood increases (Chamberlain & Wallace, 2016).

Other Residential Insecurities

Frequent moves to and within disadvantaged neighborhoods are not the only forms of residential hardship returning citizens face. Although they have received less attention from researchers, other forms of insecurity, such as skipping rent payments or moving in with others to reduce costs, known as "doubling up," are more common than frequent moves among individuals exiting prison (Geller & Curtis, 2011).

Geller and Curtis (2011) leveraged data from the Fragile Families Study, an urban, disadvantaged sample of parents, to examine these phenomena. They documented higher rates of housing insecurity for formerly incarcerated men than never-incarcerated men, including whether a person skipped rent or mortgage payments, doubled up, lived with others without paying rent, or was evicted. Of these, skipping payments and doubling up were the most common. For instance, 11% of ever-incarcerated men doubled up compared to 3% of never-incarcerated men, and 15% and 8% skipped a payment, respectively. After controls were included, men released from prison in the past five years were considerably more likely to experience any insecurity, net of any insecurity prior to incarceration. Yet when these forms of insecurity were examined separately, incarceration is only associated with living with others without paying rent. Nonetheless, this work helps illuminate individuals' regression toward more severe forms of housing instability, further down the housing continuum.

Additional work by Geller and Franklin (2014) demonstrated that these insecurities are not limited to the formerly incarcerated individual. The authors found that mothers with recently incarcerated partners were 50% more likely to experience housing insecurities compared to other mothers. The most common insecurities faced by these women were skipping a rent or mortgage payment (15%) and living with others without paying rent (11%). Moreover, the authors showed that this effect was concentrated among women who had been living with the father prior to his incarceration. This suggests that, rather than reductions in household income, increases in maternal mental stress, or restrictive housing policies, it is the removal of the father from the household via incarceration that drives housing insecurities among current or former partners (Geller & Franklin, 2014).

Thus, while it is clear that formerly incarcerated individuals and their families are at an elevated risk of experiencing housing insecurities outside of residential mobility, there is a need for additional research in this area. We outline some potential pathways below. In contrast, more research has examined the most extreme form of housing insecurity: homelessness.

Homelessness

Scholars have long highlighted the conceptual overlap between the incarcerated and homeless populations. For instance, today both populations are disproportionately comprised of single, low skill men of color with weak social ties and elevated rates of mental illness and substance use (Metraux & Culhane, 2004; Metraux et al., 2008; Petersilia, 2003; Roman & Travis, 2006; Travis, 2005). Moreover, both populations expanded considerably since the 1980s, until recently beginning to plateau or decrease (B. A. Lee et al., 2010; Wakefield & Uggen, 2010). Homelessness and incarceration also share a historical connection dating back to Colonial America. During this period, vagrants were sent to "poor houses," one of the earliest forms of prison (Rothman, 1971; Snow & Anderson, 1993). Today, the United States continues to have exceptionally high rates of homelessness and incarceration (Walmsley, 2015; Wright, Rubin, & Devine, 1998). Perhaps because the data demands are considerable for this transient population, research to date has focused on estimating the scope of the problem, usually by matching administrative prison and shelter use records.

Estimates from around the United States find that between 4.7% and 11.4% of individuals released from prison rely on homeless shelters within the first two years post-release (California Department of Corrections, 1997; Hombs, 2002; Metraux & Culhane, 2004; Metraux et al., 2008; Remster, 2017; Rossman, Gouvis, Buck, & Morley, 1999). In general, studies using samples comprised of all individuals released from prison find higher rates of homelessness than those using samples limited to individuals released on parole, as individuals who serve their full sentence (i.e., max out), are often most at risk (Herbert et al., 2015; Remster, 2017). Nonetheless, these rates are generally higher than one year prevalence estimates for the general population and similar to individuals exiting other institutions including the military, foster care, and psychiatric facilities (Remster, 2013). For instance, in a disadvantaged sample of urban fathers, Geller and Curtis (2011) found that 4% of formerly incarcerated men had stayed at a shelter compared to 1% of never-incarcerated men. Furthermore, formerly incarcerated men were approximately 2.68 times more likely to stay at a shelter than never-incarcerated men, net of prior disadvantage, housing insecurity, and a range of other controls.

With the elevated risk of homelessness well established, recent work shifted attention to how formerly incarcerated persons experience homelessness, particularly the timing of homelessness after release. Like the bulk of reentry challenges, homelessness had been originally characterized as a temporary obstacle occurring early in the reentry process (Petersilia, 2003; Travis, 2005). For instance, using two years of administrative data in New York, Metraux and Culhane (2004) found that over half of individuals who used homeless shelters did so in the first 30 days. However, research using data on men released from Pennsylvania prisons found that while the risk wanes with time since release, some individuals did not become homeless for the first time until years after release (Remster, 2017). More specifically, with nearly eight years of data post-release, 50% of those who used homeless shelters did so more than two years after release. In fact, 27% became homeless for the first time four or more years later.

Such delayed homelessness is consistent with qualitative research. Based on five years of interviews with homeless men in San Francisco and St. Louis, Gowan (2002) found that delayed homelessness among formerly incarcerated men was not uncommon as it took time for reintegration challenges to unfold and accumulate. Before experiencing literal homeless, Gowan's respondents cycled through many temporary, unstable forms of housing, sliding further down the housing continuum, which often involved burning through weak ties and limited resources. In one respondent's words, "I was getting to be more and more homeless" and another stated "I started to realize I was homeless" (2002, p. 514). Hence, Gowan writes that sometimes "marginality did not manifest itself as literal homelessness for a long time" (2002, p. 514). Harding and colleagues' (2014) research, which explored reintegration more broadly using interviews of individuals released in Michigan, echoes Gowan's conclusions; many experienced struggle after struggle, some ending in homelessness. Lenora's case is illustrative:

> She first landed in a halfway house in Detroit, and for four months the state's prisoner reentry initiative covered food and rent. At the halfway house, she and the other residents were required to be out of the house for the entire day, searching for jobs. She stopped by a university in Detroit, and discovered that she qualified for financial aid. She signed up, believing that financial aid could be her 'ticket out,' a financial resource that would allow her to establish permanent housing and buy a car. Over the following months she took advantage of jobs skills training at Goodwill Industries, free clothing at a local charity, a short-term position subsidized by the reentry initiative, and supports and services offered from a number of other Detroit area charities. And yet her frustration at not being able to get a full-time, permanent job led to a several month bout of relapse and retail fraud that ended when she was assigned to inpatient drug treatment. Both the relapse and the inpatient residence disrupted her educational plans, compromising her chance for additional loans and grants. Following her completion of the inpatient treatment program, she stayed on as a resident trainee for four months, earning $75 a week plus room and board. She hoped to be hired on to a permanent position. She was not, and thereafter moved in with her nephew, paying $300 in rent a month and subsisting on food stamps and sporadic temporary employment. The last we saw of Lenora, her nephew's house was being foreclosed upon and she was planning to move, possibly into a homeless shelter.
>
> (Harding et al., 2014, p. 458)

Beyond timing, though, qualitative work like Gowan's raises questions about how individuals experience homelessness. In addition to delayed homelessness, Gowan's (2002) subjects often experienced repeated and/or prolonged homelessness. Such findings stand in stark contrast to the reentry literature's characterization of homelessness as a fleeting, temporary state until individuals obtain more stable housing (e.g., Petersilia, 2003; Travis, 2005). Recent quantitative work corroborates this; for some, homelessness is lasting. With nearly eight years of data post-release, Remster (2017) found that the majority of formerly incarcerated men who relied on shelters did so more than once. And rather than a brief hang-up, stays averaged approximately two months. Moreover, these stays were spread out over time as the average time between spells was over a year. Although it is often the least common form of insecurity, homelessness is an enduring impediment to reintegration for some. Further, such patterns of lengthy and repeated homelessness were more common among individuals who have been incarcerated than individuals in the general population who become homeless (Remster, 2013).

Indeed, research on patterns of homelessness among the general population as well as among the formerly incarcerated demonstrates that homelessness is not a uniform phenomenon, rather there are distinct "types" (Kuhn & Culhane, 1998; Remster, 2013; Weber, 2004). In the general population, there are three types of homelessness: transitional, episodic, and chronic. The bulk of homelessness is considered transitional (80%); individuals in this group stay only temporarily in shelters and often only once in their lifetime. Approximately 10% of the homeless cycle in and out (i.e., episodic), and another 10% are considered chronic, representing long-term homelessness. Remster's (2013) work on formerly incarcerated men in Pennsylvania found similar types of homelessness, but added a fourth group who did not experience homelessness until years after release from prison. Formerly incarcerated persons in the chronic class were the most intensive: they became homeless soon after release, experienced many spells, and spent a considerable portion of the observation period homeless. Those in the episodic class experienced a few spells spread throughout the observation period that totaled several months in shelters. The late onset class was characterized by delayed yet lasting homelessness, and the transitional group experienced a short spell long after release.

Similar to other forms of residential insecurity, mobility and attainment in particular, race is central to understanding homelessness. Blacks exiting prison are more likely to become homeless and experience more spells and/or lengthier spells than whites (Gowan, 2002; Metraux & Culhane, 2004; Remster, 2017). Given the concentration of disadvantage among people of color, this is not surprising (Wilson, 1987). In other words, the most vulnerable individuals experience more residential hardship post-release than their peers. Expanding on this, Gowan (2002) argues that homelessness among formerly incarcerated men of color perpetuates their marginality.

The risk of homelessness also extends to kin and again is structured by race. Using the Fragile Families data, Wildeman (2014) found that children who experienced paternal incarceration, but not maternal, were at an increased risk of homelessness. Children of recently incarcerated fathers were about 3 times more likely to have been homeless in the past year than children who did not experience this event (Wakefield & Wildeman, 2014). Wildeman hypothesized that this is due to family hardship associated with paternal incarceration whereas maternal incarceration often results in the placement of children with relatives or in foster care, reducing the risk of homelessness. Furthermore, these trends were concentrated among African American children, with evidence of smaller and non-significant associations between paternal incarceration and child homelessness among other children (Wildeman, 2014).

Mechanisms

Existing research has made it clear that formerly incarcerated individuals experience considerable residential hardship upon release. They reside in disadvantaged areas, are highly mobile, and some experience downward mobility into increasingly disadvantaged neighborhoods. Moreover, they are more likely to skip rent payments and live with others to reduce costs. They are also more likely to become homeless and experience repeated and/or lengthy bouts of homelessness. Scholars draw on a variety of explanations to understand these patterns including (1) the stigma of incarceration, (2) the collateral consequences of incarceration, (3) intermediate sanctions during community supervision, (4) the stress of the reentry transition, and (5) traditional correlates of housing insecurities and residential outcomes.

The stigma attached to a criminal conviction has been implicated in a number of reintegration challenges, including employment (Pager, 2003), earnings (Western, 2002), and health (Massoglia, 2008). This explanation has also been extended to residential hardship. Like employers, landlords can legally discriminate on the basis of a criminal record, and access to such information is commonplace (Lageson, 2016). For instance, Helfgott (1997) found that most Seattle landlords inquired about criminal history on rental applications and 43% reported they would likely reject an applicant for a criminal conviction. Stigma may also impede achieving housing in desirable neighborhoods (Warner, 2016) and can help push individuals towards homelessness. Indeed, Gowan's (2002) interviewees named the stigma of incarceration as a reason for their homelessness; many could not endure interactions with potential employers and landlords.

Collateral consequences, which impose restrictions on individuals convicted of a felony, also impact housing. For example, many states prohibit individuals convicted of certain offenses, especially drug and sex offenses, from living in public housing. The impact of such policies is clear as Hipp, Turner, and colleague (2010) demonstrated that sex offenders are more likely to live in disadvantaged neighborhoods post-release than individuals convicted of other offenses. Other public housing rules that affect residential insecurity are not offense specific. For instance, most public housing authorities have "one strike" rules or "discretionary eviction" for non-criminal disruptive behavior, meaning that a guest or household member's misbehavior places the entire family at risk of eviction. In one case, a Pennsylvania woman was evicted because her son was arrested (*Housing Authority of the City of Pittsburgh v. Fields*, 2003). As civil petitions, the burden of proof is comparatively low and discretion high, resulting in risks many families cannot afford. Importantly, such rules impact a considerable number as an estimated one-quarter of incarcerated persons lived in public housing prior to incarceration (Travis, 2005). Geller and Curtis's (2011) research supports this phenomenon; individuals living in public housing prior to their incarceration were more likely to be evicted after release. Moreover, the paternal incarceration–homelessness relationship was partially explained by loss of such institutional support (Wildeman, 2014).

Criminal justice institutions themselves also drive housing insecurity after prison. This is especially the case for behaviors (such as drug use) and rule violations (such as missing meetings or curfew violations) that trigger sanctions resulting in short-term institutional confinement, but fall short of full revocation. As an example, a person on parole using drugs may be sent to a drug treatment center and then released back to community supervision, rather than being sent back to prison (in a sense creating at least two moves). Other types of violations may trigger short stays in jail but are not otherwise treated as revocation or recidivism. Such punishments involve short-term custody in correctional institutions or residential treatment centers, and have been termed "intermediate sanction residences" (Harding et al., 2013). The short period of confinement (given no other violations) is followed by a continuation of community supervision. Thus intermediate sanction residences create substantial residential insecurities due to the frequent and short-term transitions between the community and the facilities. By some estimates, up to one-quarter of all post-prison moves can be attributed to moves into and out of intermediate sanction residences (Harding et al., 2013; Herbert et al., 2015). Herbert and colleagues suggest that most individuals on parole experience these sanctions, and mobility due to intermediate sanctions may also funnel individuals into poorer neighborhood contexts. Such sanctions could ultimately trigger additional sanctions if surveillance is higher in such neighborhoods (K. Lee et al., 2017).

Another explanation for post-release housing insecurities is the "stress of transition." Characterized as the material hardship combined with feelings of anxiety and isolation individuals face, approximately 40% of respondents in the Boston Reentry Study reported social anxiety in the first week post-release (Western, Braga, Davis, & Sirois, 2015). Anxiety often stemmed from new technologies and routines; navigating crowded public places, for instance, and figuring out the new transit pass system were overwhelming for one respondent. As multiple studies suggest that housing insecurity is highest soon after release (K. Lee et al., 2017; Metraux & Culhane, 2004; Warner & Sharp, 2016), the multifaceted stress individuals experience as they transition out of prison and into the community may influence housing insecurities.

Finally, it is important to note that many of the same correlates of residential insecurities in the general population drive insecurities among the formerly incarcerated. For example, individuals are less likely to experience insecurities after prison while working, earning higher wages, or living with a romantic partner, and the same applies to never-incarcerated persons (Geller & Curtis, 2011; Huebner & Pleggenkuhle, 2015; B. A. Lee et al., 2010; South & Deane, 1993). Personal vulnerabilities including mental illness and substance abuse or dependence are also associated with residential instability among populations with and without a history of incarceration (Herbert et al., 2015; Larson,

Bell, & Young, 2004; Remster, 2017). Regarding demographic characteristics, older individuals and blacks are often most at risk, as are individuals with less social and human capital (Herbert et al., 2015; Metraux & Culhane, 2004; South & Deane, 1993; Western et al., 2015).

Such overlaps in correlates of insecurities between those with and without a history of incarceration also highlight selection effects in regard to both incarceration and residential outcomes. As Wheelock and Uggen (2008) state, incarceration "sustains and exacerbates" prior disadvantages, entrenching individuals in poverty. Disadvantaged populations move at high rates to begin with, and the quality of the pre-prison neighborhood is an important driver of post-prison neighborhood quality (K. Lee et al., 2017). In other words, a mobile population with high exposure to poverty is over-represented in the prison population to begin with. The same applies to instability and homelessness (Remster, 2017). All things considered, the most vulnerable persons experience the most residential hardship post-release.

Future Research

While recent research has provided valuable insights into housing and residential outcomes following prison, lingering questions remain. It is clear that formerly incarcerated people are more residentially unstable than the never incarcerated, and more so than before prison, but despite considerable theorizing, it is less clear *why* this is the case. The larger literature on residential mobility distinguishes between moves that are voluntary or involuntary. Incarceration creates what Clear (2007) termed "coercive mobility" as individuals are removed from their communities through incarceration and then subsequently released, and recent studies using data on returning citizens in Michigan demonstrate that coercive mobility continues during reentry via institutional sanctions. But this still leaves a large share of mobility unaccounted for. Future research should empirically assess the reasons behind post-prison moves. To the extent that mobility is tied to hardship or stigma, this would indicate additional involuntary mobility. However, to the extent that mobility is tied to attempts at successful reintegration, such as human or social capital opportunities, then it may be that returning citizens are highly mobile because they need to make prosocial changes in relatively short time periods (Huebner & Pleggenkuhle, 2015).

Researchers should also further examine how incarceration affects family members of the incarcerated. One of the few studies to date (Geller & Franklin, 2014) found that disadvantaged urban women with incarcerated partners are more likely to experience housing insecurities such as doubling up, missing rent/mortgage payments, or moving frequently. If these women are at an increased risk for housing insecurities, then it may follow that their neighborhood quality is also compromised. This may be another way incarceration reproduces inequality, through children growing up in disadvantaged neighborhoods. As such, research should examine the types of neighborhoods that women and children live in before, during, and after family member incarceration.

Aside from women as partners of the incarcerated, little is known about women's residential insecurities after they themselves have been incarcerated. Most studies are limited to men, who make up the bulk of the prison population, but women leaving prison likely have different residential circumstances than men. Indeed, some work suggests that reintegration in general is more challenging for women than men, in part because the stigma of incarceration differs by gender (Huebner & Pleggenkuhle, 2015; Massoglia, Pare, Schnittker, & Gagnon, 2014; Richie, 2001). Notions of criminality are inconsistent with traditional ideas of femininity and motherhood (Schur, 1984), which may limit residential opportunities. Additionally, given the prevalence of female headed households, women exiting prison may have fewer places to go than men (who rely heavily on their families), as their household may have been dissolved when they were incarcerated. Yet some work suggests that men are more likely to become homeless than women post-release (Metraux & Culhane, 2004). Thus research examining women's risk for housing insecurities is an important avenue for future work, particularly given that the female incarceration rate grew faster than the overall rate during the prison boom and remains high, despite recent declines in the overall rate (Carson & Anderson, 2016).

In this chapter we focused on residential outcomes following felony convictions, but pretrial detention and misdemeanors and their resulting jail spells may also influence residential outcomes. With the injurious and broad effects of incarceration increasingly well-documented, researchers should shift their attention to these lesser forms of criminal justice contact. Recent work suggests that such contact indeed disrupts lives (Kohler-Hausmann, 2013). Regarding mobility specifically, Herbert and colleagues (2015) found that jail spells as intermediate sanctions directly contributed to residential insecurity. The cycling in and out of jails in particular may impact residential insecurities yet little is known about this phenomenon, particularly beyond mobility.

Another important avenue for future research is how housing insecurities are related to other reintegration challenges. Post-prison housing is often termed the "lynchpin" holding reentry together because it is said that addressing other reentry needs is difficult without access to stable housing (Bradley, Oliver, Richardson, & Slayter, 2001). Little research, however, directly examines the relationship between housing and other reentry outcomes such as employment or access to treatment resources. For instance, post-prison residential hardship is an unexplored pathway that could contribute to poor health among individuals with a history of incarceration. That is, given that residents of poor neighborhoods generally have worse health outcomes than do residents of affluent neighborhoods (Ross, 2000; Ross & Mirowsky, 2001), increased exposure to such neighborhoods (and other forms of residential hardship) could hasten post-prison health issues. Where individuals live after prison, and in particular where they spend their time, is also important for access to employment (Sugie & Lens, 2017), but additional work is needed in this area. Finally, while it is clear that neighborhood quality affects recidivism (Hipp, Petersilia, & Turner, 2010; Kubrin & Stewart, 2006), the role of housing insecurities is less clear. The few studies that have accounted for residential mobility have yielded mixed results, with some evidence of protective effects (Huebner & Pleggenkuhle, 2015; Kirk, 2009), and other evidence of mobility as a risk factor (Makarios, Steiner, & Travis, 2010). As such, unpacking how housing and residential outcomes following incarceration drive other consequences of incarceration would make important empirical and policy-related contributions.

Policy Implications

While much work remains to be done, and is by no means limited to the suggestions above, millions of formerly incarcerated individuals face residential hardships each year (Shannon et al., 2017). Hence we close with a few concrete policy suggestions. In our view, the literature provides several key takeaways. First, because residential insecurities, ranging from mobility to homelessness, are greatest in the early periods of reentry, housing assistance or interventions should target the first few months post-release. Indeed, housing is most salient in the minds of returning citizens in the first days following release from prison (Garland, Wodahl, & Mayfield, 2011). At the same time, emerging research, as demonstrated above by mobility and homelessness studies, suggests that individuals leaving prison remain at risk for these challenges long after the traditional reentry period. Increased awareness of this extended risk highlights the prolonged consequences of current penal policies and reminds practitioners that some individuals may require help later.

Second, even among a disproportionately disadvantaged population, clear risk factors have emerged for who is most at risk for housing insecurities. Targeting those most at risk can help maximize limited reentry resources. For example, individuals with mental illness and substance use issues are at a higher risk. Because of the correlation between race and poverty, blacks experience higher rates of housing insecurities than whites, as do older individuals. The latter in particular has implications given the growing number of older prisoners, referred to as the "graying" of the prison population. With an increasing number of older individuals exiting prison at an elevated risk of housing insecurities, practitioners and policy makers should prepare for these issues (ACLU, 2012). Similarly, the types of neighborhoods that are most likely to receive individuals exiting prison are well established. Particularly in light of recent research suggesting that influxes of returning citizens can have a negative impact (Chamberlain, 2016; Hipp & Yates, 2009), extra resources should be dedicated to said neighborhoods to reduce the burden.

Regarding current policies, a good place to begin would be lifting barriers to housing for individuals with a felony record or offense-specific restrictions. Rather than blanket bans, perhaps housing authorities could consider applications on a case by case basis. This low cost change would allow many to apply for the very services in place to help Americans in need. Additionally, jurisdictions should reassess their policies on intermediate sanctions, especially those that create mobility. Certainly there are cases where a move to a treatment facility is warranted, but research suggests that up to one-quarter of post-prison moves are tied to intermediate sanctions (Harding et al., 2013). Residential insecurities are a risk factor for successful reentry (Metraux & Culhane, 2004; Steiner et al., 2015), and jurisdiction should take a close look at an individual's residential history and residential options when considering the available sanctions for a violation during community supervision. In other words, attempts to address some risk factors may inadvertently create others related to housing insecurities.

More broadly, "housing first" approaches are gaining empirical support to reduce acute housing insecurities in the general population (Tsemberis, Gulcur, & Nakae, 2004). Such platforms prioritize housing over other services, arguing that access to stable housing facilitates other challenges, such as mental illness or employment. Recent work suggests that such approaches are also effective for formerly incarcerated persons, and so we close by highlighting some of these approaches. Two promising programs from Washington State specifically target those at the most insecure end of the housing continuum. The Reentry Housing Pilot Program (RHPP), for example, provides up to 12 months of housing support for high-risk individuals released from prison without a place to live. An evaluation of this program found that participants had lower levels of convictions, revocations, and readmissions to prison than a similarly situated control group (Lutze et al., 2014). Also from the state of Washington, the Housing Voucher Program provides rent expenses for up to three months for individuals who have remained in prison past their earned release date because of failures to secure housing. Compared to a matched-sample control group, participants in the Housing Voucher Program committed fewer recidivist events but did commit more technical violations (likely stemming from enhanced supervision as part of program participation) (Hamilton, Kigerl, & Hays, 2015). But even with increased technical violations, the program was found to save 7 dollars for every 1 dollar spent towards housing vouchers (Hamilton et al., 2015). Finally, the provision of housing to high-risk individuals may help set the stage for future stability. Pleggenkuhle and colleagues (2016) evaluated the Solid Start program, a faith-based program in St. Louis that provides three full months of rent followed by stepped-down rent support for up to nine more months. The authors noted the program "facilitated feelings of stability and independence" (p. 392) and that participants felt integrated into their communities.

Such programs, and subsequent evaluations, are important because they are helping to separate the provision of housing with the provision of other services. That is, many programs provide housing support as part of a larger package of services (i.e., wraparound services such as therapy or a caseworker), and it is unknown whether access to stable housing in and of itself produces positive outcomes. While such wraparound services may increase the likelihood of successful reintegration, the programs above make it clear that stable housing remains a core component of reintegration. Additional implementation and evaluation of such housing first programs are still needed, however, to fully understand how housing shapes reentry.

References

ACLU. (2012). *At America's Expense: The Mass Incarceration of the Elderly*. New York, NY: American Civil Liberties Union. Retrieved from www.aclu.org/report/americas-expense-mass-incarceration-elderly

Bradley, K. H., Oliver, R. B. M., Richardson, N. C., & Slayter, E. M. (2001). *No place like home: Housing and the ex-prisoner*. Boston, MA: Community Resources for Justice.

California Department of Corrections. (1997). *Preventing parolee failure program: An evaluation*. Sacramento, CA: California State Department of Corrections.

Carson, E. A., & Anderson, E. (2016). *Prisoners in 2015* (No. NCJ 250229). Washington, DC: Bureau of Justice Statistics.

Chamberlain, A. W. (2016). From prison to the community: Assessing the direct, reciprocal, and indirect effects of parolees on neighborhood structure and crime. *Crime & Delinquency, 64*, 166–200. Retrieved from https://doi.org/10.1177/0011128716678194

Chamberlain, A. W., & Wallace, D. (2016). Mass reentry, neighborhood context and recidivism: Examining how the distribution of parolees within and across neighborhoods impacts recidivism. *Justice Quarterly, 33*(5), 912–941. Retrieved from https://doi.org/10.1080/07418825.2015.1012095

Clear, T. R. (2007). *Imprisoning communities: How mass incarceration makes disadvantaged neighborhoods worse*. New York, NY: Oxford University Press.

Dhondt, G. (2012). The bluntness of incarceration: Crime and punishment in Tallahassee neighborhoods, 1995 to 2002. *Crime, Law and Social Change, 57*(5), 521–538. Retrieved from https://doi.org/10.1007/s10611-012-9376-z

Drakulich, K. M., Crutchfield, R. D., Matsueda, R. L., & Rose, K. (2012). Instability, informal control, and criminogenic situations: Community effects of returning prisoners. *Crime, Law and Social Change, 57*(5), 493–519. Retrieved from https://doi.org/10.1007/s10611-012-9375-0

Durose, M. R., Cooper, A. D., & Snyder, H. N. (2014). *Recidivism of prisoners released in 30 states in 2005: Patterns from 2005 to 2010*. (Recidivism of Prisoners Released Series). Washington, DC: Bureau of Justice Statistics.

Garland, D. (2001). Introduction: The meaning of mass imprisonment. In D. Garland (Ed.), *Mass Imprisonment: Social Causes and Consequences* (pp. 1–3). Thousand Oaks, CA.

Garland, B., Wodahl, E. J., & Mayfield, J. (2011). Prisoner reentry in a small metropolitan community: Obstacles and policy recommendations. *Criminal Justice Policy Review, 22*(1), 90–110. Retrieved from https://doi.org/10.1177/0887403409359804

Geller, A., & Curtis, M. A. (2011). A sort of homecoming: Incarceration and the housing security of urban men. *Social Science Research, 40*(4), 1196–1213. Retrieved from https://doi.org/10.1016/j.ssresearch.2011.03.008

Geller, A., & Franklin, A. W. (2014). Paternal incarceration and the housing security of urban mothers. *Journal of Marriage and Family, 76*(2), 411–427. Retrieved from https://doi.org/10.1111/jomf.12098

Gowan, T. (2002). The nexus: Homelessness and incarceration in two American cities. *Ethnography, 3*(4), 500–534.

Hamilton, Z., Kigerl, A., & Hays, Z. (2015). Removing release impediments and reducing correctional costs: Evaluation of Washington state's housing voucher program. *Justice Quarterly, 32*(2), 255–287. Retrieved from http://dx.doi.org/10.1080/07418825.2012.761720

Harding, D. J., Morenoff, J. D., & Herbert, C. W. (2013). Home is hard to find neighborhoods, institutions, and the residential trajectories of returning prisoners. *The Annals of the American Academy of Political and Social Science, 647*(1), 214–236.

Harding, D. J., Wyse, J. B., Dobson, C., & Morenoff, J. D. (2014). Making ends meet after prison. *Journal of Policy Analysis and Management, 33*, 440–470.

Helfgott, J. (1997). Ex-offender needs versus community opportunity in Seattle, Washington. *Federal Probation, 61*(2), 12.

Herbert, C. W., Morenoff, J. D., & Harding, D. J. (2015). Homelessness and housing insecurity among former prisoners. *Russell Sage Foundation Journal of the Social Sciences, 1*(2), 44–79. Retrieved from https://doi.org/10.7758/RSF.2015.1.2.04

Hipp, J. R., Petersilia, J., & Turner, S. (2010). Parolee recidivism in California: The effect of neighborhood context and social service agency characteristics. *Criminology, 48*(4), 948–979.

Hipp, J. R., Turner, S., & Jannetta, J. (2010). Are sex offenders moving into social disorganization? Analyzing the residential mobility of California parolees. *Journal of Research in Crime and Delinquency, 47*(4), 558–590. Retrieved from https://doi.org/10.1177/0022427810381093

Hipp, J. R., & Yates, D. K. (2009). Do returning parolees affect neighborhood crime? A case study of Sacramento. *Criminology, 47*(3), 619–656. Retrieved from https://doi.org/10.1111/j.1745-9125.2009.00166.x

Hombs, M. E. (2002). Massachusetts housing and shelter alliance's research on corrections and homelessness. Presented at the Annual Meeting of the National Alliance to End Homelessness, Washington, DC, July 18.

Housing Authority of the City of Pittsburgh v. Fields, No. 816 A.2d 1099 (Pennsylvania Supreme Court 2003).

Huebner, B. M., & Pleggenkuhle, B. (2015). Residential location, household composition, and recidivism: An analysis by gender. *Justice Quarterly, 32*(5), 818–844. Retrieved from https://doi.org/10.1080/07418825.2013.827231

Ihrke, D. M. & Faber, C. S. (2012). *Geographical Mobility: 2005 to 2010. (Population Characteristics).* Washington, DC: U.S. Census Bureau. Retrieved from https://www.census.gov/library/publications/2012/demo/p20-567.html

Kirk, D. S. (2009). A natural experiment on residential change and recidivism: Lessons from Hurricane Katrina. *American Sociological Review, 74*(3), 484–505.

Kohler-Hausmann, I. (2013). Misdemeanor justice: Control without conviction. *American Journal of Sociology, 119*(2), 351–393. Retrieved from https://doi.org/10.1086/674743

Kubrin, C. E., & Stewart, E. A. (2006). Predicting who reoffends: The neglected role of neighborhood context in recidivism studies. *Criminology, 44*(1), 165–197.

Kuhn, R., Culhane, D. P. (1998). Applying cluster analysis to test a typology of homelessness by pattern of shelter utilization: Results from the analysis of administrative data. *American Journal of Community Psychology, 26,* 207–232.

La Vigne, N. G., Shollenberger, T. L., & Debus-Sherrill, S. (2009). *One year out: The experiences of male returning prisoners in Houston, Texas.* Washington, DC: Urban Institute.

La Vigne, N. G., Visher, C., & Castro, J. (2004). *Chicago prisoners' experiences returning home.* Washington, DC: Urban Institute.

Lageson, S. E. (2016). Found out and opting out the consequences of online criminal records for families. *The ANNALS of the American Academy of Political and Social Science, 665*(1), 127–141. Retrieved from https://doi.org/10.1177/0002716215625053

Larson, A., Bell, M., & Young, A. F. (2004). Clarifying the relationships between health and residential mobility. *Social Science & Medicine, 59*(10), 2149–2160. Retrieved from https://doi.org/10.1016/j.socscimed.2004.03.015

Lee, B. A., & Hall, M. S. (2009). Residential mobility, adulthood. In *Encyclopedia of the Life Course and Human Development, Volume 2: Adulthood* (pp. 371–377). Detroit, MI: Palgrave Macmillan.

Lee, B. A., Tyler, K. A., & Wright, J. D. (2010). The new homelessness revisited. *Annual Review of Sociology, 36*(1), 501–521. Retrieved from https://doi.org/10.1146/annurev-soc-070308-115940

Lee, K., Harding, D. J., & Morenoff, J. D. (2017). Trajectories of neighborhood attainment after prison. *Social Science Research, 66,* 211–233. Retrieved from https://doi.org/10.1016/j.ssresearch.2016.12.004

Lutze, F. E., Rosky, J. W., & Hamilton, Z. K. (2014). Homelessness and reentry: A multisite outcome evaluation of Washington state's reentry housing program for high risk offenders. *Criminal Justice and Behavior, 41*(4), 471–491. Retrieved from https://doi.org/10.1177/0093854813510164

Makarios, M., Steiner, B., & Travis, L. F. (2010). Examining the predictors of recidivism among men and women released from prison in Ohio. *Criminal Justice and Behavior, 37*(12), 1377–1391. Retrieved from https://doi.org/10.1177/0093854810382876

Massoglia, M. (2008). Incarceration as exposure: The prison, infectious disease, and other stress-related illnesses. *Journal of Health and Social Behavior, 49*(1), 56–71.

Massoglia, M., Firebaugh, G., & Warner, C. (2013). Racial variation in the effect of incarceration on neighborhood attainment. *American Sociological Review, 78*(1), 142–165. Retrieved from https://doi.org/10.1177/0003122412471669

Massoglia, M., Pare, P.-P., Schnittker, J., & Gagnon, A. (2014). The relationship between incarceration and premature adult mortality: Gender specific evidence. *Social Science Research, 46,* 142–154.

Metraux, S., & Culhane, D. P. (2004). Homeless shelter use and reincarceration following prison release. *Criminology & Public Policy, 3*(2), 139–160. Retrieved from https://doi.org/10.1111/j.1745-9133.2004.tb00031.x

Metraux, S., Roman, C. G., & Cho, R. S. (2008). Incarceration and homelessness. In *The 2007 National Symposium on Homelessness Research.* Washington, DC: U.S. Department of Health and Human Services, Office of Policy, Development, and Research, U.S. Department of Housing and Urban Development.

Pager, D. (2003). The mark of a criminal record. *American Journal of Sociology, 108*(5), 937–975.

Petersilia, J. (2003). *When prisoners come home: Parole and prisoner reentry.* New York, NY: Oxford University Press.

Pettit, B., & Western, B. (2004). Mass imprisonment and the life course: Race and class inequality in U.S. incarceration. *American Sociological Review, 69,* 151–169.

Pleggenkuhle, B., Huebner, B. M., & Kras, K. R. (2016). Solid start: Supportive housing, social support, and reentry transitions. *Journal of Crime and Justice, 39*(3), 380–397. Retrieved from https://doi.org/10.1080/0735648X.2015.1047465

Reardon, S. F., Fox, L., & Townsend, J. (2015). Neighborhood income composition by household race and income, 1990–2009. *The ANNALS of the American Academy of Political and Social Science, 660*(1), 78–97. Retrieved from https://doi.org/10.1177/0002716215576104

Remster, B. (2017). A life course analysis of homeless shelter use among the formerly incarcerated. *Justice Quarterly*. doi.org/10.1080/07418825.2017.1401653.Remster, B. (2013). *Invisible men: A longitudinal analysis of homelessness among ex-inmates* (Unpublished Doctoral Dissertation). State College: Pennsylvania State University.

Renauer, B. C., Cunningham, W. S., Feyerherm, B., O'Connor, T., & Bellatty, P. (2006). Tipping the scales of justice: The effect of overincarceration on neighborhood violence. *Criminal Justice Policy Review, 17*(3), 362–379. Retrieved from https://doi.org/10.1177/0887403406286488

Richie, B. E. (2001). Challenges incarcerated women face as they return to their communities: Findings from life history interviews. *NCCD News, 47*(3), 368–389. Retrieved from https://doi.org/10.1177/0011128701047003005

Roman, C. G., & Travis, J. (2006). Where will I sleep tomorrow? Housing, homelessness, and the returning prisoner. *Housing Policy Debate, 17*(2), 389–418.

Rose, D. R., & Clear, T. R. (1998). Incarceration, social capital, and crime: Implications for social disorganization theory. *Criminology, 36*(3), 441–479.

Ross, C. E. (2000). Neighborhood disadvantage and adult depression. *Journal of Health and Social Behavior, 41*(2), 177–187.

Ross, C. E., & Mirowsky, J. (2001). Neighborhood disadvantage, disorder, and health. *Journal of Health and Social Behavior, 42*(3), 258–276.

Rossi, P. H. (1980). *Why families move*. Beverley Hills, CA: SAGE Publications.

Rossman, S. B., Gouvis, C., Buck, J., & Morley, E. (1999). *Impact of the opportunity to succeed: OPTS aftercare program for substance-abusing felons. Comprehensive final report*. Washington, DC: Urban Institute.

Rothman, David J. (1971). *The discovery of the asylum: Social order and disorder in the new republic*. Boston, MA: Little Brown and Company.

Sampson, R. J., & Loeffler, C. (2010). Punishment's place: The local concentration of mass incarceration. *Daedalus, 139*(3), 20–31. Retrieved from https://doi.org/10.1162/DAED_a_00020

Schur, E. M. (1984). *Labeling women deviant gender stigma, and social control* (1st ed.–4th Printing ed.). New York, NY: McGraw-Hill Companies.

Shannon, S., Uggen, C., Schnittker, J., Thompson, M., Wakefield, S., & Massoglia, M. (2017). The growth, scope, and spatial distribution of people with Felony records in the United States, 1948-2010. *Demography, 54,* 1795–1818.

Snow, David A., & Anderson, Leon. (1993). *Down on their luck: A study of homeless street people*. Berkeley, CA: University of California Press.

Solomon, A. L., Visher, C., Vigne, N. G. L., & Osborne, J. (2006). *Understanding the challenges of prisoner reentry: Research findings from the Urban institute's prisoner reentry portfolio*. Washington, DC: Urban Institute. Retrieved from www.urban.org/research/publication/understanding–challenges–prisoner–reentry

South, S. J., & Deane, G. D. (1993). Race and residential mobility: Individual determinants and structural constraints. *Social Forces, 72*(1), 147–167.

Steiner, B., Makarios, M. D., & Travis, L. F. (2015). Examining the effects of residential situations and residential mobility on offender recidivism. *Crime & Delinquency, 61*(3), 375–401. Retrieved from https://doi.org/10.1177/0011128711399409

Sugie, N. F., & Lens, M. C. (2017). Daytime locations in Spatial mismatch: Job accessibility and employment at reentry from prison. *Demography,* 1–26. Retrieved from https://doi.org/10.1007/s13524-017-0549-3

Travis, J. (2005). *But they all come back: Facing the challenges of prisoner reentry*. Washington, DC: The Urban Institute.

Tsemberis, S., Gulcur, L., & Nakae, M. (2004). Housing first, consumer choice, and harm reduction for homeless individuals with a dual diagnosis. *American Journal of Public Health, 94*(4), 651–656. Retrieved from https://doi.org/10.2105/AJPH.94.4.651

Visher, C., & Courtney, S. (2007). *One year out: Experiences of prisoners returning to Cleveland*. Washington, DC: Urban Institute.

Wakefield, S., & Uggen, C. (2010). Incarceration and stratification. *Annual Review of Sociology, 36,* 387–406.

Wakefield, S., & Wildeman, C. (2014). *Children of the prison boom: Mass incarceration and the future of American inequality*. Oxford: Oxford University Press.

Walmsley, Roy. (2015). *World prison population list* (11th ed.). International Centre for Prison Studies. Retrieved August 25, 2017, from prisonstudies.org/sites/default/files/resources/downloads/world_prison_population_list_11th_edition_0.pdf

Warner, C. (2015). On the move: Incarceration, race, and residential mobility. *Social Science Research, 52,* 451–464. Retrieved from https://doi.org/10.1016/j.ssresearch.2015.03.009

Warner, C. (2016). The effect of incarceration on residential mobility between poor and nonpoor neighborhoods. *City & Community, 15*(4), 423–443. Retrieved from https://doi.org/10.1111/cico.12207

Warner, C., & Sharp, G. (2016). The short- and long-term effects of life events on residential mobility. *Advances in Life Course Research, 27,* 1–15. Retrieved from https://doi.org/10.1016/j.alcr.2015.09.002

Weber, Max. (2004). Class, status, party. In D. B. Grusky (Ed.), *Social stratification: Class, race, and gender in sociological perspective* (2nd ed., pp. 132–142). Boulder, CO: Westview Press.

Western, B. (2002). The impact of incarceration on wage mobility and inequality. *American Sociological Review, 67*(4), 526–546.

Western, B., Braga, A. A., Davis, J., & Sirois, C. (2015). Stress and hardship after prison. *American Journal of Sociology, 120*(5), 1512–1547. Retrieved from https://doi.org/10.1086/681301

Wheelock, D., & Uggen, C. (2008). Race, poverty and punishment: The impact of criminal sanctions on racial, ethnic, and socioeconomic inequality. In A. C. Lin & D. Harris (Eds.), *The colors of poverty: Why racial and ethnic disparities persist.* New York, NY: Russell Sage Foundation.

Wildeman, C. (2014). Parental incarceration, child homelessness, and the invisible consequences of mass imprisonment. *The ANNALS of the American Academy of Political and Social Science, 651*(1), 74–96. Retrieved from https://doi.org/10.1177/0002716213502921

Wilson, W. J. (1987). *The truly disadvantaged.* Chicago, IL: University of Chicago Press.

Wright, J. D., Rubin, B. A., & Devine, J. A. (1998). *Beside the golden door: Policy, politics, and the homeless.* New York, NY: Aldine de Gruyter.

5

IMPACT OF INCARCERATION ON EMPLOYMENT PROSPECTS

Robert Apel and Anke Ramakers

Introduction

At this point in history, incarceration represents unprecedented government intervention in the lives of millions of Americans, especially poor, undereducated, and minority citizens. Punishment scholars have introduced terms such as "mass imprisonment" (Garland, 2001) and the "prison boom" (Wakefield & Wildeman, 2013) to characterize the scale of incarceration and its growth in the last two generations. Although aggregate prison growth in the United States slowed in the 2000s and even reversed direction around 2008, the incarceration rate nevertheless remains at historic levels and will remain so for a much longer time to come.

One "collateral consequence" that has acquired sustained scholarly attention, especially in the last 15 years, is the employment barrier for formerly incarcerated individuals. A number of excellent reviews of the incarceration–employment relationship already exist and are essential reading for scholars in this tradition (Uggen, Wakefield, & Western, 2005; Wakefield & Uggen, 2010; Western, Kling, & Weiman, 2001; Wildeman & Muller, 2012). Our objective in this chapter is to consider this research in quite a bit more detail than has heretofore been possible. Our review draws together two broad types of incarceration–employment scholarship: research on formerly incarcerated individuals and employer-focused research. Within these broad areas, we categorize what we believe are distinct strands of each research type, summarize individual studies within each category, and characterize overall findings and patterns.

Review of Research Findings on Formerly Incarcerated Individuals

One frustration that is bound to be experienced by a scholar who reviews extant research on the incarceration–employment relationship is the seeming lack of consistency in the findings. It is not difficult to find persuasive evidence that incarceration corrodes employment prospects, but it is also not difficult to find equally persuasive evidence that incarceration bears no relationship with employment, and possibly even improves employment prospects in the short term. That being said, and at the risk of making what must seem like a nonsensical observation, there is consistency in the inconsistencies concerning the incarceration–employment relationship.

In the paragraphs that follow, we classify existing research into five broad categories: non-representative research, administrative research, survey research, reentry research, and cross-national research. Within each of these categories, it is possible to draw more dependable conclusions about

Findings From Non-Representative Research

One prominent strand of research on the incarceration-employment relationship utilizes a variety of high-risk but non-representative samples comprising adjudicated delinquents as well as individuals recently released from prison (Gottfredson & Barton, 1993; Laub & Sampson, 2003; Matsueda, Gartner, Piliavin, & Polakowski, 1992; Nagin & Waldfogel, 1995; Sampson & Laub, 1993). These studies typically benefit from having a comparison (non-incarcerated) sample that is demonstrably at high risk of incarceration, lending more weight to the interpretation of any differences in employment or earnings as attributable to the incarceration experience. On the other hand, the results from these kinds of studies are far less likely to generalize, not to mention that findings about the impact of incarceration on employment tend to be as frustratingly mixed as the study designs.

Matsueda et al. (1992) re-analyzed data from the subsamples of recently incarcerated individuals and individuals addicted to drugs in the National Supported Work Demonstration. They observed no difference between the two groups in the likelihood of employment as well as mean earnings (although there was a surprisingly positive correlation of the number of weeks spent in jail with employment and earnings). On the other hand, recently incarcerated individuals reported significantly higher probability and amount of illegal income earning. They also discovered that recently incarcerated individuals rated certain professional occupations (e.g., teacher, construction worker, factory worker) significantly less favorably than individuals addicted to drugs, despite the fact that both groups were chronically unemployed.

Sampson and Laub (1993; see also Laub & Sampson, 2003) re-analyzed data from a sample of youth sentenced to a Boston-area reform school matched to school-going youth, finding that length of juvenile and adolescent incarceration was inversely correlated with adult job stability. In contrast, Needels (1996) re-analyzed data from formerly incarcerated men in Georgia in the Transitional Aid Research Project, finding no relationship between the length of incarceration and earnings once she adjusted for time free in the community.

Gottfredson and Barton (1993) exploited the closing of the Montrose Training School in Maryland as a natural experiment for studying the effect of residential placement on juvenile experiences. When they compared youth who were institutionalized to youth who were supervised in the community but would have been institutionalized had the facility remained open, they failed to find any differences in post-release work experiences between the two groups. Although a study of conviction rather than incarceration, Nagin and Waldfogel (1995) did find in the Cambridge Study of Delinquent Development—a study of white men from working-class London—that conviction exacerbated work instability by increasing unemployment, decreasing tenure, and increasing the number of jobs held. Unexpectedly, conviction was also associated with significantly higher weekly earnings by more than 10 percent above the sample average. To explain this apparent contradiction, they argued that criminal conviction relegates individuals to less stable but higher-paying "spot market jobs" rather than "career jobs."[1]

In sum, non-representative research yields a somewhat mixed set of findings about the relationship between incarceration and employment, indicating either an adverse effect or a null relationship. Null findings tend to characterize studies of youth with criminal justice contacts, as well as studies that utilize incarceration length as the criterion measure. On the other hand, adverse effects of incarceration on employment prospects tend to characterize studies of men who had criminal justice contacts during adulthood (or studies that follow youth with criminal justice contacts into adulthood), and studies that utilize more diverse employment measures than employment status. Although there are a number of mixed findings from this research tradition, one notable characteristic of these

5 Incarceration and Employment Prospects

data sources is that they were collected prior to the 1980s, a period that witnessed substantial growth in the prison population.

Findings From Administrative Research

A second strand of research on the incarceration-employment relationship analyzes earnings data from administrative sources. One such administrative source includes presentence investigation (PSI) and probation/parole reports on individuals convicted in federal courts (Benson, 1984; Kerley & Copes, 2004; Kerley, Benson, Lee, & Cullen, 2004; Kling, 2004, 2006; Lott, 1992a, 1992b; Waldfogel, 1994). A second administrative source comprises data from state correctional and state unemployment insurance (UI) systems for samples of recently arrested or incarcerated individuals, including California (Grogger, 1995), Florida (Kling, 2004, 2006), Ohio (Sabol, 2007), Washington State (Pettit & Lyons, 2007, 2009), and Illinois (Cho & LaLonde, 2008; Jung, 2011; Loeffler, 2013). A distinct advantage of administrative studies is that they are frequently capable of compiling data on employment and earnings for as few as eight and as many as 20 quarters prior to and following incarceration. On the other hand, they are frequently limited to studying only the correlation between incarceration length and employment, conditional on incarceration. They also rely exclusively on official measures of employment, which can lead to distortion if formerly incarcerated individuals are frequently employed in "uncovered jobs." We return to this latter point after considering the research findings.

Lott (1992a) failed to find any relationship between prison incarceration and earnings among individuals federally convicted of drug crimes, net of their conviction. On the other hand, he found in a companion study that incarceration reduced earnings among persons convicted for larceny but not among those convicted for fraud (Lott, 1992b). In Waldfogel's (1994) study, individuals with a federal conviction experienced a relative decline of 9 percent in their employment likelihood and a 16 percent penalty in their monthly earnings. Grogger (1995) showed that individuals arrested in California also experienced a sizable penalty for jail confinement that persisted for at least six quarters following release. Specifically, the relative (to the sample mean) erosion in employment was over 15 percent, whereas the relative penalty in earnings was 14 percent.

An unexpected finding that often emerges in many state administrative datasets is that the probability of employment actually increases relative to pre-prison employment, and is unexpectedly higher among those who serve longer sentences. For example, Kling (2004, 2006) observed in Florida that employment rates were 40 percent among those incarcerated for one year, and more than 50 percent among those incarcerated for four years. Similarly, mean earnings in the peak quarter were approximately $800 among those incarcerated for one year and $1,600 among those incarcerated for four years. These differentials were relatively short lived, however, as employment and earnings converged after two years elapsed. Furthermore, Kling observed that post-prison employment rates eventually returned to their pre-prison level, irrespective of incarceration length.

Pettit and Lyons (2007, 2009; Lyons & Pettit, 2011) similarly reported that incarceration length was positively and significantly correlated with employment rates among formerly incarcerated men in Washington State. As in the Florida study, there was a tendency for employment to return to pre-prison levels within two years. Jung (2011) reported the same kind of convergence at the two-year mark among males in Cook County, Illinois (see Cho & LaLonde, 2008, for evidence on formerly incarcerated females in the same jurisdiction). Also like the Florida study, significant earnings differentials were found in favor of those who served longer terms of confinement in Washington State and Illinois, but these differentials disappeared over time.

Loeffler (2013) employed a unique research design to study the impact of incarceration on UI employment among individuals convicted of felonies in Cook County, Illinois. Specifically, he took advantage of the fact that cases are randomly assigned to circuit court judges, each of whom has a peculiar tendency to sentence differently from his or her judicial peers (on average, at least). In light of random assignment to judges, these inter-judge differences become the source of exogenous variation in the likelihood of imprisonment and a powerful way of overcoming selection bias. Using a set of unique judge identifiers as "instrumental variables" for incarceration, then, Loeffler found that there was no relationship between incarceration and five-year employment rates.[2]

To summarize the findings from administrative data sources, among individuals convicted by the federal government, incarceration seems to worsen employment prospects relative to other criminal justice sanctions. On the other hand, somewhat unexpectedly, in studies of individuals serving state prison terms, those who serve longer terms tend to have better prospects with respect to both employment and earnings than those who serve shorter terms. It is very possible that this finding is due, in part, to the conditions of community supervision for formerly incarcerated individuals with different lengths of confinement, or else to differential exposure to prison programs that emphasize job skills (in which case individuals with longer "exposure" to prison are administered a larger "dosage" of in-prison programming). However, it is noteworthy that these differentials systematically erode with the passage of time.[3] A notable feature of most of these studies is that the subjects serve a sentence longer than one year in state prisons; in fact, the average subject in these studies served approximately two years behind bars. The estimates should therefore be interpreted as the correlation between imprisonment length and employment prospects, conditional on serving a prison sentence much longer than one year.

There is one important qualification to the paradoxical finding that longer versus shorter prison terms are correlated with better employment and earnings prospects, at least in the short run. Administrative earnings data come from state tax records and are based on the earnings reported by employers to the state UI system. They therefore fail to capture income from "uncovered jobs"—for example, self-employment income and out-of-state income.[4] Comparisons of self-reported and administrative data indicate that survey earnings are routinely higher than UI earnings, although program impacts tend to be similar (Kornfeld & Bloom, 1999). The singular exception is for young males with a criminal record, for whom the discrepancy between survey and UI earnings is greatest, and for whom program impact estimates qualitatively differ depending on the source (Schochet, Burghardt, & McConnell, 2008). These males are precisely the subjects of interest in the studies cited previously, suggesting that post-prison employment prospects measured from tax records miss many sources of income for samples entangled in the criminal justice system—self-employment, informal employment, short-term employment, and employment that is cash only or "off the books." Similar findings have been reported among formerly incarcerated men in the Netherlands, wherein informal employment seemed a plausible explanation for the discrepancy between self-report and official data sources (Ramakers, Nobbe, Nieuwbeerta, & Dirkzwager, 2017).

In short, if the tendency to work in UI-covered jobs varies systematically by the length of time served in prison, then the positive correlation between incarceration length and employment will partially be an artifact of the tendency to work in covered jobs relative to uncovered jobs. This finding suggests that self-reported employment and earnings, although undoubtedly subject to their own peculiar sources of measurement error, probably yield fewer biases in samples of formerly incarcerated individuals (see also Ramakers, Apel, Nieuwbeerta, Dirkzwager, & van Wilsem, 2014).

Findings From Survey Research

A third prominent strand of research on the incarceration-employment relationship employs the National Longitudinal Survey of Youth 1979 (NLSY79), until recently the only large-scale, self-report survey permitting scholars to study the incarceration-employment relationship in a representative sample (Bound & Freeman, 1992; Davies & Tanner, 2003; Fagan & Freeman, 1999; Freeman, 1992; Huebner, 2005; Maroto, 2015; Monk-Turner, 1989; Raphael, 2007; Western, 2002, 2006; Zaw, Hamilton, & Darity, 2016). One distinct advantage of the NLSY79 is that the survey has been ongoing since its inception, allowing very long-term follow-up of respondents into their 50s. However, this advantage is offset by limitations in the measurement of incarceration, which can only be ascertained by the location of the interview and which is consequently likely to capture confinement in prison rather than jail. A more recent survey now exists in the form of the National Longitudinal Survey of Youth 1997 (NLSY97), comprising annual self-report information about incarceration in either jail or prison, and permitting the study of the incarceration-employment relationship in a contemporary sample of young people surveyed into their early 30s (Apel & Sweeten, 2010). While the NLSY79 and NLSY97 have become common fixtures in research on the incarceration-employment relationship, there are other recent and notable data sources that also provide broad generalizability. These include the Fragile Families and Child Wellbeing Study (Geller, Garfinkel, & Western, 2006; Turney & Schneider, 2016; Western, 2006), the Survey of Income and Program Participation (Sykes & Maroto, 2016), and the National Longitudinal Study of Adolescent Health (Brayne, 2014; Dennison & Demuth, in press).

Freeman was among the first to explore the relationship between incarceration and employment in the NLSY79 (Bound & Freeman, 1992; Fagan & Freeman, 1999; Freeman, 1992). In a study of just the male high school dropouts in the sample, for instance, he documented a shockingly large 21-point reduction in the likelihood of employment between ages 18 and 26 (a 34 percent relative decline from the sample mean), and a 17-point disparity five years later between ages 23 and 31 (a 22 percent relative decline from the sample mean) (Bound & Freeman, 1992). In a companion study, the relative differences were even larger among young black male high school dropouts compared to the differences for all male high school dropouts (Freeman, 1992).

The use of the NLSY79 to study the incarceration-employment relationship has been reinvigorated by Western (2002; see also Western, 2006), who used the dataset to estimate the effect of incarceration on wage levels and wage growth. Prior incarceration had a significantly depressive effect on current wages, creating a wage gap of about 16 percent between non-incarcerated individuals and those with a history of incarceration. Importantly, Western also found that incarceration deflected individuals onto a much flatter wage trajectory, slowing wage growth by 31 percent relative to high-risk men who were never incarcerated.[5]

Huebner (2005) further confirmed that a history of incarceration led to significant erosion in the long-term likelihood of employment, after controlling for an extensive set of confounding variables. Raphael (2007) explored a variety of statistical models and found that having ever been incarcerated was correlated with a significant reduction in the annual number of weeks worked, as well as a significant decline in hourly wages of about 15 percent. Jung (2015) explored whether age of first confinement in the NLSY79 moderated the incarceration-employment relationship. He found that incarceration in a youth correctional facility was correlated with significant reductions in wages and labor supply (e.g., number of weeks worked) by age 40, whereas first incarceration during the 20s was correlated with a significant wage penalty but no impact on labor supply.

Also using the NLSY79, Maroto (2015; see also Zaw et al., 2016) documented substantial differences in wealth accumulation between individuals who had ever been incarcerated and their never-incarcerated peers. For example, in a well-controlled model, she estimated a mean difference in net worth (assets less debts) on the order of $42,000. Furthermore, the difference grew substantially over time, from $19,000 among those incarcerated in the previous year to $105,000 among those incarcerated more than 10 years ago. The primary mechanism for the size of the wealth disparity was attributable to the differences in home ownership, which was exacerbated by the differences in marriage and earnings.[6]

Apel and Sweeten (2010) utilized the NLSY97 to explore a number of facets of the incarceration-employment relationship. Using a variety of different statistical methods, they estimated the employment likelihood to be about 11 percent lower among individuals who were incarcerated following their first criminal conviction, compared to comparably high-risk individuals who were also convicted of a crime for the first time but were not incarcerated. This effect was persistent for up to six years following incarceration. When they further probed the employment differential, they discovered that most of the difference was due to the fact that incarcerated individuals dropped out of the labor force (and for a significantly longer number of weeks), meaning they were neither employed nor looking for work. Interestingly, there was no difference in the likelihood or duration of unemployment, referring to a state in which someone was not employed but was actively searching for a job. The overall pattern of results compelled Apel and Sweeten to conclude that incarceration caused sustained withdrawal and detachment from work. Further comparisons showed a wage disparity of 9 percent among those who were employed, and although this estimate was not statistically significant, there was evidence of deterioration in wages over time for the comparatively young sample.

Geller et al. (2006; see also Western, 2006) performed an analysis of the incarceration-employment relationship among new fathers surveyed in the Fragile Families and Child Wellbeing Study (FFCWS).[7] Men who had ever been incarcerated possessed a relative employment rate about 4 percent lower than non-incarcerated men, as well as a wage rate about 31 percent lower. However, the magnitude and significance of these differences varied a great deal depending on what statistical adjustments were applied, not to mention that sensitivity analysis indicated the results were not particularly robust to confounding by unobserved variables. Even more recent FFCWS research by Turney and Schneider (2016) found significant disparity in the accumulation of assets—including a bank account, a vehicle, and home ownership—that was not only limited to formerly incarcerated individuals but extended to their romantic partners, as well.

Sykes and Maroto (2016) creatively merged data from multiple sources, but primarily the Survey of Income and Program Participation (SIPP), to study the relationship between incarceration and wealth. Their important results showed that incarceration (as proxied by a measure of institutionalization) led to significant erosion in household wealth, producing a 64 percent decline in assets as well as an 86 percent decline in debts. While the latter finding would not seem to be obviously problematic at first glance, in fact it suggests that households impacted by incarceration are locked out of opportunities to obtain credit and thus to build wealth. Sykes and Maroto further estimated substantial differences in the likelihood of employment among households with an incarcerated family member, suggesting spillover effects of incarceration.

Brayne (2014) utilized the National Longitudinal Study of Adolescent Health (Add Health) to investigate the degree to which various forms of criminal justice involvement resulted in "system avoidance," or the curtailing of involvement with surveilling institutions. Having been incarcerated was correlated with significant withdrawal from the labor market, and in fact other forms of criminal justice contact (e.g., arrest, conviction) were uncorrelated with employment. Dennison and Demuth (in press) also utilized Add Health to evaluate the impact of incarceration on socioeconomic status (a composite variable including educational attainment and occupational status). They treated incarceration as the most extreme status on a continuum of criminal justice involvement and found that formerly incarcerated individuals possessed significantly lower socioeconomic achievement, over and above less serious forms of criminal justice involvement.

To summarize the findings from survey research, it should be clear that this research tradition exhibits a great deal of consistency in the finding that incarceration is correlated with worse employment and socioeconomic prospects. The employment differential tends to fall between 10 and 20 percent, which is a relative difference in the probability of working between incarcerated and non-incarcerated individuals. The wage disparity is more variable and tends to be between 5 and 30 percent, although the differential is not always statistically significant. The most recent research examines wealth disparity and provides estimates that are statistically significant and quite large.

There are a number of contributions and advantages of the survey research tradition for the questions that interest us here. First, the available samples are large and nationally representative, which ensure that the results generalize to known populations. Second, the surveys are frequently longitudinal, which facilitates the study of not only short-term consequences of incarceration but long-term erosion in employment. Third, the employment outcomes are manifold, which allows unpacking of some of the complexities of the incarceration-employment relationship. Fourth, there is a great deal of attention devoted to the selection problem, which strengthens causal inference. Yet true to the adage that there is no such thing as a free lunch, one important tradeoff of these advantages is the fact that survey research is frequently limited in the available measures of incarceration and criminal justice involvement generally. For example, with possibly one exception (the NLSY97), researchers working in the survey tradition are unable to distinguish jail from prison confinement, to measure length of confinement, and to study the "filtering" of criminal suspects from arrest, through intermediate criminal justice decisions (e.g., charging, prosecution, conviction), to incarceration as the final disposition (one wave of Add Health allows these filtering distinctions as well).

Findings From Reentry Research

One final, much more recent research tradition that speaks to the nature of the incarceration-employment relationship is composed of samples of incarcerated individuals who have recently left jail or prison (Freudenberg, Daniels, Crum, Perkins, & Richie, 2005; Sugie & Lens, 2017; Visher, Debus-Sherrill, & Yahner, 2011; Western, Braga, David, & Sirois, 2015). These reentry studies are not evaluations of the impact of incarceration on employment and earnings, *per se*, simply because they lack comparison samples of individuals who were not recently incarcerated. They nevertheless allow consideration of how circumstances change before and after confinement for those who experience incarceration. They also speak with some authority to the manifold reentry challenges that recently incarcerated individuals face in the labor market and other domains, especially in the more volatile months immediately following their release.

Freudenberg et al. (2005) conducted before/after comparisons of employment among adolescent men and adult women incarcerated in New York City jails. Relative to their employment status prior to the arrest leading to their incarceration, neither group exhibited any significant change in employment about 15 months after release. What is notable, however, is that no more than one-third of either sample was employed at either time period. Notably, the adult women reported significantly more reliance on government sources and family members for income following release, whereas adolescent men reported significantly less reliance on these sources. The adult women also reported a significant increase in health problems (e.g., depression, anxiety) and emergency room visits, while adolescent men again reported significant reductions in all of these experiences.

Visher et al. (2011) reported results from the Returning Home project, a three-state, longitudinal study of individuals leaving state prisons. About two-thirds (68 percent) of the respondents held a job prior to prison, but only 31 percent reported current employment after two months in the community, and just 45 percent reported current employment after eight months in the community. At both time periods, about 75 percent reported actively searching for a job, but a large share (71 percent) felt that their criminal record had affected their job search. An examination of income sources at the eighth-month interview revealed that a higher percentage reported income from informal work (47 percent) and family and friends (48 percent), as opposed to legal work (41 percent). In a regression model of the total percentage of time employed since release, Visher et al. found that the pre-prison work history was an important correlate of post-prison employment, as was in-prison work experience and arrangement of a job prior to release. Drug use, however, was inversely correlated with post-release employment, as were physical and mental health conditions.[8]

Western et al. (2015; see also Western, Braga, Hureau, & Sirois, 2016) oversaw the Boston Reentry Study, a longitudinal study of men and women who were recently incarcerated in Massachusetts state prisons. Immediately following release, respondents did not report heavy work-related activity (e.g., employment, job search), and although labor force participation increased steadily it reached only about 15 percent by the end of the first week. Rather, about half of the sample was idle and reported no activity at all during this time. After two months, 43 percent reported paid employment, and after six months this figure increased to 53 percent.[9] Many of the reported jobs were classified as "day labor" (e.g., construction, home improvement, snow removal), suggesting a high degree of instability and seasonality. Interestingly, public assistance was far more common than employment and characterized over 70 percent of the sample at both time periods. In a regression model of employment, Western et al. reported that respondents who were more socially isolated during the first week—spending time without family and involved in no productive activity—were less likely to be employed, a result that was marginally significant.

Sugie and Lens (2017) conducted a three-month smartphone study of self-report daily employment among men who were recently released from New Jersey state prisons. The novel use of smartphones allowed them to incorporate global positioning system (GPS) tracking of the respondents' daytime whereabouts. In a model of the timing of first employment, Sugie and Lens found that only the density of low-skill, low-wage job openings in proximity to a respondent's residence was significantly correlated with his employment likelihood, suggesting "spatial mismatch" between where formerly incarcerated individuals live and where good-paying work opportunities are available. On the other hand, any kind of job availability in proximity to daytime activity spaces was strongly correlated with job acquisition, suggesting that efforts to subsidize transportation to job-rich areas might hold promise as an employment-focused intervention for individuals who have recently left prison.

In sum, research from reentry studies points to a number of challenges that face formerly incarcerated individuals in the very first few months during their return to the community. Among the challenges that have been identified in the studies reviewed above are substance use and abuse, relatively unstable and inaccessible work opportunities, mental and physical health problems, and overall social isolation (especially among formerly incarcerated males). These are challenges that are likely to severely restrict employment prospects. Yet these by no means exhaust all of the challenges, as very recent attention has been devoted to the problems of legal debt accumulation (Cook, Kang, Braga, Ludwig, & O'Brien, 2015; Harris, Evans, & Beckett, 2010) and housing insecurity (Geller & Curtis, 2011; Harding, Morenoff, & Herbert, 2013).

Findings From Cross-National Research

Lest the review thus far leave the impression that research on the relationship between incarceration and employment is limited to the United States, it is worth drawing attention to a vibrant tradition of similar research in Western Europe. One point of contrast between the U.S. and Europe is the typical length of confinement, as prison sentences in Europe are far shorter than their American counterparts. In fact, European prison confinement resembles American jail confinement with respect to its length. A second point of contrast concerns the legal system itself, as most European legal systems are inquisitorial rather than adversarial. By comparison, the U.S. represents the quintessential adversarial system of justice. A third point of contrast is related to the conditions of prison confinement, which are far more humane in Europe than in the U.S. (Johnston, 2000). A fourth point of contrast concerns the presence of a more liberal welfare state that provides for a stronger social safety net for all individuals, including the formerly incarcerated.[10] Findings from these contexts can speak to the generalizability of the large body of work based on American samples and provide insight into whether theoretical mechanisms are context-specific or universal.

A distinct advantage of cross-national research is that European scholars frequently have access to population-wide digital registries on many individual circumstances, including education, marriage and cohabitation, fertility, military service, and residence, in addition to criminal justice involvement and employment. To date, the most rigorous research on the incarceration-employment relationship outside the U.S. has been performed in the Netherlands (Ramakers et al., 2014; Ramakers, van

5 Incarceration and Employment Prospects

Wilsem, & Apel, 2012; Van der Geest, Bijleveld, Blokland, & Nagin, 2016; Verbruggen, 2016) and the Nordic countries (Aaltonen et al., 2017; Andersen, 2015; Landersø, 2015).

Using administrative data from the Netherlands, Ramakers et al. (2012) estimated the timing of employment of formerly incarcerated individuals compared to unemployed to-be-incarcerated individuals. These groups were selected from the population of incarcerated males who entered Dutch penitentiaries within a two-year window and were in the risk pool for employment (i.e., they were recently employed). They found that individuals who were recently incarcerated had a significantly higher probability of employment than unemployed individuals who had not yet been incarcerated. Specifically, the employment likelihoods were 80 and 55 percent, respectively. Recently incarcerated individuals also obtained a job more quickly—12 months versus 18 months, respectively.

In another recent study of Dutch males surveyed for the Prison Project, Ramakers et al. (2014) examined the relationship between incarceration length and a variety of self-report employment outcomes within the six-month window following release. The most consistent finding was that, for prison spells longer than six months in duration, the likelihood of employment declined with incrementally longer incarceration length. For prison spells shorter than six months, on the other hand, longer incarceration length was uncorrelated with employment. This threshold relationship was not explained by differences in in-prison programming or post-release recidivism. Interestingly, there was no clear relationship between incarceration length and measures of job quality such as wages and occupational status, nor with measures of job stability, among men who obtained employment. One suggestive finding from this study was that re-employment by pre-prison employers was partly able to explain these differentials, as males who were imprisoned for short periods of time were more likely to maintain their employment ties.

Van der Geest et al. (2016) combined treatment files on Dutch males treated in a juvenile justice institution with administrative data until age 32. He first estimated different adult employment trajectories for the sample ("normative," "delayed onset," "dropouts," and "non-participants"), and then documented heterogeneity in the incarceration–employment relationship. Among the roughly 64 percent of the sample characterized by normative and delayed onset employment trajectories, incarceration resulted in a substantial decline in the probability of employment in the subsequent year, over and above the impact of conviction. There was no incarceration–employment relationship for the balance of the sample. Verbruggen (2016) used the same dataset and included both the men and women from this high-risk sample. She found that neither a conviction nor a prison spell had any impact on employment chances for men once unemployment history was taken into account. Among women, recent conviction (but not incarceration) was associated with a significantly lower employment likelihood, and like the men, unemployment history was strongly related to current employment.

Aaltonen et al. (2017) investigated employment before and after incarceration in four Nordic welfare states: Denmark, Finland, Norway, and Sweden. The samples were composed of individuals imprisoned for the first time for a maximum of one year, and differed considerably in the degree of labor market attachment prior to incarceration as well as employment prospects following incarceration. To illustrate, 39 percent of Finnish individuals (aged 25–30 at the time of incarceration) earned any income in the year prior to their imprisonment, and this increased to 48 percent in the year after imprisonment. By comparison, the corresponding employment changes were 72 to 74 percent in Denmark, 68 to 43 percent in Sweden, and 78 to 71 percent in Norway. In all four countries, however, employment rates exhibited an overall downward trend starting five years prior to incarceration and spanning five years following incarceration.

Andersen (2015) investigated the effect of community service versus incarceration by exploiting a policy reform in Denmark, which made a large number of criminal offenses newly eligible for community service as punishment (e.g., misdemeanors, drunk driving, simple violence). Her results indicated that, for up to three years following conviction, individuals given custodial sentences exhibited the same levels of income and social welfare dependence as those sentenced to community service. On the other hand, there was a significant divergence in long-run prospects, as those sentenced to incarceration had lower income and higher social welfare dependency. For example, five years after conviction, the formerly incarcerated individuals earned 17 percent lower income and experienced 25 percent longer duration of welfare dependency.[11]

Landersø (2015) exploited another Danish reform that increased incarceration length by roughly one month, to obtain causal estimates of the effects of incarceration length on unemployment and earnings. Focusing on individuals incarcerated for violent offenses, most of whom were confined for two months or less, he compared those incarcerated after the reform to those incarcerated prior to the reform. The results indicated that the longer prisons sentences actually lowered unemployment rates for up to two years (but not beyond), and although earnings were also higher, the differences were not statistically significant. Landersø suggested that the reform may have reduced unemployment by enabling incarcerated individuals to participate in and benefit from rehabilitation programs versus merely experiencing the costs of incarceration, since participation rates for prison rehabilitation programs increased steeply with incarceration length.

To summarize the findings from cross-national research, the mix of negative, positive, and null effects of incarceration on employment is also evident in Western contexts other than the United States, namely in the Netherlands and the Nordic countries. Null findings are evident from long-term studies of high-risk samples, namely individuals confined in reform institutions as juveniles (Netherlands). Evidence that incarceration improves employment prospects, for at least some period of time following release, stems from studies of shocks to incarceration length among individuals with very short sentences (Denmark), and from studies comparing incarceration spells to unemployment spells (Netherlands). Evidence that incarceration worsens employment prospects is strongest in studies comparing prison sentences to non-custodial punishments (Denmark), and in studies comparing prison sentences longer than six months to comparatively shorter sentences (Netherlands). The latter set of findings suggest that collateral consequences in the labor market are not exclusive to contexts like the U.S., with its dissimilarity in many social and legal respects to Western Europe.

Review of Research Findings on Employers

A great deal of research on the incarceration-employment relationship implicitly concerns the "supply side" of the labor market, referring to the skills and work experiences possessed by potential job seekers that make them more or less attractive hires to employers. A supply-side explanation of the incarceration-employment relationship emphasizes simply that formerly incarcerated individuals are objectively less employable than their non-incarcerated counterparts. For instance, this might be because of erosion in their human capital due to time behind bars and thus being out of the labor market, which makes them less experienced, less productive, or less capable employees. Or it might be because of erosion in their social capital, which might constrain access to job referral networks. Yet there is another tradition of research that focuses on the "demand side" of the labor market, referring to the willingness of employers to knowingly hire formerly incarcerated individuals. This shifts the analytical focus from employees to employers and emphasizes the stigmatizing effect of incarceration and what it represents about a formerly incarcerated individual's reputation, reliability, or trustworthiness.

Clear evidence for exclusion of formerly incarcerated individuals in the labor market is the variety of statutory restrictions that prohibit employment in certain sectors (e.g., public employment), catering to certain vulnerable clientele (e.g., children), and professional licensing and bonding in certain occupations (Burton, Cullen, & Travis, 1987; Dale, 1976; Harris & Keller, 2005). Beyond these statutory exclusions, however, there is also a compelling body of research based on employers themselves that criminal justice involvement (even if it does not culminate in incarceration) stigmatizes

Experimental Audits and Correspondence Studies

Experimental audits or correspondence studies are used in a variety of disciplines to test for discrimination. In a typical study of employment, for example, a pair of applicants, known as "auditors" or "testers," applies for the same job. Relevant background characteristics of the tester pair (e.g., gender, race, education, work history) are matched as best as possible while the key characteristic under study—namely, possession of some kind of criminal history—is randomly varied between the testers. In an audit study, the testers apply in person for posted job openings, whereas in a correspondence study, résumés or applications with fictitious credentials are submitted. The key outcome in an audit or correspondence study is the "callback," or any form of favorable follow-up from an employer to a tester (e.g., offer of hire, invitation for an interview, solicitation of more information).

In what is probably the earliest version of a correspondence study, Schwartz and Skolnick (1962) solicited the assistance of a confederate to disseminate employment folders to business establishments in the Catskill region of New York State. They documented a much lower callback rate for employment files reporting a conviction and sentence for assault (4 percent), relative to files reporting no criminal record (36 percent).[12] Remarkably, despite the fact their sample size was too small for conventional statistical tests, the difference in those percentages was statistically significant (this was determined by our calculation of Fisher's exact test from Schwartz and Skolnick's data).

In a widely read experimental audit, Pager (2003; see also Pager, 2007) conducted a Milwaukee study of matched pairs and found that employers advertising entry-level job openings were less than half as likely to call back applicants who reported a prison record—a felony conviction with prison time—relative to temporary employment.[13] Specifically, the callback rates were 10 percent and 23 percent, respectively, for applicants with and without a prison record. Her conclusion was that "criminal records close doors in employment situations" (p. 956). In a replication of the audit design in New York City, Pager, Western, and Sugie (2009; see also Pager, 2007; Pager, Western, & Bonikowski, 2009) again found a significantly lower callback rate among men with a prison record. Specifically, callback rates were 15 percent and 28 percent, respectively, among applicants with and without a prison record. One important finding from their analysis concerned opportunities for applicants to establish rapport. Applicants who were given a chance to interact with a hiring manager experienced greatly improved hiring chances, and this was especially true for applicants with a prison record. This finding led Pager and colleagues to conclude that "[p]ersonal contact thus seems to play an important role in mediating the effects of criminal stigma in the hiring process" (p. 200).

One additional finding that has consistently emerged from Pager's series of audit studies concerns the influence of racial discrimination as well as the dual influence of race and incarceration (Pager, 2003, 2007; Pager et al., 2009; Pager, Western, & Sugie, 2009). Namely, black applicants received significantly fewer callbacks than white applicants, but most alarming was her finding that black applicants without a prison record had a similar callback rate to white applicants with a prison record. This provided evidence of racial discrimination that intersected in a complicated way with incarceration, in such a way that being black and possessing a prison record constituted a "double jeopardy" in low-wage labor markets (Pager, 2005, 2007).

Galgano (2009) carried out a correspondence study in Chicago, with a design very similar to Pager (2003) but involving the submission of online applications rather than in-person applications. Her testers were also female rather than male. She did not observe any difference in callback rates, suggesting that "a criminal history is not as universally stigmatizing for women" (p. 33). Decker, Ortiz, Spohn, and Hedberg (2015) replicated Pager's (2003) design in Phoenix using both an audit study and a correspondence study. Interestingly, there was no difference in the chance of a callback in the correspondence portion (online applications) of the study—8 percent of the applicants in the control group received a callback compared to 7 percent of the applicants with a prison record. On the other hand, in the audit portion of the study (in-person applications), 18 percent of the applicants in the control group received a callback compared to 10 percent of the applicants with a prison record, a difference that was statistically significant.

In sum, audit studies consistently find that the rate of callback is lower for formerly incarcerated males who apply in person for job postings, relative to men reporting no criminal record. Indeed, their callback rate is about one-half the size of the callback rate among men without any criminal history. By comparison, there does not seem to be any relationship between incarceration and callback in the correspondence studies conducted to date, for either men or women. The audit research tradition also points to the joint influence of race and criminal history. Formerly incarcerated black job applicants are especially disadvantaged, in such a way that black applicants with no criminal history tend to experience fewer callbacks than white applicants who have recently been incarcerated. However, the interaction of race with criminal history is frequently not statistically significant; thus, this joint relationship is suggestive but has not yet been definitively established.

Employer Willingness to Hire

Another strand of employer-focused research surveys the perceptions and attitudes of business owners or hiring personnel towards individuals formerly involved in the criminal justice system. To this end, multiple measures with Likert-type scales are typically used and are sometimes combined with hiring vignettes. An obvious downside of this approach is that responding to a hypothetical job applicant could produce different outcomes than authentic hiring situations. Indeed, in a follow-up survey of employers in the Milwaukee audit, Pager and Quillian (2005) documented no racial difference in employer expressions of willingness to hire in a vignette involving an applicant with a prison record, despite their finding of a racial difference in the likelihood of a callback to an applicant with a prison record. This suggests that there could be a large discrepancy between what employers say they would do (as measured by survey responses) versus what employers actually do (as measured by callback rates). While surveys might not be suitable for revealing the degree of discrimination, this method can nevertheless examine how a wide range of characteristics of the applicant, the employer, or the organizational context relate to willingness to hire from this disadvantaged group. This line of work helps to reveal these biases and understand why employers hold a generally unfavorable attitude toward these individuals.[14]

Finn and Fontaine (1983) surveyed individuals enrolled in personnel management classes and found that respondents preferred applicants without a criminal record over those with different forms of criminal records, and especially those who had served time. Good job qualifications overcame the disadvantages of a criminal record but only when they substantially exceeded the qualifications of applicants without a record.[15] In a later study, Finn and Fontaine (1985) extended their investigation to include more students (N=225) as well as different types of crime, types of employment, and the sex of the applicant. While they found no evidence for a gender bias, significantly lower scores were given to applicants who attempted armed robbery (versus no crime, drugs possession, and shoplifting) and applicants for salesperson jobs (versus hand packager, general clerk).

Albright and Denq (1996) concluded that a college degree and certain types of educational prison programs increased the willingness of employers to hire formerly convicted individuals in Houston and Dallas. The employers were very opposed to hiring individuals convicted of violent crimes but were more likely to hire formerly convicted individuals when government incentives were available and no relationship existed between the crime and the job to be filled. Albright and Denq furthermore concluded that "[e]mployers in this study indicated that the more information they received about the applicant . . . the more likely they are to consider hiring them" (p. 133). In a small-scale study in Baltimore, Giguere and Dundes (2002) examined employers' willingness to hire using a vignette that described an individual who was recently released from prison and had applied for an entry-level job. They identified people skills and customer discomfort as major employer concerns about hiring from this group. They also showed that employers who had (non-business related) contact with formerly convicted individuals held more favorable attitudes towards them, and concluded social contact with this group "helps to offset the stigma" (p. 404).

Haslewood-Pócsik, Brown, and Spencer (2008) examined several topics related to employing formerly convicted individuals in northwest England and found support for many of the above-mentioned factors.[16] Noteworthy is that, next to job skills, several "soft skills" such as honesty and reliability were rated as highly relevant characteristics. Their study furthermore revealed that employers rated a mentor most useful among a wide variety of support options. A sizeable proportion of the respondents (43 percent) had prior experience with employing formerly convicted individuals, enabling the researchers to compare the views of employers with and without this experience. Remarkably, they concluded that employers with such prior experience were more concerned about the practical risks such an employee might pose, but were also less averse to consider hiring them, regardless of their criminal record. These employers were also more likely to rate educational and professional qualifications as less critical.

Lukies, Graffam, and Shinkfield (2011; see also Graffam, Shinkfield, & Hardcastle, 2007) were the first to examine the relative importance of the criminal history of the job-seeker, personal characteristics of the employer, and organizational context variables for employer attitudes. Based on questionnaires completed by Australian employers, they concluded that the nature of the criminal history was the most salient correlate of perceived employability, although employer and organizational characteristics were also relevant correlates. While industry type and firm location had no influence on attitudes, importantly, employers in larger organizations and those who previously employed individuals involved in the criminal justice system showed a significantly more favorable attitude toward this group.

In a very recent Australian study, Reich (2017) administered vignettes to a large number of employers. She examined the role of several of the abovementioned objective factors as well as employers' subjective beliefs and found that "belief in redeemability" was a significant determinant of the willingness to hire (in her study, persons were convicted but sentenced to community service rather than to prison).[17] She also found that applicants who possessed a variety of hard and soft skills were perceived more favorably.[18]

In sum, individuals involved in the criminal justice system in general, and formerly incarcerated persons in particular, not only face a variety of statutory restrictions that categorically prohibit certain types of employment, but must also confront the seemingly intractable attitudes of hiring personnel about their unemployability. On a more positive note, several hard and soft skills appear to mitigate employers' attitudes, implying that other job qualifications might serve as fruitful targets for intervention to improve employment prospects. Furthermore, having access to more information about the applicant and prior experience with hiring from this worker pool are related to more favorable employer attitudes. While these findings are often based on small unrepresentative samples, they add a great deal of nuance to the blunter conclusion that employers possess biases against hiring formerly convicted persons.

Concluding Remarks

This chapter has been limited in scope to a review of the quantitative relationship between incarceration and employment. Out of necessity, there are several strands of research and commentary that we have had to omit in order to be as exhaustive as possible in our review. First, we did not include forms of criminal punishment other than incarceration. The rare exceptions (e.g., conviction) are for findings that help provide greater understanding of mechanisms for the relationship between incarceration and employment, but it goes without saying that other forms of punishment such as arrest and probation are worthy of review in their own right. Second, we did not include qualitative research findings. This does not stem from a lack of interest in the findings from this research tradition, but rather from the sheer number of quantitative studies that exist, coupled with the need to bring some coherence to seemingly disparate conclusions from the quantitative tradition. There are very good examples of qualitative studies that draw out some of the mechanisms that quantitative scholars are incapable of measuring, and these mechanisms are essential for theoretical clarity about the incarceration-employment relationship. Third, we did not include a lengthy policy discussion. Given the length of the current chapter, there was little space to devote to an extensive consideration of policy proposals or to the promise and pitfalls of employment-focused programs for formerly incarcerated individuals. Although existing research establishes the basic nature of the incarceration-employment relationship, policy proposals have not been met with a great deal of success; yet these challenges should not deter continued effort in the future.

As is probably obvious from this chapter, there is a healthy volume of quantitative research on the incarceration-employment relationship. We have sought to identify the key lines of inquiry, to summarize most of the key studies and results, and to point out the divergent findings and possible sources of the discrepancies. Overall, there is remarkable consistency in the finding that incarceration is highly disruptive for certain aspects of the employment experience—even relative to other highly disadvantaged individuals and even in countries with far more liberal and humane justice systems, formerly incarcerated individuals experience a great deal of instability in the labor market. Moreover, two related lines of quantitative inquiry, for which there was insufficient space in this review, imply that the collateral consequences of mass incarceration extend beyond the lives of those individuals who experience incarceration. First, aggregate research shows that the effects of mass incarceration lead to distortion in measures of the economic health of the country, particularly among the young African American men who fill the nation's prisons (e.g., Western & Beckett, 1999; Pettit & Western, 2004). To illustrate, the Current Population Survey (CPS) is used to provide estimates of the racial gap in high school dropout and wages, but it misses a sizable fraction of socially marginalized men, by design, because they reside in prisons rather than households.

Second, findings concerning statistical discrimination imply that mass incarceration can sabotage the employment prospects of all young black males. One obvious solution to the reported employer discrimination experienced by formerly incarcerated individuals could seem to impose statutory limits on the availability of criminal history information. It is possible, however, that employers who are denied access to such information might use demographic information in a statistically discriminatory way (Solinas-Saunders, Stacer, & Guy, 2015). Recent studies suggest that some employers indeed use an applicant's race (along with gender and age) as a demographic marker for possession of a criminal record, and this prejudicial exclusion is worsened if employers lack access to criminal history information (Bushway, 2004; Holzer, Raphael, & Stoll, 2006). This puts advocates in the uncomfortable position of having to decide between the social good that derives from restricting employer access to criminal history repositories or employer ability to inquire about criminal histories on job applications (e.g., "Ban the Box"), and thus improving the employment chances of formerly incarcerated individuals, versus the social harm done by statistical discrimination toward young male African American job applicants who have no criminal justice involvement.

Despite all that has been learned from the research reviewed herein, there is still a great deal of room for advancement of this research tradition. In our concluding comments, we just focus on three of these. First, it is essential to avoid treating employment in isolation from other life domains, since evidence is building that incarceration touches many aspects of an individual's life other than his or her employment prospects, including housing (Kirk in Chapter 3) health (Fahmy & Wallace in Chapter 6, LeBel & Richie in Chapter 7), and family life (Northcutt Bohmert & Wakefield in Chapter 8) (see also Wakefield & Uggen, 2010; Wildeman & Muller, 2012). This suggests that efforts to estimate the incarceration-employment relationship in a longitudinal setting will be complicated by the fact that non-employment aspects of a formerly incarcerated individual's life might actually serve as mediators between incarceration and later employment prospects. If so, standard panel designs risk underestimating the incarceration-employment relationship by treating these non-employment aspects as control variables rather than as causal mediators (e.g., Baćak & Kennedy, 2015).

Second, it is probably a good time to move beyond point estimation altogether, or efforts to identify the "average effect" of incarceration controlling for confounders, and to instead focus future efforts on estimation of heterogeneity in the effects of incarceration. Despite the fact that formerly incarcerated individuals tend to be drawn disproportionately from the lower rungs of the social ladder, there is still likely to be considerable heterogeneity in effects. Heterogeneity can come in manifold forms. It can refer to *groupwise heterogeneity* resulting from measureable characteristics of punished individuals that can moderate incarceration effects, for example, the severity of an individual's background risk (e.g., Wakefield & Powell, 2016). Yet it can also refer to *distributional heterogeneity* resulting from a shift in the location or scale of an outcome for punished individuals relative to their non-punished counterparts. For instance, formerly incarcerated individuals might not only exhibit lower mean wages, but also experience compression in their wage distribution, relative to non-incarcerated individuals.

Third and finally, most existing research is concerned with prison incarceration, which is quite natural given the greater ease of access to state correctional data. But it is also important to develop a much better understanding of the consequences of jail incarceration, or the impact of comparatively short sentences of incarceration. The jail population on any given day tends to be about one-half the size of the prison population—the prison incarceration rate is about 500 per 100,000 (roughly 1.5 million people) and the jail incarceration rate is about 250 per 100,000 (roughly 750,000 people). However, the average daily jail population underestimates by a very large margin the number of individuals who actually pass through the nation's jails in a given year, which the Bureau of Justice Statistics estimates at slightly less than 13 million in 2010 (Minton, 2011). Accounting for the fact that a little less than 40 percent of individuals are in jail serving a sentence (rather than awaiting trial) still yields approximately 5 million who are incarcerated in jail for a crime in a given year. Short sentences of incarceration are clearly the norm, yet they continue to be the least studied form of incarceration.

Notes

1 This is a distinction that roughly corresponds with work in the secondary and primary labor markets, respectively.
2 Our interpretation of Loeffler's (2013) study suggests more ambiguity in the key finding than what is reported. Although the details are somewhat technical, one limitation of instrumental variables models is their tendency to be inefficient, so much so that they can frequently be no better than standard regression models, especially when the instruments are only weakly correlated with the "causal" variable. In Loeffler's sample, the point estimates for incarceration barely differed between the standard regression model and the instrumental variables model, while the standard errors were considerably inflated in the latter model and therefore rendered the incarceration effect non-significant. In the standard regression model, on the other hand, incarceration was associated with a significant four-point reduction in the probability of employment. Given a roughly 18-percent mean employment rate, this amounts to about a 20-percent relative difference in employment.
3 Similar findings of short-term improvement followed by long-term erosion have even been observed for very short custody spells for post-prison parole violations (Harding, Siegel, & Morenoff, in press).
4 These studies can also suffer from a substantial amount of missing data due to inability to match individuals across state correctional and employment databases. For example, Kling (2004) reported the loss of up to 42 percent of his sample (individuals involved in the federal criminal justice system) because of match difficulty.

5 It should be pointed out that most but not all NLSY79 studies find that incarceration has a robust impact on employment. For one exception, see Monk-Turner (1989), who found no relationship between incarceration in a juvenile institution and occupational status among white males in the NLSY79.
6 For state-level evidence on the homeownership gap, see Schneider and Turney (2015).
7 The Fragile Families and Child Wellbeing Study is a nationally representative study of non-marital childbirths in large cities.
8 In their model, Visher et al. (2011) also estimated a significantly positive relationship between employment and possession of photo identification at the time of release. Although it is impossible to ignore the possibility of selection bias, this finding does point to one inexpensive strategy for prison pre-release programming.
9 These estimates were driven by the male respondents, as females reported just 27 percent employment at both time periods.
10 For cross-national evidence on the use of imprisonment, see Lappi-Seppälä (2011).
11 For additional evidence on social welfare dependency, see Andersen and Andersen (2014).
12 The most alarming finding from the Schwartz and Skolnick (1962) study was that employment files reporting a trial and acquittal—in other words, an applicant who was accused of assault but proclaimed to be without guilt—also exhibited a lower callback rate (18%) than files reporting no criminal record. This suggests that individuals who have even minor brushes with the law can experience hiring difficulty if potential employers are able to find out about it. For even more recent evidence to this effect, see Vuolo, Lageson and Uggen (2017).
13 In Pager's (2003) study, the individual involved in the criminal justice system was assigned a felony cocaine trafficking conviction with 18 months total prison time, the last six months of which included employment in a prison industry (which was reported in the application filled out at the workplace). To account for the same sequence of 12 months of labor force non-participation followed by six months of employment, the other individual was assigned 12 months of schooling (after being held back one year) followed by six months of employment in low-skill jobs for a temp agency.
14 Type of punishment (e.g., custodial versus non-custodial) is not always specified in these studies. More often, studies measure employers' attitude towards hiring formerly convicted individuals in general, and distinguish between different types of crime (e.g., violent, non-violent).
15 See Varghese, Hardin, Bauer, and Morgan (2010) for a similar approach and findings. In their study, college students rated applicants with different charges and job qualifications. Severity of charge lowered employability, and qualifications could increase employability among applicants with a misdemeanor but not among those with a felony record.
16 Haslewood-Pócsik et al. (2008) found that offense type influenced employer attitudes, and concluded that the potential risk an individual might pose to staff or customers was the most important employer concern. They also concluded that many employers wanted to know about the criminal record of the applicant in the earliest stage of the hiring process, and found that most employers had little knowledge about the rules concerning the disclosure of criminal convictions.
17 In Reich's (2017) study, employer belief in redeemabilty was measured by responses to the following four items: "Most offenders can go on to lead productive lives with help and hard work"; "even the worst young offenders can grow out of criminal behavior"; "most offenders really have little hope of changing for the better"; and "some offenders are so damaged that they can never lead productive lives."
18 Reich (2017) operationalized two types of skill sets that she referred to as "desistance signals" in her study. Hard skills were measured by an applicant's willingness to openly disclose details about past offending, completion of an employment program following conviction, and receipt of a certificate of rehabilitation, among others. Soft skills were measured by self-presentation, communication ability, and positive attitude, among others.

References

Aaltonen, M., Skardhamar, T., Nilsson, A., Andersen, L. H., Bäckman, O., Estrada, F., & Danielsson, P. (2017). Comparing employment trajectories before and after first imprisonment in four Nordic countries. *British Journal of Criminology, 57*, 828–847.

Albright, S., & Denq, F. (1996). Employer attitudes toward hiring ex-offenders. *Prison Journal, 76*, 118–137.

Andersen, S. H. (2015). Serving time or serving the community? Exploiting a policy reform to assess the causal effects of community service on income, social benefit dependency and recidivism. *Journal of Quantitative Criminology, 31*, 537–563.

Andersen, L. H., & Andersen, S. H. (2014). Effect of electronic monitoring on social welfare dependence. *Criminology and Public Policy, 13*, 349–379.

5 Incarceration and Employment Prospects

Apel, R., & Sweeten, G. (2010). The impact of incarceration on employment during the transition to adulthood. *Social Problems, 57*, 448–479.

Baćak, V., Kennedy, E. H. (2015). Marginal structural models: An application to incarceration and marriage during young adulthood. *Journal of Marriage and Family, 77*, 112–125.

Benson, M. L. (1984). The fall from grace: Loss of occupational status as a consequence of conviction for a white-collar crime. *Criminology, 22*, 573–593.

Bound, J., & Freeman, R. B. (1992). What went wrong? The erosion of relative earnings and employment among young black men in the 1980s. *The Quarterly Journal of Economics, 107*, 201–232.

Brayne, S. (2014). Surveillance and system avoidance: Criminal justice contact and institutional attachment. *American Sociological Review, 79*, 367–391.

Burton, V. S., Jr., Cullen, F. T., & Travis, L. F., III. (1987). The collateral consequences of a felony conviction: A national study of state statutes. *Federal Probation, 51*, 52–60.

Bushway, S. D. (2004). Labor market effects of permitting employer access to criminal history records. *Journal of Contemporary Criminal Justice, 3*, 276–291.

Cho, R. M., & LaLonde, R. J. (2008). The impact of incarceration in state prison on the employment prospects of women. *Journal of Quantitative Criminology, 24*, 243–265.

Cook, P. J., Kang, S., Braga, A. A., Ludwig, J., & O'Brien, M. E. (2015). An experimental evaluation of a comprehensive employment-oriented prisoner re-entry program. *Journal of Quantitative Criminology, 31*, 355–382.

Dale, M. W. (1976). Barriers to the rehabilitation of ex-offenders. *Crime and Delinquency, 22*, 322–337.

Davies, S., & Tanner, J. (2003). The long arm of the law: Effects of labeling on employment. *Sociological Quarterly, 44*, 385–404.

Decker, S. H., Ortiz, N., Spohn, C., & Hedberg, E. (2015). Criminal stigma, race, and ethnicity: The consequences of imprisonment for employment. *Journal of Criminal Justice, 43*, 108–121.

Dennison, C. R., & Demuth, S. (in press). The more you have, the more you lose: Criminal justice involvement, ascribed socioeconomic status, and achieved SES. *Social Problems.*

Fagan, J., & Freeman, R. B. (1999). Crime and work. In Tonry, M. (Ed.), *Crime and justice: A review of research* (Vol. 25, pp. 225–290). Chicago, IL: University of Chicago Press.

Finn, R. H., & Fontaine, P. A. (1983). Perceived employability of applicants labeled as offenders. *Journal of Employment Counseling, 20*, 139–144.

Finn, R. H., & Fontaine, P. A. (1985). The association between selected characteristics and perceived employability of offenders. *Criminal Justice and Behavior, 12*, 353–365.

Freeman, R. B. (1992). Crime and the employment of disadvantaged youths [Crime and the economic status of disadvantaged young men]. In Peterson, G. E., & Vroman, W. (Eds.), *Urban labor markets and job opportunity* (pp. 201–238). Washington, DC: Urban Institute Press.

Freudenberg, N., Daniels, J., Crum, M., Perkins, T., & Richie, B. E. (2005). Coming home from jail: The social and health consequences of community reentry for women, male adolescents, and their families and communities. *American Journal of Public Health, 95*, 1725–1736.

Galgano, S. W. (2009). Barriers to reintegration: An audit study of the impact of race and offender status on employment opportunities for women. *Social Thought and Research, 30*, 21–37.

Garland, D. (Ed.). (2001). *Mass imprisonment: Social causes and consequences.* Thousand Oaks, CA: SAGE Publications.

Geller, A., & Curtis, M. A. (2011). A sort of homecoming: Incarceration and the housing security of urban men. *Social Science Research, 40*, 1196–1213.

Geller, A., Garfinkel, I., & Western, B. (2006). *The effects of incarceration on employment and wages: An analysis of the Fragile families survey.* Working Paper No. 2006–01-FF. Princeton University.

Giguere, R., & Dundes, L. (2002). Help wanted: A survey of employer concerns about hiring ex-convicts. *Criminal Justice Policy Review, 13*, 396–408.

Gottfredson, D. C., & Barton, W. H. (1993). Deinstitutionalization of juvenile offenders. *Criminology, 31*, 591–611.

Graffam, J., Shinkfield, A. J., & Hardcastle, L. (2007). The perceived employability of ex-prisoners and offenders. *International Journal of Offender Therapy and Comparative Criminology, 52*, 673–685.

Grogger, J. (1995). The effect of arrests on the employment and earnings of young men. *Quarterly Journal of Economics, 110*, 51–71.

Harding, D. J., Morenoff, J. D., & Herbert, C. W. (2013). Home is hard to find: Neighborhoods, institutions, and the residential trajectories of returning prisoners. *Annals of the American Academy of Political and Social Science, 647*, 214–236.

Harding, D. L., Siegel, J. A., & Morenoff, J. D. (in press). Custodial parole sanctions and earnings after release from prison. *Social Forces.* Harris, A., Evans, H., & Beckett, K. (2010). Drawing blood from stones: Legal debt and social inequality in the contemporary United States. *American Journal of Sociology, 115*, 1753–1799.

Harris, P. M., & Keller, K. S. (2005). Ex-offenders need not apply: The criminal background check in hiring decisions. *Journal of Contemporary Criminal Justice, 21*, 6–30.

Haslewood-Pócsik, I., Brown, S., & Spencer, J. (2008). A not so well-lit path: Employers' perspectives on employing ex-offenders. *The Howard Journal, 47*, 18–30.

Holzer, H. J., Raphael, S., & Stoll, M. A. (2006). Perceived criminality, criminal background checks, and the racial hiring practices of employers. *Journal of Law and Economics, 49*, 451–480.

Huebner, B. M. (2005). The effect of incarceration on marriage and work over the life course. *Justice Quarterly, 22*, 281–303.

Johnston, N. (2000). *Forms of constraint: A history of prison architecture*. Chicago, IL: University of Illinois Press.

Jung, H. (2011). Increase in the length of incarceration and the subsequent labor market outcomes: Evidence from men released from Illinois state prisons. *Journal of Policy Analysis and Management, 30*, 499–533.

Jung, H. (2015). The long-term impact of incarceration during the teens and 20s on the wages and employment of men. *Journal of Offender Rehabilitation, 54*, 317–337.

Kerley, K. R., Benson, M. L., Lee, M. R., & Cullen, F. T. (2004). Race, criminal justice contact, and adult position in the social stratification system. *Social Problems, 51*, 549–568.

Kerley, K. R., & Copes, H. (2004). The effects of criminal justice contact on employment stability for white-collar and street-level offenders. *International Journal of Offender Therapy and Comparative Criminology, 48*, 65–84.

Kling, J. R. (2004). *Incarceration length, employment, and earnings*. Working Paper No. 494. Princeton University.

Kling, J. R. (2006). Incarceration length, employment, and earnings. *American Economic Review, 96*, 863–876.

Kornfeld, R., & Bloom, H. S. (1999). Measuring program impacts on earnings and employment: Do unemployment insurance wage reports from employers agree with surveys of individuals? *Journal of Labor Economics, 17*, 168–197.

Landersø, R. (2015). Does incarceration length affect labor market outcomes? *Journal of Law and Economics, 58*, 205–234.

Lappi-Seppälä, T. (2011). Explaining imprisonment in Europe. *European Journal of Criminology, 8*, 303–328.

Laub, J. H., & Sampson, R. J. (2003). *Shared beginnings, divergent lives: Delinquent boys to age 70*. Cambridge, MA: Harvard University Press.

Loeffler, C. E. (2013). Does imprisonment alter the life course? Evidence on crime and employment from a natural experiment. *Criminology, 51*, 137–166.

Lott, J. R., Jr. (1992a). An attempt at measuring the total monetary penalty from drug convictions: The importance of an individual's reputation. *Journal of Legal Studies, 21*, 159–187.

Lott, J. R., Jr. (1992b). Do we punish high income criminals too heavily? *Economic Inquiry, 20*, 583–608.

Lukies, J., Graffam, J., & Shinkfield, A. J. (2011). The effect of organizational context variables on employer attitudes toward employability of ex-offenders. *International Journal of Offender Therapy and Comparative Criminology, 55*, 460–475.

Lyons, C. J., & Pettit, B. (2011). Compounded disadvantage: Race, incarceration, and wage growth. *Social Problems, 58*, 257–280.

Maroto, M. L. (2015). The absorbing status of incarceration and its relationship with wealth accumulation. *Journal of Quantitative Criminology, 31*, 207–236.

Matsueda, R. L., Gartner, R., Piliavin, I., & Polakowski, M. (1992). The prestige of criminal and conventional occupations: A subcultural model of criminal activity. *American Sociological Review, 57*, 752–770.

Minton, T. D. (2011). *Jail inmates at midyear 2010—Statistical tables*. Document No. 233431. Washington, DC: Bureau of Justice Statistics.

Monk-Turner, E. (1989). Effect of high school delinquency on educational attainment and adult occupational status. *Sociological Perspectives, 32*, 413–418.

Nagin, D., & Waldfogel, J. (1995). The effects of criminality and conviction on the labour market status of young British offenders. *International Review of Law and Economics, 15*, 109–126.

Needels, K. E. (1996). Go directly to jail and do not collect? A long-term study of recidivism, employment, and earnings patterns among prison releasees. *Journal of Research in Crime and Delinquency, 33*, 471–496.

Pager, D. (2003). The mark of a criminal record. *American Journal of Sociology, 108*, 937–975.

Pager, D. (2005). Double jeopardy: Race, crime, and getting a job. *Wisconsin Law Review, 2005*, 617–662.

Pager, D. (2007). *Marked: Race, crime, and finding work in an era of mass incarceration*. Chicago, IL: University of Chicago Press.

Pager, D., & Quillian, L. (2005). Walking the talk: What employers say versus what they do. *American Sociological Review, 70*, 355–380.

Pager, D., Western, B., & Bonikowski, B. (2009). Discrimination in a low-wage labor market: A field experiment. *American Sociological Review, 79*, 777–799.

5 Incarceration and Employment Prospects

Pager, D., Western, B., & Sugie, N. (2009). Sequencing disadvantage: Barriers to employment facing young Black men and White men with criminal records. *Annals of the American Academy of Political and Social Sciences, 623,* 195–213.

Pettit, B., & Lyons, C. J. (2007). Status and the stigma of incarceration: The labor-market effects of incarceration, by race, class, and criminal involvement. In S. Bushway, M. A. Stoll, & D. F. Weiman (Eds.), *Barriers to reentry? The labor market for released prisoners in post-industrial America* (pp. 203–226). New York, NY: Russell Sage Foundation.

Pettit, B., & Lyons, C. J. (2009). Incarceration and the legitimate labor market: Examining age-graded effects on employment and earnings. *Law & Society Review, 43,* 725–756.

Pettit, B., & Western, B. (2004). Mass imprisonment and the life course: Race and class inequality in U.S. incarceration. *American Sociological Review, 69,* 151–169. Ramakers, A., Apel, R., Nieuwbeerta, P., Dirkzwager, A., & van Wilsem, J. (2014). Imprisonment length and post-prison employment prospects. *Criminology, 52,* 399–427.

Ramakers, A., Nobbe, P., Nieuwbeerta, P., & Dirkzwager, A. (2017). Zwart werk na vrijlating. *Mens en Maatschappij, 92,* 7–33.

Ramakers, A., van Wilsem, J., & Apel, R. (2012). The effect of labour market absence on finding employment: A comparison between ex-prisoners and unemployed future prisoners. *European Journal of Criminology, 9,* 442–461.

Raphael, S. (2007). Early incarceration spells and the transition to adulthood. In S. Danziger & C. E. Rouse (Eds.), *The price of independence: The economics of early adulthood* (pp. 278–305). New York, NY: Russell Sage Foundation.

Reich, S. E. (2017). An exception to the rule: Belief in redeemability, desistance signals, and the employer's decision to hire a job applicant with a criminal record. *Journal of Offender Rehabilitation, 56,* 110–136.

Sabol, W. J. (2007). Local labor-market conditions and post-prison employment experiences of offenders released from Ohio state prisons. In S. Bushway, M. A. Stoll, & D. F. Weiman (Eds.), *Barriers to reentry? The labor market for released prisoners in post-industrial America* (pp. 257–303). New York, NY: Russell Sage Foundation.

Sampson, R. J., & Laub, J. H. (1993). *Crime in the making: Pathways and turning points through life.* Cambridge, MA: Harvard University Press.

Schochet, P. Z., John Burghardt, J., & McConnell, S. (2008). Does job corps work? Impact findings from the national Job Corps study. *American Economic Review, 98,* 1864–1886.

Schneider, D., & Turney, K. (2015). Incarceration and black—White inequality in homeownership: A state-level analysis. *Social Science Research, 53,* 403–414.

Schwartz, R. D., & Skolnick, J. H. (1962). Two studies of legal stigma. *Social Problems, 10,* 133–142.

Solinas-Saunders, M., Stacer, M. J., & Guy, R. (2015). Ex-offender barriers to employment: Racial disparities in labor markets with asymmetric information. *Journal of Crime and Justice, 38,* 249–269.

Sugie, N. F., & Lens, M. C. (2017). Daytime locations in spatial mismatch: Job accessibility and employment at reentry from prison. *Demography, 54,* 775–800.

Sykes, B. L., & Maroto, M. (2016). A wealth of inequalities: Mass incarceration, employment, and racial disparities in U.S. household wealth, 1996 to 2011. *Russell Sage Foundation Journal of the Social Sciences, 2,* 129–152.

Turney, K., & Schneider, D. (2016). Incarceration and household asset ownership. *Demography, 53,* 2075–2103.

Uggen, C., Wakefield, S., & Western, B. (2005). Work and family perspectives on reentry. In J. Travis & C. Visher (Ed.), *Prisoner reentry and crime in America* (pp. 209–243). New York, NY: Cambridge University Press.

Van der Geest, V. R., Bijleveld, C. C. J. H., Blokland, A. A. J., & Nagin, D. S. (2016). The effects of incarceration on longitudinal trajectories of employment. A follow-up in high-risk youth from ages 23 to 32. *Crime and Delinquency, 62,* 107–140.

Varghese, F. P., Hardin, E. E., Bauer, R. L., & Morgan, R. D. (2010). Attitudes toward hiring offenders: The roles of criminal history, job qualifications, and race. *International Journal of Offender Therapy and Comparative Criminology, 54,* 769–782.

Verbruggen, J. (2016). Effects of unemployment, conviction and incarceration on employment: A longitudinal study on the employment prospects of disadvantaged youths. *British Journal of Criminology, 56,* 729–749.

Visher, C., Debus-Sherrill, S. A., & Yahner, J. (2011). Employment after prison: A longitudinal study of former prisoners. *Justice Quarterly, 28,* 698–718.

Vuolo, M., Lageson, S., & Uggen, C. (2017). Criminal record questions in the era of "Ban the Box." *Criminology and Public Policy, 16,* 139–165.

Wakefield, S., & Powell, K. (2016). Distinguishing petty offenders from serious criminals in the estimation of family life effects. *Annals of the American Academy of Political and Social Science, 665,* 195–212.

Wakefield, S., & Uggen, C. (2010). Incarceration and stratification. *Annual Review of Sociology, 36,* 387–406.

Wakefield, S., & Wildeman, C. (2013). *Children of the prison boom: Mass incarceration and the future of American inequality.* New York, NY: Oxford University Press. Waldfogel, J. (1994). The effect of criminal conviction on income and the trust "reposed in the workmen." *Journal of Human Resources, 29,* 62–81.

Western, B. (2002). The impact of incarceration on wage mobility and inequality. *American Sociological Review, 67,* 526–546.

Western, B. (2006). *Punishment and inequality in America.* New York, NY: Russell Sage Foundation.

Western, B., & Beckett, K. (1999). How unregulated is the U.S. labor market? The penal system as a labor market institution. *American Journal of Sociology, 104,* 1030–1060.

Western, B., Braga, A. A., Davis, J., & Sirois, C. (2015). Stress and hardship after prison. *American Journal of Sociology, 120,* 1512–1547.

Western, B., Braga, A. A., Hureau, D., & Sirois, C. (2016). Study retention as bias reduction in a hard-to-reach population. *Proceedings of the National Academy of Sciences, 113,* 5477–5485.

Western, B., Kling, J. R., & Weiman, D. F. (2001). The labor market consequences of incarceration. *Crime and Delinquency, 47,* 410–427.

Wildeman, C., & Muller, C. (2012). Mass imprisonment and inequality in health and family life. *Annual Review of Law and Social Science, 8,* 11–30.

Zaw, K., Hamilton, D., & Darity, W. (2016). Race, wealth and incarceration: Results from the national longitudinal survey of youth. *Race and Social Problems, 8,* 103–115.

6

INCARCERATION, REENTRY, AND HEALTH

Chantal Fahmy and Danielle Wallace

The health of current and former prisoners and how their health impacts a host of social phenomena is an overlooked area of research. Research focusing on pre-arrest and pre-incarceration tends to be on the theoretical aspects of criminality while the research on post-incarceration tends to study recidivism. However, both physical and mental health can play a significant role in pre- and post-incarceration outcomes. It is important that scholars examine how prisoners' health status not only affects this group that consists of millions of Americans, but also how the collateral consequences of mass incarceration and the related health issues affect their families, friends, neighborhoods, and social networks.

The framework for the chapter is as follows. First, we outline the relationship between health—both physical and mental—and incarceration. We also discuss the spillover effects of deleterious health outcomes of former prisoners on their loved ones. Next, we detail how former prisoners' health is impacted upon release from prison and how that affects not only their reentry outcomes, but relationships with family, friends, neighborhoods, and personal networks. Moreover, we argue that understanding the links between reentry outcomes and health, as well as the barriers and facilitators of good health post-release, is of utmost importance to criminologists, health scholars, policy makers, and epidemiologists working to ensure public health issues are minimal. We continue to an overview on the theoretical perspectives, specifically emphasizing the stress process theory, general strain theory, and the fundamental causes perspective, which are used to understand the links between health, incarceration, and reentry outcomes. We examine how and why those who are disproportionality imprisoned bear the biggest burden of health disparities and how many of these health problems can be answered by turning to the nation's structural—social, economic, and political—factors. Lastly, we detail sources of public data that can be used to examine the relationship between incarceration, reentry, and health, and conclude with a call for more research and data collection in this arena.

Incarceration and Health

Over the last few decades, an unprecedented number of American citizens have found themselves in custody (Dumont, Brockmann, Dickman, Alexander, & Rich, 2012). Jails and prisons have largely housed those who are deprived, socially marginalized, and medically underserved, as well as those who carry a plethora of health issues. Incarceration keeps individuals' health issues unchanged or worse—functioning as a catalyst for deteriorating health during imprisonment

Dedicated to the memory of Marie L. Griffin.

(Brinkley-Rubinstein, 2013). This is due, in part, to the tendency for prisons to house individuals most at risk for experiencing multiple predictors of health disparities such as exposure to violence, substance use, mental health issues, and chronic diseases (Brinkley-Rubinstein, 2013; Heron et al., 2009; Schnittker, Massoglia, & Uggen, 2012).

As a result, rates of mental and physical health illnesses are much higher for those who have been incarcerated than that of the general population (Dumont et al., 2012; Schnittker & John, 2007). Massoglia (2008b) found that individuals who have ever been imprisoned are far more likely to suffer from a host of stress-related illnesses such as depression (Schnittker et al., 2012; Turney, Wildeman, & Schnittker, 2012), as well as diseases such as hypertension and heart disease, than individuals never imprisoned. However, these groups appear to be similar on other health-related outcomes, lending credence to the idea that incarceration has a direct relationship with health for the types of illnesses that are conceivably driven by imprisonment.

Physical Health

The physical health of the incarcerated population, although an important collateral consequence of imprisonment, is somewhat overlooked in comparison to other, broader outcomes such as the overall impact of incarceration on families. Nearly 25% of United States prisoners have a latent tuberculosis infection, which is 6 to10 times greater that of the general population (Bick, 2007; Dumont et al., 2012). Similarly, HIV infection is 10 to 20 times more prevalent among the incarcerated population compared to the general population (Bick, 2007; Brinkley-Rubinstein, 2013; Maruschak, 2012). Approximately 1.5% of prisoners are HIV positive, compared to only 0.3% of the non-incarcerated population (Maruschak, 2012). AIDS status in prisoners is at least 5 times greater than the general population (Bick, 2007), with AIDS remaining one of the most common causes of illness-related deaths among prisoners (Hammett, Harmon, & Rhodes, 2002; Noonan, 2016). Sexually transmitted diseases are also elevated in the incarcerated population due to the risk factors detailed below (Bick, 2007; Ousey, 2017). For instance, although syphilis was near complete suppression, Freudenberg (2002) found a rate of more than 1,000-fold for women in New York jails compared to non-incarcerated women.

In the case of chronic viral hepatitis infections, hepatitis B virus (HBV) prevalence estimates show that about 30% of those who have the infection have been previously incarcerated, with these estimates tremendously elevated compared to the general population (Bick, 2007; Weinbaum, Sabin, & Santibanez, 2005). Regarding hepatitis C virus (HCV), the numbers are similar in that between 29% and 43% of prisoners demonstrate serologic evidence of infection by the virus (Bick, 2007; Dumont et al., 2012; Hammett et al., 2002; Ruiz et al., 1999; Weinbaum et al., 2005). Because of the asymptomatic nature of these two chronic infections, approximately 65% and 75% of those with HBV and HCV, respectively, are unaware they have been infected until much later when cirrhosis or liver cancer appeared, making the in-prison prevalence rate difficult to estimate (Colvin & Mitchell, 2010; Varan, Mercer, Stein, & Spaulding, 2014). However, cases of HIV and hepatitis C have declined since the turn of the 21st century (Massoglia & Pridemore, 2015; Varan et al., 2014). HIV/AIDS rates showed a decline of an average 3% per year between 2001 and 2010 (Maruschak, 2012) with the state prisoner mortality rate for HIV/AIDS down from about 10% in 2001 to 1.8% in 2014 (Noonan, 2016).

The disease profile of prisoners has primarily focused on infectious diseases since they have the highest likelihood of spreading to other prisoners, correctional staff, and to the general public upon release. By comparison, chronic, non-infectious diseases and illness, although prevalent, have received far less attention in the literature (Dumont et al., 2012). Other, non-infectious diseases and illnesses such as asthma, cancer, arthritis, anemia, and hypertension are prevalent in the incarcerated population; hypertension is particularly known to be higher among those faced with stressful situations (Binswanger, Krueger, & Steiner, 2009; Brinkley-Rubinstein, 2013; Olubodun, 1996). For example,

6 Incarceration, Reentry, and Health

in a study with a matched in-prison control group, prisoners' blood pressure was higher compared to the control group and seemed to increase with the length of incarceration, after controlling for hard drug use, diet history, medical history, salt intake, and smoking (Olubodun, 1996). This finding may explain part of the increased risk of heart disease in prisoners (Wang et al., 2009). Similarly, Wang and colleagues (2009, p. 689) found that even after adjusting for age, sex, race, poverty, drug use, and alcohol use, "the relationship between incarceration and hypertension was particularly pronounced and statistically significant" especially for Black men and less-educated individuals. Moreover, former prisoners were more likely to lack treatment for their hypertension seven years later compared to a non-incarcerated subsample (Wang et al., 2009).

Other research has found chronic illness within the incarcerated population to be persistently elevated compared to the non-incarcerated population (Dumont et al., 2012; Wilper et al., 2009). Approximately 38% of federal prisoners, 43% of state prisoners, and 39% of local jail inmates reported having at least one chronic medical condition, which included rates of diabetes, hypertension, myocardial infarction (heart attack), and persistent asthma (Wilper et al., 2009). Binswanger and colleagues (2009) found that the odds of having asthma, arthritis, cervical cancer, obesity, and diabetes are higher among incarcerated individuals than their non-incarcerated counterparts. Chronic conditions will likely receive more attention as particular developing trends in the incarcerated population continue to emerge. Based on the fact that younger people are contracting diabetes more frequently, partly stemming from the obesity epidemic, and because of the aging population of prisoners— especially because of longer mandatory minimum sentences from the late 1980s and 1990s (Dumont et al., 2012; Noonan, 2016; Rich et al., 2013; B. A. Williams, Goodwin, Baillargeon, Ahalt, & Walter, 2012)—future research will inevitably focus on non-infectious chronic conditions as well.

Mental Health

Although physical health outcomes are an important component in the incarceration-reentry-health link, the widespread impact of mental health issues on prisoners must be underscored. With the many intersecting categories of disadvantage that this population finds itself in, it is to be expected that the association between incarceration and mental health is considerable (Brinkley-Rubinstein, 2013; Draine, Salzer, Culhane, & Hadley, 2002). Put another way, those with mental illness are also members of other groups who are at a high risk of being arrested and incarcerated, primarily attributed to social, political, and economic factors that contribute to both mental health and selection into prison (Schnittker et al., 2012). In 2005, more than half of all state prison, federal prison, and jail inmates had a mental health problem and nearly a quarter of that group had served three or more prison terms (James & Glaze, 2006). Female prisoners had higher rates of mental health problems (73%) compared to male prisoners (55%; James & Glaze, 2006), and this rate has increased in Western countries over the last 15 years (Adams & Ferrandino, 2008; Yang, Kadouri, Révah-Lévy, Mulvey, & Falissard, 2009).

As early as the 1960s, Goffman (1961) conceptualized the potential for mental health issues among those incarcerated based on the psychological effects of living in a total institution. Consistent with the premise that denial of freedom coupled with an identity change presumes high levels of anxiety and distress, the prevalence of mental health-related issues and psychiatric disorders is high in the institutionalized population (Schnittker et al., 2012; Wilper et al., 2009). Comorbidity of mental illness and addiction is quite common for prisoners, especially those who use substances as a coping strategy for their mental health issues (Rich et al., 2013). Using 62 surveys from 12 countries that included nearly 23,000 prisoners, Fazel and Danesh (2002) reported that about 4% of prisoners were diagnosed with a psychotic illness, about 11% of prisoners suffered from major depression, and 47% of male prisoners and 21% of female prisoners were diagnosed with antisocial personality disorder. Thus, the incarcerated population carries 2 times the burden of psychotic illnesses, 4 times for major depression, and nearly 10 times more diagnoses of antisocial personality disorder compared with the non-incarcerated population in the United States and Great Britain (Fazel & Danesh, 2002).

The deinstitutionalization of the mentally ill in the United States is partially responsible for the large population of incarcerated prisoners with untreated mental illness (Al-Rousan, Rubenstein, Sieleni, Deol, & Wallace, 2017). But past research has indicated that incarceration is independently related to emotional instability, such as severe anxiety, and elicits stronger responses with every subsequent incarceration (Schnittker et al., 2012), findings that hold in a French prison (Blanc, Lauwers, Telmon, & Rougé, 2001). Additionally, the incarcerated population has disproportionately higher levels of depression, antisocial personality disorder, and psychiatric disorders like schizophrenia (Brinkley-Rubinstein, 2013; Fazel & Danesh, 2002; Mallik-Kane & Visher, 2008; Schnittker et al., 2012; Wilper et al., 2009).

Although some research has observed the, now discredited, "healthy prisoner hypothesis" (e.g., Baćak & Wildeman, 2015), which states that those who are imprisoned or criminal cannot be in poor health based on the fact that many crimes require strength and/or tenacity to carry out, "the fact remains that most prisoners are less healthy than we would expect a matched individual of the same age, sex, race, and class from the free population to be" (Wildeman, 2015, p. 2). However, given that many prisoners come from disadvantaged areas, it is not surprising that this group likely experiences poor health regardless of their incarceration (Wildeman, 2015; Wildeman & Muller, 2012).

Pathways Linking Incarceration and Health

In their recent review, Massoglia and Pridemore (2015) outlined three major pathways linking incarceration to negative effects on health. First, they discuss exposure to infectious diseases, followed by how incarceration itself is an acute and chronic stressor, and finally, they end with an explanation on how incarceration can be an impediment to social integration, and thus social support, by the time the prison term is completed. Incarceration acts as a direct effect on health in the form of exposure to infectious disease (Massoglia, 2008b; Massoglia & Pridemore, 2015). Although many inmates enter prison with infections at the outset of their sentence, prison places undue stress on the body and leaves them at an increased risk of acquiring an infectious disease. In that sense, long stints of incarceration act as a chronic stressor (Pearlin, 1989) with the initial shock of loss of freedom and liberty acting as an acute stressor, causing negative repercussions for health almost immediately (Massoglia & Pridemore, 2015; Thoits, 1995). The prison environment facilitates the spread of disease transmission through shared bathroom facilities, poor nutrition, inadequate health care, overcrowding, unsatisfactory ventilation, delayed diagnosis, lack of proper infection control, inaccessible harm reduction strategies such as condom use, insufficient laundering of clothing, the sharing of personal hygienic materials such as razors and soap, and the use of unsanitary needles for tattooing, piercing, and drug use (Bick, 2007; Binswanger et al., 2009; Dumont et al., 2012; Massoglia & Pridemore, 2015; Polonsky et al., 1994). For the third pathway linking incarceration to bad health, Massoglia and Pridemore (2015) explain that imprisonment functions in a way that impedes the chances of social integration and social support from loved ones throughout the prison term and during reintegration. Incarceration disrupts prosocial bonds and stable family and friendship networks by creating a wedge between the incarcerated individual and their loved one through the stigmatization of prison. These effects are pronounced but only fully manifest after release, explicating a potential mediating factor between incarceration and deleterious health outcomes (Massoglia & Pridemore, 2015).

Spillover Effects

Another branch of research related to incarceration and health outcomes considers the spillover effects or collateral consequences felt by the family, friends, and neighbors of the previously and currently incarcerated (Schnittker, Uggen, Shannon, & McElrath, 2015; Wakefield & Wildeman, 2013; Wildeman & Wang, 2017). These effects may be especially damaging to the romantic partners and children of ex-prisoners (see Chapter 8 in this volume; Wildeman, 2015). For example, children of incarcerated fathers score significantly higher on aggression measures and attention problems as well as significantly lower on verbal ability measures than children whose fathers have not been incarcerated. However, child health assessments, based on mother reports, do not see any significant differences with regard to physical health and internalizing behaviors (Geller, Cooper, Garfinkel, Schwartz-Soicher, & Mincy, 2012). Women whose family members are absent because of incarceration have an increased chance of cardiovascular risk factors (H. Lee & Wildeman, 2013; H. Lee, Wildeman, Wang, Matusko, & Jackson, 2014), and romantic partners are more likely to have major depressive disorder, decreased overall happiness, and diminished life satisfaction (Wildeman, Schnittker, & Turney, 2012). Specifically, women bearing this burden of their family member's incarceration reported 1.88 times the odds of being obese, 2.68 times the odds of having diabetes, 2.44 times the odds of having a heart attack or stroke, and 3.27 times the odds of reporting fair or poor health outcomes compared to women without a family member incarcerated (H. Lee et al., 2014). This area of study is of grave importance since the majority of incarcerated individuals return to their communities, contributing to worsening public health outcomes.

Reentry and Health

As the section before demonstrates, correctional facilities are not a place of good health nor do they have healthy people in them. Most of those individuals, however, leave prison at some point in time. Approximately 2,000 former prisoners are released per day across the nation (Guerino, Harrison, & Sabol, 2011) and more than four million individuals are under community supervision (Kaeble, Maruschak, & Bonczar, 2015). Former prisoners bring their health and health circumstances back into the community when they return from prison. As such, ex-prisoners' personal health is likely an important component of post-release life and outcomes. A substantial body of work is still building on the health status of individuals who have returned from prison, as well as what the barriers and facilitators to successful reentry are as they relate to health. In this section, we review what is known about the impact of post-release health on reentry outcomes, such as substance abuse and reincarceration.

Overview of Health and Reentry

To begin with, the mortality rate of individuals returning from prison is dire. For all the research demonstrating that prison is a violent place (Catalano, 2005; Wolff, Blitz, Shi, Siegel, & Bachman, 2007), scholars have shown that for many former prisoners mortality rates are higher after being released from prison (Binswanger et al., 2007; Patterson, 2010; Rosen, Schoenbach, & Wohl, 2008; Rosen, Wohl, & Schoenbach, 2011; Spaulding et al., 2011; Wildeman & Muller, 2012). The first few weeks after release are a particularly dangerous time, where many former prisoners are at risk of homicide, suicide, and drug overdose (Binswanger et al., 2007). Binswanger and colleagues (2007) note that in the first two weeks after release, former prisoners have a 12.7 times higher risk of death than their counterparts; this translates into a death rate of 2,589 per 100,000 person years.

From another perspective, researchers have suggested incarceration may actually *improve* health outcomes for this population. Specifically, for Black men, whose socioeconomic status typically inhibits them from having good access to health care for a variety of reasons, prison gives them the health care that they need. For instance, Mumola (2007) finds that from 2001 to 2004, Black men in state prisons had a mortality rate that was 57% lower than their counterparts in the general population. Thus, for Black males, prison was as a protective factor, which lowered their mortality. In 2014, the leading cause of death for Black males in the U.S. aged 15–34 was homicide (Centers for Disease Control, 2010), showing that life outside of prison is particularly violent and dangerous for Black males.

Once individuals lose access to health care, including medication, and room and board, it is likely that former prisoners' health declines. One of the most comprehensive examinations of the health of formerly incarcerated persons is by Mallik-Kane and Visher (2008) who conducted a representative survey of 1,100 returning prisoners, targeting understanding the health and reentry needs of returning prisoners. Findings surrounding former prisoners' health were dismal (p. 1):

- "One-half of men and two-thirds of women had been diagnosed with chronic physical health conditions such as asthma, diabetes, hepatitis, or HIV/AIDS.
- Fifteen percent of men and over one-third of women reported having been diagnosed with depression or another mental illness.
- Returning prisoners often had more than one type of health problem. Roughly 4 in 10 men and 6 in 10 women reported a combination of physical health, mental health, and substance abuse conditions."

Other scholars note additional health issues for former imprisoned persons, like sleep problems (Testa & Porter, 2017), depression (Schnittker et al., 2012; Turney et al., 2012), and diseases such as hypertension and heart disease, are more severe and more prevalent than in the never-imprisoned population (Massoglia, 2008a). Mental health problems are common among both current prisoners and former prisoners. Nearly 15% of male and 33% of female former prisoners reported having depression or some other diagnosed mental illness (Mallik-Kane & Visher, 2008). Lastly, former prisoners do not engage in healthy behaviors. Porter (2014) finds that individuals who were incarcerated in their youth tend to smoke and eat unhealthy food, such as fast food, more than their counterparts. This relationship is partially due to the lower socioeconomic status of many former prisoners (Porter, 2014). As such, poor health when leaving prison and poor health behaviors likely collude to keep former prisoners in poor health or facing chronic health conditions.

When former prisoners are released, even if they have adequate reentry plans, they have a number of hurdles to face in finding health care in the community and often do not have insurance (Hamilton & Belenko, 2015; Hammett, Roberts, & Kennedy, 2001; Vail, Niyogi, Henderson, & Wennerstrom, 2017). Indeed, being uninsured may be "the single biggest barrier" to receiving satisfactory care upon release (Massoglia & Schnittker, 2009, p. 41). Medicaid benefits are suspended while individuals are incarcerated, often taking months to restore eligibility (Hammett et al., 2001; O'Grady & Swartz, 2016; Spillman, Clemans-Cope, Mallik-Kane, & Hayes, 2017). Additionally, since many insurance policies do not cover existing conditions, existing conditions create additional obstacles for those attempting to gain insurance coverage (Massoglia & Schnittker, 2009; Vail et al., 2017).

With all of the above, former prisoners tend to rate their health well (Mallik-Kane & Visher, 2008; S. A. Wallace, Strike, Glasgow, Lynch, & Fullilove, 2016). Wallace et al. (2016) find that formerly incarcerated Black males rate their health as good or excellent. However, the authors also note that this rating comes in spite of many respondents also reporting having a tangible health problem. This finding is also confirmed in other studies that examined health among Blacks, Whites, and Hispanics (Mallik-Kane & Visher, 2008). Other studies have reported that prisoners had generally optimistic expectations for maintaining their health once released (La Vigne & Parthasarathy, 2005), unfortunately, their optimism did not translate into better or even consistent health (Binswanger et al., 2011; Mallik-Kane & Visher, 2008). Linking prisoners with continued care in the community seemed to be rare (La Vigne & Parthasarathy, 2005).

6 Incarceration, Reentry, and Health

Collateral Consequences of Poor Health

Prisoners are, in general, an unhealthy population, which gives rise to the concern that health status upon release impacts reentry outcomes, like recidivism, employment, or finding housing. Prisoners have a constitutional right to health care, which is likely behind some of the better in-prison mortality rates (Binswanger et al., 2007; Mumola, 2007; Patterson, 2010; Rosen et al., 2008, 2011; Spaulding et al., 2011; Wildeman & Muller, 2012). Yet, upon release, these rights evaporate, leaving former prisoners to gain health care and service their own health needs without support. Obtaining insurance once released from prison is difficult, especially given that the availability of insurance is often tied to employment. Mallik-Kane and Visher (2008) reported that 68% of male and 58% of female former prisoners do not have health insurance eight to 10 months after release from prison, though these individuals also tend to use a number of health services in the form of emergency room visits and hospitalizations.

It is highly plausible that a host of health conditions impacts many reentry outcomes, however, very little research exists that tests this premise (for exceptions, see Binswanger et al., 2011; Mallik-Kane & Visher, 2008). Currently, what is known about the relationships between post-release health conditions and reentry outcomes is descriptive. For instance, Binswanger and colleagues (2011) report a number of challenges former prisoners have with obtaining housing, both immediately and in the long term. In one poignant quote, a subject describes his first night out of prison:

> It was terrible . . . I took a van from the facility to the bus station and they just kind of kicked you out of the van and said, 'Bye, have fun!' . . . [We] get into [the city] and it's too late to do anything. So . . . I couldn't get any shelters . . . of course the parole office is closed . . . I spent my first night just walking around . . . I had no idea where to go. I mean they don't tell you where to go or what to do. They don't tell you any of that.
>
> (Binswanger et al., 2011, p. 251)

Mallik-Kane and Visher (2008) report similar findings with individuals struggling with homelessness, especially if they suffer from mental illness or substance abuse. These same individuals are also less likely to be able to turn to their families for housing (Mallik-Kane & Visher, 2008).

Individuals with health problems upon release also struggle finding employment (see Chapter 5 in this volume). Mallik-Kane and Visher (2008) found that "men and women with mental health conditions had been less likely to find any employment, worked for fewer post-release months, and were less likely to have current employment at each of the post-release interviews" (p. 38). While it is difficult for any returning prisoner to find employment (Freudenberg et al., 2005; Uggen & Staff, 2001; Visher, Winterfield, & Coggeshall, 2005; Western, Kling, & Weiman, 2001), former prisoners with health issues—including mental health issues and substance abuse—generally never catch up to their pre-imprisonment employment levels (Mallik-Kane & Visher, 2008).

As for recidivism, which is typically the most studied reentry outcome, and its relationship to health and health outcomes, there too is very little scholarly work in this area. Mallik-Kane and Visher (2008) report that for men, physical health issues were not related to recidivism, however, for women, this was not the case. Women with physical health ailments were more likely to report criminal activity post-release (Mallik-Kane & Visher, 2008). Similar findings hold for men and women with mental health problems (Mallik-Kane & Visher, 2008). However, both men and women with substance abuse problems reported more post-release criminal activity and were more likely to be reincarcerated than their peers without substance abuse problems (Mallik-Kane & Visher, 2008). One potential reason for this lack of information on the relationship between health and recidivism, or rather information from only one study, is available data

(Ahalt, Binswanger, Steinman, Tulsky, & Williams, 2012). In the final section of this chapter, we discuss data limitations.

Family, Friends, and Networks

While there is an increasing number of scholars examining the collateral consequences of incarceration on families and relationships (Turney, 2014a; Wildeman, 2010; Wildeman, Lee, & Comfort, 2013; Wildeman & Muller, 2012), few scholars have examined how the *health* of those previously incarcerated impacts family, friends, and other relationships. We do know, for example, that poor family support post-release goes on to have a negative impact on mental health (D. Wallace et al., 2016) and recidivism (Breese, Ra'el, & Grant, 2000), however, it is unknown if this relationship is the same for physical health or specific health conditions. Conversely, when family support is high, it helps former prisoners stay on positive pathways to success (Nelson, Deess, & Allen, 1999). Former prisoners with substance abuse problems are more likely to have family members with their own problems with drugs or alcohol (Mallik-Kane & Visher, 2008). Moreover, the health of family members who have incarcerated loved ones is compromised (H. Lee & Wildeman, 2013; H. Lee et al., 2014; Wildeman et al., 2013, 2012). Clearly, the work of the above scholars suggests that the health of formerly incarcerated individuals likely plays a role in the core functioning of relationships, families, and networks in general. Scholars would do well to examine this area in the future.

Neighborhoods

Given that 15% of individuals with HIV have passed through correctional facilities and 40% of all people with hepatitis C had contact with correctional facilities (Travis, Solomon, & Waul, 2001), the spread of infectious diseases from the correctional population to the general public is a real concern. However there is little causal proof that incarceration and reentry are related to outbreaks of infectious disease in communities. For example, in North Carolina, as incarceration rates increase so do rates of teenage pregnancy and sexually transmitted diseases (Thomas & Torrone, 2006). While this is only an association, it does suggest that incarceration impacts communities in more ways than just crime fighting or removing individuals from the community.

Some neighborhoods see concentrated prisoner reentry (Chamberlain & Wallace, 2015; Harding, Morenoff, & Herbert, 2013). And, due to the very common health problems facing returning prisoners, they are likely also to see concentrations of unhealthy former prisoners. Neighborhoods experiencing concentrated reentry are also likely poor communities (Harding et al., 2013; Kirk, 2009). As such, these communities do not have the resources that former prisoners need to succeed (D. Wallace, 2015), particularly health resources (D. Wallace, Eason, & Lindsey, 2015; D. Wallace & Papachristos, 2014). Finally, the concentration of parolees in neighborhoods is associated with increases in recidivism (Chamberlain & Wallace, 2015). It is highly likely that the health—particularly substance abuse problems—of these clusters of parolees plays a part in larger neighborhood dynamics. Given the dearth of research on the community health consequences of returning prisoners, additional research in this area needs to be done.

Theory and Health

As noted previously, there is an important overlap between criminal justice involvement and disparate health outcomes: both are related to stratification, racial disparities, discrimination, segregation, and spatial division of resources more generally. In that sense, imprisonment can be viewed as a mechanism by which social inequalities are mutually generated and reinforced (Schnittker & John, 2007; Wakefield & Uggen, 2010; Western, 2006; D. R. Williams & Collins, 1995), increasing the list of stratifying institutions such as the educational system and labor market (Wakefield & Uggen, 2010).

For instance, minorities, particularly Blacks and Latinos, are overrepresented in the criminal justice system (London & Myers, 2006; Schnittker & John, 2007), but these numbers are not necessarily driven by a reflection of their involvement in crime (Beckett, Nyrop, & Pfingst, 2006; Zimring & Hawkins, 1993). Nevertheless, one report shows that Black males have a 1 in 4 chance of going to prison in their lifetime and Latino males have a 1 in 6 chance; conversely, White males have a 1 in 23 chance of being incarcerated (Bonczar & Beck, 1997; Pettit & Western, 2004; Western & Wildeman, 2009). The statistics on health disparities are similarly bleak. Blacks are much more likely to have disparities in sexually transmitted diseases (including HIV), according to Healthy People 2010, which is a comprehensive nationwide assessment launched by the Centers for Disease Control and Prevention (CDC) (Keppel, 2007). The rate of new cases of gonorrhea is 2,757 times higher in the non-Hispanic Black population than other races (Keppel, 2007). Blacks face a number of disparities in health when compared to the population at large: Blacks are more likely to suffer drug-induced deaths, injury and death related to firearms, and tuberculosis, to name a few. Relatedly, drug-induced deaths, contracting syphilis or tuberculosis, exposure to air pollutants, cirrhosis, lack of health care, and low rate of high school completion are named as the largest contributors to health disparities among Hispanics (Keppel, 2007). In essence, the overrepresentation of minorities in the criminal justice system and the drastic health disparities they experience are related to the same social processes (Brinkley-Rubinstein, 2013; Wildeman & Wang, 2017).

To understand these processes, we turn to the theory of fundamental causes, stress process theory, and from criminology, the general strain theory. First, the fundamental cause perspective purports that there are collective and structural factors inherent in society that both work to illuminate and facilitate the racial and ethnic disparities in physical and mental health. Link and Phelan (1995) introduced the idea that disease may be linked to more broad, societal causes rather than just individual risk factors. Since incarceration, race, and community-level factors are independently associated with health and mortality, it created a new line of research linking these all-encompassing "fundamental causes" to multiple sociological processes (Link & Phelan, 1995; London & Myers, 2006). This literature has primarily linked structural factors in the form of social and economic disadvantage to racial and ethnic disparities in disease and illness (Bowman & Travis, 2012; Sampson & Loeffler, 2010; Walker, Spohn, & Delone, 2012).

According to the theory, a fundamental social cause of health inequality must include four primary elements: (1) it must influence multiple disease outcomes; it cannot only affect one or two illnesses, for instance; (2) it must affect these disease outcomes through multiple risk factors; (3) a fundamental cause impacts access to resources that may mitigate the consequences or avoid risks of the diseases once it occurs; and (4) the relationship between the fundamental cause and health must be replicated over time in different situations by substituting the intervening mechanisms in the pathway (Link & Phelan, 1995; Phelan, Link, & Tehranifar, 2010). Socioeconomic status (SES), which plays a dramatic role in health disparities, can be used to elucidate this theory. For the past two decades, research in this area has shown that not only are inequalities in health based on SES for adults, SES-related health inequalities are also present in children and become more pronounced into adulthood (Adler, 2007; Case, Lubotsky, & Paxson, 2002). Data from a Dutch cohort of children found that family SES accounted for at least 10% of the variation in health disparities later in life (van de Mheen, Stronks, Looman, & Mackenbach, 1998). Once incarceration as a fundamental cause is added into this equation, it is not surprising that this cycle of inequality in health is repeated through generations (Adler, 2007; Case et al., 2002; Phelan et al., 2010; van de Mheen et al., 1998; Wildeman, 2015).

Stress process theory (Pearlin, Aneshensel, & Leblanc, 1997) is particularly helpful in understanding how incarceration is a long-term stressor with multiple consequences impacting health and other areas of reentry (Graffam, Shinkfield, & Lavelle, 2004; Pearlin, 1989). At the core of the stress process theory are the intertwined ideas of stress proliferation and primary and secondary stressors. Stress proliferation occurs when a major life event or stressor (primary stressor) generates other stressors (secondary stressors) because so many aspects of individuals' lives are interrelated (Pearlin, 1989; Thoits, 1995). In this sense, a primary and chronic stressor like incarceration (Massoglia, 2008b; Thoits, 1995; Turney et al., 2012) generates a number of other secondary stressors like health issues or difficulty in areas of reentry. Specifically, the prolonged exposure to stress vis-à-vis incarceration that is subsequently followed by reentry and its associated struggles, mentally and physically exhausts the body's ability to regulate healthy functioning and appropriately react to new stressors, thereby increasing the risk of deleterious health outcomes (Fazel & Baillargeon, 2011; Massoglia, 2008b; Pridemore, 2014; Schnittker & John, 2007). Thus, between incarceration and reintegration, the former prisoner is put at a much greater risk for stress-related illnesses such as heart disease and hypertension (Massoglia, 2008b; Pridemore, 2014; Schnittker, 2014).

Relating health to recidivism or other criminological outcomes like substance abuse requires also thinking about criminological theories. One such theory is general strain theory, which posits that when individuals experience stressors or strains, such as incarceration and poor health, they sometimes cope with them in criminal ways (Agnew, 1992, 2001). Poor health can generate strain in a number of ways given that it can negatively affect goal attainment, which is at the core of the general strain theory. We use employment here as an example. When individuals suffer from poor health it weakens their ability to obtain and maintain employment as well as limits what jobs they can do (Baćak & Wildeman, 2015; Pelkowski & Berger, 2004). Poor health also creates stress and strain through an ever-present noxious stimuli in the forms of pain, limited mobility, fatigue, or other similar indicators of poor health. Finally, health issues lessen or even remove the more positive aspects of life, such as having an active social life (J. Lee, 2012). Because these stimuli are tied to negative emotions (Schroeder, Hill, Haynes, & Bradley, 2011), criminally coping with these stimuli is more likely. The ability to cope prosocially with these stressful life events and daily strains wrought with challenges is vital to understanding ways to reduce recidivism.

Data on the Health of Returning Prisoners

As we and many others suggest, there remains a significant amount of work to be done in the arena of incarceration, reentry, and health. While there are a number of studies that researchers can use to examine this link, there are many missed opportunities to study the relationship between incarceration and health in several nationally representative data collection efforts (Ahalt et al., 2012). Below we detail the most commonly used datasets that are publically available.

The Fragile Families and Child Wellbeing (FFCW) data are ideal for studying incarceration, reentry, and health as well as other collateral consequences of incarceration (for example see (Geller, Garfinkel, Cooper, & Mincy, 2009; Reichman, Teitler, Garfinkel, & Mclanahan, 2001; Turney, 2014a; Wildeman, 2010; Wildeman & Western, 2010). The FFCW data "follows a cohort of new parents and their children and provides previously unavailable information about the conditions and capabilities of new unwed parents and the wellbeing of their children" (Reichman et al., 2001, p. 303), capturing approximately 4,700 births, about 3,600 of which are non-marital births, in 20 U.S. cities. While not the original intent of the study, a significant number of subjects in the FFCW data have experienced incarceration: 42% of surveyed fathers and 7% of surveyed mothers have experience with incarceration (Geller et al., 2009). Due to this, linking incarceration to parental, relationship, or childhood outcomes becomes possible. The FFCW data are publically available (see http://opr.princeton.edu/archive/ff/).

Data from the National Longitudinal Survey of Adolescent Health (Add Health) (Harris et al., 2009) has also produced a number of studies examining the relationship between incarceration, reentry, and health (for example see, Foster & Hagan, 2009; Roettger & Boardman, 2012; Teplin, Mericle, Mcclelland, & Abram, 2003; Viljoen, O'Neill, & Sidhu, 2005). The Add Health data are valuable in that they contain measures on the adolescent subjects' health, but also information regarding their personal networks and parental information.

Next, the Serious and Violent Offender Reentry Initiative (SVORI) data are aimed at understanding the effectiveness of reentry programing in reducing recidivism among those individuals mostly likely to reoffend. SVORI is a longitudinal dataset that employs four waves of surveys, with the first survey taking place in prison about one month prior to release (Lattimore, Visher, Winterfield, Lindquist, & Brumbaugh, 2005b). The other three waves take place at three, nine, and 15 months post-release. Currently the SVORI data have not been used to their full potential, with only a few studies employing the data and with the primary focus being on reentry programing (Lattimore & Visher, 2009; Lattimore, Visher, Winterfield, Lindquist, & Brumbaugh, 2005a; Stansfield, Mowen, & O'Connor, 2017; Stansfield, Mowen, O'Connor, & Boman, 2016; D. Wallace et al., 2016). SVORI is notable in that it includes a number of questions on health, health status, disease diagnoses, treatment, and validated scales such as the short form of the SF-36 Health Scale (Ware, Kosinski, & Keller, 1996). Moreover, SVORI has measures on a number of reentry outcomes, like self-reported offending and incarceration, drug use, housing, employment, family relationships, and financial status. A major drawback of SVORI, however, is the lack of administrative data on reoffending, whether incarceration or arrest. While administratve data was originally collected along with the interviews, that data is no longer available (see https://www.icpsr.umich.edu/icpsrweb/NACJD/studies/27101/version/1).

Next the Prison Inmate Network Study (PINS) (Kreager, Bouchard, et al., 2015) is a data collection effort geared towards understanding "the structure and implications of inmate network ties for in-prison health and rehabilitation and post-release recidivism" and whether "an inmate's position within the unit's informal network structure relates to his out-of-prison ties and community reentry" (http://justicecenter.psu.edu/research/projects/prison-inmate-networks-study-pins). Currently, a limited amount of data from PINS is publically available on the study's website. Publications using this data are just starting to emerge (see Kreager et al., 2017; Kreager, Schaefer, et al., 2015).

Other surveys that have been employed to study incarceration, reentry, and health include the National Survey of Children's Health (Turney, 2014b) and the Coronary Artery Risk Development in Young Adults (Wang et al., 2009). Additionally, Ahalt et al. (2012) identify the Midlife in the United States (MIDUS) as being a potential dataset that can be used to study incarceration, reentry, and health. Other studies have employed local administrative data or smaller studies (see Turney, Lee, & Comfort, 2013; Wildeman et al., 2013, for example) to examine these phenomena conjointly.

Conclusion

Above we have detailed the numerous ways in which current and former prisoners are unhealthy and how these health issues have a number of collateral consequences. Our efforts here are by no means exhaustive of the research on the health of incarcerated and formerly incarcerated individuals, but to expose some holes in the existing research. For instance, while the health of returning prisoners is often framed as a public health problem for reasons related to infectious disease, we have yet to understand if and how this transmission of disease to the general population actually occurs. Moreover, understanding how the health of someone incarcerated or formerly incarcerated affects their networks and families has yet to be fully explored. Additionally, there is little information on how the health of current and former prisoners impacts macro-level neighborhood processes. We urge researchers to continue to expand research in this field as there are many questions left unanswered.

References

Adams, K., & Ferrandino, J. (2008). Managing mentally ill inmates in prisons. *Criminal Justice and Behavior*, *35*(8), 913–927.

Adler, N. E. (2007). Health disparities: What's optimism got to do with it? *Journal of Adolescent Health*, *40*(2), 106–107. Retrieved from http://doi.org/10.1016/j.jadohealth.2006.12.003

Agnew, R. (1992). Foundation for a general strain theory of crime and delinquency. *Criminology*, *30*(1), 47–87.

Agnew, R. (2001). Building on the foundation of general strain theory: Specifying the types of strain most likely to lead to crime and delinquency. *Journal of Research in Crime and Delinquency*, *38*(4), 319–361.

Ahalt, C., Binswanger, I. A., Steinman, M., Tulsky, J., & Williams, B. A. (2012). Confined to ignorance: The absence of prisoner information from nationally representative health data sets. *Journal of General Internal Medicine*, *27*(2), 160–166.

Al-Rousan, T., Rubenstein, L., Sieleni, B., Deol, H., & Wallace, R. B. (2017). Inside the nation's largest mental health institution: A prevalence study in a state prison system. *BMC Public Health*, *17*(1), 342. Retrieved from http://doi.org/10.1186/s12889-017-4257-0

Baćak, V., & Wildeman, C. (2015). An empirical assessment of the "healthy prisoner hypothesis." *Social Science and Medicine*, *138*, 187–191.

Beckett, K., Nyrop, K., & Pfingst, L. (2006). Race, drugs, and policing: Understanding disparities in drug delivery arrests. *Criminology*, *44*(1), 105–137. Retrieved from http://doi.org/10.1111/j.1745-9125.2006.00044.x

Bick, J. A. (2007). Infection control in jails and prisons. *Clinical Infectious Diseases*, *45*(8), 1047–1055.

Binswanger, I. A., Krueger, P. M., & Steiner, J. F. (2009). Prevalence of chronic medical conditions among jail and prison inmates in the USA compared with the general population. *Journal of Epidemiology and Community Health*, *63*(11), 912–919.

Binswanger, I. A., Nowels, C., Corsi, K. F., Long, J., Booth, R. E., Kutner, J., & Steiner, J. F. (2011). "From the prison door right to the sidewalk, everything went downhill,": A qualitative study of the health experiences of recently released inmates. *International Journal of Law and Psychiatry*, *34*(4), 249–255.

Binswanger, I. A., Stern, M. F., Deyo, R. A., Heagerty, P. J., Cheadle, A., Elmore, J. G., & Koepsell, T. D. (2007). Release from prison- A high risk of death for former inmates. *The New England Journal of Medicine*, *356*(2), 157–165.

Blanc, A., Lauwers, V., Telmon, N., & Rougé, D. (2001). The effect of incarceration on prisoners' perception of their health. *Journal of Community Health*, *26*(5), 367–381. Retrieved from http://doi.org/10.1177/1557988310385104

Bonczar, T. P., & Beck, A. J. (1997). *Lifetime likelihood of going to state or federal prison.* Washington, DC: U.S. Department of Justice, Bureau of Justice Statistics.

Bowman, S., & Travis, R. (2012). Prisoner reentry and recidivism according to the formerly incarcerated and reentry service providers: A verbal behavior approach. *The Behavior Analyst Today*, *13*(3–4), 9–19.

Breese, J. R., Ra'el, K., & Grant, G. K. (2000). No place like home: A qualitative investigation of social support and its effects on recidivism. *Sociological Practice: A Journal of Clinical and Applied Research*, *2*(1), 1–21.

Brinkley-Rubinstein, L. (2013). Incarceration as a catalyst for worsening health. *Health & Justice*, *1*(3), 1–17. Retrieved from http://doi.org/10.1186/2194-7899-1-3

Case, A., Lubotsky, D., & Paxson, C. (2002). Economic status and health in childhood: The origins of the gradient. *The American Economic Review*, *92*(5), 1308–1334.

Catalano, S. (2005). *Criminal victimization, 2004 (No. NCJ 210674).* Washington, DC: U.S. Department of Justice, Bureau of Justice Statistics.

Centers for Disease Control. (2010). *Leading causes of death, black males 2014.* Retrieved from www.cdc.gov/men/lcod/2014/black/index.htm

Chamberlain, A. W., & Wallace, D. (2016). Mass reentry, neighborhood context and recidivism: Examining how the distribution of parolees within and across neighborhoods impacts recidivism. *Justice Quarterly*, 1–30. Retrieved from http://doi.org/10.1080/07418825.2015.1012095

Colvin, H. M., & Mitchell, A. E. (2010). *Hepatitis and liver cancer: A national strategy for prevention and control of hepatitis B and C.* Washington, DC: The National Academies Press.

Draine, J., Salzer, M. S., Culhane, D. P., & Hadley, T. R. (2002). Role of social disadvantage in crime, joblessness, and homelessness among persons with serious mental illness. *Psychiatric Services*, *53*(5), 565–573. Retrieved from http://doi.org/10.1176/appi.ps.53.5.565

Dumont, D. M., Brockmann, B., Dickman, S., Alexander, N., & Rich, J. D. (2012). Public health and the epidemic of incarceration. *Annual Review of Public Health*, *33*(1), 325–339.

Fazel, S., & Baillargeon, J. (2011). The health of prisoners. *The Lancet*, *377*(9769), 956–965.

Fazel, S., & Danesh, J. (2002). Serious mental disorder in 23,000 prisoners: A systematic review of 62 surveys. *The Lancet, 359*, 545–550.

Foster, H., & Hagan, J. (2009). The mas incarceration of parents in America: Issues of race/ethnicity, collateral damage to children, and prisoner reentry. *The ANNALS of the American Academy of Political and Social Science, 623*(1), 179–194. Retrieved from http://doi.org/10.1177/0002716208331123

Freudenberg, N. (2002). Adverse effects of U.S. jail and prison policies on the health and well-being of women of color. *American Journal of Public Health, 92*(12), 1895–1899.

Freudenberg, N., Daniels, J., Crum, M., Perkins, T., & Richie, B. E. (2005). Coming home from jail: The social and health consequences of community reentry for women, male adolescents, and their families and communities. *American Journal of Public Health, 95*(10), 1725–1736.

Geller, A., Cooper, C. E., Garfinkel, I., Schwartz-Soicher, O., & Mincy, R. B. (2012). Beyond absenteeism: Father incarceration and child development. *Demography, 49*(1), 49–76.

Geller, A., Garfinkel, I., Cooper, C. E., & Mincy, R. B. (2009). Parental Incarceration and Child Well-Being: Implications for Urban Families. *Social Science Quarterly, 90*(5), 1186–1202. Retrieved from http://doi.org/10.1111/j.1540-6237.2009.00653.x

Goffman, E. (1961). *Asylums: Essays on the social situation of mental patients and other inmates.* Garden City, NY: Anchor Books.

Graffam, J., Shinkfield, A., & Lavelle, B. (2004). Variables affecting successful reintegration as perceived by offenders and professionals. *Journal of Offender Rehabilitation, 40*(1–2), 147–171.

Guerino, P., Harrison, P. M., & Sabol, W. J. (2011). *Prisoners in 2010.* Washington, DC: U.S. Department of Justice, Bureau of Justice Statistics.

Hamilton, L., & Belenko, S. (2015). Effects of pre-release services on access to behavioral health treatment after release from prison. *Justice Quarterly.* Retrieved from http://doi.org/10.1080/07418825.2015.1073771

Hammett, T. M., Harmon, M. P., & Rhodes, W. (2002). The burden of infectious disease among inmates of and reliasees from US correctional facilities, 1997. *American Journal of Public Health, 92*(11), 1789–1794.

Hammett, T. M., Roberts, C., & Kennedy, S. (2001). Health-related issues in prisoner reentry. *Crime & Delinquency, 47*(3), 390–409.

Harding, D. J., Morenoff, J. D., & Herbert, C. W. (2013). Home is hard to find: Neighborhoods, institutions, and the residential trajectories of returning prisoners. *The ANNALS of the American Academy of Political and Social Science, 647*(1), 214–236. Retrieved from http://doi.org/10.1177/0002716213477070

Harris, K. M., Halpern, C. T., Whitsel, E., Hussey, J. M., Tabor, J., Entzel, P., & Udry, J. R. (2009). *The National Longitudinal Study of Adolescent and Adult Health: Research Design.* Retrieved from http://www.cpc.unc.edu/projects/addhealth/design

Heron, M., Hoyert, D. L., Murphy, S. L., Xu, J., Kochanek, K. D., & Tejada-Vera, B. (2009). Deaths: Final data for 2006. *National Vital Statistics Report, 57*(7), 1–136.

James, D. J., & Glaze, L. E. (2006). *Mental health problems of prison and jail inmates.* Washington, DC: U.S. Department of Justice.

Kaeble, D., Maruschak, L. M., & Bonczar, T. P. (2015). *Probation and parole in the United States, 2014.* Washington, DC: U.S. Department of Justice, Bureau of Justice Statistics.

Keppel, K. G. (2007). Ten largest racial and ethnic health disparities in the United States based on Healthy People 2010 objectives. *American Journal of Epidemiology, 166*(1), 97–103. Retrieved from http://doi.org/10.1093/aje/kwm044

Kirk, D. S. (2009). A natural experiment on residential change and recidivism: Lessons from Hurricane Katrina. *American Sociological Review, 74*(3), 484–505. Retrieved from http://doi.org/10.1177/000312240907400308

Kreager, D. A., Bouchard, M., Haynie, D., Schaefer, D. R., Soyer, M., Wakefield, S., . . . Zajac, G. (2015). *The prison inmate network study (PINS), Wave 1, 1995.* State College, PA: Justice Center for Research, Penn State University.

Kreager, D. A., Schaefer, D. R., Bouchard, M., Haynie, D. L., Wakefield, S., Young, J., & Zajac, G. (2015). Toward a criminology of inmate networks. *Justice Quarterly*, 1–29.

Kreager, D. A., Young, J. T. N., Haynie, D. L., Bouchard, M., Schaefer, D. R., & Zajac, G. (2017). Where "old heads" prevail: Inmate hierarchy in a men's prison unit. *American Sociological Review*, 1–34. Retrieved from http://doi.org/10.1177/0003122417710462

La Vigne, N., & Parthasarathy, B. (2005). *Returning home Illinois policy brief: Health and prisoner reentry.* Washington, DC: Urban Institute.

Lattimore, P. K., & Visher, C. A. (2009). *The multi-site evaluation of SVORI: Summary and synthesis.* Washington, DC: National Institute of Justice.

Lattimore, P. K., Visher, C. A., Winterfield, L., Lindquist, C., & Brumbaugh, S. (2005a). Implementation of prisoner reentry programs: Findings from the serious and violent offender reentry initiative multi-site evaluation. *Justice Research and Policy, 7*(2), 87–110.

Lattimore, P. K., Visher, C. A., Winterfield, L., Lindquist, C., & Brumbaugh, S. (2005b). Implementation of prisoner reentry programs: Findings from the serious and violent offender reentry initiative multi-site evaluation. *Justice Research and Policy, 7*(2), 87–110. Retrieved from http://doi.org/10.3818/JRP.7.2.2005.87

Lee, H., & Wildeman, C. (2013). Things fall apart: Health consequences of mass imprisonment for African American women. *Review of Black Political Economy, 40*(1), 39–52. Retrieved from http://doi.org/10.1007/s12114-011-9112-4

Lee, H., Wildeman, C., Wang, E. A., Matusko, N., & Jackson, J. S. (2014). A heavy burden: The cardiovascular health consequences of having a family member incarcerated. *American Journal of Public Health, 104*(3), 421–427.

Lee, J. (2012). Wounded: Life after the shooting. *The ANNALS of the American Academy of Political and Social Science, 642*(1), 244–257. Retrieved from http://doi.org/10.1177/0002716212438208

Link, B. G., & Phelan, J. (1995). Social conditions as fundamental causes of disease. *Journal of Health and Social Behavior, 35*(1995), 80–94.

London, A. S., & Myers, N. A. (2006). Race, incarceration, and health: A life-course approach. *Research on Aging, 28*(3), 409–422.

Mallik-Kane, K., & Visher, C. A. (2008). *Health and prisoner reentry: How physical, mental, and substance abuse conditions shape the process of reintegration.* Washington, DC: Urban Institute, Justice Policy Center.

Maruschak, L. M. (2012). *HIV in prisons, 2001–2010.* Washington, DC: U.S. Department of Justice, Bureau of Justice Statistics.

Massoglia, M. (2008a). Incarceration, health, and racial disparities in health. *Law & Society Review, 42*(2), 275–306.

Massoglia, M. (2008b). Incarceration as exposure: The prison, infectious disease, and other stress-related illnesses. *Journal of Health and Social Behavior, 49*(1), 56–71.

Massoglia, M., & Pridemore, W. A. (2015). Incarceration and health. *Annual Review of Sociology, 41*, 291–310.

Massoglia, M., & Schnittker, J. (2009). No real release. *Contexts, 8*, 38–42. Retrieved from http://doi.org/10.1525/ctx.2009.8.1.38.winter

Mumola, C. J. (2007). *Medical causes of death in state prisons, 2001–2004.* Washington, DC: Bureau of Justice Statistics, U.S. Department of Justice.

Nelson, M., Deess, P., & Allen, C. (1999). *The first month out: Post-incarceration experiences in New York City.* New York, NY: Vera Institute of Justice.

Noonan, M. E. (2016). *Mortality in state prisons, 2001–2014—Statistical tables.* Washington, DC: Bureau of Justice Statistics, U.S. Department of Justice.

O'Grady, C. L., & Swartz, J. A. (2016). The effects of insurance status and medical need on community-based health care access among jail detainees with serious mental illnesses. *Criminal Justice and Behavior, 1*–20. Retrieved from http://doi.org/10.1177/0093854816642814

Olubodun, J. (1996). Prison life and the blood pressure of the inmates of a developing community prison. *Journal of Human Hypertension, 10*(4), 235–238.

Ousey, G. C. (2017). Crime is not the only problem: Examining why violence and adverse health outcomes co-vary across large U.S. counties. *Journal of Criminal Justice, 50*, 29–41. Retrieved from http://doi.org/10.1016/j.jcrimjus.2017.03.003

Patterson, E. J. (2010). Incarcerating death: Mortality in U.S. state correctional facilities, 1985–1998. *Demography, 47*(3), 587–607.

Pearlin, L. I. (1989). The sociological study of stress. *Journal of Health and Social Behavior, 30*(3), 241–256.

Pearlin, L. I., Aneshensel, C. S., & Leblanc, A. J. (1997). The forms and mechanisms of stress proliferation: The case of AIDS caregivers. *Journal of Health and Social Behavior, 38*(3), 223. Retrieved from http://doi.org/10.2307/2955368

Pelkowski, J. M., & Berger, M. C. (2004). The impact of health on employment, wages, and hours worked over the life cycle. *The Quarterly Review of Economics and Finance, 44*(1), 102–121. Retrieved from http://doi.org/10.1016/j.qref.2003.08.002

Pettit, B., & Western, B. (2004). Mass imprisonment and the life course: Race and class inequality in U.S. incarceration. *American Sociological Review, 69*(2), 151–169.

Phelan, J. C., Link, B. G., & Tehranifar, P. (2010). Social conditions as fundamental causes of health inequalities: Theory, evidence, and policy implications. *Journal of Health and Social Behavior, 51*(Spring), 28–40.

Polonsky, S., Kerr, S., Harris, B., Gaiter, J., Fichtner, R. R., & Kennedy, M. G. (1994). HIV prevention in prisons and jails: Obstacles and opportunities. *Public Health Reports, 109*(5), 615–625.

Porter, L. C. (2014). Incarceration and post-release health behavior. *Journal of Health and Social Behavior, 55*(2), 234–249.

Pridemore, W. A. (2014). The mortality penalty of incarceration: Evidence from a population-based case-control study of working-age males. *Journal of Health and Social Behavior, 55*(2), 215–233.

Reichman, N. E., Teitler, J. O., Garfinkel, I., & Mclanahan, S. S. (2001). Fragile families: Sample and design. *Children and Youth Services Review, 23*(45), 303–326.

Rich, J. D., DiClemente, R., Levy, J., Lyda, K., Ruiz, M. S., Rosen, D. L., & Dumont, D. (2013). Correctional facilities as partners in reducing HIV disparities. *Journal of Acquired Immune Deficiency Syndromes, 63*(Suppl. 1), S49–S53.

Roettger, M. E., & Boardman, J. D. (2012). Parental incarceration and gender-based risks for increased body mass index: Evidence from the national longitudinal study of adolescent health in the United States. *American Journal of Epidemiology, 175*(7), 636–644. Retrieved from http://doi.org/10.1093/aje/kwr409

Rosen, D. L., Schoenbach, V. J., & Wohl, D. A. (2008). All-cause and cause-specific mortality among men released from state prison, 1980–2005. *American Journal of Public Health, 98*(12), 2278–2284.

Rosen, D. L., Wohl, D. A., & Schoenbach, V. J. (2011). All-cause and cause-specific mortality among black and white North Carolina state prisoners. *Annals of Epidemiology, 21*(10), 719–726.

Ruiz, J. D., Molitor, F., Sun, R. K., Mikanda, J., Facer, M., Colford, J. M., . . . Ascher, M. S. (1999). Prevalence and correlates of hepatitis C virus infection among inmates entering the California correctional system. *The Western Journal of Medicine, 170*(3), 156–160.

Sampson, R. J., & Loeffler, C. (2010). Punishments place: The local concentration of mass incarceration. *Daedalus, 139*(3), 20–31.

Schnittker, J. (2014). The psychological dimensions and the social consequences of incarceration. *The ANNALS of the American Academy of Political and Social Science, 651*(1), 122–138.

Schnittker, J., & John, A. (2007). Enduring stigma: The long-term effects of incarceration on health. *Journal of Health and Social Behavior, 48*(2), 115–130.

Schnittker, J., Massoglia, M., & Uggen, C. (2012). Out and down: Incarceration and psychiatric disorders. *Journal of Health and Social Behavior, 53*(4), 448–464.

Schnittker, J., Uggen, C., Shannon, S. K. S., & McElrath, S. M. (2015). The institutional effects of incarceration: Spillovers from criminal justice to health care. *The Milbank Quarterly, 93*(3), 516–560.

Schroeder, R. D., Hill, T. D., Haynes, S. H., & Bradley, C. (2011). Physical health and crime among low-income urban women: An application of general strain theory. *Journal of Criminal Justice, 39*(1), 21–29. Retrieved from http://doi.org/10.1016/j.jcrimjus.2010.09.009

Spaulding, A. C., Seals, R. M., McCallum, V. A., Perez, S. D., Brzozowski, A. K., & Steenland, N. K. (2011). Prisoner survival inside and outside of the institution: Implications for health-care planning. *American Journal of Epidemiology, 173*(5), 479–487.

Spillman, B., Clemans-Cope, L., Mallik-Kane, K., & Hayes, E. (2017). *Connecting justice-involved individuals with health homes at reentry: New York and Rhode Island.* Washington, DC: Urban Institute.

Stansfield, R., Mowen, T. J., & O'Connor, T. (2017). Religious and spiritual support, reentry, and risk. *Justice Quarterly*, 1–26. Retrieved from http://doi.org/10.1080/07418825.2017.1306629

Stansfield, R., Mowen, T. J., O'Connor, T., & Boman, J. H. (2016). The role of religious support in reentry: Evidence from the SVORI data. *Journal of Research in Crime and Delinquency, 54*(1), 111–145.

Teplin, L. A., Mericle, A. A., Mcclelland, G. M., & Abram, K. M. (2003). HIV and AIDS risk behaviors in juvenile detainees: Implications for public health policy. *American Journal of Public Health, 93*(6), 906–912.

Testa, A., & Porter, L. C. (2017). No rest for the wicked? The consequences of incarceration for sleep problems. *Society and Mental Health*, 1–13. Retrieved from http://doi.org/10.1177/2156869317707002

Thoits, P. A. (1995). Stress, coping, and social support processes: Where are we? What next? *Journal of Health and Social Behavior, 35*, 53–79.

Thomas, J. C., & Torrone, E. (2006). Incarceration as forced migration: Effects on selected community health outcomes. *American Journal of Public Health, 96*(10), 1762–1765. Retrieved from http://doi.org/10.2105/AJPH.2005.081760

Travis, J., Solomon, A. L., & Waul, M. (2001). *From prison to home: The dimensions and consequences of prisoner reentry.* Washington, DC: Urban Institute, Justice Policy Center.

Turney, K. (2014a). Stress proliferation across generations? Examining the relationship between parental incarceration and childhood health. *Journal of Health and Social Behavior, 55*(3), 302–319.

Turney, K. (2014b). The intergenerational consequences of mass incarceration: Implications for children's contact with grandparents. *Social Forces, 93*(1), 299–327. Retrieved from http://doi.org/10.1093/sf/sou062

Turney, K., Lee, H., & Comfort, M. (2013). Discrimination and psychological distress among recently released male prisoners. *American Journal of Men's Health, 7*(6), 482–493.

Turney, K., Wildeman, C., & Schnittker, J. (2012). As fathers and felons: Explaining the effects of current and recent incarceration on major depression. *Journal of Health and Social Behavior*, *53*(4), 465–481.

Uggen, C., & Staff, J. (2001). Work as a turning point for criminal offenders. *Work*, *5*(4), 1–16.

Vail, W. L., Niyogi, A., Henderson, N., & Wennerstrom, A. (2017). Bringing it all back home: Understanding the medical difficulties encountered by newly released prisoners in New Orleans, Louisiana—A qualitative study. *Health & Social Care in the Community*, *25*(4), 1448–1458.

van de Mheen, D., Stronks, K., Looman, C. W. N., & Mackenbach, J. P. (1998). Does childhood socioeconomic status influence adult health through behavioural factors? *International Journal of Epidemiology*, *27*(3), 431–437. Retrieved from http://doi.org/10.1093/ije/27.3.431

Varan, A. K., Mercer, D. W., Stein, M. S., & Spaulding, A. C. (2014). Hepatitis C seroprevalence among prison inmates since 2001: Still high but declining. *Public Health Reports*, *129*(2), 187–195.

Viljoen, J. L., O'Neill, M. L., & Sidhu, A. (2005). Bullying behaviors in female and male adolescent offenders: Prevalence, types, and association with psychosocial adjustment. *Aggressive Behavior*, *31*(6), 521–536. Retrieved from http://doi.org/10.1002/ab.20036

Visher, C. A., Winterfield, L., & Coggeshall, M. B. (2005). Ex-offender employment programs and recidivism : A meta-analysis. *Journal of Experimental Criminology*, 295–315.

Wakefield, S., & Uggen, C. (2010). Incarceration and stratification. *Annual Review of Sociology*, *36*(1), 387–406.

Wakefield, S., & Wildeman, C. (2013). *Children of the prison boom: Mass incarceration and the future of American inequality*. New York, NY: Oxford University Press.

Walker, S., Spohn, C., & Delone, M. (2012). *The color of justice: Race, ethnicity, and crime in America* (5th ed.). Belmont, CA: Wadsworth, Cengage Learning.

Wallace, D. (2015). Do neighborhood organizational resources impact recidivism? *Sociological Inquiry*, 1–24.

Wallace, D., Eason, J. M., & Lindsey, A. M. (2015). The influence of incarceration and re-entry on the availability of health care organizations in Arkansas. *Health and Justice*, *3*(3), 1–11. Retrieved from http://doi.org/10.1186/s40352-015-0016-4

Wallace, D., Fahmy, C., Cotton, L., Jimmons, C., McKay, R., Stoffer, S., & Syed, S. (2016). Examining the role of familial support during prison and after release on post-incarceration mental health. *International Journal of Offender Therapy and Comparative Criminology*, *60*(1), 3–20. Retrieved from http://doi.org/10.1177/0306624X14548023

Wallace, D., & Papachristos, A. V. (2014). Recidivism and the availability of health care organizations. *Justice Quarterly*, *31*(3), 588–608.

Wallace, S. A., Strike, K. S., Glasgow, Y. M., Lynch, K., & Fullilove, R. E. (2016). "Other than that, I"m good': Formerly incarcerated young black men's self-perceptions of health status. *Journal of Health Care for the Poor and Underserved*, *27*(2A), 163–180. Retrieved from http://doi.org/10.1353/hpu.2016.0056

Wang, E. A., Pletcher, M., Lin, F., Vittinghoff, E., Kertesz, S. G., Kiefe, C. I., & Bibbins-Domingo, K. (2009). Incarceration, incident hypertension, and access to health care: Findings from the Coronary Artery Risk Development in Young Adults (CARDIA) Study. *Archives of Internal Medicine*, *169*(7), 687–693.

Ware, J. E., Kosinski, M., & Keller, S. D. (1996). A 12-item short-form health survey: Construction of scales and preliminary tests of relibaility and validity. *Medical Care*, *34*(3), 220–233.

Weinbaum, C. M., Sabin, K. M., & Santibanez, S. S. (2005). Hepatitis B, hepatitis C, and HIV in correctional populations: A review of epidemiology and prevention. *AIDS*, *19 Suppl*(3), S41–S46.

Western, B. (2006). *Punishment and inequality in America*. New York, NY: Russell Sage Foundation.

Western, B., Kling, J. R., & Weiman, D. F. (2001). The labor market consequences of incarceration. *Crime & Delinquency*, *47*(3), 410–427.

Western, B., & Wildeman, C. (2009). The black family and mass incarceration. *The ANNALS of the American Academy of Political and Social Science*, *621*(1), 221–242.

Wildeman, C. (2010). Paternal incarceration and children's physically aggressive behaviors: Evidence from the Fragile families and child wellbeing study. *Social Forces*, *89*(1), 285–310.

Wildeman, C. (2015). Incarceration and health. In R. A. Scott & S. M. Kosslyn (Eds.), *Emerging trends in the social and behavioral sciences* (Vol. 41, pp. 291–310). John Wiley & Sons. Retrieved from http://doi.org/10.1002/9781118900772

Wildeman, C., Lee, H., & Comfort, M. (2013). A new vulnerable population? The health of female partners of men recently released from prison. *Women's Health Issues*, *23*(6), e335—e340.

Wildeman, C., & Muller, C. (2012). Mass imprisonment and inequality in health and family life. *Annual Review of Law and Social Science*, *8*(1), 11–30. Retrieved from http://doi.org/10.1146/annurev-lawsocsci-102510-105459

Wildeman, C., Schnittker, J., & Turney, K. (2012). Despair by association? The mental health of mothers with children by recently incarcerated fathers. *American Sociological Review*, *77*(2), 216–243. Retrieved from http://doi.org/10.1177/0003122411436234

Wildeman, C., & Wang, E. A. (2017). Mass incarceration, public health, and widening inequality in the USA. *The Lancet, 389*(10077), 1464–1474. Retrieved from http://doi.org/10.1016/S0140-6736(17)30259-3

Wildeman, C., & Western, B. (2010). Incarceration in fragile families. *Future of Children, 20*(2), 157–177. Retrieved from http://doi.org/10.1353/foc.2010.0006

Williams, B. A., Goodwin, J. S., Baillargeon, J., Ahalt, C., & Walter, L. C. (2012). Addressing the aging crisis in U.S. criminal justice health care. *Journal of the American Geriatrics Society, 60*(6), 1150–1156. Retrieved from http://doi.org/10.1111/j.1532-5415.2012.03962.x

Williams, D. R., & Collins, C. (1995). US socioeconomic and racial differences in health: Patterns and explanations. *Annual Review of Sociology, 21*, 349–386.

Wilper, A. P., Woolhandler, S., Boyd, J. W., Lasser, K. E., McCormick, D., Bor, D. H., & Himmelstein, D. U. (2009). The health and health care of US prisoners: Results of a nationwide survey. *American Journal of Public Health, 99*(4), 666–672.

Wolff, N., Blitz, C. L., Shi, J., Siegel, J., & Bachman, R. (2007). Physical violence inside prisons. *Criminal Justice and Behavior, 34*(5), 588–599. Retrieved from http://doi.org/10.1177/0093854806296830

Yang, S., Kadouri, A., Révah-Lévy, A., Mulvey, E. P., & Falissard, B. (2009). Doing time: A qualitative study of long-term incarceration and the impact of mental illness. *International Journal of Law and Psychiatry, 32*(5), 294–303. Retrieved from http://doi.org/10.1016/j.ijlp.2009.06.003

Zimring, F. E., & Hawkins, G. (1993). *The scale of imprisonment.* Chicago, IL: University of Chicago Press.

7

THE PSYCHOLOGICAL EFFECTS OF CONTACT WITH THE CRIMINAL JUSTICE SYSTEM

Thomas P. LeBel and Matt Richie

Introduction

The structural impediments to successful reentry and reintegration are well known and summarized by many scholars (see e.g., LeBel & Maruna, 2012; Travis, Western, & Redburn, 2014; in this volume see Apel & Ramakers, Chapter 5; Kirk, Chapter 3). Recently, researchers have begun to argue that psychosocial strains and psychological influences should be focused on as barriers to successful reentry and reintegration (Garland & Wodahl, 2014, p. 404; Schnittker, 2014, p. 123). Maruna, Immarigeon, and LeBel (2004, p. 5; Visher & Travis, 2003) state that "[m]ore broadly, re-entry is also a long-term process." Under this definition, prisoner reentry includes many processes that begin before the individual is sent to prison, experiences while incarcerated, issues faced at the moment of release and during the first months out, and encounters during the (re)integration process of the first few years in the community (Irwin, 1970; Mears, Cochran, & Cullen, 2015; Visher & Travis, 2003). Additionally, very little is known about the life experiences of formerly incarcerated persons five or more years after release from prison.

This chapter examines potential long-term psychological effects of varying levels of contact and experiences with the criminal justice system. The use of the term "contact" describes a gradient from a dip of the toe in the shallow end (arrest, probation) of the criminal justice system, to incarceration in prison and release to the community from the darkest depths (supermax prison, after serving a life sentence, or after exoneration from death row) of the proverbial ocean of the carceral state. We have clustered the key themes emerging from this research about psychological effects into (interrelated) sections dealing with the following areas: the pains of imprisonment (including post-traumatic stress disorder, solitary confinement, trauma and victimization, and community supervision), and perceptions of and responses to stigma in the community.[1] Gonnerman (2004, p. 10) argues that "the true story of America's exodus of ex-cons cannot be told only with numbers." In response, our discussion gives voice to the perspectives and experiences of currently incarcerated adults, persons who have returned to the community from state and federal prisons, and young persons incarcerated in juvenile prisons and later released. The final sections provide a summary of key findings, implications for policy and practice, and directions for future research.

The Pains of Imprisonment

Sykes's (1958) seminal book, *The Society of Captives*, highlighted the deprivations and pains of imprisonment (i.e., limited liberty, autonomy, goods and services, heterosexual relationships, and security).

Haney (2003, p. 37) later noted that "more people have been subjected to the pains of imprisonment for longer periods and under conditions that threaten greater psychological distress and potential long-term dysfunction." Most recently, Fleury-Steiner and Longazel (2014. p. 58), in their book *The Pains of Mass Imprisonment*, conclude that the United States has a humanitarian "crisis behind bars" with prisoners "locked in a system that disregards their human dignity by subjecting them to containment, exploitation, coercion, isolation, and brutality." Harsh conditions experienced by many incarcerated individuals include frequent body searches (pat, strip, and cavity) by staff, prolonged isolated confinement, physical and sexual assault by other prisoners and staff, supervised showers, and forced usage of toilets without doors. Haney (2012, p. 2) mentions three important Ds of incarceration that can have a damaging psychological impact: "danger, dehumanization, and deprivation." More importantly, Haney (2003) argues that in adapting to survive the pains of living in prison, "many people are permanently changed" (2003, p. 38). Roman, a formerly incarcerated person who served 17 years behind bars explains that "[i]t doesn't help people; what it *does* is it helps people to become *dysfunctional* because it helps you to become functional in a dysfunctional environment" (Stern, 2014, p. 113, italics in original).

Some researchers have noted the iatrogenic effects of placement and experiences in deeper levels of the correctional system (Gatti, Tremblay, & Vitaro, 2009; Lerman, 2009). For example, Gatti and colleagues (2009) report that placement of a juvenile in more restrictive and intense settings, especially in an institution, had the greatest negative impact on criminal behavior as an adult. Similarly, Lerman's (2009, p. 164) research with adults found that "placement in a higher-security prison appears to have a criminogenic effect on both cognitions and personality," especially for prisoners with a less extensive criminal history. In particular, using the Correctional Offender Management Profiling for Alternative Sanctions (COMPAS), a risk and needs assessment, she found that placement in a higher-security prison predicted increases in scales for criminal involvement, criminal personality, and criminal cognitions (Lerman, 2009).

Several researchers and formerly incarcerated persons have discussed the importance of fear in shaping responses to prison life (see e.g., Grounds, 2005; McCorkle, 1992; Stern, 2014). Bernstein (2014, p. 23) ominously notes that "[f]ear is omnipresent inside a youth prison, hanging over the place like a persistent fog." McCorkle's (1992) study of a maximum security prison found that due to fear of victimization, over 40% of prisoners avoid some areas and about an equal percentage isolate themselves in their cells. Leslie Rodgers, after serving over a decade in prisons in New York State, poignantly reported that "it's about *fear*—and the *feared*. But no one can *show* the fear" (Stern, 2014, p. 110). To survive in prison, Haney (2003; see also Bernstein, 2014 about youth) describes the "prison mask" that many put on to project a steely image and protect their emotions and deter others from attempting to victimize them. More than 40 years ago, Archie Connett (1973, p. 113), a formerly incarcerated person, succinctly summarized the impact of serving time in prison by stating that "it seems certain they create in many feelings of dependence, inadequacy, unworthiness, guilt, self-hatred, insecurity, frustration, alienation, fear, apathy, rage, and confusion."

Posttraumatic Stress Disorder (PTSD)

In 2013, the American Psychiatric Association revised the PTSD diagnostic criteria in the fifth edition of its *Diagnostic and Statistical Manual of Mental Disorders* (*DSM-5*). PTSD now includes criteria involving exposure to traumatic event, event is persistently re-experienced, avoidance of trauma-related stimuli, negative thoughts or feelings that began or worsened after the trauma, trauma-related arousal and reactivity that began or worsened after the trauma, symptoms lasting for more than 1 month, symptoms that create distress or functional impairment (e.g., social, occupational), and at least one avoidance symptom. Haney (2003, p. 45; see also Liem, 2016) argues that "[f]or some prisoners, incarceration is so stark and psychologically painful that it represents a form of trauma severe enough to produce posttraumatic stress reactions in the free world." Anderson, Geier, and Cahill (2016) utilized The National Survey of American Life to examine the impact of incarceration on PTSD. In this study of a nationally representative sample of 5,008 Black Americans, they found that those with incarceration histories had elevated rates of exposure to potentially traumatic experiences and were more likely to be suffering with PTSD than their peers who had not been incarcerated. In particular, persons with a history of incarceration were about twice as likely to meet diagnostic criteria for PTSD when assessed in the 12 months prior to the interview.

Schnittker (2014) examined the impact of incarceration (ever spent time in prison, jail, or a correctional facility) using The National Comorbidity Survey Replication (NCS-R), a national representative survey that assessed the prevalence and correlates of psychiatric disorders. Schnittker (2014) found that for both mood and anxiety disorders, the prevalence rate among former inmates is about twice what is found among persons without a history of incarceration. He also found that former inmates are more likely to suffer from two or more psychiatric disorders simultaneously (comorbidity). The NCS-R also allowed for an examination of core attachment styles involving trusting others. Schnittker (2014) found that former prisoners were much more likely to report avoidant or anxious styles indicating more discomfort in getting close with others or "avoiding other people altogether" (p. 133). These findings led Schnittker (2014) to conclude that "the lasting damage of incarceration rests with how it reshapes beliefs, perceptions, and mindsets" (p. 135).

Several scholars have suggested new diagnostic categories for previously incarcerated persons (Herman, 1992; Gorski, 2001; Liem, 2016). For example, Judith Herman (1992) coined the term "complex PTSD" and suggested that it be used to describe the syndrome that can result from "prolonged, repeated trauma or the profound deformations of personality that occur in captivity" (Herman, 1992, p. 119). Similarly, Gorski (2001) suggests that "Post Incarceration Syndrome (PICS)" is "caused by being subjected to prolonged incarceration in environments of punishment with few opportunities for education, job training, or rehabilitation." Liem and Kunst (2013; Liem, 2016) suggest that PICS constitutes a discrete subtype of PTSD that results from long-term imprisonment. Based on in-depth interviews with 25 released "lifers" who had served an average of 19 years in prison, they concluded that their narratives indicated a specific conglomeration of symptoms including each of the four characteristic PTSD feature clusters (intrusion, hyper arousal, persistent avoidance, and emotional numbing) (Liem & Kunst, 2013, p. 335).

In a study involving prisoners serving sentences of 5 years or longer in about a dozen European countries, Dudeck et al. (2011) found that 14% developed PTSD subsequent to traumatic events experienced in prison. Freudenberg and colleagues (2005) compared 476 women's mental health prerelease and post-release from New York City jails and reported women's symptoms of anxiety and depression significantly worsened post-release. While Lynch and Heath (2017) found that about one-third (32% at initial interview while incarcerated and 29% at post-release) of women in their study met the criteria for clinical levels of PTSD symptoms. Moreover, there are also many studies of prisoners and former prisoners that do not clinically measure PTSD but report symptoms suggestive of the disorder (i.e., hypervigilance, aggression, irritability, depression, nightmares, flashbacks, and problems with closeness and intimate relationships) (see e.g., Grounds, 2005; Irwin & Owen, 2005; Munn, 2011).

Grounds (2005) used the ICD-10 developed by the World Health Organization (1992) to examine the impact of the miscarriage of justice and long-term imprisonment on 18 men released after serving many years in prison for wrongful convictions. The ICD-10 includes an additional diagnostic category that adds to the PTSD definition, "enduring personality change following catastrophic experience." This requires a primary "stressor" criterion that specifies that the person must have experienced an event or situation of an exceptionally threatening or catastrophic nature, likely to cause pervasive distress in almost anyone. The diagnostic guidelines for enduring personality change include the presence of features not previously seen in the person that are present for at least two years, such as: a hostile or mistrustful attitude towards the world; social withdrawal; feelings of emptiness or hopelessness; a chronic feeling of being "on edge" as if constantly threatened; and estrangement. Importantly, the change may be seen as a reaction to prolonged traumatic experience, such as long-term incarceration (Grounds, 2005, p. 14). Grounds (2005) found that for 14 of the 18 men the personality change fit the ICD-10 diagnostic category of enduring personality change after catastrophic experience. These men had marked features of estrangement, loss of capacity for intimacy, moodiness, loss of a sense of purpose and direction, and a pervasive attitude of mistrust toward the world (for similar research findings about exonerees see Flowers, 2016; Westervelt & Cook, 2012; Wildeman et al., 2011). Grounds (2005, p. 44) also noted that these psychiatric conditions and changes in personality were persistent and long term with some difficulties still evident, and possibly worse, more than 10 years after release from prison.

Solitary Confinement

Arrigo and Bersot (2015) note that solitary confinement is generally defined as housing that restricts individuals to their cell for 23 hours a day with an hour allotted for exercise. Estimates suggest that approximately 100,000 state and federal prisoners are in solitary confinement of some sort at any one time (Frost & Monteiro, 2016; Mears, 2013; Shalev, 2009). Moreover, Sedlak and McPherson (2010; see also HRW & ACLU, 2012) report that 24% of youth were placed in solitary confinement at some point during their incarceration. In their recent comprehensive review, Frost and Monteiro (2016) conclude that "from the limited studies conducted to date, little good empirical evidence shows that time spent in isolation has demonstrable negative effects on psychological or behavioral outcomes for most inmates subjected to it" (p. 25). In particular, quantitative studies, using matched comparison or control groups, do not show a long-term impact of solitary confinement on recidivism (see esp. Labrecque, 2015; Mears & Bales, 2009; Smith, Gendreau, & Labrecque, 2015). However, Lovell, Johnson, and Cain (2007) found that prisoners released to the community directly from a supermax facility (69%) were more likely to commit new felonies within three years as compared to their non-supermax peers (51%) and later-released supermax inmates (53%).

Qualitative studies, in contrast, especially those involving persons who have spent many years in solitary confinement and/or in supermax prisons, are more likely to indicate deleterious, and sometimes long-term, psychological effects from this form of isolation (Frost & Monteiro, 2016; Grassian, 1983; Haney, 2003; HRW & ACLU, 2012; Irwin, 2005; Shalev, 2009). Grassian (1983) for example, identified a psychopathological condition that he referred to as "SHU syndrome" among prisoners that served a considerable length of time in solitary confinement. For Grassian (1983; see also Haney, 2003), SHU syndrome is characterized by factors such as perceptual changes; affective disturbance; hypersensitivity; cognitive dysfunction; anger, aggression, and/or rage; helplessness and hopelessness; chronic depression; anxiety and panic attacks; problems with impulse control; emotional breakdowns; and extreme paranoia. More recently, based on his extensive research career and involvement as an expert witness in numerous class action lawsuits, Grassian (2016) asserts that many prisoners will likely suffer permanent harm as a result of solitary confinement.

The narratives of persons who have spent years in solitary confinement are especially poignant in regard to the long-term psychological impact of these negative prison experiences. Brian Nelson (2016), who spent 23 years in solitary confinement, reports that "[n]o one wants to admit that we are weak as motherfuckers, that our brains beat us up" (p. 119). Although now living in the community, he says "I hate it out here. I'm afraid every fucking day" (p. 118). Importantly, Brian would be viewed by many people as a success because he has a good job working for the Uptown People's Law Center in Chicago, and has been out of prison for 5 years.

Trauma and Victimization

Before incarceration, many prisoners have experienced interpersonal trauma (physical, sexual, and/or crime-related) of some sort. Research with incarcerated women and youth indicates that the vast majority experienced physical and/or sexual abuse as children and/or as an adult (see e.g., Beck, Harrison, & Guerino, 2010; Browne, Miller, & Maguin, 1999; Green, Miranda, Daroowalla, & Siddique, 2005; Kao et al., 2014; Sedlak & McPherson, 2010). Bernstein (2014, p. 153), for example, reports that "[w]alking onto a juvenile unit is like entering a trauma ward, an emotional MASH unit where the gore is no less visceral for being interior." Notably, the majority of adult males have also experienced trauma before incarceration, especially physical and crime-related trauma (Carlson, Shafer, & Duffee, 2010; Kao et al., 2014; Komarovskaya, Loper, Warren, & Jackson, 2011; Maschi, Viola, Morgen, & Koskinen, 2015). Haney (2012, p. 12; see also Covington, 2003; Kupers, 2005) argues that "imprisonment represents a form of 'retraumatization' for many prisoners."

Several studies report rates of victimization in correctional facilities for adults (Listwan et al., 2013; Schappell et al., 2016; Schneider et al., 2011; Wolff et al., 2007) and youth (Sedlak & McPherson, 2010; Sedlak et al., 2013; HRW & ACLU, 2012). When including witnessing victimization with direct victimization, nearly all of those surveyed (98% in Listwan et al., 2012; and 89% in Schappell et al., 2016) report experiencing victimization of some sort. In Listwan and colleagues' (2013) study of the experiences of 1,616 prisoners released to halfway houses in Ohio, the majority (58.3%) reported some type of direct victimization in the last 12 months of their incarceration with 23% indicating theft and 29% physical fighting. In Wolff and colleagues' (2007, Wolff & Shi, 2009) epidemiological survey of thousands of prisoners in one state, approximately 40% of male and female prisoners experienced sexual or physical violence in the 6 months prior to the assessment. Meanwhile, Schneider and colleagues (2011) found that about one-third (34%) of male prisoners in New South Wales and Queensland had experienced physical assault. These findings support Sykes's (1958) quote from a prisoner saying, "The worst thing about prison is you have to live with other prisoners" (p. 77).

The Survey of Youth in Residential Placement (SYRP) is the first study to assess rates of victimization for youth in custody (Sedlak & McPherson, 2010; Sedlak et al., 2013). SYRP's findings are based on confidential interviews with a nationally representative sample of 7,073 youth in custody during spring 2003, and it assessed victimization experiences for theft, robbery, physical assault, and sexual assault. Among the key findings of the study is that more than half (56%) of incarcerated youth experienced one or more of the types of victimization (Sedlak et al., 2013), and more than one-third (38%) fear attack by someone (Sedlak & McPherson, 2010, p. 6). Many youth report being victimized repeatedly, and often for more than one type of violence, at the hands of staff as well as their peers (Bernstein, 2014, p. 301; Sedlak et al., 2013). Incarcerated juveniles interviewed by Bernstein (2014, p. 33) were quoted as saying that staff "treat you like dogs." Moreover, Irwin (2005, p. 164) reports that many prisoners are "psychologically scarred" by the "hostility and contempt directed at them" by criminal justice personnel.

Understandably, then, many prisoners are wary of others attacking or exploiting them, which can lead to hypervigilance and distrust (Haney, 2003). Essentially, inmates cannot easily escape dangerous situations, and thus must always be on "high alert." With such a heavy emphasis on avoiding victimization while incarcerated, a concern for many prisoners upon release is letting their guard down. In a study of 100 male ex-offenders released from prison for an average of 23 months, Schappell and colleagues (2016) determined that victimization and feeling unsafe during incarceration was associated with increased antisocial behavior, post-traumatic stress, and emotional distress. Similarly, Listwan and colleagues (2012, 2013) found that prisoners who scored higher on a coercion index, based on victimization experiences (especially violent) and perceptions of the prison environment as threatening and hostile, were more likely to be rearrested or reimprisoned after release. Moreover, experiencing victimization in prison was significantly related to psychological well-being, that is, post-traumatic cognitions and symptoms, such as elevated levels of depression and anxiety (Listwan et al., 2012). Other studies have also reported that victimization in prison is related to depression, anxiety, and/or posttraumatic stress symptoms (including anger) following release (Hochstetler, Murphy, & Simons, 2004; Wolff & Shi, 2009).

Zweig and colleagues (2015) analyzed data from the multi-site evaluation of the Serious and Violent Offender Reentry Initiative to assess the impact of victimization on a variety of reentry outcomes. This study involved interviews with 543 men and 168 women in 12 states before prison release and three times after release. Zweig and colleagues' (2015) analyses determined that prisoners who are physically assaulted or threatened have negative emotional reactions including hostility and depression, and that these emotional reactions increase recidivism (especially violent criminal behavior) and substance use up to 15 months post-release. Importantly, because this study is longitudinal in nature, it is able to specify that victimization experiences in prison are the cause of these negative effects. There is little doubt that experiencing these pains of imprisonment has a negative impact on persons coming in contact with the criminal justice system.

What Happens in Prison Doesn't Stay in Prison

Research results do not indicate a clear negative or positive impact of the imprisonment experience in relation to post-release recidivism (Frost & Monteiro, 2016; Mears et al., 2015; Rydberg & Clark, 2016). However, many people who would be considered a success in terms of non-recidivism report dealing with the psychological effects of their incarceration, sometimes more than five years after release from prison. Irwin (2005, p. 191), for example, argues that even though "[m]ost parolees *eventually* stay out of prison," neither formerly incarcerated persons nor the general public would consider this a successful outcome. Austin and Irwin (2000, 156; Irwin, 2005, p. 197) compound this negative prognosis by estimating that more than 25% of released prisoners "eventually end up on the streets, where they live out a short life of dereliction, alcoholism, and drug abuse."

Importantly, what happens in prison doesn't always stay in prison, and thus the "effects of incarceration extend beyond the prison walls" (Kazemian & Travis, 2015, p. 370). Munn (2011, p. 235), for example, notes that a man in his early 30s who has been in the community for five years after serving a 10-year sentence reported "I went to jail and I've seen things that nobody else will ever see . . . and like I have a lot of disturbing memories from a lot of things I've seen" (p. 235). Despite earning a doctorate in clinical psychology 13 years after serving a 7-year sentence, Dailey (2001, p. 260) states that "I still experience residual effects from my incarceration. I have occasional nightmares and sometimes grind my teeth when I sleep. Inside buildings, I am most comfortable sitting with my back against the wall, facing the door." In discussing the negative impact of time spent in prison, Zamble and Porporino (1988, p. 153) talk of becoming "frozen developmentally." Grounds (2005) reports that all of the exonerees in his study felt that time had stopped while they were incarcerated. For example, one man explained that "I'm thirty-five but I'm twenty in my head" (p. 46).

As mentioned earlier, Haney (2003) describes emotional numbing and the "prison mask" that prisoners use to protect themselves. Several researchers have reported on how methods of coping in prison can become maladaptive after release. Munn (2011, p. 236; see also Liem, 2016) provides the example of Luc, who served over 30 years in prison on a life sentence and had been out for more than a decade. Luc remarked that

> [w]hile incarcerated, we pick up all kinds of masks that we put on to survive in jail and . . . these masks work . . . so it's very easy when you're out in the community and

things . . . don't work out the way you want them, to . . . put back some of these masks again. It doesn't work.

(Munn, 2011, p. 236)

Similarly, a 37-year-old male released lifer exclaimed that

[y]ou have to build like this shell around you, to protect you from your environment. So if you keep on doing this for so long, then once you get let out, it's kind of difficult to bring it down, because it's ingrained in you.

(Liem & Kunst, 2013, p. 335)

Building a wall, or wearing a "prison mask" to keep people out, may eventually become what keeps a person in, and unable to interact in positive ways with the social environment (Haney, 2003; Liem, 2016). Hypervigilance and being constantly watchful and suspicious is another characteristic of many released prisoners. A formerly incarcerated youth interviewed by Bernstein (2014) noted that in prison "Anything could happen at any time. You're watching everybody and everybody's watching you. You're *watching* everybody watch you watch them" (p. 194). This hypervigilance often extends after release in a variety of social interactions (Garland, Wodahl, & Mayfield, 2011; Victor & Waldram, 2015).

Pains of Post-Prison Supervision

In a sense, community supervision may be thought of as an extension of the pains of imprisonment. Carson (2015) reports that about 70% of inmates released from state prisons in 2014 will be under some form of post-custody community supervision. Failure rates on supervision are high with only about half (50%) of parolees successfully completing supervision without violating a condition of release, absconding, or committing a new crime (Maruschak & Bonczar, 2015). Consequently, it is not surprising that many parolees express great fear of being returned to prison for a revocation due to a "technical violation" (Bernstein, 2014; Best, Wodahl, & Holmes, 2014; Goffman, 2009; Liem, 2016; Munn, 2011) and use avoidance strategies to remain in the community. Goffman (2009), for example, uses the term "on the run" in describing persons with supervision violations pending or outstanding warrants for minor offenses. She describes these persons using a coping strategy in which they "avoid dangerous places, people, and interactions entirely" (p. 353). Liem (2016, p. 5) used the term "fragile freedom" to refer to the constant fear that lifers had of being returned to prison and reported that some avoided seeking help for various issues for this reason. This fear is not unreasonable, as Rydberg and Clark (2016) found that those serving longer prison sentences had a higher likelihood of parole revocations and were returned to prison for a revocation sooner after release than their peers with shorter sentences.

Far from endorsing a "seamless" transition from prison control to community control, "convict criminologists" Mobley and Terry (2002; see also Dailey, 2001) write, "No one wants the separation of prison and parole more urgently than do prisoners. When people 'get out,' they want to *be out*. Any compromise or half-measure, any 'hoops' or hassles placed in their path, breeds resentment." Parole conditions that include prohibitions against associating with fellow formerly incarcerated persons or entering drinking establishments (both of which are nearly impossible to enforce) often undermine the perceived legitimacy of the entire parole process. Another source of aggravation and frustration for parolees is the frequent handing-off of supervision responsibility from one parole officer to another with each having a unique supervision style and enforcement of conditions (Austin & Irwin, 2000, Gonnerman, 2004).

In interviews with parole-eligible inmates, Best, Wodahl, and Holmes (2014) found that about one-third (36%) feared revocation of parole, and one-fourth (28%) reported a sense of anxiety relating to feelings of having become institutionalized. For one participant, parole was not really freedom and in many ways, is eerily similar to prison:

> They hang your freedom over your head. Yet, they can search your house and your car, and make you pay for your own UA [urinalysis]. They watch you like a hawk and steal your money. If you screw up, they'll send you back. That's not freedom, if you ask me.
>
> (Best et al., 2014, p. 335)

Similarly, Munn (2011, p. 238) discusses how parolees "felt a pervasive sense of omniopticism (being watched by multiple others) and were always cognizant that they were being surveilled." Bucklen and Zajac (2009) found that many parole violators have "tunnel vision, seeing no alternatives" (p. 258). Moreover, many parolees who fail tend to "crash and burn" with about three-fourths indicating some sort of negative emotion (i.e., frustrated, worried, depressed, angry, stressed, etc.) in the 48 hours before violating their parole (Bucklen & Zajac, 2009).

Perceptions of and Responses to Stigma

It is now generally understood that formerly incarcerated persons are stigmatized and discriminated against in society (see e.g., LeBel, 2012a; Petersilia, 2003; Travis et al., 2014). Petersilia (2003) for example, suggests that the plight of felons is best summed up as "a criminal conviction—no matter how trivial or how long ago it occurred—scars one for life (p. 19)." Similarly, Bernstein (2014, p. 186) suggests that "[t]he scarlett C, mark of the convict, can never be erased." Many researchers have assessed perceptions of "ex-con" stigma from the perspective of currently or formerly incarcerated persons (see e.g., Gunnison & Helfgott, 2013; Harding, 2003; Halsey et al., 2016; Irwin, 1970, 2005; LeBel, 2012a, 2012b; Munn, 2012; Uggen, Manza, & Behrens, 2004; Winnick & Bodkin, 2009). Irwin (2005), based on 40 years of research with prisoners and former prisoners, argues that "doing good" in a post-prison lifestyle is "very difficult for ex-convicts to achieve because of their debilitating prison experiences and their ex-convict stigma" (p. 192).[2]

LeBel (2012a) developed a 9-item scale measuring perceptions of stigma that included many stereotypes of formerly incarcerated persons (e.g., dangerous, dishonest, untrustworthy), as well as indicators for being feared, discriminated against, and looked down on. LeBel (2012a, 2012b; see also Winnick & Bodkin, 2009) reported that nearly two-thirds (65%) believe they have been discriminated against because of their status as former prisoner, but that there is a substantial amount of variation in the formerly incarcerated persons' perception of being personally stigmatized by society. This finding fits with Pinel's (1999) construct of "stigma consciousness," which indicates that respondents from the same stereotyped group may differ from one another in perceptions of stigmatization.

Findings of perceptions of stigma have been reinforced in considerable qualitative research with ex-prisoners: "You are labeled as a felon, and you're always gonna be assumed and known to have contact with that criminal activity and them ethics. And even when I get off parole, I'm still gonna have an 'F' on my record" (Uggen et al., 2004, p. 283). Importantly, stigma appears to have real consequences, as research results reveal that soon-to-be released prisoners' perception of "social prejudice against ex-convicts" is a strong predictor of recidivism (LeBel, Burnett, Maruna, & Bushway, 2008) and that higher perceptions of personal stigma are negatively related to belief in the American Dream and self-esteem (see LeBel, 2012b, LeBel, Richie, & Maruna, 2015).

Perhaps the most damaging long-term psychological effects of having a felony record and/or serving time in prison is the perception that stigmatization based on one's criminal past will never end. LeBel and colleagues (2015) examined perceptions of the stability of stigmatization in a study involving about 225 formerly incarcerated persons who were asked to respond with their level of agreement to the statement, "Society will never fully accept that former prisoners have paid their debt to society." They found that formerly incarcerated persons receiving reentry services were very pessimistic and that the majority (56%) agreed or strongly agreed that one's debt to society can never be paid. These clients were also quite pessimistic in their agreement (47%) that former prisoners will "always be treated with suspicion."

These findings lend credence to the qualitative evidence suggesting that many former prisoners believe that people will *always* treat them with suspicion and will *never* fully accept that they have paid their debt to society (see e.g., Bernstein, 2014; Hunter, 2011). A white-collar offender lamented that "you've been found guilty and you pay your debt to society but *it never ends*, you know society will never let you forget that" (Hunter, 2011, p. 232, emphasis added). For those incarcerated in juvenile prison, Bernstein (2014, pp. 185–186) reports that

> these young people who walk out the gates and into a wall learn that 'paying their debt to society' is a fool's errand, that debt, many learn, will be with them forever, accruing compound interest and blocking their prospects everywhere they turn.

An important examination of the long-term psychological effects of stigma is provided in Farrall and colleagues' (2014) longitudinal study of probationers. They noted that a key component of "interviewees' emotional trajectories was that of frustration—of the feeling that one's future was being unnecessarily impeded because of what one had done in the past" (p. 282). For those 10 to 13 years post-conviction, "intermittent reminders of their past returned to haunt them in the course of trying to achieve normal objectives" (Farrall et al., 2014, p. 211; see also Gunnison & Helfgott, 2013, p. 140).

Many researchers note that the belief in one's ability to "go straight," or one's sense of self-efficacy, self-confidence, optimism, or hope, may be a necessary, if not sufficient, condition for an individual to be able to succeed after prison and desist from crime more generally (see e.g., Farrall et al., 2014; LeBel et al., 2008; Maruna, 2001; Visher & O'Connell, 2012). For some former prisoners, the perceived stability in how they're stigmatized and negatively treated by society may influence them to lose hope. Socio-cognitive research with former prisoners suggests that long-term, persistent offenders tend to lack feelings of agency, experiencing their lives as being largely determined for them in a fatalistic mind-set, which Maruna (2001, p. 74; see also Halsey et al., 2016; Irwin, 2005; Liem, 2016) refers to as being "doomed to deviance, " and finds to be similar to the "learned helplessness" theory of depression described by Abramson, Seligman, and Teasdale (1978). To remedy this dire situation, Tromanhauser (2003, p. 93) argues, "By far, the greatest need is emotional and psychological support." As Farrall and colleagues (2014; see also LeBel et al., 2008) suggest in their longitudinal study of probationers, "Perhaps the principal lesson to be drawn is that those working with people trying to desist should recognize the need to engender hope first and foremost" (p. 215).

Reactive and Protective Stigma Management Strategies

In managing information about his or her criminal past, a formerly incarcerated person must decide "to display or not to display; to tell or not to tell; to let on or not to let on; to lie or not to lie; and in each case, to whom, how, when, and where" (Goffman, 1963, p. 42). In fact, the process of if, when, and how to disclose or conceal one's "ex-con" status (or criminal past) may be an ever-present and ongoing dilemma for those who have had contact with the criminal justice system. Stigma coping strategies have been described along a "reactive-proactive continuum" (Siegel et al., 1998) and with a hierarchy of disclosure strategies from complete social avoidance and secrecy to "coming out proud" and broadcasting one's identity (see Corrigan & Rao, 2012; Goffman, 1963; Jones et al., 1984; LeBel, 2009; Link, Mirotznik, & Cullen, 1991; Winnick & Bodkin, 2009).

Research has consistently found that stigmatized individuals attempt to "pass" as normal (Goffman, 1963), or more generally strive to keep their stigmatized status a secret from others (e.g., Jones et al., 1984; Link et al., 1991). According to Irwin (1970, p. 137), "Most ex-convicts can 'pass' with ease" if they so desire. In several qualitative studies of formerly incarcerated persons, "passing" behavior or concealment of one's criminal past was found to be the most often used stigma management strategy (Harding, 2003; Munn, 2012). LeBel (2016) examined formerly incarcerated persons' use of concealment and assessed the potential impact of concealing one's criminal past on psychological well-being and an avoidance coping strategy more generally. Essentially, this study examined if, how, and why perceptions of, and protective and defensive responses to, stigma matter. Overall, there was substantial variation in the use of concealment with some attempting to keep their identity as a former prisoner completely secret, while others were more open and discussed their criminal past more freely. LeBel (2016) also assessed concealment on applications with the question: "Have you avoided indicating on written applications (for jobs, licenses, housing, school, etc.) that you have a felony conviction for fear that information will be used against you?" More than one-third (36.7%) reported that they had often or very often avoided disclosure or concealed their criminal history on applications, while about one-third of the sample indicated *never* concealing it.

Many studies indicate that a higher perception of stigma is positively associated with the use of concealment as a management strategy (see e.g., Chronister et al., 2013; Link et al., 1991, 1997; Luoma et al., 2007). In a study involving medium-security prisoners, Winnick and Bodkin (2009) found that greater perceptions of stigma are related to the expected use of concealment after release from prison, especially as the perceived difficulty of finding employment increased. As expected, LeBel's (2016) research also found that perceptions of personal stigma have a positive and statistically significant impact on the defensive and reactive strategy of concealment. These findings suggest that former prisoners conceal their criminal history partly because of the belief that society will look at them personally, as a former prisoner, with great suspicion.

Similar to concealment, an avoidance coping strategy is also largely protective and defensive in nature. A coping strategy of avoidance can involve physical, social, or psychological withdrawal from a variety of social interactions where the person might be rejected because of their stigma (Miller & Kaiser, 2001). For example, Munn (2012) found that some of the formerly incarcerated men in her study "maintain both spatial and social/emotional distance" from others to "evade judgement" (p. 168). This sort of avoidant strategy is also similar to Irwin's (2005, p. 198) description of the post-prison lifestyle of "drifting on the edge" or "laying low."

There is substantial consensus among researchers that stigmatized individuals who conceal their condition face the constant risk of discovery and may therefore worry excessively about whether, when, and how they should reveal it (Frable et al., 1998; Goffman, 1963; Jones et al., 1984; Smart & Wegner, 2000). Persons who conceal might suffer from intrusive thoughts about the stigma, may lose the benefits provided by affiliating with other stigmatized persons such as social support and the opportunity for social comparison, and may have difficulty developing long-term social relationships (Major, Quinton, McCoy, & Schmader, 2000; Smart & Wegner, 2000). Some additional costs of disclosing include: others may disapprove and react negatively to the discreditable condition/status or the disclosure of it; others may exclude you from social gatherings; others may exclude you from work, housing, and other opportunities; you may worry about what people are thinking about you; family members and "wise" friends may be angry you disclosed; and moving forward, you may have difficulty keeping track of who knows and who doesn't (Goffman, 1963; Newheiser & Barreto, 2014; Quinn et al., 2014). For example, Kevin, a convicted sex offender with a good job, reported "I'm definitely more anxious than I used to be. It's a rare day that goes by where I don't worry that somebody's going to find out about my past and then, you know, will I lose my job?" (Victor & Waldram, 2015, p. 111). Researchers also emphasize the dilemma of a "double-reaction" if one does not divulge their criminal past (Munn, 2012, p. 166). As an example, a formerly incarcerated sex offender struggled with whether or not to disclose his past, "Is it safe to lie through life or be truth-ful? What do people want?" (Victor & Waldram, 2015, p. 112).

According to Goffman (1963), the person who passes "must necessarily pay a great psychological price . . . in living a life that can be collapsed at any moment" (p. 87). In support of this assertion, the coping strategy that a stigmatized person uses is related to psychological and behavioral out-comes. Many researchers, studying a variety of stigmatized identities, have consistently found that the use of reactive and defensive coping strategies (i.e., concealment and avoidance) are harmful in terms of psychological well-being (i.e., depression, anxiety, self-esteem, life satisfaction/quality of life), employment status, and health status (see e.g., Chronister et al., 2013; Corrigan et al., 2006, Jones et al., 1984; Link et al., 1991, 2002; Quinn et al., 2014; Smart & Wegner, 2000; Wahl, 1999). LeBel's (2016) research with formerly incarcerated persons also found that those with higher scores for concealment had lower self-esteem and were less satisfied with their lives. These findings suggest that the greater use of concealment in one's personal life and in filling out applications might have a potentially harmful impact on facilitating the successful reentry and reintegration of a substantial number of formerly incarcerated persons.

Proactive Stigma Management Strategies

As discussed above, underpinning many concerns of persons with contact with the criminal justice system is the issue of stigma. Maruna and LeBel (2009) suggest that perhaps the primary chal-lenge facing the returning prisoner is the need to prove him or herself to be worthy of forgiveness. Researchers have begun to recognize a more proactive and strengths-based stigma management strategy among recovering substance users and formerly incarcerated persons involving becoming a "professional ex-" (Brown, 1991) or a "wounded healer" (LeBel, 2007; LeBel et al., 2015; Maruna, 2001). Brown (1991) asserts that it is important to consider how one might "adopt a legitimate career premised upon an identity that embraces one's deviant history" (p. 220).

Although impossible to measure the true extent of the wounded healer or professional ex- phe-nomenon, Maruna (2001) argues that "the desisting self-narrative frequently involves reworking a delinquent history into a source of wisdom to be drawn from while acting as a drug counselor, youth worker, community volunteer, or mutual-help group member" (p. 117). This role is often accomplished by sharing one's experiences, strength, and hope; acting as a role model; mentoring others; and, for some, making a career of assisting others who are not as far along in the recovery and/or reintegration process. Many formerly incarcerated persons, across a wide range of roles (e.g., "life coaches," Schinkel & Whyte, 2012), and by type of offender (lifers, Liem, 2016, Munn, 2011; white-collar offenders, Hunter, 2015; exonerees, Westervelt & Cook, 2012), express an interest and/or active involvement in roles helping others. In particular, preliminary evidence suggests that many staff members working for prisoner reentry programs are, in fact, formerly incarcerated persons (see e.g., Irwin, 2005; LeBel et al., 2015).

Maruna and LeBel (2009; see also Aresti, Eatough, & Brooks-Gordon, 2010; LeBel, 2012a) posit that these strengths-based efforts work primarily as a form of stigma management or reverse "labe-ling" (Braithwaite, 1989). The purported benefits of assuming the role of helper include the rein-forcement of personal learning, increased feelings of interpersonal competence, a sense of meaning and purpose in their lives, improved self-esteem, a sense of accomplishment, and social approval (see e.g., Aresti et al., 2010; Brown, 1991; Maruna, 2001; Toch, 2000). Thus, becoming a professional ex-or wounded healer may allow stigmatized individuals to overcome the "ex-con" label and reconcile with society for their past crimes, while also contributing to changes in the person's self-identity. Importantly, Hunter (2015, p. 140) argues that a person "[m]ust disclose to be a professional-ex; but still might conceal in other parts of life," and that "this coping mechanism is also about *being seen to do good*, thereby showing the world change has taken place" (p. 131, italics in original).

LeBel and colleagues (2015) examined if, how, and why formerly incarcerated staff members of prisoner reentry programs differ from the clients. A current staff position as a professional-ex or wounded healer was positively related to perceiving less personal stigma, having more prosocial attitudes/beliefs, using active coping strategies such as advocacy, self-esteem, satisfaction with life, and having more positive relationships with family members (LeBel et al., 2015). Moreover, staff members were much less likely to forecast that they will get arrested in the next three years. Therefore, the professional-exes appear to have undergone a remarkable change in their self-identities and worldviews. These findings suggest that this stigma management strategy assists some in overcoming the trauma and psychological effects of incarceration and the reentry process (LeBel et al., 2015; Maruna & LeBel, 2009).

The transformation of formerly incarcerated individuals from being part of the problem into part of a solution requires mechanisms in which their lives can become useful and purposeful. If helping others has adaptive consequences, then an argument can be made to make opportunities to engage in reciprocal processes of mutual support (i.e., mutual-help groups and volunteering) more widely available to prisoners and former prisoners (Maruna et al., 2003). Concrete steps that corrections could adopt include sponsoring altruistic behavior through opportunities to voluntarily engage in public service work that the larger community needs and wants, and fostering the development of peer mentors (Maruna et al., 2003). For example, successful formerly incarcerated persons can provide newly released prisoners with an introduction to life in the community and help them to deal with problems related to reentry and reintegration such as resisting peer pressure and environmental influences that promote offending, negotiating the hazards of being a former prisoner in a "high-risk" neighborhood, providing information about receptive places to find employment, introducing individuals with substance use histories to support groups (e.g., AA/NA), and providing guidance to successfully complete community supervision. In addition, to create more professional exes, policies can be developed to reduce legal restrictions to employment for felons, and to provide monetary support to promote the completion of certification programs (e.g., substance abuse counseling) and college degrees. Based on the potential benefits of pro-social peer groups for released prisoners, correctional administrators should also consider changing non-contact supervision policies for interacting with persons with felony convictions (LeBel et al., 2015).

Maruna and LeBel (2009; see also LeBel, 2009) have discussed going a "third mile" as moving beyond the helping roles of the professional-ex/wounded healer to engaging in more direct efforts at stigma reduction through advocacy/activism in ex-prisoner issues on a political level. They argue that this is a natural next step in efforts towards destigmatization of formerly incarcerated persons. In contrast to the use of reactive and protective stigma management strategies, empowerment-oriented, proactive, and collective attempts to change public perceptions and create a more positive identity are increasingly being thought to be stigmatized persons' "most effective and enduring route to reducing prejudice" (Major et al., 2000, p. 217). A benefit of activism over individualistic strategies such as concealment and avoidance is that any improved treatment will spill over across a variety of situations and improve the lives of other similarly stigmatized persons (Major et al., 2000). Of course, it is important to keep in mind that only a relatively small cadre of individuals likely participate in "third mile" forms of activism.

Becoming involved in advocacy-related activities that contribute to pro-social change may aid formerly incarcerated persons in shedding the negative connotations of the "ex-convict" identity, while also giving their lives purpose and meaning (see Burton & Lynn, 2017). Moreover, some persons who have had extensive contact with the criminal justice system may experience posttraumatic growth (Tedeschi & Calhoun, 2004), and adapt resiliently and more proactively by becoming advocates for reform in the criminal justice system. The involvement of exonerees in policy work to bring about reform in the criminal justice system is especially notable (Grounds, 2005; Konvisser & Werry, 2017; Westervelt & Cook, 2012).

Some reentry organizations, such as The Fortune Society (2017) in New York City, engage in both proactive roles, with ex-prisoners working as professional-exes in counseling other prisoners, as well as doing advocacy work to change laws restricting ex-prisoner access to jobs. Others have gone further and suggested that the perspective of formerly incarcerated persons should be at the forefront of the wider policy debate regarding criminal justice reform and reentry. Indeed, many contemporary ex-prisoner advocacy groups align themselves with the wider criminal justice reform movements (e.g., Ban-the-Box, Black Lives Matter, ending the death penalty, dismantling the prison-industrial complex), and some portray themselves as more militant campaigners against a corrupt justice system (see e.g., Burton & Lynn, 2017; LSPC, 2017).

Formerly incarcerated persons are increasingly speaking out, as a group (LeBel, 2009), and becoming politically active (see Maruna & LeBel, 2009). Organizations like All of Us or None and the Women's Prison Association (WPA) seek to develop "a group of leaders equipped to craft solutions to the problems facing incarcerated and formerly incarcerated persons" (Women's Prison Association, 2017). These grassroots organizations provide a voice to formerly incarcerated persons and the opportunity to be engaged in attempts to change public policy. For example, All of Us or None is a national organizing initiative of formerly incarcerated persons and persons in prison. On its website and in its brochure, this organization states that, "Advocates have spoken for us, but now is the time for us to speak for ourselves" (LSPC, 2017). This organization has argued, "It's OUR responsibility to stop the discrimination, and to change the public policies that discriminate against us, our families, and our communities."

A recent entry into the realm of advocacy work is JustLeadershipUSA (JLUSA) (2017), with formerly incarcerated person, Glenn Martin as the President and Founder. The JLUSA website indicates that the "goal is to amplify the voice of the people most impacted, and to position them as reform leaders. . . . JLUSA is based on the principle that people closest to the problem are also the people closest to its solution." JLUSA attempts to accomplish these goals through advocacy campaigns, leadership training, and member engagement. In academia, a similar movement called "Convict Criminology," largely consisting of ex-prisoner academics, has made strides in changing the way in which crime and justice issues are researched and taught at the university level (Jones, Ross, Richards, & Murphy, 2009). In addition, Witness to Innocence describes itself as "the nation's only organization dedicated to empowering exonerated death row survivors to be the most powerful and effective voice in the struggle to end the death penalty in the United States" (Witness to Innocence, 2017).

These types of organizations are important because research results indicate that "greater levels of outness" are related to more positive outcomes for those with concealable stigmatized identities (Quinn et al., 2014, p. 2; Corrigan, Kosyluk, & Rusch, 2013; Rusch et al., 2014). Similar to the altruism of the wounded healer orientation, there may be discernible personal benefits for engaging in advocacy work. In research among other stigmatized groups, Wahl (1999, p. 476; Link et al., 2002) found that "involvement in advocacy and speaking out are self-enhancing, and the courage and effectiveness shown by such participation help to restore self-esteem damaged by stigma." In addition, like helping behaviors, becoming involved in advocacy-related activities can give meaning, purpose, and significance to a formerly incarcerated person's life (Connett, 1973, p. 114).

LeBel's (2009) quantitative research provides evidence of the benefits of involvement in advocacy as a coping orientation for ex-prisoners. His survey research with formerly incarcerated persons found that an advocacy orientation is positively correlated with one's psychological well-being, and in particular satisfaction with life as a whole. He found a strong negative correlation between one's advocacy orientation and criminal attitudes and behavior, indicating that this coping strategy may help to maintain a person's prosocial identity and facilitate ongoing desistance from crime. These findings suggest that involvement in advocacy-related activities might have potential in facilitating the successful reintegration of some formerly incarcerated persons. There is also potential for political organizing among recently released prisoners as many are supportive of advocacy. Moving forward, research is needed to learn how and why formerly incarcerated persons become involved in advocacy-related activities, to study leaders of these advocacy organizations, and to document the development of this growing social movement.

Directions for Future Research and Policy

The successful reintegration of former prisoners requires addressing stigma and discrimination in mainstream society in order to give former prisoners a realistic "second chance" at becoming law-abiding, tax-paying citizens. This will involve education of the public in the harm of current practices of exclusion as well as fostering the idea that former prisoners, through the consistent display of prosocial behavior, can earn their way back to full citizenship status. In effect, this would recognize formerly incarcerated persons' debt to society as fully paid and give them official permission to legally move on from the past (Maruna, 2001). For this to occur, communities in America will need to halt the accumulation of stigmatizing laws and reduce the dissemination of discrediting information to the public.

Recently, in order to foster successful reintegration and desistance from crime, Maruna (2014) has expanded on his argument for an official destigmatization process and

> started to believe that a "certificate of rehabilitation" is probably preferable than legal re-biographing. Rather than having one's criminal past buried or "knifed-off," such policies instead formally and legally declare the person to be "rehabilitated," whilst still providing relief from all legal penalties and disqualifications.
>
> (p. 134)

Garretson (2016) reports that 10 states have some sort of certificate of rehabilitation legislation, with New York and Connecticut having additional legislation prohibiting discrimination based on a criminal record when used jointly with these certificates. Research appears to support the assertion that certificates can reduce the stigma of a felony conviction. Leasure and Anderson (2016) examined Ohio's Certificate of Qualification for Employment (CQE), created in 2012, and found that individuals with a one-year-old felony drug conviction holding a CQE received nearly 3 times as many job offers or invitations for interviews as compared to persons with identical criminal records and qualifications but no CQE. Garretson (2016) argues that to make the use of certificates of rehabilitation more effective moving forward, "legislation must exist with a strong education component, an expectation of use, and be utilized with legislation that gives certificates teeth" (p. 41).

Many social psychologists now consider the consequences of (and responses to) stigma to be primarily context-specific (e.g., Major et al., 2002). A person by situation approach is thought to be important because coping strategies (e.g., concealment or advocacy) that might be effective in reducing stigma or improving psychological well-being in certain social contexts may be less helpful, or possibly detrimental, in other situations (Major et al., 2002). To address the negative consequences of stigma, it is believed that a holistic approach is needed that is multifaceted and multilevel (Link & Phelan, 2001), targeting individuals with stigma, specific groups like employers and landlords who might discriminate against a specific group, and attempting to change the attitudes and beliefs of the general public that perpetuate stigma and discrimination. At the individual level, there is preliminary evidence that counseling approaches (Brown et al., 2003) and cognitive therapy (Corrigan & Calabrese, 2005) are effective in helping persons to overcome the negative consequences of perceptions of stigma. Scholars have suggested that specialized training modules in coping skills for stigma can be incorporated into treatment programs for stigmatized persons such as those with mental disorders (see Corrigan & Calabrese, 2005; Link et al., 2002). This training is designed to help persons to more effectively cope with stigma and maintain and enhance self-esteem and self-efficacy.

More coordinated and structural anti-stigma interventions, including legal and policy initiatives, are needed to make a lasting impact (see e.g., Heijnders & Van Der Meij, 2006; Link et al., 2002). Research findings suggest that the public's stigmatizing attitudes might be improved using education strategies and through contact with persons with the stigma (see e.g., Corrigan et al., 2002). Educational campaigns using stigmatized group members as speakers that inform the general public by providing facts and dispelling myths has shown positive results for improving attitudes and behaviors of audience members toward persons with mental illness (see e.g., Corrigan et al., 2002), and may also be advantageous for persons with criminal records.

Conclusion

A review of the literature pertaining to the long-term psychological effects of contact with the criminal justice system reinforces the idea that success must expand beyond the myopic focus on recidivism to examine the "more subtle, hidden kinds of psychological and emotional disability" (Grounds, 2005, p. 48) that it may cause. Reentry and reintegration is a long-term process with many ups and downs even for those "doing good" (Irwin, 2005; Maruna et al., 2004). As Schnittker (2014, p. 136) argues, "The psychological consequences of incarceration are easy to overlook," and so is the seemingly never ending struggle to overcome the stigma of a criminal past (LeBel, 2012a). Consequently, moving forward, longitudinal research, using longer assessment time-frames, combining qualitative, quantitative, and more interdisciplinary work is needed to provide a more in-depth understanding of the psychological effects of contact with the criminal justice system (Kazemian & Travis, 2015; see also Liem & Kunst, 2013).

A policy to address the potential long-term psychological effects of contact with the criminal justice system could be more consistent screening for victimization and trauma (especially PTSD and PICS symptoms) at all levels of the criminal justice system, but especially in corrections (see Zweig et al., 2015). Similarly, a more concerted focus on implementing "what works" in trauma informed care is warranted (see e.g., Maschi et al., 2015; Najavits, 2002). Moreover, as suggested by Gunnison and Helfgott (2013, p. 145; see also Grounds, 2005), "[e]xamining the differences in the postprison life experiences of ex-offenders as they move further out in the survival curve" is essential.

Braithwaite and Braithwaite (2001) suggest that our criminal justice system should jettison the use of stigmatization because it may make the offender a "permanent outcast" (p. 36). Moving forward, more research is needed to examine why and how perceptions of stigma and responses to it matter. It appears to be especially important for researchers to focus on how individuals with prolonged contact with the criminal justice system cope with stigma and how it affects their psychological well-being and ability to maximize their human potential.

Notes

1 This review does not focus attention on specific populations covered elsewhere in this volume: for sex offenders see Kras, McGuirk, Pleggenkuhle, & Huebner, 2008; and for women see Bohmert, Galasso, & Cobbina, 2008.
2 Research findings indicate that persons with felony convictions face considerable discrimination in competing for jobs, leading to reduced prospects for obtaining even low-wage employment (Decker, Ortiz, Spohn, & Hedberg, 2015; Pager, 2007). For more about the collateral consequences of incarceration and felony convictions for employment, see Apel and Ramakers, Chapter 5 in this volume.

References

Abramson, L.Y., Seligman, M. E., & Teasdale, J. D. (1978). Learned helplessness in humans: Critique and reformulation. *Journal of Abnormal Psychology, 87*(1), 49–74.
American Psychiatric Association. (2013). *Diagnostic and statistical manual of mental disorders* (5th ed.). Washington, DC: American Psychiatric Association.

Anderson, R. E., Geier, T. J., & Cahill, S. P. (2016). Epidemiological associations between posttraumatic stress disorder and incarceration in the National Survey of American Life. *Criminal Behaviour and Mental Health*, *26*, 110–123.

Aresti, A., Eatough, V., & Brooks-Gordon, B. (2010). Doing time after time: An Interpretative Phenomenological Analysis of reformed ex-prisoners' experiences of self-change, identity and career opportunities. *Psychology, Crime & Law*, *16*(3), 169–190.

Arrigo, B. A., & Bersot, H. Y. (2015). Revisiting the mental health effects of solitary confinement on prisoners in supermax units: A psychological jurisprudence perspective. In S. C. Richards (Ed.), *The Marion experiment: Long-term solitary confinement and the supermax movement* (pp. 175–200). Carbondale, IL: Southern Illinois University Press.

Austin, J., & Irwin, J. (2000). *It's about time: America's imprisonment binge* (3rd ed.). Belmont, CA: Wadsworth.

Beck, A. J., Harrison, P. M., & Guerino, P. (2010). *Special report: Sexual victimization in juvenile facilities reported by youth, 2008–2009.* Washington, DC: U.S. Department of Justice, Bureau of Justice Statistics.

Bernstein, N. (2014). *Burning down the house: The end of juvenile prison.* New York, NY: The New Press.

Best, B. L., Wodahl, E. J., & Holmes, M. D. (2014). Waiving away the chance of freedom: Exploring why prisoners decide against applying for parole. *International Journal of Offender Therapy and Comparative Criminology*, *58*(3), 320–347.

Bohmert, M. N., Matthew Galasso, M., & Cobbina, J. (2018). The collateral consequences of punishment for women. In B. M. Huebner & N. Frost (Eds.), *ASC Division on Corrections and Sentencing Volume 3: Handbook on the consequences of sentencing and punishment decisions.* New York: Routledge.

Braithwaite, J. (1989). *Crime, shame, and reintegration.* Cambridge: Cambridge University Press.

Braithwaite, J., & Braithwaite, V. (2001). Part I: Shame, shame management and regulation. In E. Ahmed, N. Harris, J. Braithwaite, & V. Braithwaite (Eds.), *Shame management through reintegration.* Cambridge: Cambridge University Press.

Brown, J. D. (1991). The professional ex-: An alternative for exiting the deviant career. *Sociological Quarterly*, *32*, 219–230.

Brown, L., Macintyre, K., & Trujillo, L. (2003). Interventions to reduce HIV/AIDS stigma: What have we learned? *AIDS Education and Prevention*, *15*, 49–69.

Browne, A., Miller, B., & Maguin, E. (1999). Prevalence and severity of lifetime physical and sexual victimization among incarcerated women. *International Journal of Law and Psychiatry*, *22*(3), 301–322.

Bucklen, K. B., & Zajac, G. (2009). But some of them don't come back (to prison!): Resource deprivation and thinking errors as determinants of parole success and failure. *The Prison Journal*, *89*(3), 239–264.

Burton, S., & Lynn, C. (2017). *Becoming Ms. Burton: From prison to recovery to leading the fight for incarcerated women.* New York, NY: The New Press.

Carlson, B. E., Shafer, M. S., & Duffee, D. E. (2010). Traumatic histories and stressful life events of incarcerated parents II: Gender and ethnic differences in substance abuse and service needs. *Prison Journal*, *90*(4), 494–515.

Carson, E. A. (2015). *Prisoners in 2014.* NCJ Bulletin 248955. Washington, DC: U.S. Department of Justice, Bureau of Justice Statistics.

Chronister, J., Chou, C., & Liao, H. (2013). The role of stigma coping and social support in mediating the effect of societal stigma on internalized stigma, mental health recovery, and quality of life among people with serious mental illness. *Journal of Community Psychology*, *41*(5), 582–600.

Connett, A. V. (1973). Epilogue. In R. J. Erickson, W. J. Crow, L. A. Zurcher, & A. V. Connett, *Paroled but not free* (pp. 106–116). New York, NY: Behavioral Publications.

Corrigan, P. W., & Calabrese, J. D. (2005). Strategies for assessing and diminishing self-stigma. In P. W. Corrigan (Ed.), *On the stigma of mental illness: Practical strategies for research and social change* (pp. 239–256). Washington, DC: American Psychological Association.

Corrigan, P. W., Kosyluk, K. A., & Rusch, N. (2013). Reducing self-stigma by coming out proud. *American Journal of Public Health*, *103*, 794–800.

Corrigan, P. W., & Rao, D. (2012). On the self-stigma of mental illness: Stages, disclosure, and strategies for change. *Canadian Journal of Psychiatry*, *57*(8), 464–469.

Corrigan, P. W., Rowan, D., Green, A., Lundin, R., River, L. P., Uphoff-Wasowski, K., White, K., & Kubiak, M. A. (2002). Challenging two mental illness stigmas: Personal responsibility and dangerousness. *Schizophrenia Bulletin*, *28*, 293–309.

Corrigan, P. W., Watson, A. C., & Barr, L. (2006). The self-stigma of mental illness: Implications for self-esteem and self-efficacy. *Journal of Social and Clinical Psychology*, *25*, 75–84.

Covington, S. S. (2003). A woman's journey home: Challenges for female offenders. In J. Travis & M. Waul (Eds.), *Prisoners once removed: The impact of incarceration and reentry on children, families, and communities* (pp. 67–103). Washington, DC: The Urban Institute Press.

Dailey, L. (2001). Reentry: Prospects for postrelease success. In D. Sabo, T. A. Kupers, & W. London (Eds.), *Prison masculinities* (pp. 255–264). Philadelphia, PA: Temple University Press.

Decker, S. H., Ortiz, N., Spohn, C., & Hedberg, E. (2015). Criminal stigma, race, and ethnicity: The consequences of imprisonment for employment. *Journal of Criminal Justice, 43*(2), 108–121.

Dudeck, M., Drenkhahn, K., Spitzer, C., Barnow, S., Kopp, D., Kuwert, P., . . . Dünkel, F. (2011). Traumatization and mental distress in long-term prisoners in Europe. *Punishment & Society, 13*, 403–423.

Farrall, S., Hunter, B., Sharpe, G., & Calverley, A. (2014). *Criminal careers in transition: The social context of desistance from crime.* Oxford: Oxford University Press.

Fleury-Steiner, B., & Longazel, J. (2014). *The pains of mass imprisonment.* New York, NY: Routledge.

Flowers, A. (2016). *Exoneree diaries: The fight for innocence, independence, and identity.* Chicago, IL: Haymarket Books.

Fortune Society. (2017). *Homepage.* Retrieved from https://fortunesociety.org/

Frable, D. E. S., Platt, L., & Hoey, S. (1998). Concealable stigmas and positive self-perceptions: Feeling better around similar others. *Journal of Personality and Social Psychology, 74*, 909–922.

Freudenberg, N., Daniels, J., Crum, M., Perkins, T., & Richie, B. E. (2005). Coming home from jail: The social and health consequences of community reentry for women, male adolescents, and their families and communities. *American Journal of Public Health, 95*(10), 1725–1736.

Frost, N., & Monteiro, C. E. (2016). *Administrative segregation in U.S. prisons* (NCJ 249749). Washington, DC: U.S. Department of Justice, Office of Justice Programs, National Institute of Justice.

Garland, B., & Wodahl, E. (2014). Coming to a crossroads: A critical look at the sustainability of the prisoner reentry movement. In M. S. Crow & J. O. Smykla (Eds.), *Offender reentry: Rethinking criminology and criminal justice* (pp. 399–422). Burlington, MA: Jones & Bartlett.

Garland, B., Wodahl, E., & Mayfield, J. (2011). Prisoner reentry in a small metropolitan community: Obstacles and policy recommendations. *Criminal Justice Policy Review, 22*, 90–110.

Garretson, H. J. (2016). Legislating forgiveness: A study of post-conviction certificates as policy to address the employment consequences of a conviction. *Boston University Public Interest Law Journal, 25*(1), 1–41.

Gatti, U., Tremblay, R. E., & Vitaro, F. (2009). Iatrogenic effect of juvenile justice. *Journal of Child Psychology and Psychiatry, 50*, 991–998.

Goffman, A. (2009). On the run: Wanted men in a Philadelphia ghetto. *American Sociological Review, 74*, 339–357.

Goffman, E. (1963). *Stigma: On the management of spoiled identity.* Englewood Cliffs, NJ: Prentice-Hall.

Gonnerman, J. (2004). *Life on the outside: The prison odyssey of Elaine Bartlett.* New York, NY: Farrar, Straus and Giroux.

Gorski, T. T. (2001). *Post incarceration syndrome and relapse.* Retrieved June 1, 2017, from www.tgorski.com/criminal_justice/cjs_pics_&_relapse.htm.

Grassian, S. (1983). Psychopathological effects of solitary confinement. *American Journal of Psychiatry, 140*(11), 1450–1454.

Grassian, S. (2016). Psychiatric effects of solitary confinement. In J. Casella, J. Ridgeway, & S. Shourd (Eds.), *Hell is a very small place: Voices from solitary confinement* (pp. 155–161). New York, NY: The New Press.

Green, B. L., Miranda, J., Daroowalla, A., & Siddique, J. (2005). Trauma exposure, mental health functioning, and program needs of women in jail. *Crime & Delinquency, 51*(1), 133–151.

Grounds, A. T. (2005). Understanding the effects of wrongful imprisonment. *Crime and Justice, 32*, 1–58.

Gunnison, E., & Helfgott, J. B. (2013). *Offender reentry: Beyond crime & punishment.* Boulder, CO: Lynne Rienner Publishers.

Halsey, M., Armstrong, R., & Wright, S. (2016). "F★ck it!": Matza and the mood of fatalism in the desistance process. *British Journal of Criminology.* doi:10.1093/bjc/azw041

Haney, C. (2003). The psychological impact of incarceration: Implications for post-prison adjustment. In J. Travis & M. Waul (Eds.), *Prisoners once removed: The impact of incarceration and reentry on children, families, and communities* (pp. 33–66). Washington, DC: Urban Institute Press.

Haney, C. (2012). Prison effects in the era of mass incarceration. *Prison Journal.* doi:10.1177/0032885512448604

Harding, D. J. (2003). Jean Valjean's dilemma: The management of ex-convict identity in the search for employment. *Deviant Behavior, 24*, 571–595.

Heijnders, M., & Van Der Meij, S. (2006). The fight against stigma: An overview of stigma—reduction strategies and interventions. *Psychology, Health, and Medicine, 11*, 353–363.

Herman, J. L. (1992). *Trauma and recovery.* New York, NY: Basic.

Hochstetler, A., Murphy, D. S., & Simons, R. L. (2004). Damaged goods: Exploring predictors of distress in prison inmates. *Crime & Delinquency, 50*, 436–457.

Human Rights Watch & American Civil Liberties Union. (2012). *Growing up locked down: Youth in solitary confinement in jails and prisons across the United States.* New York, NY: Human Rights Watch.

Hunter, B. (2011). I can't make my own future. In S. Farrall, M. Hough, S. Maruna, & R. Sparks (Eds.), *Escape routes* (pp. 221–239). Abingdon, UK: Routledge.

Hunter, B. (2015). *White-collar offenders and desistance from crime: Future selves and the constancy of change*. New York, NY: Routledge.

Irwin, J. (1970). *The felon*. Englewood Cliffs, NJ: Prentice Hall.

Irwin, J. (2005). *The warehouse prison: Disposal of the new dangerous class*. Los Angeles, CA: Roxbury Publishing Company.

Irwin, J., & Owen, B. (2005). Harm and the contemporary prison. In A. Liebling & S. Maruna (Eds.), *The Effects of Imprisonment*. Portland, OR: Willan Publishing.

Jones, E. E., Farina, A., Hastorf, A. H., Markus, H., Miller, D. T., & Scott, R. A. (1984). *Social stigma: The psychology of marked relationships*. Hillsdale, NJ: Erlbaum.

Jones, R. S., Ross, J. I., Richards, S. C., & Murphy, D. S. (2009). The first dime: A decade of convict criminology. *The Prison Journal, 89*, 151–171.

JustLeadershipUSA. (2017). *About us*. Retrieved from www.justleadershipusa.org/about-us/

Kao, J. C., Chuong, A., Reddy, M. K., Gobin, R. L., Zlotnick, C., & Johnson, J. E. (2014). Associations between past trauma, current social support, and loneliness in incarcerated populations. *Health and Justice, 2*(7), 1–10.

Kazemian, L., & Travis, J. (2015). Imperative for inclusion of long termers and lifers in research and policy. *Criminology & Public Policy, 14*(2), 355–395.

Komarovskaya, I. A., Loper, A. B., Warren, J., & Jackson, S. (2011). Exploring gender differences in trauma exposure and the emergence of symptoms of PTSD among incarcerated men and women. *Journal of Forensic Psychiatry & Psychology, 22*(3), 395–410.

Konvisser, Z. B., & Werry, A. (2017). Exoneree engagement in policy reform work: An exploratory study of the Innocence Movement Policy Reform Process. *Journal of Contemporary Criminal Justice, 33*(1), 43–60.

Kras, K.R., McGuirk, M., Pleggenkuhle, B., & Huebner, B.M. (2018). Compounded stigmatization: Collateral consequences of a sex offense conviction. In B.M. Huebner & N. Frost (Eds.), *ASC Division on Corrections and Sentencing Volume 3: Handbook on the consequences of sentencing and punishment decisions*. New York: Routledge.

Kupers, T. A. (2005). Posttraumatic stress disorder in prisoners. In S. Stojkovic (Ed.), *Managing special populations in jails and prisons* (pp. 10-1–10-21). Kingston, NJ: Civic Research Institute.

Labrecque, R. M. (2015). *The effect of solitary confinement on institutional misconduct: A longitudinal evaluation*. Washington, DC: U.S. Department of Justice.

Leasure, P., & Andersen, T. S. (2016). The effectiveness of certificates of relief as collateral consequence relief mechanisms: An experimental study. *Yale Law and Policy Review Inter Alia, 35*(11), 11–22.

LeBel, T. P. (2007). An examination of the impact of formerly incarcerated persons helping others. *Journal of Offender Rehabilitation, 46*(1/2), 1–24.

LeBel, T. P. (2009). Formerly incarcerated persons' use of advocacy/activism as a coping orientation in the reintegration process. In B. M. Veysey, J. Christian, & D. J. Martinez (Eds.), *How offenders transform their lives* (pp. 165–187). Cullompton: Willan Publishing.

LeBel, T. P. (2012a). Invisible stripes? Formerly incarcerated persons' perceptions of stigma. *Deviant Behavior, 33*, 89–107.

LeBel, T. P. (2012b). "If one doesn't get you another one will": Formerly incarcerated persons' perceptions of discrimination. *The Prison Journal, 92*(1), 63–87.

LeBel, T. P. (2016). *To tell or not to tell? Formerly incarcerated persons' use of concealment as a stigma management strategy*. Invited paper and presentation at Prisoner Reentry and Reintegration Workshop. Newark, NJ: Rutgers University. April 15, 2016.

LeBel, T. P., Burnett, R., Maruna, S., & Bushway, S. (2008). The "chicken and egg" of subjective and social factors in desistance from crime. *European Journal of Criminology, 5*(2), 130–158.

LeBel, T. P., & Maruna, S. (2012). Life on the outside: Transitioning from prison to the community. In J. Petersilia & K. Reitz (Eds.), *The Oxford handbook of sentencing and corrections* (pp. 657–683). New York, NY: Oxford University Press.

LeBel, T. P., Richie, M., & Maruna, S. (2015). Helping others as a response to reconcile a criminal past: The role of the wounded healer in prisoner reentry programs. *Criminal Justice and Behavior, 42*(1), 108–120.

Legal Services for Prisoners with Children (LSPC). (2017). *All of us or none*. Retrieved from www.prisonerswith children.org/our-projects/allofus-or-none/

Lerman, A. E. (2009). The people prisons make: Effects of incarceration on criminal psychology. In S. Raphael & M. A. Stoll (Eds.), *Do prisons make us safer? The benefits and costs of the prison boom* (pp. 151–176). New York, NY: Russell Sage Foundation.

Liem, M. (2016). *After life imprisonment: Reentry in the era of mass incarceration*. New York, NY: New York University Press.

Liem, M., & Kunst, M. (2013). Is there a recognizable post-incarceration syndrome among released "lifers"? *International Journal of Law and Psychiatry, 36*(3–4), 333–337.

Link, B. G., Mirotznik, J., & Cullen, F. T. (1991). The effectiveness of stigma coping orientations: Can negative consequences of mental illness labeling be avoided? *Journal of Health and Social Behavior, 32*, 302–320.

Link, B. G., & Phelan, J. C. (2001). Conceptualizing stigma. *Annual Review of Sociology, 27*, 363–385.

Link, B. G., Struening, E. L., Neese-Todd, S., Asmussen, S., & Phelan, J. C. (2002). On describing and seeking to change the experience of stigma. *Psychiatric Rehabilitation Skills, 6*(2), 201–231.

Link, B. G., Struening, E. L., Rahav, M., Phelan, J. C., & Nuttbrock, L. (1997). On stigma and its consequences: Evidence from a longitudinal study of men with dual diagnosis of mental illness and substance abuse. *Journal of Health and Social Behavior, 38*, 177–190.

Listwan, S. J., Hanley, D., & Colvin, M. (2012). *The prison experience and reentry: Examining the impact of victimization on coming home.* Washington, DC: Report submitted to the National Institute of Justice. Doc. No. 238083.

Listwan, S. J., Sullivan, C. J., Agnew, R. Cullen, F. T., & Colvin, M. (2013). The pains of imprisonment revisited: The impact of strain on inmate recidivism. *Justice Quarterly, 30*, 144–168.

Lovell, D., Johnson, L. C., & Cain, K. C. (2007). Recidivism of supermax prisoners in Washington State. *Crime & Delinquency, 53*, 633–656.

Luoma, J. B., Twohig, M. P., Waltz, T., Hayes, S. C., Roget, N., Padilla, M., & Fisher, G. (2007). An investigation of stigma in individuals receiving treatment for substance abuse. *Addictive Behaviors, 32*, 1331–1346.

Lynch, S., & Heath, N. (2017). Predictors of incarcerated women's postrelease PTSD, depression, and substance-use problems. *Journal of Offender Rehabilitation, 56*(3), 157–172.

Major, B., Quinton, W. J., & McCoy, S. K. (2002). Antecedents and consequences of attributions to discrimination: Theoretical and empirical advances. In M. P. Zanna (Ed.), *Advances in experimental social psychology* (pp. 251–330). Boston, MA: Academic Press.

Major, B., Quinton, W. J., McCoy, S. K., & Schmader, T. (2000). Reducing prejudice: The target's perspective. In S. Oskamp (Ed.), *Reducing prejudice and discrimination* (pp. 211–237). Mahwah, NJ: Lawrence Erlbaum.

Maruna, S. (2001). *Making good: How ex-convicts reform and reclaim their lives.* Washington, DC: American Psychological Association.

Maruna, S. (2014). Reintegration as a right and the rites of reintegration: A comparative review of de-stigmatization practices. In J. A. Humphrey & P. Cordella (Eds.), *Effective interventions in the lives of criminal offenders* (pp. 121–138). New York, NY: Springer.

Maruna, S., Immarigeon, R., & LeBel, T. P. (2004). Ex-offender reintegration: Theory and practice. In S. Maruna & R. Immarigeon (Eds.), *After crime and punishment: Pathways to offender reintegration* (pp. 3–26). Cullompton: Willan Publishing.

Maruna, S., & LeBel, T. (2009). Strengths-based approaches to reentry: Extra mileage toward reintegration and destigmatization. *Japanese Journal of Sociological Criminology, 34*, 58–80.

Maruna, S., LeBel, T. P., & Lanier, C. (2003). Generativity behind bars: Some "redemptive truth" about prison society. In E. de St. Aubin, D. McAdams, & T. Kim (Eds.), *The generative society: Caring for future generations* (pp. 131–151). Washington, DC: American Psychological Association.

Maruschak, L. M., & Bonczar, T. P. (2015). *Probation and parole in the United States, 2012.* Washington, DC: U.S. Department of Justice, Bureau of Justice Statistics.

Maschi, T., Viola, D., Morgen, K., & Koskinen, L. (2015). Trauma, stress, grief, loss, and separation among older adults in prison: The protective role of coping resources on physical and mental well-being. *Journal of Crime and Justice, 38*(1), 113–136.

McCorkle, R. (1992). Personal precautions to violence in prison. *Criminal Justice and Behavior, 19*, 160–173.

Mears, D. P. (2013). Supermax prisons. *Criminology & Public Policy, 12*(4), 681–719.

Mears, D. P., & Bales, W. D. (2009). Supermax incarceration and recidivism. *Criminology, 47*(4), 1131–1166.

Mears, D. P., Cochran, J. C., & Cullen, F. T. (2015). Incarceration heterogeneity and its implications for assessing the effectiveness of imprisonment on recidivism. *Criminal Justice Policy Review, 26*(7), 691–712.

Miller, C. T., & Kaiser, C. R. (2001). Implications of mental models of self and others for the targets of stigmatization. In M. R. Leary (Ed.), *Interpersonal rejection* (pp. 189–212). New York, NY: Oxford University Press.

Mobley, A., & Terry, C. (2002). *Dignity, resistance and re-entry: A convict perspective.* Unpublished paper.

Munn, M. (2011). Living in the aftermath: The impact of lengthy incarceration on post-carceral success. *Howard Journal of Criminal Justice, 50*(3), 233–246.

Munn, M. (2012). The mark of criminality: Rejections and reversals, disclosure and distance: Stigma and the ex-prisoner. In S. Hannem & C. Bruckert (Eds.), *Stigma revisited: Implications of the mark* (pp. 147–169). Ottawa, Canada: University of Ottawa Press.

Najavits, L. (2002). *Seeking safety.* New York, NY: Guilford Press.

Nelson, B. (2016). Weak as motherfuckers. In J. Casella, J. Ridgeway, & S. Shourd (Eds.), *Hell is a very small place: Voices from solitary confinement* (pp. 117–120). New York, NY: The New Press.

Newheiser, A., & Barreto, M. (2014). Hidden costs of hiding stigma: Ironic interpersonal consequences of concealing a stigmatized identity in social interactions. *Journal of Experimental Social Psychology, 52*, 58–70.

Pager, D. (2007). *Marked: Race, crime, and finding work in an era of mass incarceration.* Chicago, IL: University of Chicago Press.

Petersilia, J. (2003). *When prisoners come home: Parole and prisoner reentry.* New York, NY: Oxford University Press.

Pinel, E. C. (1999). Stigma consciousness: The psychological legacy of social stereotypes. *Journal of Personality and Social Psychology, 76*, 114–128.

Quinn, D. M., Williams, M. K., Quintana, F., Gaskins, J. L., Overstreet, N. M., . . . Chaudoir, S. R. (2014). Examining effects of anticipated stigma, centrality, salience, internalization, and outness on psychological distress for people with concealable stigmatized identities. *PLoS ONE, 9*(5), 1–15.

Rusch, N., Abbruzzese, E., Hagedom, E., Hartenhauer, D., Kaufman, I., Curschellas, J., . . . Corrigan, P. W. (2014). Efficacy of coming out proud to reduce stigma's impact among people with mental illness: Pilot randomized controlled trial. *British Journal of Psychiatry, 204*, 391–397.

Rydberg, J., & Clark, K. (2016). Variation in the incarceration length-recidivism dose-response relationship. *Journal of Criminal Justice, 46*, 118–128.

Schappell, A., Docherty, M., & Boxer, P. (2016). Violence and victimization during incarceration: Relations to psychosocial adjustment during reentry to the community. *Violence and Victims, 31*(2), 361–378.

Schinkel, M., & Whyte, B. (2012). Routes out of prison using life coaches to assist resettlement. *The Howard Journal of Criminal Justice, 51*(4), 359–371.

Schneider, K., Richters, J., Butler, T., Yap, L., Richards, A., Grant, L., . . . Donovan, B. (2011). Psychological distress and experience of sexual and physical assault among Australian prisoners. *Criminal Behaviour and Mental Health, 21*, 333–349.

Schnittker, J. (2014). The psychological dimensions and social consequences of incarceration. *The Annals of the American Academy of Political and Social Science, 651*(1), 122–138.

Sedlak, A. J., & McPherson, K. S. (2010). Conditions of confinement: Findings from the Survey of Youth in Residential Treatment. *Juvenile Justice Bulletin.* Washington, DC: U.S. Department of Justice, Office of Justice Programs, Office of Juvenile Justice and Delinquency Prevention.

Sedlak, A. J., McPherson, K. S., & Basena, M. (2013). Nature of risk and victimization: Findings from the Survey of Youth in Residential Treatment. *Juvenile Justice Bulletin.* Washington, DC: Office of Juvenile Justice and Delinquency Prevention.

Shalev, S. (2009). *Supermax: Controlling risk through solitary confinement.* Portland, OR: Willan Publishing.

Siegel, K., Lune, H., & Meyer, I. H. (1998). Stigma management among gay/bisexual men with HIV/AIDS. *Qualitative Sociology, 21*(1), 3–23.

Smart, L., & Wegner, D. M. (2000). The hidden costs of hidden stigma. In T. F. Heatherton, R. E. Kleck, M. R. Hebl, & J. G. Hull (Eds.), *Stigma: Social psychological perspectives* (pp. 220–242). New York, NY: Guilford.

Smith, P., Gendreau, P., & Labrecque, R. M. (2015). *The impact of solitary confinement on inmate behavior: A meta-analytic review.* Paper presented at the North American Correctional and Criminal Justice Psychology (N3) Conference, Ottawa, Canada. Retrieved from http://media.wix.com/ugd/7fc458_2efc5654e7ea4d27a9d45 a64f331fec5.pdf

Stern, K. (2014). *Voices from American prisons: Faith, education, and healing.* New York, NY: Routledge.

Sykes, G. M. (1958). *The society of captives: A study of a maximum-security prison.* Princeton, NJ: Princeton University Press.

Tedeschi, R. G., & Calhoun, L. G. (2004). Posttraumatic growth: Conceptual foundations and empirical evidence. *Psychological Inquiry, 15*, 1–18.

Toch, H. (2000). Altruistic activity as correctional treatment. *International Journal of Offender Therapy and Comparative Criminology, 44*, 270–278.

Travis, J., Western, B., & Redburn, S., Eds. (2014). *The growth of incarceration in the United States: Exploring causes and consequences.* Washington, DC: National Academies Press.

Tromanhauser, E. (2003). Comments and reflections on forty years in the criminal justice system. In J. I. Ross & S. C. Richards (Eds.), *Convict criminology* (pp. 81–94). Belmont, CA: Wadsworth.

Uggen, C., Manza, J., & Behrens, A. (2004). "Less than the average citizen": Stigma, role transition and the civic reintegration of convicted felons. In S. Maruna & R. Immarigeon (Eds.), *After crime and punishment: Pathways to offender reintegration* (pp. 261–293). Cullompton: Willan Publishing.

Victor, J., & Waldram, J. B. (2015). Moral habilation and the new normal: Sexual offender narratives of post-treatment community integration. In L. Presser & S. Sandberg (Eds.), *Narrative criminology: Understanding stories of crime* (pp. 96–121). New York: New York University Press.

Visher, C. A., & O'Connell, D. J. (2012). Incarceration and inmates' self perceptions about returning home. *Journal of Criminal Justice, 40*, 386–393.

Visher, C. A., & Travis, J. (2003). Transitions from prison to community: Understanding individual pathways. *Annual Review of Sociology, 29*, 89–113.

Wahl, O. F. (1999). *Telling is risky business: Mental health consumers confront stigma.* New Brunswick, NJ: Rutgers University Press.

Westervelt, S. D., & Cook, K. J. (2012). *Life after death row: Exonerees' search for community and identity.* New Brunswick, NJ: Rutgers University Press.

Wildeman, J., Costelloe, & Schehr, R. (2011). Experiencing wrongful and unlawful conviction. *Journal of Offender Rehabilitation, 50*, 411–432.

Winnick, T. A., & Bodkin, M. (2009). Stigma, secrecy, and race: An empirical examination of black and white incarcerated men. *American Journal of Criminal Justice, 34*(1/2), 131–150.

Witness to Innocence. (2017). *Meet our exoneree members.* Retrieved from www.witnesstoinnocence.org/exonerees.html

Wolff, N., Blitz, C. L., Shi, J., Siegel, J., & Bachman, R. (2007). Physical violence inside prisons: Rates of victimization. *Criminal Justice and Behavior, 34*, 588–599.

Wolff, N., & Shi, J. (2009). Type, source, and patterns of physical victimization: A comparison of male and female inmates. *The Prison Journal, 89*, 172–191.

Women's Prison Association. (2017). *Homepage.* Retrieved from www.wpaonline.org/

World Health Organization. (1992). *The ICD-10 classification of mental and behavioural disorders: Clinical descriptions and diagnostic guidelines.* Geneva: World Health Organization.

Zamble, E., & Porporino, F. J. (1988). *Coping, behavior, and adaptation in prison inmates.* New York, NY: Springer.

Zweig, J. M., Yahner, J., Visher, C. A., & Lattimore, P. K. (2015). Using general strain theory to explore the effects of prison victimization experiences on later offending and substance use. *The Prison Journal, 95*(1), 84–113.

8
IMPACTS OF INCARCERATION ON CHILDREN AND FAMILIES

Miriam Northcutt Bohmert and Sara Wakefield

Introduction

The effects of incarceration are felt both by those who experience it directly as inmates as well as by those sociologist Megan Comfort has described as legal bystanders (Comfort, 2007). Legal bystanders experience incarceration indirectly through their connections to the incarcerated—and such connections prove to be both common and highly consequential. Among the most studied legal bystanders to mass incarceration are the partners and children of the imprisoned and many studies connect incarceration to family disruption and decreases in well-being (see, for example, Apel, 2016; Massoglia, Remster, & King, 2011; Turney, 2014, 2015; Wakefield & Wildeman, 2011; Wildeman, 2009). The difficulties for families imposed by incarceration are also not limited to the time while incarcerated and last long afterward. Former inmates experience substantial disadvantages, including under-employment, housing instability, poor health and mental health problems, substance abuse, homelessness, and poor access to transportation (Northcutt Bohmert, 2016; Petersilia, 2003; Travis, 2005; Western, 2006).

Estimates vary but most find that a (slight) majority of the incarcerated have children (Glaze & Maruschak, 2008; Travis, Cincotta, & Solomon, 2003) and approximately half of these parents had children who were living with them prior to incarceration (Geller, 2013). Nationwide, about 3%, or 2.1 million, children have an incarcerated father, (Western, 2006) but the likelihood of experiencing parental incarceration is sharply racialized. Whereas less than 2% of white children had an incarcerated parent in 2008, more than 3.5% of Latino children and a startling 11% of African-American children had experienced parental incarceration (Western & Pettit, 2010; see also, Wildeman, 2009). The modal child of an incarcerated parent is 8 years old, from a family that earns less than $1,000 per month, and is most likely black or Hispanic (Mumola, 2000). More than half a million African-American children, or approximately half of the children born to African-American men without high school diplomas, will experience parental incarceration (Western & Wildeman, 2009). Finally, it is notable that the racial disparity in parental incarceration *within* the United States is larger than the prevalence of parental incarceration when comparing between the United States and Denmark, a country with a much lower incarceration rate (Wildeman & Andersen, 2015).

Estimating the number of children who have *ever* had a parent incarcerated is much more difficult; a recent estimate suggests more than 5 million (Murphey & Cooper, 2015), but this is surely an undercount because it was restricted to residential parents. Whatever the true number, it is abundantly clear that children of incarcerated parents represent a large and, unfortunately, hidden population in the United States. Such large estimates also have implications for marriage. Among inmates with children, roughly 20–30% of men and 10–20% of women were living with a spouse just prior to their incarceration (see also Apel, 2016; Massoglia et al., 2011). The racial disparity in the likelihood of experiencing parental incarceration during childhood also has important consequences for a host of important developmental outcomes (Wakefield & Wildeman, 2013). Such racial disparities are not limited to parental incarceration; black men and women often have numerous family members bound up in the criminal justice system (H. Lee, McCormick, Hicken, & Wildeman, 2015; Wildeman & Wakefield, 2014).

The main focus of this chapter is on the effects of incarceration for children but also on the family. Most research focuses on issues of child well-being (Wildeman, Wakefield, & Turney, 2013), but some has looked at adult women's well-being (Wildeman, Schnittker, & Turney, 2012), financial well-being (Geller, Garfinkel, & Western, 2011), or family outcomes more broadly. The chapter is organized by outcomes including health (e.g., mental health problems, antisocial behavioral problems, infant mortality), economic insecurity (e.g., homelessness, financial hardship, system disengagement), family relationships and dissolution, attainment (e.g., school performance and outcomes), and delinquency. As we review these areas, where possible, we forefront the latest and best research but also address inconsistencies in findings, specifically related to heterogeneity of effects, differences in race/ethnicity, and differences between maternal or parental incarceration. Along this vein, we highlight new gaps in research where appropriate. In the last sections of the chapter, we highlight emerging research and discuss promising policies and practices.

Effects of Parental Incarceration

The balance of research shows that parental incarceration is harmful for children, but research on the effects of paternal, relative to maternal, incarceration is more extensive, rigorous with respect to selection bias, and consistent. With regard to paternal incarceration, the balance of evidence suggests that it is harmful across a wide variety of outcomes. The effects range in size across studies and outcomes, but our summation of the literature is that paternal incarceration results in small to moderate effects in the direction of harm. Taken together, paternal incarceration effects are largest on children's behavior and mental health problems for externalizing, delinquent, violent, and physically aggressive behaviors (Craigie, 2011; Wakefield & Wildeman, 2011, 2013). Internalizing behaviors and mental health problems as well as minor forms of delinquency are evident at older ages (Roettger & Swisher, 2011; Swisher & Roettger, 2012; Wakefield & Wildeman, 2013). This summation is not to suggest that every study finds harmful effects, however. Several studies find that the removal of an abusive or otherwise harmful parent results in null effects for children, and may even benefit them (Giordano, 2010; Siegel, 2011; Wakefield & Powell, 2016; Wakefield & Wildeman, 2013; Wildeman, 2010). Research that further explores how paternal incarceration effects are conditioned by experiences prior to prison or the conditions of confinement is sorely needed (Turney, 2017). It is notable, for example, that after almost two decades of intensive focus on children of incarcerated parents, the literature has produced little knowledge that clearly shows how, for whom, or under what conditions it is most harmful.

Research on the effects of maternal incarceration is much less clear-cut and remains contested. There is also much less of it because of substantial data infrastructure problems—few large surveys or administrative datasets exist with sufficient numbers of incarcerated women to study and the literature is, as a result, more reliant on small sample descriptive studies. In large sample work, several studies find null effects of maternal imprisonment for children (Cho, 2009b; Turney & Wildeman, 2015) and very large differences in methodological rigor are apparent. That said, there are good reasons to believe that the effects of maternal incarceration are more complicated and often indirect (Foster & Hagan, 2015; Hagan & Foster, 2015). In the text to follow, we take care to note important differences

8 Impact of Incarceration on Kids and Families

in maternal and paternal incarceration effects. Such caveats should not discourage more research into both populations, but we hope to sensitize readers to the very different population distributions from which male and female inmates are drawn and how this may influence the interpretation of current research findings.

Research and the Identification of Causal Effects

Early research on parental incarceration suggested consequential problems but largely consisted of small samples with few clear comparison groups (Braman, 2004; Hairston, 2007; Johnston, 2006; Kampfner, 1995; Nurse, 2002; Sack, 1977). Small sample descriptive studies are hugely important for detailing potential causal mechanisms and focusing attention on the population of children unlikely to be found in large surveys (for example, those in child welfare)—yet such studies are not able to clearly distinguish effects that follow imprisonment from those that precede it. In a review of research, Johnson and Easterling (2012) show that research on the effects of parental incarceration on child well-being had not sufficiently controlled for selection bias. Because children of incarcerated parents differ from other children on so many dimensions, they concluded that it is difficult to infer whether problems observed among these children are due to a parent's incarceration or to other circumstances surrounding the child. Giordano (2010) and Sampson (2011) have also raised similar concerns that social context prior to incarceration may be driving the observed effects; as a result, the obstacles to causal inference are high.

In a response to these criticisms, Wildeman and colleagues (2013) described 12 exemplar research studies from criminal justice, sociology, psychology, and economics to illustrate that, while there are studies of less rigor, there also are studies using relatively sophisticated matching techniques (Cho, 2009b; Craigie, 2011; Foster & Hagan, 2007, 2009; Geller, Cooper, Garfinkel, Schwartz-Soicher, & Mincy, 2012; R. Johnson, 2009; Murray, Loeber, & Pardini, 2012; Roettger & Swisher, 2011; Roettger, Swisher, Kuhl, & Chavez, 2011; van de Rakt, Murray, & Nieuwbeerta, 2012; Wakefield & Wildeman, 2011; Wildeman, 2010). More recent work does adjust for selection bias by using more than one comparison group, covariate adjustment, propensity-score matching, fixed effects (or other approaches that control for unobserved yet stable traits), strategic comparisons between those who are incarcerated and those will become incarcerated in the future, and placebo regressions. When these 12 studies are included, one draws substantively different conclusions and a number of works published since then more firmly establish the research base on the harmful effects of parental incarceration, at least with respect to fathers. Although research is less clear on how parental incarceration compares to parental divorce, it is more clear on how it relates to parental absence—parental incarceration is worse than absence in terms of increases in aggressive behavior (Geller et al., 2012) as well as greater risks of antisocial personality disorder and self-reported delinquency at age 18 (Murray & Farrington, 2005). Similarly, Uggen & McElrath (2014) suggest making use of naturally occurring comparison groups and others employing such strategic comparisons show both null and harmful effects of paternal incarceration (for example, Porter & King, 2012).

The literature has rapidly evolved, utilizing sophisticated comparison groups and large, rich representative datasets like the Fragile Families and Child Wellbeing Study (Geller, 2013; Geller et al., 2011; Turney & Wildeman, 2015; Wildeman et al., 2012), the National Longitudinal Study of Adolescent Health (Burgess-Proctor, Huebner, & Durso, 2016; Foster & Hagan, 2013; R. D. Lee, Fang, & Luo, 2013; Mears & Siennick, 2016; Muftic, Bouffard, & Armstrong, 2016; Porter & King, 2012), the National Longitudinal Survey of Youth (Huebner & Gustafson, 2007), the Cambridge Study in Delinquent Development (Murray & Farrington, 2008a), and the Project on Human Development in Chicago Neighborhoods (Wakefield, 2015; Wakefield & Wildeman, 2011). Still, where randomized experiments are largely impossible and researchers have access to a very limited set of (mostly survey) datasets (Wakefield, Lee, & Wildeman, 2016), the available avenues for overcoming significant challenges to causality remain severely constrained. Moreover, it remains the case that incarcerated mothers are difficult to study using the aforementioned surveys because small cells sizes limit our ability to analyze them in complex ways.

We return to differences in research findings on maternal and paternal incarceration below in our review but wish to remind readers here that a focus on the causal effect of incarceration is important but should not obscure the vulnerability of children of incarcerated parents more generally. Incarceration of a parent is a strong signal of disadvantage—but it signals (1) significant vulnerability and disadvantage that may culminate in the incarceration of a parent as well as (2) the difficulties that flow from experiencing parental incarceration. While nailing down the causal effect of incarceration on partners and children, the presence or absence of such effects in some contexts or conditions does not imply that the criminal justice system is unimportant for understanding the American stratification system or that criminal justice involvement is irrelevant to understanding child welfare.

Type of Parental Incarceration

Research on maternal and paternal incarceration has developed along different paths. Some of this is driven by available data—while women's incarceration rates have increased more rapidly than men's (Kruttschnitt, 2010), the number of incarcerated women remains low relative to men and, as a result, most surveys are plagued by small-cell problems. Some studies have combined fathers and mothers (Arditti & Savla, 2015; Murray & Farrington, 2008b; Nichols & Loper, 2012; Phillips, Erkanli, Keeler, Costello, & Angold, 2006) or focused exclusively on paternal incarceration with much less focus on maternal incarceration. For our purposes, it is notable that the literature on paternal and maternal incarceration initially developed along largely different paths, with few scholars tackling both. This is much less true today, a change we argue is much needed in order to develop a full accounting of the complicated relationships between pre-prison experiences and incarceration effects.

A major gap in this body of research is that the number of children with both parents incarcerated is under researched. About two-thirds of the time maternal incarceration co-occurs with paternal incarceration (Garfinkel, Geller, & Cooper, 2007; Phillips et al., 2006; Wildeman & Wakefield, 2014), and we know little about these situations. Separating out the effects of paternal and maternal incarceration, when both co-occurring, is challenging. Muftic and colleagues (2016) attempt to address this using Add Health data and propensity score matching. They show that maternal incarceration impacts future criminal behavior of children, even after controlling for effects of paternal incarceration. However, due to small sample sizes of both maternal incarceration and co-occurring incarcerations, the authors were not able to align samples using propensity score matching and thus are unable to strongly assert that the effects of maternal incarceration exist beyond the effect of paternal incarceration. Another paper (that we would characterize as substantially more rigorous) that is able to address co-occurring incarcerations as well as maternal from paternal separately finds that poor outcomes for children are driven by paternal, not maternal, incarceration (Wildeman & Turney, 2014).

Such differential findings are open to several plausible interpretations, but it is clear that the more rigorous the study with respect to selection bias, the more likely it is that maternal incarceration effects become null while paternal incarceration effects survive attempts to net out such bias. It could be that maternal incarceration effects are more likely to be indirect (Hagan & Foster, 2015). The pre-prison circumstances of children who have a mother incarcerated relative to a father are vastly different, and this may blunt the effect of maternal incarceration because everything that comes before it is already so damaging (Giordano, 2010). Finally, the selection process into prison for men versus women results in substantially different profiles of incarcerated men and women—and such differences are likely important for thinking about effects on children. We take no firm position on the debate here except to note that those who hope to compare the *causal* effect of maternal versus paternal incarceration should account for large variation in methodological rigor across studies and, put bluntly, they rarely compare favorably. Largely owing to data infrastructure problems, the research base is simply much stronger on paternal incarceration effects on children.

Research has also been relatively silent on caregivers and extended family who care for children of incarcerated parents. Several qualitative studies suggest that understanding caregivers is crucial to understanding effects on children (Siegel, 2011; Turnanovic, Rodriguez, & Pratt, 2012), and several quantitative studies suggest that caregiver stress is an important part of understanding declines in child well-being (Turney, 2014; Wakefield, 2015), but few are able to rigorously estimate or compare variation in caregiving circumstances. Research should investigate coping resources, material resources, and stability of arrangements, among other concerns to see how these arrangements differ from parental guardianship. Finally, the outcomes for children who land in the child welfare system (disproportionately the children of incarcerated mothers) remain a largely hidden population because none of the most often used datasets to study parental incarceration in the United States are able to follow children who enter foster care (but see Andersen and Wildeman [2014] for example using Danish register data and Berger, Cancian, Cuesta, and Noyes [2016] for a study using administrative data from carceral and child welfare systems in Wisconsin).

Paternal Incarceration

Rates of paternal incarceration vary from 2% of all children (Western, 2006) to 11% (Foster & Hagan, 2013), or even higher. Part of the variation is due to whether rates represent daily risk or risk of ever having a parent incarcerated; however, the rates also vary tremendously by demographic factors (Wakefield & Wildeman, 2013). As mentioned earlier, paternal incarceration affects children of less educated fathers and black (and Hispanic and Native) children at much higher rates than white children whose parents have higher levels of education (Wakefield & Wildeman, 2013). Due to the nationwide increase in mass incarceration, the number of men in prison has increased and along with it, the number of children who experience paternal incarceration. Nationwide, about 3%, or 2.1 million, children have an incarcerated father (Western, 2006). And research tells us that approximately 40% of these children lived with their fathers just prior to incarceration (Geller, 2013).

Much of the research on children of incarcerated parents has focused on paternal incarceration (Foster & Hagan, 2007; Murray & Farrington, 2008a; Roettger & Boardman, 2012; Wakefield & Wildeman, 2011). Paternal incarceration is typically harmful to children (Wakefield & Uggen, 2010; Wakefield & Wildeman, 2013) except in very specific circumstances such as when a father is engaged in domestic violence ~~or was convicted of a violent offense~~ in which case it is unclear if paternal incarceration helps or harms children (Wakefield & Wildeman, 2013; Wildeman, 2010). More recent analyses also find that children with parents who were least likely to be incarcerated are most harmed by the experience (Turney, 2017) and that children with fathers with major substance abuse and mental health problems may benefit from paternal incarceration (Wakefield & Powell, 2016). Studies that further flesh out how and for whom paternal incarceration is most consequential are sorely needed. Again, however, such efforts are substantially constrained by the available data sources, and papers that explore such questions often have fairly severe methodological problems.

An early concern, raised by Johnson and Easterling (2012) was that researchers were misinterpreting the effects of paternal absence as paternal incarceration. However, careful research has examined this claim and found that the effects of paternal incarceration are not the same as paternal absence, for example, divorce. Geller and colleagues (2012) compared 5-year-old children of incarcerated fathers to children who had experienced paternal absence and found that paternal incarceration was associated with significantly greater increases in aggressive behaviors. Similarly, Murray and Farrington (2005) examined several types of paternal absences and found that paternal incarceration was associated with significantly greater risks of antisocial personality disorder and delinquency than paternal absence unless fathers were hospitalized or had died. The suddenness and irreversibility of these types of absences, which are similar to prison, may be different than other types of paternal absence. Thus, research has shown that paternal incarceration is most likely worse than separation for kids, except in limited circumstances.

The best evidence for harmful paternal incarceration effects are focused on children's behavior and mental health problems for externalizing, delinquent, violent, and physically aggressive behaviors (Foster & Hagan, 2007; Roettger & Boardman, 2012; Wakefield & Wildeman, 2011, 2013). Studies of older children also find smaller effects for internalizing problems (Wakefield & Wildeman, 2011) and minor forms of delinquency (Porter & King, 2015; Roettger & Swisher, 2011). Research has also clearly demonstrated other deleterious effects such as increased marijuana use (Roettger et al., 2011) and poor educational outcomes (Hagan & Foster, 2012b, 2012a; Haskins, 2014; Haskins & Jacobsen, 2017; Turney & Haskins, 2014).

Health Outcomes

Some of the most common measures of child well-being are related to health outcomes such as mental and behavioral health. Research has shown that internalizing behaviors such as stress, sadness, fear or depression (La Vigne, Davies, & Brazell, 2008) are common among children of incarcerated parents. This research has been supported by others who have also found mental health concerns such as separation anxiety, depression, and sadness resulting from parental incarceration (Dallaire & Wilson, 2010; Murray & Farrington, 2008a; Poehlmann, 2005). Related to externalizing behaviors, Murray and Farrington (2005), using the Cambridge Study in Delinquent Development, show paternal incarceration is associated with significantly greater risks of antisocial personality disorder and self-reported delinquency at age 18. Gaston (2016) investigates the long-term effects of parental incarceration on depressive symptoms, using Add Health data, and has found that, for children who experience parental incarceration at a young age, parental incarceration is associated with depressive symptoms. Both Gaston (2016) and Swisher and Roettger (2012) have investigated whether the effect on mental health varies by race or ethnicity and have not found support for this idea.

In a meta-analytic review of 40 studies including over 7,000 children of incarcerated parents, Murray, Farrington, and Sekol's (2012) findings complicate this picture. They find that children of incarcerated parents are at a higher risk for antisocial behavior but not for mental health problems. Wakefield and Wildeman (2014) provide some clarity to these mixed results. They find, for internalizing and externalizing behaviors, across all age groups, paternal incarceration increases problems in children. Internalizing behavioral problems also seem to be more commonly found in samples of children in older age groups (Geller, 2013).

Moving from behavioral health, paternal incarceration also appears to harm physical health. Infant mortality, or death within the first year of life, is a commonly used indicator of overall population health. Several studies find that infants of recently incarcerated parents are much more likely to die in their first year than other infants, although the incidence is still quite low, roughly seven per 1,000 compared to four per 1,000 for infants whose parents were not incarcerated (Light & Marshall, Forthcoming; Wakefield & Wildeman, 2013; Wildeman, 2012). Further underscoring the level of disadvantage for children of incarcerated children, the mothers of these infants were less likely to have had a previous healthy birth, were more likely to have smoked or received public assistance, and were more likely to have reported being abused by the father of the child. Even after controlling for these and other risk factors, the effect of parental incarceration is associated with a 49% increase in the odds of early infant mortality, and mass incarceration is a significant factor in the racial gap in infant mortality in the United States (Wakefield & Wildeman, 2013; see also Wildeman, 2016).

Economic Insecurity

To understand how indicators of economic insecurity such as homelessness and financial hardship are impacted by parental incarceration, cumulative disadvantage theory is instructive (Foster & Hagan, 2007; Merton, 1968; Sampson & Laub, 2004). This theory posits that individuals' lives are shaped by decisions and events that are both positive (advantages) and negative (disadvantages). Advantages and disadvantages, occurring at various levels, shape an individual's path. Advantaged individuals experience opportunities and benefits that propel them toward college, professional degrees, and successful careers; they readily shake off the occasional disadvantage. However, for the disadvantaged, who face an accumulation of constraints and deficits, shaking off the occasional problem is less easily accomplished; each additional hardship serves to accumulate and severely restrict future opportunities (Sampson & Laub, 2004). Individuals who are involved in the criminal justice system are already disadvantaged. Yet, for families that have lost a member to incarceration, their already precarious situation, and the well-being of their children, is likely worsened by the increased risk of financial and housing instability.

Compatible with cumulative disadvantage theory, research shows that, before going to prison, 60% of fathers are employed full time; 68% of those fathers report that their wages are the primary source of income for their families (Travis et al., 2003). Children living in these homes are likely to experience financial strain due that loss of income or loss of child support payments (Hairston, 1998). Children with incarcerated fathers were more likely to experience financial hardship than children with never-incarcerated, never-resident fathers (Garfinkel et al., 2007). Similarly, using a small sample from rural North Carolina, Phillips and colleagues (2006) find that, even after controlling for parents' substance abuse, mental health, education, and race, children of incarcerated parents were 80% more likely to live in a household with economic strain. Paternal incarceration is more broadly associated with greater material insecurity (Schwartz-Soicher, Geller, & Garfinkel, 2011) and public assistance receipt (Sugie, 2012).

At the extreme of material disadvantage, paternal incarceration is also associated with a much greater risk of homelessness (Wakefield & Wildeman, 2013; Wildeman, 2014). Homelessness is also one of the few areas where there is a clear racial difference in the effects of paternal incarceration. In most studies, black and white children (this is the most common comparison) respond similarly to parental incarceration, but racial gaps result from the much greater prevalence of parental incarceration among black children. For homelessness, however, paternal incarceration increases the risk of homelessness almost exclusively for black children. Using data from the Fragile Families study, the authors control for a variety of other factors known to influence homelessness (e.g., parental demographic characteristics, housing risk factors, mother's depression, and prior incarceration) and find that father's incarceration increases the odds of child homelessness by 95%. Such results are also compatible with cumulative disadvantage theory in that children with added social disadvantages fare worse than other children. Further, the authors were able to explain that the effect of paternal incarceration on child homelessness is explained in large part due to destabilizing of finances and housing but not, as some have suggested, by impacting maternal well-being (Wakefield & Wildeman, 2013).

Family Relationships and Dissolution

Early research on family relationships and dissolution focused on the partners of inmates (usually female partners and male inmates). On balance, incarceration appears to play a larger role in breaking up intact families (Apel, Blokland, Nieuwbeerta, & van Schellen, 2010; Charles & Luoh, 2010; Lopoo & Western, 2005; Massoglia et al., 2011; Turney, 2015; Turney, Schnittker, & Wildeman, 2012) than in reducing the marriageability of single men. Notably, the incarceration effect for relationship dissolution happens rather quickly and with often very short spells of incarceration (Apel, 2016).

Beyond dissolution, parental incarceration leads to changes in living arrangements and parent-child relationships (LaVigne et al., 2008). Disruptions in care such as temporary or informal childcare are destabilizing (Glaze & Maruschak, 2008; Travis et al., 2003).

Even if fathers and children had positive relationships when the incarceration event occurred, maintaining that relationship is riddled with difficulties. According to LaVigne and colleagues (2008), prisons are located, on average, 100 miles away from where fathers were living at the time of arrest. Arrangements to visit prison are time-consuming and expensive. Men's prisons often lack nurseries, separate areas for visits with children, or programs that offer parenting classes. Thus, children may find the experience intimidating, uncomfortable, and humiliating (Comfort, 2007; Hairston & Rollin, 2006; Travis et al., 2003). Despite the hurdles in place, more than half of incarcerated parents report receiving at least one in-person visit from their children and 40% of fathers report weekly contact via phone or letters (Travis et al., 2003). It is important to note that, for some families, the separation may be good for children (Giordano, 2010; Wildeman, 2010). If children were living with a father who was drug-addicted, abusive, or neglectful, removal of the father may increase child well-being under some circumstances (Murray & Farrington, 2008b; Western & Wildeman, 2009).

Educational Attainment

Research on educational attainment has looked at a variety of outcomes such as school academic performance, school behavior, and grade retention. Foster and Hagan (2007), using Add Health data and working within the cumulative disadvantage framework, assert that father's educational attainment and incarceration, in combination with the associated absence and financial loss, negatively impact the educational success of their children. Using Fragile Families & Child Wellbeing Study data, Turney and Haskins (2014) have similarly found negative effects of paternal incarceration on grade retention, particularly in early schooling that cannot be explained by test scores or behavior problems but may be influenced by teachers' perceptions of children's academic proficiencies. Among younger children, paternal incarceration is associated with declines in non-cognitive skills such as school readiness, increases in special education placement, early grade retention, and less parental engagement in children's schooling activities (Haskins, 2014; Haskins & Jacobsen, 2017; Turney & Haskins, 2014). Though not focused exclusively on the children of incarcerated parents, Hagan and Foster (2012a) examine whether the concentration of fathers and mothers (2012b) who have been incarcerated in a school impacts the attainment of all students. They find that, in schools with as little as 2.5% percent parental incarceration, students without incarcerated parents are significantly less likely to attend college.

Delinquency

Research has found that having an incarcerated father was associated with higher levels of self-reported delinquency (Murray & Farrington, 2005), as well as marijuana use and other drugs throughout late adolescence (Roettger et al., 2011). Geller et al. (2012), using the Fragile Families and Child Wellbeing study, found paternal incarceration was associated with significantly greater increases in aggressive behaviors than in paternal absence in 5-year-old children. Father's incarceration has also been associated with more serious forms of delinquency such as theft (Murray, Loeber, et al., 2012), arrest (Roettger & Swisher, 2011), and conviction (van de Rakt et al., 2012). Challenging these studies, and searching for mechanisms that underlie the relationship, Porter and King (2012) utilize a unique comparison group, children whose father will be incarcerated in the future, to show that the effect of an incarcerated father on instrumental delinquency is spurious. The authors define instrumental delinquency as offending that has the potential to result in monetary gain. But, the effect on delinquency is intact for expressive forms of delinquency such as fighting and destroying property.

Maternal Incarceration

Although the number of women incarcerated remains much smaller than men's incarceration, the number of children with incarcerated mothers has increased substantially in recent years. Approximately 1 to 3% of children in the United States have an incarcerated mother based on Add Health data (Foster & Hagan, 2013; Muftic et al., 2016). The number of children under age 18 with a mother in prison more than doubled from 1991 to 2007, increasing 131%, with approximately 147,400 children having a mother in prison in the year 2007 (Glaze & Maruschak, 2008). During this same time, the number of children with a father only increased by 77% (La Vigne et al., 2008). Similar to paternal incarceration, maternal incarceration is much more common for black children of less educated parents (Wildeman, 2009).

Health Outcomes

Research has found maternal incarceration is associated with health problems and antisocial behavior in young adulthood, child depression, and internalizing symptoms (Foster & Hagan, 2013; Turney & Wildeman, 2015). Foster and Hagan (2013) find that maternal incarceration increases depressive symptoms for young adults. Turney and Wildeman (2015) find that maternal incarceration is associated negatively with internalizing and externalizing behaviors and early childhood delinquency only for children of mothers who are unlikely to experience incarceration. Lee, Fang, and Luo (2013) find few effects for maternal incarceration on physical and mental health, in comparison to paternal incarceration, but caution that small sample sizes for maternal incarceration may be hiding significant effects. Nonetheless, the authors find a significant association with depression; the odds of depression for individuals who experience this event are 1.6 times that of individuals with no parental incarceration. No effects were found for a host of other health conditions such as asthma, migraine, PTSD, anxiety, obesity, HIV/AIDS, or diabetes. Related, in a sample of 33 children with incarcerated mothers, Kampfner (1995) found evidence of chronic sleeplessness, difficulties concentrating, and depression.

Economic Insecurity

Garfinkel and colleagues (2007) find that, similar to children with incarcerated fathers, children with incarcerated mothers were more likely to experience financial hardship than children with never-incarcerated, never-resident mothers, in part, because 39% of mothers were employed prior to imprisonment. Maternal incarceration is also strongly associated with entry into foster care (Dworsky, Harden, & George, 2011; E. I. Johnson & Waldfogel, 2004; Swann & Slyvester, 2006). Very few studies have followed children who enter foster care as a result of maternal incarceration so it is difficult to assess effects for this population, though studies of children in foster care more broadly suggest poor outcomes (Doyle Jr., 2007, 2008).

Family Relationships and Dissolution

Whereas 88% of children with incarcerated fathers continue to live with their mothers, only 37% of children with incarcerated mothers live with their fathers (Glaze & Maruschak, 2008). More often, children go to live with grandparents (42% of children), other relatives, friends, or non-family guardians (Glaze & Maruschak, 2008; Hanlon, Carswell, & Rose, 2007). Mothers were 5 times more likely than fathers to report that children were in the care of a foster home or other agency (Glaze & Maruschak, 2008). These living arrangements, coupled with incarcerated mothers typically being incarcerated 60 miles farther away, than fathers, from where they were arrested (Travis et al., 2003), contribute to 40% of mothers reporting no visits from children while in prison (Christian, 2005; Mumola, 2000). However, unlike men's prisons, women's prisons often have better visitation facilities as well as prison-based parenting programs and sometimes prison nurseries. These can help mitigate the effects of parental absence as well as improve parenting deficits where they exist. Similar to fathers, 60% of mothers report weekly contact via phone or letters (Travis et al., 2003).

Educational Attainment

In a series of articles examining educational outcomes, Cho (2009a, 2009b, 2010) used matched data to find that maternal incarceration has no effect on children's reading or math standardized test scores (Cho, 2009b; see also Turney & Wildeman, 2015) *and that it improves grade retention* (Cho, 2009a). However, accounting for timing, dosage, and gender of the child, Cho (2010) finds that male children who experience maternal incarceration between ages 11 and 14 are 25% more likely to drop out of school and 55% more likely to drop out due to incarceration. However, for daughters, timing of maternal incarceration did not significantly impact drop out. Boys' average dropout rate increases with additional maternal incarcerations until it peaks at four incarcerations and drops off, but this same effect was not observed for girls. Girls were more sensitive to length of incarceration than number of incarcerations.

Delinquency

Limited research exists on the effects of maternal incarceration on children's delinquency. The best research to date has found a null effect on delinquency (Turney & Wildeman, 2015) when comparing children of incarcerated parents to similar children whose parents are not incarcerated—thus controlling for other factors known to be related to delinquency such as poverty, substance abuse, or housing instability.

Beyond delinquency and into adulthood, Muftic and colleagues (2016) find that maternal incarceration significantly impacts likelihood of children experiencing arrest, conviction, or incarceration as an adult. Even after controlling for maternal absence and paternal incarceration and using propensity score matching, respondents whose mothers had ever been incarcerated were nearly twice as likely to experience arrest, conviction, and incarceration themselves as adults. However, due to small cell sizes and incomplete matching, additional studies with, for example, larger cell sizes are needed to further investigate effects on adult criminal behavior.

Maternal Versus Paternal

As research has begun to isolate and examine the impact of maternal incarceration (Cho, 2010; Muftic et al., 2016; Turney & Wildeman, 2015), the findings have been much less consistent and more nuanced than studies of paternal incarceration. Some research finds that maternal incarceration, on average, harms children (Huebner & Gustafson, 2007; Muftic et al., 2016). Yet, other research has found maternal incarceration has a null effect on children (Turney & Wildeman, 2015) or improves outcomes (Cho, 2009b, 2009a).

Giordano (2010) raised issues of contextualized maternal incarceration effects early on in a qualitative sample, laying out hypotheses that could later be tested with a larger sample. She suggested that the effects of maternal incarceration are likely more complicated and that there was no theoretical reason to suspect maternal incarceration should have uniform effects on children. Other work has raised similar concerns that researchers must consider the contexts surrounding the incarceration such as demographic characteristics (e.g., race, ethnicity, sex, age), family context (e.g., household socioeconomic status, parental separation, number of siblings), and neighborhood context (e.g., poverty rate, levels of crime) (see also Poehlmann, 2005).

Turney and Wildeman (2015) tested the heterogeneity hypothesis with quantitative data. The authors rely on data from the Fragile Families study (n=3197), a birth cohort survey of new parents in urban areas. Using these data, they find no average effect of maternal incarceration on child well-being for the four measures they examine: internalizing behavior, externalizing behavior, Peabody Picture Vocabulary Test (PPVT) scores, and early childhood delinquency. Importantly, they find that effects of maternal incarceration are highly heterogeneous by propensity to experience maternal incarceration. Specifically, children whose mothers are least likely to be incarcerated experience the most pronounced effects on internalizing and externalizing behaviors and early childhood delinquency, compared to those without incarcerated mothers.

Children with mothers who are least likely to be incarcerated may have been subject to fewer disadvantages and thus traumatic experiences like having a mother incarcerated may be more novel (and therefore more harmful). These assumptions are also supported by literature on parental separation—that abrupt and unexpected events like a hospitalization or death of a parent is more damaging to a child than an incarceration event—all of which are characterized by a higher level of irreversibility and lack of control (Murray & Farrington, 2005). However, other types of absences (divorce) that are more predictable and more reversible have smaller effects on children.

Perhaps some of the heterogeneity effects can be addressed with dosage information such as how long the mother was in prison or the extent of her prior involvement in the criminal justice system. The longer her relationship with the criminal justice system, the less disruptive or traumatic an incarceration would be on children. Similarly, developmental stage information such as whether a mother was in prison during a critical developmental stage for the child (Muftic et al., 2016; Turney & Wildeman, 2015) should be examined. Psychologists assert that some stages require more parental involvement than others (Koepke & Denissen, 2012). In their 2003 Urban Institute Report, Travis and colleagues show the effects of parental arrest and incarceration by developmental stage from birth through age 18 (adapted from Gabel & Johnston, 1997). For example, although middle childhood (ages 7 to 10 years) is characterized by increased independence from caregivers, the effects of separation still present in terms of poor self-concept and impaired ability to overcome future trauma (Gabel & Johnston, 1997; Travis et al., 2003). Cho (2010) has examined the influence of timing and dosage on children's high school dropout rate and risk of incarceration. Using data on 9,563 children between the ages of 5 and 17 and a sibling-pair sample, Cho finds that boys are more sensitive to frequency of incarceration but girls are more sensitive to length—with both experiencing negative school outcomes. Studies such as these, across a greater range of outcomes, will help illuminate heterogeneity effects.

Parental sex may also explain some of the inconsistent findings related to average effect of maternal incarceration. Turney and Wildeman (2015) suggest that mother-daughter or mother-son pairings may be impacted differently by maternal incarceration. Combining these together in one model likely masks these gender pairing effects. Burgess-Proctor and colleagues (2016) found that parental sex does matter; incarcerated mothers have greatest effect on daughters, and incarcerated fathers have large effects on sons. Cross-gender pairings did not significantly affect criminal behavior in adult children. Apart from these two studies, research on parental incarceration (whether maternal or paternal) does not have a strong set of theories anticipating gendered effects. On balance, many studies find larger effects for boys, but this may be driven by a focus on outcomes that are of most interest to criminologists. Research that takes stock of the pattern of gendered results across a broad set of outcomes would advance knowledge considerably.

Emerging Trends in Parental Incarceration

In roughly 15 years, researchers have expanded knowledge on the consequences of incarceration for family life considerably. The partners and children of inmates were previously a largely hidden population, ignored for the most part by researchers and the public, and certainly playing no large role in discussions of punishment policy. In this brief essay, we have taken stock of what is known about incarceration and family life, but much work remains. To conclude, we offer several suggestions for broadening the lens and deepening knowledge.

Developing a Broader View

In order to extend knowledge about the intersection between criminal justice contact and family life, Uggen and McElrath (2014) push researchers to also consider the effects of parental arrest, conviction, and criminal records on children and families. Chapter 2 in this volume addresses the impacts of conviction—extending this work to children would be an important next step. For example, restrictions on housing, SNAP benefits, and automatic revocations of benefits and driving licenses for those with felonies directly impact and disadvantage children. See also Chapters 3 and 5 of this volume for discussions of how conviction impacts housing and employment. Further, particular types of conviction may have more impact than others; for example, drug convictions (Chapter 10 of this volume) and sex offense convictions (Chapter 11 of this volume) carry additional penalties for receipt of social services or employment.

We might also broaden the lens to include less visible consequences that flow from criminal justice contact and expand research to other forms of correctional control beyond incarceration (Kohler-Hausmann, 2013). As an example, Northcutt Bohmert (2016) details how the loss of driving licenses results in missed school and doctor's appointments for children of mothers on probation and parole. Such research is in line with other studies that consider how felony convictions and incarceration histories contribute to detachment from family life and parental engagement (Haskins & Jacobsen, 2017; Lageson, 2016). Research along these lines would also bring connections to the family more fully into emerging discussions of criminal justice reform outside of the incarceration realm.

Taking a Longer View

Beyond broadening our view to other forms of criminal justice contact and consequences, current research is limited insofar as it is typically focused on the period just following incarceration. Giordano (2010) and others have called for a life course approach to examining whether the harms of parental incarceration persist over time and throughout the life course (see also Uggen & McElrath, 2014). Mears and Siennick (2016), using Add Health data, find that the negative effects of parental incarceration do indeed extend well beyond childhood into adulthood. Some research cited here, for example, Muftic and colleagues (2016), examines how parental incarceration impacts children's arrests as adults. Investigating how other areas of children's' adult lives are impacted, such as long-term physical and mental health problems, would be a promising avenue of research.

Developing a More Cohesive and Interdisciplinary Theoretical Framework

Citing early theorists' reliance on strain, socialization, and stigma theories, Foster and Hagan (2015, p. 137) present a multilevel model that ties together findings from the most recent research. Their model incorporates direct and indirect pathways between state and cross-national factors (i.e., political climate, index crime rates, state welfare supports), school factors (i.e., parental incarceration rates, policies), and individual and family factors that cause and are caused by incarceration and that ultimately lead to social exclusion. This theoretical model suggests many areas of future work (i.e., hypotheses and pathways that could be tested). For example, given low levels of state funding for public schools and social services, as well as high rates of parental incarceration in schools, one could investigate which individual and family level factors protect children of incarcerated parents from social exclusion. Social exclusion of children can be exacerbated via stigmatizing contacts with the criminal justice system such as arrests, convictions, and incarcerations (Brayne, 2014) or even online criminal histories that document minor brushes with the law (Lageson, 2016). Thus, we know that parents, especially fathers (Haskins & Jacobsen, 2017), avoid surveilling institutions such as schools to the detriment of their children's education but we do not yet understand the family-level protective factors that can encourage parental attachment to schooling or the individual-level factors that buffer children from the effects of social exclusion and system avoidance.

Further development of theories to interpret incarceration effects should better incorporate knowledge from multiple disciplines (including but not limited to family demography, developmental psychology, life course criminology, and economics). Importantly, the development of such theories would be better able to differentiate between maternal and paternal incarceration effects, anticipate (and explain) gendered findings, and lead to more effective policy interventions for the children and families of the incarcerated. Absent such innovation, the literature may simply continue to expand by offering ever more outcomes influenced by incarceration—while such a path may prove useful, it is unlikely to lend itself to greater understanding and intervention.

Promising Reforms and Policies in Parental Incarceration

Despite growing research on the deleterious effects of parental incarceration on children, virtually none of this research has translated into clear policy proscriptions. Aside from the typical criminal justice calls to increase prison parenting programs, make prison visitation easier, and to offer additional social services for financial and housing support, few recommendations have been tailored to the unique problems created when parents go to prison. Above and beyond effects of socioeconomic status, children of incarcerated parents encounter far worse outcomes, even as infants, that still must be addressed in policy and practice.

Such interventions would also have to overcome the substantial complexities imposed by interactions between the criminal justice system and other social institutions. The spillover of problems imposed by mass incarceration for the child welfare system, for example, are well documented (Berger et al., 2016; E. I. Johnson & Waldfogel, 2002). But mass incarceration has bled into other institutions as well, in more pernicious ways. Consider the educational system. Schools represent a potentially important site of intervention for vulnerable children. Yet the research evidence shows that children of incarcerated parents are more likely to be relegated to special education programs (Haskins, 2014), held back or drop out (Hagan & Foster, 2012a, 2012b; Turney & Haskins, 2014) and that teachers evaluate students with incarcerated parents more poorly (independent of their performance or behavior) (Dallaire, Ciccone, & Wilson, 2010; Wildeman, Scardamalia, Walsh, O'Brien, & Brew, 2017). Simply documenting problems in school for children with incarcerated parents offers little guidance on how to address the problem; indeed, what little research exists suggests that the last thing we should do is make this experience more visible to teachers. As another example, significant literature exists on easing visitation between children and their parents while they are incarcerated, but it is worth remembering that the occasional visit is likely a weak intervention and does not address the constellation of problems that remain once a parent is released. In our view, the greatest weakness of the literature on children of incarcerated parents is that very little of it has been translated into interventions designed to undo the many harms detailed here.

Conclusion

Partners and children of inmates now receive greater attention from researchers and the public and occupy a central role in the criminal justice policy reform discussion. This is important and something few researchers likely could have imagined just two decades ago. Research on incarceration and family is no longer a niche area, and the literature is more broadly-defined, focused on complexity, and tackling more difficult questions today than it did in its infancy. No longer does research simply focus exclusively on parental or paternal incarceration, for example. It has also expanded far beyond the narrow criminological question of how the punishment influences the criminal behavior of their children, considering health, education, housing, and the socio-economic consequences of parental incarceration.

Worth emphasizing is also that what we have learned is startling. For a majority of incarcerated individuals, the effects of their incarceration last far beyond prison impacting children and caretakers by way of under-employment, unstable housing, poor health and mental health problems, substance abuse, poor access to transportation, and homelessness. Nationwide more than 5 million children have at one time had an incarcerated parent. On average, these children are 8 years old, from a family that earns less than $1,000 per month, and are most likely black or Hispanic (Mumola, 2000). Shocking disparities by race/ethnicity exist—11% of African-American children and 3.5% of Hispanic children, compared to 2% of white children experience parental incarceration.

Yet, more work is needed to advance knowledge in this area. Throughout we have noted areas in which additional research is particularly needed. For example, under what conditions paternal incarceration helps or harms children—likely related to a parent's experiences prior to confinement—is needed. Rigorous research is needed to investigate temporal ordering of event related to incarceration, to examine timing of incarcerations in children's developmental stages, to tease out the relationship between maternal and paternal incarceration, as well as to examine gender pairings of parents and children. For example, some evidence suggests boys are impacted more by greater frequency of incarcerations while girls are more impacted by duration—yet we do not understand why. Related, longitudinal research that follows children into foster care, and other living arrangements, is needed to understand the longer-term impacts of incarceration. More broadly, we suggest researchers and practitioners expand beyond parental incarceration to consider parental arrest and conviction. We suggest utilizing life course approaches to capture context for both children and parents. Incorporating knowledge from multiple disciplines will be necessary to understand the multi-layered effects of incarceration. Most importantly, we hope that this review encourages researchers with a range of interest to consider the familial connections of those bound up in the criminal justice system as they design interventions or seek policies that reduce the footprint of the criminal justice system on American family life.

References

Andersen, S. H., & Wildeman, C. (2014). The effect of paternal incarceration on children's risk of foster care placement. *Social Forces, 93*(1), 269–298.

Apel, R. (2016). The effects of jail and prison confinement on cohabitation and marriage. *The Annals of the American Academy of Political and Social Science, 665*(1), 103–126.

Apel, R., Blokland, A. A. J., Nieuwbeerta, P., & van Schellen, M. (2010). The impact of imprisonment on marriage and divorce: A risk set matching approach. *Journal of Quantitative Criminology, 26*, 269–300.

Arditti, J. A., & Savla, J. (2015). Parental incarceration and child trauma symptoms in single caregiver homes. *Journal of Child and Family Studies, 24*, 551–561. Retrieved from https://doi.org/10.1007/s10826-013-9867-2

Berger, L. M., Cancian, M., Cuesta, L., & Noyes, J. L. (2016). Families at the intersection of the criminal justice and child protective services systems. *The ANNALS of the American Academy of Political and Social Science, 665*(1), 171–194. Retrieved from https://doi.org/10.1177/0002716216633058

Braman, D. (2004). *Doing time on the outside: Incarceration and family life in urban America.* Ann Arbor, MI: University of Michigan Press.

Brayne, S. (2014). Surveillance and system avoidance: Criminal justice contact and institutional attachment. *American Sociological Review, 79*(3), 367–391. Retrieved from https://doi.org/10.1177/0003122414530398

Burgess-Proctor, A., Huebner, B. M., & Durso, J. M. (2016). Comparing the effects of maternal and paternal incarceration on adult daughters' and sons' criminal justice system involvement: A gendered pathways analysis. *Criminal Justice and Behavior, 43*(8), 1034–1055. Retrieved from https://doi.org/10.1177/0093854816643122

Charles, K. K., & Luoh, M. C. (2010). Male incarceration, the marriage market, and female outcomes. *Review of Economics and Statistics, 92*, 614–627.

Cho, R. M. (2009a). Impact of maternal imprisonment on children's probability of grade retention. *Journal of Urban Economics, 65*(1), 11–23. Retrieved from https://doi.org/10.1016/j.jue.2008.09.004

Cho, R. M. (2009b). The impact of maternal imprisonment on children's educational achievement: Results from children in Chicago public schools. *Journal of Human Relations, 44*(3), 772–797.

Cho, R. M. (2010). Maternal incarceration and children's adolescent outcomes: Timing and dosage. *Social Service Review, 84*(2), 257–282. Retrieved from https://doi.org/10.1086/653456

Christian, J. (2005). Riding the bus: Barriers to prison visitation and family management strategies. *Journal of Criminal Justice, 21*(1), 31–48.

Comfort, M. (2007). Punishment beyond the legal offender. *Annual Review of Law and Social Science, 3*(1), 271–284.

Craigie, T.-A. L. (2011). The effect of paternal incarceration on early child behavioral problems: A racial comparison. *Journal of Ethnicity in Criminal Justice, 9*(3), 179–199.

Dallaire, D. H., Ciccone, A., & Wilson, L. C. (2010). Teachers' experiences with and expectations of children with incarcerated parents. *Journal of Applied Developmental Psychology, 31*(4), 281–290. Retrieved from https://doi.org/10.1016/j.appdev.2010.04.001

Dallaire, D. H., & Wilson, L. (2010). The relation of exposure to parental criminal activity, arrest, and sentencing to children's maladjustment. *Journal of Family Studies, 19*, 404–418.

Doyle Jr., J. J. (2007). Child protection and child outcomes: Measuring the effects of foster care. *The American Economic Review, 97*(5), 1583–1610.

Doyle Jr., J. J. (2008). Child protection and adult crime: Using investigator assignment to estimate causal effects of foster care. *Journal of Political Economy, 116*(4), 746–770.

Dworsky, A., Harden, A., & George, R. (2011). The relationship between maternal incarceration and foster care placement. *The Open Family Studies Journal, 4*(2), 117–121.

Foster, H., & Hagan, J. (2007). Incarceration and intergenerational social exclusion. *Social Problems, 54*(4), 399–433. Retrieved from https://doi.org/10.1525/sp.2007.54.4.399

Foster, H., & Hagan, J. (2009). The mass incarceration of parents in America: Issues of race/ethnicity, collateral damage to children, and prisoner reentry. *Annals of the American Academy of Political and Social Science, 623*, 179–194.

Foster, H., & Hagan, J. (2013). Maternal and paternal imprisonment in the stress process. *Social Science Research, 42*, 650–669.

Foster, H., & Hagan, J. (2015). Punishment regimes and the multilevel effects of parental incarceration: Intergenerational, intersectional, and interinstitutional models of social inequality and systematic exclusion. *Annual Review of Sociology, 41*, 135–158.

Gabel, K., & Johnston, D. (1997). *Children of incarcerated parents.* New York, NY: Lexington Books.

Garfinkel, I., Geller, A., & Cooper, C. (2007). *Parental incarceration in Fragile Families: Summary of three year findings* (A report to the Annie E. Casey Foundation, Sept 4). Unpublished.

Gaston, S. (2016). The long-term effects of parental incarceration: Does parental incarceration in childhood or adolescence predict depressive symptoms in adulthood? *Criminal Justice and Behavior, 43*(8), 1056–1075. Retrieved from https://doi.org/10.1177/0093854816628905

Geller, A. (2013). Paternal incarceration and father-child contact in fragile families. *Journal of Marriage and Family, 75*, 1288–1295.

Geller, A., Cooper, C. E., Garfinkel, I., Schwartz-Soicher, O., & Mincy, R. B. (2012). Beyond absenteeism: Father incarceration and child development. *Demography, 48*, 49–76.

Geller, A., Garfinkel, I., & Western, B. (2011). Incarceration and support for children in fragile families. *Demography, 48*, 25–47.

Giordano, P. C. (2010). *Legacies of crime: A follow-up of children of highly delinquent girls and boys.* New York, NY: Cambridge University Press.

Glaze, L. E., & Maruschak, L. (2008). *Parents in prison and their minor children.* Washington, DC: United States Department of Justice Printing Office.

Hagan, J., & Foster, H. (2012a). Children of the American prison generation: Student and school spillover effects of incarcerating mothers. *Law & Society Review, 46*(1), 37–69.

Hagan, J., & Foster, H. (2012b). Intergenerational educational effects of mass imprisonment in America. *Sociology of Education, 85*(3), 259–286.

Hagan, J., & Foster, H. (2015). Review of children of the prison boom: Mass incarceration and the future of American inequality. *American Journal of Sociology, 120*(5), 1557–1559.

Hairston, C. F. (1998). The forgotten parent: Understanding the forces that influence incarcerated fathers' relationships with their children. *Child Welfare, 77*(5).

Hairston, C. F. (2007). *Focus on children of incarcerated parents: An overview of the research literature.* (Annie E. Casey Foundation, Ed.). Baltimore, MD: Annie E. Casey Foundation.

Hairston, C. F., & Rollin, J. (2006). Prisoner reentry: Social capital and family connections. In R. Immarigeon (Ed.), *Women and girls in the criminal justice system: Policy issues and practices* (Chapter 4). Kingston, NJ: Civic Research Institute.

Hanlon, T. E., Carswell, S. B., & Rose, M. (2007). Research on the caretaking of children of incarcerated parents: Findings and their service delivery implications. *Children and Youth Services Review, 29,* 348–362.

Haskins, A. (2014). Unintended consequences: Effects of paternal incarceration on school readiness and later special education placement. *Sociological Science, 1,* 141–158.

Haskins, A., & Jacobsen, W. (2017). Schools as surveilling institutions? Paternal incarceration, system avoidance and parental involvement in schooling. *American Sociological Review, 82*(4), 657–684. Retrieved from https://doi.org/10.1177/0003122417709294

Huebner, B. M., & Gustafson, R. (2007). The effect of maternal incarceration on adult offspring involvement in the criminal justice system. *Journal of Criminal Justice, 35,* 283–296.

Johnson, E. I., & Easterling, B. (2012). Understanding the unique effects of parental incarceration on children: Challenges, progress, and recommendations. *Journal of Marriage and Family, 74,* 342–356.

Johnson, E. I., & Waldfogel, J. (2002). Parental incarceration: Recent trends and implications for child welfare. *Social Service Review, 76*(3), 460–479. Retrieved from https://doi.org/10.1086/341184

Johnson, E. I., & Waldfogel, J. (2004). Children of incarcerated parents: Multiple risks and children's living arrangements. In M. E. Patillo, D. F. Weiman, & B. Western (Eds.), *Imprisoning America: The social effects of mass incarceration* (pp. 97–131). New York, NY: Russell Sage Foundation.

Johnson, R. (2009). Ever-increasing levels of parental imprisonment and consequences for children. In S. Raphael & M. A. Stoll (Eds.), *Do prisons make us safer? The benefits and costs of the prison boom* (pp. 177–206). New York, NY: Russell Sage Foundation.

Johnston, D. (2006). The wrong road: Efforts to understand the effects of parental crime and incarceration. *Criminology & Public Policy, 5*(4), 703–719.

Kampfner, C. J. (1995). Post-traumatic stress reactions of children of incarcerated mothers. In K. Gabel & D. Johnston (Eds.), *Children of Incarcerated Parents.* New York, NY: Lexington Books.

Koepke, S., & Denissen, J. J. A. (2012). Dynamics of identity development and separation—Individuation in parent—Child relationships during adolescence and emerging adulthood—A conceptual integration. *Developmental Review, 32*(1), 67–88. Retrieved from https://doi.org/10.1016/j.dr.2012.01.001

Kohler-Hausmann, I. (2013). Misdemeanor justice: Control without conviction. *American Journal of Sociology, 119*(2), 351–393.

Kruttschnitt, C. (2010). The paradox of women's imprisonment. *Daedalus, 139*(3), 32–42.

La Vigne, N., Davies, E., & Brazell, D. (2008). *Broken bonds: Understanding and addressing the needs of children with incarcerated parents.* Washington, DC: Urban Institute Justice Policy Center.

Lageson, S. E. (2016). Found out and opting out: The consequences of online criminal records for families. *The ANNALS of the American Academy of Political and Social Science, 665*(1), 127–141. Retrieved from https://doi.org/10.1177/0002716215625053

Lee, H., McCormick, T., Hicken, M. T., & Wildeman, C. (2015). Racial inequalities and connectedness to imprisoned individuals in the Unites States. *Du Bois Review,* 1–14. Retrieved from https://doi.org/10.1017/S1742058X15000065

Lee, R. D., Fang, X., & Luo, F. (2013). The impact of parental incarceration on the physical and mental health of young adults. *Pediatrics, 131*(4), 1188–1195. Retrieved from https://doi.org/10.1542/peds.2012-0627

Light, M. T., & Marshall, J. (Forthcoming). On the weak morality returns to the prison boom: Comparing infant mortality and homicide in the incarceration ledger. *Journal of Health and Social Behavior.*

Lopoo, L. M., & Western, B. (2005). Incarceration and the formation of stability of marital unions. *Journal of Marriage and the Family, 67*(3), 721–734.

Massoglia, M., Remster, B., & King, R. D. (2011). Stigma or separation? Understanding the incarceration-divorce relationship. *Social Forces, 90*(1), 133–155.

Mears, D. P., & Siennick, S. E. (2016). Young adult outcomes and the life-course penalties of parental incarceration. *Journal of Research in Crime and Delinquency, 53,* 3–35.

Merton, R. K. (1968). The Matthew effect in science: The reward and communication systems of science are considered. *Science, 159*(3810), 56–63.

Muftic, L. R., Bouffard, L., & Armstrong, G. S. (2016). Impact of maternal incarceration on the criminal justice involvement of adult offspring: A research note. *Journal of Research in Crime and Delinquency, 53,* 93–111.

Mumola, C. (2000). *Incarcerated parents and their children.* Washington, DC: Bureau of Justice Statistics Government Printing Office.

Murphey, D., & Cooper, P. M. (2015). *Parents behind bars: What happens to their children?* Washington, DC: Child Trends.

Murray, J., & Farrington, D. P. (2005). Parental imprisonment: Effects on boys' antisocial behavior and delinquency throughout the life-course. *Journal of Child Psychology and Psychiatry, 46*, 1269–1278.

Murray, J., & Farrington, D. P. (2008a). Parental imprisonment: Long-lasting effects on boys' internalizing problems through the life course. *Development and Psychopathology, 20*, 273–290.

Murray, J., & Farrington, D. P. (2008b). The effects of parental imprisonment on children. *Crime and Justice: A Review of Research, 37*, 133–206.

Murray, J., Farrington, D. P., & Sekol, L. (2012). Children's antisocial behavior, mental health, drug use, and educational performance after parental incarceration: A systematic review and meta-analysis. *Psychological Bulletin, 138*, 175–210.

Murray, J., Loeber, R., & Pardini, D. (2012). Parental involvement in the criminal justice system and the development of youth theft, depression, marijuana use, and poor educational performance. *Criminology, 50*, 255–302.

Nichols, E. B., & Loper, A. B. (2012). Incarceration in the household: Academic outcomes of adolescents with an incarcerated household member. *Journal of Youth and Adolescence, 41*(11), 1455–1471.

Northcutt Bohmert, M. (2016). The role of transportation disadvantage for women on community supervision. *Criminal Justice and Behavior, 43*(11), 1522–1540.

Nurse, A. (2002). *Fatherhood arrested: Parenting from within the juvenile justice system.* Nashville, TN: Vanderbilt University Press.

Petersilia, J. (2003). *When prisoners come home: Parole and prisoner reentry.* New York, NY: Oxford University Press.

Phillips, S. D., Erkanli, A., Keeler, G. P., Costello, J., & Angold, A. (2006). Disentangling the risks: Parent criminal justice involvement and children's exposure to family risks. *Criminology & Public Policy, 5*(4).

Poehlmann, J. (2005). Children's family environments and intellectual outcomes during maternal incarceration. *Journal of Marriage and Family, 67*, 1275–1285.

Porter, L., & King, R. D. (2012). *Reconsidering the relationship between paternal incarceration and delinquency* (Working Paper Series WP-12–08). Bowling Green, OH: National Center for Family and Marriage Research.

Porter, L., & King, R. D. (2015). Absent fathers or absent variables? A new look at paternal incarceration and delinquency. *Journal of Crime and Delinquency, 52*(3), 414–443.

Roettger, M., & Boardman, J. D. (2012). Parental incarceration and gender-based risks for increased body mass index: Evidence from the national longitudinal study of adolescent health in the united states. *American Journal of Epidemiology, 175*(7), 636–644. Retrieved from https://doi.org/10.1093/aje/kwr409

Roettger, M., & Swisher, R. R. (2011). Associations of fathers' history of incarceration with son's delinquency and arrest among Black, White, and Hispanic males in the United States. *Criminology, 49*, 1109–1147.

Roettger, M., Swisher, R. R., Kuhl, D. C., & Chavez, J. (2011). Paternal incarceration and trajectories of marijuana and other illegal drug use from adolescence into young adulthood: Evidence from longitudinal panels of males and females in the United States. *Addiction, 106*(1), 121–132.

Sack, W. (1977). Children of imprisoned fathers. *Psychiatry, 40*, 163–174.

Sampson, R. J. (2011). The incarceration ledger: Toward a new era in assessing societal consequences. *Criminology & Public Policy, 10*, 819–828.

Sampson, R. J., & Laub, J. H. (2004). A life-course theory of cumulative disadvantage and the stability of delinquency. In T. P. Thornberry (Ed.), *Developmental theories of crime and delinquency* (Vol. 7). Brunswick, NJ: Harvard University Press.

Schwartz-Soicher, O., Geller, A., & Garfinkel, I. (2011). The effect of parental incarceration on material hardship. *Social Service Review, 85*(3), 447–473.

Siegel, J. (2011). *Disrupted childhoods: Children of women in prison.* New Brunswick, NJ: Rutgers University Press.

Sugie, N. (2012). Punishment and welfare: Paternal incarceration and families' receipt of public assistance. *Social Forces, 90*(4), 1403–1427.

Swann, C., & Slyvester, M. S. (2006). The foster care crisis: What caused caseloads to grow? *Demography, 43*(2), 309–335.

Swisher, R. R., & Roettger, M. E. (2012). Father's incarceration and youth delinquency and depression: Examining differences by race and ethnicity. *Journal of Research on Adolescence, 22*(4), 597–603. Retrieved from https://doi.org/10.1111/j.1532-7795.2012.00810.x

Travis, J. (2005). *But they all come back: Facing the challenges of prisoner reentry* (1st ed.). Washington, DC: Urban Institute Press.

Travis, J., Cincotta, E. M., & Solomon, A. L. (2003). *Families left behind: The hidden costs of incarceration and reentry.* Washington, DC: The Urban Institute.

Turnanovic, J. J., Rodriguez, N., & Pratt, T. C. (2012). The collateral consequences of incarceration revisited: A qualitative analysis of the effects of caregivers of children of incarcerated parents. *Criminology*, *50*(4), 913–959.

Turney, K. (2014). The consequences of paternal incarceration for maternal neglect and harsh parenting. *Social Forces*, *92*(4), 1607–1636. Retrieved from https://doi.org/10.1093/sf/sot160

Turney, K. (2015). Liminal men: Incarceration and relationship dissolution. *Social Problems*, *0*, 1–30.

Turney, K. (2017). The unequal consequences of mass incarceration for children. *Demography*, *54*(1), 361–389.

Turney, K., & Haskins, A. (2014). Falling behind? Children's early grade retention after paternal incarceration. *Sociology of Education*, *87*(4), 241–258.

Turney, K., Schnittker, J., & Wildeman, C. (2012). Those they leave behind: Paternal incarceration and maternal instrumental support. *Journal of Marriage and Family*, *74*(5), 1149–1165. Retrieved from https://doi.org/10.1111/j.1741-3737.2012.00998.x

Turney, K., & Wildeman, C. (2015). Detrimental for some? Heterogeneous effects of maternal incarceration on child wellbeing. *Criminology & Public Policy*, *14*(1), 125–156.

Uggen, C., & McElrath, S. (2014). Parental incarceration: What we know and where we need to go. *Journal of Criminal Law and Criminology*, *104*, 597–604.

van de Rakt, M., Murray, J., & Nieuwbeerta, P. (2012). The long-term effects of parental imprisonment on criminal trajectories of children. *Journal of Research in Crime and Delinquency*, *49*, 81–108.

Wakefield, S. (2015). Accentuating the positive or eliminating the negative? Paternal incarceration and caregiver-child parenting quality. *Journal of Criminal Law and Criminology*, *104*(4), 905–928.

Wakefield, S., Lee, H., & Wildeman, C. (2016, May). Tough on crime, tough on families? Criminal justice and family life in America. *The Annals of the American Academy of Political and Social Science*, 8–21.

Wakefield, S., & Powell, K. (2016). Distinguishing "petty offenders" from "serious criminals" in the estimation of family life effects. *The Annals of the American Academy of Political and Social Science*, *665*(1), 195–212.

Wakefield, S., & Uggen, C. (2010). Incarceration and stratification. *Annual Review of Sociology*, *36*, 387–406.

Wakefield, S., & Wildeman, C. (2011). Mass imprisonment and racial disparities in childhood behavioral problems. *Criminology & Public Policy*, *10*(3), 793–817.

Wakefield, S., & Wildeman, C. J. (2013). *Children of the prison boom: Mass incarceration and the future of American inequality*. New York, NY: Oxford University Press.

Western, B. (2006). *Punishment and inequality in America*. New York, NY: SAGE Publications.

Western, B., & Pettit, B. (2010). Incarceration & social inequality. *Daedalus*, *139*(3), 8–19.

Western, B., & Wildeman, C. (2009). The Black family and mass incarceration. *Annals of the American Academy of Political and Social Science*, *621*, 221–242.

Wildeman, C. (2009). Paternal imprisonment, the prison boom, and the concentration of childhood advantage. *Demography*, *46*, 265–280.

Wildeman, C. (2010). Parental incarceration and children's physically aggressive behaviors: Evidence from the Fragile Families and Child Wellbeing Study. *Social Forces*, *89*, 285–310.

Wildeman, C. (2012). Imprisonment and infant mortality. *Social Problems*, *59*(2), 228–259.

Wildeman, C. (2014). Parental incarceration, child homelessness, and the invisible consequences of mass imprisonment. *The Annals of the American Academy of Political and Social Science*, *651*(1), 74–96.

Wildeman, C. (2016). Incarceration and population health in wealthy democracies. *Criminology*, *54*(2), 360–382.

Wildeman, C., & Andersen, L. H. (2015). Cumulative risks of paternal and maternal incarceration in Denmark and the United States. *Demographic Research*, *32*, 1567–1580.

Wildeman, C., Scardamalia, K., Walsh, E. G., O'Brien, R. L., & Brew, B. (2017). Paternal incarceration and teachers' expectations of students. *Socius: Sociological Research for a Dynamic World*, *3*, 237802311772661. Retrieved from https://doi.org/10.1177/2378023117726610

Wildeman, C., Schnittker, J., & Turney, K. (2012). Despair by association? The mental health of mothers with children by recently incarcerated fathers. *American Sociological Review*, *77*, 216–243.

Wildeman, C., & Turney, K. (2014). Positive, negative, or null? The effects of maternal incarceration on children's behavioral problems. *Demography*, *51*(3), 1041–1068.

Wildeman, C., & Wakefield, S. (2014). The long arm of the law: The concentration of incarceration in families in the era of mass incarceration. *Journal of Gender, Race, and Justice*, *17*, 367–389.

Wildeman, C., Wakefield, S., & Turney, K. (2013). Misidentifying the effects of parental incarceration? A comment on Johnson and Easterling (2012). *Journal of Marriage and Family*, *75*(1), 252–258.

9

IMPACTS OF CONVICTION AND IMPRISONMENT FOR WOMEN

Miriam Northcutt Bohmert, Matthew Galasso, and Jennifer Cobbina

Introduction

"Collateral consequences" are constraints imposed by the state and federal government on individuals who offend as the result of an arrest, conviction, or imprisonment. These additional restrictions are civil consequences of conviction, outside the realm of the criminal process (Johnson, 2001; Pinard, 2010), and are considered indirect penalties of having a felony offense (Pinard, 2006). Generally said to be "unintended," these consequences continue to impact an individual long after she has served her sentence term. In this chapter, we present a description of the challenges that women involved with the criminal justice system experience—whether as a result of a criminal conviction or incarceration. Of course, women who have not been incarcerated differ from those who have been to jail or prison for an extended period of time. The added burden of being incarcerated pre- or post-conviction (that is, going to jail or prison to either be held, await trial, or to serve a sentence) means these women have spent time away from family, friends, and employment and are likely to have fractured these important networks in ways that have consequences beyond just the conviction.

Over the past 30 years, women have been a fast growing population in corrections—prison incarcerations have increased over 700 percent since 1980 (The Sentencing Project, 2015). In fact, since 2010, the female jail population has been the fastest growing correctional population, increasing by an average annual rate of 3.4 percent (Glaze & Kaeble, 2014). Just from 2009 to 2013, the number of women in jail increased 48 percent (Minton, Ginder, Brumbaugh, Smiley-McDonald, & Rohloff, 2015). Although parole numbers appear to be stabilizing or slightly declining (Glaze & Bonczar, 2009; Maruschak & Parks, 2012), between 2000 and 2010, the female probation population increased by 17 percent, or an average of 1.5 percent annually (Glaze & Kaeble, 2014). On any given day, 1.2 million women are under the authority of the criminal justice system (Kaeble, Glaze, Tsoutis, & Minton, 2016); approximately 1 million are sentenced to community supervision, 111,495 are incarcerated in a state or federal prison (Carson & Anderson, 2016), and another 100,940 are in local jails (Minton et al., 2015).

The typical female involved in the criminal justice system has had a drug or property offense (25 percent and 28 percent, respectively; Carson & Anderson, 2016), is a victim of child and adult sexual and intimate partner violence (Scroggins & Malley, 2010; Verona, Murphy, & Javdani, 2016), exhibits mental health problems (James & Glaze, 2006), is drug or alcohol dependent (Mumola & Karberg, 2006), is unemployed or economically marginalized (Morash, Kashy, Northcutt Bohmert, Cobbina, & Smith, 2015), and is the mother of a minor child (The Sentencing Project, 2015). Black women are more than twice as likely, and Hispanic women are 1.2 times as likely, as White women to be incarcerated (The Sentencing Project, 2015). Although Black and Hispanic women experience higher rates of imprisonment than White women, the gap has closed dramatically between 2000 and 2014—for example, the rate of imprisonment for Black women fell 47 percent while it increased 56 percent for White women.

Evidence that collateral consequences have impacted women in profound ways is also found in their high rates of recidivism. About 25 percent of women released from prison fail within six months (i.e., have an arrest for a new crime), 33 percent fail within a year, and 68 percent fail within five years of release (Snyder, Durose, Cooper, & Mulako-Wangota, 2016). Similarly, failure rates for individuals on probation or parole have remained consistent over time at approximately 18 to 20 percent (Kaeble & Bonczar, 2016; see Tables 3 and 5). These data indicate women are having a hard time getting their lives back together after conviction and incarceration events. In this chapter, we review the most common collateral consequences experienced after conviction—with attention to how these consequences may be worse for women who have been incarcerated.

Pathways Into Crime

To understand how collateral consequences of conviction and incarceration impact women, it is important to first appreciate the context in which they are occurring. Women involved in the criminal justice system, as is the case with men as well, are not experiencing the punishment of a conviction in isolation. Instead, the penalties accompanying conviction are most often interlaced with a host of other challenges women experienced prior to their most recent criminal justice system involvement. And the new hardships are likely not additive, but rather multiplicative, or interactive to the hardships they are already managing. This sheds light on how the new challenges of a felony conviction or serving time behind prison walls will impact those who already have a criminal conviction.

The gendered pathways paradigm first developed by Kathleen Daly (1992) delineated five main pathways women take to criminal behavior: Harmed-and-Harming, Street, Drug-Connected, Battered, and Other. To develop these pathways, or profiles of women, Daly collected and analyzed 40 women's pre-sentence investigation reports. Until Daly's study, the dominant narrative was that women who engaged in offending behavior were all "street women"—women who had run away from abusive households, had gotten involved in petty hustles, became drug addicted, and engaged in prostitution, theft, or selling drugs to support a drug habit; however, in Daly's study these women only comprised 25 percent of the sample. Instead, the most common type of women (37.5 percent) who engaged in criminal activity were harmed-and-harming women who had psychological problems and an inability to cope with current circumstances. Many of these women were abused or neglected as children, used drugs or alcohol, and may become violent when doing so.

Daly's framework has since been refined by others who have confirmed the presence of multiple pathways women take into crime. However, the number and composition of those pathways have varied (Brennan, Breitenbach, Dieterich, Salisbury, & Voorhis, 2012; Chesney-Lind, 1997; B. A. Owen, 1998; Reisig, Holtfreter, & Morash, 2006; Salisbury & Van Voorhis, 2009). For instance, utilizing data from interviews, risk assessments, and criminal history data from 718 women, Brennan and colleagues (2012) identified eight pathways nested in four superordinate pathways: *normal functioning but drug-abusing females* (34.7 percent) who have more positive vocational and educational resources, less poverty and abuse, and fewer mental health problems; *battered women* (23.6 percent) who have experienced lifetimes of physical and sexual abuse but are average in other areas; *socialized subcultural pathways, women* (28.5 percent) who are severely socially marginalized and have serious deficits in education and vocational skills, live in higher crime neighborhoods, have stronger antisocial attitudes, and whose drug use and drug trafficking suggested subcultural crime networks but who did not experience sexual or physical abuse; and *aggressive antisocial women* (12.9 percent) who had the most extreme risk and need profiles combined with lifelong sexual and physical abuse, antisocial personality, antisocial families, mental health issues, and homelessness.

The gendered pathways model highlights several considerations relevant to the study of collateral consequences. First, the paths women take into crime are diverse—some women may have been pushed into crime by histories of victimization while others entered crime as a result of severe economic marginalization and residence in a high crime neighborhood. Second, as a result, women on each pathway have shared challenges as well as resources at their disposal. Some women need extensive counseling and addiction treatment, others do not; some need educational and vocational training while others do not; some need the safety and opportunities afforded to those who live in better neighborhoods while other women already reside in such places. Thus, types of collateral consequences, and the severity, that women experience as a result of having a conviction, will vary tremendously by the path she took into crime as well as the tools she has available to respond. For example, the normal-functioning female with drug addiction who already has a job and lives in a nice neighborhood will not be as impacted by housing, employment, and social service practices that disqualify those with felony records as a more socially and economically marginalized woman. In short, the collateral consequences outlined in this chapter will not be experienced in the same ways, to the same extent, for all women who have been convicted or incarcerated. This body of research lays the groundwork for understanding how collateral consequences may impact some women more harshly than others. We will review the major collateral consequences in the following sections.

Collateral Consequences

Finding Employment

Even in an era of relative financial stability, finding stable and worthwhile employment can be difficult, especially for those with a felony conviction who may often face restricted access to particular jobs or opposition from employers (Pager, 2003). Mauer (2005, p. 609) noted:

> Once a prison term is completed, the transition back to the community is almost always laden with difficulty. What in many cases is a situation of limited connections with the world of work becomes even more problematic with the stigma of imprisonment attached to former offenders. And particularly in an economy increasingly diverging into a high skills/high technology sector and a broad low skill service economy, few offenders have promising prospects for advancing out of the bottom rungs of the job ladder.

Women who have been to prison may have difficulty functioning emotionally and/or interpersonally in the employment setting (Harper, 2011). Employers generally expect their employees to work and communicate well with others, follow instructions, adapt to change, and accomplish organizational goals (Herr & Cramer, 1996; Neff, 1977). In her examination of the role of prisonization on employability for men and women, Harper (2011) found that the development of interactional processes was disrupted as a result of prisonization's psychological impact. Thus, the experiences learned and implemented in prison themselves serve as a collateral consequence to successful prison reentry; these may need to be un-learned or retooled for individuals to find success during reentry.

Moreover, for those who have been incarcerated, employment opportunities are further restricted because many former prisoners typically have few work skills, low levels of education, and limited work history. Between 1991 and 1997, 68 percent of inmates in state prison did not have a high school degree or their General Educational Development (GED; Harlow, 2003). A multi-state analysis of reentry outcomes revealed that about one-third of women have secured employment six months post-release (Mallik-Kane & Visher, 2008). Lack of childcare, discrimination, and conflict with employers have been identified as primary factors to women's low employment rate following release from prison (Harm & Phillips, 2001; Richie, 2001; Schram, Koons-Witt, Williams, & McShane, 2006).

Yet, employment may serve as a particularly important path out of crime for many women. Holtfreter, Reisig, and Morash (2004) found that economic marginalization is a prominent reason why women commit crimes, suggesting they may have additional deficits in this area that have likely been worsened by new convictions or incarcerations. They suggest that employment may serve as a particularly important path out of crime for many women. The authors point to state-sponsored resources such as employment assistance or childcare as helpful in providing economically marginalized women with the necessary resources to survive without having to commit crime.

The impact of a conviction or incarceration on women's employment is shaped by the economic conditions present in the current historical epoch. Factors such as availability of jobs or social service programs impact women's success. Research by Morash and colleagues (2015) found that changes in the availability of social services (loss of monetary assistance or housing) increased certain types of recidivism for 345 women on probation and parole in one Midwestern state. Women who had high and unmet needs were at greater risk for recidivism, mental illness, and substance abuse, highlighting the relationships between economic context and women's reentry success.

Success in securing employment and navigating economic hardship has also been linked to strong ties and family support. However, women involved in the criminal justice system have what Desmond (2012) has called disposable or weak ties—unstable and short-lived relationships forged with new acquaintances to gain access to needed resources and provide some measure of companionship and comfort. Poor inner-city women often travel in isolated, small social circles, which inhibits them from developing strong social ties that may provide employment opportunities post-release (Reisig, Holtfreter, & Morash, 2002). Further complicating women's ability to obtain or maintain employment is the collateral consequences often tied to driving licenses. At least 16 states require at least a six-month suspension of driver's license for drug possession charges (Cauchon, 2014). The loss of a license and the enormous financial fees required to reinstate the license may compound women's problems obtaining employment (Northcutt Bohmert & DeMaris, 2017). Though employment is one way that formerly incarcerated women can establish a new post-incarceration identity, many find it difficult to secure a decent paying job.

Securing Housing

Finding suitable housing is the lynchpin to successfully transitioning into the free world (Petersilia, 2003; Visher & Courtney, 2006). Bradley and colleagues (2001, p. 7) detail the role that housing plays in shaping the reentry process:

> For the returning prisoner, the search for permanent, sustainable housing is more than simply a disagreeable experience. It is a daunting challenge—one that portends success or failure for the entire reintegration process. . . . Housing is the lynchpin that holds the reintegration process together. Without a stable residence, continuity in substance abuse and mental health treatment is compromised. Employment is often contingent upon a fixed living arrangement. And, in the end, a polity that does not concern itself with the housing needs of returning prisoners finds that it has done so at the expense of its own public safety.

A stable home environment provides social and emotional support and structure that is conducive to positive reentry transitions (Sullivan, Mino, Nelson, & Pope, 2002). In their investigation of 570 male and female parolees, Cobbina, Huebner, and Berg (2012) found that women with prosocial relationships with an intimate partner or who had strong ties with their parents had a lower risk for recidivism and re-offense; this effect held regardless of prior criminal history. While finding a place to live is one of the pressing concerns returning prisoners encounter, it is often permeated with numerous barriers.

First, many women have limited personal or private sources of support upon release. As a result, most women returning home from prison will stay with family members; however, evidence suggests that family are less supportive of women who return home than men (Mallik-Kane & Visher, 2008). Moreover, the stay with loved ones may be temporary if their ties have weakened or if her presence poses a threat to housing stability for the family. While some returning prisoners will stay with their extended network of friends and relatives, parole agencies typically prohibit parolees from associating with anyone with a criminal record. This restriction, which includes family and friends who may be willing to take the person in, further limits housing options.

Second, while the private housing market is also available, this option is often cost-prohibitive, as most cannot afford first and last month's rent, plus a security deposit. Most former prisoners leave prison without enough money for a security deposit and those that do provide vouchers may, at the most, provide only a few weeks of housing (Center for Public Policy Research, 2007).

Third, even though public housing is an option, there are a number of policies that have effectively restricted access to public housing for significant numbers of individuals who formerly engaged in crime. Convicted drug and sex felons are prohibited from residing in subsidized housing, which further depletes their housing options (Lutze, Rosky, J.W., & Hamilton, 2014; Wheelock, 2005). Individuals' status as ex-convicts often provides landlords reason to rent to another applicant, even if they do not have a drug or sex offense. Even if they do qualify, waiting lists can be as long as two or three years for subsidized housing (Petersilia, 2001).

Fourth, though homeless shelters are an option for housing, many shelters are often overcrowded with long waiting lists and limit the number of days they can remain in residence. Some do not accept children, which is problematic, especially for women who are trying to mother their children (Petersilia, 2001). Given that shelters may be temporary or restrictive, living with family or friends may be for short periods of time, and rent may be unaffordable, it is not surprising that a proportion of individuals returning home from prison experience homelessness. Approximately 10 percent of people who enter prison have experienced homelessness and it is estimated that at least the same percent will experience homelessness upon their release (Roman & Travis, 2006).

Obtaining Social Services

The 1996 federal welfare law prohibits anyone convicted of a drug-related felony from receiving federally funded food stamps and cash assistance (also known as TANF—Temporary Assistance for Needy Families). This is a lifetime ban for drug felony offenses regardless of whether that person is a minor or a first offender. While states have the option of passing legislation to limit the ban or eliminate it altogether, most states restrict at least some people with drug felony convictions from being eligible for federally funded public assistance and food stamps. The Legal Action Center (2004) reports that 17 states have adopted the federal drug felon ban without modification; 21 states have limited the ban in some way to enable those with drug felony convictions to get public assistance if they meet certain conditions, such as participating in alcohol or drug treatment; 12 states have eliminated the ban entirely, having detrimental effects on those with lower socioeconomic status.

Reductions in assistance to the poor primarily impact female-headed families with dependent children (Bloom, Owen, & Covington, 2004; United States Government Accountability Office, 2005). Specifically, it limits access to economic aid through TANF by setting time limits for receipt of financial assistance and requiring states to involve minimum percentages of welfare caseloads in work preparation and employment. Research conducted in multiple states showed that sanctions for non-compliance to guidelines primarily affected clients who are Black, have mental illness, limited education and disabilities, and victims of domestic violence and Black clients (Alfred & Chlup, 2009; Monnat, 2010). As already mentioned, many women engaged in offending behavior have the characteristics of those most negatively affected by sanctions; thus, they would be likely to experience the increasingly punitive welfare system.

Moreover, one-quarter of women are serving a sentence of a drug crime (Carson & Anderson, 2016), and 62 percent of state, and 63 percent of federally, incarcerated women are mothers (Glaze & Maruschak, 2008). Prior to incarceration about one-third of mothers in prison were unemployed. Moreover, 36 percent of mothers (and nearly 10 percent of fathers) in prison received welfare benefits prior to imprisonment (Glaze & Maruschak, 2008). Children of incarcerated parents who are denied economic aid are at risk of neglect, experiencing hardships, and having involvement with the criminal justice system due to the prospect of reduced family income support (Allard, 2002).

Managing Child and Family Responsibilities

Criminal records can prohibit women with felony convictions from retaining parental rights. In 1997, Congress passed the Adoption and Safe Families Act (ASFA), which was intended to move children into permanent placement within certain time frames to ensure foster children were not staying in foster care for prolonged periods of time. However, the ASFA guidelines have served as barriers to reunification between imprisoned women and their children. Approximately 52 percent of women in prison reported being single parents, which increases the odds that their children will enter the child welfare system upon their arrest (Glaze & Maruschak, 2008). Moreover, 6 percent of children in foster care entered the system as a result of parental incarceration (Allard & Lu, 2006). Although welfare workers are required to make a "reasonable effort" to reunite children with their parents when children enter the welfare system, the passage of the ASFA in several states shortened the time frame for initiating the process of terminating parental rights for foster children from 15 months to 12 months (Travis, 2003). Since the average time incarcerated women serve in prison is 18 months in prison, most are at risk of losing their parental rights (Christian, 2009).

To prevent the termination of their parental rights, incarcerated women face several challenges. First, it is impossible for women to maintain regular contact with a child in foster care, given her imprisonment. Thus, the onus would be on the child welfare caseworker to arrange for visitation between the child and incarcerated mother. With high caseloads, some may abandon the prospects of reunification with an imprisoned mother even though courts are less likely to terminate the rights of a mother who can demonstrate continual positive contact with her child and involvement in his or her life (Christian, 2009). Second, involvement in children's dependency proceedings (i.e., case planning, hearings, and court orders) demonstrates a willingness to be reunited with children and can help to avoid termination of rights. However, mothers are often dependent on caseworkers for information and guidance to navigate the dependency proceedings. Unfortunately, evidence suggests that caseworkers rarely communicate with parents in prison, inform them of hearings, or involve them in case planning (Christian, 2009).

Living in Disadvantaged Neighborhood Contexts

People in prison are concentrated in a relatively small number of predominantly economically distressed neighborhoods (see, for example, Lynch & Sabol, 2001). For instance, Harding, Morenoff, and Herbert (2013) found that a small proportion of impoverished areas in Michigan tend to house the vast majority of formerly incarcerated female and male individuals. Given the constraints on former prisoners, they often have little choice but to return to communities that are spatially proximate to criminally involved individuals in their former social network (Holtfreter et al., 2004).

Most women, particularly women of color, return to disenfranchised communities with high levels of crime. These urban areas are characterized by high levels of poverty, segregation, unemployment, and racial isolation (Massey & Denton, 1993; Massey & Fisher, 2010). For instance, in their examination of how women engaged in criminal activity navigate neighborhood crime, Cobbina, Morash, Kashy, and Smith (2014) found that Black women were more likely to describe more crime in their neighborhood and lived in census tracts with higher disadvantage and lower affluence and residential stability than White women. Women of color often reside in economically distressed neighborhoods with limited political, social, and economic resources and consequently often report a lack of access to neighborhood programs and services (Owen & Bloom, 1995; Richie, 2001). Consequently, women of color who return home from prison often report feelings of marginalization within the context of an economically distressed neighborhood, making successful reintegration more difficult.

Drawing on in-depth interviews from 37 women returning to impoverished St. Louis, Missouri, neighborhoods, Berg and Cobbina (2016) examined the intersection of cognitive transformation and ecological context on post-release success; they hoped to learn *how* neighborhoods matter. They found that women returning to the same structurally disadvantaged neighborhood contexts were not predestined to the same outcome. Women's commitments to prosocial identities, when the "upfront work" of thoroughly constructing a plan for change was completed earlier, enabled them to desist from crime despite poor residential contexts. However, the authors did also find that neighborhood effects remained quite powerful. Berg and Cobbina discovered that while neighborhoods did possess illicit lures most also contained prosocial resources. This mixture poses challenges for even the most committed women returning home from prison and makes it difficult to abstain from crime.

Recently, Huebner and Pleggenkuhle (2015), using a large sample of men and women to provide a rigorous test of gender, did just that by examining several contexts: parenting, family support, neighborhood, and residential mobility. Compared to men, women who cared for children were less likely to be reconvicted for a subsequent crime; however, women were more likely to incur a technical violation and fail more quickly than men within four years of release. Living with family was important in helping women desist but was not as important for men. Longer periods of residence, and in more disadvantaged neighborhoods, functioned to increase recidivism for both men and women. However, in their examination of women released from prison, Huebner et al. (2010) found no significant effects of community conditions on recidivism for either African American or White women. Thus, the effect of context at many levels should continue to be examined for women in the criminal justice system.

Promising Reforms and Policies in Collateral Consequences for Justice-Involved Women

Gender-Responsive Programming

Researchers are developing new policies to support women with convictions and incarcerations (Swavola, Riley, & Subramanian, 2016). One promising strategy for addressing the interconnectedness of women's unique needs (substance abuse, trauma, violence, homelessness, caretaking responsibilities) that considers agency as well as her social structural position is gender-responsive programming (Bloom, Owen, & Covington, 2006). Gender-responsive programming acknowledges the following: (1) gender makes a difference; (2) fosters an environment based on safety, respect, and dignity; (3) promotes healthy connections to children, family, significant others and the community; (4) addresses the web of appropriate social services; (5) address economic needs; and (6) improves coordination between community services (Bloom et al., 2006). Bloom et al. (2006) provide implementation steps for each arena of gender-responsive programming as well as recommend the use of restorative justice techniques and greater focus on community support to accomplish these goals.

Putting these principles to work, the National Institute of Corrections funded the University of Cincinnati to examine existing procedures for classifying women engaged in illicit activity on the basis of risk and needs. Research was conducted in four states (Colorado, Missouri, Minnesota, and Hawaii), including four institutional samples, four probation samples, and one pre-release sample (Van Voorhis, Wright, Salisbury, & Baumann, 2010; Wright, Salisbury, & Van Voorhis, 2007). While the assessments were designed for men and applied to women, with little concern for their appropriateness, the studies found that the original, gender-neutral assessments were valid for women. However, the research also found that they could be improved with the addition of a number of gender-responsive factors that were found to be predictive of institutional misconducts and community recidivism. To further improve how women are treated, the following gender-responsive needs should be assessed: mental health history, depression/anxiety, psychosis, child abuse, adult victimization, relationship dysfunction, parental stress, and housing safety. Strengths should also be examined including self-efficacy, parental involvement, family support, and educational assets.

The National Institute of Corrections has initiated the development of the Women's Offender Case Management Model (WOCMM), which is being used on a specialized caseload of medium- to high-risk adult women in the state of Connecticut. The WOCM approach relies on a team of service providers, family, community supports, and women themselves to identify women's needs, strengths, goals, and required community services (Millison, Robinson, & Van Dieten, 2010), all of which are vital to the success of women involved in the criminal justice system.

Wrap-Around Services

Several methods of caseload management have focused on providing women with comprehensive wrap-around reentry support. For example, two programs in California provide a variety of wrap-around services such as intensive case management, peer support, primary care, transportation, employment services, parenting classes, and counseling to high-risk women (Bloom, 2015). In providing for women's constellation of needs, wrap-around services should evaluate whether programs are appropriate for women, seek parity, commit to women-appropriate services, consider community, and include family and children (Bloom et al., 2006). Research evaluating the effectiveness of 'wrap-around' curricula for integrated, gender-responsive, trauma-informed treatment services within residential facilities found that, after successful completion, women reported less substance abuse, less depression, and fewer trauma symptoms (e.g., anxiety) (Covington, Burke, Keaton, & Norcott, 2008). Research of similar programs, with women not involved in the criminal justice system but with co-occurring disorders, utilizing meta-analysis of 17 studies and 10 treatment protocols, provides tentative support for the utility of trauma-informed, integrated programming but calls attention to the lack of methodologically rigorous treatment trials; the authors call for additional work in this area (van Dam, Vedel, Ehring, & Emmelkamp, 2012).

At the same time as there is a push to consider women's multiple contexts and to increase programming and services to meet needs holistically, there is also a push to have less intervention in order to improve women's outcomes during reentry (O'Brien & Ortega, 2015; Phelps, 2016). Northcutt Bohmert and DeMaris (2017) examine the experiences of women on probation and parole and find that the wrap-around services provided by attentive and well-meaning supervision agents may create additional hardships for women who have poor transportation. The authors conclude that, although wrap-around services are required to address women's multiple needs, sometimes less services, and less travel, may be appropriate so women are not set up to fail.

Similarly, Phelps (2016) details the ways in which the local, state, and national attempts at smarter correction have involved both expanding and contracting the penal state. For example, increasing the use of diversion options for low-level and drug offenses, in particular, has limited the growth of women's incarceration. However, increased punitiveness on drug offenses has expanded the carceral state. Simplifying the reach of the system, at the macro level, by politicians and criminal justice administrators, as well as on the micro level—in everyday interactions between community supervision agents and service providers—would serve to increase success for women with convictions and incarcerations.

Specialty Courts

Another promising approach is reentry-focused courts that simultaneously consider substance abuse, mental health, homelessness, and past trauma alongside women's sentences. Upon successful completion of court-ordered treatment, these courts have the ability to reduce or dismiss charges. Although reentry courts have been operating in some jurisdictions, predominantly for men, for many years (Fetsco, 2013; Maruna & LeBel, 2002), with some success in reducing new convictions but also associations with higher revocations (Hamilton, 2010), they have not been as widely utilized, or studied, for women. Legal scholars have reviewed, and advocated for, the anticipated benefits of these courts (McGrath, 2012), but rigorous evaluation research is sorely needed to determine the effectiveness of reentry court outcomes for female participants.

Conclusion

Recent empirical work has situated women who commit crimes within the web of factors such as neighborhood context, family environments, and economic climates, which together constrain their agency. Yet, as collateral consequences of imprisonment such as finding employment, securing housing and social services, overcoming transportation problems, and navigating disadvantaged neighborhoods continue to bear down on individuals, developments in research, theory, and policy remain important. Promising new policies such as gender responsive programming, wrap-around services, and specialty courts provide an important intersection of strong theory and rigorous empirical work—in a tangible way that improves the lives of those who have contact with the criminal justice system.

References

Alfred, M. V., & Chlup, D. T. (2009). Neoliberalism, illiteracy, and poverty: Framing the rise in black women's incarceration. *Western Journal of Black Studies, 33*, 240–249.

Allard, P. (2002). *Life sentences: Denying welfare benefits to women convicted of drug offenses.* Washington, DC: The Sentencing Project.

Allard, P., & Lu, L. D. (2006). *Rebuilding families, reclaiming lives: State obligations to children in foster care and their incarcerated parents.* New York, NY: Brennan Center for Justice, New York University School of Law.

Berg, M. T., & Cobbina, J. E. (2016). Cognitive transformation, social ecological settings, and the reentry outcomes of women offenders. *Crime & Delinquency, Online First*, 1–25.

Bloom, B. (2015). *Meeting the needs of women in California's County Justice Systems: A toolkit for policy makers and practitioners* (p. 18). Oakland, CA: Californians for Safety and Justice.

Bloom, B., Owen, B., & Covington, S. (2004). Women offenders and the gendered effects of public policy. *Review of Policy Research, 21*, 31–48.

Bloom, B., Owen, B., & Covington, S. (2006). Gender responsive strategies: Theory, policy, guiding principles and practice. In R. Immarigeon (Ed.), *Women and girls in the criminal justice system: Policy issues and practices* (pp. 1–21). Kingston, NJ: Civic Research Institute.

Bradley, K., Richardson, N., Oliver, R. B. M., & Slayter, E. (2001). *No place like home: Housing and the ex-prisoner. Policy Brief.* Boston, MA: Community Resources for Justice. Retrieved from www.crj.org/cji/entry/publication_noplacelikehome

Brennan, T., Breitenbach, M., Dieterich, W., Salisbury, E. J., & Voorhis, P. van. (2012). Women's pathways to serious and habitual crime: A person-centered analysis incorporating gender responsive factors. *Criminal Justice and Behavior, 39,* 1481–1508.

Carson, E. A., & Anderson, E. (2016). *Prisoners in 2015.* Washington, DC: Bureau of Justice Statistics.

Cauchon, D. (2014). States that suspend drivers' licenses for drug possession: A list. Retrieved from http://clemencyreport.org/states-suspend-drivers-license-drug-possession-list/

Center for Public Policy Research. (2007). *State policies and procedures regarding "gate money."* Retrieved from www.cdcr.ca.gov/Adult_Research_Branch/Research_Documents/Gate_Money_Oct_2007.pdf

Chesney-Lind, M. (1997). *The female offender: Girls, women, and crime.* Thousand Oaks, CA: SAGE Publications.

Christian, S. M. (2009). *Children of incarcerated parents.* Denver, CO: National Conference of State Legislatures.

Cobbina, J. E., Huebner, B. M., & Berg, M. T. (2012). Men, women, and postrelease offending: An examination of the nature of the link between relational ties and recidivism. *Crime & Delinquency, 58,* 331–361.

Cobbina, J. E., Morash, M., Kashy, D. A., & Smith, S. W. (2014). Race, neighborhood danger, and coping strategies among female probationers and parolees. *Race and Justice, 4,* 3–28.

Covington, S., Burke, C., Keaton, S., & Norcott, C. (2008). Evaluation of a trauma-informed and gender-responsive intervention for women in drug treatment. *Journal of Psychoactive Drugs, 5,* 387–398.

Daly, K. (1992). Women's pathways to felony court: Feminist theories of lawbreaking and problems of representation. *Southern California Review of Law & Women's Studies, 2,* 11–52.

Desmond, M. (2012). Disposable ties and the urban poor. *American Journal of Sociology, 117,* 1295–1335.

Fetsco, D. M. (2013). Reentry courts: An emerging use of judicial resources in the struggle to reduce the recidivism of released offenders. *Wyoming Law Review, 13,* 591–614.

Glaze, L. E., & Bonczar, T. P. (2009). *Probation and parole in the United States, 2008* (Bulletin). Washington DC: United States Department of Justice, Bureau of Justice Statistics.

Glaze, L. E., & Kaeble, D. (2014). *Correctional populations in the United States, 2013* (Bureau of Justice Statistics Bulletin No. NCJ 248479). Washington, DC: United States Department of Justice, Bureau of Justice Statistics.

Glaze, L. E., & Maruschak, L. (2008). *Parents in prison and their minor children.* Washington, DC: United States Department of Justice Printing Office.

Hamilton, Z. (2010). *Do reentry courts reduce recidivism?* New York, NY: Center for Court Innovation Research. Retrieved from www.proceduraljusticeinstitute.org/sites/default/files/Reentry_Evaluation.pdf

Harding, D. J., Morenoff, J. D., & Herbert, C. W. (2013). Home is hard to find: Neighborhoods, institutions, and the residential trajectories of returning prisoners. *The ANNALS of the American Academy of Political and Social Science, 647,* 214–236.

Harlow, C. W. (2003). *Education and correctional populations (Bureau of Justice Statistics Special Report No. NCJ 195670).* Washington, DC: United States Department of Justice, Bureau of Justice Statistics.

Harm, N. J., & Phillips, S. D. (2001). You can't go home again: Women and criminal recidivism. *Journal of Offender Rehabilitation, 32,* 3–21.

Harper, J. (2011). *The effects of prisonization on the employability of former prisoners: First-hand voices.* University of Pennsylvania, ProQuest Dissertations Publishing, Philadelphia, PA.

Herr, E. L., & Cramer, S. H. (1996). *Career guidance and counseling through the lifespan. Systematic approaches* (5th ed.). New York, NY: Harper Collins.

Holtfreter, K., Reisig, M. D., & Morash, M. (2004). Poverty, state capital, and recidivism among women offenders. *Criminology & Public Policy, 3,* 185–208.

Huebner, B. M., DeJong, C., & Cobbina, J. E. (2010). Women coming home: Long-term patterns of recidivism. *Justice Quarterly, 27,* 225–254.

Huebner, B. M., & Pleggenkuhle, B. (2015). Residential location, household composition, and recidivism: An analysis by gender. *Justice Quarterly, 32,* 818–844.

James, D. J., & Glaze, L. E. (2006). *Mental health problems of prison and jail inmates* (No. NCJ 213600). U.S. Department of Justice: United States Department of Justice, Bureau of Justice Statistics.

Johnson, R. M. A. (2001). Collateral consequences. *Criminal Justice, 16,* 32–33.

Kaeble, D., & Bonczar, T. P. (2016). *Probation and parole in the United States, 2015* (No. NCJ 250230). Washington, DC: United States Department of Justice, Bureau of Justice Statistics.

Kaeble, D., Glaze, L. E., Tsoutis, A., & Minton, T. (2016). *Correctional populations in the United States, 2015* (No. NCJ 249513). Washington, DC: United States Department of Justice, Bureau of Justice Statistics.

Legal Action Center. (2004). *After prison: Roadblocks to reentry—A report on legal barriers facing people with criminal records.* Retrieved from www.lac.org/roadblocks.html

Lutze, F. E., Rosky, J. W., & Hamilton, Z. K. (2014). Homelessness and reentry. *Criminal Justice and Behavior, 41*, 471–491.

Lynch, J. P., & Sabol, W. J. (2001). *Prisoner reentry in perspective.* (Crime Policy Report). Washington, DC: Urban Institute Justice Policy Center.

Mallik-Kane, K., & Visher, C. (2008). *Health and prisoner reentry: How physical, mental, and substance abuse conditions shape the process of reintegration.* Washington, DC: Urban Institute.

Maruna, S., & LeBel, T. P. (2002). Welcome home- examining the reentry court concept from a strengths-based perspective. *Western Criminology Review, 4*, 91–107.

Maruschak, L., & Parks, E. (2012). *Probation and Parole in the United States, 2011* (Bulletin). Washington, DC: Bureau of Justice Statistics.

Massey, D. S., & Denton, N. A. (1993). *American apartheid: Segregation and the making of the underclass.* Cambridge, MA: Harvard University Press.

Massey, D. S., & Fisher, M. J. (2010). How segregation concentrated poverty. *Ethnic and Racial Studies, 23*, 670–691.

Mauer, M. (2005). Thinking about prison and its impact in the twenty-first century. *Ohio State Journal of Criminal Law, 2*, 607–618.

McGrath, E. (2012). Reentry courts: Providing a second chance for incarcerated mothers and their children. *Family Court Review, 50*, 113–127.

Millison, B., Robinson, D., & Van Dieten, M. (2010). *Women offender case management model: The Connecticut model* (pp. 6–7). Washington, DC: U.S. Department of Justice, National Institute of Corrections.

Minton, T., Ginder, S., Brumbaugh, S. M., Smiley-McDonald, H., & Rohloff, H. (2015). *Census of jails: Population changes, 1999–2013* (No. NCJ 248627). Washington, DC: United States Department of Justice, Bureau of Justice Statistics.

Monnat, S. M. (2010). The color of welfare sanctioning: Exploring the individual and contextual roles of race on TANF case closures and benefit reductions. *The Sociological Quarterly, 51*, 678–707.

Morash, M., Kashy, D., Northcutt Bohmert, M., Cobbina, J. E., & Smith, S. (2015). Women at the nexus of correctional and social policies: Implications for recidivism risk. *British Journal of Criminology, 57*, 441–462.

Mumola, C., & Karberg, J. (2006). *Drug use and dependence, State and federal prisoners, 2004* (No. NCJ 213530). Washington, DC: U.S. Department of Justice.

Neff, W. S. (1977). *Work and human behavior.* Oxford: Aldine.

Northcutt Bohmert, M., & DeMaris, A. (2017). Cumulative disadvantage and the role of transportation in community supervision. *Crime & Delinquency, Online First.* Retrieved from http://journals.sagepub.com/doi/abs/10.1177/0011128716686344

O'Brien, P., & Ortega, D. M. (2015). Feminist Transformation: Deconstructing prisons and reconstructing justice with criminalized women. *Affilia: Journal of Women and Social Work, 30*, 141–144.

Owen, B. A. (1998). *In the mix: Struggle and survival in a women's prison.* Albany, NY: SUNY Press.

Owen, B., & Bloom, B. (1995). Profiling women prisoners: Findings from national surveys and a California sample. *The Prison Journal, 75*, 165–185.

Pager, D. (2003). The mark of a criminal record. *American Journal of Sociology, 108*, 937–975.

Petersilia, J. (2001). Prisoner reentry: Public safety and reintegration challenges. *The Prison Journal, 81*, 360–375.

Petersilia, J. (2003). *When prisoners come home: Parole and prisoner reentry.* New York, NY: Oxford University Press.

Phelps, M. S. (2016). Possibilities and contestation in twenty-first-century us criminal justice downsizing. *Annual Review of Law and Social Science, 12*, 153–170.

Pinard, M. (2006). An integrated perspective on the collateral consequences of criminal convictions and reentry issues faced by formerly incarcerated individuals. *BUL Review, 86*, 623.

Pinard, M. (2010). Reflections and perspectives on reentry and collateral consequences. *Journal of Criminal Law and Criminology, 100*, 1213–1224.

Reisig, M. D., Holtfreter, K., & Morash, M. (2002). Social capital among women offenders: Examining the distribution of social networks and resources. *Journal of Contemporary Criminal Justice, 18*, 167–187.

Reisig, M. D., Holtfreter, K., & Morash, M. (2006). Assessing recidivism risk across female pathways to crime. *Justice Quarterly, 23*, 384–405.

Richie, B. (2001). Challenges incarcerated women face as they return to their communities: Findings from life history interviews. *Crime & Delinquency, 47*, 368–389.

Roman, C., & Travis, J. (2006). Where will I sleep tomorrow? Housing, homelessness, and the returning prisoner. *Housing Policy Debate, 17*, 389–418.

Salisbury, E. J., & Van Voorhis, P. (2009). Gendered pathways: A quantitative investigation of women probationers' paths to incarceration. *Criminal Justice and Behavior, 36*, 541–566.

Schram, P., Koons-Witt, B., Williams, F., & McShane, M. (2006). Supervision strategies and approaches for female parolees: Examining the link between unmet needs and parole outcome. *Crime & Delinquency, 52*, 450–471.

Scroggins, J. R., & Malley, S. (2010). Reentry and the (unmet) needs of women. *Journal of Offender Rehabilitation*, *49*, 146–163.

The Sentencing Project. (2015). *Incarcerated women and girls*. Retrieved from www.sentencingproject.org/doc/publications/Incarcerated-Women-and-Girls.pdf

Snyder, H. N., Durose, M. R., Cooper, A., & Mulako-Wangota, J. (2016). *Recidivism rates of prisoners with selected characteristics released from prisons in 30 States in 2005—Female and male* (Generated using the Prisoner Recidivism Analysis Tool—2005 (PRAT-2005).). United States Department of Justice, Bureau of Justice Statistics. Retrieved from www.bjs.gov/recidivism_2005_arrest/

Sullivan, E., Mino, M., Nelson, K., & Pope, J. (2002). *Families as a resource in recovery from drug abuse: An evaluation of La Bodega de La Familia*. New York, NY: Vera Institute of Justice.

Swavola, E., Riley, K., & Subramanian, R. (2016). *Overlooked: Women and jails in an era of reform*. New York, NY: Vera Institute of Justice.

Travis, J. (2003). *Prisoners once removed: The impact of incarceration and reentry on children, families, and communities*. Washington, DC: Urban Institute.

United States Government Accountability Office. (2005). *Adult drug courts: Evidence indicates recidivism reductions and mixed results for other outcomes* (No. GAO-05-219). Washington, DC: United States Government Accountability Office.

van Dam, D., Vedel, E., Ehring, T., & Emmelkamp, P. M. G. (2012). Psychological treatments for concurrent posttraumatic stress disorder and substance use disorder: A systematic review. *Clinical Psychology Review, 32*, 202–214.

Van Voorhis, P., Wright, E. M., Salisbury, E. J., & Baumann, A. (2010). Women's risk factors and their contributions to existing risk/needs assessment: The current status of a gender responsive supplement. *Criminal Justice and Behavior, 37*, 261–288.

Verona, E., Murphy, B., & Javdani, S. (2016). Gendered pathways: Violent childhood maltreatment, sex exchange, and drug use. *Psychology of Violence, 6*, 124–134.

Visher, C., & Courtney, S. M. E. (2006). *Cleveland prisoners' experiences returning home*. Washington, DC: Urban Institute.

Wheelock, D. (2005). Collateral consequences and racial inequality: Felons status restrictions as a system of disadvantage. *Journal of Contemporary Criminal Justice, 21*, 82–90.

Wright, E. M., Salisbury, E. J., & Van Voorhis, P. (2007). Predicting the prison misconducts on women offenders: The importance of gender-responsive needs. *Journal of Contemporary Criminal Justice, 23*, 310–340.

PART III

Consequences of Sentencing Decisions

10

PUNISHED FOR BEING PUNISHED

Collateral Consequences of a Drug Offense Conviction

Ashley Nellis

An estimated 1.7 million Americans were under some form of correctional supervision in 2015 because of a drug conviction (Kaeble & Glaze, 2016; The Sentencing Project, 2017). After their release from supervision, they join the ranks of those who experience a range of legislatively erected barriers that obstruct their ability to regain a foothold in society.

Post-conviction exclusions and restrictions, some of which are lifelong, are felt not only by the convicted persons themselves but by their children, spouses, and other family members (see North-cutt Bohmert & Wakefield, Chapter 8; Vallas et al., 2015). In some instances, even innocent family and friends may be punished by the actions of another.

Over the past four decades, the goals of reintegration have increasingly become subverted by the collateral consequences returning citizens face on release from correctional supervision (Travis, 2005). They have increased both in volume and complexity as one of the far-reaching effects of the America's forty-year prison build-up (Kaiser, 2016; Mauer & Chesney-Lind, 2002). The breadth of collateral consequences is obscured by the scattered placement of restrictions and exclusions across jurisdictional codes and enforcement across diverse and disconnected agencies. This makes it nearly impossible to have an accurate sense of the type and number of collateral consequences to be faced post-conviction. Because collateral consequences are "civil" rather than criminal punishments, legal counsel and courts are typically not required to reveal their nature or extent (Chin, 2002). Moreover, some collateral consequences are automatically attached to specific crimes while others are established on a case-by-case basis. And while some consequences are lifelong others eventually expire.

A single, first-time, felony-level drug offense, for example, may result in some or all of the following: exclusion from federally funded education assistance, a temporary loss of one's driver's license, licensing and employment disqualifications, and an inability to purchase a firearm. This single conviction may also result in a ban from joining the military, loss of the right to vote, and the loss of the opportunity to sit on a jury. Finally, a felony conviction can result in deportation for noncitizens (Padilla v. Kentucky (130 S. Ct. 1473 [2010]).

Within five years of release, more than three quarters of formerly incarcerated prisoners have been rearrested (Durose, Cooper, & Snyder, 2014). This is partly due to these barriers (Travis, 2005).

The present chapter reflects on two collateral consequences that are particularly relevant for people convicted of drug offenses: eviction from public housing and exclusion from public assistance. In addition to barriers in gaining employment, voting, and earning a higher education described in other chapters of this book, people convicted of a drug offense are faced with the reality that they have also been specifically excluded from these two critical forms of assistance.

Because the primary target of the country's infamous "war on drugs" was placed on inner city communities, the impact of the collateral consequences of a drug conviction has fallen disproportionately on people of color, especially African Americans (Clear, 2008; Rubenstein & Mukamal, 2002; Western, 2006). Tracking the overall impact of these sanctions on the affected populations is nearly impossible given diverse, disconnected agencies responsible for carrying them out and the low priority around monitoring them (Travis, 2005).

In Michelle Alexander's seminal book on race and the criminal justice system, she argues,

> The uncomfortable reality is that convictions for drug offenses—not violent crime—are the single most important cause of the prison boom in the United States, and people of color are convicted of drug offenses at rates out of proportion to their drug crimes.
>
> (Alexander, 2010, p. 102)

Though some analysts fail to find such a strong relationship between the war on drugs and the prison boom (Pfaff, 2015), many agree that the heightened focus on incarceration for drug possession and sales certainly accelerated of mass incarceration(Rubenstein & Mukamal, 2002). Because of the enduring patterns of over-policing, over-prosecuting, and over-sentencing African Americans for drug offenses, African Americans have been disproportionately impacted by the collateral consequences associated with a drug conviction. Women, too, have faced a disparate share of the burdens imposed by these bans because of their lower income levels and their disparate share of the drug-offender population.

Collateral Consequences of a Drug Conviction

Individuals who are arrested and convicted for drug offenses find themselves in a maze of non-criminal civil sanctions that impede their ability to move beyond the mistakes of their past. The number of collateral consequences has multiplied over the past several decades (Love, 2011; Petersilia, 2003; Pinard, 2010a, 2010b). Today more than 46,000 separate collateral consequences have been documented, with as many as 70% impacting the ability to obtain a job (National Inventory of Collateral Consequences, 2017).

Scholars, practitioners, and advocates generally conclude that while some post-conviction civil restrictions are necessary in some circumstances, the extensive spread of collateral consequences has failed to fulfill any public safety goal (Uggen & Stewart, 2015). Instead, collateral consequences marginalize those with a conviction, which has the effect of challenging successful reintegration and increasing the likelihood of recidivism. They serve to further punish those who already have paid their debt to society. In addition to the collateral consequences explored throughout this volume, there are two civil penalties that have been established solely for those convicted of drug crimes: barriers to living in certain housing establishments and lifetime bans from receiving public assistance such as Temporary Assistance to Needy Families (TANF) and Supplemental Nutritional Assistance Program (SNAP).

Beginning in the 1980s and extending to the mid-1990s, a new derivative of cocaine—crack—besieged many inner cities. The availability of crack was accompanied by a rise in violence in inner cities as sellers fought to establish their markets, and the violence was facilitated by easy access to handguns (Mauer, 2006). The rise in violence led to increased worries about crime, especially in communities of color: a poll from 1995 found that 28 percent of African Americans considered drug abuse to be a crisis in their neighborhoods and schools, compared to just 9 percent of white respondents (Pew Research Center, 2014). Both policy makers and community members responded by merging the rising drug addiction with larger community crime problems, as well as to attach it to a crumbling urban landscape and extensive social and economic problems. Both substance users and dealers were caught in the aggressive policing, prosecution, and sentencing that followed as part of an acceleration of drug-related law enforcement and prosecution as part of the "war on drugs." The effects of these efforts were disproportionately felt by African Americans, particularly black men.

The new drugs laws aimed to remove drug kingpins from the marketplace, but the day-to-day implementation of the law focused on everyone from managers to low-level dealers. These strategies were destined to fail for two reasons: first, removing drug sellers from the street through incarceration caused replacement of new drug sellers to the street rather than acting as a deterrent to potential recruits (Blumstein2003). Second, the law swept up drug possessors and dealers at all levels of the market because of concentrated enforcement tactics and aggressive prosecutions across all drug crimes rather than the high-level managers of the drug trade. The result was an unprecedented rise in incarceration for people convicted of drug offenses (Mauer, 2006). In 1980, there were 40,900 people incarcerated in prisons and jails for a drug conviction, but by 2015 this number had risen to 469,545 (The Sentencing Project, 2017).

Mass incarceration has disproportionately burdened the African American community. Imprisonment of black males outpaces that of white males by nearly six-to-one (Carson & Anderson, 2016). Because the efforts of the drug war have been concentrated most heavily in African American communities, it is the members of these communities who have been most affected by the collateral sanctions of drug conviction.

The racial effects of the war on drugs were not accidental. Consider as evidence the following interview excerpt with Richard Nixon's domestic policy advisor, John Ehrlichman (Baum, 2016), who admitted to the racially explicit aim of the war on drugs:

> The Nixon campaign in 1968, and the Nixon White House after that, had two enemies: the antiwar left and black people. . . . We knew we couldn't make it illegal to be either against the war or black, but by getting the public to associate the hippies with marijuana and blacks with heroin. And then criminalizing both heavily, we could disrupt those communities. We could arrest their leaders, raid their homes, break up their meetings, and vilify them night after night on the evening news. Did we know we were lying about the drugs? Of course we did.

Grasping the racialized impact of incarceration for drug offenses is necessary to gain a full appreciation of collateral consequences of a drug conviction. Relying on the criminal justice system to address drug addiction is an exclusively American approach, one that has been more effectively handled as a public health problem in many other countries. The effects of a punitive strategy for drug addiction have fallen disproportionately on people of color, who are more likely to encounter challenges in obtaining stable housing, employment, and participation in democracy even in the absence of a felony drug conviction.

Housing

More than 2 million Americans live in public housing, and another 4.7 million participate in the Housing Choice Voucher program, formerly named "Section 8" housing. People exiting prison often do so with few resources, which makes availability of public housing a key component for reintegration to society. Housing instability often leads to reoffending (Ehman & Reosti, 2015; Fontaine & Biess, 2012; Kirk, Chapter 3; Thompson, 2008). Despite its relevance for desisting from crime, individuals with a criminal conviction face obstacles in securing housing. Public housing authorities can deny admission to "applicants whose habits and practices reasonably may be expected to have a detrimental effect on the residents or the project environment" (24 CFR 960.202).

Housing restrictions were part of the 1988 Anti-Drug Abuse Act, known best for its establishment of a five-year mandatory minimum federal prison sentence for first-time simple possession of 5 grams of crack cocaine (Mauer, 2006). The law required public housing authorities to terminate or evict potential or existing tenants if it was discovered that they were engaging in criminal activities "on or near public housing premises" (Silva, 2015). The law stipulated that, at the discretion of the housing agents, both tenants and their family members *or guests*[1] could be subject to termination and eviction (Silva, 2015).

Following the 1988 Anti-Drug Abuse Act was the 1990 Cranston-Gonzalez National Affordable Housing Act, which expanded the authority granted to public housing authorities beyond "any criminal activity" to any "drug-related criminal activity," and added a prohibition against receiving public housing for a period of three years following an original determination (Silva, 2015). Drug-related criminal activity included simple possession and was defined as "the manufacture, sale, distribution, or use of a drug, or the possession of a drug with intent to manufacture, sell, distribute or use the drug" (24 C.F.R. §5.100; The Controlled Substances Act, 21 U.S.C.§ 802 [2012]).

In his 1996 State of the Union address, President Bill Clinton urged housing authorities nation-wide to adopt a "one-strike policy" to combat drug crimes in public housing. "[C]riminal gang members and drug dealers are destroying the lives of decent tenants. From now on, the rule for residents who commit crime and pedal drugs should be one strike and you're out" (White House, 1996).

Federal regulations (CFR §966.4) subsequently authorized public housing agents to terminate a resident's tenancy for "any criminal activity that threatens the health, safety, or quiet enjoyment of the PHS's ... premises ... or (2) any drug-related criminal activity on or near the premises."

Public housing authorities are afforded broad discretion in detecting and enforcing policies (Silva, 2015). Unlike law enforcement agents and prosecutors, authorities in public housing are not required to meet a standard of proof to determine that an individual is engaged in criminal activity. They instead have nearly unrestrained authority to deny housing for "any drug-related or violent criminal activity or any other criminal activity that would adversely affect the healthy, safety, or right to peaceful enjoyment of the premises by other residents if the criminal activity occurred a 'reasonable' time before the person seeks admission" (Rubinstein & Mukamal, 2006).

Arrest and conviction are not necessary conditions for eviction, just suspicion on the part of the public housing agent (Pinard, 2010b; Rubinstein & Mukamal, 2002). The guidance offered provided simply that "some sort of evidence will be required" to terminate a household (Silva, 2015: p. 796).

At the time, the "one strike" policy had broad public support among community members, including among those impacted by the rise of drug-related crime in their environment. A national survey conducted in 1995 found that 88 percent of African American respondents supported eviction of individuals convicted of drug possession or sales (Hellegers, 1999). Though federally subsidized housing was already restricted in the abovementioned ways for those with a felony-level drug conviction, the policy that became part of the 1996 Housing Opportunity Program Extension Act of 1996 (42 USC § 1437 (d)(I)(6)) extended prohibitions further, urging public housing authorities to extend their reach to residents both on *and off* public housing property and to allow the prohibition for every member of the individual's household.[2] In 1998, the Quality Housing and Work Responsibility Act extended many of these same restrictions on public housing to Housing Choice Voucher programs.

In the first six months following passage of the "one strike" policy, HUD reported 19,405 applicants turned down for federal housing opportunities on mere suspicions of drug-based criminal activity (Silva, 2015). In 1997, 43 percent of the housing application rejections were because of the policy; in this year the PHA denied admission to 45,079 applicants (Travis, 2005).

The housing ban described here is exceptional in comparison to the other collateral consequences because of its direct impact on innocent family members and associates of the convicted individual. Though litigation challenging the constitutionality of evicting family members or guests of individuals with a drug conviction has been mounted in a number of cases, the U.S. Supreme Court ultimately upheld the policy via its ruling in *Department of Housing and Urban Development v. Rucker* (535 U.S. 125, 130 [2002]). Evictions of blameless family members have also been upheld when the offense was convicted in juvenile court rather than criminal court. In an Ohio case, a 15-year-old's minor marijuana possession conviction was sufficient to have his grandmother, with whom he lived, evicted (*Cincinnati Metropolitan Housing Authority v. Browning*, Ohio Court of Appeals [2002]).

Not all states enforce the policy equally, and some modest modifications have been made to the policy. Some states, for example, have enacted a "right to cure" clause that allows tenants to remedy the lease infraction that is accused of them and possibly prevent eviction (Silva, 2015).

Some promising developments at the federal level have been made. In 2015, the Obama Administration issued guidance offered based on the advice of its Federal Interagency Reentry Council, a cabinet-level agency designed to ease the transition from incarceration, support public safety, and encourage cross-agency coordination. Principal among these recommendations was the modification of the "one strike" policy, aiming to remedy the punitive nature with the goal of improving reentry and reintegration of those returning from incarceration (White House, 2015). Based on the advice of the Council, the Department of Housing and Urban Development established that arrest alone, in the absence of a conviction, should not suffice as evidence of criminal activity and thus qualify one for eviction (U.S. Department of Housing and Urban Development, 2015). The Administration directed public housing agencies to loosen some of the restrictions for people with criminal convictions (U.S. Department of Housing and Urban Development, 2015).

Housing restrictions on those with criminal convictions or suspected of criminal activity that were initially enacted at the federal level have provoked similar restrictions in the private rental housing market. This places people with a drug conviction at an even greater disadvantage since they are less favorable applicants for public housing. A 2005 survey of the largest rental market associations reported that four out of five landlords screened potential tenants for criminal records and made their decision based on results (Uggen & Stewart, 2015). The prevalence of criminal records accessible through online searches has made it virtually impossible to keep past criminal acts private. Neighborhood associations and community groups, too, use online forums to organize opposition to tenants with criminal convictions (Oyama, 2009). Online searches for criminal records are frequently rife with errors, either through reporting outdated information or expunged arrests and convictions (Oyama, 2009).

Leasing companies justify their background searches on the basis that they could be held liable if a tenant with a criminal record in their past harms another tenant. In reality, liability could be a factor whether one has a criminal record or not, but this justification has been used successfully to bar individuals from renting. It should be noted that there is no empirical support for the relationship between having a criminal record and failure to meet the requirements of a rental agreement (Vallas & Dietrich, 2014).

African Americans have been disproportionately impacted by the war on drugs and mass incarceration more broadly, which means this segment of the population has been more acutely affected by collateral consequences that follow a drug conviction. The combined effect of a criminal record with the well-documented bias that African Americans already face when applying for housing means that racial minorities suffer disproportionately from exclusionary housing policies (Oyama, 2009). Because of disproportionate impact of criminal records on people of color, some argue that the liability claim could violate the Fair Housing Act (Ehman & Reosti, 2015; Oyama, 2009).

Public Assistance

The massive prison build-up of the past forty years has devastated the potential for many communities to thrive (Clear, 2008). Arrest, conviction, and incarceration are now a common experience for large segments of these communities (Clear, 2008; Sampson & Loeffler, 2010). Scholars note that the scale of use of incarceration itself has had profound effects on socioeconomic stability, shifted large segments of African American communities into poverty (Wakefield & Uggen, 2010). A resulting "pernicious feedback loop" has become entrenched in inner city communities with high concentrations of returning prisoners. These barriers make return to prison more likely (Morenoff & Harding, 2014).

When people exit a period of incarceration, they typically struggle financially to meet their financial obligations and support their family. Two supports that people turn to are SNAP (Supplemental Nutrition Assistance Program) and TANF (Temporary Assistance for Needy Families). Both SNAP and TANF are federally funded grant programs that give money to states through block grants. SNAP supports food assistance and TANF provides cash assistance to needy families, promotes stable family structure, and supports job preparation programs. Broad discretion is afforded to each state to design the components of its individual grant program including the amount a family can receive, conditions for receipt, and the period for which a family can receive benefits.

Americans have a long history of turning to government support as a temporary safety net in the absence of other income sources. The mark of a criminal conviction already presents substantial barriers to employment (see Apel & Ramakers, Chapter 5 in this volume; Pager, 2003; Pager, 2007), which makes access to public assistance even more necessary. Yet a substantial rewrite of the public welfare law in 1996 eliminated this safety net for people convicted of drug crimes.

The problematic component of the Personal Responsibility and Work Opportunity Reconciliation Act (PRWORA) was the lifetime denial of public assistance for those convicted of possession, use, or distribution of a controlled substance (Rubenstein & Mukamal, 2002). Notably, the scale of this Act's provision was afforded hardly any consideration during the congressional voting process. After only two minutes of debate (one for Democrats and one for Republicans), the so-called felony drug ban was adopted through unanimous voice vote as part of the PRWORA that ultimately passed (The Sentencing Project, 2013). As this and other chapters in this volume attempt to establish, these "hidden" punishments that make up the collateral consequences often last far past the original one imposed by the criminal justice system. In the case of those convicted of felony drug offenses, these punishments are lifelong.

Denying public assistance limits individuals' capacity to reestablish a footing in society and maintain a financially stable household. In addition to increasing the chances for committing a new crime, this leads to a greater likelihood of losing custody of one's children, which is in turn associated with heavier foster care dependence (Swann & Sylvester, 2006). This is especially true for women, as they are less likely to be employed before incarceration and are more likely to rely on public assistance (Schirmer, Nellis, & Mauer, 2009; The Sentencing Project, 2013). Data from 2009 show that 86 percent of the adult TANF recipients were female; women are also twice as likely to rely on food stamp benefits at some point during their lifetime (Loprest, 2012; Morin, 2013). The denial of benefits is also especially problematic for women because of their growing representation in prison populations: the rise of female incarceration has outstripped male incarceration, particularly among those convicted of drug offenses. Between 1980 and 2010 the number of women in prison rose by 646 percent compared to a 419 percent increase among men. (The Sentencing Project, 2013). In addition, data from 2015 show that 25.1 percent of women in state prison had been convicted of a drug offense, compared to 14.9 percent of men (Carson & Anderson, 2016).

States can opt out of the felony drug ban, and many have either partially or fully done so. As of early 2017, fourteen states had fully opted out of the bans and in an additional twenty-four states had adopted modifications to either the TANF ban, the SNAP ban, or both for persons convicted of felony drug crime. In states that have modified the ban, modifications include allowing benefits for those who pass a drug test, allowing benefits for a drug possession conviction (but not for those convicted of intent to distribute drugs), and/or exempting those who agree to enter drug treatment. A complete ban of both programs remains in place in Arizona, Mississippi, North Dakota, South Carolina, and West Virginia (Mohan, L., Palacio, V., & Lower-Basch, E., 2017). In 2016, New Jersey Governor Chris Christie vetoed a bill that would have allowed childless drug offenders to receive cash assistance amounting to $140 a month (Livio, 2016).

As noted, women are especially vulnerable under the ban to public assistance. An analysis of the lifetime potential impact of the TANF ban on women in the twelve states with a full TANF ban estimates that 180,100 women have been denied assistance between 1996 and 2011 (The Sentencing Project, 2013). Separately, sociologists Chris Uggen and Melissa Thompson studied female arrest rates in each of the three types of states: states that had opted out of the ban completely, those that had partially opted out, and those that preserved the full ban. Their findings showed a statistically significantly greater increase in arrests among states that had imposed the ban compared to those that partially imposed it as well as those states that had opted out. Though conclusions about causation are limited, these findings comport with analyses elsewhere that show fewer instances of drug and property crimes among women receiving assistance during the periods in which they receive assistance. Their preliminary findings suggest that a ban on felony drug offenders could have the unintended consequence of increasing crime rates (Uggen & Stewart, 2015).

Registries for People Convicted of Drug Offenses

So-called "offender registries" are most known as a requirement for individuals convicted of a sex offense. The general rationale behind registries is to keep better track of potential perpetrators' whereabouts and ensure public safety. Arming citizens with information about their neighbors is a popular and widely used tactic, but the evidence for improving public safety is not clear. For the most part, studies on the effectiveness of registries deterrence, recidivism and public safety are unconvincing (Tewksbury, 2007). Nearly all research to date has focused on the effects of sex offender registries—the most prevalent form of registry—on recidivism, stigma, housing, and other factors. Housing restrictions are a main component of sex offender registries. Research in this area shows impairments to individual mobility and harmful social stigma on registrants (Tewksbury, 2007). At the same time, public safety benefits are not evident using offender registries. The explanation for this lies in the fact that most sex offenses occur within the offender's home against another resident in the home (Tewksbury, 2007).

Despite lack of empirical evidence, some states have recently moved to expand the registries to other types of offenses. At least six states—Illinois, Kansas, Minnesota, New Hampshire, Oklahoma, and Tennessee—have proposed or passed legislation that would require people with a drug conviction to place themselves on an offender registry with law enforcement (Lu, R., Raju, J., Scholz-Bright, R., 2016). In 2013, Oklahoma enacted the Methamphetamine Offender Registry Act, which requires that anyone convicted of possession, manufacture, distribution, or trafficking of methamphetamine and/or its precursors list themselves on the registry. Individuals convicted of a methamphetamine-related offense are prohibited from purchasing or possessing pseudoephedrine, even if they have been prescribed this medication by a doctor (Oklahoma Statute § 2–701). Kansas and Tennessee have similar registries, and these have the added feature of being publicly accessible.

In 2016, New Hampshire legislators introduced a bill that would require placement on a drug offender registry for a term of four years upon one's third conviction for possession, manufacture, or intent to sell a long list of controlled substances (House Bill 1603). This bill received media attention in part because of the state's ongoing struggle with heroin use but ultimately did not pass.

The stated purpose of drug offender registries is to inhibit the opportunities for registrants to do further harm through increasing supervision not only by law enforcement but by public citizens with access to registries. As with all offender registries, law enforcement officials are notified when a registered person moves to their jurisdiction, which is anticipated to assist police with surveillance, detection, and prevention of drug-law violations.

Deportation

Deportation of noncitizens can result from criminal convictions, even in cases where the conviction is a misdemeanor and may have occurred in the past. Though drug crimes have always been just cause for deportation, statutes in the 1980s as part of the "war on drugs" intensified the post-conviction punishments for noncitizens, including deportation. The 1986 Anti-Drug Abuse Act authorized the use of detention for individuals arrested for a drug crime while awaiting immigration custody. Federal law allows deportation for simple possession, possession with intent to sell, and distribution of a controlled substance. Data from the Immigration and Customs Enforcement (ICE) analyzed by Human Rights Watch (HRW) identified a 43 percent increase in deportations for persons convicted of drug possession between 2007 and 2012 (Meng, 2015). The stepping up of deportations for those with even minor drug convictions, sometimes years old, stands at odds with the broad bipartisan recognition that nonviolent drug convictions have unnecessarily filled our prisons but failed to deter involvement in the drug trade or promote public safety (Meng, 2015).

Deportations of those with previous encounters with the law were enhanced under the Obama Administration. Between 2014 and 2016, 59 percent of the 235,413 people who were deported had criminal convictions (Wiltz, 2016). Analysis of the crime data shows, however, that most of the crimes were low-level offenses (Meng, 2015). Eleven percent of crime-related deportations were for nonviolent drug convictions and 33 percent of the drug convictions were marijuana-related (Thompson & Flagg, 2016).

Obama voiced an emphasis in his Administration on "felons not families." Deportations for those with criminal convictions were identified as a priority in his public comments on immigration reform in 2014:

> Even as we are a nation of immigrants, we're also a nation of laws. Undocumented workers broke our immigration laws, and I believe that they must be held accountable—especially those who may be dangerous. That's why, over the past six years, deportations of criminals are up 80 percent. And that's why we're going to keep focusing enforcement resources on actual threats to our security. Felons, not families. Criminals, not children. Gang members, not a mom who's working hard to provide for her kids. We'll prioritize, just like law enforcement does every day.
>
> (White House, 2014)

Under the Trump Administration, deportations for noncitizens with criminal records are likely to accelerate because of the Administration's heavy focus on immigration. Deportation policies announced in early 2017 called for only an emphasis on "anyone who has committed an act that constitute a chargeable criminal offense" (Wiltz, 2016). In other words, one not even have been charged with an offense to be become the focus for deportation. The authority of immigration officers has also been expanded under the Trump Administration to simply their "judgment" to determine whether a person poses a risk to public safety or national security (Wiltz, 2016).

Contrary to the rules for other collateral consequences, attorneys must be aware of and inform their clients of the possibility of deportation that accompanies a guilty plea for noncitizens. The major Supreme Court case ruling in favor of informing defendants of civil punishments is *Padilla v.*

Kentucky (599 US 256 [2010]). *Padilla* argued that effective assistance of counsel must include a warning to clients of the possibility of deportation upon a guilty plea. In its ruling, the Court acknowledged the "seriousness of deportation as a consequence of a criminal plea, and the concomitant impact of deportation on families living lawfully in [the United States]" (Pinard, 2010a). Through *Padilla*, deportation represents the only collateral consequence to date on which the Supreme Court has granted some form of protection for those facing post-conviction collateral consequences.

Conclusion

For the roughly 19 million Americans with a felony record (Shannon et al., 2017), opportunities in housing, employment, education, public assistance, and civic engagement become limited by a wide range of collateral consequences. For people with a drug conviction, estimated at 1.7 million, the penalties can be even more severe.

Though the aim of collateral consequence is public safety, a broad range of criminological studies shows that most individuals who engage in crime mature out of their criminal behavior. Someone with a felony conviction is at approximately the same risk of offending as someone without any conviction after about seven years (Blumstein & Nakamura, 2009). This reality suggests that, while time-limited sanctions can be an appropriate and necessary response to crime, long-term collateral consequences serve no public safety benefit.

The stigma and civil penalties that follow "formal" punishment frustrate attempts to reintegrate into society through employment, access to temporary income support, and obtaining or maintaining secure housing. In most cases, collateral consequences do not protect public safety; instead they threaten it. These consequences are frequently compounded by preexisting racial and ethnic inequalities.

Collateral consequences stand at odds with the recently renewed focus on bolstering individuals through reentry programming and supports. The juxtaposition of release from imprisonment followed by the start of a "hidden punishment" (Kaiser, 2016) was scrutinized in the courts more than a century ago in *Weems v. United States* (217 U.S. 349, 366 [1910]):

> His prison bars and chains are removed, it is true . . . but he goes from them to a perpetual limitation of his liberty . . . subject to tormenting regulations that, if not so tangible as iron bars and stone walls, oppress as much by their continuity, and deprive essential liberty.

Evidence of the renewed interest in prisoner reentry is shown through the Second Chance Act, which was signed into law in 2007 by President George W. Bush and received broad bipartisan support. Through the authorization of this Act funds are provided to local jurisdictions to support citizens returning from incarceration. Upon signing the bill, President Bush emphasized the importance of redemption (White House, 2008):

> The country was built on the belief that each human being has limitless potential and worth. Everybody matters. We believe that even those who have struggled with a dark past can find brighter days ahead. One way we act on that belief is by helping former prisoners who've paid for their crimes—we help them build new lives as productive members of our society.
>
> The work of redemption reflects our values. It also reflects our national interests. Each year, approximately 650,000 prisoners are released from jail. Unfortunately, an estimated two-thirds of them are rearrested within three years. The high recidivism rate places a huge financial burden on taxpayers, it deprives our labor force of productive workers, and it deprives families of their daughters and sons, and husbands and wives, and moms and dads.

The extent to which a criminal act follows an individual through life is not easily identified. Collateral consequences are typically developed in an ad hoc manner by legislatures rather than imposed by the courts. Civil sanctions are scattered around a jurisdiction's code rather than identifiable in one central location (Chin, 2002). Because collateral consequences are not defined as part of the punishment they are mostly exempt from constitutional provisions around criminal proceedings. They are considered regulatory rather than punitive.

Defense attorneys are often unaware of—and, with few exceptions, under no obligation to learn—the full list of sanctions that their clients could face upon conviction, thus complicating a fully informed plea. Judges, too, are rarely aware of the full implications of a sentence (Chin, 2002; Chin, 2012). "Most state legislatures attempt to make the punishment fit the crime, but this task is impossible if no one knows what the punishment is" (Chin, 2002, p. 277).

Recent years have brought about some encouraging developments. Vocal, nonpartisan legal bodies including the American Bar Association, the American Law Institute, and the Uniform Law Commission have urged broader awareness about the spread of collateral consequences and their impact (Uggen & Stewart, 2015). Experts advocate for a streamlined repository of collateral consequences for use by attorneys, judges, and defendants. They advocate for better acquaintance with the mandatory and potential collateral consequences associated with a conviction, as well as call for restriction of collateral consequences to only those that clearly promote public safety.

The American Law Institute's Model Penal Code recommends that sentencing commissions "compile, maintain, and publish a compendium of all collateral consequences contained in [the jurisdiction's] statutes and administrative regulations." The ALI further recommends that each crime in state codes should be accompanied by a regularly updated compendium of all collateral consequences that are authorized by the statute, regulations, and federal law (The American Law Institute, 2017, p. 241).

In addition to these developments, some state lawmakers and executive officials have taken the initiative to change the policies or practices that work to keep people with convictions from full reintegration to society. Some changes have come about in the areas of restoration of voting rights (i.e., Virginia and Alabama). In other states, policy makers have pressed for the partial or full opting out of the felony welfare ban. In the last several years we have seen modifications to overly punitive drug laws take place in more than three quarters of the states (Pew Research Center, 2014). These changes will surely assist in reducing collateral consequences of a drug conviction.

Public sentiment is also shifting around substance use, punishment for drug offenses, and addiction treatment. According to a public opinion poll released by the Pew Research Center in 2014, the majority (54 percent) of the public now supports marijuana legalization and nearly three quarters of the public feels that those caught with small amounts of marijuana should not be incarcerated. Moreover, the public supports a less punitive response to drug offenses than it did in 2001. Polling shows that as of 2014, 63 percent support eliminating mandatory minimums for nonviolent drug crimes whereas only 47 percent were in support in 2001. And finally, 76 percent of Americans believe the U.S. government should prioritize treatment over punishment for illegal drug use, with only one quarter of Americans supporting prosecution. Importantly, the view of drug abuse as a crisis or serious problem has not changed considerably between 1995 and 2014, but a greater share of the public has abandoned the main principles behind the "war on drugs."

At the same time of these developments, America is in the middle of a new drug crisis. Overdoses from heroin and other opioids have soared and are now the leading cause of death among individuals under 50 years old (Katz, 2017). There was a 300 percent increase in heroin related deaths between 1999 and 2015 (Centers for Disease Control and Prevention, 2017). The misuse of prescription painkillers is at an all-time high. This new era of addiction presents an opportunity to choose different policies than those of the crack epidemic.

10 Punished for Being Punished

The impulse reaction by some policy makers has been to seek tougher penalties such as new mandatory minimums and other punitive approaches that once again use the criminal justice system as the primary tool to respond to this latest public health crisis. Some of the proposed solutions are following the same spirit as the failed "war on drugs" and with a reminiscent rationale for doing so. Fortunately, policy makers have the benefit of hindsight to make informed decisions this time around.

Notes

1 According to federal regulations, a "guest" is defined as an individual who is "temporarily staying in the unit with the consent of a tenant or other member of the household who has express or implied authority to so consent on behalf of the tenant." 24 §Section 5.100 (2017).
2 Specifically, 42 USC § 1437 (d)(1)(B)(iii) states: "Any criminal activity that threatens the health, safety or right to peaceful enjoyment of the premises by other tenants or any drug-related criminal activity on or off such premises, engaged in by a public housing tenant, any member of the tenant's household, or any guest or other person under the tenant's control, shall be cause for termination of tenancy."

References

Alexander, M. (2012). *The new jim crow: Mass incarceration in the age of colorblindness*. New York: The New Press.
Baum, D. (2016). Legalize it all: How to win the war on drugs. *Harper's Magazine*. Retrieved from https://harpers.org/archive/2016/04/legalize-it-all/
Blumstein, A., & Nakamura, K. (2009). Redemption in the presence of widespread criminal background checks. *Criminology, 47*(2), 327–339.
Blumstein, A. (2003). The notorious 100:1 Crack: powder disparity--the data tell us that it is time to restore the balance. *Federal Sentencing Reporter, 16*(1): 87–92.
Carson, E. A., & Anderson, E. (2016). *Prisoners in 2015*. Washington, DC: Bureau of Justice Statistics.
Carson, E. A. & Anderson, E. (2011). *Prisoners in 2010*. Washington, DC: Bureau of Justice Statistics.
Centers for Disease Control and Prevention. (2017). *Wonder*. Retrieved June 2, 2017, from https://wonder.cdc.gov/
Chin, G. (2002). Race, the war on drugs, and the collateral consequences of a criminal conviction. *Journal of Gender, Race and Justice* (6), 255–278.
Chin, G. (2012). The new civil death: Rethinking punishment in the era of mass conviction. *University of Pennsylvania Law Review, 160*, 1789–1833.
Clear, T. (2008). The effects of high imprisonment rates on communities. *Crime and Justice, 37*(1): 91–132.
Durose, M. R., Cooper, A. D., & Snyder, H. N. (2014). *Recidivism of prisoners released in 30 states in 2005: Patterns from 2005 to 2010 – Update*. Washington, DC: Bureau of Justice Statistics.
Ehman, M., & Reosti, A. (2015). Tenant screening in an era of mass incarceration: A criminal record is no crystal ball. *New York University Journal of Legislation and Public Policy Quorum*, 1–109.
Fontaine, J., & Biess, J. *Housing as a platform for formerly incarcerated persons*. Washington, DC: Urban Institute.
Hellegers, A. P. (1999). Reforming HUD's 'One Strike' public housing evictions through tenant participation. *The Journal of Criminal Law and Criminology, 90*(1), 323–362.
Kaeble, D., & Glaze, L. (2016). *Correctional populations in the U.S, 2015*. Washington, DC: Bureau of Justice Statistics.
Katz, J. (2017) The first count of fentynl deaths in 2016: Up 540% in three years. *The New York Times*. Retrieved from https://www.nytimes.com/interactive/2017/09/02/upshot/fentanyl-drug-overdose-deaths.html
Kaiser, J. (2016). Revealing the hidden sentence: How to add transparency, legitimacy, and purpose to "collateral" punishment policy. *Harvard Law and Policy Review, 10*, 124–184.
Livio, S. K. (2016, November 30). Christie: Convicted drug offenders will not get welfare. *NJ.com*.
Loprest, P. J. (2012). *How has the TANF caseload changed over time?* Washington, DC: U.S. Department of Health and Human Services Administration for Children and Families.
Love, M. G. (2011). Paying their debt to society: Forgiveness, redemption, and the Uniform Collateral Consequences of Conviction Act. *Howard Law Journal, 54*(3), 753–793.
Lu, R., Raju, J., & Scholz-Bright, R. (2016). *Establishing a drug dealer registry in New Hampshire*. Hanover: The Nelson A. Rockefeller Center at Dartmouth College.
Mauer, M., & Chesney-Lind, M. (2002). *The collateral consequences of mass imprisonment*. New York: The New Press.
Mauer, M. (2006). *Race to Incarcerate*. New York: The New Press.

Meng, G. (2015). *A price to high: U.S. families torn apart by deportations*. San Francisco: Human Rights Watch. Retrieved from www.hrw.org/report/2015/06/16/price-too-high/us-families-torn-apart-deportations-drug-offenses

Mohan, L., Palacio, V., & Lower-Basch, E. (2017). *No more double punishments*. Washington, DC: Center for Law and Social Policy.

Morenoff, J. D., & Harding, D. J. (2014). Incarceration, prisoner reentry, and communities. *Annual Review of Sociology, 40,* 411–429.

Morin, R. (2013). *The politics and demographics of food stamp recipients*. Washington, DC: Pew Research Center.

Oyama, R. (2009). Do not (re)enter: The rise of criminal background tenant screening as a violation of the Fair Housing Act. *Michigan Journal of Race and Law, 15,* 181–222.

Padilla v. Kentucky, 130 S. Ct. 1473 (2010).

Pager, D. (2003). The mark of a criminal record. *American Journal of Sociology, 108*(5), 937–975.

Pager, D. (2007). *Marked: Race, crime, and finding work in an era of mass incarceration*. Chicago, IL: University of Chicago Press.

Petersilia, J. (2003). *When prisoners come home: Parole and prisoner reentry*. Oxford: Oxford University Press.

Pew Charitable Trusts: Pew Center on the States. (2010). *Collateral costs: Incarceration's effect on economic mobility*. Washington, DC: Author.

Pew Research Center. (2014). *America's new drug policy landscape: Two thirds favor treatment, not jail, for use of heroin, cocaine*. Washington, DC: Author.

Pinard, M. (2010a). Reflections and perspectives on reentry. *Journal of Criminal Law and Criminology, 100*(3), 1213–1224.

Pinard, M. (2010b). Collateral consequences of criminal consequences: Confronting issues of race and dignity. *New York University Law Review, 85*(2), 457–534.

Rubenstein, G. and Mukumal, D. (2002). Welfare and housing--Denial of benefits to drug offenders. In M. Mauer & M. Chesney-Lind (Eds.), *Invisible punishment: The collateral consequences of mass imprisonment*. New York, The New Press.

Sampson, R., & Loeffler, C. (2010). Punishment's place: The local concentration of mass incarceration. *Deadalus, 139,* 20–31.

Schirmer, S., Nellis, A., & Mauer, M. (2009). *Incarcerated parents and their children*. Washington, DC: The Sentencing Project.

The American Law Institute (2017). *Model Penal Code: Sentencing*. Philadephia: The American Law Institute.

The Sentencing Project. (2013). *A lifetime of punishment: The impact of the felony drug ban on welfare benefits*. Washington, DC: The Sentencing Project.

The Sentencing Project. (2017). *Trends in U.S. corrections*. Washington, DC: The Sentencing Project.

Shannon, S. K. S., Uggen, C., Schnittker, J., Thompson, M., Wakefield, S., & Massoglia, M. (2017). The growth, scope, and spatial distribution of people with felony records, 1948 to 2010. *Demography. 54*(5), 1795–1818.

Silva, L. R. (2015). Collateral damage: A public housing consequences of the "war on drugs." *University of California Irvine Law Review, 5,* 783–811.

Swann, C., & Sylvester, M. (2006). The foster care crisis: What caused caseloads to grow? *Demography, 43*(2), 309–355.

Tewksbury, R. (2007). Exile at home: The unintended consequences of sex offender residency requirements. *Harvard Civil Rights-Civil Liberties Law Review, 42,* 531–540.

Thompson, A. C. (2008). *Releasing prisoners, redeeming communities: Reentry, race and politics*. New York, NY: New York University Press.

Thompson, C., & Flagg, A. (2016). *Who is ICE deporting? Obama's promise to focus on 'felons not families' has fallen short*. The Marshall Project. Retrieved from www.themarshallproject.org/2016/09/26/who-is-ice-deporting?utm_medium=email&utm_campaign=newsletter&utm_source=opening-statement&utm_term=newsletter-20160927-594#.1tHM7EJGr

Travis, J. (2005). *But they all come back: Facing the challenges of prisoner reentry*. Washington, DC: Urban Institute Press.

Uggen, C. and Stewart, R. (2015). Piling on: Collateral consequences and community supervision. *Minnesota Law Review, 99,* 1871–1910.

U.S. Department of Housing and Urban Development. *Guidance for Public Housing Agents – Owners of federally assisted housing on excluding the use of arrest records in housing decisions*. Washington, DC: U.S. Department of Housing and Urban Development. Retrieved from https://www.hud.gov/sites/documents/PIH2015-19.PDF

Vallas, R., Boteach, M., West, R., & Odum, J. (2015). *Removing barriers to opportunities for parent with a criminal record and their children*. Washington, DC: Center for American Progress.

Vallas, R., & Dietrich, S. (2014). *One strike and you're out: How we can eliminate barriers to economic security and mobility for people with criminal records*. Washington, DC: Center for American Progress.

Wakefield, S., & Uggen, C. (2010). Incarceration and stratification: *Annual Review of Sociology, 36*, 387–406.

Western, B. (2006). *Punishment and inequality in America*. New York: Russell Sage Foundation.

White House (1996). 1996 State of the Union Address. Retrieved May 2, 2018, from https://www.c-span.org/video/?69496-1/1996-state-union-address

White House (2008). *President Bush Signs H.R. 1593 the Second Chance Act of 2007*. Washington, DC: The White House. Retrieved May 2, 2018, from https://georgewbush-whitehouse.archives.gov/news/releases/2008/04/20080409-2.html

White House. (2014, November 20). *Remarks by the President in the address to the nation on immigration*. Washington, DC: The White House. Retrieved September 30, 2017, from https://obamawhitehouse.archives.gov/the-press-office/2014/11/20/remarks-president-address-nation-immigration

White House. (2015, November 2). *Fact sheet: President Obama announces new actions to promote rehabilitation and reintegration for the formerly-incarcerated*. Washington, DC: The White House. Retrieved September 30, 2017, from https://obamawhitehouse.archives.gov/the-press-office/2015/11/02/fact-sheet-president-obama-announces-new-actions-promote-rehabilitation

Wiltz, T. (2016). What crimes are eligible for deportation. *Stateline*. Washington, DC: The Pew Charitable Trusts. Retrieved May 29, 2017, from www.pewtrusts.org/en/research-and-analysis/blogs/stateline/2016/12/21/what-crimes-are-eligible-for-deportation

11

COMPOUNDED STIGMATIZATION

Collateral Consequences of a Sex Offense Conviction

Kimberly R. Kras, Morgan McGuirk, Breanne Pleggenkuhle, and Beth M. Huebner

Introduction

The mark of a criminal record is far reaching and can impact nearly every facet of a convicted person's life (Pager, 2003; Petersilia, 2003; Travis, 2005). There is evidence that individuals convicted of a sexual crime are doubly marked—first by the conviction itself and second by the additional requirements placed on this class of offenses. Control-focused legislation emerging in part as a result of the populist punitivism movement of the 1990s, rested on the public's perception of sex offenses as the most egregious (Simon, 1998). In 1994, Congress passed the Jacob Wetterling Crimes Against Children and Sexually Violent Offender Registration Act (42 USC 14071) mandating community registration for individuals convicted of sex offenses. This act has been amended to include mandatory dissemination of registry information, Megan's Law in 1996, and lifetime registration for serious offenders and recidivists, Pam Lychner Act 1996, and was replaced by the Adam Walsh Act (AWA) of 2006. Legislation mandates a broad scope of requirements for individuals convicted of a sex offense including residency restrictions, public registries, GPS monitoring, mandated treatment, and civil commitment, thereby broadening the stigma of a conviction.

Consistent with larger trends in mass incarceration, there has been a substantial rise in correctional control of individuals convicted of sex offenses. Between 1980 and 1994, the number of individuals convicted and incarcerated for a sex offense increased 300% (Greenfield, 1997), and in 2015, 12.4% of all state prisoners were incarcerated for sexual assault or rape (Carson & Anderson, 2016). According to the Center for Sex Offender Management (CSOM, 2007), individuals convicted of sex offenses serve, on average, almost twice as much actual prison time compared to individuals convicted of non-sexual offenses. In the community, the number of people with a sex offense conviction registered on public websites has grown nearly 30% in the 10 years since the passage of the AWA (National Center for Missing and Exploited Children [NCMEC], 2016). There are 859,500 individuals convicted of sexual offenses currently on state and federal registries (NCMEC, 2016).

The collateral consequences of a felony conviction are well documented, including housing challenges, family disruption, employment obstacles, economic strain, and stigma (please refer to Whittle, Chapter 2). For individuals convicted of sex offenses, these consequences do not exist singularly; rather they compound to produce intense, long-lasting, and far-reaching effects on the individual's ability to successfully reintegrate into society. In this chapter, we present the most recent

188

developments in understanding the collateral consequences of a sex offense conviction. First, we briefly review the current literature, then discuss the impacts of legislation and restrictions on the post-conviction experience. We consider the impact of collateral consequences on emerging populations of study including women, juveniles, and tribal groups. Finally, we conclude the chapter by examining trending policy developments, especially those aimed at improving the reintegration of individuals convicted of sex offenses in the context of the compounded stigmatization they face.

Collateral Consequences of a Sex Offense Conviction

A wealth of research recognizes the costs of a sex offense conviction, including housing, family disruption, employment obstacles, and economic strain (Jennings, Zgoba, & Tewksbury, 2012; Levenson & Cotter, 2005; Levenson, D'Amora, & Hern, 2007; Levenson & Hern, 2007; Tewksbury, Jennings, & Zgoba, 2012; Tewksbury & Mustaine, 2007). Research also documents the unique experience of stigma among this population (Robbers, 2009; Tewksbury, 2005). The stigma attached to a sexual crime remains a barrier to many aspects of reentry, but especially identity change and desistance. The following sections detail the extant research in this area.

Housing

Scholars advocate that secure, stable housing is a prerequisite for success and is the foundation on which other treatment modalities can be built (for a full review, refer to Kirk, Chapter 3). Despite the importance of stable housing, returning individuals convicted of sex offenses face both legal and extra-legal challenges in accessing a home plan. Nearly every state in the U.S. has some measure of residency restriction aimed at preventing sex offenses against children by restricting individuals previously convicted of such crimes from locales in which children congregate (Socia & Stamatel, 2010), such as schools, parks, and daycares—typically around 1,000 feet (Levenson & Cotter, 2005). Despite research indicating residency restrictions are not associated with declines in sexually-related offenses (Huebner et al., 2014; Socia, 2014; Zandbergen, Levenson, & Hart, 2010), the public and government officials express support for these laws (Meloy, Curtis, & Boatwright, 2013; Pickett, Mancini, & Mears, 2013; Socia & Harris, 2016).

Research suggests that residency restrictions and registration requirements negatively impact the ability of individuals convicted of sex offenses to find a home. Individuals report restricted access to housing, separation from family, and high residential mobility (Burchfield & Mingus, 2008; Rydberg, Grommon, Huebner & Bynum, 2014). Landlords and community members are reluctant to allow individuals convicted of sex offenses to reside in their neighborhoods (Burchfield & Mingus, 2008; Levenson, D'Amora, & Hern, 2007). For example, Levenson and Hern (2007) found that 30% of their sample reported being denied a rental property by a landlord because of their sex offender status and 21% reported moving because a neighbor or landlord found out about their status.

Consequently, individuals convicted of sex offenses are more likely than those with non-sex offense convictions to reside in areas of concentrated disadvantage (Burchfield & Mingus, 2008, 2014; Hipp, Petersilia, & Turner, 2010; Mustaine, Tewksbury, & Stengel, 2006; Socia, 2013, 2016). Socia (2016) found that registered individuals, as compared to the general public, were more likely to cluster in areas of concentrated disadvantage with more affordable housing. Similarly, Huebner and colleagues (2013) found that available housing options in areas of concentrated disadvantage were substandard, but these rentals were both outside the restricted areas and in structures where the landlord was willing to rent to someone with a sex offense conviction, making them one of the only viable options for many citizens.

Residency restriction laws are also associated with higher levels of transience and homelessness (Rolfe, Tewksbury, & Schroeder, 2016; Socia et al., 2015). One study in Florida found that communities with local-level restrictions encompassing wide geographic areas also had a higher proportion of transients (Levenson, Ackerman, Socia, & Harris, 2015; see also Socia, Levenson, Ackerman, & Harris, 2015). In some jurisdictions, corrections departments assign homeless individuals to transitional housing facilities, but research has shown that these locales can have deleterious effects on reintegration because they exist in disadvantaged areas and separate individuals from social supports (Dum, 2016; Kras, Pleggenkuhle, & Huebner, 2016).

Employment and Economy

Employment is a central aspect of reentry as it is associated with strong social support and capital and lower rates of recidivism (for a full review refer to Apel & Ramakers, Chapter 5). Individuals convicted of sex offenses derive the same benefits from employment as other convicted persons. Individuals convicted of sex offenses with stable employment histories show lower likelihoods of recidivism for all types of offending, generally (Hanson & Harris, 2000; Kruttschnitt, Uggen, & Shelton, 2000; Willis & Grace, 2009), while unemployment is associated with increased sexual recidivism specifically (Hanson & Morton-Bourgon, 2005).

Despite its importance, the "mark of a criminal record" makes obtaining stable employment challenging (Pager, 2003). The stigma associated with a criminal conviction and the experience of incarceration is linked with fewer job prospects and reduced wages (Huebner, 2005; Pager, 2003; Western, 2002). Individuals convicted of a sexual offense often have additional conditions of community supervision that may interfere with sustained employment (Daly, 2008). Persons convicted of sex offenses are more likely to be sentenced to electronic monitoring (EM) and have mandated participation in community treatment, both of which can interfere with employment responsibilities.

Employers can formally bar individuals convicted of a sex offense from certain employment sectors where the risk for interacting with potential victims is greater, such as retail clerk, security guard, hotel employee, or medical worker (CSOM, 2007). In surveys of employers, half reported they would not consider hiring an individual with a sex offense history, prioritizing perceived risk to staff and customers, as well as considering negative publicity over the potential capabilities and skills of the applicant (Brown, Spencer, & Deakin, 2007). As a result, most individuals with a sex offense conviction rely on factory or manual labor, and in some cases, individuals seek self-employment or begin their own business as a way to sidestep employment restrictions and stigma (Brown et al., 2007). Overall, research suggests individuals convicted of sex offenses experience downward movement in employment and earnings. For example, Bensel and Sample (2016) found that participants earned half their annual salary following a sex offense conviction.

Individuals convicted of sex offenses experience other unique burdens related to employment. Studies have documented the financial hardship and difficulty securing employment due to residency restrictions (Levenson, 2008; Levenson & Cotter, 2005; Levenson & Hern, 2007; Mercado et al., 2008). Levenson and Hern (2007) reported that 37% of their sample lived far away from employment prospects because of residency restrictions. Tewksbury and Zgoba (2010) found that participants' highest levels of reported stress were related to the job search with 42% reporting employment difficulties.

Stigma can also be compounded by an individual's presence on the registry. Online public registries have made it especially challenging to obtain and maintain employment for individuals with a sex offense conviction (Robbers, 2009; Tewksbury & Lees, 2006). Registered individuals experience low self-esteem and lack of confidence in their employment search (Brown et al., 2007; Tewksbury & Lees, 2006). In interviews with 153 men convicted of sex offenses, Robbers (2009) found that being labeled a sex offender was the most challenging part of reintegration because of the impact on employment opportunities. Levenson and Cotter (2005) found in their study of registered individuals in Florida over one quarter had lost a job due to their presence on the registry.

Stigma and Social Relationships

Social support upon reentry from prison is associated with attaining stable housing and employment, and reducing recidivism (Bahr, Harris, Fisher, & Harker Armstrong, 2010; Berg & Huebner, 2011; Visher, Knight, Chalfin, & Roman, 2009; Willis & Grace, 2008). A criminal conviction can disrupt familial relationships (see Northcutt Bohmert & Wakefield, Chapter 8), which is often amplified for individuals convicted of sex offenses because the stigma of a sex offense conviction can be a barrier to building prosocial relationships and social capital. Individuals convicted of sex offenses may be legally barred from interacting with minor children including their own (CSOM, 2007). In Robbers' (2009) study, more than half of the sample of individuals convicted of a sexual offense reported losing relationships with their family and children because of legal restrictions and the sex offender label. Moreover, research suggests those who have weak social bonds are at an increased risk of sexual reoffending (Hanson & Bussiere, 1998; Hanson & Harris, 2000). Negative environments, characterized by abuse or family dysfunction, magnify deficits in social skills and encourage rumination on the sexually deviant thoughts and feelings that are associated with increases in sexual recidivism (Duwe, Donnay, & Tewksbury, 2008; Hanson & Morton-Bourgon, 2005).

Family members also report experiencing stigma resulting from a loved one's conviction, and this tension can weaken social bonds (Tewksbury & Lees, 2006; Tewksbury & Zgoba, 2010). Intimate partners may exacerbate relationship tension because of the strains they experience from the offense and incarceration, as well as experience stigma from the nature of their loved one's conviction (Tewksbury & Levenson, 2009). Some studies report that the families of individuals convicted of sex offenses experience increased shame, stigma, embarrassment, and harassment because of their loved one's sex offender label (Levenson & Cotter, 2005; Robbers, 2009; Spraitz et al., 2015; Tewksbury & Levenson, 2009). Additionally, Bensel and Sample (2016) found family members of individuals convicted of sex offenses share a collective identity as a stigmatized group. The stigma associated with the sex offender label may also diminish friendship prospects, as two studies found that nearly half of participants reported losing friends due to restrictions and stigma (Mercado et al., 2008; Tewksbury, 2005). In another study, participants reported having limited social capital and few friends, and admitted to avoiding relationships to minimize the stigma and shame associated with disclosing their offense (Burchfield & Mingus, 2008).

The stigma and shame of being labeled a sex offender can also influence one's identity. Most individuals convicted of a sex offense report experiencing psychosocial stress and emotional hardship because of residency restriction policies, including having to live farther away from family and other sources of social support (Levenson, 2008; Levenson & Hern, 2007; Mercado et al., 2008). Social stigma can reinforce maladaptive identities of the sex offender label by ostracizing and isolating individuals from prosocial alternatives (Gobbels, Ward, & Willis, 2012). Mingus and Burchfield's (2012) study found most participants convicted of sex offenses believe they are devalued and discriminated against by society, and emerging research suggests the label has similar effects of individuals incarcerated outside of the U.S. In interviews with individuals imprisoned for sex offenses in Israel, Elisha and colleagues (2012) found participants experienced negative labeling, social exclusion, and rejection due to the nature of their crime.

In totality, the collateral consequences faced by persons convicted of sex offenses are cumulative and often hinder the reentry process. The broad and long-lasting effects of these visible and invisible punishments on individuals, their loved ones, and the community lead scholars, practitioners, and policy makers to reframe approaches to crime prevention. However, efforts to blend policies aimed at improving public safety with effective reintegration have been slow.

New Directions in Research and Policy

The compounded stigmatization experienced by individuals convicted of sex offenses, alongside the growing body of research regarding the efficacy of policies and practices (Huebner et al., 2014; Tewsbury & Jennings, 2010; Tewksbury, Jennings, & Zgoba, 2012), has been the impetus for recent shifts in research and policy. The following sections denote new directions in policy including enhancements to treatment and community supervision and emerging applied work on sex offender registry policies and practice.

Treatment and Supervision Strategies

While there are a multitude of cumulative, negative effects associated with a sex offense conviction, there has been little research to better understand how public policy could be altered to mitigate the stigma while maintaining community safety. One of the predominant models of supervision of individuals convicted of a sex offense is the containment model, which promotes a victim-centered philosophy triangulating treatment, supervision, and polygraph testing with the goal of reducing sexual behavior and recidivism (English, Pullen, & Jones, 1997). The model has a heavy reliance on coordination between the treatment provider and the criminal justice system to manage risk and reduce recidivism.

Most treatment involves cognitive behavioral therapy (CBT) aimed at restructuring the cognitive distortions supporting sexual deviance (Yates, 2004). Despite public opinion that individuals convicted of sex offenses are not amenable to treatment (Schiavone & Jeglic, 2009), studies demonstrate effectiveness in reducing sexual recidivism (Hanson et al., 2002; Losel & Schmucker, 2005; Kim, Benekos, & Merlo, 2016). In one meta-analysis, Losel and Schmucker (2005) found that participants who completed sex offender treatment had a recidivism rate of 11%, while those untreated had a recidivism rate of 17.5%, and this difference was significant. Further, participation in treatment signals to the community that the individual is working towards reform, potentially reducing risk and stigma (Waldram, 2010).

Despite the body of research supporting the use of treatment for those who have committed sexual crimes, much remains to be done to improve outcomes. First, Schmucker and Losel (2015) highlight the need for more randomized controlled trials to demonstrate the effectiveness of treatment and for whom. Further, treatment has followed the same CBT model for decades focusing heavily on risk reduction and management; however, current programs, like the Good Lives Model (GLM), suggest refocusing efforts toward building one's strengths as a method of improving psychosocial well-being and reducing risk (Ward & Gannon, 2006). The GLM is an extension of CBT focusing on the positive attributes of the person rather than solely focusing on deficits. This model emphasizes the development of one's primary goods, such as agency and relatedness to others, which act as protective factors against sexual recidivism. Although the research is in its infancy, the GLM shows promise to engage individuals convicted of all types of sex offenses in the process of desistance (Laws & Ward, 2011).

One facet of a strengths-building treatment orientation is engagement with community actors who support the reentering individual in reintegration. Circles of Support and Accountability (COSA) is an emerging intervention involving restorative justice practices. COSA highlights the role of the community and focuses on mitigating the shame and stigma of a criminal conviction in order for individuals to fully reintegrate (Braithwaite, 1989; Wilson & McWhinnie, 2016). COSAs are comprised of volunteer community members who have been trained in sex offending issues to act as a social support group providing mechanisms of "restorative reentry" for high-risk individuals convicted of sex offenses who often lack social supports and are not fully prepared to encounter stigmatization upon release (Fox, 2014). COSAs assist individuals in acquiring housing, finding employment, and obtaining services, as well as providing a social network for the daily accountability necessary for reform.

COSAs have potential for mitigating the effects of compounded stigmatization by assisting individuals in rejecting the sex offender label, and helping practice and adopt a prosocial identity as modeled by the circle members (Hudson, Taylor, & Henley, 2015). These types of support groups may be better suited to assist participants in shedding their deviant sexual identities and transforming into productive members of society as evaluation research demonstrates COSAs have been successful at reducing recidivism and assisting participants with meaningful community transitions (Elliott, Beech, & Mandeville-Norden, 2013; Fox, 2014; Wilson et al., 2007).

While COSAs operate predominately in Canada, Australia, and the UK, there is evidence that this treatment model can be successfully implemented in the U.S. In an evaluation of the Minnesota COSA program, Duwe (2013) found rearrests were lowered by 62% and returns to prison by 84%. In Bohmert et al.'s (2016) case study of Minnesota's program, 70% of reentering individuals reported receiving instrumental support and all reported receiving expressive support from COSA members. The predominance of expressive support is aligned with the restorative justice philosophy and proved to be a key factor in improving reentry circumstances for participants.

However, there are challenges to fully implementing COSAs. In Fox's (2014) study of COSAs in New Zealand, she found that corrections officials, despite aligning with their role as a social support for individuals under supervision, felt conflicted about how much support they could offer. Rather, they felt it important to identify a "receptive community" to assist individuals with reentry (Fox, 2014, p. 242; see also Willis & Grace, 2009). Similarly, the applicability of COSAs in the U.S., given the current social and political climate concerning individuals convicted of sex offenses, remains tenuous. In a study of various professionals who interact with this population, Call (2016) found a majority agreed individuals convicted of sex offenses experience collateral consequences of loss, emotional and psychological issues, and residency restrictions; however, there was great variation in the sample and many held negative orientations toward individuals convicted of sex offenses (Call, 2016; Mustaine, Tewksbury, Connor, & Payne, 2015). Similar reluctance is seen in community samples. In a study conducted in the UK, many individuals reported a willingness to volunteer for a COSA program even though they understood the efficacy of these models (McAvoy, 2012; see also Hoing et al., 2016). Greater public education is warranted to better inform the public of the potential of COSAs for improving reentry (Richards & McCartan, 2017).

Gender Responsive Programming

While scholars acknowledge the importance of gender responsive programming in reentry, there remains a dearth of literature regarding gendered strategies to sex offending and reentry. Women comprise approximately 10% of sex offense convictions in the U.S. (CSOM, 2007) and are most likely to offend against children, offend with a male co-defendant, and to have experienced sexual abuse and trauma as compared to individuals convicted on a non-sexual offense (Comartin, Burgess-Proctor, Kubiak, & Kernsmith, 2017; Levenson, Willis, & Prescott, 2015; Strickland, 2008; Wijkman, Bijleveld, & Hendriks, 2010).

Most treatment modalities implemented for individuals convicted of a sexual offense were developed for males. For example, risk assessment instruments have focused on male samples, but validating these instruments on female populations is challenging due to the low numbers (CSOM, 2007). Similarly, attention to gender-specific risk and protective factors has been limited, though scholars suggest the same factors associated with criminality in general for women may be associated with female sex offending (CSOM, 2007). More research in this area is sorely needed as more women are convicted of sex offenses and subject to restrictions and stigmatization.

Researchers have also documented women's unique experiences with a sex offense conviction. Tewksbury (2004) provided perspectives on 40 women on the Kentucky sex offender registry. Participants reported losing jobs, housing, social supports, and being harassed at similar rates of those found in men's studies (Tewksbury, 2004). In a study of females convicted of sex offenses in Florida, Klein and colleagues (2014) found women experienced increased alienation from prosocial supports, including family and community members, as a consequence of their sex offense conviction. Many women reported experiencing increased shame being on the sex offender registry (Tewksbury, 2004). This shame is likely linked to the public perceptions and stereotypes about women as more vulnerable, especially to co-offending with male partners (DeCou, Cole, Rowland, Kaplan, & Lynch, 2015). Many typologies, as well as the media, focus on women sex offending while in caregiver roles such as teacher or babysitter, thereby decreasing the perception of the behavior as criminal (CSOM, 2007; Hayes & Baker, 2014). This attitude neglects women's etiology of sex offending, victim's experiences, and potential for desistance.

Technology and Monitoring

Technology, including global positioning system (GPS) monitoring, electronic monitoring (EM), and internet and cell phone surveillance, has become a vital tool in community supervision. In fact, GPS monitoring has been legislated as part of the terms of community supervision for individuals convicted of a sex offense in a number of states (Padgett, Bales, & Blomberg, 2006; Turner, Chamberlain, Jennetta, & Hess, 2015), conveying to the public the idea that this "virtual prison" prohibits individuals from recidivating (Gies, 2015b, p. 1).

Evidence suggests that GPS monitoring has the potential to be effective in surveilling individuals with a sex offense conviction. For instance, Turner and colleagues (2015) compared GPS to traditional monitoring for parolees convicted of sex offenses in California. Those not assigned to GPS monitoring were 3 times more likely to abscond or fail to register, and 16% more likely to be convicted of a new crime. Similarly, in another California study, Gies and colleagues (2012) found parolees convicted of sex offenses who were not under GPS supervision were 3 times more likely to incur a sexually-related technical violation and 2 times more likely to be arrested than those under GPS supervision.

Despite evidence supporting the potential benefits of GPS monitoring, this type of surveillance has been criticized for being too pervasive, while not specifying whether it is a means of punishment, prevention, or control (Button, DeMichele, & Payne, 2009). Button, DeMichele, and Payne (2010) suggest the extent of lifetime registration and supervision laws means the net of those under GPS monitoring will continue to widen. Other critics suggest the unreliable technology results in increased workload for community corrections officials and difficulties for individuals under GPS supervision (Button et al., 2009; Payne & DeMichele, 2011). For example, Armstrong and Freeman (2011) found that up to 37% of alerts were caused by loss of signal or power disconnection. Overall, they find GPS alerts in response to non-violations take up "an inordinate amount of an agency's resources—resources that could be better directed to other case management activities" (Armstrong & Freeman, 2011, p. 180).

While proponents of GPS monitoring see it as a tool to implement constant supervision and deter potential criminal activity, this focus redirects attention away from rehabilitative efforts that may be more effective (Gies, 2015b). A review of EM for individuals convicted of sex offenses found little scientific research supporting this as a stand-alone practice; rather it is most efficacious with high-risk individuals when combined with a CBT component (Button et al., 2009). For example, a quasi-experimental study of EM in combination with an intensive CBT program found promising results for high-risk individuals (Bonta, Wallace-Capretta, & Rooney, 2000). Recidivism rates were 20% lower for high-risk individuals who received treatment as compared to controls.

Newer technological developments utilize mobile applications (apps) for tracking individuals convicted of sex offenses. For example, the National Sex Offender Public Website (NSOPW, 2016) created a smartphone app allowing members of the general public to search public registries for a person's name or by location. While the Adam Walsh Act (AWA) mandates the creation of a database with information about individuals convicted of sex offenses, 34 states have failed to meet these requirements due to implementation costs and doubts about effectiveness (Harris, Lobanov-Rostovsky, & Levenson, 2016b). Therefore, apps reflect incomplete data, resulting in an inaccurate depiction of registrant information (Mowlabocus, 2016). Scholars also suggest apps locating and identifying registrants fail to capture or abate risk as most victims are known to the offender (Mowlabocus, 2016). The difference between information and entertainment becomes less clear when the public uses these apps and are potentially relying on inaccurate information. Easy access to registry data potentially increases fear of sexual crime among residents who access these databases, furthering the "othering" of this population (Beck & Travis, 2004).

There is some evidence to support the utility of registration for sex offenses. In a survey of individuals convicted of sex offenses, one-third (33%) denoted that the restrictions increased their willingness to manage their risk, be more honest with themselves, and some indicated it decreased their access to potential victims (Levenson & Cotter, 2005). Additionally, contact with the criminal justice system can also bring people in contact with treatment services to which they may not otherwise have access. Currently, in many states in the U.S., reentry policies mandate in-prison and post-incarceration treatment attendance, including psychological evaluations, assessments, and individual and group therapy (see Gies, 2015b). These efforts, especially in conjunction with promising new treatment modalities like the GLM and reentry efforts like COSA, may do more to reform individuals convicted of sex offenses than the current surveillance-focused tactics.

New Developments in Sex Offender Registry Policy

Registries have been a primary contributor to the compounded stigma experienced by individuals convicted of sex offenses. Recently, there has been movement away from traditional registries that do not differentiate registrants by offense type. For example, the AWA required states to classify individuals convicted of sex offenses by tiers based on the nature of the crime, which makes comparison across states easier. However, most states have not implemented AWA as intended, and research suggests that the tiered system has done little to mitigate the negative experiences of individuals on the registry and increase the efficacy of cross-state comparison (Harris et al., 2016b). There is evidence that the use and scope of registries has continued to broaden. The following sections denote the use of the registries for juveniles and tribal groups as well as expansion outside of the U.S.

Juvenile Registries

Justice system responses to juveniles convicted of sexual offenses have garnered much attention. Estimates suggest that the majority of crimes (65%) for which juveniles are incarcerated are sexual offenses (Finkelhor & Ormrod, 2001), though the sexual recidivism rate is low. One meta-analysis followed 11,219 juveniles who committed sexual offenses over a 59-month period and found that only 7% committed a new sex offense while 43% recidivated for any crime (Caldwell, 2010; see also, Lussier & Cale, 2013). Consequently, more effort has been made to mitigate collateral consequences for juveniles convicted of sex offenses.

While the AWA has been revised to remove juveniles from public registries and offer registration relief, some juvenile sex offenses fall under lifetime registration requirements (Harris & Lobanov-Rostovsky, 2010). Currently, 38 states include juveniles on the registry, while the remaining 12 include only those convicted in adult court (Beitsch, 2015). Advocates of removing juveniles from registration cite research showing registered juveniles are more likely to be rearrested and convicted of new non-sexual crimes than their non-registered peers (Beitsch, 2015). Najdowski, Cleary, and Stevenson (2016) suggest juvenile registration for sexual offenses has little deterrent effect, as most adolescents are likely unaware of what registration entails. Those who are aware of the registration requirements are still likely not deterred due to various developmental issues including psychosocial immaturity and normalizing nonviolent sexual offenses.

Emerging research examines the collateral consequences experienced by youth convicted of sexual offenses. Hackett and colleagues (2015) interviewed 117 juveniles convicted of sex offenses regarding their experiences. Nearly 20% reported feeling they had no control over their offense information and who it would reach, and feared negative reactions from the local community. Harris and colleagues (2016), in a survey of youth treatment providers, found that most believe juveniles experience negative consequences and potential harm due to registration and notification requirements. Most providers noted that juveniles are mistreated by the criminal justice system, experience school problems such as having to switch or not attend school, and are forced to live in group homes due to their public registration. Additionally, a majority of providers believe notification requirements make juveniles more likely to experience mental health problems; feel shame, embarrassment, and loneliness; and experience harassment (Harris et al., 2016a). Continued research regarding juveniles who commit sex offenses, amid a shifting climate away from populist punitivism and the recognition of the deleterious effects of compounded stigmatization on minors, is warranted.

Tribal Registries

Another population of interest regarding sex offender registries and the collateral consequences of conviction are tribal registrants. Approximately 3 million U.S. citizens are Native American, yet there are relatively few statistics about the prevalence of sexual offending among this population (Wiseman, 2015). The U.S. Department of Justice (DOJ, 2000) finds Native Americans are 2.5 times more likely than any other race to be victims of sexual assault, and one out of three Native American women has reported being raped (Davis & Washburn, 2008). Thus, more comprehensive understanding of the incidence and prevalence of the consequences of sex offenses in Native American communities is needed.

The AWA included provisions for tribes to access the national and state-level sex offender registries. The Office of Sex Offender Sentencing, Monitoring, Apprehending, Registering, and Tracking (SMART) indicates 109 federally recognized tribes in 35 states have registry and notification laws. Participating tribes submit registrant biographical data, including biometrics, for inclusion in federal databases like the National Sex Offender Registry (NSOR) (Office of Justice Programs, "NASOM," n.d.). In August 2015, the DOJ initiated the Tribal Access Program for National Crime Information (TAP) allowing tribes access to national crime information so they can better protect and serve their communities. Tribes must comply with various auditing, policy, technical, personal, and physical requirements, as well as provide high-speed internet access and pay fees to the Federal Bureau of Investigation's (FBI) Criminal Justice Information Services (CJIS) for background checks on fingerprints and names. Tribes establish policy and procedure for what data are shared with law enforcement (Office of Justice Programs, "NASOM," n.d.).

The SMART Office's Native American Sex Offender Management (NASOM) offers assistance to tribes interested in creating their own registries (Office of Justice Programs, "NASOM," n.d.). Strides have been made in better documenting the prevalence of sexual offending on tribal lands, but little is known about the experience of those on the registries in tribal communities. As SMART engages tribal groups in management of Native Americans convicted of sex offenses, additional research is needed to better understand the specific needs of tribes in monitoring these individuals in their communities.

Registries in Other Countries

Sex offender registries have also grown globally. Since the U.S. implemented the first national sex offender registration law in 1994, 18 countries including Argentina, Australia, Bermuda, Canada, France, Germany, Ireland, Jamaica, Jersey, Kenya, Maldives, Malta, Pitcairn Islands, South Africa, South Korea, Taiwan, Trinidad & Tobago, and the UK have passed registry legislation (SMART, 2014). The nature of the registries and registration requirements vary widely. For example, the UK developed an assessment and three-tiered management system in the early 2000s for individuals who have committed sexual offenses. Level 1 involves management by a single agency for low to medium risk individuals; Level 2 uses multiple social service agencies to manage high to very high risk individuals; Level 3 is reserved for the "critical few" at risk for serious harm, and relies on multiple agencies and senior level oversight (Hudson, Taylor, & Henley, 2015, p. 59). Kenya passed legislation in 2006 requiring lifetime registration. The registry, which became public in 2012, includes information on the citizen's address, employment status and location, and school enrollment. France enacted its law in 2004, but without public disclosure of information. Individuals must register for 10 to 20 years depending on the offense, and verify and maintain their address.

Research has not been conducted on the efficacy of international registration laws, but there is evidence of growing public support for these types of controls. Australia implemented a national registry in 2004 with each territory and state also maintaining registries, and has taken measures to utilize this information to prevent sexual crimes (SMART, 2014). Australia recently proposed a law to revoke passports of registrants convicted of child sex offenses in an attempt to mitigate the growing child sex trade in Asia. If passed, this law would be the first of its kind worldwide, affecting 20,000 currently registered individuals living in Australia (Haag, 2017). Additional research regarding cultural differences in registry use and stigma experienced by registrants is needed.

Conclusion

Individuals convicted of sex offenses experience compounded stigma as a result of being doubly marked—first by their criminal record and second by their "sex offender" status, which is further reinforced by laws and restrictions. This compounded stigmatization is felt through myriad reentry aspects such as housing, employment, and social engagement, and the cumulative effects of these collateral consequences can lead to psychosocial distress and instability, ultimately impeding reintegration. Recent research suggests these complex post-conviction experiences impact the identity transformation process (to someone other than a "sex offender") and finally achieve desistance. To this end, we make several recommendations about how research, policy, and practice should advance.

First, scholars and policy makers should continue to reconsider the registration and registry requirements as a function of post-conviction remedies. Much research demonstrates the ineffectiveness of current policies aimed at addressing sexual recidivism and preventing sex offending (Chajewski & Mercado, 2009; Huebner et al., 2014; Levenson & Cotter, 2005; Socia, 2013), yet these remain central in containment strategies of individuals supervised for sex offense convictions.

Numerous efforts to improve the efficacy of policy and practice have been undertaken suggesting a slow shift in public and government support for evidence-based approaches in reintegrating individuals convicted of sex offenses. One shift has been the modification of AWA in response to research findings in order to improve management of individuals convicted of sex offenses. This is evidenced by removing registration requirements for juveniles convicted of certain sexual offenses, as well as providing support to tribal groups to address the problem of sex offending in their jurisdictions. States should work to comply with policies advanced by AWA, however, leading policy makers should continue to evaluate data of registrants, community members, and professionals working with this population to determine if the strategies are achieving intended goals.

While the U.S. serves as a model to other countries regarding legislation and an array of restrictions, legislators should heed the warnings of scholars about the challenges in legislating and implementing them, as well as identify realistic and evidence-based expectations about outcomes. As more countries work to address the issue of sexual offending within their borders, accompanying research needs to evaluate these policies and practices.

Second, as scholars and policy makers enhance the evidence base for effective practices regarding the management of individuals convicted of sex offenses in the community, more work remains in developing effective treatment modalities to support these moves. In particular, treatment programs should attend to the cognitive distortions linked with sex offending, alongside the post-conviction experience that may counter therapeutic gain. The compounded stigmatization experiences when returning to the community after a sex offense conviction should be considered in the development of these modalities. While the Good Lives Model (GLM) is a promising alternative to the current risk-focused programs, more theoretical work will inform how best to mitigate the negative experience of stigma upon conviction and in the face of the broad and long-lasting effects of collateral consequences.

Some international reentry models, like Circles of Support and Accountability (COSAs), have shown success by providing clients with the tools to address the stigma of a conviction through restorative justice principles. Rather than reserving post-conviction surveillance to registries and justice system actors, trained and supportive community could provide real time, and perhaps more impactful, assessments of a reentering individual's risk for reoffending. More importantly, and as new treatment modalities such as the GLM would emphasize, addressing the compounded stigmatization of being a sex offender by providing actual instrumental and emotional support may produce more efficacious outcomes than just addressing shame through strengths-building. That is, relying on both formal and informal support actors such as those in COSAs to redirect public shaming in positive ways might achieve better results.

In addition, integrating such community responses in reducing the stigma of being a "felon" and a "sex offender" with the use of new technology to surveil behavior in meaningful ways may provide a more comprehensive approach to attending to the very behaviors treatment and supervision aim to reduce. There remains room for additional research regarding technological advances in both efficacy and ethics. In particular, future research should explore the ways in which surveillance data are captured and used to better inform the supervision process and reduce erroneous alerts that currently add to staff's workload and individual stigma.

Finally, ongoing research should work to deepen our knowledge of sexual offending and offenders. At present, there are few longitudinal studies of post-conviction experiences of individuals with a sex offense conviction, so much remains to be learned about the etiology of sex offending behavior once detected, the long-term efficacy of treatment interventions, and desistance. Further, most studies investigate sex offending with male samples, neglecting the experience of women who commit sex offenses and their victims. As gender-responsiveness evolves in regard to general offending behavior, future research should consider how women might differ from men in risk and protective factors related to sex offending (refer to Northcutt Bohmert et al., Chapter 9).

The experience of compounded stigmatization may also be mitigated by reducing the universal application of sex offender laws, particularly registration and residency restrictions. The aim of such laws is to prevent harm to the public, and most individuals convicted of sex offenses agree this risk needs to be curbed (Huebner et al., 2013). While emerging policies work to reduce the number of juveniles present on the registry and provide continuity of designation among adult registrants, scholars suggest more work needs to be done in providing relief from registration for certain offenses or after certain periods of time. Overall, relief from effects of compounded stigmatization via public registries is the most pressing issue for returning citizens convicted of sex offenses.

In conclusion, the experience of compounded stigmatization by returning individuals convicted of sex offenses poses a threat to prosocial reentry and ultimately desistance. Current research and policy work suggests there is a trend to modify approaches by considering emerging findings about efficacy, theoretical developments, and learning from the lived experiences of returning individuals to better inform research, policy, and practice.

References

Armstrong, G. S., & Freeman, B. C. (2011). Examining GPS monitoring alerts triggered by sex offenders: The divergence of legislative goals and practical application in community corrections. *Journal of Criminal Justice, 39*, 175–182.

Bahr, S. J., Harris, L., Fisher, J. K., & Harker Armstrong, A. (2010). Successful reentry: What differentiates successful and unsuccessful parolees? *International Journal of Offender Therapy and Comparative Criminology, 54*(5), 667–692.

Beck, V.S., & Travis, L. F. (2004). Sex offender notification and fear of victimization. *Journal of Criminal Justice, 32*, 455–463.

Beitsch, R. (2015). *States slowly scale back juvenile sex offender registries*. Washington, DC: The Pew Charitable Trusts.

Bensel, T., & Sample, L. L. (2016). The influence of sex offender registration and notification laws on fostering collective identity among offenders. *Journal of Crime and Justice*, 1–15.

Berg, M. T., & Huebner, B. M. (2011). Reentry and the ties that bind: An examination of socialties, employment, and recidivism. *Justice Quarterly, 28*(2), 382–410.

Bonta, J., Wallace-Capretta, S., & Rooney, J. (2000). A quasi-experimental evaluation of an intensive rehabilitation supervision program. *Criminal Justice and Behavior, 27*(3), 312–329.

Braithwaite, J. (1989). *Crime, shame and reintegration*. Cambridge University Press.

Brown, K., Spencer, J., & Deakin, J. (2007). The reintegration of sex offenders: Barriers and opportunities for employment. *The Howard Journal of Criminal Justice, 46*(1), 32–42.

Burchfield, K. B., & Mingus, W. (2008). Not in my neighborhood: Assessing registered sex offenders' experiences with local social capital and social control. *Criminal Justice and Behavior, 35*(3), 356–374.

Burchfield, K. B., & Mingus, W. (2014). Sex offender reintegration: Consequences of the local neighborhood context. *American Journal of Criminal Justice, 39*(1), 109–124.

Button, D. M., DeMichele, M., & Payne, B. K. (2009). Using electronic monitoring to supervise sex offenders. *Criminal Justice Policy Review, 20*(4), 414–436.

Caldwell, M. F. (2010). Study characteristics and recidivism base rates in juvenile sex offender recidivism. *International Journal of Offender Therapy and Comparative Criminology, 54*(2), 197–212.

Call, C. (2016). The collateral consequences of sex offender management policies: Views from professionals. *International Journal of Offender Therapy and Comparative Criminology*. doi:0306624X16653978

Carson, E. A., & Anderson, E. (2016). Prisoners in 2015. *Bureau of Justice Statistics*. Office of Justice Programs. U.S. Department of Justice. NCJ250229, pp. 1–35.

Center for Sex Offender Management (CSOM). (2007). Retrieved from http://csom.org/

Chajewski, M., & Mercado, C. C. (2009). An evaluation of sex offender residency restriction functioning in town, county, and city-wide jurisdictions. *Criminal Justice Policy Review, 20*(1), 44–61.

Comartin, E. B., Burgess-Proctor, A., Kubiak, S., & Kernsmith, P. (2017). Factors related to co-offending and coerced offending among female sex offenders: The role of childhood and adult trauma histories. *Violence and Victims, 33*(1), 53–74.

Daly, K. (2008). Setting the record straight and a call for radical change: A reply to Annie Cossins on "restorative justice and child sex offences". *British Journal of Criminology, 48*(4), 557–566.

Davis, V., & Washburn, K. (2008). Sex offender registration in Indian country. *Ohio State Journal of Criminal Law, 6*(3), 3–23.

DeCou, C. R., Cole, T. T., Rowland, S. E., Kaplan, S. P., & Lynch, S. M. (2015). An ecological process model of female sex offending: The role of victimization, psychological distress, and life stressors. *Sexual Abuse, 27*(3), 302–323.

Dum, C. P. (2016). *Exiled in America: Life on the margins in a residential motel*. New York, NY: Columbia University Press.

Duwe, G. (2013). Can circles of support and accountability (COSA) work in the United States? Preliminary results from a randomized experiment in Minnesota. *Sexual Abuse, 25*(2), 143–165.

Duwe, G., Donnay, W., & Tewksbury, R. (2008). Does residential proximity matter? A geographic analysis of sex offense recidivism. *Criminal Justice and Behavior, 35*(4), 484–504.

Elisha, E., Idisis, Y., & Ronel, N. (2012). Window of opportunity: Social acceptance and life transformation in the rehabilitation of imprisoned sex offenders. *Aggression and Violent Behavior, 17*(4), 323–332.

Elliott, I. A., Beech, A. R., & Mandeville-Norden, R. (2013). The psychological profiles of internet, contact, and mixed internet/contact sex offenders. *Sexual Abuse*, *25*(1), 3–20.

English, K., Pullen, S. K., & Jones, L. (1997). *Managing adult sex offenders in the community: A containment approach*. Washington, DC: U.S. Department of Justice, Office of Justice Programs, National Institute of Justice.

Finkelhor, D., & Ormrod, R. (2001). Offenders incarcerated for crimes against juveniles. *Juvenile Justice Bulletin*. Office of Juvenile Justice and Delinquency Prevention. NCJ 191028, 14p.

Fox, K. J. (2014). Restoring the social: Offender reintegration in a risky world. *International Journal of Comparative and Applied Criminal Justice*, *38*(3), 235–256.

Gies, S., Gainey, R., Cohen, M., Healy, E., Duplantier, D., Yeide, M., Bekelman, A., Bobnis, A., & Hopps, M. (2012). *Monitoring high-risk sex offenders with GPS technology: An evaluation of the California supervision program final report*. Washington, DC: U.S. Department of Justice, National Institute of Justice.

Gies, S. V. (2015a). A tale of two studies: Lessons learned from GPS supervision in California corrections. *Corrections Today*, *77*(7), 20–22.

Gies, S. (2015b). GPS supervision in California: One technology, two contrasting goals. *NIJ Journal*, *275*, 10–17.

Göbbels, S., Ward, T., & Willis, G. M. (2012). An integrative theory of desistance from sex offending. *Aggression and Violent Behavior*, *17*(5), 453–462.

Greenfield, L. A. (1997). *Sex offenses and offenders: An analysis of data on rape and sexual assault*. Washington, DC: National Institute of Justice.

Haag, M. (2017, May 30). Australia plans to revoke child sex offenders' passports to combat sex tourism. *The New York Times*. Retrieved from www.nytimes.com/2017/05/30/world/australia/australia-passports-sex- trade. html?_r=0

Hackett, S., Masson, H., Balfe, M., & Phillips, J. (2015). Community reactions to young people who have sexually abused and their families: A shotgun blast, not a rifle shot. *Children & Society*, *29*(4), 243–254.

Hanson, R. K., & Bussiere, M. T. (1998). Predicting relapse: A meta-analysis of sexual offender recidivism studies. *Journal of consulting and clinical psychology*, *66*(2), 348.

Hanson, R. K., Gordon, A., Harris, A. J., Marques, J. K., Murphy, W., Quinsey, V. L., & Seto, M. C. (2002). First report of the collaborative outcome data project on the effectiveness of psychological treatment for sex offenders. *Sexual Abuse*, *14*(2), 169–194.

Hanson, R. K., Gordon, A., Harris, A. J., Marques, J. K., Murphy, W., Quinsey, V. L., & Seto, M. C. (2002). First report of the collaborative outcome data project on the effectiveness of psychological treatment for sex offenders. *Sexual Abuse*, *14*(2), 169–194.

Hanson, R. K., & Harris, A. J. (2000). Where should we intervene? Dynamic predictors of sexual offense recidivism. *Criminal Justice and Behavior*, *27*(1), 6–35.

Hanson, R. K., & Morton-Bourgon, K. E. (2005). The characteristics of persistent sexual offenders: A meta-analysis of recidivism studies. *Journal of Consulting and Clinical Psychology*, *73*(6), 1154.

Harris, A. J., Levenson, J. S., Lobanov-Rostovsky, C., & Walfield, S. M. (2016a). Law enforcement perspectives on sex offender registration and notification effectiveness, challenges, and policy priorities. *Criminal Justice Policy Review*. doi:0887403416651671

Harris, A. J., & Lobanov-Rostovsky, C. (2010). Implementing the Adam Walsh Act's sex offender registration and notification provisions: A survey of the states. *Criminal Justice Policy Review*, *21*(2), 202–222.

Harris, A. J., Lobanov-Rostovsky, C., & Levenson, J. S. (2016b). *Law enforcement perspectives on sex offender registration and notification: Supplemental report: Open-ended responses on policy recommendations*. Lowell, MA: University of Massachusetts Lowell.

Harris, A. J., Walfield, S. M., Shields, R. T., & Letourneau, E. J. (2016). Collateral consequences of juvenile sex offender registration and notification: Results from a survey of treatment providers. *Sexual Abuse*, *28*(8), 770–790.

Hayes, S., & Baker, B. (2014). Female sex offenders and pariah femininities: Rewriting the sexual scripts. *Journal of Criminology*, *2014*.

Hipp, J. R., Petersilia, J., & Turner, S. (2010). Parolee recidivism in California: The effect of neighborhood context and social service agency characteristics. *Criminology*, *48*(4), 947–979.

Höing, M. A., Petrina, R., Hare Duke, L., Völlm, B., & Vogelvang, B. (2016). Community support for sex offender rehabilitation in Europe. *European Journal of Criminology*, *13*(4), 491–516.

Hudson, K., Taylor, C., & Henley, A. (2015). Trends in the management of registered sexual offenders across England and Wales: A geographical approach to the study of sexual offending. *Journal of Sexual Aggression*, *21*(1), 56–70.

Huebner, B. M. (2005). The effect of incarceration on marriage and work over the life course. *Justice Quarterly*, *22*(3), 281–303.

Huebner, B. M., Bynum, T. S., Rydberg, J., Kras, K., Grommon, E., & Pleggenkuhle, B. (2013). *An evaluation of sex offender registry restrictions in Michigan and Missouri*. Washington, DC: National Institute of Justice.

11 Compounded Stigmatization

Huebner, B. M., Kras, K. R., Rydberg, J., Bynum, T. S., Grommon, E., & Pleggenkuhle, B. (2014). The effect and implications of sex offender residence restrictions. *Criminology & Public Policy, 13*(1), 139–168.

Jennings, W. G., Zgoba, K. M., & Tewksbury, R. (2012). A comparative longitudinal analysis of recidivism trajectories and collateral consequences for sex and non-sex offenders released since the implementation of sex offender registration and community notification. *Journal of Crime and Justice, 35*(3), 356–364.

Kim, B., Benekos, P. J., & Merlo, A. V. (2016). Sex offender recidivism revisited: Review of recent meta-analyses on the effects of sex offender treatment. *Trauma, Violence, & Abuse, 17*(1), 105–117.

Klein, J. L., Tolson, D., & Collins, C. (2014). Expressing strain: A qualitative evaluation of the testimonies of female sex offenders. *Journal of Qualitative Criminal Justice and Criminology, 2*, 119–147.

Kras, K. R., Pleggenkuhle, B., & Huebner, B. M. (2016). A new way of doing time on the outside: Sex offenders' pathways in and out of a transitional housing facility. *International Journal of Offender Therapy and Comparative Criminology, 60*(5), 512–534.

Kruttschnitt, C., Uggen, C., & Shelton, K. (2000). Predictors of desistance among sex offenders: The interaction of formal and informal social controls. *Justice Quarterly, 17*(1), 61–87.

Laws, D. R., & Ward, T. (2011). *Desistance from sex offending: Alternatives to throwing away the keys.* New York, NY: Guilford Press.

Levenson, J., Ackerman, A. R., Socia, K. M., & Harris, A. J. (2015). Where for art thou? Transient sex offenders and residence restrictions. *Criminal Justice Policy Review, 26*(4), 319–344.

Levenson, J. S. (2008). Collateral consequences of sex offender residence restrictions. *Criminal Justice Studies, 21*(2), 153–166.

Levenson, J. S., & Cotter, L. P. (2005). The effect of Megan's Law on sex offender reintegration. *Journal of Contemporary Criminal Justice, 21*(1), 49–66.

Levenson, J. S., D'Amora, D. A., & Hern, A. L. (2007). Megan's law and its impact on community re-entry for sex offenders. *Behavioral Sciences & the Law, 25*(4), 587–602.

Levenson, J. S., & Hern, A. L. (2007). Sex offender residence restrictions: Unintended consequences and community reentry. *Justice Policy and Research, 9*(1), 59–73.

Levenson, J. S., Willis, G. M., & Prescott, D. S. (2015). Adverse childhood experiences in the lives of female sex offenders. *Sexual Abuse, 27*(3), 258–283.

Lösel, F., & Schmucker, M. (2005). The effectiveness of treatment for sexual offenders: A comprehensive meta-analysis. *Journal of Experimental Criminology, 1*(1), 117–146.

Lussier, P., & Cale, J. (2013). Beyond sexual recidivism: A review of the sexual criminal career parameters of adult sex offenders. *Aggression and Violent Behavior, 18*(5), 445–457.

McAvoy, J. (2012). Birds of a feather? Irish public attitudes towards sex crime and sex offender reintegration. Is there a publically perceived scale of sexual deviance? (Unpublished master's thesis). Dublin Institute of Technology, Dublin.

Meloy, M., Curtis, K., & Boatwright, J. (2013). The sponsors of sex offender bills speak up: Policy makers' perceptions of sex offenders, sex crimes, and sex offender legislation. *Criminal Justice and Behavior, 40*(4), 438–452.

Mercado, C. C., Alvarez, S., & Levenson, J. (2008). The impact of specialized sex offender legislation on community reentry. *Sexual Abuse: A Journal of Research and Treatment, 20*(2), 188–205.

Mingus, W., & Burchfield, K. B. (2012). From prison to integration: Applying modified labeling theory to sex offenders. *Criminal Justice Studies, 25*(1), 97–109.

Mowlabocus, S. (2016). 'Y'all need to hide your kids, hide your wife': Mobile applications, risk and sex offender databases. *New Media & Society, 18*(11), 2469–2484.

Mustaine, E. E., Tewksbury, R., Connor, D. P., & Payne, B. K. (2015). Criminal justice officials' views of sex offenders, sex offender registration, community notification, and residency restrictions. *Justice System Journal, 36*(1), 63–85.

Mustaine, E. E., Tewksbury, R., & Stengel, K. M. (2006). Social disorganization and residential locations of registered sex offenders: Is this a collateral consequence? *Deviant Behavior, 27*(3), 329–350.

Najdowski, C. J., Cleary, H., & Stevenson, M. C. (2016). Adolescent sex offender registration policy: Perspectives on general deterrence potential from criminology and developmental psychology. *Psychology, Public Policy, and Law, 22*(1), 114.

National Center for Missing and Exploited Children (NCMEC). (2016). Retrieved from http://www.missing kids.com/ourwork/publications/exploitation/so-map

National Sex Offender Public Website (NSOPW). (2016). Retrieved from www.nsopw.gov/

Northcutt Bohmert, M., Duwe, G., & Hipple, N. K. (2016). Evaluating restorative justice circles of support and accountability: Can social support overcome structural barriers? *International Journal of Offender Therapy and Comparative Criminology, 62*(3), pp. 739–758.

Office of Justice Programs (2017). Office of Sex Offender Sentencing, Monitoring, Apprehending, Registering, and Tracking (SMART). Native American Sex Offender Management (NASOM) Project. Retrieved from www.smart.gov/nasom.htm

Office of Justice Programs. Office of Sex Offender Sentencing, Monitoring, Apprehending, Registering, and Tracking (SMART). Tribal Access Program (TAP). Retrieved from www.smart.gov/tap.htm

Office of Sex Offender Sentencing, Monitoring, Apprehending, Registering, and Tracking (SMART). (2014). Global overview of sex offender registration and notification systems. Retrieved from https://smart.gov/pdfs/GlobalOverview.pdf

Pager, D. (2003). The mark of a criminal record. *American Journal of Sociology*, *108*(5), 937–975.

Padgett, K. G., Bales, W. D., & Blomberg, T. G. (2006). Under surveillance: An empirical test of the effectiveness and consequences of electronic monitoring. *Criminology & Public Policy*, *5*(1), 61–91.

Payne, B. K., & DeMichele, M. T. (2010). Electronic supervision for sex offenders: Implications for work load, supervision goals, versatility, and policymaking. *Journal of Criminal Justice*, *38*(3), 276–281.

Payne, B. K., & DeMichele, M. (2011). Sex offender policies: Considering unanticipated consequences of GPS sex offender monitoring. *Aggression and Violent Behavior*, *16*(3), 177–187.

Petersilia, J. (2003). *When prisoners come home: Parole and prisoner reentry*. Oxford: Oxford University Press.

Pickett, J. T., Mancini, C., & Mears, D. P. (2013). Vulnerable victims, monstrous offenders, and unmanageable risk: Explaining public opinion on the social control of sex crime. *Criminology*, *51*(3), 729–759.

Richards, K., & McCartan, K. (2017). Public views about reintegrating child sex offenders via circles of support and accountability (COSA): A qualitative analysis. *Deviant Behavior*, 1–17.

Robbers, M. L. (2009). Lifers on the outside sex offenders and disintegrative shaming. *International Journal of Offender Therapy and Comparative Criminology*, *53*(1), 5–28.

Rolfe, S. M., Tewksbury, R., & Schroeder, R. D. (2016). Homeless shelters' policies on sex offenders: Is this another collateral consequence? *International Journal of Offender Therapy and Comparative Criminology*. doi:0306624X16638463

Rydberg, J., Grommon, E., Huebner, B. M., & Bynum, T. (2014). The effect of statewide residency restrictions on sex offender post-release housing mobility. *Justice Quarterly*, *31*(2), 421–444.

Schiavone, S. K., & Jeglic, E. L. (2009). Public perception of sex offender social policies and the impact on sex offenders. *International Journal of Offender Therapy and Comparative Criminology*, *53*(6), 679–695.

Schmucker, M., & Lösel, F. (2015). The effects of sexual offender treatment on recidivism: An international meta-analysis of sound quality evaluations. *Journal of Experimental Criminology*, *11*(4), 597–630.

Simon, J. (1998). Managing the monstrous: Sex offenders and the new penology. *Psychology, Public Policy, and Law*, *4*(1–2), 452.

Socia, K. (2016). Examining the concentration of registered sex offenders in upstate New York census tracts. *Crime & Delinquency*, *62*(6), 748–776.

Socia, K. M. (2013). Too close for comfort? Registered sex offender spatial clustering and recidivistic sex crime arrest rates. *Sexual Abuse*, *25*(6), 531–556.

Socia, K. M. (2014). Residence restrictions are ineffective, inefficient, and inadequate: So now what? *Criminology & Public Policy*, *13*(1), 179–188.

Socia, K. M., & Harris, A. J. (2016). Evaluating public perceptions of the risk presented by registered sex offenders: Evidence of crime control theater? *Psychology, Public Policy, and Law*, *22*(4), 375.

Socia, K. M., Levenson, J. S., Ackerman, A. R., & Harris, A. J. (2015). Brothers under the bridge: Factors influencing the transience of registered sex offenders in Florida. *Sexual Abuse*, *27*(6), 559–586.

Socia, K. M., & Stamatel, J. P. (2010). Assumptions and evidence behind sex offender laws: Registration, community notification, and residence restrictions. *Sociology Compass*, *4*(1), 1–20.

Spraitz, J. D., Frenzel, E. D., Bowen, K. N., Bowers, J. H., & Phaneuf, S. (2015). Adam Walsh Act compliance in Pennsylvania: What does the future hold? A research note. *Criminal Justice Policy Review*, *26*(3), 252–261.

Strickland, S. M. (2008). Female sex offenders exploring issues of personality, trauma, and cognitive distortions. *Journal of Interpersonal Violence*, *23*(4), 474–489.

Tewksbury, R. (2004). Experiences and attitudes of registered female sex offenders. *Federal Probation*, *68*, 30.

Tewksbury, R. (2005). Collateral consequences of sex offender registration. *Journal of Contemporary Criminal Justice*, *21*(1), 67–81.

Tewksbury, R., & Jennings, W. G. (2010). Assessing the impact of sex offender registration and community notification on sex-offending trajectories. *Criminal Justice and Behavior*, *37*(5), 570–582.

Tewksbury, R., Jennings, W. G., & Zgoba, K. M. (2012). A longitudinal examination of sex offender recidivism prior to and following the implementation of SORN. *Behavioral Sciences & the Law*, *30*(3), 308–328.

Tewksbury, R., & Lees, M. (2006). Perceptions of sex offender registration: Collateral consequences and community experiences. *Sociological Spectrum*, *26*(3), 309–334.

Tewksbury, R., & Levenson, J. (2009). Stress experiences of family members of registered sex offenders. *Behavioral Sciences & the Law, 27*(4), 611–626.

Tewksbury, R., & Mustaine, E. E. (2007). Collateral consequences and community re-entry for registered sex offenders with child victims: Are the challenges even greater? *Journal of Offender Rehabilitation, 46*(1–2), 113–131.

Tewksbury, R., & Zgoba, K. M. (2010). Perceptions and coping with punishment: How registered sex offenders respond to stress, internet restrictions, and the collateral consequences of registration. *International Journal of Offender Therapy and Comparative Criminology, 54*(4), 537–551.

Travis, J. (2005). *But they all come back: Facing the challenges of prisoner reentry.* Washington, DC: Urban Institute.

Turner, S., Chamberlain, A. W., Jannetta, J., & Hess, J. (2015). Goes GPS improve recidivism among high risk sex offenders? Outcomes for California's GPS pilot for high risk sex offender parolees. *Victims & Offenders, 10*(1), 1–28.

Visher, C. A., Knight, C. R., Chalfin, A., & Roman, J. K. (2009). *The impact of marital and relationship status on social outcomes for returning prisoners.* Washington, DC: Urban Institute.

Waldram, J. B. (2010). Moral agency, cognitive distortion, and narrative strategy in the rehabilitation of sexual offenders. *Ethos, 38*(3), 251–274.

Ward, T., & Gannon, T. A. (2006). Rehabilitation, etiology, and self-regulation: The comprehensive good lives model of treatment for sexual offenders. *Aggression and Violent Behavior, 11*(1), 77–94.

Western, B. (2002). The impact of incarceration on wage mobility and inequality. *American Sociological Review,* 526–546.

Wijkman, M., Bijleveld, C., & Hendriks, J. (2010). Women don't do such things! Characteristics of female sex offenders and offender types. *Sexual Abuse: A Journal of Research and Treatment, 22*(2), 135–156.

Willis, G. M., & Grace, R. C. (2008). The quality of community reintegration planning for child molesters' effects on sexual recidivism. *Sexual Abuse: A Journal of Research and Treatment, 20*(2), 218–240.

Willis, G. M., & Grace, R. C. (2009). Assessment of community reintegration planning for sex offenders: Poor planning predicts recidivism. *Criminal Justice and Behavior, 36*(5), 494–512.

Wilson, R. J., & McWhinnie, A. J. (2016). Circles of support & accountability: The role of the community in effective sexual offender risk management. In *Sexual Offending* (pp. 745–754). New York, NY: Springer.

Wilson, R. J., McWhinnie, A., Picheca, J. E., Prinzo, M., & Cortoni, F. (2007). Circles of support and accountability: Engaging community volunteers in the management of high-risk sexual offenders. *The Howard Journal of Crime and Justice, 46*(1), 1–15.

Wiseman, J. (2015). Incidence and prevalence of sexual offending. Washington, DC: U.S. Department of Justice, Office of Justice Programs.

Yates, P. (2004). Treatment of adult sexual offenders: A therapeutic cognitive-behavioural model of intervention. *Journal of Child Sexual Abuse, 12*(3–4), 195–232.

Zandbergen, P. A., Levenson, J. S., & Hart, T. C. (2010). Residential proximity to schools and daycares: An empirical analysis of sex offense recidivism. *Criminal Justice and Behavior, 37*(5), 482–502.

12

THE HIDDEN CONSEQUENCES OF VISIBLE JUVENILE RECORDS

Megan C. Kurlychek and Riya Saha Shah

> The juvenile court planners envisaged a system that would practically immunize juveniles from "punishment" for "crimes" in an effort to save them from youthful indiscretions and stigmas due to criminal charges or convictions.
> —*In re Gault, 387. S. 1, 60 (1967) (J. Black concurring)*

The Basis for Confidentiality in the Early Juvenile Court

Before the first juvenile court was founded in Chicago in 1899, marking a new way of treating children under the law,[1] youth misconduct was traditionally treated as equivalent to adult crime. Legal scholar William Blackstone described a formula for determining culpability for youth who commit crimes.[2] Children under age 7 were presumed incapable of criminal intent and therefore immune from liability in the justice system and children above age 14 were treated as adults under the law—subject to the same procedures and punishments (Thompson & Morris, 2016).

Advocates of the juvenile court movement were "appalled by adult procedures and penalties, and by the fact that children could be given long prison sentences."[3] Therefore, rather than imposing adult penalties and process on young people who were accused of misconduct, the juvenile court system was established as a separate and more paternalistic system for youth charged with criminal offenses. Grounded in the belief that juvenile misconduct was attributable to the environment or heredity more than choice, the court sought to "spare juveniles from the harsh proceedings in adult court" and "the stigma of being branded criminal" (Office of Juvenile Justice and Delinquency Prevention, 1997). Rather, the court embraced a less punitive and more therapeutic approach.

Keeping confidential the records of a less-than-culpable child was essential to a regime of rehabilitation. This meant that juvenile proceedings generally were closed to the public, records of juvenile crime were not disseminated or disclosed beyond what was necessary to provide supervision and rehabilitation to the child, and the child could be released from court without the stigma of criminality. The early founders of the court thought this important because without confidentiality, the public might brand a delinquent child as a criminal and stymie the youth's readjustment in the community (Henning, 2004).[4] In envisioning the ideal system, Julian Mack, one of the first judges to preside over a juvenile court, wrote:

> To get away from the notion that the child is to be dealt with as a criminal; to save it from the brand of criminality, the brand that sticks to it for life; to take it in hand and instead of first stigmatizing and then reforming it, to protect it from the stigma.
>
> (Mack, 1909)

Here we see not only the notion of rehabilitation protecting the child from the punitive nature of the adult system at the core of the juvenile courts, but also the realization that a criminal record, and the stigma that accompanies it, are indeed a form of a life sentence.

The notion of stigma, first developed by sociologist Erving Goffman, refers to any feature of an individual being physically or socially constructed that causes others to judge and shun the given individual (Goffman, 2009). This concept has been widely accepted by criminologists, particularly through labeling theory, which focuses on how the label of "criminal" breaks down traditional social bonds and opportunities to form such bonds as the label becomes a formal stigma separating the "delinquent" youth from normal youth. One of the earliest renditions of labeling theory was presented in 1938 by Frank Tannenbaum. In his book, *Crime and the Community*, Tannenbaum objected to the dichotomy that youth who commit delinquent acts or who are adjudicated delinquent for such acts by the courts are in some way fundamentally different from other youths. He called this the dualistic fallacy. According to Tannenbaum, youth are often at odds with the adults in their community for things as simple as playing music too loud or hanging out. As conflicts between young people and adults grow, the adults tend to think of the children themselves as bad rather than disapproving of their behaviors. Through this process he called the "dramatization of evil," the label of "bad" is transferred from the act to the young person (Tannenbaum, 1938).

Such a label is not without consequence of its own. Writing some 13 years later, Edwin Lemert developed these early ideas into a formal labeling theory proposing the ideas of primary deviance—those adolescent mistakes all youth make—and secondary deviance—that deviance that occurs after someone internalizes the label of delinquent or "evil" put upon them by society. Thus the label becomes a self-fulfilling prophecy (Lemert, 1951).

The popularity of these theories during the 1960s and 1970s led to the extension of even further protections to youth and provided the framework for the evolution of record sealing and expungement statutes (Funk, 1996). Thus, in addition to a youth being spared the onus of an adult criminal record through juvenile court processing, the juvenile court record could be officially sealed from view, or even expunged upon reaching the age of maturity. In this way the youth could avoid "an eternal blot on [the] youth's record because of an immature, impulsive act" (Snow, 1992).

In addition to state efforts to further protect the confidentiality of juvenile records, the ABA adopted formal juvenile justice standards recommending that access to, and the use of, juvenile records be strictly controlled to limit the risk that disclosure would result in the misuse or misinterpretation of information or the unnecessary denial of opportunities and benefits to youth.[5]

The Erosion of Confidentiality

Despite these philosophical, legal, and theoretical concerns about acquiring a criminal record at such a young age that were entwined with the development of the juvenile court and its policies, the juvenile court was not immune from political influence and indeed as our nation entered into a proposed "war on drugs" and "war on crime" the juvenile court and its practices of confidentiality were about to come under attack. These attacks came in three distinct waves, each of which played a particular role in the erosion of the confidentiality of juvenile court records.

Wave 1: State Policy Choice Versus Constitutional Protection

Early criticisms of confidentiality noted the juvenile court's lack of due process. The ideal of rehabilitation had manifested in a court philosophy of *parens patriae*, which translates as state as father, in which the court operated in an informal, non-adversarial fashion with the primary focus of the proceeding as determining the best interests of the child (Nelson, 1998). Reformers believed that when the court acted in this capacity there was no risk of a young person being deprived of life, liberty, or property, and therefore due process protections such as the right to an attorney and the right against self-incrimination were not needed (Blum, 1996). In fact, it was argued that such procedural protections could obstruct the court's efforts to act in a child's best interest.

However, when the juvenile court failed to reach its idealistic goals of protection and rehabilitation, the system was challenged in a set of court cases that has come to be known as the Due Process Movement (Bernard & Kurlychek, 2010). The landmark Supreme Court case to begin this movement was *In re Gault*.[6] While this case is probably best known for granting certain due process rights to juveniles—such as the right to counsel and the opportunity to confront witnesses—the Court also reasoned that due process protections were not only consistent with the purpose of the juvenile court but could work in concert with the need to protect the confidentiality of juvenile proceedings.[7] The court reasoned that "the policy of the juvenile law is to hide youthful errors from the full gaze of the public and bury them in the graveyard of the forgotten past."[8] However, even the Court saw this claim as problematic.

> [t]his claim of secrecy, however, is more rhetoric than reality. Disclosure of court records is discretionary with the judge in most jurisdictions. Statutory restrictions almost invariably apply only to the court records, and even as to those the evidence is that many courts routinely furnish information to the FBI and the military, and on request to government agencies and even to private employers. Of more importance are police records. In most States the police keep a complete file of juvenile 'police contacts' and have complete discretion as to disclosure of juvenile records. Police departments receive requests for information from the FBI and other law-enforcement agencies, the Armed Forces, and social service agencies, and most of them generally comply. Private employers word their application forms to produce information concerning juvenile arrests and court proceedings, and in some jurisdictions information concerning juvenile police contacts is furnished private employers as well as government agencies.[9]

In the next decade, the Court revisited the issue of confidentiality, characterizing it as a state "policy interest," and not a constitutional right.[10] Thereafter, a series of First Amendment cases further reduced children's interest in confidentiality with the Court deciding that confidentiality could not prevent journalists from publishing sensitive information about juvenile matters, as long as the information was lawfully obtained.[11] By formally establishing that confidentiality of juvenile court records is a privilege given by states and not a constitutional right, and by allowing for the lawful release and use of such records in the cases noted above, the Supreme Court, "paved the way for states to rescind their earlier promises to protect juveniles from social stigmas" (Blum, 1996).

Wave 2: The Get Tough Movement

In the late 1980s and early 1990s, a second wave of attacks on the juvenile justice system arose from "concerns about deteriorating public safety and the need for accountability" (Henning, 2004). A stark increase in juvenile violence, and particularly homicides committed by youth, in certain inner cities in America sparked the notion of a national juvenile crime wave (Snyder & Sickmund,

1999). The media further fanned these flames promoting an image of a new breed of "juvenile super predator" as a sociopathic youth with no moral conscience (Dilulio, 1995). The public perceived the increase in serious crime by juveniles as a failure of the policies of the juvenile court (Melli, 1996; Rossum, 1995). Legislators and policy makers took a new stance to "get tough" on juvenile crime that led to a greater number of youth being tried in the adult criminal justice system, resulting in the complete availability of the records of their criminal conduct as well as an assault on many of the rehabilitative policies of the juvenile court, including the confidentiality of records (Torbet, Gable, Montgomery, & Hurst, 1996). In addition, states began modifying the preambles to their juvenile codes to diminish the prominence of rehabilitation and reflect a greater emphasis on accountability and punishment (Feld, 1988). As one scholar noted,

> The juvenile court's original commitment to rehabilitation and protection of minors had been eclipsed by commitment to community protection and the 'public's right to know.' Support for forgiving and forgetting juvenile misconduct had significantly diminished, while support for governmental and judicial transparency had significantly increased.
>
> (Jacobs, 2013)

Wave 3: The War on Terror

In 2001, after the terror attacks in New York City on September 11, state policies reflected the fear of the unknown. Across the country, state legislatures enacted provisions in their codes to create transparency, open records, and share information broadly. At this time, the juvenile justice system experienced yet another attack to confidentiality. More states lessened protections afforded to minors, and the number of FBI background checks increased significantly. Law enforcement began collecting and disseminating more information under a philosophy of the public's right to know. These efforts were aided by the rise of the digital information age that "makes possible the collection, classification and retrieval of vastly more information than the juvenile court founders could have imagined" (Jacobs, 2013).[12]

As accountability was the rhetoric of the Get Tough era, public safety was the new catch phrase of the War on Terror. This new language vastly overshadowed rehabilitation as the guiding principle of juvenile court. Under this final attack, confidentiality lost its critical role in the juvenile justice system (Henning, 2004). The myth underlying this public sentiment was that youth who break the law would undoubtedly commit other crimes in the future, even if they have no prior record. Almost 20% of people believe a youth is "almost certain" to re-offend, another 50% believe a youth will "probably" re-offend (Soler, 2001). Thus, states moved toward opening juvenile proceedings to the public and limiting the universal confidentiality protections once enjoyed by youth in juvenile court (Henning, 2004; Torbet et al., 1996). States also began moving toward the increased collection of juvenile DNA and fingerprint information and greater accessibility to juvenile record information by law enforcement, the media, and schools.[13] At last count, a recent study also showed that at least thirty-three states and the District of Columbia have statutory provisions allowing for the release of otherwise confidential juvenile record information to school personnel (Juvenile Law Center, 2014).

The Consequences of a Visible Record

The original philosophy and policies were meant to shield youth from the potential negative impacts of having a criminal record. Perhaps what is, or should be, most concerning is that at the very same time these protections were, and are, eroding, the consequences of having a record are also becoming more severe. These consequences go far beyond criminal justice system processing—such as sentence enhancements based on prior records—to infiltrate almost every aspect of social life. Often referred to as the collateral consequences of a criminal record, the social stigma, sanctions, and exclusion that accompany a visible criminal record have been coined "The Punishment Without End" (Butts & Mitchell, 2000) and represent one of today's most prominent social stigmas (Goffman, 2009). In the following sections we detail some of the most prominent impacts the label of criminal can have on these young individuals.

Education

Primary and Secondary Education

Our nation has come to rely on public education as the backbone of our economy by preparing youth for entry into the labor market. While the system was originally developed to provide education to poor children and children of immigrants who could not afford private education, the system evolved over the centuries to include all youth, regardless of socio-economic class, race, or ethnicity (Cremin, 1961). However, school outcomes have been far from equal across these groups with research showing that immigrant youth, youth of color, and youth from lower socio-economic backgrounds are more at risk of school failure and drop out (Wiggan, 2007). These poor outcomes can lead these same vulnerable populations to be the most at risk of obtaining a juvenile record, which can be released to the child's school, adding yet another layer of disadvantage (Leone, Christle, Nelson, Skiba, Frey, & Jolivette, 2003; Lynam, Moffitt, & Stouthamer-Loeber, 1993).

The self-fulfilling prophecy suggested by labeling theory (Lemert, 1951) can be replicated in schools when juvenile record information is readily made available to school personnel. These youth may first face challenges early on at school due to their poor home environment (Cohen, 1955). These challenges may lead the youth to fall behind in school and ultimately to delinquency (Lynam et al., 1993). In an almost ironic fashion, this school failure and delinquency then leads to further school failure and delinquency (Elliott & Voss, 1974; Thornberry et al., 1985). From a justice system perspective, these same processes are perhaps better known as the "school to prison pipeline" (Kim, Losen, & Hewitt, 2010; Wald & Losen, 2003).

This pattern of development is perhaps best theoretically presented by John Laub and Robert Sampson in their depiction of the age-graded theory of crime (Sampson & Laub, 1995). This theory proposes that each youth is born into certain structural features of society such as their gender, race, and family's social economic status, and these factors can impact early school development and the accumulation of pro-social bonds (Hirschi, 1969). If the youth, due to these structural characteristics and the challenges faced, fails to attach to school and positive peers this can lead to a cycle of delinquency that further limits opportunity and the development of pro-social bonds, which in turn spurs more delinquency. While Lemert (1951) would have proposed that this later, or secondary deviance, was due to the acceptance of the deviant label, the age-graded theory proposes a slightly different etiology that places a greater emphasis on the exclusion of the youth from pro-social opportunities. Thus, the youth is more pushed into crime through social exclusion than actively choosing to continue on a path of delinquency (Sampson & Laub, 2005).

Despite this important function of primary and secondary education in the lives of American youth and the suggested heightened importance of inclusion, it is perhaps here that the deviant label has its first and more significant impact. One of the most common exceptions to confidentiality of juvenile court records is their release to school personnel. At least thirty-three states and the District of Columbia have statutory provisions allowing for the release of *otherwise confidential* juvenile court records to school personnel. [14]

However, the criteria for release vary drastically across states. Some states, such as Mississippi and Kentucky, allow access to records for nearly all crimes to any school employee with very little protection offered to the student as to how these records will be stored and used. [15] Other states have more strict requirements for access. For example, Indiana's statute allows for juvenile records to only be released to the school superintendent or administrator upon written request. The request must be reviewed by the court, and it must be determined that the information requested is necessary for the school to serve the educational needs of the juvenile or to protect the safety or health of students and employees.[16] Some states also restrict how long the information can be retained by the school or how is can be used.[17]

The release of juvenile record information to schools has several potential negative consequences from the stigmatization of the youth and differential treatment by administrators and educators to the actual suspension and expulsion of the student. For example, in Washington State authorities are required to inform the school if a student is arrested for any of the following:

- a violent offense as defined in RCW 9.94A.030;
- a sex offense as defined in RCW 9.94A.030;
- inhaling toxic fumes under chapter 9.47A RCW;
- a controlled substance violation under chapter 69.50 RCW;
- a liquor violation under RCW 66.44.270; and
- any crime under RCW's 9.41 (firearms), 9A.36 (assault), 9A.40 (kidnapping), 9A.46 (harassment), and 9A.48 (arson).

Upon notification the school is required to consider disciplinary action, which can include long-term suspension or expulsion. And Washington is not alone. Missouri law allows schools to suspend or expel students who were charged with a felony, even if they are not convicted of the offense.[18] And North Carolina permits schools to suspend or expel students charged, convicted, or adjudicated delinquent of a criminal offense or an offense that would be criminal if they were an adult regardless of where the offense occurred.[19]

Importantly, in most states the release of juvenile record information to schools does not depend on whether the offense occurred on school property or has any implication on the young person's school attendance or progress. This blurring of the line between school discipline and court action may further perpetuate the school to prison pipeline.

Post-Secondary Education

The impact of justice system involvement does not end with high school. The impact of a juvenile or adult criminal record can have lasting educational implications beyond secondary school. A recent survey found that more than half of universities collect criminal justice information during the admissions process.[20] As of 2006, the Common Application, which is used by more than 600 schools across the country, began asking applicants to disclose their past adjudications and convictions.

Another survey of 273 colleges and universities conducted by the Center for Community Alternatives found that although a majority of schools reported collecting and using criminal history information in their acceptance process (66%), less than half of these schools that collect and use criminal justice information have written policies in place to guide decision-making and only 40% had any training for staff on how to use or interpret such information. In addition, it was reported that a broad array of adjudications/convictions, including drug and alcohol convictions, misdemeanor convictions, and youthful offender adjudications, negatively impact the acceptance decision (Weismann et al., 2010).

Because obtaining a higher education degree is so important to successful labor market participation in today's economy, denying individuals such opportunities based on youthful misconduct can set them up for a lifetime of failure. Moreover, even if the youth can gain admission to college, there are another set of barriers when attempting to pay for this education. For example, youth can be temporarily barred from receiving federal financial aid for college if convicted of certain drug-related offenses. Although this restriction is imposed only upon individuals with drug convictions in the adult criminal justice system, not for records of juvenile adjudications, it nevertheless affects many young people. During the Get Tough movement described above, laws were amended to transfer the prosecution of young people charged with drug offenses to the adult system. Youth of color as well as youth who live in urban areas are more likely to be subject to continuous law enforcement patrol, making it more likely that police will detect this behavior (Saul, 2016). Felony drug charges are disproportionately imposed on young people of color, and therefore this particular bar on financial aid for individuals convicted of drug offenses has a disproportionate effect on the ability of young people of color to attain a college education.

Employment

The blight of an early criminal record does not end with limited education but follows the individual into the employment sector. While criminal background screenings have been traditionally conducted for certain types of public positions in society such as police officer or teacher, the information age has ushered in a newfound ease of conducting such checks, which, in turn, has led to more and more employers adopting screening mechanisms regardless of the duties of the job for which the individual is to be hired (Bushway, Briggs, Taxman, Tanner, & Van Brakle, 2007). For example, a survey by Holzter (Holzer, Raphael, & Stoll, 2006) found that upwards of half of all companies surveyed indicated that they perform a criminal background check before hiring an individual and another study found that almost 80% of the nation's largest companies reported performing such checks (Burke, 2004). Even when compared to other traditionally stigmatized labor market groups, such as individuals on welfare, those with less than college education, or job applicants with gaps in employment, employers express the strongest aversion to hiring individuals who have criminal records.

In some cases this aversion is "informal" and can be hidden as discretion, and in other cases it reflects actual laws or mandates against hiring individuals with criminal backgrounds for certain positions. For example, individuals with felony convictions are prohibited from more than 800 occupations due to laws and licensing rules (NELP, 2015; Wright, 2003), and many others are disqualified from employment in licensed or professional occupations such as jobs in health care, public sector employment, or working with vulnerable populations (EEOC, 2012). Although these prohibitions typically only apply to adult convictions, young people with juvenile records are nevertheless routinely denied similar opportunities. In many cases, individual advocacy is required to educate licensing boards to look past a young person's juvenile adjudication.

This literature also points to racial disparities in employment based on screening by criminal records. An audit study examined the behavior of employers who were presented résumés from graduate students posing as potential employees who were the same in every aspect except for the fact that one set of résumés indicated a criminal record and the other did not found that the mark of the criminal record served as more of a hindrance to employment for minority males when compared to white males (Pager, 2003).

In response to this growing use of criminal records in employment decisions and the potential of such practices to discriminate against protected populations, the EEOC promulgated new guidelines in 2012 to limit the ability of employers to employ blanket bans against the employment of individuals with a criminal record and to instead require individualized assessments (EEOC, 2012). These assessments are to consider age at the first offense, time since last offense, and evidence of rehabilitation, among other things.

While much of this information is commonly discussed when addressing reentry of adult offenders, it is often overlooked when thinking about the impact of a juvenile record as not all juveniles seek work and some even believe that work for youth can be counterproductive to their staying in school (National Research Council, 1998). However, there is a growing body of evidence showing that jobs are important for youth because they not only help to better prepare them for the adult labor force, but they actually can reduce delinquency, particularly formal work that provides hours of structured and supervised activity (Apel, Paternoster, Bushway, & Brame, 2006; Apel, Bushway, Paternoster, Brame, & Sweeten, 2008; Osgood, 1999).

However, youth with records seeking employment are at a double disadvantage. They have often not yet even formally entered the labor market before the stigma of their record attaches. Thus, while potential employers often consider experience, education, and other references in their employment decisions, and such factors might help to counterbalance a criminal record, a youth with a criminal record may be prevented from ever gaining such experience and education in the first place. Moreover, the very factors suggested to be considered by the EEOC, such as age at offense and time since last offense, suggest that it may be a long time until these youth are viewed as "redeemed" and ready for employment.

The inability of a youth to enter the labor market can have major consequences for the individual youth as well as for society. Research clearly shows a link between unemployment and crime. For example, research indicates that youth who work are more likely to finish school and less likely to be delinquent (Apel et al., 2007). From a life course perspective, Sampson and Laub (Laub & Sampson, 1993; Sampson & Laub, 1993; Sampson & Laub, 2003) assert that adult social bonds such as employment and marriage can be key turning points in an individual's life that help him/her desist from crime. Thus, by making a juvenile's youthful transgressions public and using these records to limit the opportunity to begin forming adult social bonds such as employment, these policies are actually making society less safe by promoting criminality over desistance. Employment or the ability to gain employment during the transition to adulthood may be a key factor in promoting desistance. For example, one study also found a direct link between the ability to find employment and desistance from delinquency. In a study of youth in a community-based reentry program in a large urban county in the Western U.S., Abrams and colleagues found that over half of individuals between the ages of 18 and 25 with former juvenile justice system involvement who were unemployed reported at least one new conviction in the adult system, compared to only 28% of similar individuals in that age bracket with part- or full-time employment (Abrams, Terry, & Franke, 2011). Using data from the National Longitudinal Survey of Youth, Apel and Sweeten also find that youth who are incarcerated at a young age are less likely to participate in the formal job market and more likely to have illegal earnings and unstable employment (Apel & Sweeten, 2010). Using the same data, another study finds these instabilities continue across a young person's lifespan impacting the formation of the adult social bonds of both employment and marriage (Huebner, 2005).

Housing

Just as employers are afforded latitude to protect their interests so are landlords allowed to deny housing based on criminal background. In the case of publicly assisted housing, federal law permits denial of subsidized housing for three categories of individuals:

1. those who have been evicted from subsidized housing because of drug-related activity are ineligible for a three-year period from the date of their eviction,
2. any household member who is subject to a lifetime registration requirement under a state sex offender registration program is permanently banned, and
3. any individual convicted of manufacturing or producing methamphetamine on the premise of federally assisted housing is permanently banned.

In addition, the law allows the local public housing authority the right to ban other applicants based on criminal history with no guidance or restrictions on what information can be utilized. While no formal studies of this process were found, anecdotal evidence suggests that it is commonplace for such housing authorities to deny applicants for any criminal record (Bradley, Oliver, Richardson, & Slayter, 2001).

Moreover, the United States Supreme Court has upheld Public Housing Authorities' abilities to evict residents based on not only their criminal records, but the offenses of their relatives. Thus, if a child receives a juvenile adjudication, especially for a drug or sex offense, the entire family may be prevented from seeking public housing and/or may be evicted from their current housing.[21] In some situations the family can only receive housing if the child lives elsewhere. This policy can lead to the breakup of families and even homelessness, both which can have deleterious outcomes for not only the youth, but the entire family.

As such, these policies thus go against everything known to psychological and sociological literature on the importance of family attachments and stability. The formation of strong attachment to parents and family is key to successful adolescent development (Hirschi, 1969), and the breakdown of social bonds is also highly correlated with the emergence of and persistence in delinquency (Glueck & Glueck, 1950; Sampson & Laub, 1993; Li, 2004; Wright et al., 1999).

As bleak as the situation may be in public housing, it can be worse for private housing. First and foremost, if the individual is not able to find employment as he/she transitions to adulthood, it is difficult to even afford any private housing option. Second, private landlords may deny housing based on any evidence of a criminal record and there are no existing regulations on what questions can be asked or what information considered on a private rental application. While there is no database that formally assesses the practices of private landlords a 2005 survey of landlords of multi-housing units found that 80% of private landlords reported asking questions about criminal histories on their rental applications (Delgado, 2005).

Other Impacts

Although there are a myriad of additional negative consequences that accompany a criminal record, this article highlights the salient ones that have significant immediate and long-lasting implications for youths. Other consequences not touched on deeply include the loss of driving privileges, which can prevent young people from working or attending school, and implications for naturalization of immigrant youth. For example, a juvenile adjudication can be used to deny U.S. citizenship to an immigrant youth as the applicant is required to be of good moral character. Current law allows the attorney general to consider juvenile adjudications as indicators of moral character.[22]

Notably, the vast amount of collateral consequences attendant to juvenile or criminal convictions exist without empirical research demonstrating that retention of records or public availability of records actually increases public safety. Rather, the research that is available suggests that they work to create a lasting stigma on the individual and erect barriers to productive civic involvement. In line with labeling theory, the criminal history record can act as a "brand of inferiority" that literally works to exclude the individual from mainstream society and instead lock the individual into a life of crime (Kessler, 2015). With the ever-increasing availability and use of records to enact such consequences, one scholar has called this the "perfect storm" of collateral consequences (Bell, 2014). It would seem then as a society we should be interested in removing the stigma of a criminal record from individuals, particularly our societies youngest and most vulnerable.

Removing the Stigma

Return to Confidentiality

One of the key philosophies behind the origin of the juvenile court was confidentiality to ensure youth move past their court involvement to become productive citizens. While this philosophy was based on observation of youthful behavior and common sense, recent scientific evidence further supports that adolescent brains are different than adult brains and that their behavior as a youth is not necessarily indicative of the adult they will become.

For example, research on adolescent brain development finds that the left frontal cortex of the brain does not fully develop until around age 21 for females and age 24 for males (Lenroot & Giedd, 2006). This is responsible for rational decision-making and impulse control. This is the first purely scientific evidence that juveniles are not capable of the type of rational choice upon which our adult system of justice is so heavily premised. Without the ability to reason in an adult-like function, research shows that adolescents' decision-making is controlled by the amygdala, which is the part of the brain responsible for emotions (Baird, Johnathon, & Fugelsang, 2004). These studies were the first to suggest that there are clear biological reasons youth may not be as responsible or culpable for their actions as adults.

Research further demonstrates that these differences lead young people to make decisions that are clearly different than adults in notable ways. First, their decision-making is characterized by a short temporal focus, making them less likely to understand long-term consequences of their actions. Second, in social situations they have been found to be more likely to be highly influenced by their peers than adults (Steinberg & Cauffman, 1996).

This research has been widely accepted by the court system, most notably in a series of landmark juvenile cases before the United States Supreme Court. [23] The logic underpinning the United States Supreme Court decisions in the death penalty and life sentencing cases should apply to youth with juvenile records as well. Youth are incapable of making decisions based on reason and forethought of the consequences attendant to their actions. They act impulsively and without regard for the risks involved. While they must be held accountable for their actions, they need not be denied the opportunity to demonstrate their growth beyond that moment in time. That is, we suggest a return to the logic and wisdom of the progressives in the founding of the juvenile court and the confidential nature of its handling of youth.

The American Bar Association recently adopted a policy consistent with this principle addressing the collateral consequences facing individuals adjudicated delinquent or convicted of a crime:

> Laws, rules, regulations and policies that require disclosure of juvenile adjudications can lead to numerous individuals being denied opportunities as an adult based upon a mistake(s) made when they were a child. The ABA recognizes the language used by the United States Supreme Court in *Roper v. Simmons*, 543 U.S. 551 that children are different than adults because of: 'A lack of maturity and an underdeveloped sense of responsibility are found in youth more often than in adults and are more understandable among the young. These qualities often result in impetuous and ill-considered actions and decisions.' Therefore, the ABA is recommending that the collateral consequences of committing a crime as a youth be severely reduced by reducing barriers to education and vocational opportunities because of a juvenile incident. Furthermore there should be limited exceptions that only exist when the incident is directly relevant to the position sought or a concern of a school.[24]

However, today, only ten states fully protect the confidentiality of juvenile records as originally intended by the court and as promoted by legal, medical, and sociological evidence.[25] Moreover, given that the current political climate may not be supportive of a logical and scientific approach to justice, we suggest that states enact laws that provide for the sealing and expungement of juvenile records and/or restrict the ability of schools, employers, landlords, and others to utilize such records to discriminate against individuals with juvenile records.

Sealing/Expunging

Sealing generally refers to the practice by which the court keeps a record on a youthful arrest, adjudication, or conviction, but the record is "sealed" from the view of most individuals in the public, including landlords, employers, and educators. The records can however often be used for criminal justice purposes such as sentencing enhancements and counts of prior records depending on state policy. Expungement is a step further in which the actual record is destroyed and cannot be viewed by anyone or used for any purpose against the accused or convicted individual. Most states maintain at least some provision by which juvenile records can be sealed from view and/or expunged after a given time period. For example, New York maintains confidentiality of juvenile court records, and even for youth processed in adult court, if the offense was committed before his/her 19th birthday the judge can offer a "Youthful Offender Seal" at the time of adjudication.[26] Unfortunately, there is often a lengthy waiting period, and in many cases the youth must apply for the sealing or expungement, and in some cases even have legal representation and/or pay a fee (SEARCH, 2010).

Because of the vast immediate and lifelong consequences of juvenile records, states should seal most juvenile records from view to anyone outside of the immediate juvenile justice system or workers treating the youth and provide for their swift and barrier-free expungement. A 2014 Report by Juvenile Law Center recommended that states should "ensure that access to juvenile record information is limited to individuals connected to the case" [27] and provide for automatic expungement of records once the youth has reached a given age or after a given time period.

However, sealing and expungement are not a fix all in the current world of prolific access to personal information. In addition to the limited nature of sealing and expungement (e.g., different practices in different jurisdictions, long waiting periods, and legal fees etc.), expungement can be difficult to enforce. For example, even if a record is sealed at the courthouse, it still exists and a recorder for a Credit Reporting Agency (CRA) could erroneously input the data, or could have entered the data before it was sealed. Once the record exists publically, it is difficult if not impossible to eliminate its impact (Bushway et al., 2007). While an individual may have the right to appeal any negative educational, employment, or housing decision in some states/cases, even if the individual informs the decision-maker that the record was sealed, the damage may have already been done.

Of even greater concern is the fact that even if the file is properly sealed and/or expunged, some licensing boards, employers, landlords, and others may request disclosure of expunged convictions. For example, while New York State holds one of the most liberal sealing policies in the country, (Kurlychek, Martin, & Durose, 2017), the New York State judicial committee that oversees bar admissions requires applicants to divulge arrests as well as convictions, whether juvenile or adult, *even if they have been expunged*. Specifically question 12 asks the candidate to divulge any prior arrest or conviction specifying that "although a conviction may have been expunged from the records by an order of a court, it nevertheless should be disclosed in the answer to this question." [28]

Thus, simply sealing or expunging an already existing record is not a safeguard against its use to discriminate against these youth.

Restricted Use

For records that remain and do not enjoy confidentiality protections, we suggest that better policies be implemented to guide the use of these records and to limit civil consequences. Current efforts by the EEOC provide some first best practices in this direction restricting the use of blanket bans on the hire of individuals with criminal records and instead requiring individualized assessments that consider not only circumstances surrounding the conviction, but also allow for the consideration of positive and rehabilitative factors (EEOC, 2012). Yet much more must be done to provide life opportunities to these youth starting with their immediate educational and housing settings.

Noting that the youth who come into contact with the system are already often facing multiple hardships (Abram, Teplin, McClelland, & Dulcan, 2003; Ko et al., 2008) and limited educational opportunities (Osher, Woodruff, & Sims, 2002) the use of a juvenile record, particularly for offenses committed outside of the school, to suspend, expel, or otherwise restrict educational access seems entirely unwarranted and counterproductive to the purpose of reducing delinquency and molding these youth into law abiding citizens. College and other institutions of higher learning need also not access an individual's criminal record, let alone one acquired while a juvenile, when assessing an individual's credentials for admission. No research exists to support that having that information at admission ensures public safety on campuses. In fact existing research finds that most campus crime is not committed by students with criminal records but rather is related to drinking, Greek life, and sports teams (Center for Community Alternatives, 2015). In addition to not promoting safety, this report criticizes the practices for inadvertently discriminating against youths of color who are more likely to have run-ins with the law. Moreover, the mere presence of such a question might discourage someone from applying to college or for a job. For example, despite administrator comments that the question is not used to necessarily exclude students, a recent report found that of the 2,924 applicants to the SUNY system in a year who check "yes" to the box disclosing a felony, only 1,828 go on to finish the application (Center for Community Alternatives, 2015).

Similar to the "ban the box" movement in the employment industry, many are calling for colleges and universities to remove the criminal history question from their applications. We suggest that such efforts should not only continue but should be applied to the multiple contexts (housing, employment, naturalization) that combine to limit opportunity and trap, rather than exonerate, youth from a life of crime.

Removing the Stigma

As unlikely as a return to the past confidentiality procedures is, it is probably also unlikely that jurisdictions across the country will come together to uniformly pass policies that seal and expunge records and/or restrict the use of records in a meaningful way. Why? Possibly because individuals with criminal records in general have very little political clout. While many adults with criminal records are banned from voting because of their record for a period of time, or even for life, juveniles have never even gained the right to vote at the time they are subject to formal social controls, thus they have little to no political power and must rely on others to represent their interests.

Beyond recommending the formal social policy changes noted above, we also would like to reiterate and emphasize that words and labels have powerful meanings and define not only social situations but the individuals in them (Mahoney, 1974). Reverting back to the original words of Tannenbaum as he proclaimed the "dramatization of evil" as the process by which the act defines the individual actor, we suggest a change in words and rhetoric may be important.

In recognition of this simple fact, the United States Department of Justice issued a proclamation that directs researchers and practitioners to use the term "individuals with criminal records" rather than such derogatory terminology as "ex-con" or "ex-offender." This simple change in language highlights the individual over the status assigned. With research showing that over one-third of the population has a criminal record by early adulthood (Brame, Turner, Paternoster, & Bushway, 2012) and that individuals from minority populations are more likely to accumulate a formal record despite self-report similarities in many offending behaviors (Brame, Bushway, Paternoster, & Turner, 2014) it is important to remember that system measures of arrest and conviction are not necessarily measures of morality and not predictive instruments for measuring whether a youth will become an adult criminal.

Beyond words, actions are also required to remove the stigma. The juvenile justice system has historically utilized diversionary programs that attempt to keep youth from penetrating the juvenile justice system. Such diversionary programs can happen at arrest or at the time of court processing. Some of the emerging best practices in the juvenile system indeed involve restorative justice diversionary programs that work to hold a youth accountable for the harm done by his/her actions, yet maintain the youth in the community and strengthen not weaken community ties. In a comprehensive review of restorative justice practices with both youth and adults, Sherman and Strang (2007) find that offenders who receive restorative justice practice instead of standard practices reoffend less often with this result being strongest for violent offenders, and that victims who are exposed to the restorative justice practice also fair better than victims who must go through the traditional criminal justice process (p. 88). We highlight this last finding here to re-emphasize our point that what is best for youth is most often what is best for society in general, including victims of, or potential victims of, crime.

Conclusions

In the end, our society has a clear choice as to whether it will: (1) hold any contact with the justice system against growing and maturing individuals to limit opportunities or (2) provide meaningful chances for development, rehabilitation, and redemption. This choice is an important one that should *not* be dominated by political rhetoric and symbolic misrepresentations of youth that reduce their existence to mere statistics on a rap-sheet, but rather it should be dominated by the same common sense that drove the original progressive movement and the emerging scientific evidence of maturational differences between youth and adults to provide not only the best outcomes for society's youth, but the best outcome for our society as a whole.

Notes

1 *Juvenile Justice History*, Center on Juvenile and Criminal Justice, www.cjcj.org Education/Juvenile-Justice-History.html
2 Commentaries on the Laws of England.
3 *In re Gault*, 387 U.S. 1, 15 (1967).
4 See also *Smith v. Daily Mail Publ'g Co.*, 443 U.S. 97, 107–08 (1979) (Rehnquist, J., concurring).
5 IJA-ABA Standards Relating to Juvenile Records and Information Services, Part XV: Access to Juvenile Records (1980).
6 *In re Gault*, 387 U.S. 1 (1967).
7 *In re Gault*, 387 U.S. at 25 ("In any event, there is no reason why, consistently with due process, a State cannot continue if it deems it appropriate, to provide and to improve provision for the confidentiality of records of police contacts and court action relating to juveniles.").
8 *In re Gault*, 387 U.S. at 32.
9 *Gault*, 387 U.S. at 24–25. See also *McKeiver v. Pennsylvania*, 403 U.S. 528, 567–68 (1971).
10 *Davis v. Alaska*, 415 U.S. 308, 320 (1974) ("The State's policy interest in protecting the confidentiality of a juvenile offender's record cannot require yielding of so vital a constitutional right as the effective cross-examination for bias of an adverse witness.").
11 *Globe Newspaper Co. v. Superior Court*, 457 U.S. 596, 607–09 (1982) (holding that it was unconstitutional for the state to require judges to exclude the press and public from criminal trials involving juvenile sex-crime victims without a showing that closure served compelling state interest); *Smith v. Daily Mail Publ'g Co.*, 443

U.S. 97, 104–06 (1979) (holding that a statute prohibiting the publication of an alleged juvenile delinquent's name violated the First and Fourteenth Amendments); *Oklahoma Publ'g Co. v. Dist. Court*, 430 U.S. 308, 311–12 (1977) (prohibiting the trial court from enjoining a newspaper's publication of a juvenile's name when the press was present at the hearing and no objections were made).

12 Jacobs points to gang databases as an example. State and federal government authorize the collection and dissemination of information related to gang affiliation and suspected gang affiliation to aid law enforcement and other government agencies to identify and monitor suspected gang members who, it is assumed, pose a high risk of current and future criminality.

13 See, e.g., Del. Code tit. 10, § 1063(b) and Ga. Code § 15–11–83(f).

14 Alabama (Ala. Code § 12–15–134, Ala. Code § 12-15-133); Alaska (Alaska Stat. § 47.12.310(c)); Arkansas (Ark. Code. §§ 9-27-309(k)-(1)); Colorado (Colo. Rev. Stat. § 19–1–304); Connecticut (Conn. Gen. Stat. § 10–233h); District of Columbia (D.C. Code §16–2331(c)); Florida (Fla. Stat. § 985.04 (1)); Georgia (Ga. Code § 15-11-82(e)); Illinois (705 Ill. Comp. Stat. 405/1-7); Indiana (Ind. Code 31-39-2-13.8.); Iowa (Iowa Code § 232.147); Kansas (Kan. Stat. §38–2310); Kentucky (Ky. Rev. Stat. § 610.340); Louisiana (La. Child. Code. art. 412); Maine (Me. Rev. Stat. tit. 15,§ 3308); Maryland (Md. Educ. Code § 7–303); Minnesota (Minn. Stat. § 260B.171); Mississippi (Miss. Code § 43-21-255); Missouri (Mo. Rev. Stat. § 211.321); Montana (Mont. Code § 41-5-215); New Jersey (N.J. Stat. § 2A:4A-60); New Mexico (N.M. Stat. § 32A-2-32); New York (N.Y. Crim. Proc. § 720.35); North Carolina (N.C. Gen. Stat. § 7B-3101); North Dakota (N.D. Cent. Code. §27-20-51, N.D. Cent. Code § 27-20-52); Oklahoma (Okla. Stat. tit. 10A, §2-6-102); Oregon (Or. Rev. Stat. § 419A.255); South Carolina (S.C. Code § 63-19-2020, S.C. Code § 63–19–2030);Tennessee (Tenn. Code. § 49-6-3051); Texas (Tex. Fam. Code § 58.0051);Virginia (Va. Code § 16.1-300,Va. Code § 16.1–301);Washington (Wash. Rev. Code § 13.50.050);Wisconsin (Wis. Stat. § 938.396,Wis. Stat. § 938.396(1) (a)(2));Wyoming (Wyo. Stat. § 14-6-203).

15 Minn. Stat. § 43–21–255, Ky. Rev. Stat. § 610.340.

16 Ind. Code 31-39-2-13.8.

17 N.Y. Crim. Proc. § 720.35, Md. Educ. Code § 7-303

18 Mo. Rev. Stat. § 167.115,164 (2000)

19 N.C.G.S § 7B-3101 (a)(2), (a)(3), (a)(5).

20 Boxed Out, *supra* note 32, at ii.

21 National Affordable Housing Act, Pub. L. No. 104–120, 110 Stat. 836q (1996) and *Department of Housing and Urban Development v. Rucker*, 535 U.S. 125 (2002).

22 8. U.S.C.A. § 1427(e).

23 Roper v Simmons 543 U.S. 551, 2005; Graham v. Florida 560 U.S. 48, 2010; *Miller V Alabama* 567 U.S. 460, 2012.

24 Report to the House of Delegates. Am. Bar Ass'n, Criminal Justice Section, Committee on Homelessness and Poverty, Standing Committee on Legal Aid and Indigent Defense, at 14 (2010) at www.americanbar.org/content/dam/aba/publishing/criminal_justice_section_newsletter/crimjust_policy_midyear2010_102a.authcheckdam.pdf.

25 The only states that fully protect juvenile record information are California (Cal. Rules of Court, Rule 5.552); Illinois (705 Ill. Comp. Stat. § 405(C)); Nebraska (Neb. Rev. Stat. § 43–2,108); New Mexico (N.M. Stat. § 32A-2–32); New York (N.Y. Fam. Ct. § 381.3); North Carolina (N.C. Gen. Stat. § 7B-3000); North Dakota (N.D. Cent. Code § 27-20-52); Ohio (Ohio Rev. Code Ann. § 2151.18); Rhode Island (R.I. Gen. Laws § 14-1-64; R.I. Gen. Laws § 14-1-30); and Vermont (Vt. Stat. tit., 33 § 5117).

26 New York C.P.L. § 720.20(1)(a)

27 National Review, *supra* note 22, at 20. Cal. Penal Code Ann. § 1203.4 (West 2005); *see also* Darren T. Kavinoky, *Expungement 1* () J, www.1800duilaws.com/article/expungement 10 I.asp (accessed Oct. 6, 2006).

28 New York Supreme Court Appellate Division, *Application for Admission to Practice as an Attorney . . . and Counselor-at-Law in the State of New York,* www.nybarexam.org/admform.pdf (Revi,ed, Oct. 20(2).

References

Abram, K. M., Teplin, L. A., McClelland, G. M., & Dulcan, M. K. (2003). Comorbid psychiatric disorders in youth in juvenile detention. *Archives of General Psychiatry, 60*(11), 1097–1108.

Abrams, L. S., Terry, D., & Franke, T. M. (2011). Community-based juvenile reentry services: The effects of service dosage on juvenile and adult recidivism. 50 *Journal of Offender Rehabilitation, 50*(8), 492–510.

Apel, R., Bushway, S., Brame, R., Haviland, A. M., Nagin, D. S., & Paternoster, R. (2007). Unpacking the relationship between adolescent employment and antisocial behavior: A matched samples comparison. *Criminology, 45*(1), 67–97.

Apel, R., Bushway, S. D., Paternoster, R., Brame, R., & Sweeten, G. (2008). Using state child labor laws to identify the causal effect of youth employment on deviant behavior and academic achievement. *Journal of Quantitative Criminology, 24*(4), 337–362.

Apel, R., Paternoster, R., Bushway, S. D., & Brame, R. (2006). A job isn't just a job: The differential impact of formal versus informal work on adolescent problem behavior. *Crime & Delinquency, 52*(2), 333–369.

Apel, R., & Sweeten, G. (2010). The impact of incarceration on employment during the transition to adulthood. *Social problems, 57*(3), 448–479.

Baird, A., Johnathon, A., & Fugelsang A. (2004). The emergence of consequential thought: Evidence from neuroscience. *Philosophical Transactions of the Royal Society B, 359*, 1797–1804.

Bell, S. D. (2014). The long shadow: Decreasing barriers to employment, housing, and civic participation for people with criminal records will improve public safety and strengthen the economy, 42 *W. St. L. Rev.* 1, 11

Bernard, T.J. & Kurlychek, M. (2010). *The Cycle of Juvenile Justice* (2nd ed.). Oxford: Oxford University Press.

Blum, A. R. (1996). Disclosing the identities of juvenile felons: Introducing accountability to juvenile justice, 27 *Loy. U. Chi. L. J.* 349, 371

Bradley, K. H., Oliver, R. B., Richardson, N. C., & Slayter, E. M. (2001). No Place like Home: Housing and the ex-prisoner. Community Resources for Justice Policy Brief. Retrieved June 2017, from www.crj.org/page/-/cjifiles/No_Place_Like_Home.pdf

Brame, R., Bushway, S. D., Paternoster, R., & Turner, M. G. (2014). Demographic patterns of cumulative arrest prevalence by ages 18 and 23. *Crime & Delinquency, 60*(3), 471–486.

Brame, R., Turner, M. G., Paternoster, R., & Bushway, S. D. (2012). Cumulative prevalence of arrest from ages 8 to 23 in a national sample. *Pediatrics, 129*(1), 21–27.

Bushway, S. D., Briggs, S., Taxman, F., Tanner, M., & Van Brakle, M. (2007). Private providers of criminal history records: Do you get what you pay for? In S. Bushway, M. Stoll, & D. Weiman (Eds.), *Barriers to Reentry?: The Labor Market for Released Prisoners in Post-Industrial America* (pp. 174–200). New York, NY: Russell Sage Foundation.

Butts, J. A., & Mitchell, O. (2000). Brick by brick: Dismantling the border between juvenile and adult justice. *Criminal justice, 2*, 167–213.

Burke, M.E. (2004). *Reference and Background Checking Survey Report: A Study by the Society for Human Resource Management.* Alexandrea, VA: Society for Human Resoure Management.

Center for Community Alternatives. (2010). *The use of criminal records in college applications reconsidered.* Syracuse, NY. Retrieved from www.communityalternatives. org/pdf/reconsidered-criminal-hist-recs-in-college-admissions.pdf

Cohen, A. (1955). *Delinquent boys: The Culture of the Gang.* New York, NY: Free Press p. 84.

Commonwealth. v. Fisher, 213 Pa. 48, 53 (1905).

Cremin, L. A. (1961). The transformation of the school: Progressivism in American education, 1876–1957. *British Journal of Educational Studies, 10*(1), 106.

Deitch, M. (1995, November) *From time out to hard time: Young children in the adult criminal justice system*, Austin, TX: The University of Texas at Austin, LBJ School of Public Affairs (2009) citing John Dilulio, The coming of the super predators, *The Weekly Standard, 1*(11).

Delgado, J. (2005, July 9). Security survey shows current premise protection practices of M-H owners. *Multi-Housing News.*

EEOC. (2012). *EEOC enforcement guidance: Consideration of arrest and conviction records in employment decisions under title VII of the civil rights act of 1964.* Washington, DC: U.S. EEOC. Retrieved from www.eeoc.gov/laws/guidance/upload/arrest_conviction.pdf

Elliott, D. S., & Voss, H. L. (1974). *Delinquency and dropout.* Lenox, MA: Heath.

Feld, B. C. (1988). The juvenile court meets the principle of offense: Punishment, treatment, and the difference it makes. 68 *Boston University Law Review*, 821, 841–844.

Funk, M. T. (1996). A mere youthful indiscretion? Reexamining the policy of expunging juvenile delinquency records. 29 *University Of Michigan Journal Law Reform*, 885, 901.

Glueck, S., & Glueck, E. (1950). *Unraveling juvenile delinquency.* New York, NY: The Commonwealth Fund.

Goffman, E. (2009). *Stigma: Notes on the management of spoiled identity.* New York: Simon and Schuster.

Henning, K. (2004). Eroding confidentiality in delinquency proceedings: Should schools and public housing authorities be notified? 79 *New York University of Law Review*, 520, 526–527.

Hirschi, T. (1969). *Causes of delinquency.* Berkeley, CA: University of California Press.

Holzer, H. J., Raphael, S., & Stoll, M. S. (2006). Perceived criminality, criminal background checks, and the racial hiring practices of employers. *Journal of Law and Economics, 49*, 451–480.

Huebner, B. M. (2005). The effect of incarceration on marriage and work over the life course. *Justice Quarterly, 22*(3), 281–303.

Jacobs, J. B. (2013). *Juvenile criminal record confidentiality.* New York University Public Law and Legal Theory Working Papers (2013). Paper 403. Retrieved from http://lsr.nellco.org/nyu_plltwp/403 at 9–10.

Juvenile Law Center, Juvenile Records: A National Review of State Laws on Confidentiality, Sealing, and Expungement. (2014). Retrieved from http://jlc.org/juvenilerecords

Kessler, A. (2015). Excavating expungement law: A comprehensive approach. 87 *Temple Law Review*, 403, 404–405.

Kim, C. Y., Losen, D. J., & Hewitt, D. T. (2010). *The school-to-prison pipeline: Structuring legal reform.* New York, NY: New York University Press.

Ko, S. J., Ford, J. D., Kassam-Adams, N., Berkowitz, S. J., Wilson, C., Wong, M., & Layne, C. M. (2008). Creating trauma-informed systems: Child welfare, education, first responders, health care, juvenile justice. *Professional Psychology: Research and Practice, 39*(4), 396.

Kurlychek, M. C., Martin, K., & Durose M. (2017). Bureau of Justice Statistics, Office of Justice Programs, Washington, DC: United States Department of Justice.

Laub, J. H., & Sampson, R. J. (1993). Turning points in the life course: Why change matters to the study of crime. *Criminology, 31*, 301–325.

Lemert, E. M. (1951). Social Pathology; A systematic approach to the theory of sociopathic behavior. New York, NY: McGraw Hill.

Lenroot, R. K., & Giedd, J. N. (2006). Brain development in children and adolescents insights from anatomical magnetic resonance imaging. *Neuroscience and Biobehavioral Reviews, 30*(6), 718–729.

Leone, P. E., Christle, C. A., Nelson, C. M., Skiba, R., Frey, A., & Jolivette, K. (2003). School failure, race, and disability: Promoting positive outcomes, decreasing vulnerability for involvement with the juvenile delinquency system. *Juvenile Justice*, 12–13.

Li, S. D. (2004). The impacts of self-control and social bonds on juvenile delinquency in a national sample of midadolescents. *Deviant Behavior, 25*(4), 351–373.

Lynam, D., Moffitt, T., & Stouthamer-Loeber, M. (1993). Explaining the relation between IQ and delinquency: Class, race, test motivation, school failure, or self-control? *Journal of Abnormal Psychology, 102*(2), 187.

Mack, J. W. (1909). The juvenile court. 23 *Harvard Law Review*, 104–109.

Mahoney, A. R. (1974). The effect of labeling upon youths in the juvenile justice system: A review of the evidence. *Law & Society Review, 8*(4), 583–614.

Melli, M. S. (1996). Juvenile justice reform in context. *Wisconsin Law Review*, 375, 390–91.

National Employment Litigation Project. (2015). The consideration of criminal records in occupational licensing. Retrieved July 1, 2017, from www.nelp.org/content/uploads/TheConsiderationofCriminalRecordsin OccupationalLicensing.pdf

National Research Council, Committee on Health and Safety Implication of Child Labor. (1998). *Protecting youth at work: Health safety and development of working children and Adolescents in the United States.* Washington, DC: National Academy Press.

Nelson, K. E. (1998). The release of juvenile records under Wisconsin's juvenile justice code: A new system of false promises. 81 *Marquette Law Review*, 1101, 1115.

Oestreicher, S. E., Jr. (2001). Toward fundamental fairness in the kangaroo courtroom: The due process case against statutes presumptively closing juvenile proceedings. 54 *Vanderblit Law Review*, 1751, 1761 n.44.

Office of Juvenile Justice and Delinquency Prevention, Juvenile Justice Reform Initiatives in the States: 1994–1996, at 36. (1997). Retrieved from www.ncjrs.gov/pdffiles/reform.pdf

Osgood, D. W. (1999). Having the time of their lives: All work and no play. *Transitions to Adulthood in a Changing Economy: No Work, No Family, No Future*, 176–186.

Osher, D., Woodruff, D., & Sims, A. E. (2002). Schools make a difference: The overrepresentation of African American youth in special education and the juvenile justice system. *Racial Inequity in Special Education*, 93–116.

Pager, D. (2003). The mark of a criminal record. *American Journal of Sociology, 108*, 937–975.

Pager, D (2007). *Marked: Race, crime, and finding work in an era of mass incarceration.* Chicago, IL: University of Chicago Press.

Rossum, R. A. (1995). *Holding Juveniles Accountable: Reforming America's "Juvenile Injustice System,"* 22 Pepp. L. Rev. 907, 909.

Sampson, R. J., & Laub, J. H. (1995). *Crime in the making: Pathways and turning points through life.* Cambridge, MA: Harvard University Press.

Sampson, R. J., & Laub, J. H. (2003). Desistance over the life course. Chapter 14. In J. T. Mortimer & M. J. Shanahan (Eds.), *The handbook of the lifecourse. Springer Science and Business Media* (pp. 295–309).

Sampson, R. J., & Laub, J. H. (2005). A general age-graded theory of crime: Lessons learned and the future of life-course criminology. *Integrated Developmental and Life Course Theories of Offending, 14*, 165–182.

Saul, S. (2016, January 28). Colleges that ask applicants about brushes with the law draw scrutiny. *New York Times*. Retrieved from www.nytimes.com/2016/01/29/us/colleges-that-ask-applicants-about-brushes-with-the-law-draw-scrutiny.html?mtrref=www.nytimes.com&_r=2&mtrref=www.nytimes.com&gwh=1AADB7A8170F20415CAE152281639D47&gwt=pay

SEARCH. (2010). *Survey of state criminal record sealing and expungement practices*. Retrieved February 12, 2017, from www.search.org/files/pdf/Criminal_record_sealing_expungement_survey_March_2010.pdf

Sherman, L., & Strang, H. (2007). *Restorative justice: The evidence*. London, UK: The Smith Institute.

Snow, C. J. (1992). Expungement and employment law: The conflict between an employer's need to know about juvenile misdeeds and an employee's need to keep them secret. 41 *Washington University Journal of Urband and Contemporary Law*, 3, 16.

Snyer, H., & Sickmund, H. (1999). *Juvenile offenders and victims: A national report*. Washington, DC: Office of Juvenile Justice and Delinquency Prevention, Office of Justice Programs, U.S. Department of Justice.

Soler, M. (2001). *Public opinion on youth, crime, and race: A guide for advocates*. Washington, DC: Building Blocks for Youth.

Steinberg, L., & Cauffman, E. (1996). Maturity of judgment in adolescence: Psychosocial factors in adolescent decision making. *Law and Human Behavior, 20*(3), 249.

Tannenbaum, F. (1938). *Crime and the Community*. Boston, MA: Ginn.

Thompson, K. C., & Morris, R. J. (2016). *Juvenile Delinquency and Disability*. New York, NY: Springer.

Thornberry, T. P., Moore, M., & Christenson, R. L. (1985). The effect of dropping out of high school on subsequent criminal behavior. *Criminology, 23*(1), 3–18.

Torbet, P., Gable, R., Montgomery, I., & Hurst, H. (1996). *State responses to serious & violent juvenile crime*. Collingdale, PA: DIANE Publishing.

Wald, J., & Losen, D. J. (2003). Defining and redirecting a school-to-prison pipeline. *New Directions for Youth Development, 2003*(99), 9–15.

Weissman, M. Rosenthal, A., Warth, P., Wolf, E., & Messina-Yauchzy, M. (2010). The use of criminal history records in college admissions. Retrieved from Center for Community Alternatives, Inc. website: www.communityalternatives.org/pdf/reconsidered-criminal-hist-recs-in-college-admissions.pdf.college

Wiggan, G. (2007). Race, school achievement, and educational inequality: Toward a student-based inquiry perspective. *Review of Educational Research, 77*(3), 310–333.

Wright, R. G. (2003). Sex offender registration and notification: Public attention, political emphasis, and fear. *Criminology & Public Policy, 3*(1), 97–104.

Wright, B.R., Caspi, A., Moffit, T.E. & Sliva, P.A. (1999). Low self-control, social bonds, and crime: Social causation, social selection or both? *Criminology, 37*(3), 479–514.

13

DEPORTATION AS A COLLATERAL CONSEQUENCE

Carlos E. Monteiro

In February 2017, Guadalupe Garcia de Rayos's name was featured in every major news outlet and her story became the rallying call for immigrant advocacy groups hoping to push back against the new deportation guidelines set by the Trump administration (Almasy, Grinberg, & Sanchez, 2017; Riley, 2017; Santos, 2017). Guadalupe's story was unique given the circumstances that brought her immigrant experience to an abrupt ending. A 36-year-old mother of two, Guadalupe immigrated to the United States in 1995 at the age of 14 (Nevarez, 2017). Guadalupe was among the first individuals deported under the new administration's shift in immigration policy. Guadalupe's deportation can be traced back to 2008, when she was arrested in a workplace raid, was charged with using a fake social security number, and pled guilty to a lesser felony charge of criminal impersonation, a class 6 low-level felony (Schmidt & Larimer, 2017). Guadalupe spent six months in a detention center and was then permitted to remain in the United States on the condition that she check in with Immigration and Customs Enforcement (ICE) on an annual basis. On February 8, 2017, she checked in with ICE as was her norm, unsuspecting that she would be detained and repatriated back to Mexico within 24 hours (Domonoske, 2017). Guadalupe's story, while seemingly extreme, is quite common today, as criminal histories that are at times decades old are drawn on as grounds for removal.

Introduction

The literature on reentry catalogues an assortment of intersecting laws and policies applying to individuals with criminal convictions, which overtime have become known for their unintended consequences of hindering the reintegration process (Love, 2006; Pinard, 2010; Travis, 2005; Turanovic, Rodriguez, & Pratt, 2012). While most of these post-conviction mandates such as housing access restrictions, employment limitations, voting disenfranchisement, loss of public aid, and a host of the other sanctions and disqualifications covered in the other chapters of this book are indeed quite punitive, they at the very least permit the individuals facing such sanctions to reenter the community from which they came. Deportation, on the other hand, serves as one of the only collateral consequences of criminal convictions to have a transformative permanent outcome, ultimately eliminating the possibility of a return to the United States.

The policy of deporting non-citizens convicted of crimes has been a longstanding practice for a wide range of countries, including Russia, France, England, Germany, Italy, and others (Aas & Bosworth, 2013; C. Anderson, 2007; Cook, 2003; Gentes, 2009; Kingston, 2005; N. Morris & Rothman,

1995; Pike, 1983). Internationally there is a strong consensus in favor of continuing this form of civil sanctioning (C. Anderson, 2007; Fekete, 2011; Martin, 1987). In the United States, the practice continues at near record pace. In 2015, deportations triggered by prior criminal convictions accounted for roughly 42 percent (139,950) of the total number of all deportations. Between 2009 and 2014, the United States deported a total of 2.4 million people, with more deportations in 2013 (435,000) than any other year (*Yearbook of Immigration Statistics*, 2017). While reasons for deportation vary, the removal of non-citizens on the basis of criminal offenses is purported to be a priority for the U.S. Immigration and Customs Enforcement agency (Eagly, 2017).

The U.S. immigration detention infrastructure is not always discussed in the context of deportation; however, it is arguably the single most critical component in immigration enforcement. Evidence of its relevance is best demonstrated through its expansion in size and cost over the last two decades. In 1995 there were approximately 85,000 people held in immigration detention facilities across the country (Meissner, Kerwin, Chishti, & Bergeron, 2013); by 2012 that number reached a record of 477,523 detentions (*United States Immigration Detention Profile*, 2016). The latest detention numbers covering fiscal year 2015 indicate a 30 percent drop since the 2012 record (*Yearbook of Immigration Statistics*, 2017). Detention costs also continue to be a matter of controversy in the immigration debate as the growing numbers have created burdens on tax expenditures. In 2009, Congress further complicated the issue of expenditure when it appropriated U.S. Department of Homeland Security's (DHS) funding to maintaining a bed quota of 34,000 detention beds a day (Sinha, 2016). The mandate, which was lowered to 30,543 in FY 2015 (DHS, 2015), has received extensive pushback as advocates expressed concerns over the growing privatization of the U.S. immigration detention system (Conlon & Hiemstra, 2014; Miroff, 2013).

Although immigration enforcement as a federal policy has affected millions of people, there has been very little research on the practice of deportation as it applies to criminal convictions. This chapter provides an overview of the current state of knowledge on specific aspects of deportation policies, focusing primarily on detention and expulsions that result from criminal convictions. Although much is known about border enforcement, visa controls, travel screenings, and other legal policies that facilitate deportation (B. Anderson, Gibney, & Paoletti, 2011; Ngai, 2003), there has been very little research into the effects of those policies on crime, on communities, or on individuals.

For context and to better understand deportation policies in the United States, it is first necessary to fully understand the practice, from the origins of expulsion as a localized strategy for immigration control to the expansive process that is the norm today. The chapter begins with a brief review of U.S. deportation policies, chronicling how this sanctioning tactic has evolved, before turning to an analysis of the major implications. While the historical component builds the context for understanding deportation policies, the chapter's main goal is to provide a current state of knowledge on deportations that result as a collateral consequence of criminal convictions. In using this state of the field approach, this chapter reviews what is known about this collateral consequence from social science research, with an emphasis on what we know and still do not know.

Origins of Deportation

With the potential for global effects, deportation is an increasingly polarizing issue. The policy of deportation is not new, nor is the consternation about this form of sanction (Bhabha, 1998; Boswell, 2007b). The practice of community removal has been around for centuries with roots going back to the age-old sanctions of banishment and transportation (De Beaumont & De Tocqueville, 1833). Even a cursory review of the historical literature suggests that the practice has been mired in controversy with debates over its morality, its status as a punishment or a civil remedy, and its potentially deleterious effects on individuals and communities.

The Nation's First Deportation Laws

The Alien and Sedition Laws of 1789 were America's first attempts to control the arrival, settlement, and removal of immigrants since gaining independence (Navasky, 1958; Newman, 1993). Designed and directed at aliens, the laws consisted of three acts: the Alien Act, the Alien Enemies Act, and the Naturalization Act. Citing national security as the driving force, Congress first enacted the Naturalization Act, which increased the period of residence required for naturalization from five to 14 years ("Naturalization Act," 1798). Congress then passed the Alien Act that was modeled after the British Alien Act of 1793, which authorized the removal of any alien deemed dangerous (Elkins & McKitrick, 1995). The Alien Act provided the president with broad discretion and with broad authority to specify removal orders and dates for any alien. Failure to comply with the order would result in criminal prosecution and imprisonment for up to three years, or to the satisfaction of the sitting president.

Congress passed the final component of the Alien and Sedition Acts in July 1798, entitled the Alien Enemies Act. The Alien Enemies Act focused on enemies of the state and authorized the arrest, detention, and expulsion of suspected aliens of an enemy nation (*Alien and Sedition Acts*, 1798). Moreover, the Alien Enemies Act broadened the president's discretion over aliens, authorizing the indefinite detention and removal of aliens, without any judicial oversight or hearings (Wasserman, 1953). Debates over the constitutionality of the Alien and Sedition Laws of 1789 continued well into the 20th century, with numerous landmark cases (including *Fong Yue Ting v. United States* [1893], *Li Sing v. United States* [1901], *United States ex rel. Bilokumsky v. Tod* [1923] and *Zakonaite v. Wolf* [1912]) challenging the sweeping authority granted by the three acts. Despite the challenges, federal courts have consistently affirmed the legality of the three statutes; authorizing the deportation of individuals thought to pose a danger to the public's welfare or to national security (see *Carlson v. Landon* [1952]; *Galvan v. Press* [1954]; *Harisiades v. Shaughnessy* [1952]; *Kleindienst v. Mandel* [1972]; *Zadvydas v. Davis* [2001]).

The decisions from two U.S. Supreme court cases, *Chae Chan Ping v. United States* (1889) and *Fong Yue Ting v. United States* (1893), established precedent for the federal government's complete jurisdiction over deportation proceedings. In deciding these two landmark cases, the Court upheld the Chinese Exclusion Act and established the "plenary power doctrine" in regulating immigration, which meant that courts would have a policy of nonintervention in immigration cases, instead, granting Congress and the executive branch complete power over such matters (Wasserman, 1953). Crucially, the justices characterized deportation as an administrative process that would be placed far outside of constitutional protections. Through these decisions, the Court ruled that deportation proceedings would not fall under constitutional protections, indicating that individuals deemed deportable would not be afforded due process or any other constitutional protection. Most importantly, the justices in the landmark exclusion cases specified that deportation is not a punishment, an important distinction that would establish precedent allowing for the incarceration and detention of individuals awaiting deportation. With regard to new deportation laws, legislators remained largely inactive in the years following the Chinese Exclusion Act; and it was not until the Immigration and Nationality Acts of 1953 and 1990 when Congress would make the next major shifts in deportation legislation.

Although deportation was a norm for much of U.S. history, the Alien Act is recognized for establishing precedent for the federal government's authority to deport (Hutchinson, 1981) and the cases surrounding the Chinese Exclusion Act affirmed the executive branch's jurisdiction. Today deportation operates independent of many state and local jurisdictions and just outside of the many due process protections afforded to individuals facing other governmental mandates (Golash-Boza, 2015).

Crime and Deportation Laws

Deportation as a collateral consequence of a criminal conviction was and continues to be a driving theme in political discourse, with vocal segments of the public demanding stricter immigration legislation and regular calls for removal of non-citizens living in the U.S. with current and past records of criminal involvement. The call to place greater focus on non-citizens with a criminal background dates back to the 1907 Immigration Act, which in addition to broadening the categories for removals, also added the "crimes involving moral turpitude clause" (CIMT) as a basis for deporting anyone with a criminal conviction ("An act to regulate the immigration of aliens into the United States, 1907," 1907). In 1910, a critical amendment to the Act reinforced deportation decrees by adding the stipulation that even minor offenses such as prostitution could be classified as crimes involving moral turpitude and would qualify in establishing grounds for deportations (Farrelly, 2011; Nolan, 1975). In 1913, the U.S. Supreme Court heard arguments in a case challenging the deportation of a prostitute on the basis that she violated the moral turpitude clause (see *Bugajewitz v. Adams* [1913]). The justices ruling established the first instance where the federal government can pass laws limiting a person's visa solely based on past criminal convictions. The case provided even greater support for deportations based on past criminal involvement.

Although legal challenges to early deportation laws were quite common (see *Bugajewitz v. Adams* [1913]; *Ekiu v. United States* [1892]; *Li Sing v. United States* [1901]; *Turner v. Williams* [1904]), successful challenges were few and far between as courts often deferred to the "*plenary power doctrine*," which granted Congress and the executive branch absolute authority over immigration affairs. In 1917, deportation advocates enjoyed a small victory when Congress enacted the Judicial Recommendations Against Deportation (JRAD), which offered potential recourses for individuals found guilty under the crimes involving moral turpitude clause (Farrelly, 2011). Designed as a potential alternative to deportation, JRADs placed removal discretion in the hands of the sentencing judge who Congress believed knew the circumstances of the defendant's case and could best determine if deportation was warranted (Taylor & Wright, 2002). The measure was incorporated into the Immigration and Naturalization Act given the growing concerns over the severity of deportations for minor offenses that fell under the crimes against moral turpitude clause.

Rulings made in many of the legal challenges not only solidified the federal government's authority over deportation proceedings, but also created separate jurisdiction for deportations that would be independent of judicial reviews. Under this new jurisdiction, deportations would operate free from the constraints of procedural due process principles that generally govern other aspects of American society.

The Supreme Court decisions in the Chinese Exclusion cases created a more direct shift for immigration laws to target aliens involved in criminal activity. The focus on criminals or "criminal aliens" continued to grow throughout the early to mid-20th century. For instance, in his message to Congress on December 2, 1930, President Herbert Hoover raised the issue of "strengthening our deportation laws so as to more fully rid ourselves of criminal aliens" (Hoover, 1930). In that same year, New York and Chicago were among a number of cities focused on removing non-citizens living in the United States who had criminal records. Furthermore, on December 19, 1930, the New York City Police Department established a bureau of detectives charged with rounding up and investigating all non-citizens with criminal records for the purposes of initiating deportation proceedings (Clark, 1931; "Police to Round Up Criminal Aliens Here; New Bureau to Get Evidence for Mulrooney," 1930). Over the next several decades, concern about criminality continued to drive immigration control policy.

The Buildup Toward Stricter Deportation Laws

The Immigration Act of 1952 signaled a major turning point in the country's policy of exclusion and removal (Griffith, 1999; Ngai, 2003). The 1952 Act for the first time provided some relief from the removal process by allowing Congress and the judicial branch to set aside and suspend certain deportation orders (Ngai, 2003; Saggiomo III, 1981). Although the framework for modern day deportation laws was established with the enactment of the 1952 Immigration Act, it was not until the 1980s that immigration laws began expediting deportations based on criminal convictions.

Between 1980 and 1990, Congress amended the INA to include a number of important reforms aimed at restricting immigration and expediting deportations (Finch Jr, 1990). In 1986, Congress developed the Criminal Alien Program, which was established in conjunction with the Immigration Reform and Control Act of 1986 (Rodriguez, 2005). The Criminal Alien Program allowed for the expediting of deportations by holding removal hearings while the individuals were still detained (Lasch, 2008). The 1986 Act initiated specific grounds of deportability based primarily on criminal involvement. For example, non-citizens convicted of crimes of moral turpitude that carried sentences of a year or longer were subject to deportation, provided the offense was committed within five years of admission into the country. Similarly, the Act stipulated that any noncitizen with two or more criminal convictions of moral turpitude would be deportable regardless of when the offense took place ("Immigration Reform and Control Act," 1986).

The expansion of deportation continued with the passage of the Anti-Drug Abuse Acts of (ADAA) 1986 and 1988, which included a list of criminal offenses for which a conviction would subject the offender to deportation proceedings (Baker, 1997). Although the much broader ADAA is known mainly as the policy that catapulted America's war on drugs, the laws also added deportation conditions for a number of other offenses, beginning with classification of all controlled substances as prohibited drug offenses that could lead to removal. Also included in the ADAA was the provision that offenders convicted of firearms violations, domestic violence, and other miscellaneous offenses related to "national security" were all subject to deportation (Hernandez, 2014). The ADAA's introduction of the "aggravated felonies provision" was by far one of the more punitive and most popular in terms of immigration enforcement. Convictions for aggravated felonies did not have a sunset provision, meaning that noncitizens with such convictions could face deportations regardless of the conviction or offense date (Weld et al., 1987). The original list of aggravated felonies, which included murder and drug and weapons trafficking, was continuously expanded during the Immigration Acts of the 1980s and 1990s. In 1988, for example, Congress coupled the aggravated felony provision for deportation with crimes that were normally found in the crimes involving moral turpitude clause (Schuck & Williams, 1998). The new list of deportable convictions included offenses such as rape, money laundering, drug trafficking, and tax evasion convictions, but the more damaging aspect was that the expanded list also absorbed any conviction that "could have resulted in punishment lasting over a year" (Farrelly, 2011).

The introduction of immigration detainers in the 1986 ADAA drastically changed the future of deportation enforcement. Immigrations detainers were embedded into the ADAA of 1986 and provided local and state law enforcement with the authority to maintain custody of persons who were arrested or convicted of controlled substance-related offenses (Weld et al., 1987). Prior to 1986, federal authorities did issue detainers on the basis of sovereignty and national security; however, the 1986 ADAA provided specific guidelines for funneling potentially deportable noncitizens into federal custody as a means of expediting removal proceedings. Additionally, under the provisions, law enforcement could hold individuals for up to 48 hours beyond the individual's scheduled time of release.

The Nexus Between Immigration Enforcement and the Criminal Justice System

By the early 1990s, the nexus between deportation enforcement and the criminal justice system was closer than at any time in U.S. history. Building on the crime and drug war that was the hallmark of the punitive era, Congress creatively revamped its efforts to increase deportation well into the 1990s, with strategies that simultaneously embedded deportation provisions in many new crime bills.

In 1990, for example, Congress allocated $25 million for "criminal investigations and the expeditious deportation of criminal aliens from detention" ("Crime Control Act," 1990). In the same year, Congress passed the Immigration Act of 1990, which also focused on the expeditious removal of noncitizens who were already in the criminal justice system. In an effort to ensure a more streamlined removal process, the 1990 Act emboldened immigration officers by arming them in the literal sense and also by broadening their warrantless arrest powers (Hernandez, 2014). More specifically, the 1990 INA increased the enforcement powers by authorizing officers to carry firearms and make warrantless arrests for certain crimes ("S.358—Immigration Act of 1990," 1990). At the same time, the 1990 Immigration Act terminated the discretionary relief measures that were offered through the Judicial Recommendation Against Deportation (JRAD) requests. As highlighted in the previous section, JRAD allowed judges to forego deportation orders on a case-by-case basis, thereby affording judges greater discretion over removal proceedings (Farrelly, 2011). In addition to repealing JRAD and nullifying all existing relief requests, the 1990 Immigration Act also stripped judges of their discretion in cases where noncitizens were convicted of an aggravated felony, a drug-related offense, a firearm charge, or a range of crimes involving moral turpitude (Farrelly, 2011).

Over time, the threshold for deportations was lowered with the passage of each new piece of immigration legislation. Most notable in this long list of legislation was the Antiterrorism and Effective Death Penalty Act (AEDPA) and Illegal Immigration Reform and Immigrant Responsibility Act of 1996 (IIRIRA), which collectively formed the most sweeping reforms to U.S. deportation policies to date. The two bills introduced mandatory statutes provision and a series of other mandates that placed increased emphasis on expedited removal proceedings. Congress passed the AEDPA on April 24, 1996, with the intention of combatting terrorism, particularly after the bombings in 1993 and 1996 of the World Trade Center and the federal building in Oklahoma City (Kanstroom & Lykes, 2015; Salinas, 2004).

The final IIRIRA bill was comprised of distinct sections that sought to (1) heighten immigration enforcement through increased funding for border security; (2) add a variety of enhanced provisions for combating alien smuggling, document fraud, and unauthorized workers; (3) overhaul U.S. deportation proceedings; and (4) implement stricter eligibility requirements for federal public benefits to legal residents living in the United States for at least five years (Fragomen, 1997). Together, these four broad sections of the 1996 IIRIRA, coupled with the AEDPA (hereinafter referred to as the 1996 immigration laws) radically altered the course of U.S. immigration enforcement, implementing a legislative framework that allowed for a streamlined detention and deportation process.

The most unique and lasting aspect of the 1996 immigration laws was that the new laws largely removed discretion in deportation, establishing instead, a compulsory system with mandatory detention and mandatory deportation as consequences of criminal convictions (Chicco & Congress, 2015; Morawetz, 2000). Under these new bills, grounds for deportations were broadened to include a more expansive list of minor offenses that never before warranted intervention by immigration authorities. To accomplish this, Congress doubled down on the "Aggravated Felonies" designation that was introduced in the 1988 ADAA, redefining the term so that an even greater list of offenses—that were neither serious enough to be deemed aggravated nor felonies—would now trigger deportation proceedings (Golash-Boza, 2015; Marley, 1998). A brief overview of the evolution of the "Aggravated Felonies" designation is necessary to understand the divergence between the 1988 ADAA and the 1996 IIRIRA. Under the original 1988 bill, only serious offenses such as murder, drug trafficking, and firearms trafficking, would be considered aggravated felonies. By 1996, a more expansive definition classified a much larger segment of the immigrant population as aggravated felons. Foreign-born individuals, both documented and undocumented, would be labeled as aggravated felons for offenses such as low-level money laundering, tax evasion, failing to appear in court, perjury, gambling, obstruction of justice, alien smuggling ("assisting family members with clandestine entry into the U.S."), and passport alteration and document fraud (Marley, 1998, p. 866; Trinh, 2004). Additionally, the enactment of the 1996 IIRIRA labeled simple battery, petty theft, and receiving stolen goods as aggravated felonies that warranted deportation proceedings. Lastly, the 1996 bill modified the length of sentence requirement for an offense to qualify as an aggravated felony, adjusting the term to just one year, regardless if the sentence term was served or suspended. What is most punitive in lowering the qualifying sentence length for an aggravated felony is that some state misdemeanor offenses would be considered deportable offenses so long as the sentence triggered could be at least one year.

Of all the components of the 1996 immigration bills, the retroactive application of the laws proved to be the most consequential for foreign-born individuals living in the U.S. The retroactive feature expanded the scope of deportations by making criminal involvement (including arrests and convictions that occurred prior to the 1996 enactments) the only necessary criterion for initiating removal proceedings, with detention and deportation as potential outcomes. The retroactive aspect immediately changed the status of foreign-born individuals living in the United States, as many, as a result of their background, were deemed deportable. Under the retroactive clause, qualifying offenses committed by foreign-born and non-naturalized individuals would be considered as grounds for deportation, regardless of when the offenses took place.

The impact of the 1996 immigration laws is readily apparent when reviewing the actual numbers of individuals removed as a result of these policy changes. A review of immigration statistics before and after the 1996 immigration laws illustrates a sharp increase in deportation numbers in only a short period of time. In 1995, the Department of Homeland Security reported that a total of 50,924 individuals were deported (*Statistical Yearbook of the Immigration and Naturalization Service, 1998*, 2000). In 1996, deportations increased only marginally to a total of 69,680 individuals. By 1997, just a year after the laws were enacted, deportations more than doubled to a total of 114,432. In 2007, roughly 10 years after the 1996 immigration laws were fully implemented, the number of deportations increased by 358 percent to a total of 319,382 removals (*2014 Yearbook of Immigration Statistics*, 2016).

The 1996 immigration laws revamped immigration in the United States; however, immigrant enforcement practices are always evolving and have expanded greatly since then, with the enactment of several policies such as the Patriot Act, the National Fugitive Operations Program, and the Secure Communities and 287(g) program, all aimed at prioritizing immigration enforcement. Although there is growing literature on the effects of the expansion of these enforcement programs, there are very few that have focused on broader impacts of these enforcement policies on individuals, families, and communities.

The Emerging Field of Deportation Studies

Deportations rose to unprecedented levels in the years after the 1996 immigration laws. While the literature on deportations has documented the increase and the direct and indirect impact on the American criminal justice system (Chacón, 2012; Ewing, Martínez, & Rumbaut, 2015), finding that it undermined the integrity of the criminal justice system and attributed to the nations burgeoning correctional population, relatively few scholarly works have been published on the unintended consequences of deportation. Indeed, the overwhelming number of scholarly works involving deportation has been descriptive or exploratory, focusing on the intake of immigrants rather than the removal (*Budgeting for immigration enforcement: A path to better performance*, 2012; Chacón, 2012; Morton, 2010; Motivans, 2012; Passel, Director, & Lopez, 2009; *Yearbook of Immigration Statistics*, 2017). The impact of deportation on criminal justice systems, communities (both domestic and foreign), and children and families remains a nascent but overlooked field of study.

Criminologist Susan Bibler Coutin (2015) introduces the claim that the new field emerged in the early 2000s with the intersection of immigration and security studies. Coutin and others (see Boswell, 2007a; Hollifield, Martin, & Orrenius, 2014; Martinez, Stowell, & Cancino, 2008; Perea, 1997; Stowell, Messner, Barton, & Raffalovich, 2013; Walters, 2002) were motivated by the policy decisions on behalf of the United States and other popular immigrant destinations to intensify their enforcement strategies, to restrict employment and service access, and to expand sanctioning legislation. These shifts in emphasis motivated researchers to begin more in-depth explorations about these enforcement tactics, with deportation outcomes as an emerging topic of study.

Some of the earliest research on deportation focused on explaining the reasons for increased calls for immigration enforcement. The researchers note that concerns associated with racism, terrorism, and economic insecurity (job displacement) were primarily to blame for the increased restriction and expulsion efforts (Christensen, Read, Sullivan, & Walth, 2000; Hernández, 2008; Jaret, 1999; Rizer III, 2016; Welch, 2002, 2003, 2006). These scholars noted that politicians fueled moral panics about immigrants endangering American society, despite the evidence that showed the contrary (Kubrin, Ousey, Reid, & Adelman, 2017). Ewing et al. (2015) described the extent to which discourse surrounding immigration ignored empirical evidence and honed in on fear and stereotypes to ascribe the stigma of criminality in guiding immigration enforcement, with detention and deportation as the primary mechanism of social control.

Social disorganization theory has been commonly used in understanding immigrant communities, with much of the research interest focused on the link between immigration and crime (Bursik, 2006; Martinez, Stowell, & Lee, 2010; Polczynski-Olson, Laurikkala, Huff-Corzine, & Corzine, 2009; Stowell & Martinez, 2007). Social science literature, nonetheless, has consistently found evidence that immigration has a negative or null effect on crime (Kubrin et al., 2017; Kubrin, Zatz, & Martinez, 2012; Martinez et al., 2008; Sampson, Morenoff, & Raudenbush, 2005; Stowell, Messner, McGeever, & Raffalovich, 2009). Despite these findings, proponents of stricter immigration policies continue their efforts at linking crime and immigration. Studies examining the effect of these enforcement policies including deportation have been done; however, a considerable gap in knowledge exist in this area.

While the discourse surrounding immigrant criminality persists, and the literature on immigration and crime is now quite expansive, data regarding the numbers of individuals, the crimes they committed, and the reasons for their detention and deportation have not been as available to inform these conversations. In 2013, the Department of Homeland Security published a report with estimates of the numbers of deportable individuals with prior criminal records (DHS, 2013). In the report, DHS estimated that there were 1.9 million convicted criminals among the entire immigrant noncitizen population, accounting for both legal and unauthorized individuals. The number (1.9 million) was used repeatedly by politicians including President Donald Trump to continue stoking the flames of moral panic of immigrant criminality (Park & Griggs, 2017).

Overall, the research on deportation has been scant, with the majority of the work relying on descriptive and qualitative methodologies. The few descriptive analyses rely mainly on limited data provided by policy advocates, think tanks, the Department of Homeland Security and a few other government agencies. The United States Sentencing Commission (USSC) is one of the agencies that serves as a reliable source for data and research on deportation in the federal sentencing system. In their examination of nearly 68,000 federal criminal cases, Schmitt and Jones (2017) of the USSC found that immigration-related cases were the second most common type of federal cases after drug cases, accounting for roughly a third of the federal caseload. Of the immigration-related cases, roughly 83 percent of the offenses involved unlawful reentry into the United States or for remaining in the country beyond the granted visa date. Their analysis also revealed that 92 percent of the cases not involving immigration received parole or some form of supervised release, whereas only 58 percent of the immigration cases received sentences that were accompanied by a period of supervised release. Schmitt and Jones noted that this was indicative of the fact that many of the individuals in the system for immigration offenses are ordered deported once their sentence is completed.

In another recent report, researchers from the USSC (2015) examined a representative sample (1,897 cases) of all 18,498 persons who were previously removed from the United States only to return and be convicted and sentenced in 2013 for illegal reentry. One of the key findings from their report was that over 96 percent of the 1,897 illegal reentry offenders examined had at least one prior criminal conviction, with 4.4 prior convictions as the average. Although the report provided a number of important statistics, such as the fact that the average offender had 3.2 prior deportations, the methodology described suggests that deportation data are not readily available and the available data required extensive criminal history coding.

Other investigations into the associations between criminal convictions and deportations have indicated similar data challenges often revealing an incomplete picture surrounding the key drivers of deportations in the United States (Motivans, 2012). Rosenblum (2015) used data obtained by the *New York Times* through a Freedom of Information Act request to provide detailed information regarding the outcomes of the roughly 3.7 million deportations that took place over the course of 11 years, between fiscal years 2003–2013 (Thompson & Cohen, 2014). An important element in this work was that the researchers provided detailed information about the removals through their analysis of what was previously unpublished data on deportees' characteristics and enforcement histories (Rosenblum & McCabe, 2014). In addition to identifying descriptive outcomes such as the gender breakdown of deportees, with males accounting for 91 percent of all removals, the study also revealed insight into the driving factors behind deportations resulting from criminal convictions. Convictions for immigration offenses, once again, were the largest category of convictions for criminal deportees comprised of 18 percent of the 1.5 million criminal removals, followed by FBI Part 1 and then Part 2 crimes, which together accounted for approximately 29 percent of the deportations. In noting the study limitations, Rosenblum and McCabe make a plea for DHS to (1) make immigration enforcement data more publicly available and to (2) offer a more complete dataset that allows researchers to analyze repeat removals. The researchers noted that the data that are publicly available such as the Yearbook on Immigration Statistics are restricted to those who were ultimately deported, which results in a one-sided analysis and does not allow for an understanding of the role prosecutorial discretion plays in the process (Rosenblum & McCabe, 2014).

Immigration detention orders, also known as detainers, offer another important area for research that has been neglected in the broader topic of understanding deportations as a collateral consequence of criminal convictions. Detainers are formal requests by the Immigration and Customs Enforcement to local, state, and federal law enforcement agencies to hold noncitizens for possible deportation. The ACLU conducted a detailed analysis of the use of detainers as part of a class action lawsuit (see *Rodriguez v. Robbins* [2015]) challenging prolonged immigration detention in California. As part of the lawsuit, 1,026 class member cases were reviewed revealing an average detention length of 404 days per detainee (ACLU, 2016). In addition to highlighting the prolonged detention period, the ACLU study also included cost analyses using data provided by ICE. Using these data, the ACLU analysis revealed that with a $164 daily cost of detention estimate, the federal government was spending over $2 billion annually to detain individuals (*Rodriguez, et al. v. Robbins, et al.* [2015]). In a 2013 report, TRAC (2013) reported that legal noncitizens are detained for the longest period, usually because they are challenging the deportation decision that led to the detention.

The Effects of Deportation and Immigration Enforcement Policies

It is well known that the immigration enforcement laws of the 1980s and 1990s drastically affected deportation numbers, leading to marked increases in a short period of time; however, the underlying impact of these laws is not strictly limited to numbers of removals. Although deportation is arguably the penalty feared most by undocumented immigrants, the relentless efforts to ward off removals leads to a new dimension of effects that deportation scholarship has yet to cover. The widening of the immigration enforcement net over the last two decades has resulted in effects that span vastly different domains. The impact of these policies has not been fully documented in the nascent scholarship on deportation but is contextualized through individual, familial, health, economic, and a range of other social challenges.

One of the emergent areas for deportation scholarship focuses on the practice's impact on people's lives as they negotiate the broad immigration enforcement landscape. Coutin (1993) was able to demonstrate—through ethnographic work on the legalization status of Salvadoran immigrants—that immigration enforcement practices produce a concept of nonexistence among undocumented immigrants that features the social exclusion, isolation, withdrawal, and repression experienced by the undocumented as they circumnavigate the dragnet immigration laws passed in '80s and '90s. Coutin (1993, 1998) was among the first to introduce such a theoretical framework discussing the extent to which immigration law structured the experiences of the undocumented, discouraging undocumented immigrants from making definitive long-term plans given the uncertainties resulting from the possibility of deportation (De Genova, 2002).

In discussing the potential social effects of deportation, both Coutin (1998) and De Genova (2002) expand the theoretical framework, stating that enforcement imperatives, coupled with anti-immigrant sentiment, instill "deportability," which is distress and concern in the minds of those at risk for removal. Deportability, according to De Genova, is the awareness of the possibility of being deported, which creates a sense of fear and vulnerability, and a willingness to withdraw from actions that could publicly expose the individual in any way (Coutin, 2015). Asch, Leake, and Gelberg's (1994) study was one of the earliest to examine the broad impact of immigration enforcement on the vulnerability and deportability of immigrants. The researchers were responding to physician groups and their concern that possible legislation mandating medical staff to report undocumented patients to immigration authorities would cause serious delay in curative care for infectious diseases. Asch et al. interviewed 313 patients with active tuberculosis from 95 different facilities in California and found that only 6 percent reported fear of immigration enforcement as a result of their medical visit but noted that these respondents were 4 times more likely to delay seeking care. The researchers concluded that this fear of seeking medical care because of the undocumented immigration status could potentially impact the spread of infectious diseases (Asch et al., 1994).

The outcome in Berk and Schur's (2001) study provides additional support for De Genova's deportability principle. Berk and Schur examined the extent to which undocumented immigrants avoid seeking medical care because of their immigration status and found that 39 percent of the undocumented adult immigrants sampled expressed fear of receiving medical care. Moreover, those reporting fear of receiving care because of their undocumented status were also more likely to report challenges acquiring other medical services including dental care and prescription drugs. More recently, Watson (2014) found robust evidence that expansion in immigration enforcement practices reduces Medicaid participation among immigrant children, regardless of their citizenship or legal status.

Capps and Fortuny (2006) demonstrate that the habit of avoiding important safety net services out of fear of detection and immigration enforcement is not limited to just medical care but extends to other important areas that could help curb the hardship already facing immigrants as a whole and the undocumented more specifically. In their assessment report, Capps and Fortuny focused on the impact of child- and family-related policies on immigrant populations and noted that immigrants, including undocumented, are fearful of interacting with public agencies. Although discussing the hardships confronting immigrants more broadly is beyond the scope of this review essay, it is important to note that immigration enforcement strategies such as the Personal Responsibility and Work Opportunity Reconciliation Act of 1996 (Welfare Act) intensify the hardships and create a context of disadvantage that disproportionately impacts individuals most fearful of deportation.

Capps and Fortuny noted that deportation concerns, for example, have often deterred undocumented parents from applying for public assistance and services, including Temporary Assistance for Needy Families (TANF), food stamps, housing, and medical care (Holcomb, Tumlin, Koralek, Capps, & Zuberi, 2003). Logically, the hardships faced by immigrant parents are passed down to their children, who may be citizens and thus qualify for a variety of public benefit programs. In their assessment of child and family policies, Capps and Fortuny also found that despite higher poverty and hardship rates, children in immigrant families are less likely than children from non-immigrant families to participate in public benefit programs including public housing, voucher programs, and TANF. The stark reality is that even when the children of undocumented immigrants are citizens or have legal residency statuses making them eligible for these program, their parents avoid seeking help out of fear of deportation (Capps, Hagan, & Rodriguez, 2004).

In an effort to expand the literature on the relationship between deportability and its effects on families, Brabeck and Xu (2010) conducted a quantitative exploration of immigrant families' legal vulnerability and examined the impact of the threat and experience of detention and deportation on the family context. Brabeck and Xu measured parent legal vulnerability through a series of questions as to whether the parent: is undocumented or not, has been previously deported or has a current removal order, has a relative who had been deported, was previously in immigration detention, or has a family member currently in detention. Results from their analyses indicate that parent legal vulnerability and history and experience with detention and deportation significantly impact the family's emotional and financial well-being, including the well-being of involved children. Although these listed hardships shift the discussion point from a deportation matter to the much larger issue of immigration and poverty, they nonetheless make up a significant part of the social effects of the immigration laws passed in the 1980s and 1990s.

Evidently, the emerging literature does indicate that the social and psychological effects of removal policies are not only limited to the individuals at risk for deportations, but also extend to their children, spouses, and other close relatives (Capps, Castañeda, Chaudry, & Santos, 2007; Mendoza & Olivos, 2009; J. E. Morris & Palazuelos, 2015; Parker, 2009). In one example, Capps et al. (2016) examined two years of in-depth interviews conducted of parents and their children during and after the deportation and detention proceedings, and found evidence of significant trauma and stress, and also noted anxiety, mental health, and physical health challenges were common outcomes. Capps and colleagues also found that loss of earnings, increased dependence on public assistance and charity, and increased family hardships were commonly reported. Lastly, the researchers not only found that mental health was a challenge for the parents experiencing deportation and detention, but also for the children who exhibited signs of anxiety and other important behavioral changes. In a similar study, Hagan and colleagues (2010) found that anxiety, stress, confusion, and fear were quite common for immigrants and their family members in those communities.

Other researchers have also documented the fear of family separation, which happens frequently to deportees (Dreby, 2012; Horner et al., 2014; Mendoza & Olivos, 2009; Parker, 2009). Horner and colleagues (2014) used in-depth interviews and focus groups with 20 children who themselves were at risk of deportation and/or whose parents had been deported or were also at risk of deportation and identified experiences of isolation, exclusion, and conflicted realities that prevent the children from being fully incorporated into American society. Horner and colleagues found that these children were living in high stress environments, facing conditions analogous to post-traumatic stress. Evidence from social and psychological research indicates that forced parent-child separation and parental loss are potentially traumatic events (PTE) (Finkelhor, Ormrod, Turner, & Hamby, 2005; Finkelhor, Ormrod, & Turner, 2009). Emerging research in this subject area has indicated that parental detention and deportation heightens the risk for adverse child mental health effects, including possibilities for psychological distress, anxiety, and depression (Allen, Cisneros, & Tellez, 2015; Zayas, Aguilar-Gaxiola, Yoon, & Rey, 2015). In a more recent study, Rojas-Flores, Clements, Hwang Koo, and London (2017) compared citizen children of detained and deported parents to peers whose parents have never had contact with immigration enforcement authorities and found higher levels of PTSD symptoms as reported by the parent in the former. The findings revealed heightened PTSD symptoms following the detention or deportation of a parent.

The Impact on Children and Families

The effects of immigration enforcement practices continue to be an area rife for scholarly research, with avenues for building on the work of the more established prison and policing scholarship. In correctional research, for example, parental incarceration is critical for understanding the broader consequences of incarceration (see Chapter 8 for a review). Similarly, the effects of parental deportation and detention on children are critical for understanding the broader impacts of United States policy on immigration matters more generally.

A 2010 report by the University of California Berkley and Davis Schools of Law reviewed 10 years' worth of data (1997–2007) and found that roughly 88,000 U.S. citizen children lost a legal permanent resident parent to deportation (Baum, Jones, & Barry, 2010; Brabeck & Xu, 2010). Wessler (2011) also examined this issue of family separation due to detention and deportation. The report found that at least 5,100 children were living in foster care as a result of parental detention and deportation. The report noted that in the first six months of 2011, roughly 46,000 mothers and fathers of children born in the United States were detained or deported. Wessler (2012) obtained data from the Immigration and Customs Enforcement that highlighted that approximately 205,000 deportations of parents of United States citizen children in the two years between 2010 and 2012. A more recent report revealed an estimated increase to approximately 500,000 U.S. citizen children who experienced the apprehension, detention, and deportation of at least one parent between 2011 and 2013 (Capps et al., 2015; *U.S. Citizen Children Impacted by Immigration Enforcement*, 2017).

An important takeaway from Wessler's report was the realization of the gap in literature involving parental immigration detention and the risks of losing their children to foster care given the federal mandates terminating parental rights after 15 months of a parent being incarcerated. The mandates were enacted in 1997 under the federal Adoption and Safe Families Act (ASFA) and require states to file petitions to terminate parental rights of children in foster care for 15 of the most recent 22 months (Phillips & Mann, 2013). Although there is a sizeable body of empirical literature on parental incarceration including comprehensive reviews of ASFA (see, for example, Halperin & Harris, 2004; Murray & Farrington, 2005; Smith & Young, 2003; Wakefield & Wildeman, 2013; Wildeman, 2014), a significant gap in literature remains involving parents in detention and deportation proceedings. Wessler's report closes with a discussion of the potential for social developmental and social integration problems for separated children regardless if they are left in foster care or with relatives.

The Impact of Deportation on Communities

The empirical literature consistently reveals that deportation policies debilitate and destabilize the family unit; however, there is ample evidence suggesting that effects of these policies extend well beyond into other social institutions. The concept of avoidance or immigrant flight, for example, is a documented response to rising immigration enforcement policies (Baum et al., 2010; Singer, Wilson, & DeRennzis, 2009). With the expansion of enforcement policies, immigrants concerned with their legal status take precautions including calculated steps to avoid detection by immigration authorities. An evaluation of a 2008 immigration law passed in Prince William County, Virginia, found a substantial decrease in the population of both documented and undocumented immigrants after passage of the law. In addition to the evidence pointing to population attrition, the report also found that turnover was slow as many potential new immigrants avoided the area as a result of the restrictive policies.

In a related study, Hagan, Rodriguez, and Castro (2011) conducted 359 interviews with a sample of largely young males (over a third of whom reported living in the United States for more than 10 years) to document the social and human costs of the U.S. deportation system. Amongst a host of findings, the research also uncovered that it was common practice for individuals at risk for deportations to withdraw from the community and avoid public spaces such as restaurants and hospitals, with some even taking steps to avoid unnecessary expenditures (expensive furniture and cars) that could tie them to life in America. While Hagan and colleagues' work did not differentiate deportations on the basis of criminal convictions, it serves as a template for future researchers to consider following when more precisely examining deportations that result from criminal convictions and the impact on families. Hagan and colleagues (2010) noted that not only did rampant deportation policies break up families, but they also led to heightened sense of suspicion, fear, and distrust in immigrant communities (Hagan et al., 2010). From a criminological perspective, the work by Hagan and colleagues highlights many of the factors commonly linked in models for understanding the social disorganization of communities. Rose and Clear's (1998) coercive mobility thesis, for example, serves as an ideal framework for understanding how deportations can effectively destabilize a community. As a model, coercive mobility identifies the value of each community and treats the removal of residents for incarceration as a major destabilizing factor for community self-regulation.

Leyro (2013, 2017) builds on this social disorganization model through an in-depth examination of the relationship between immigration enforcement and crime. More specifically, Leyro's key research questions focused on whether deportation concerns, including fear and vulnerability to removal, disrupted protective mechanisms necessary for effective community self-regulation. Leyro was able to demonstrate, through qualitative interviews with noncitizens living in the U.S., that deportability (e.g., fear and vulnerability) leads to a breakdown of social ties and cohesion, thus impeding collective efficacy and blocking integration of residents in affected communities. Leyro's research introduces deportation as a key indicator in the social disorganization framework, particularly as it applies to immigration enforcement.

Other scholars have sought to examine the extent to which immigration enforcement practices including deportation may affect violence levels in ways that are not widely considered. Stowell et al. (2013) were among the first to examine crime levels in the context of deportation. In their work, Stowell and colleagues focus on how rates of violence are shaped by patterns of deportation. The researchers did not find evidence of a relationship between deportation activity and violent crime rates. More specifically, Stowell et al. found that initially, increased levels of deportation accompanied an increase in violence; however, when deportation activity stagnated, violent crime rates started to decline. Additionally, the researchers found no compelling evidence that deportation, measured as either an in- or out-flow process, results in elevated levels of violence.

In a more recent study, Wong (2017) used ICE data to do a comparative analysis across a range of social and economic indicators between sanctuary and non-sanctuary counties. The concept of a sanctuary county or city refers to jurisdictions that do not make it a priority to help with immigration control (Villazor, 2010). More specifically, communities that carry the sanctuary distinction do not assist federal immigration enforcement officials by detaining people in custody beyond their release date. In comparing sanctuary and non-sanctuary counties, Wong (2017) found that sanctuary counties have crime rates that are statistically significantly lower, and perform better on economic measures such as higher median household income, less poverty, and less reliance on public assistance to higher labor force participation, higher employment-to-population ratios, and lower unemployment.

Detention and Deportation Data Challenges

The evidence included in this chapter raises some important challenges for future scholarship. First, the collateral consequence of deportation resulting from criminal conviction is relatively unspecified given the lack of comprehensive publicly available data. Many of the descriptive reports highlighted in this chapter discussed the data challenges, underscoring that obtaining data was difficult, often requiring requests through the Freedom of Information Act.

It is quite evident when reviewing immigration statistics that inconsistencies in definitions and data used for reporting deportations, particularly when examining specific grounds for deportations, stand as a major challenge for advancing scholarship in this area. As an example, terms such as removals and deportations have been used interchangeably at various points in the past. The enactment of the 1996 IIRIRA, for instance, introduced removal as the suitable term, swapping out the more common term of deportation (Morawetz, 2000). Despite the change, government reports by the *Yearbook of Immigration Statistics* and the Department of Homeland Security website continued to use both terms, further confounding the issue. While this may seem trivial, the inconsistency matters a great deal in providing accurate data with potentially broad policy implications. Moreover, the inconsistency in the definitions and data is a major roadblock for disaggregating grounds for deportations.

Reviews of the literature on immigration statistics, including assessments of official government figures, raise many more questions than they answer regarding the issue of deportation as a collateral consequence of criminal convictions. Disaggregating deportations resulting from criminal convictions in these data is particularly challenging. The *Yearbook of Immigration Statistics* is a compendium of data on foreign individuals who entered, attempted to enter, or were removed from the United States. One of the goals of the yearbook is to provide data on immigration enforcement including deportations. The yearbooks prior to 2005 made significant efforts to disaggregate the data, while the reports after 2005 condensed major data components making it nearly impossible to parse out what lies behind the numbers, particularly behind deportations figures. For example, prior to 2005, the *Yearbook of Immigration Statistics* provided information on a number of data points regarding deportations including criminal, administrative, formal, worksite enforcement, fraud, and anti-smuggling activities. These distinctions allowed for a better understanding of the different grounds for deportations. Deportations based on criminality are handled differently in the post-2005 reports as these data are dichotomized on criminal status. Through this approach, the reports do not disaggregate the grounds for deportations; instead, deportations are simply distinguished as criminal or non-criminal, with the former referring to persons with a criminal record who are removed. Certainly grouping into criminal and non-criminal categories offers an unambiguous representation of deportations figures; however, this approach has limitations as there is no way to determine on what basis the removal occurred.

These data limitations raise attention to the lasting impact of the 1996 immigration laws. More specifically, the lack of clarity in the data highlighted above can be traced directly back to the implementation of the 1996 laws. The laws made it nearly impossible to accurately track deportations because they introduced countless overlapping clauses. Researchers from the Syracuse University-based Transactional Records Access Clearinghouse, better known as TRAC, report that very little is known about how some of the provisions of the 1996 immigration laws are used and about how that information is tracked and reported by the federal government (TRAC, 2006). TRAC noted that the federal government has yet to publish data on the number of individuals deported or put through deportation proceedings as a result of the aggravated felony provision of the 1996 laws. Other reports have also raised concerns regarding a lack transparency in immigration statistics (Ercolani, 2013; HRC, 2017). Warner noted that a lack of transparency by the Office of Immigration Statistics has made it nearly impossible to determine what specific grounds for deportations are being used for individuals with the criminal alien designation (Warner, 2005). Wiltz (2016) pointed to this in her reporting, which acknowledged that federal data on criminal deportees do not classify the types of crimes committed or the number of deportees who were undocumented, making it hard to get a clear picture of the factors driving deportation.

The Path Forward in Deportation Research

The challenge going forward is for researchers to continue advancing the literature on deportation, with targeted studies that (1) more accurately account for the extent of deportations that result from criminal convictions; (2) shift the focus of deportation research toward investigations related to post-removal outcomes, both for deportees and the communities that expel and absorb them; and (3) investigate the residual effects of deportations, including investigations related to the economic, political, and familial impacts.

First, although data limitations are important to overcome, the future of scholarship involving deportation proceedings will also require more evidence related to the financial and social costs of deportations resulting from criminal convictions. Deportation proceedings are slow and take months to complete. Throughout this period, individuals and their families face mounting financial burdens as a result of their absence. Other noteworthy avenues for scholarship include explorations of the impact of detention and deportation proceedings on processes within the criminal justice system, such as guilty pleas by noncitizen individuals that were conceded because of the deportability and vulnerability mind-set. Moreover, the lengthy deportation process also means a heavy burden on tax dollar-backed correctional budgets at both the state and federal level. The burden on correctional systems that resulted largely from mass incarceration, more generally, and the ratcheting of immigration enforcement played a major role in the privatization of the U.S. immigration detention infrastructure. The policies and practices guiding immigration detention, such as the bed quota mandates, detention lengths, and plea bargaining, remain as underdeveloped areas of study.

Last, deportation research seems to fade when the individual is removed, which unfortunately means that many opportunities have been missed in capturing the policy's full impact. For example, deportees do return to the United States, as highlighted above, but not much is known in terms of social science research about this cyclical process. The experiences of deportees have not been covered extensively in social science research, and very little research exists covering the impact of deportees on the receiving countries. For example, a number of the countries with higher deportation activity have major socioeconomic challenges including poverty that make the implications of deportation for these nations an important topic.

Additionally, the work of Brotherton and Barrios (2011) serves as a reminder of the vast areas of research that remain unexplored at the back end of deportation. Brotherton and Barrios were two of the earliest criminologists to examine deportation outcomes. Through five years of ethnographic research on deportees in the Dominican Republic, Brotherton and Barrios (2009) examined how deportees fared after being returned to their birth nation. The researchers found that in addition to the economic and other social hardships, deportees also face stigmatization that keeps them excluded from both societies, with other effects that remain largely unexplored. Future deportation scholarship can build on the work in the broader immigration and enforcement literature to potentially evaluate crime rates in receiving countries, with the hopes of better understanding how deportations resulting from criminal convictions shape crime patterns within those communities.

This chapter opened with the unfortunate story of Guadalupe Garcia de Rayos, Alas, similar tragic stories of deportees have become all too common in news articles, law review journals, and book chapters. What is not often shared is what happens on the back end of deportation. As a closing memo, an unfinished story is presented as a prompt for researchers to follow. The story begins at Boston's Logan Airport, where two ICE officers accompany a young man who is handcuffed and carrying a small backpack. The young man immigrated to the United States at the age of 3 but is being deported because of a criminal conviction. Since arriving in the United States, the young man has spoken only English and he has never stepped foot in any other country. The officers and the young man board the airplane, take a six-hour flight and land in Praia, Cape Verde, a small nation on the West Coast of Africa. After landing, the young man's handcuffs are removed and he and the officers exit the plane and go their separate ways. Stories such as this one are common for deportees, but the end of these stories have not been very well documented in social science research. The transition or reentry of deportees is an unknown area that welcomes more scholarship. Countries such as Cape Verde have no systems in place to identify, supervise, or assist these individuals. In Cape Verde, deportees depend on relatives, if they have them, to help with the transition process.

Conclusion

Although deportation has emerged as a popular theme across popular culture, with films like *Babel* and *The Visitor* vividly depicting the plight of immigrants subject to an increasingly unforgiving deportation machine, deportation has only recently emerged as a subject of empirical research. Studies of immigration and crime continue to far outnumber the studies of crimes leading to deportation. From a social science perspective, very little is known about deportations resulting from a criminal conviction, particularly as it applies to the post-deportation effects on the individual and his or her new community. As a consequence, we know very little about the impacts of deportation or its imposition as one of the many collateral consequences of sentencing decisions. This makes deportation in the context of criminology an area ripe for future research.

References

2014 Yearbook of Immigration Statistics. (2016). Washington, DC. Retrieved from www.dhs.gov/sites/default/files/publications/DHS 2014 Yearbook.pdf

Aas, K. F., & Bosworth, M. (2013). *The Borders of Punishment: Migration, Citizenship, and Social Exclusion*. New York, NY: Oxford University Press.

ACLU. (2016). *Prolonged detention fact sheet*. Retrieved from ACLU www.aclu.org/sites/default/files/assets/prolonged_detention_fact_sheet.pdf

Alien and Sedition Acts. (1798).

Allen, B., Cisneros, E. M., & Tellez, A. (2015). The children left behind: The impact of parental deportation on mental health. *Journal of Child and Family Studies, 24*(2), 386–392.

Almasy, S., Grinberg, E., & Sanchez, R. (2017). 'I did it for love,' says mother deported in Arizona immigration case. *CNN*. Retrieved from CNN.com website: www.cnn.com/2017/02/09/us/arizona-guadalupe-garcia-de-rayos-protests/index.html

An act to regulate the immigration of aliens into the United States. (1907). *The American Journal of International Law, 1*(2), 238–258.

Anderson, B., Gibney, M. J., & Paoletti, E. (2011). Boundaries of belonging: Deportation and the constitution and contestation of citizenship. *Citizenship Studies, 15*(5), 543–545.

Anderson, C. (Ed.) (2007). *Sepoys, servants and settlers: Convict transportation in the Indian Ocean, 1787–1945*. Ithaca, NY: Cornell University Press.

Asch, S., Leake, B., & Gelberg, L. (1994). Does fear of immigration authorities deter tuberculosis patients from seeking care? *Western Journal of Medicine, 161*(4), 373.

Baker, S. G. (1997). The "amnesty" aftermath: Current policy issues stemming from the legalization programs of the 1986 immigration reform and control act. *International Migration Review, 31*(1), 5–27.

Baum, J., Jones, R., & Barry, C. (2010). *In the child's best interest?: The consequences of losing a lawful immigrant parent to deportation*. Berkley, CA: International Human Rights Law Clinic.

Berk, M. L., & Schur, C. L. (2001). The effect of fear on access to care among undocumented Latino immigrants. *Journal of Immigrant Health, 3*(3), 151–156. doi:10.1023/a:1011389105821

Bhabha, J. (1998). "Get back to where you once belonged": Identity, citizenship, and exclusion in Europe. *Human rights quarterly., 203*, 592–627.

Boswell, C. (2007a). Migration control in Europe after 9/11: Explaining the absence of securitization. *JCMS: Journal of Common Market Studies, 45*(3), 589–610.

Boswell, C. (2007b). Migration control in Europe after 9/11: Explaining the absence of Securitization★. *JCMS: Journal of Common Market Studies, 45*(3), 589–610. doi:10.1111/j.1468–5965.2007.00722.x

Brabeck, K., & Xu, Q. (2010). The impact of detention and deportation on Latino immigrant children and families: A quantitative exploration. *Hispanic Journal of Behavioral Sciences, 32*(3), 341–361. doi:10.1177/0739986310374053

Brotherton, D. C., & Barrios, L. (2009). Displacement and stigma: The social-psychological crisis of the deportee. *Crime, Media, Culture, 5*(1), 29–55.

Brotherton, D. C., & Barrios, L. (2011). *Banished to the homeland: Dominican deportees and their stories of exile*. New York, NY: Columbia University Press.

Budgeting for immigration enforcement: A path to better performance. (2012). Washington DC: National Academies Press.

Bugajewitz v. Adams No. 228 U.S. 585 (1913).

13 Deportation as a Collateral Consequence

Bursik, R. (2006). Rethinking the Chicago school of criminology. In R. Martinez & A. J. Valenzuela (Eds.), *Immigration and Crime: Ethnicity, Race, and Violence* (pp. 20–35). New York, NY: New York University Press.

Capps, R., Castañeda, R. M., Chaudry, A., & Santos, R. (2007). *Paying the price: The impact of immigration raids on America's children.* Washington, DC: The Urban Institute.

Capps, R., Chaudry, A., Pedroza, J. M., Castañeda, R. M., Santos, R., & Scott, M. M. (2016). US children with parents in deportation proceedings. In *Migration in an Era of Restriction and Recession* (pp. 75–98). New York, NY: Springer.

Capps, R., & Fortuny, K. (2006). *Immigration and child and family policy:* Urban Institute Washington, DC.

Capps, R., Hagan, J., & Rodriguez, N. (2004). Border residents manage the U.S. immigration and welfare reforms. In P. Kretsedemas & A. Aparicio (Eds.), *Immigrants, welfare reform, and the poverty of policy* (pp. 229–250). Westport, CT: Praeger Publishers.

Capps, R., Koball, H., Campetella, A., Perreira, K., Hooker, S., & Pedroza, J. M. (2015). *Implications of immigration enforcement activities for the wellBeing of children in immigrant families.* Washington, DC: Urban Institute and Migration Policy Institute.

Carlson v. Landon, No. 342 U.S. 524, 527 n.3, 543–44 (1952).

Chacón, J. M. (2012). Overcriminalizing immigration. *Journal of Criminal Law & Criminology, 102,* 613.

Chae Chan Ping v. United States, 130 U.S. 581 (1889)

Chicco, J., & Congress, E. P. (2015). Legal and social work responses to the detained and deported: Interdisciplinary reflections and actions. In D. Kanstroom & M. B. Lykes (Eds.), *The New Deportations Delirium: Interdisciplinary Responses.* New York, NY: New York University Press.

Christensen, K., Read, R., Sullivan, J., & Walth, B. (2000). Unchecked power of the INS shatters American dream. *The Oregonian:* December 9: 1–8.

Clark, J. P. (1931). *Deportation of Aliens from the United States to Europe.* New York, NY: Arno Press.

Conlon, D., & Hiemstra, N. (2014). Examining the everyday micro-economies of migrant detention in the United States. *Geographica Helvetica, 69*(5), 335.

Cook, M. (2003). Banished for minor crimes: The aggravated felony provision of the immigration and nationality act as human rights violation. *Boston College Third World Law Journal, 23*(2), 293–330.

Coutin, S. B. (1993). *The culture of protest: Religious activism and the U.S. sanctuary movement.* Boulder, CO: Westview Press.

Coutin, S. B. (1998). From refugees to immigrants: The legalization strategies of Salvadoran immigrants and activists. *International Migration Review,* 901–925.

Coutin, S. B. (2015). Deportation studies: Origins, themes and directions. *Journal of Ethnic and Migration Studies, 41*(4), 671–681.

Crime Control Act, (1990).

De Beaumont, G., & De Tocqueville, A. (1833). *On the penitentiary system in the United States: And its application in France; with an appendix on penal colonies, and also, statistical notes.* Philadelphia, PA: Carey, Lea & Blanchard.

De Genova, N. P. (2002). Migrant "illegality" and deportability in everyday life. *Annual Review of Anthropology, 31*(1), 419–447.

DHS. (2013). *U.S. immigration and customs enforcement salaries and expenses, Fiscal Year 2013 congressional submission.* Retrieved from www.dhs.gov/dhs-budget

DHS. (2015). *Budget-in-brief Fiscal Year 2015.* Retrieved from www.dhs.gov/sites/default/files/publications/FY15BIB.pdf

Domonoske, C. (2017). After years of uneventful check-ins, Arizona woman is arrested, deported. *NPR.* Retrieved from npr.com: www.npr.org/sections/thetwo-way/2017/02/09/514299631/after-years-of-uneventful-check-ins-arizona-woman-is-arrested-faces-deportation

Dreby, J. (2012). The burden of deportation on children in Mexican immigrant families. *Journal of Marriage and Family, 74*(4), 829–845.

Eagly, I. V. (2017). Criminal justice in an era of mass deportation. *New Criminal Law Review: In International and Interdisciplinary Journal, 20*(1), 12–38.

Ekiu v. United States, No. 142 US 651 (1892).

Elkins, S., & McKitrick, E. (1995). *The age of federalism: The early American republic, 1788–1800.* New York, NY: Oxford University Press.

Ercolani, S. P. (2013). Why are immigrants being deported for minor crimes? *The Atlantic.* Retrieved from www.theatlantic.com/national/archive/2013/11/why-are-immigrants-being-deported-for-minor-crimes/281622/

Ewing, W. A., Martínez, D. E., & Rumbaut, R. G. (2015). *Special report: The criminalization of immigration in the United States.* The American Immigration Council.

Farrelly, J. J. (2011). Denying formalism's apologists: Reforming immigration law's CIMT analysis. *University Of Colorado Law Review, 82,* 877.

Fekete, L. (2011). Accelerated removals: The human cost of EU deportation policies. *Race and Class, 52*(4), 89–97.

Finch Jr, W. A. (1990). The immigration reform and control act of 1986: A preliminary assessment. *Social Service Review, 64*(2), 244–260.

Finkelhor, D., Ormrod, R. K., & Turner, H. A. (2009). Lifetime assessment of poly-victimization in a national sample of children and youth. *Child Abuse & Neglect, 33*(7), 403–411.

Finkelhor, D., Ormrod, R., Turner, H., & Hamby, S. L. (2005). The victimization of children and youth: A comprehensive, national survey. *Child Maltreatment, 10*(1), 5–25.

Fong Yue Ting v. United States, 149 U.S. 698 (1893).

Fragomen, A. T. (1997). The illegal immigration reform and immigrant responsibility act of 1996: An overview. *The International Migration Review, 31*(2), 438–460.

Galvan v. Press, No. 347 U.S. 522 (1954).

Gentes, A. A. (2009). *Russia's penal colony in the far east a translation of Vlas Doroshevich's"Sakhalin.* New York, NY: Anthem Press.

Golash-Boza, T. M. (2015). *Deported: Immigrant policing, disposable labor, and global capitalism.* New York, NY: New York University Press.

Griffith, E. (1999). The transition between suspension of deportation and cancellation of removal for nonpermanent residents under the immigration and nationality act: The impact of the 1996 reform legislation. *Drake Law Review, 48*(1), 79–136.

Hagan, J. M., Castro, B., & Rodriguez, N. (2010). The effects of US deportation policies on immigrant families and communities: Cross-border perspectives. *North Carolina Law Review, 88,* 1799.

Hagan, J. M., Rodriguez, N., & Castro, B. (2011). Social effects of mass deportations by the United States government, 2000–10. *Ethnic and Racial Studies, 34*(8), 1374–1391.

Halperin, R., & Harris, J. L. (2004). Parental rights of incarcerated mothers with children in foster care: A policy vacuum. *Feminist Studies,* 339–352.

Harisiades v. Shaughnessy, No. 342 U.S. 580 (1952).

Hernandez, C. C. G. (2014). Immigration detention as punishment. *UCLA Law Review, 61*(5), 1346–1414.

Hernández, D. M. (2008). Pursuant to deportation: Latinos and immigrant detention. *Latino Studies, 6*(1–2), 35–63.

Holcomb, P. A., Tumlin, K., Koralek, R., Capps, R., & Zuberi, A. (2003). The application process for TANF, food stamps, medicaid and SCHIP. *Issues for Agencies and Applicants and Limited English Speakers,* 7.

Hollifield, J., Martin, P. L., & Orrenius, P. (2014). *Controlling immigration: A global perspective* (3rd ed.). Stanford, CA: Stanford University Press.

Hoover, H. (1930). Annual message to the congress on the state of the inion. Retrieved from www.presidency. ucsb.edu/ws/?pid=22458

Horner, P., Sanders, L., Martinez, R., Doering-White, J., Lopez, W., & Delva, J. (2014). I put a mask on" the human side of deportation effects on Latino youth. *Journal of Social Welfare and Human Rights, 2*(2), 33–47.

HRC. (2017). *Systemic indifference: Dangerous and substandard medical care in US immigration detention.* Retrieved from www.hrw.org/sites/default/files/report_pdf/usimmigration0517_web_0.pdf

Hutchinson, E. P. (1981). *Legislative history of American immigration policy, 1798–1965.* Philadelphia, PA: University of Pennsylvania Press.

Immigration Reform and Control Act, S. 1200 (1986).

Jaret, C. (1999). Troubled by newcomers: Anti-immigrant attitudes and action during two eras of mass immigration to the United States. *Journal of American Ethnic History,* 9–39.

Kanstroom, D., & Lykes, M. B. (2015). *The new deportations delirium: Interdisciplinary responses.* New York, NY: New York University Press.

Kingston, R. (2005). The unmaking of citizens: Banishment and the modern citizenship regime in France. *Citizenship Studies, 9*(1), 23–40.

Kleindienst v. Mandel, No. 408 U.S. 753 (1972).

Kubrin, C., Ousey, G. C., Reid, L., & Adelman, R. (2017). Immigration and crime: What does the research say? *The Conversation.* Retrieved from https://theconversation.com/immigration-and-crime-what-does-the-research-say-72176

Kubrin, C., Zatz, M. S., & Martinez, R. (2012). *Punishing immigrants: Policy, politics, and injustice.* New York, NY: New York University Press.

Lasch, C. N. (2008). Enforcing the limits of the executive's authority to issue immigration detainers *William Mitchell Law Review, 35*(1), 164.

Leyro, S. P. (2013). Exploring deportation as a causal mechanism of social disorganization. In D. C. Brotherton, D. L. Stageman, & S. P. Leyro (Eds.), *Outside justice: Immigration and the criminalizing impact of changing policy and practice* (pp. 133–148). New York, NY: Springer.

Leyro, S. P. (2017). *The fear factor: Exploring the impact of the vulnerability to deportation on immigrants' lives.* City University of New York, Available from ProQuest Dissertations & Theses Global.

Li Sing v. United States, 180 486, 493 (1901).

Love, M. C. (2006). *Relief from the collateral consequences of a criminal conviction: A state-by-state resource guide.* William S. Hein.

Marley, B. R. (1998). Exiling the new felons: The consequences of the retroactive application of aggravated felony convictions to lawful permanent residents. *San Diego Law Review, 35*(3), 855–895.

Martin, D. A. (1987). *Major issues in immigration law* (Vol. 87). Federal Judicial Center.

Martinez, R., Stowell, J. I., & Cancino, J. M. (2008). A tale of two border cities: Community context, ethnicity, and homicide. *Social Science Quarterly, 89*(1), 1–16.

Martinez, R., Stowell, J. I., & Lee, M. T. (2010). Immigration and crime in an era of transformation: A longitudinal analysis of homicides in San Diego neighborhoods, 1980–2000. *Criminology, 48*(3), 797–829.

Meissner, D. M., Kerwin, D. M., Chishti, M., & Bergeron, C. (2013). *Immigration enforcement in the United States: The rise of a formidable machinery.* Washington, DC: Migration Policy Institute.

Mendoza, M., & Olivos, E. M. (2009). Advocating for control with compassion: The impacts of raids and deportations on children and families. *Oregon Review of International Law, 11*, 111.

Miroff, N. (2013). Controversial quota drives immigration detention boom. Retrieved from www.washington post.com/world/controversial-quota-drives-immigration-detention-boom/2013/10/13/09bb689e-214c-11e3-ad1a-1a919f2ed890_story.html?utm_term=.a4eda77698b7

Morawetz, N. (2000). Understanding the impact of the 1996 deportation laws and the limited scope of proposed reforms. *Harvard Law Review, 113*(8), 1936–1962. doi:10.2307/1342314

Morris, J. E., & Palazuelos, D. (2015). The health implications of deportation policy. *Journal of Health Care for the Poor and Underserved, 26*(2), 406–409.

Morris, N., & Rothman, D. J. (1995). *The Oxford history of the prison: The practice of punishment in western society.* London, UK: Oxford University Press.

Morton, J. (2010). *Civil immigration enforcement: Priorities for the apprehension, detention, and removal of aliens.* Retrieved from www.ice.gov/doclib/news/releases/2011/110302washingtondc.pdf

Motivans, M. (2012). *Immigration Offenders in the Federal Justice System, 2010.* Washington, DC: Department of Justice. Retrieved from www.bjs.gov/content/pub/pdf/iofjs10.pdf

Murray, J., & Farrington, D. P. (2005). Parental imprisonment: Effects on boys' antisocial behaviour and delinquency through the life-course. *Journal of Child Psychology and psychiatry, 46*(12), 1269–1278.

Naturalization Act (1798).

Navasky, V. (1958). Deportation as punishment. *University of Kansas City Law Review, 27*, 213–233.

Neuman, G. L. (1993). The Lost Century of American Immigration Law (1776-1875). *Columbia Law Review, 93*(8), 1833–1901.

Nevarez, G. (2017). Arizona woman deported to Mexico despite complying with immigration officials. *The Guardian.* Retrieved from theguardian.com www.theguardian.com/us-news/2017/feb/09/arizona-guadalupe-garcia-de-rayos-deported-protests

Ngai, M. M. (2003). The strange career of the illegal alien: Immigration restriction and deportation policy in the United States, 1921–1965. *Law and History Review, 21*(1), 69–108.

Nolan, R. (1975). Deportation as punishment: Plenary power re-examined. *Chicago Kent Law Review, 52*(2), 466.

Park, H., & Griggs, T. (2017). Could trump really deport millions of unauthorized immigrants? *The New York Times.* Retrieved from www.nytimes.com/interactive/2016/11/29/us/trump-unauthorized-immigrants.html?mcubz=0

Parker, A. (2009). *Forced apart (by the numbers): Non-citizens deported mostly for nonviolent offenses.* New York, NY: Human Rights Watch.

Passel, J. S., Director, P. T., & Lopez, M. H. (2009). *A Portrait of Unauthorized Immigrants in the United States.* Pew Hispanic Center: Washington DC. Retrieved from www.pewhispanic.org/2009/04/14/a-portrait-of-unauthorized-immigrants-in-the-united-states/

Perea, J. F. (1997). *Immigrants out!: The new nativism and the anti-immigrant impulse in the United States.* New York, NY: New York University Press.

Phillips, C. M., & Mann, A. (2013). Historical analysis of the adoption and safe families act of 1997. *Journal of Human Behavior in the Social Environment, 23*(7), 862–868.

Pike, R. (1983). *Penal servitude in early modern spain.* Madison: University of Wisconsin Press.

Pinard, M. (2010). Collateral consequences of criminal convictions: Confronting issues of race and dignity. *NYUL Rev., 85*, 457.

Polczynski-Olson, C., Laurikkala, M. K., Huff-Corzine, L., & Corzine, J. (2009). Immigration and violent crime: Citizenship status and social disorganization. *Homicide Studies, 13*(3), 227–241.

Police to Round Up Criminal Aliens Here; New Bureau to Get Evidence for Mulrooney. (1930, December 20, 1930). *The New York Times*.

Riley, K. (2017). Arizona mother deported to Mexico after living in U.S. For 21 years. *Time*. Retrieved from http://time.com/4665860/arizona-deportation-mexico-guadalupe-garcia-de-rayos/

Rizer III, A. L. (2016). The ever-changing bogeyman: How fear has driven immigration law and lolicy. *Louisiana Law Review*, 77, 243.

Rodriguez, S. A. (2005). Exile and the not-so-lawful permanent resident: Does international law require a humanitarian waiver of deportation for the non-citizen convicted of certain crimes. *Georgetown Immigration Law Journal*, 20(3), 483.

Rodriguez v. Robbins (9th Circuit 2015).

Rodriguez, et al. v. Robbins, et al. (2015). [Press release]. Retrieved from www.aclu.org/cases/rodriguez-et-al-v-robbins-et-al

Rojas-Flores, L., Clements, M. L., Hwang Koo, J., & London, J. (2017). Trauma and psychological distress in Latino citizen children following parental detention and deportation. *Psychological Trauma: Theory, Research, Practice, and Policy*, 9(3), 352.

Rose, D. R., & Clear, T. R. (1998). Incarceration, social capital, and crime: Implications for social disorganization theory. *Criminology*, 36(3), 441–480.

Rosenblum, M. R. (2015). *Understanding the Potential Impact of Executive Action on Immigration Enforcement*. Washington, DC: Migration Policy Institute.

Rosenblum, M. R., & McCabe, K. (2014). Deportation and discretion: Reviewing the record and options for change. Washington, DC: Migration Policy Institute.

S.358—Immigration Act of 1990, S.358 (1990).

Saggiomo III, R. A. B. (1981). Exclusion or deportation of aliens for the conviction of foreign crimes involving moral turpitude: Grand problems with the petty offense exception. *Cornell International Law Journal*, 14, 135.

Salinas, L. S. (2004). Deportations, removals and the 1996 immigration acts: A modern look at the ex post facto clause. *Boston University International Law Journal*, 22, 245.

Sampson, R. J., Morenoff, J. D., & Raudenbush, S. (2005). Social anatomy of racial and ethnic disparities in violence. *American Journal of Public Health*, 95(2), 224–232.

Santos, F. (2017). She showed up yearly to meet immigration agents. Now they've deported her. *The New York Times*. Retrieved from www.nytimes.com/2017/02/08/us/phoenix-guadalupe-garcia-de-rayos.html

Schmidt, S., & Larimer, S. (2017). For years, immigration authorities gave this Arizona mother a pass. Now she has been deported. *The Washington Post*. Retrieved from washingtonpost.com: www.washingtonpost.com/news/morning-mix/wp/2017/02/09/for-decades-immigration-authorities-gave-this-mother-a-pass-wednesday-when-she-checked-in-with-them-they-seized-her/?utm_term=.2c7d7ad9ed38

Schmitt, G. R., & Jones, E. (2017). *Overview of federal criminal cases: Fiscal year 2016*. Washington, DC: United States Sentencing Commission. Retrieved from www.ussc.gov/sites/default/files/pdf/research-and-publications/research-publications/2017/FY16_Overview_Federal_Criminal_Cases.pdf

Schuck, P. H., & Williams, J. (1998). Removing criminal aliens: The pitfalls and promises of federalism. *Harvard Journal of Law & Public Policy*, 22, 367.

Singer, A., Wilson, J. H., & DeRennzis, B. (2009). *Immigrants, politics, and local response in suburban*. Washington, DC: Metropolitan Policy Program, Brookings Institution.

Sinha, A. (2016). Arbitrary detention: The immigration detention bed quota. *Duke Journal of Constitutional Law & Public Policy*, 12, 77.

Smith, C. J., & Young, D. S. (2003). The multiple impacts of TANF, ASFA, and mandatory drug sentencing for families affected by maternal incarceration. *Children and Youth Services Review*, 25(7), 535–552.

Statistical Yearbook of the Immigration and Naturalization Service, 1998. (2000). Washington, DC. Retrieved from www.ins.usdoj.gov/graphics/aboutins/statistics/index.html

Stowell, J. I., & Martinez, R. (2007). Displaced, dispossessed, or lawless? Examining the link between ethnicity, immigration, and violence. *Aggression and Violent Behavior*, 12(5), 564–581.

Stowell, J. I., Messner, S. F., Barton, M. S., & Raffalovich, L. E. (2013). Addition by subtraction? A longitudinal analysis of the impact of deportation efforts on violent crime. *Law & Society Review*, 47(4), 909–942. doi:10.1111/lasr.12042

Stowell, J. I., Messner, S. F., McGeever, K. F., & Raffalovich, L. E. (2009). Immigration and the recent violent crime drop in the united states: A pooled, cross-sectional time-series analysis of metropolitan areas. *Criminology*, 47(3), 889–928.

Taylor, M. H., & Wright, R. F. (2002). The sentencing judge as immigration judge. *Emory Law Journal*, 51, 1131.

Thompson, G., & Cohen, S. (2014, April 6, 2014). More deportations follow minor crimes, records show. *The New York Times*. Retrieved from www.nytimes.com/2014/04/07/us/more-deportations-follow-minor-crimes-data-shows.html

TRAC. (2006). How often is the aggravated felony statute used? Retrieved August 29, 2017 from http://trac.syr.edu/immigration/reports/158/

TRAC. (2013). Legal Noncitizens Receive Longest Ice Detention. NY. Retrieved from http://trac.syr.edu/immigration/reports/321/

Travis, J. (2005). *But they all come back: Facing the challenges of prisoner reentry*. Washington, DC: The Urban Institute.

Trinh, Y. H. (2004). The impact of new policies adopted after September 11 on lawful permanent residents facing deportation under the AEDPA and IIRIRA and the hope of relief under the Family Reunification Act. *The Georgia Journal of International and Comparative Law, 33*, 543.

Turanovic, J. J., Rodriguez, N., & Pratt, T. C. (2012). The collateral consequences of incarceration revisited: A qualitative analysis of the effects on caregivers of children of incarcerated parents. *Criminology, 50*(4), 913–959.

Turner v. Williams, No. 194 U.S. 279, 290 (1904).

U.S. Citizen Children Impacted by Immigration Enforcement. (2017). Washington, DC. Retrieved from www.americanimmigrationcouncil.org/sites/default/files/research/us_citizen_children_impacted_by_immigration_enforcement.pdf

United States ex rel. Bilokumsky v. Tod, 263 U.S. 149, 150, 152 n.1 (1923).

United States Immigration Detention Profile. (2016). USSC. (2015). *Illegal reentry offenses.* Retrieved from www.ussc.gov/sites/default/files/pdf/research-and-publications/research-projects-and-surveys/immigration/2015_Illegal-Reentry-Report.pdf

Villazor, R. C. (2010). Sanctuary cities and local citizenship. *Fordham Urban Law Journal, 37*, 573.

Wakefield, S., & Wildeman, C. (2013). *Children of the prison boom: Mass incarceration and the future of American inequality.* Oxford: Oxford University Press.

Walters, W. (2002). Deportation, expulsion, and the international police of aliens. *Citizenship Studies, 6*(3), 265–292.

Warner, J. A. (2005). The social construction of the criminal alien in immigration law, enforcement practice and statistical enumeration: Consequences for immigrant stereotyping. *Journal of Social and Ecological Boundaries, 1*(2), 56–80.

Wasserman, J. (1953). The immigration and nationality act of 1952-our new alien and sedition law. *Temple Law Quarterly, 27*, 62.

Watson, T. (2014). Inside the refrigerator: Immigration enforcement and chilling effects in Medicaid participation. *American Economic Journal: Economic Policy, 6*(3), 313–338.

Welch, M. (2002). *Detained: Immigration laws and the expanding INS jail complex.* Philadelphia, PA: Temple University Press.

Welch, M. (2003). Ironies of social control and the criminalization of immigrants. *Crime, Law and Social Change, 39*(4), 319–337.

Welch, M. (2006). *Scapegoats of September 11th: Hate crimes & state crimes in the war on terror.* New Brunswick, NJ: Rutgers University Press.

Weld, W. F., Saphos, C. S., Zeldin, M., Harbin, H., Schneider, G., & Hollenhorst, T. M. (1987). *Handbook on the anti-drug abuse act of 1986.* Washington, DC.

Wessler, S. F. (2011). *Shattered families: The perilous intersection of immigration enforcement and the child welfare system.* Applied Research Center.

Wessler, S.F. (2012). Nearly 205K deportations of parents of U.S. citizens in just over two years. *The Color Line.* Retrieved from www.colorlines.com/articles/nearly-205k-deportations-parents-us-citizens-just-over-two-years

Wildeman, C. (2014). Parental incarceration, child homelessness, and the invisible consequences of mass imprisonment. *The ANNALS of the American Academy of Political and Social Science, 651*(1), 74–96. Wiltz, T. (2016). *What Crimes Are Eligible For Deportation? The Pew Charitable Trusts.* Retrieved from http://www.pewtrusts.org/en/research-and-analysis/blogs/stateline/2016/12/21/what-crimes-are-eligible-for-deportation

Wong, T. K. (2017). *The effects of sanctuary policies on crime and the economy.* Washington, DC: Center For American Progress.

Yearbook of Immigration Statistics. (2017). Washington, DC. Retrieved from www.dhs.gov/immigration-statistics/yearbook

Zadvydas v. Davis, No. 533 U.S. 678, 725 (2001).

Zakanaite v. Wolf, No. 226 U.S. 678, 725 (2001).

Zayas, L. H., Aguilar-Gaxiola, S., Yoon, H., & Rey, G. N. (2015). The distress of citizen-children with detained and deported parents. *Journal of Child and Family Studies, 24*(11), 3213–3223.

PART IV

Institutional Contexts

14

MASS JAIL INCARCERATION AND ITS CONSEQUENCES

Joshua C. Cochran and Elisa L. Toman

... the American jail operates as an archaic, unacceptable social institution; it needs to be changed fundamentally.

—Goldfarb (1975, p. 418)

Social scientists, like the general public, have shown a great interest in the prison but have almost completely ignored the jail.

—John Irwin's The Jail *(1985, p. xi)*

Two themes pervade the literature on local jails. The first is their importance; paradoxically, the second is their neglect by social scientists.

—Klofas (1990, p. 69)

... inquiries into the social role of jails, the internal social structure of these places, and kindred questions, have been rare indeed.

—Backstrand et al. (1992, p. 220)

Introduction

Early corrections scholarship identified jails as a central component of the criminal justice system, but one we knew little about (Bales & Garduno, 2016; Goldfarb, 1975; Irwin, 1985; Klofas, 1990; Mattick, 1974). By the early 1980s, jails housed millions of individuals every year for diverse reasons and lengths of time (Baunach & Kline, 1987). Knowledge about the experiences individuals had in jails indicated that they were heterogeneous, salient, and potentially more adverse than the experiences of state prisoners (Irwin, 1985; Klofas, 1987; Mays & Thompson, 1988; Senese & Kalinich, 1993). Earlier work also identified that, by contrast to prisons, our understanding of jail experiences and their effects was limited and that dramatically more research was needed to understand the implications of the expanding jail systems in the United States along with potential avenues for reform (Backstrand et al., 1992). John Irwin (1985, p. 118) acknowledged as much in his book *The Jail*, where he wrote that academics knew little about the effects and collateral harms of jails and that "[p]rogress on this agenda," that is, the agenda of rethinking the criminal justice system and the role of jails in it, "if it occurs at all, will necessarily be slow."

And slow it has been. Now, more than three decades later, the state of jail research is little improved. With some exceptions (see, Freudenberg et al., 2005; May et al., 2014; Solomon et al., 2008), we have only a limited understanding of the typical sets of experiences individuals have in jail, how those experiences vary across groups and contexts, how they compare to the typical experiences of individuals incarcerated in state prisons, and, generally, the short- and long-term consequences of spending time in a jail. By extension, and unlike prison scholarship, we know little about the relative effectiveness of jail as a correctional sanction (Cochran et al., 2014), about the potential collateral consequences of jail (Pogrebin et al., 2001; Weisheit & Klofas, 1990), or about the extent to which jails lead to or exacerbate social and economic inequalities (e.g., Western & Pettit, 2010). Indeed, although scholars have argued that prison experiences and their effects constitute a "black box" (Mears, 2008; DeLisi, Trulson, Marquart, Drury, & Kosloski, 2011; see also, Nagin et al., 2009; Sampson, 2011), the state of knowledge surrounding jail effects is by comparison more anemic and, in keeping with the metaphor, exists in a box further devoid of light.

These research gaps were problematic in the 1980s and earlier, but the stakes today are even higher. When John Irwin's book was published in 1985, the stock population of U.S. jails was approximately 223,000 inmates with over 8 million admissions to jails per year (Baunach & Kline, 1987; Henrichson et al., 2015). Today, the stock population in U.S. jails is over 700,000 inmates and there are nearly 11 million jail admissions every year (Minton & Zeng, 2016). The U.S. was spending approximately $5.7 billion on jails annually in the early 1980s but spends more than $22 billion today (Henrichson et al., 2015). And, as of 2017, it appears as if jails will continue to expand well into the foreseeable future. This is due, at least in part, to a perpetually expanding use of pretrial detention, expanding use of jails as "bed rentals" for state and federal institutions (Aiken, 2017), and perhaps also as a result of state-level decarceration efforts that have to date operated by utilizing local jails as an outlet for inmates who otherwise would have been held in a prison (California Department of Corrections and Rehabilitation, 2013a; Caudill et al., 2014; Petersilia & Snyder, 2013).

Thus, the overall lack of research on jail experiences and their effects is anomalous given the large-scale, expanding use of jails and, in turn, the potential salience of jail experiences for individuals, families, and communities. It is anomalous, too, given the relatively voluminous body of research centered on prisons.[1] Jails admit—and conceivably affect—substantially more individuals than state prisons do. In turn, policy implications stemming from jail research may stand to make more appreciable impacts. The gap is even more anomalous given that jail experiences may be worse, or have more adverse implications, compared to the typical experiences inherent to state prisons. Limited existing studies and inmate accounts suggest, for example, that experiences in jail may be more chaotic and tumultuous and elicit greater pains than those stemming from a stay in prison (e.g., George, 2010; Gibbs, 1987; Irwin, 1985; May et al., 2014). Not least, theory and research suggest that jail incarceration may operate via a host of mechanisms to not only be harmful to individuals, families, and communities, but to also be especially harmful to already disadvantaged groups (Pettit & Western, 2004).

This Chapter

Against this backdrop, the goal of this chapter is twofold. First, and broadly, we revive an old argument—that jail incarceration and, now, *mass* jail incarceration has unique and salient implications, but we know little about them. Although both jails and prisons contribute to the large-scale use of incarceration in the U.S., jails may elicit different effects on recidivism and different, or worse, intended and unintended consequences. Thus, jails deserve a research agenda that is substantially more coherent and robust than what currently exists.

Second, we construct a conceptual framework that seeks to advance development of such a research agenda and, specifically, a better understanding of jail experiences and their effects. Towards this goal, the framework identifies four key dimensions on which future studies will ideally focus. Namely: (1) heterogeneity in jail experiences, (2) the effectiveness of jail as a correctional sanction, (3) collateral consequences of mass jail incarceration, and (4) the contribution of mass jail incarceration to inequality. We argue that each of these dimensions constitutes an important, but relatively overlooked research domain, includes consideration of micro- and macro-level phenomena, and will require creative and cutting-edge qualitative and quantitative research efforts. Taken together, the framework provides a detailed roadmap for informing future theory and research and for developing evidence-based jail policies that increase the fairness and effectiveness of jails. It is a roadmap that we hope contributes to spurring on a surge of jail-centric studies and funded projects.

The chapter proceeds in three corresponding parts. It begins with a discussion of the unique attributes of mass jail incarceration. Specifically, we highlight key comparative statistics that emphasize the scale of jail use compared to prisons. We then turn to the conceptual framework and its four dimensions. The chapter ends with a discussion of the broader implications and challenges that flow from consideration of the framework.

"Mass Jail Incarceration"

The phrase "mass incarceration" typically invokes thoughts of get-tough sentencing policies and the use of more, and longer, prison sentences. Jails are ignored. Dramatically expanded use of incarceration over the past four decades has, however, included dramatic expansion of both prison and jail incarceration. Indeed, local jails have experienced nearly identical changes as a result of get-tough punishment movements as prisons.

Thus, before turning to the conceptual framework, we first provide an overview of the state of mass jail incarceration in the U.S. and, specifically, how jail statistics compare to prison statistics. This is important context in and of itself, but also for establishing a primary argument of the chapter—jails detain and affect a substantial portion of society, more so than do state prisons, which makes the lack of jail research especially troubling.

Policy changes over the last four decades called on jails to increase substantially their capacity to fulfill their two principle tasks—pretrial detention and a court-designated sanction for misdemeanors and low-grade felony crimes (Aiken, 2017; California Department of Corrections and Rehabilitation, 2013a; D'alessio & Stolzenberg, 1995; Lawrence, 2016). Together, these expansions created fiscal problems and management challenges as jails, starting in the 1980s, became overcrowded and understaffed (Shelden & Brown, 1991; Mancini, 1988). In addition, as probation and parole services became tougher and more restrictive (United States Court, 2017), jails were, and continue to be, tasked with detaining substantially more probation and parole violators (Beck, 2000; James, 2004; Tonry & Lynch, 1996). And, although jail incarceration has plateaued in recent years (Minton & Zeng, 2016), there are signs that jail use may continue to expand. For example, preliminary evidence suggests that state efforts to decarcerate (e.g., Caudill et al., 2014; Petersilia & Snyder, 2013; Pragacz, 2016) may actually cause local jails to experience influxes of diverted state prison inmates.[2]

As mentioned above, the Bureau of Justice Statistics reports an average daily population of jails of about 728,000 inmates (Minton & Zeng, 2016), up from about 250,000 in the 1980s (Baunach & Kline, 1987). The jail population is, though, dwarfed by the population of state prison inmates (1.3 million; Carson & Anderson, 2016). Examination of stock populations, however, obscures the footprint or relative impact of jails on society. Instead, the wide-reaching scope of mass jail incarceration is clearer upon comparative examination of inmate flow. Here, jails reign. Roughly 20 times more individuals enter into and out of jails compared to prisons every year—10.9 million jail inmates enter into and leave jails compared to 608,000 into and out of prisons (Carson & Anderson, 2016; Minton & Zeng, 2016). Ironically, we have a growing body of scholarship centered on understanding prisoner reentry (e.g., Mears & Cochran, 2015), but no such literature that focuses on jail reentry (see, however, Crayton et al., 2010; Frost & Clear, 2012; Janetta, 2009; Miller & Miller, 2010; Solomon et al., 2008; White et al., 2012).

Inspection of longitudinal incarceration trends over the past 30 years provides a fuller picture. Figure 14.1[3] provides a comparison of jail and prison changes in average daily population (panel A) and annual admissions (panel B) since the 1980s. Inspection of the figure reveals a commonly overlooked fact: jail expansion has largely kept up with, if not exceeded, prison expansion. For example, the average daily population in prisons increased by 204 percent between 1985 and its peak in 2009,

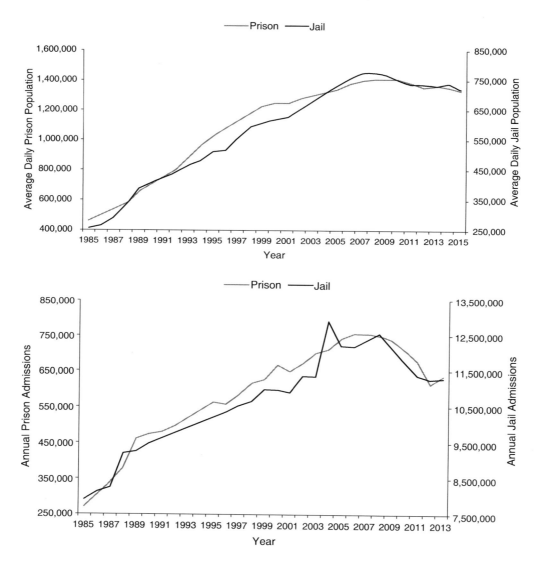

Figure 14.1 Jail and prison incarceration in the United States over time

Panel A. Average Daily Population in State Prisons and Local Jails

Panel B. Annual Admissions to State Prisons and Local Jails

14 Mass Jail Incarceration and Its Consequences

and the jail population increased by 203 percent between 1985 and its peak in 2008 (see panel A). Jail admissions have increased substantially, too (see panel B). Although the rate of jail expansion is less compared to prison, the absolute size of the expansion of jails compared to prison is substantially greater. For example, jail admissions increased 65 percent between 1985 and their peak in 2004, but admit today more than 3 million more inmates per year than they did in 1985. Comparatively, prison admissions expanded by more than 170 percent between 1985 and their peak in 2006, but have had to navigate a much smaller absolute expansion of about 350,000 admissions more per year today compared to 1985.

In short, jails affect a larger proportion of the U.S. population than do prisons in any given year and their role in the criminal justice system has increased substantially and, in some ways, just as quickly as prisons. However, especially when compared to theory and research on prison, we know little about the experiences of jail inmates or the various ways in which jails affect society.

A Conceptual Framework for Advancing Theory and Research on the Effects and Consequences of Jail

We now turn to a conceptual framework that seeks to advance a coherent and systematic body of jail research. Here, we identify four dimensions. Each dimension represents a key jail research domain. Our discussion of each dimension includes, first, describing the broad importance of that domain. Second, within each dimension, we provide a core set of specific recommendations aimed at informing future scholarship and empirical studies that work to address critical research gaps in the jail literature. To ease review and consideration of these recommendations, we have compiled them in Table 14.1. As we emphasize here and throughout the chapter, these recommendations should be viewed more as a starting point and less as a comprehensive list of the research questions that should be addressed in studies of jails. Many other questions exist. However, we view these particular recommendations as especially important pieces of what is undoubtedly a large and complicated research puzzle centered on jails and their consequences.

Dimension 1: Heterogeneity in Jail Incarceration

To date, we have limited knowledge about the experiences of inmates in jails. Most of what we do know about jail experiences originates from a handful of studies that consists primarily of early qualitative and quantitative assessments that examined a patchwork of aspects of jail inmates and their experiences. For example, a small handful of prior studies explored the different types of offenders jails hold (e.g., Irwin, 1985), the socio-economic and demographic characteristics of jail inmates (e.g., Freudenberg et al., 2007; Goldfarb, 1975; Mattick, 1974), the subcultures that exist within jails (e.g., Garofalo & Clark, 1985; Meeks, 2005; Rottman & Kimberly, 1975), experiences of jail inmates with misconduct and victimization (e.g., Fox et al., 2013; Ludwig et al., 2012; Senese & Kalinich, 1993;), and some of the methods through which jail inmates work to manage and navigate painful jail experiences (e.g., Gibbs, 1982; Rottman & Kimberly, 1975).

These studies are important because they provide initial insight into the extent to which jail experiences are heterogeneous and to which this heterogeneity may have salient implications during and after a stay in jail. However, these studies are also limited in important ways. Most existing studies, for example, are more than two or three decades old (e.g., Garofalo & Clark, 1985; Goldfarb, 1975; Irwin, 1985; Mattick, 1974; Rottman & Kimberly, 1975). Most also utilize small and non-random samples, focus on singular jail facilities, and employ bivariate analysis or other weak statistical designs (Fox et al., 2013; Freudenberg et al., 2007; Ludwig et al., 2012). These limitations raise questions

Table 14.1 A Conceptual Framework for Future Jail Theory and Research

Dimensions and core research recommendations	Example research questions
Heterogeneity in jail incarceration	
1.1 Examine who goes to jail and factors that influence jail populations	How do demographic profiles of jail inmates vary across time and place?
	How do inmate needs and challenges vary within and across jail facilities?
	What contextual factors impact jail populations?
1.2 Develop a more systematic understanding of the heterogeneous nature of jail experiences	What types of experiences are typical in jail?
	How do jail inmates maintain ties to outside social networks?
	How do importation and deprivation perspectives apply to jail inmates?
	How does jail social order compare to prison social order?
1.3 Examine contextual influences on jail experiences	How do jails differ across place?
	How do differences in jail characteristics impact jail inmates and staff?
The effectiveness of jail as a correctional sanction	
2.1 Assess the relative effects of jail on recidivism	What are the effects of jail on recidivism relative to other sanctions?
	How do jail experiences condition jail's effects on recidivism?
2.2 Assess the relative effects of jail on rehabilitation	How effective are jails, relative to other sanctions, at rehabilitation?
	How do program and treatment options differ between jails and prisons?
	What impact does the local nature of jails have on rehabilitative effects?
2.3 Explore the reentry experiences of jail inmates	What are the common challenges inherent to jail reentry?
	How do jail reentry challenges compare to prisoner reentry challenges?
	How does the local and short-term nature of jail stays impact reentry?
Collateral consequences of jails for individuals, families, and communities	
3.1 Identify the collateral consequences of jails for individuals	What are the collateral consequences of jails on life course outcomes?
	How do the collateral consequences of jail compare to those of prison?
3.2 Identify the collateral consequences of jails for families	What are the collateral consequences of jails for families?
	What are the effects of parental jail incarceration on children and partners?
3.3 Identify the collateral consequences of jails for communities	How does mass jail incarceration impact crime rates?
	Do theories about the social impacts of mass incarceration on communities apply to jails?
The contributions of mass jail incarceration to inequality	
4.1 Assess disparities in who goes to jail	How do race, ethnicity, gender, and other extralegal factors affect who goes to jail?
4.2 Assess whether jail experiences are more disadvantageous for disadvantaged groups	How do race, ethnicity, gender, and other extralegal factors affect jail experiences?
	How are jail experiences especially disadvantageous for poor and minority populations?
	Is jail reentry more challenging for disadvantaged populations and communities?

about the generalizability of prior analyses of jail inmate populations and overall highlight how little is known about jail experiences.

As we discuss further below, such limitations are more common in jail research than prison research in part because of the vast number of jail facilities that exist, limited access to comprehensive administrative jail datasets, and the fact that jails are local and so potentially more heterogeneous. In our view, these research barriers further motivate the need to understand what happens in jails, given that jails come in so many different shapes and sizes and exist within such a vast array of contexts.

Furthermore, understanding heterogeneity in who goes to jail and the experiences individuals have when they get there is critical for understanding the implications of jails and mass jail incarceration. The corrections literature has clearly emphasized this point in the context of prisons. Prison scholars underscore, for example, the importance of understanding how various prison experiences condition the extent to which a prison term leads to increased or decreased recidivism (e.g., Cullen et al., 2011; Nagin et al., 2009; Travis et al., 2014). By extension, recent examinations of prison experiences have included studies of a diverse range of experiences and their attendant effects during and after incarceration. These lines of inquiry include, but are not limited to, assessing variation in and effects of in-prison misconduct, victimization, visitation, vocational programming, drug treatment, education, social networks, and even food quality (e.g., Adams et al., 1994; Cochran, 2014; Kreager et al., 2017; Listwan et al., 2014; Mattick, 1974; Mears et al., 2002; Trulson, 2007; Welsh et al., 2007).

The literature on jail experiences is not nearly as robust. But systematic examination of heterogeneity in jail experiences is similarly if not more important for at least three reasons. First, jails entail a set of experiences distinct from prisons. One of the many reasons jail research may be so severely lagging behind prison research is the implicit assumption that experiences individuals have in jail may be similar to those that occur in prison (Klofas, 1990). If so, findings from prison research may be generalizable to jails. Theory and research suggest, however, that this is not the case (Cochran et al., 2014; Senese & Kalinich, 1993). Jails differ substantially from prisons in a range of theoretically important ways. Jails serve different purposes, feature different structural designs, utilize different administrative regimes (May et al., 2014; Newman & Price, 1977), and differ in the types of populations they house (e.g., non-convicted individuals awaiting trial, misdemeanants, less serious felony offenders) and the number of inmates they hold per year. By extension, the safer and more theoretically sound assumption is that jail experiences and their attendant effects differ in a range of ways.

Second, but related, jails are inherently more heterogeneous. For example, prisons are managed by states, but jails are managed by counties or municipalities. The local nature of jails creates heterogeneity. Compared to state-run prisons, jails operate under more limited and unstable budgets (Ortiz, 2015; Subramanian et al., 2015). Jail administrative styles and strategies may differ across contexts more dramatically. And jails will be more strongly affected by formal and informal practices of local law enforcement. For example, changes in law enforcement strategies to pursue more or less aggressively specific types of offenses and offenders (e.g., gang members, drug dealers) will influence substantially the types of individuals housed in a particular jail and, in turn, the experiences of anyone working and residing in the jail facility. A sudden police crackdown on heroin users will, in turn, create considerable strains on jail resources that target substance abuse and risk management (see, e.g., Bedell, 2015). By contrast, any given state prison population will be relatively insulated from such local-level policy changes.

Third, prior research suggests that jail experiences are more adverse and painful than prison experiences. Specifically, scholars anticipate that the typical experience in a local jail will be more chaotic and disorderly. This is due, in part, to the fact that jails house a more diverse clientele (see, generally, Minton & Zeng, 2016). For example, Minton and Zeng (2016) report that of the estimated 721,300 individuals incarcerated in local jails on an average day in 2015, roughly 37 percent were convicted (i.e., held in jail for their sanction) and 63 percent were not convicted (i.e., held pre-trial). And 68 percent of those individuals were in jail for felony crimes while 32 percent were held for non-felony crimes (p. 1). This diversity in both the seriousness and status of individuals incarcerated in jails exacerbates institutional challenges related to, at best, providing effective treatment and programming options that might improve incarcerated individuals' mental health, behavior, and demeanor and, at worst, avoiding unnecessary harms. For example, prior estimates suggest that although 60 percent of jail inmates are substance dependent and 65 percent are mentally ill, only 12 percent of jail inmates report participating in substance abuse treatment and 17 percent report receiving mental health counseling (James & Glaze, 2006).[4]

More than that, jail experiences are likely more adverse because jail populations are in constant flux. The weekly turnover rate in local jails is above 50 percent, ranging from 42 percent in the largest jurisdictions to 140 percent in the smallest jurisdictions (Minton & Zeng, 2016). This creates practical challenges for jail staff seeking to properly identify and manage inmate needs on any given day (e.g., Center for Substance Abuse Treatment, 2005; Torrey et al., 2014). Inmate churning also has other implications, such as impeding officer-inmate relationships and the ability of officers and inmates to develop rapport, which is useful for maintaining institutional social order (Conover, 2000; Crewe, 2011; Farkas, 1999). Challenges for maintaining jail social order are likely amplified by the fact that jails often house individuals during the most difficult part of their incarceration experiences—the beginning. Research suggests, for example, that the first days and weeks of incarceration are the most chaotic and painful as inmates learn how to navigate the institutional setting (Gibbs, 1982; Goffman, 1961; Harvey, 2005). This is precisely when jails house inmates. Thus, jail experiences may be especially adverse because both inmates and jail staff face greater challenges to behaving normatively and maintaining order, respectively.

To make much-needed advancements to our understanding of the heterogeneity that exists in jail experiences and the effects of this heterogeneity, we have three core research recommendations:

Recommendation 1.1—Examine Who Goes to Jail and Factors That Influence Jail Populations

Early qualitative work focused specifically on answering the question of who goes to jail. Now, the Bureau of Justice Statistics provides annual jail census data that provide national statistics on the composition of U.S. jail populations (e.g., Minton & Zeng, 2016). Research is needed, however, that extends these efforts to understand more closely how jail populations differ from prison populations and what specific needs and challenges jail populations present. Qualitative and quantitative descriptive examinations of jail populations are needed that can delve deeper into the characteristics and deficits inherent to jail populations across different jail contexts. For example, we know little about the status of jail inmates' mental health, substance abuse, social connectedness, education, or employment status and how these and other characteristics vary across time and place. Analyses are also needed that examine trends in inmate composition over time and across different jails and that can consider external factors (e.g., policing practices, local or municipal policy changes) that influence jails. How do social contextual factors influence jail populations? What role do police practices and policies have in creating jail population heterogeneity? How do any such effects vary across contexts? Answering these and other questions would allow for the development of improved theory, research, and policy aimed at understanding key challenges jails face along with the intended and unintended impacts of jails.

Recommendation 1.2—Develop a More Systematic Understanding of the Heterogeneous Nature of Jail Experiences

Research is also needed that assesses how jail experiences vary across jails and inmate populations (Carmichael, 2005; Klofas, 1990). Here, numerous questions exist. What types of experiences are typical of a jail stay? How often, for example, are jail inmates visited by family members and how do visitation rates compare to prisons? Visitation rates in jails may be higher given that jail inmates are typically closer to home (e.g., Christian, 2005). With that said, jail inmates are disproportionately poor and socioeconomic status is a key barrier to visiting (Hemmens & Stohr, 2014). When visits are impossible, how do inmates maintain connections to outside social ties (e.g., phone calls, video chats)? For example, reports and a small handful of empirical studies have focused on a recent trend in jails—the replacement of in-person visiting with video visitation or video calling technology (e.g., Martin, 2016; Rabuy & Wagner, 2015; Sturges & Al-Khattar, 2009). Video technology in jails can help reduce some of the safety risks incurred from in-person visits and, controversially, may provide revenue for private for-profit companies (Alexander, 2017; Fulcher, 2014). But we know little about the relative effectiveness of video visiting for improving jail safety and order or for otherwise allowing incarcerated individuals to maintain social connections on the outside as effectively as in-person visits. More broadly, then, how do jail inmates otherwise "survive" their isolation? How, for example, do coping or adjustment strategies compare between jail and prison inmates? And, how do jail inmates interact with jail officers and staff? How often do jail inmates engage in misconduct or receive infractions and how do jails treat or punish those who do offend?

These questions only begin to scratch the surface of existing research gaps surrounding jail experiences. Given the many possible avenues, on what experiences in particular should researchers focus? Prior incarceration theory and research provide important guidance. One broad avenue researchers should pursue is testing the extent to which theories about incarceration experiences (e.g., importation, deprivation, strain, legitimacy) apply, or not, to jail and prison incarceration. To our knowledge, no such comparative literature exists (see, however, Kellar & Wang, 2005; Senese & Kalinich, 1993). For example, importation perspectives argue that characteristics and experiences that individuals bring with them into the institution affect their behavior and experiences within the institution (Clemmer, 1940; Irwin & Cressey, 1962; Schrag, 1954). What imported characteristics are more or less common among individuals incarcerated in jails? And, what imported characteristics yield more or less salient impacts on, say, misconduct in the jail environment compared to the prison environment?

Similarly, relative to prison studies, limited empirical knowledge exists about the typical deprivations and strains that individuals face in jails (e.g., Blevins et al., 2010; Morris et al., 2012; Sykes, 1958; Sykes & Messinger, 1960). Prior research suggests assertively that jail experiences are more adverse and painful than prison experiences (Center for Substance Abuse Treatment, 2005; May et al., 2014; May & Wood, 2010; Ortiz, 2015; Subramanian et al., 2015; Torrey et al., 2014). Irwin (1985:xi) argued that jails, as opposed to prisons, "impose the cruelest form of punishment in the United States." And Goldfarb (1975, p. 5) wrote, after conducting research on prisons and jails, that "[o]ur prisons are used to incarcerate men convicted of serious crimes and our jails primarily hold people who are awaiting trial, who have been convicted of nothing; yet our jails are far worse than our prisons."

Empirical studies are needed that can bring data to bear on questions about the relative adversity individuals incarcerated in jails face. Using deprivation perspectives as a theoretical lens, we need a detailed empirical portrait of the kinds of pains individuals experience, assessment of who is more likely to experience them, and consideration of how those experiences might differ across place and time. Do jails offer fewer or lower quality treatment and programs compared to state prisons? Mattick (1974, p. 819) wrote, for example, about the "curse of idleness" in jails that results in part from the absence, generally, of useful work and rehabilitative programs in most jail facilities (see, also, Rottman & Kimberly, 1975). What is the current state of idleness among jail inmates and how does it compare to those incarcerated in state prisons? Furthermore, do jail inmates pose greater treatment needs and behavioral problems than typical prison inmates? And, are jail facilities properly equipped to diagnose and assess those needs?

A host of other questions that go beyond social support, misconduct, strains, and programming exist and are important. Answering these and other questions about the heterogeneous nature of jail experiences is a critical task for informing future studies that seek, among other goals, to understand the effects of jail. As the prison scholarship has emphasized (e.g., Mears et al., 2015), the heterogeneous nature of jail experiences will likely determine the potentially diverse impacts of jail on individuals, families, and communities. Ideally, researchers can use existing theory as a guidepost for determining the most salient experiences to examine. From there, studies should focus on domains of incarcerated life that are theoretically linked to important short- and long-term outcomes. Studies should prioritize, for example, examinations of jail experiences that impact health, social support, employment, inequality, perceptions of legitimacy, and, not least, public safety.

Recommendation 1.3—Examine Contextual Influences on Jail Experiences

Studies are needed that also consider how context influences jail populations and experiences. This is a natural extension of the recommendations above because it underscores, again, the strong possibility that substantial heterogeneity exists in jails and jail experiences, yet we know little about it. Jail populations and experiences likely vary not only between any given jail facilities, but also across other macro-level units, such as states and regions (Mattick, 1974). For example, jails in eastern Pennsylvania may very well differ substantially in form and function compared to jails in western Pennsylvania. At the same time, Pennsylvania jails may differ substantially from New York jails. And jails in northeastern states likely differ across a range of dimensions compared to southern jails.

Given the local and autonomous nature of jails (Goldfarb, 1975), jail facilities and administrations will theoretically be more sensitive to community contextual variation than prisons. Jails located in rural contexts will differ substantially from urban jails because, among other reasons, the context influences heavily the cultures, demographics, and prior experiences of the incarcerated individuals and officers that reside and work, respectively, within the facility (Applegate & Sitren, 2008) as well as the capacity and utilization of the facility (Mattick, 1974).[5] Macro-level and multilevel research frameworks will be important tools for this line of inquiry. Generally, how does context influence facility, officer, and inmate characteristics? How, directly or indirectly, does context influence incarcerated individuals' behavior, facility order/disorder, programming, and other jail experiences (e.g., Huebner, 2003; Lahm, 2008; Steiner, 2009)?

Dimension 2: The Effectiveness of Jail as a Correctional Sanction

A varying proportion of jail inmates are housed there because they are convicted misdemeanants or low-level or non-violent felony offenders and are serving their punishment (Minton & Zeng, 2016).[6] How effective, though, are jails as a correctional sanction? Are jails more or less effective at reducing recidivism relative to other sanctioning options? Are they effective at rehabilitating individuals?

The current body of research on jail sanction effects provides little basis for answering these questions. Indeed, recent reviews and meta-analyses have identified glaring weaknesses in the state of research on how incarceration affects recidivism relative to non-incarcerative sanctions (e.g., Gendreau et al., 1996; Mears et al., 2015; Nagin et al., 2009). These studies and reviews, though, uniformly focus on how *prison* affects recidivism. Thus, the state of knowledge on the effects of *jails* on recidivism is even weaker (Frost & Clear, 2012). For example, only a handful of studies, to our knowledge, assess the effects of jail on recidivism (e.g., Deyoung, 1997; Wodahl et al., 2015) and fewer still do so by employing advanced methodological designs, such as those that can rigorously account for potential sources of confounding or that compare jail effects to theory- and policy-relevant counterfactual scenarios (e.g., jail effects compared to prison, probation, fines, etc.; see, e.g., Cochran et al., 2014; Mitchell et al., 2017; Nagin et al., 2009).

14 Mass Jail Incarceration and Its Consequences

What is needed, then, is the development of a systematic body of research that examines the relative effects of spending time in jail on key correctional outcomes, including recidivism and rehabilitation. It is here where we focus our next set of recommendations.

Recommendation 2.1—Assess the Relative Effects of Jail on Recidivism

Studies are needed that examine jail effects on recidivism relevant to alternative sanction options. Consider, for example, the deliberations of a prosecutor and judge about a given convicted individual. In theory, most individuals incarcerated in jails could have conceivably received a range of alternative sanctions, such as a fine, restitution, probation, intensive probation, or a short prison term (e.g., Mears et al., 2015).[7] What basis exists, however, to know if and when jail is an appropriate option? Put differently, when, in the interests of public safety, should courts opt for a jail term instead of a community sanction? Or when should courts be lenient and give a shorter jail sentence instead of a longer prison sentence? Theoretically, when does a jail sentence provide too much, too little, or just enough deterrence?

Assessments of jail effects on recidivism along the lines of deterrence and other theoretical perspectives are needed and should use recent studies of prison effects as a model. Here, scholars have begun to utilize a range of advanced statistical techniques to identify more accurate estimates of the causal impacts of prison stays on recidivism relative to other sanction options. For example, recent studies have utilized propensity score matching methodologies to account more rigorously for observed sources of confounding (Bales & Piquero, 2012; Loughran et al., 2009). Scholars have also identified opportunities to use instrumental variables and regression discontinuity designs, which theoretically perform better at accounting for sources of unmeasured or unobserved confounding and, in turn, provide more accurate estimates of sanction effects (Green & Winik, 2010; Loeffler, 2013; Mitchell et al., 2017; Pelissier et al., 2003). Similar opportunities likely exist to assess the effects of jails.

In addition, and by extension to dimension 1, studies of jail effects on recidivism will need to consider variation in jail effects that might be caused by heterogeneity in jail experiences (Mears et al., 2015). For example, when does jail reduce recidivism and when does it increase it, or have no effect? For which types of jail inmates or jail experiences? Similarly, how do community and jail contexts contribute not only to jail experiences, but also to the effectiveness of jails for reducing recidivism?

Research that assesses these and related questions stands to make critical contributions to theory and policy. Such studies will, for example, contribute to our understanding of jail effects on recidivism and, more broadly, how deterrence and the selection of severity of punishment affects convicted individuals' future behavior. Specifically, for policy, a more robust understanding of the relative effects of jail as a sanction will provide valuable insight into the public safety benefits of jail as opposed to potentially more affordable, if not more humane, opportunities to allow individuals to remain in the community under supervision. Such studies, in turn, will provide an important evidence-based platform for informing efforts to reevaluate the use of jail, prison, and community-based sanctions.

Recommendation 2.2—Assess the Relative Effects of Jail on Rehabilitation

Similarly, research is needed that assesses the effectiveness of jails for achieving a different correctional goal—rehabilitation. This, too, is a natural extension of dimension 1. Here, though, the focus turns to understanding how experiences in jail—and, in particular, experiences with rehabilitative treatments and programs in jail—lead or contribute to successful rehabilitation.

Scholarship on jail rehabilitation should focus both specifically and broadly. We need studies and evaluations of specific programs and specific aspects of jail facilities (e.g., Arditti, 2003; Linhorst et al., 2009; Swartz et al., 1996) that can determine what kinds of programs are effective and what types of rehabilitative needs (e.g., mental health, substance abuse, employment) jails and jail programs can successfully address and for which kinds of jail populations. At the same time, research is needed that takes on a "bird's eye view" of jails relative to other sanction options. That is, how, generally, do jails compare to other sanction options in their overall functionality as a rehabilitative mechanism (see, e.g., Mears & Cochran, 2015)? For example, does the local nature of jails improve their effectiveness at achieving offender rehabilitation? Or, are there components unique to jails that make them relatively less than ideal environments for rehabilitation? Jail stays are typically shorter than prison stays. A typical jail stay averages about 23 days (Subramanian et al., 2015), while an average prison term is as high as three years (Pew Center on the States, 2012). Jails themselves, due to budget or staffing constraints, may offer fewer or lower quality programs (Subramanian et al., 2015). Thus, it may be that jails provide fewer or less effective rehabilitative opportunities relative to prisons.

Recommendation 2.3—Explore the Reentry Experiences of Jail Inmates

There is also a broader need to explore the reentry experiences of jail inmates (Frost & Clear, 2012; Solomon et al., 2008). The existing prisoner reentry literature has focused primarily on the experiences of ex-prisoners leaving state and sometimes federal prisons (e.g., Mears & Cochran, 2015; Petersilia, 2003; Travis, 2005; Visher et al., 2004). Here, again, a straightforward approach for research involves developing a comparative body of literature with an emphasis on jails. For example, what are the common challenges and barriers that ex-jail inmates face? Where do jail inmates go immediately after release? Are they more or less likely than ex-prisoners to struggle with reuniting with family, obtaining employment, connecting to healthcare, or the vast array of other challenges inherent to prisoner reentry (e.g., Mears & Cochran, 2015; Hammett et al., 2001)? And, how do inherent differences in jail incarceration, such as shorter lengths of stay and remaining in closer proximity to the community, affect, if at all, reentry experiences?

Systematic exploration of jail reentry experiences will be critical not only for documenting unique barriers and challenges that individuals and their families face, it will also shed light on the causal mechanisms that explain identified effects in studies of recidivism and rehabilitation. When formerly jail-incarcerated individuals recidivate, what contributed to that recidivism? Was it a particular reentry challenge? Or, if desistance happens, what was the cause? Successful rehabilitation programs in jail? Family reunification? Change in demeanor or attitude (e.g., Maruna, 2001)? Generally, then, a focus on jail reentry can provide a more robust view of the overall effects of a jail term and the factors that contribute to them.

Dimension 3: Collateral Consequences of Jails for Individuals, Families, and Communities

Jails also deserve a dedicated body of scholarship aimed at understanding other effects and potential collateral harms stemming from jail incarceration. This body of research should include a focus on both the consequences resulting from stays in pretrial detention and the use of jail as a sanction. Such research should also use theory and prior studies of the collateral consequences of prison to consider the many and multifaceted ways in which jail incarceration might harm individuals, families, and communities.

There is a growing and relatively rich existing empirical literature that examines how prisons and mass prison incarceration have led to collateral harms. Prison incarceration is linked to a range of adverse effects on individuals' future life course outcomes including reduced opportunities for employment and lowered earnings (e.g., Apel & Sweeten, 2010; Kling, 2006; Western, 2006), worsened mental and physical health (e.g., Massoglia, 2008; Schnittker & John, 2007), reduced access to social ties and social capital (e.g., Rose & Clear, 2003; Wolff & Draine, 2004), and more. For families, imprisonment can be lead to marriage dissolution (Lopoo & Western, 2005; Siennick, Stewart, & Staff, 2014) and generational transmission of crime and incarceration to incarcerated individuals' children (e.g., Murray, Loeber, & Pardini, 2012; Roettiger & Swisher, 2011). More broadly, mass prison incarceration has been linked to a range of adverse impacts on communities including salient impacts on economies and labor markets (Wacquant, 2000; Western & Beckett, 1999) and community social integration (Clear, Rose, & Ryder, 2001; Rose & Clear, 1998). Studies find, for example, that high rates of incarceration in the United States reduces the population of working-age men and increases unemployment rates by creating barriers to stable employment after incarceration (e.g., Western & Beckett, 1999). At the same time, communities that experience high rates of incarceration amongst its members become more socially disorganized. For example, a high concentration of imprisoned community members operates not only to affect employment rates, but also to breakdown family structures and other sources of informal social control (Rose & Clear, 1998). A range of other community consequences stem from mass incarceration. Researchers suspect that high concentrations of incarcerated males in a community may lead to increased rates of sexually transmitted infections as well as increased prevalence of mental illness and incarceration among children living in those communities (for review, see Dumont et al., 2012; see also, Massoglia, 2008; Wildeman, 2016). By extension, scholars theorize that these and other adverse consequences of mass incarceration may, via a range of pathways, lead to unintended and adverse impacts on crime rates within communities with the highest incarceration rates. Mass reentry of individuals back into communities from prison without proper supports and resources—and thus a high propensity to recidivate—may result in measurable impacts on crime rates within those communities (Mears & Cochran, 2015). The concentrated, adverse impacts of parental incarceration may lead to aggregate generational transmission of crime and incarceration. And excessively high rates of imprisonment may have other impacts on community members, such as undermining citizens' perceptions of the legitimacy or fairness of the criminal justice system that, in turn, increases propensities for crime amongst community members (see, e.g., Tyler, 2010).

A parallel literature is needed that places in center focus jails and their collateral impacts. A limited, but critical body of empirical studies exists (e.g., Apel, 2016; Holsinger, 2016). We review those studies as part of our recommendations, below. The development of a substantially more robust literature is vital for understanding how the mass use of jails affects society. Here, then, the recommendations for jail scholarship are relatively straightforward. We need studies that work to disentangle the unintended impacts of jails on individuals, families, and communities.

Recommendation 3.1—Identify the Collateral Consequences of Jails for Individuals

Much work is needed that seeks to understand the collateral and unintended harms of jails on individuals across a range of short- and long-term outcomes. A focus on collateral consequences involves looking beyond typical correctional goals (e.g., recidivism, rehabilitation) and considering how a stay in jail affects critical social, economic, and health outcomes for individuals (see, e.g., in the prison literature, Apel & Sweeten, 2010; Massoglia, 2008; Wacquant, 2000). A range of qualitative and quantitative study designs can work to illuminate in various ways the impact of a jail stay on the life course of individuals by examining concrete outcomes such as employment status, mental health, and access to healthcare and prescription medication. Key model studies of jail impacts already exist but are limited in number. Freudenberg and colleagues (2005) published a study in the *American Journal of Public Health* that examined in-jail and reentry outcomes, via surveys, for more than 1,400 females and adolescent males leaving jails in New York City. Broadly, the findings indicated that individuals received limited access to services and treatment during a jail stay and that jail reentry poses a similar set of barriers and challenges to individuals in the year immediately following release. Van Olphen and colleagues (2009) assessed more closely the post-jail reintegration of substance-abusing females to assess the extent to which jail incarceration exacerbates the challenges individuals face integrating into society. Interviews with reentering females suggested that jail incarceration, like prison, creates added stigmatization and additional barriers to desisting from substance abuse as well as crime. Prior prison research and a small handful of jail-focused studies provide a template for these and similar categories of individual-level studies, as well as opportunities to compare and contrast jail consequences to those stemming from prison.

Recommendation 3.2—Identify the Collateral Consequences of Jails for Families

Similarly, we need a parallel body of scholarship that seeks to disentangle how stays in jail, either for pretrial detention or as punishment, impact inmates' families. To our knowledge, only a handful of prior studies exist that examine how a jail term affects children and partners of jail inmates. For example, Arditti and colleagues (2003) conducted interviews with family members visiting loved ones in a local jail to understand how the incarceration experience affected the visitors and their families. Their interviews uncovered a host of individual- and family-level impacts, including heightened emotional and economic strains. Pogrebin and colleagues (2001) identified similar economic impacts and suggested stronger consideration of community and work release programs that allow individuals to better maintain employment and familial roles despite a jail term. Apel (2016) examined the National Longitudinal Survey of Youth to assess how jail and prison incarceration impacts marriage and cohabitation. The findings suggest that incarceration causes an immediate and long-term disruption to partners' likelihood of cohabitation and marriage following a term of incarceration. Apart from these empirical examinations, we have little basis for determining whether and how jail incarceration may have parallel impacts on families and, in particular, children. Empirical studies of familial outcomes and children's behavior, school outcomes, future criminality, and socialization following parental jail incarceration are needed that replicate the current literature that has primarily focused on prison (e.g., Turanovic et al., 2012; Turney, 2014; Wildeman & Turney, 2014).

Recommendation 3.3—Identify the Collateral Consequences of Jails for Communities

Like with each of the earlier dimensions, current efforts to understand mass incarceration effects on communities are ongoing (e.g., Rose & Clear, 2003; Visher et al., 2004). The focus, though, has been primarily on the impacts of prison incarceration, and only a few studies exist that consider how jail incarceration affects communities (e.g., Freudenberg et al., 2005). Generically, this literature is also more limited—meaning, community-focused studies have received less attention than individual- and family-focused studies—in part because of the methodological and research challenges inherent to macro-level incarceration research (see, e.g., Spelman, 2008). What we do know is that mass prison incarceration has incurred significant social and economic costs, with poor, minority, and otherwise disadvantaged communities bearing the brunt of those costs. These include, but are not limited to, reduced community employment opportunities, increased rates of poverty, familial disruptions, increased racial and ethnic inequalities, reduced community social support, public health problems, and even increased violence in some areas (Western & Pettit, 2010; Western & Wildeman, 2009). For example, two studies, one by Western and Pettit (2010) and the other by Western and Wildeman (2009), contrast national level demographic data and demographic shifts against incarceration rates to layout the disadvantageous relationships and impacts of incarceration, at a macro-level, on communities and groups. On balance, national-level trends support the argument that imprisonment hurts the employment, housing, and familial success of those who experience it and, as both studies indicate, the communities, families, and children of those who experience it. Thus, the communities that experience the most incarceration suffer long-term consequences in their social and economic institutions. Both studies find, as do other scholars (e.g., Western, 2006), that young, minority males are disproportionately incarcerated and that, by extension, the adverse impacts of mass incarceration are disproportionately concentrated among poor, minority, and otherwise disadvantaged communities.

Despite these salient harms, has mass incarceration provided a public safety benefit? Understanding the linkages between crime rates and incarceration rates has proven to be a complicated research puzzle (e.g., Baumer, 2008; Baumer & Wolff, 2014; Uggen, 2012). For example, U.S. cities experienced a substantial decline in crime rates in the mid- to late-1990s, coinciding with continuing prison expansion and thus raising questions about whether the dramatic expansion of the prison system, perhaps due to incapacitation and deterrence impacts of imprisonment, caused or contributed substantially to the crime decline (Western, 2006; Zimring, 2007). The short answer? Probably not. Best estimates indicate substantially modest impacts of incarceration on crime rates and, if accurate, impacts that would certainly not justify the costs incurred.[8] For example, William Spelman's (2008) estimates suggest that, nationally, a 1 percent increase in the prison population results in a 0.03 to 0.05 percent reduction in crime. These impacts, though, might vary across states, such that some states might actually see modest increases in crime rates as a result of increased incarceration. Regardless, the crime reducing, or public safety, impacts of imprisonment appear to be, at worst, harmful and, at best, trifling, such that they could be easily considered a pyrrhic victory—one that has cost society members, minority groups in particular, far more than any benefits that have been received in return (Western & Pettit, 2010).[9]

Does mass jail incarceration provide a similar type of pyrrhic victory? We simply do not know. The jail literature can tell us little, currently, about how jails impact communities or how any unintended, invisible impacts might be balanced against the intended ones. We need to know the extent to which jail incarceration causes similar adverse effects on communities and the contexts under which jails lead to greater or lesser harms. In addition, we need to know whether theoretical arguments about the forces that lead to collateral harms of incarceration apply similarly to jails and prisons. For example, Daniel Nagin theorizes that overuse of incarceration can work to undermine the deterrence effects of severe punishments (1998), which, in turn, could work to desensitize community members to incarceration and potentially increase crime. How might overuse of jail incarceration have effects along these lines? Similarly, Bruce Western (2006) and others (e.g., Sampson & Loeffler, 2010; Wacquant, 2000; Western & Pettit, 2010; Wildeman, 2016) highlight various ways that mass incarceration contributes to disadvantage and social disintegration in poor, disproportionately minority communities. Here, again, how might mass *jail* incarceration lead, or not, to similar effects on community-level social and racial inequalities? (We expand on other issues related to jails and inequality directly below.)

Dimension 4: The Contribution of Mass Jail Incarceration to Inequality

It is possible, if not likely, that jails not only lead to a range of collateral, adverse effects on individuals, families, and communities, but that these effects are especially adverse for socially and economically disadvantaged populations. Poor, minority, or otherwise disadvantaged groups may be especially likely to spend time in jail, to have particularly painful experiences when they get there, and to be disproportionately disadvantaged as a result. At the individual-level, such inequalities in the experience of jails will worsen the social and economic circumstances for inmates and their families. At an aggregate level, such inequalities underscore the strong possibility that large-scale and expanding use of jail incarceration, and especially the disproportionate incarceration of poor and minority populations (Minton & Zeng, 2016; Pattillo, Western & Weiman, 2004), works to further solidify racial, ethnic, and social inequalities in communities and society.

Consideration of potential inequalities is relevant to each of the dimensions discussed above, but critical enough to warrant specific attention as its own dimension. Specifically, we have two recommendations for jail research aimed at understanding jail and inequality.

Recommendation 4.1—Assess Disparities in Who Goes to Jail

We described above the importance of understanding heterogeneity in who goes to jail and the factors that influence individuals' experiences in jail. Particular focus is needed, however, on understanding how socioeconomic status as well as race, ethnicity, gender, and other extralegal factors contribute to placement in jails. Understanding the factors that contribute to placement in jail is important for determining, then, whether economic and social disparities exist in who is most likely to experience jail and, in turn, to confront the collateral consequences of jail. For example, future studies should renew efforts to understand disparities in who receives bail, in bail amounts, and in who stays in jail because of an inability to afford bail (e.g., Free, 2001; Jones, 2013; see also, Goulette & Wooldredge, Chapter 15 of this volume). Specifically, researchers should focus on how economic disadvantage, minority status, gender, and the interaction of the three affects the likelihood of receiving pretrial detention. Similar disparities should be explored in the likelihood to receive jail versus prison versus community-based sanctions as a result of a conviction. This body of literature would be, in part, an important expansion of studies of court decisions and sentencing, which has, to date, primarily focused on factors that contribute to disparities in the receipt and length of prison sentences (e.g., Spohn & Holleran, 2000; Steffensmeier et al., 1998; Ulmer & Johnson, 2004).

Recommendation 4.2—Assess Whether Jail Experiences Are More Adverse or Disadvantageous for Already Disadvantaged Groups

The jail literature also lacks a coherent body of evidence that systematically differentiates between the kinds of experiences poor and minority individuals have in jail and how their experiences compare to those of more affluent and white individuals (see, however, Freudenberg et al., 2007). Similarly, limited research exists that explores how the experiences of females in jails compare to males (e.g., Binswanger et al., 2010) or how other social or demographic factors might operate to increase or decrease the adverse impacts stemming from a jail stay.

A more comprehensive literature on prisons highlights, however, important ways that race, ethnicity, gender, socioeconomic status, and a range of other factors shape incarceration experiences (see, e.g., Harer & Steffensmeier, 1996; Kruttschnitt & Gartner, 2003; Thomas, 1975). Unfortunately, we know little about whether these findings generalize to the experiences of jail inmates. Thus, critical opportunities exist to push forward research on the experiences of individuals in jails, the attendant effects of those experiences, and the extent to which those experiences sustain or exacerbate inequality.

Theory suggests, for example, that economically disadvantaged individuals may be especially at-risk for adverse jail experiences. Such inmates may be more likely to bring with them into the prison a host of needs and challenges (e.g., mental illness, substance abuse, educational deficits, reduced social support). These heightened needs are adverse and disadvantageous in and of themselves, and they are especially problematic if jails are indeed less well equipped than prisons or community sanctions to properly diagnose and address them (Center for Substance Abuse Treatment, 2005). By extension, social and economic disadvantage may increase the painful aspects of jail incarceration, which could, in turn, increase exposure to the collateral consequences of a jail term for social groups that happen to also be more likely to experience jail in the first place.

In addition, jail populations generally consist of a disproportionate amount of economically disadvantaged individuals because jails are partly filled with individuals awaiting trial and who could not afford bail (e.g., Goldfarb, 1975; Mattick, 1974). Meaning, jails are partly filled with individuals who are there simply because they could not afford *not* to be there.[10] This could have at least two implications deserving consideration in future research. First, the use of jails for pretrial detention means jails are filled with disproportionately impoverished individuals. Here, again, is a mechanism that works to disproportionately increase exposure of the most economically disadvantaged groups in society to any harms that stem from jail.[11] Second, this particular group of inmates may be especially agitated by and skeptical of the legitimacy of their current detainment. This may lead to a range of impacts, including but not limited to challenges to rule compliance and jail social order (e.g., Rocque, 2011; Sparks & Bottoms, 1995; Tyler, 2010).

Jail reentry, too, may be more difficult for less affluent groups (Jung et al., 2010). For example, the most disadvantaged jail inmates will be those who, if employed prior to jail, held jobs that are more tenuous and low paying than those held by more affluent jail inmates. Such jobs are precisely those that will be difficult to retain even given exceptionally short jail stays (e.g., a few days or a week). Less affluent individuals may also face greater difficulties maintaining ties to their outside social networks during a jail stay and so face greater social isolation upon release from jail (Arditti et al., 2003). For example, visitation, even to a local jail, can be arduous and expensive for friends and family members (e.g., Sitren et al., 2009). Even phone or video calls from jail can be expensive or unaffordable (e.g., Kukorowski et al., 2013). And, unique to jails, given the local nature of them, is the possibility that facilities located in particularly poor counties or municipalities may be those that can afford to provide the fewest resources and services both during and after a term of jail incarceration. Thus, individuals who spend time in such jails are not only disproportionately more likely to be already disadvantaged, they will be those who have reduced access to resources and services that might assist with reentry or otherwise protect them from the adversities stemming from time spent in jail.

Apart from broad focus on economic disadvantage, researchers should consider examinations of the unique experiences of other groups and ways in which jails might exert systematically disparate or unfair impacts. For example, gender-focused research is needed that can shed light on how female experiences with jails differ from those of males and how particular aspects of life in jail may be especially harmful for females. The prison literature highlights that females experience more mental illness, victimization, and more acute feelings of social isolation during incarceration (Greenfeld & Snell, 1999; Houck & Loper, 2002; James & Glaze, 2006; Kruttschnitt & Gartner, 2003; McClellan et al., 1997). These unique experiences then have important implications for female reentry. Similar gender effects may very well emerge during and after a jail stay. Similarly, how does race, ethnicity, and age affect, in isolation and combined, the experiences of individuals during and after jail incarceration?

Conclusions

Given the expanded size and theoretical social, economic, and public safety impacts of jails, one could easily expect that a robust body of scholarship exists dedicated to disentangling the various ways that individuals' experiences in jails are heterogeneous, how jails impact recidivism, the potentially adverse effects of jails on rehabilitation and reentry, and effects of pretrial detention and jail sanctions on individuals' families. One might easily expect, too, that scholars have systematically assessed the aggregate impacts of jail incarceration on communities and society, including the extent to which potential overuse of jails contributes to racial, ethnic, and other social inequalities.

Unfortunately, and perhaps surprisingly, no such literature exists. There is a glaring paucity of historical or contemporary empirical studies of the experiences of jail inmates and the effects of those experiences. Reviews and commentaries on the state and effects of mass incarceration commonly overlook the trends and implications of jail incarceration (see, e.g., Mears & Cochran, 2015; Parke & Clarke-Stewart, 2002; Pratt, 2009; Wakefield & Uggen, 2010). And, theoretical perspectives about the effects and potential collateral impacts of incarceration focus almost solely on prison incarceration (e.g., Blevins et al., 2010; Clemmer, 1940; Sykes, 1958; Turanovic et al., 2012; Wildeman, 2016; Wolff & Draine, 2004; see however, Pogrebin et al., 2001; Weisheit & Klofas, 1990).

We sought here to bring attention to looming theory and research gap surrounding jails, and mass jail incarceration, and to provide a series of recommendations that identify key dimensions of jails that represent pressing research needs. Specifically, we argue for the development of a substantially more coherent research agenda centered on jails that focuses on the four following dimensions: (1) heterogeneity in jail experiences, (2) the effectiveness of jail as a correctional sanction, (3) the collateral consequences of mass jail incarceration, and (4) the implications of jails for inequality. Within each of these dimensions, we worked to identify core recommendations and research questions that are specific and that would provide concrete strategies for contributing to the development of research that seeks to address each dimension.

It is important to emphasize that the research recommendations identified throughout this chapter are more than academic exercises. Each research question represents a critically important opportunity to advance theory and research about jail experiences and effects. At the same time, advancing our understanding within any of these or related research dimensions stands to make critical contributions to the development of real-world, evidence-based policy impacts. Indeed, if efforts to develop beneficial reforms that improve the fairness and effectiveness of criminal justice systems are to be successful, those efforts will require precisely the kinds of studies outlined here.

With that said, we see at least two key barriers, or existing impediments, to implementing the recommendations of this chapter. First, the development of a systematic body of jail research is especially challenging because of the diversity inherent to jails (Applegate & Sitren, 2008; Backstrand et al., 1992; Briar, 1983; Klofas, 1990). Jails vary considerably in structure, operations, administrative philosophies, officer and staff composition, inmate populations, and across local contexts. This variation creates difficulties for researchers to identify commonalities across jails. This variation also raises critical questions about the generalizability of research results that stem from a singular study or facility. Here, there is no magical solution. Instead what is needed is exactly what we argue for throughout each dimension discussed above—more and better studies that examine the experiences and impacts of jails across a range of groups, populations, and contexts.

Second, consideration of the framework and the diversity across jail settings underscores the need also for more and better data. However, obtaining jail data can pose considerable challenges. Circumstances vary, but the local nature of jails suggests that most data collection efforts will focus on singular jail facilities (Mattick, 1974). By contrast, in the prison literature, researchers commonly obtain access to large administrative datasets that include records from statewide or nationally representative samples or inmate populations. Local jails do not typically utilize overarching data systems within a state and instead operate data collections independently. Thus, collecting jail data, especially data from a sample of jails or all jails within a given state, will be cumbersome and resource-intensive.

Potential solutions for addressing these and other data challenges are complicated and, perhaps, ambitious. Currently, researcher access to jail data is seemingly sporadic and non-systematic. Not all jails will have accessible or quality data collection efforts, and obtaining access to jail data requires, among other things, researchers developing connections with data "gatekeepers" and administrators at individual jail facilities. Many other challenges and data obstructions exist. Ideally, then, collaborative efforts between jails and also between researchers can help to improve the coordination of jail data and the broader accessibility of jail data. State- and nationwide jail databases, for example, would require careful coordination and planning, but such efforts would be invaluable. Similarly, resources and efforts that help support new data collections, including studies that utilize both quantitative and qualitative data collection techniques, are needed to fill in the remaining gaps.

Overcoming these and other attendant research barriers is possible and sorely needed. For example, there are a handful of ongoing organizational efforts that we are aware of, including the Vera Institute of Justice Incarceration Trends Tool (http://trends.vera.org/incarceration-rates) and Measures for Justice (https://measuresforjustice.org), that seek to coordinate and warehouse criminal justice data across jurisdictions, counties, and states that might facilitate many of these research endeavors focused on jails. Given the salient potential impacts of mass jail incarceration on society, the time is none too soon for such efforts to ramp up.

Notes

1 Notably, however, state prison research is limited in important ways as well (Bosworth et al., 2005; Mears et al., 2015; Nagin et al., 2009; Reiter, 2014). Relative to empirical examinations of the effects of jail on recidivism and other key outcomes, however, the state of prison research can arguably be characterized as "voluminous."
2 For example, when California was tasked by Governor Brown to reduce its prison population, reports indicate that felon parole violators were not sent home, but instead were sent to reside in local jails *near* their homes (California Department of Corrections and Rehabilitation, 2013b).
3 Data for average daily jail and prison populations (panel A) come from multiple BJS sources (Baunach & Kline, 1987; Beck 2000; Beck et al. 1993, 2002; Beck & Karberg, 2001; Gilliard, 1999; Gilliard & Beck, 1996, 1997, 1998; Harrison & Beck, 2005, 2006; Harrison & Karberg, 2003, 2004; Jankowski, 1992; Kline, 1987, 1988; Minton, 2011, 2013; Minton & Zeng, 2016; Perkins et al., 1995; Sabol et al., 2007; Stephan, 1990; and Stephan & Jankowski, 1991). Data for prison admissions come from the BJS Statistical Analysis Tool (Carson & Mulako-Wangota, 2017). Data for jail admissions come from the Vera Institute of Justice's Incarceration Trends Tool (Kang-Brown, 2015). These data are based on the same BJS data sources but include interpolations calculated by Vera to account for any missing data. For more information on the Vera Institute of Justice Incarceration Trends Tool used in panel B see Kang-Brown (2015).
4 As a point of comparison, BJS reports that 40 percent of state prison inmates report receiving substance abuse treatment and 34 percent report receiving counseling for their mental health (James & Glaze, 2006).
5 Mattick (1974:789), for example, noted the following: "Rural jails are often empty; urban jails are usually severely overcrowded." More recently, though, some rural jails have become overcrowded (Kang-Brown, 2016).
6 There is some debate over the definition or characteristics of jails, and there is also important variation in the types of purposes various local jails serve. This is an important discussion, but to save space, we direct readers to prior deliberations of the defining features of jails (e.g., Mattick, 1974; Rottman & Kimberly, 1975; Klofas, 1990).
7 It is certainly the case, too, that defendants will receive a combination of sanctions and so complicate assessments further.
8 And, what are best estimates? In short, William Spelman (2008) suggests that the best estimates seek to account for the complicated causal and potentially lagged relationships between prison rates and crime. That is, because crime rates might affect incarceration rates and, at the same time, incarceration rates might affect crime rates, some sophisticated statistical gymnastics are necessary to come to unbiased estimates of the effect of increasing or decreasing the prison population. Estimating the effects of changes in the national jail population is likely to be similarly, if not more, complicated.
9 Weisberg and Petersilia (2010) provide examples of potential pyrrhic victories in punishment policies in the era of mass incarceration.
10 Disproportionate incarceration of the poor in jails due to an inability to pay bail has long been a problem endemic in jails. Goldfarb wrote, for example, in 1975 (p. 3), that "[o]ne stark fact of life is that generally people of means never see the inside of a jail."
11 Jail stays are often accompanied or caused by fees and fines incurred as a result of contact with the criminal justice system, which could work to further exacerbate the unequal impacts of jail (see, for example, Harris 2016).

References

Adams, K., Bennett, K. J., Flanagan, T. J., Marquart, J. W., Cuvelier, S. J., Fritsch, E., Longmire, D. R., & Burton, V. S. (1994). A large-scale multidimensional test of the effect of prison education programs on offenders' behavior. *The Prison Journal*, 74(4), 433–449.

Aiken, J. (2017). *Era of mass expansion: Why state officials should fight jail growth.* Northampton, MA: Prison Policy Initiative.

Alexander, B. (2017, August 10). When prisoners are a 'revenue opportunity'. *The Atlantic*. Retrieved from www.theatlantic.com/business/archive/2017/08/remote-video-visitation/535095/

Apel, R. (2016). The effects of jail and prison confinement on cohabitation and marriage. *The ANNALS of the American Academy of Political and Social Science, 665*(1), 103–126.

Apel, R., & Sweeten, G. (2010). The impact of incarceration on employment during the transition to adulthood. *Social Problems, 57*(3), 448–479.

Applegate, B. K., & Sitren, A. H. (2008). The jail and the community: Comparing jails in rural and urban contexts. *The Prison Journal, 88*(2), 252–269.

Arditti, J. A. (2003). Locked doors and glass walls: Family visiting at a local jail. *Journal of Loss and Trauma, 8*(2), 115–138.

Arditti, J. A., Lambert-Shute, J., & Joest, K. (2003). Saturday morning at the jail: Implications of incarceration for families and children. *Family Relations, 52*(3), 195–204.

Backstrand, J. A., Gibbons, D. C., & Jones, J. F. (1992). Who is in jail? An examination of the rabble hypothesis. *Crime & Delinquency, 38*(2), 219–229.

Bales, W. D., & Garduno, L. S. (2016). Confinement in local jails: Institutions and their clients neglected by criminologists. In T. G. Blomberg, J. M. Brancale, K. M. Beaver, & W. D. Bales (Eds.), *Advancing criminology and criminal justice policy*. New York, NY: Routledge.

Bales, W. D., & Piquero, A. R. (2012). Assessing the impact of imprisonment on recidivism. *Journal of Experimental Criminology, 8*(1), 71–101.

Baumer, E. P. (2008). An empirical assessment of the contemporary crime trends puzzle: A modest step toward a more comprehensive research agenda. In A. Goldberger & R. Rosenfeld (Eds.), *Understanding crime trends*. Washington, DC: National Academies Press.

Baumer, E. P., & Wolff, K. T. (2014). Evaluating contemporary crime drop(s) in America, New York City, and many other places. *Justice Quarterly, 31*(1), 5–38.

Baunach, P. J., & Kline, S. (1987). *Jail inmates, 1985*. Washington, DC: Bureau of Justice Statistics.

Beck, A. J. (2000). *Prison and jail inmates at midyear 1999*. Washington, DC: U.S. Department of Justice, Bureau of Justice Statistics.

Beck, A. J., Bonczar, T. P., & Gilliard, D. K. (1993). *Jail inmates, 1992*. Washington, DC: U.S. Department of Justice, Bureau of Justice Statistics.

Beck, A. J., & Karberg, J. C. (2001). *Prison and jail inmates at midyear 2000*. Washington, DC: U.S. Department of Justice, Bureau of Justice Statistics.

Beck, A. J., Karberg, J. C., & Harrison, P. M. (2002). *Prison and jail inmates at midyear 2001*. Washington, DC: U.S. Department of Justice, Bureau of Justice Statistics.

Bedell, J. (2015, June 13). Heroin detox in jail costing taxpayers. *WHIO TV*. Retrieved from www.whio.com/news/heroin-detox-jail-costing taxpayers/uLUQ19okBL4FKMeIg1xMsI/

Binswanger, I. A., Merrill, J. O., Krueger, P. M., White, M. C., Booth, R. E., & Elmore, J. G. (2010). Gender differences in chronic medical, psychiatric, and substance-dependence disorders among jail inmates. *American Journal of Public Health, 100*(3), 476–482.

Blevins, K. R., Listwan, S. J., Cullen, F. T., & Jonson, C. L. (2010). A general strain theory of prison violence and misconduct: An integrated model of inmate behavior. *Journal of Contemporary Criminal Justice, 26*(2), 148–166.

Bosworth, M., Campbell, D., Demby, B., Ferranti, S. M., & Santos, M. (2005). Doing prison research: Views from inside. *Qualitative Inquiry, 11*(2), 249–264.

Briar, K. H. (1983). Jails: Neglected asylums. *Social Casework, 64*, 387–393.

California Department of Corrections and Rehabilitation. (2013a). *Realignment report: An examination of offenders released from state prison in the first year of public safety realignment*. Sacramento, CA: California Department of Corrections and Rehabilitation, Office of Research.

California Department of Corrections and Rehabilitation. (2013b). *2011 Public safety realignment*. Sacramento, CA: California Department of Corrections and Rehabilitation, Office of Research.

Carmichael, J. T. (2005). The determinants of jail use across large US cities: An assessment of racial, ethnic, and economic threat explanations. *Social Science Research, 34*(3), 538–569.

Carson, E. A., & Anderson, E. (2016). *Prisoners in 2015*. Washington, DC: Bureau of Justice Statistics.

Carson, E. A., & Mulako-Wangota, J. (2017). *Bureau of justice statistics correctional statistical analysis tool—Count of total jurisdiction population*. Washington, DC: Bureau of Justice Statistics.

Caudill, J. W., Trulson, C. R., Marquart, J. W., Patten, R., Thomas, M. O., & Anderson, S. (2014). Correctional destabilization and jail violence: The consequences of prison depopulation legislation. *Journal of Criminal Justice, 42*(6), 500–506.

Center for Substance Abuse Treatment. (2005). 8 treatment issues specific to jails. *A treatment improvement protocol TIP 44*. Rockville, MD: U.S. Department of Health and Human Services.

Christian, J. (2005). Riding the bus: Barriers to prison visitation and family management strategies. *Journal of Contemporary Criminal Justice, 21*(1), 31–48.

Clear, T. R., Rose, D. R., & Ryder, J. A. (2001). Incarceration and the community: The problem of removing and returning offenders. *Crime & Delinquency, 47*(3), 335–351.

Clemmer, D. (1940). *The prison community.* New York, NY: Holt, Rinehart, and Winston.

Cochran, J. C. (2014). Breaches in the wall: Imprisonment, social support, and recidivism. *Journal of Research in Crime and Delinquency, 51*(2), 200–229.

Cochran, J. C., Mears, D. P., & Bales, W. D. (2014). Assessing the effectiveness of correctional sanctions. *Journal of Quantitative Criminology, 30*(2), 317–347.

Conover, T. (2000). *Newjack: Guarding sing sing.* New York, NY: Random House, Inc.

Crayton, A., Ressler, L., Mukamal, D. A., Janetta, J., & Warwick, K. (2010). *Partnering with jails to improve reentry: A guidebook for community-based organizations.* Washington, DC: Urban Institute.

Crewe, B. (2011). Soft power in prison: Implications for staff-prisoner relationship, liberty and legitimacy. *European Journal of Criminology, 8*(6), 455–468.

Cullen, F. T., Jonson, C. L., & Nagin, D. S. (2011). Prisons do not reduce recidivism: The high cost of ignoring science. *The Prison Journal, 91*(3), 48S–65S.

D'alessio, S. J., & Stolzenberg, L. (1995). The impact of sentencing guidelines on jail incarceration in Minnesota. *Criminology, 33*(2), 283–302.

DeLisi, M., Trulson, C. R., Marquart, J. W., Drury, A. J., & Kosloski, A. E. (2011). Inside the prison black box: Toward a life course importation model of inmate behavior. *International Journal of Offender Therapy and Comparative Criminology, 55*(8), 1186–1207.

Deyoung, D. J. (1997). An evaluation of the effectiveness of alcohol treatment, driver license actions and jail terms in reducing drunk driving recidivism in California. *Addiction, 92*(8), 989–997.

Dumont, D. M., Brockmann, B., Dickman, S., Alexander, N., & Rich, J. D. (2012). Public health and the epidemic of incarceration. *Annual Review of Public Health, 33*, 325–339.

Farkas, M. A. (1999). Correctional officer attitudes toward inmates and working with inmates in a "get tough" era. *Journal of Criminal Justice, 27*(6), 495–506.

Fox, K. A., Lane, J., & Akers, R. L. (2013). Understanding gang membership and crime victimization among jail inmates: Testing the effects of self-control. *Crime & Delinquency, 59*(5), 764–787.

Free, M. D. (2001). Racial bias and the American criminal justice system: Race and presentencing revisited. *Critical Criminology, 10*(3), 195–223.

Freudenberg, N., Daniels, J., Crum, M., Perkins, T., & Richie, B. E. (2005). Coming home from jail: The social and health consequences of community reentry for women, male adolescents, and their families and communities. *American Journal of Public Health, 95*(10), 1725–1736.

Freudenberg, N., Moseley, J., Labriola, M., Daniels, J., & Murrill, C. (2007). Comparison of health and social characteristics of people leaving New York City jails by age, gender, and race/ethnicity: Implications for public health interventions. *Public Health Reports, 122*(6), 733–743.

Frost, N. A., & Clear, T. R. (2012). New directions in correctional research. *Justice Quarterly, 29*(5), 619–649.

Fulcher, P. A. (2014). Double-edged sword of prison visitation: Claiming to keep families together while furthering the aims of the prison industrial complex. *Florida A&M University Law Review, 9*, 83–112.

Garofalo, J., & Clark, R. (1985). The inmate subculture in jails. *Criminal Justice & Behavior, 12*(4), 415–434.

Gendreau, P., Little, T., & Goggin, C. (1996). A meta-analysis of the predictors of adult offender recidivism: What works! *Criminology, 34*(4), 575–608.

George, E. (2010). *A woman doing life: Notes from a prison for women.* (Eds. R. Johnson). New York, NY: Oxford University Press.

Gibbs, J. J. (1982). Disruption and distress: Going from the street to jail. *Coping with Imprisonment, 29*–44.

Gibbs, J. J. (1987). Symptoms of psychopathology among jail prisoners: The effects of exposure to the jail environment. *Criminal Justice and Behavior, 14*(3), 288–310.

Gilliard, D. K. (1999). *Prison and jail inmates at midyear 1998.* Washington, DC: U.S. Department of Justice, Bureau of Justice Statistics.

Gilliard, D. K, & Beck, A. J. (1996). *Prison and jail inmates, 1995.* Washington, DC: U.S. Department of Justice, Bureau of Justice Statistics.

Gilliard, D. K., & Beck, A. J. (1997). *Prison and jail inmates at midyear 1996.* Washington, DC: U.S. Department of Justice, Bureau of Justice Statistics.

Gilliard, D. K., & Beck, A. J. (1998). *Prison and jail inmates at midyear 1997.* Washington, DC: U.S. Department of Justice, Bureau of Justice Statistics.

Goffman, E. (1961). On the characteristics of total institutions: The inmate world. In D. R. Cressey (Ed.), *The prison: Studies in institutional organization and change.* New York, NY: Rineheart and Winston, Inc.

Goldfarb, R. (1975). *Jails: The ultimate ghettos.* Garden City, New York, NY: Anchor Press/Doubleday.

Green, D. P., & Winik, D. (2010). Using random judge assignments to estimate the effects of incarceration and probation on recidivism among drug offenders. *Criminology, 48*(2), 357–387.

Greenfeld, L. A., & Snell, T. L. (1999). *Special report: Women offenders.* Washington, DC: Bureau of Justice Statistics.

Hammett, T. M., Roberts, C., & Kennedy, S. (2001). Health-related issues in prisoner reentry. *Crime & Delinquency, 47*(3), 390–409.

Harer, M. D., & Steffensmeier, D. J. (1996). Race and prison violence. *Criminology, 34*(3), 323–355.

Harris, A. (2016). *A pound of flesh: Monetary sanctions as punishment for the poor.* New York, NY: Russell Sage Foundation.

Harrison, P. M., & Beck, A. J. (2005). *Prison and jail inmates at midyear 2004.* Washington, DC: U.S. Department of Justice, Bureau of Justice Statistics.

Harrison, P. M., & Beck, A. J. (2006). *Prison and jail inmates at midyear 2005.* Washington, DC: U.S. Department of Justice, Bureau of Justice Statistics.

Harrison, P. M., & Karberg, J. C. (2003). *Prison and jail inmates at midyear 2002.* Washington, DC: U.S. Department of Justice, Bureau of Justice Statistics.

Harrison, P. M., & Karberg, J. C. (2004). *Prison and jail inmates at midyear 2003.* Washington, DC: U.S. Department of Justice, Bureau of Justice Statistics.

Harvey, J. (2005). Crossing the boundary: The transition of young adults into prison. In A. Liebling & S. Maruna (Eds.), *The effects of imprisonment* (pp. 232–254). New York, NY: Routledge.

Hemmens, C., & Stohr, M. K. (2014). The racially just prison. In F. T. Cullen, C. L. Jonson, & M. K. Stohr (Eds.), *The American prison: Imagining a different future.* Los Angeles, CA: SAGE Publications.

Henrichson, C., Rinaldi, J., & Delaney, R. (2015). *The price of jails: Measuring the taxpayer cost of local incarceration.* New York, NY: Vera Institute of Justice.

Holsinger, A. M. (2016). *Analyzing bond supervision survey data: The effects of pretrial detention on self-reported outcomes.* Boston, MA: Crime and Justice Institute.

Houck, K. D. F., & Loper, A. B. (2002). The relationship of parenting stress to adjustment among mothers in prison. *American Journal of Orthopsychiatry, 72*(4), 548–558.

Huebner, B. M. (2003). Administrative determinants of inmate violence: A multilevel analysis. *Journal of Criminal Justice, 31*(2), 107–117.

Irwin, J. (1985). *The jail: Managing the underclass in American society.* Berkeley, CA: University of California Press.

Irwin, J., & Cressey, D. R. (1962). Thieves, convicts, and the inmate culture. *Social Problems, 10,* 142–155.

James, D. J. (2004). *Profile of jail inmates, 2002.* Washington, DC: U.S. Department of Justice, Bureau of Justice Statistics.

James, D. J., & Glaze, L. E. (2006). *Mental health problems of prison and jail inmates.* Washington, DC: U.S. Department of Justice, Bureau of Justice Statistics.

Janetta, J. (2009). Assembling the jail reentry puzzle. *American Jails,* 9–18.

Jankowski, L. W. (1992). *Jail inmates, 1991.* Washington, DC: U.S. Department of Justice, Bureau of Justice Statistics.

Jones, C. (2013). "Give us free": Addressing racial disparities in bail determinations. *N.Y.U. Journal of Legislation & Public Policy, 16,* 919–961.

Jung, H., Spjeldnes, S., & Yamatani, H. (2010). Recidivism and survival time: Racial disparity among jail ex-inmates. *Social Work Research, 34*(3), 181–189.

Kang-Brown, J. (2015). *Incarceration trends: Data and methods for historical jail populations in U.S. counties, 1970–2014.* New York, NY: Vera Institute of Justice.

Kang-Brown, J. (2016, March 24). The rise of 1,000 small jails: New analysis shows that the growth in the jail population is happening in unexpected places. *The Atlantic.* Retrieved from www.theatlantic.com/politics/archive/2016/03/the-rise-of-1000-small-jails/475260/

Kellar, M., & Wang, H. (2005). Inmate assaults in Texas county jails. *The Prison Journal, 85*(4), 515–534.

Kline, S. (1987). *Jail inmates, 1986.* Washington, DC: U.S. Department of Justice, Bureau of Justice Statistics.

Kline, S. (1988). *Jail inmates, 1987.* Washington, DC: U.S. Department of Justice, Bureau of Justice Statistics.

Kling, J. R. (2006). Incarceration length, employment, and earnings. *The American Economic Review, 96*(3), 863–876.

Klofas, J. M. (1987). Patterns of jail use. *Journal of Criminal Justice, 15*(5), 403–411.

Klofas, J. M. (1990). The jail and the community. *Justice Quarterly, 7*(1), 69–102.

Kreager, D. A., Young, J. T. N., Haynie, D. L., Bouchard, M., Schaefer, D. R., & Zajac, G. (2017). Where "old heads" prevail: Inmate hierarchy in a men's prison unit. *American Sociological Review, 82*(4), 685–718.

Kruttschnitt, C., & Gartner, R. (2003). Women's imprisonment. *Crime and Justice, 30,* 1–81.

Kukorowski, D., Wagner, P., & Sakala, L. (2013). *Please deposit all of your money: Kickbacks, rates, and hidden fees in the jail phone industry.* Northampton, MA: Prison Policy Initiative.

Lahm, K. F. (2008). Inmate-on-inmate assault: A multilevel examination of prison violence. *Criminal Justice and Behavior, 35*(1), 131–150.

Lawrence, A. (2016). *How state legislatures are helping local jurisdictions address jail usage.* New York, NY: Vera Institute of Justice, Safety and Justice Challenge.

Linhorst, D. M., Dirks-Linhorst, P. A., & Bernsen, H. L. (2009). The development and implementation of a jail-based substance abuse treatment program. *Journal of Social Work Practice in the Addictions, 9*(1), 91–112.

Listwan, S. J., Daigle, L. E., Hartman, J. L., & Guastaferro, W. P. (2014). Poly-victimization risk in prison: The influence of individual and institutional factors. *Journal of Interpersonal Violence, 29*(13), 2458–2481.

Loeffler, C. E. (2013). Does imprisonment alter the life course? Evidence on crime and employment from a natural experiment. *Criminology, 51*(1), 137–166.

Lopoo, L. M., & Western, B. (2005). Incarceration and the formation and stability of marital unions. *Journal of Marriage and Family, 67*(3), 721–734.

Loughran, T. A., Mulvey, E. P., Schubert, C. A., Fagan, J., Piquero, A. R., & Losoya, S. H. (2009). Estimating a dose-response relationship between length of stay and future recidivism in serious juvenile offenders. *Criminology, 47*(3), 699–740.

Ludwig, A., Cohen, L., Parsons, A., & Venters, H. (2012). Injury surveillance in New York City jails. *American Journal of Public Health, 102*(6), 1108–1111.

Mancini, N. (1988). *Our crowded jails: A national plight.* Washington, DC: Bureau of Justice Statistics, U.S. Department of Justice.

Martin, E. (2016, September/October). The changing nature of correctional visitation. *Corrections Today.*

Maruna, S. (2001). *Making good: How ex-convicts reform and rebuild their lives.* Washington, DC: American Psychological Association Books.

Massoglia, M. (2008). Incarceration, health, and racial disparities in health. *Law & Society Review, 42*(2), 275–306.

Mattick, H. W. (1974). The contemporary jails of the United States: An unknown and neglected area of justice. In Daniel Glaser (Ed.), *Handbook of criminology.* Chicago, IL: Rand McNally College Publishing Company.

May, D., & Wood, P. (2010). *Ranking correctional punishments: Views from offenders, practitioners, and the public.* Raleigh, NC: Carolina Academic Press.

May, D. C., Applegate, B. K., Ruddell, R., & Wood, P. B. (2014). Going to jail sucks (And it really doesn't matter who you ask). *American Journal of Criminal Justice, 39*(2), 250–266.

Mays, G. L., & Thompson, J. A. (1988). Mayberry revisited: The characteristics and operations of America's small jails. *Justice Quarterly, 5*(3), 421–440.

McClellan, D. S., Farabee, D., & Crouch, B. M. (1997). Early victimization, drug use, and criminality: A comparison of male and female prisoners. *Criminal Justice and Behavior, 24*(4), 455–476.

Mears, D. P. (2008). Accountability, efficiency, and effectiveness in corrections: Shining a light on the black box of prison systems. *Criminology & Public Policy, 7*(1), 143–152.

Mears, D. P., & Cochran, J. C. (2015). *Prisoner reentry in the era of mass incarceration.* Thousand Oaks, CA: SAGE Publications.

Mears, D. P., Cochran, J. C., & Cullen, F. T. (2015). Incarceration heterogeneity and its implications for assessing the effectiveness of imprisonment on recidivism. *Criminal Justice Policy Review, 26*(7), 691–712.

Mears, D. P., Lawrence, S., Solomon, A., & Waul, M. (2002). Prison-based programming: What it can do and why it's needed. *Corrections Today, 64*, 66–71.

Meeks, D. (2005). Doing jail time: The socialization process of a county jail environment. *Justice Policy Journal, 2*, 2–21.

Miller, H. V., & Miller, J. M. (2010). Community in-reach through jail reentry: Findings from a quasi-experimental design. *Justice Quarterly, 27*(6), 893–910.

Minton, T. D. (2011). *Jail inmates at midyear 2010—statistical tables.* Washington, DC: U.S. Department of Justice, Bureau of Justice Statistics.

Minton, T. D. (2013). *Jail inmates at midyear 2012—Statistical tables.* Washington, DC: U.S. Department of Justice, Bureau of Justice Statistics.

Minton, T. D., & Zeng, Z. (2016). *Jail inmates in 2015.* Washington, DC: Bureau of Justice Statistics.

Mitchell, O., Cochran, J. C., Mears, D. P., & Bales, W. D. (2017). Examining prison effects on recidivism: A regression discontinuity approach. *Justice Quarterly, 34*(4), 571–596.

Morris, R. G., Carriaga, M. L., Diamond, B., Piquero, N. L., & Piquero, A. R. (2012). Does prison strain lead to prison misbehavior? An application of general strain theory to inmate misconduct. *Journal of Criminal Justice, 40*(3), 194–201.

Murray, J., Loeber, R., & Pardini, D. (2012). Parental involvement in the criminal justice system and the development of youth theft, marijuana use, depression, and poor academic performance. *Criminology, 50*(1), 255–302.

Nagin, D. S. (1998). Criminal deterrence research at the outset of the twenty-first century. *Crime and Justice, 23*(1), 1–42.

Nagin, D. S., Cullen, F. T., & Jonson, C. L. (2009). Imprisonment and reoffending. *Crime and Justice, 38*(1), 115–200.

Newman, C. L., & Price, B. R. (1977). Jails and services for inmates: A perspective on some critical issues. *Criminology, 14*(4), 501–512.

Ortiz, N. (2015). *County jails at a crossroads*. Washington, DC: National Association of Counties.

Parke, R., & Clarke-Stewart, K. A. (2002). *Effects of parental incarceration on young children*. Washington, DC: U.S. Department of Health and Human Services.

Pattillo, M., Western, B., & Weiman, D. (2004). *Imprisoning America: The social effects of mass incarceration*. New York, NY: Russel Sage Foundation.

Pelissier, B. M. M., Camp, S. D., Gaes, G. D., Saylor, W. G., & Rhodes, W. (2003). Gender differences in outcomes from prison-based residential treatment. *Journal of Substance Abuse Treatment, 24*(2), 149–160.

Perkins, C. A., Stephan, J. J., & Beck, A. J. (1995). *Jails and jail inmates, 1993–94*. Washington, DC: U.S. Department of Justice, Bureau of Justice Statistics.

Petersilia, J. (2003). *When prisoners come home: Parole and prisoner reentry*. New York, NY: Oxford University Press.

Petersilia, J., & Snyder, J. G. (2013). Looking past the hype: 10 questions everyone should ask about California's prison realignment. *California Journal of Politics and Policy, 5*(2), 266–306.

Pettit, B., & Western, B. (2004). Mass imprisonment and the life course: Race and class inequality in U.S. incarceration. *American Sociological Review, 69*(2), 151–169.

Pew Center on the States. (2012). *Time served: The high cost, low return of longer prison terms*. Washington, DC: The Pew Center on the States.

Pogrebin, M., Dodge, M., & Katsampes, P. (2001). The collateral costs of short-term jail incarceration: The long-term social and economic disruptions. *Corrections Management Quarterly, 5*(4), 64–69.

Pragacz, A. J. (2016). Is this what decarceration looks like? Rising jail incarceration in upstate New York. In William G. Martin & Joshua M. Price (Eds.), *After prisons? Freedom, decarceration, and justice disinvestment*. New York, NY: Lexington Books.

Pratt, T. C. (2009). *Addicted to incarceration: Corrections policy and the politics of misinformation in the United States*. Thousand Oaks, CA: SAGE Publications.

Rabuy, B., & Wagner, P. (2015). Screening out family time: The for-profit video visitation industry in prisons and jails. *Prison Legal News, 26*, 1–12.

Reiter, K. (2014). Making windows in walls: Strategies for prison research. *Qualitative Inquiry, 20*(4), 417–428.

Rocque, M. (2011). Racial disparities in the criminal justice system and perceptions of legitimacy: A theoretical linkage. *Race and Justice, 1*(3), 292–315.

Roettiger, M. E., & Swisher, R. R. (2011). Associations of fathers' history of incarceration with sons' delinquency and arrest among Black, White, and Hispanic males in the United States. *Criminology, 49*(4), 1109–1147.

Rose, D. R., & Clear, T. R. (1998). Incarceration, social capital, and crime: Implications for social disorganization theory. *Criminology, 36*(3), 441–480.

Rose, D. R., & Clear, T. R. (2003). Incarceration, reentry, and social capital. *The Impact of Incarceration and Reentry on Children, Families, and Communities*, 189–232.

Rottman, D. B., & Kimberly, J. R. (1975). The social context of jails. *Sociology and Social Research, 59*(4), 344–361.

Sabol, W. J., Minton, T. D., & Harrison, P. M. (2007). Prison and jail inmates at midyear 2006. Washington, DC: U.S. Department of Justice, Bureau of Justice Statistics.

Sampson, R. J. (2011). The incarceration ledger. *Criminology & Public Policy, 10*(3), 819–828.

Sampson, R. J., & Loeffler, C. (2010). Punishment's place: The local concentration of mass incarceration. *Daedalus, 139*(3), 20–31.

Schnittker, J., & John, A. (2007). Enduring stigma: The long-term effects of incarceration on health. *Journal of Health and Social Behavior, 48*(2), 115–130.

Schrag, C. (1954). Leadership among prison inmates. *American Sociological Review, 19*(1), 37–42.

Senese, J. D., & Kalinich, D. B. (1993). A study of jail inmate misconduct: An analysis of rule violations and official processing. *Journal of Criminal Justice, 16*(1), 131–147.

Shelden, R. G., & Brown, W. B. (1991). Correlates of jail overcrowding: A case study of a county detention center. *Crime & Delinquency, 37*(3), 347–362.

Siennick, S. E., Stewart, E. A., & Staff, J. (2014). Explaining the association between incarceration and divorce. *Criminology, 52*(3), 371–398.

Sitren, A. H., Smith, H. P., Applegate, B. K., & Gould, L. A. (2009). Jail visitation: An assessment of organizational policy and information availability. *The Southwest Journal of Criminal Justice, 5*(3), 207–220.

Solomon, A. L., Osborne, J. W. L., LoBuglio, S. F., Mellow, J., & Mukamal, D. A. (2008). *Life after lockup: Improving reentry from jail to the community*. Washington, DC: Urban Institute.

Sparks, R. J., & Bottoms, A. E. (1995). Legitimacy and order in prisons. *British Journal of Sociology, 46*, 45–62.

Spelman, W. (2008). Specifying the relationship between crime and prisons. *Journal of Quantitative Criminology, 24*(2), 149–178.

Spohn, C., & Holleran, D. (2000). The imprisonment penalty paid by young, unemployed Black and Hispanic male offenders. *Criminology, 38*(1), 281–306.

Steffensmeier, D., Ulmer, J., & Kramer, J. (1998). The interaction of race, gender, and age in criminal sentencing: The punishment cost of being young, Black, and male. *Criminology, 36*(4), 763–798.

Steiner, B. (2009). Assessing static and dynamic influences on inmate violence levels. *Crime & Delinquency, 55*(1), 134–161.

Stephan, J. J. (1990). *Census of local jails, 1988*. Washington, DC: U.S. Department of Justice, Bureau of Justice Statistics.

Stephan, J. J., & Jankowski, L. W. (1991). *Jail inmates, 1990*. Washington, DC: U.S. Department of Justice, Bureau of Justice Statistics.

Sturges, J. E., & Al-Khattar, A. M. (2009). Survey of jail visitors about visitation policies. *The Prison Journal, 89*(4), 482–496.

Subramanian, R., Delaney, R., Roberts, S., Fishman, N., & McGarry, P. (2015). *Incarceration's front door: The misuse of jails in America*. New York, NY: Vera Institute of Justice.

Swartz, J. A., Lurigio, A. J., & Slomka, S. A. (1996). The Impact of IMPACT: An assessment of the effectiveness of a jail-based treatment program. *Crime & Delinquency, 42*(4), 553–573.

Sykes, G. M. (1958). *The society of captives*. Princeton, NJ: Princeton University Press.

Sykes, G. M., & Messinger, S. L. (1960). The inmate social system. In R. Cloward (Ed.), Theoretical studies in social organization of the prison. New York, NY: Social Science Research Council.

Thomas, C. W. (1975). Theoretical perspectives on alienation in the prison society: An empirical test. *Sociological Perspectives, 18*(4), 483–499.

Tonry, M., & Lynch, M. (1996). Intermediate sanctions. *Crime and Justice, 20*, 99–144.

Torrey, E. F., Zdanowicz, M. T., Kennard, A. D., Lamb, H. R., Eslinger, D. F., Biasotti, M. C., & Fuller, D. A. (2014). *The treatment of persons with mental illness in prisons and jails: A state survey*. Arlington, VA: Treatment Advocacy Center.

Travis, J. (2005). *But they all come back: Facing the challenges of prisoner reentry*. Washington, DC: The Urban Institute Press.

Travis, J., Western, B., Redburn, S. (2014). *The growth of incarceration in the United States: Exploring causes and consequences*. Washington, DC: National Academy Press.

Trulson, C. R. (2007). Determinants of disruption: Institutional misconduct among state-committed delinquents. *Youth Violence and Juvenile Justice, 5*(1), 7–34.

Turanovic, J. J., Rodriguez, N., & Pratt, T. C. (2012). The collateral consequences of incarceration revisited: A qualitative analysis of the effects on caregivers of children of incarcerated parents. *Criminology, 50*(4), 913–959.

Turney, K. (2014). Stress proliferation across generations? Examining the relationship between parental incarceration and childhood health. *Journal of Health and Social Behavior, 55*(3), 302–319.

Tyler, T. R. (2010). Legitimacy in corrections: Policy implications. *Criminology & Public Policy, 9*(1), 127–134.

Uggen, C. (2012). *Crime and the great recession*. Stanford, CA: Stanford Center on Poverty and Inequality.

Ulmer, J. T., & Johnson, B. (2004). Sentencing in context: A multilevel analysis. *Criminology, 42*(1), 137–178.

United States Courts. (2017). *Probation and pretrial services history*. Washington, DC: United States Courts.

Van Olphen, J., Eliason, M. J., Freudenberg, N., & Barnes, M. (2009). Nowhere to go: How stigma limits the options of female drug users after release from jail. *Substance Abuse Treatment, Prevention, and Policy, 4*(1), 10.

Visher, C., LaVigne, N., & Travis, J. (2004). *Returning home: Understanding the challenges of prisoner reentry*. Washington, DC: Urban Institute, Justice Policy Center.

Wacquant, L. (2000). The new "peculiar institution": On the prison as surrogate ghetto. *Theoretical Criminology, 4*(3), 377–389.

Wakefield, S., & Uggen, C. (2010). Incarceration and stratification. *Annual Review of Sociology, 36*, 387–406.

Weisberg, R., & Petersilia, J. (2010). The dangers of pyrrhic victories against mass incarceration. *Daedalus, 139*(3), 124–133.

Weisheit, R. A., & Klofas, J. M. (1990). The impact of jails: Collateral costs and affective responses. *Journal of Offender Counseling Services Rehabilitation, 14*(1), 51–65.

Welsh, W. N., McGrain, P., Salamatin, N., & Zajac, G. (2007). Effects of prison drug treatment on inmate misconduct: A repeated measures analysis. *Criminal Justice and Behavior, 34*(5), 600–615.

Western, B. (2006). *Punishment and inequality in America*. New York, NY: Russell Sage Foundation.

Western, B., & Beckett, K. (1999). How unregulated is the U.S. labor market: The penal system as a labor market institution. *American Journal of Sociology, 104*(4), 1030–1060.

Western, B., & Pettit, B. (2010). Incarceration and social inequality. *Daedalus, 139*, 8–19.

Western, B., & Wildeman, C. (2009). The Black family and mass incarceration. *The ANNALS of the American Academy of Political and Social Science, 621*, 221–242.

White, M. D., Saunders, J., Fisher, C., & Mellow, J. (2012). Exploring inmate reentry in a local jail setting: Implications for outreach, service use, and recidivism. *Crime & Delinquency, 58*(1), 124–146.

Wildeman, C. (2016). Incarceration and population health in wealthy democracies. *Criminology, 54*(2), 360–382.

Wildeman, C., & Turney, K. (2014). Positive, negative, or null? The effects of maternal incarceration on children's behavioral problems. *Demography, 51*(3), 1041–1068.

Wodahl, E. J., Boman, J. H., & Garland, B. E. (2015). Responding to probation and parole violations: Are jail sanctions more effective than community-based graduated sanctions? *Journal of Criminal Justice, 43*(3), 242–250.

Wolff, N., & Draine, J. (2004). Dynamics of social capital of prisoners and community reentry: Ties that bind? *Journal of Correctional Health Care, 10*(3), 457–490.

Zimring, F. E. (2007). *The great American crime decline*. New York, NY: Oxford University Press.

15

COLLATERAL CONSEQUENCES OF PRETRIAL DETENTION

Natalie Goulette and John Wooldredge

Introduction

Scholars have long contended that the U.S. criminal justice system, particularly the criminal courts, biases against those accused of committing crimes based on their race/ethnicity or sex (see reviews by Doerner & Demuth, 2014; Ulmer, 2012). While differential treatment in case dispositions and outcomes has been noted at various stages throughout the court system, the bulk of this research has focused exclusively on investigating extra-legal disparities at the much more visible stage of sentencing[1] (see Ulmer, 2012, for a review of related research). More recently, scholars have taken a closer look at treatment disparities at earlier decision points and have discussed the possible impact of these decisions on individuals involved in the criminal justice system and their families. In particular, scholars have argued that pretrial release decisions (whether a suspect should be released on bond and the appropriate bond amount) and outcomes (whether or not a suspect remains in the custody of the court or is released prior to disposition) can have an immense impact on these individuals.

Permitting suspects to be released prior to trial stems from the due process concern that suspects should not be punished (by serving time in jail) before they have been found guilty in court. This process also helps defendants to work freely with attorneys in preparing their defense while freeing up limited jail space for convicted individuals. Pre-trial release enables defendants to continue working at their jobs and to support their families, which also reduces tax burdens by reducing a suspect's reliance on public assistance for both family support and legal fees. Yet, the system of pre-trial release reflects a basic conflict between our interests in due process (protecting the rights of the defendant) versus crime control (protecting the community), and the way the system operates in practice is far from ideal. For example, most suspects cannot afford to post their own bond and must seek assistance through a surety company or a bail bondsman. This and other aspects of the system introduce many opportunities for abusing the rights of defendants while also ignoring the interests of the community.

In this chapter we focus specifically on the collateral consequences of pretrial detention, particularly for indigent suspects who are most likely to be detained prior to trial. These "collateral consequences" include impacts of pretrial detention on other case dispositions and outcomes as well as the social, psychological, and economic impacts on accused individuals and their families. Considerations for future research are also discussed.

The Pretrial "Experience" and Possible Impacts on Case Outcomes

Once an individual is arrested, s/he is taken into custody to be booked and processed. Individuals who are suspected of committing a non-violent or less serious misdemeanor offense may be released on their own recognizance. This is a written contract between the suspect and the court that s/he will appear for future court hearings. It does not require the suspect to post any monetary bond before release (Wiseman, 2014). Some suspects may be able to post bond and are released from custody very quickly. Other suspects will wait in detention until a court hearing is scheduled. State and federal authorities are required to schedule this hearing without "unnecessary delay" (Manns, 2005; The Bail Reform Act of 1984), usually within 48 hours after arrest. It is at this initial appearance that the judge will determine whether the suspect poses a danger to either himself or the community at large, or if there is strong evidence to suggest the suspect will not appear for future court hearings. If the suspect is perceived to be dangerous or a flight risk, the judge may decide to deny the suspect bond, requiring the suspect to be held in detention until trial (Manns, 2005). Most suspects are not denied bond, however, and so in most cases a judge will require the suspect to post a specific bond amount in order to obtain release. This bond is intended to act as incentive for the suspect to return to court for all subsequent proceedings.

Suspects deemed eligible for bond are protected from having to pay "excessive bail" via a constitutional provision implied by the Eighth Amendment to the U.S. Constitution. This provision is intended to prohibit the practice of setting very high bond amounts in order to prevent defendants from being released altogether. In the first empirical study of bail practices, Foote (1954) underscored the importance of being able to balance the need to ensure the suspect's appearance at trial with the desire to avoid needless punishment given that the defendant is presumed innocent until proven guilty. However, many scholars argue that suspects with even small bond amounts face a daunting task of buying their freedom (Appleman, 2012; Manns, 2005; Wiseman, 2014). Cohen and Reaves (2007) found that higher bond amounts greatly reduced the odds of a suspect obtaining pretrial release, with only 10 percent of suspects successfully obtaining release when they were assigned bonds of $100,000 or more. Even small bond amounts can be problematic for indigent suspects, with roughly half of all suspects obtaining release when their bonds ranged between $5,000 and $9,999. While many states have a preference for nonfinancial release options written into their laws, only a small portion of suspects are able to post the necessary money to secure their release from jail (Human Rights Watch, 2010). These observations underscore how counterintuitive the process is to making sure that bond is not excessive *to the individual*. That is, any specific amount might not appear excessive relative to the crime committed, but it might be excessive to the defendant if s/he does not have the means to raise the money. Foote (1954) observed that pre-trial detainees rarely challenge their detention since defendants who cannot afford bail also cannot afford an appeal.

Despite the implications of pretrial release decisions for shaping a suspect's "punishment" prior to being found guilty, judicial discretion in these decisions has largely been ignored. Foote (1954) observed that any effort to "individualize bail determination must be plagued by the treacherous *uncertainty* inherent in predicting future human behavior" (p. 1035, emphasis added). He noted the difficulty in determining what standards magistrates applied when determining bail since the process occurred very quickly and seemed to be driven primarily by "custom." Foote (1954) also observed that magistrates set high bail in order to punish defendants who they knew would not be convicted based on the evidence and/or the crimes committed. Based on these observations, it was not surprising to Foote that different magistrates assigned different bail amounts to similarly situated defendants.

In many cases, judges who are assigning bond amounts have limited access to information related to whether a suspect resides with family, has formal education, or whether the suspect is employed (Demuth, 2003). It may be necessary for the judge to develop a way in which to quickly decide if a suspect is dangerous or likely to recidivate, if left in the community. Judges who develop a "perceptual shorthand" (Hawkins, 1981) may make decisions related to pretrial release quickly at the request of the prosecutor and without much information (see Albonetti [1987, 1991] and Steffensmeier, Ulmer, & Kramer, [1998]). Judges may make these decisions based in part on how they handled similar cases and/or suspects in the past. This process can lead judges to develop stereotypes of particular groups of individuals, and their subsequent decision-making may be influenced by these stereotypes. In short, decisions related to bond amounts and pretrial release may be made by judges based on extra-legal factors, such as a suspect's race, ethnicity, age, and/or sex (Demuth & Steffensmeier, 2004).

Research suggests that pretrial detention can impact case processing and sentencing by increasing the odds of guilty pleas, trial convictions, and prison sentences upon conviction (for evidence of one or more of these outcomes, see Appleman, 2012; Ares et al., 1963; Baumer, 2013; Bushway & Forst, 2013; Clark & Henry, 1997: Goldkamp, 1979; Gottfredson & Gottfredson, 1988; Kutateladze, Andiloro, Johnson, & Spohn, 2014; Rehavi & Starr, 2012; Reitler, Sullivan, & Frank, 2013; Spohn, 2009; Stolzenberg, D'Alessio, & Eitle, 2013; Sutton, 2013; Ulmer, 2012; Wald, 1964; Wooldredge, Frank, Goulette, & Travis, 2015). Scholars argue that pretrial detention can give prosecutors the upper hand in encouraging many suspects to plead guilty to the charges filed against them (Appleman, 2012; Manns, 2005; Sacks & Ackerman, 2012). This may be especially true for suspects who fear staying in jail will cause them to lose their jobs or cause undue stress on family members. Indigent suspects who do not have the ability to post bond, regardless of the amount, may feel overwhelmed at the prospects of waiting for trial. Suspects are likely to plead guilty if the agreement does not include any additional prison time, or if they are promised that they will be granted time served, also resulting in their release from detention (Kellough & Wortley, 2002). Hoping to get out of detention as quickly as possible, these suspects may feel compelled to take the plea agreement offered to them by the prosecutor (Appleman, 2012; Manns, 2005; McCoy, 2007; Sacks & Ackerman, 2012). While the research suggests that pleading guilty can protect suspects from facing potentially harsher punishments at trial (Sacks & Ackerman, 2012), waiving one's right to trial and being convicted of the alleged offenses can have other adverse effects on these individuals.

For defendants who opt for trial, pretrial detention can limit the quality of defense preparations and may promote images of detained defendants as more "dangerous" in the eyes of judges and jurors (Foote, 1954; Turner & Johnson, 2006). Foote (1954) observed higher conviction and imprisonment rates among detained defendants who went to trial versus those released prior to trial. He argued that the difference in imprisonment rates might lie in detainees losing their jobs prior to trial, thus providing less incentive for judges to administer probation so that convicted individuals are able to keep their jobs.

These processes whereby suspects detained prior to trial are treated more harshly at subsequent stages of case processing is sometimes referred to as "cumulative disadvantage" (e.g., Spohn, 2009; Sutton, 2013). Cumulative disadvantage occurs when prior negative events increase the odds that subsequent negative events will be experienced (Baumer, 2013; Bushway & Forst, 2013; Goulette, Wooldredge, Frank, Travis, 2015; Kutateladze et al., 2014; Rehavi & Starr, 2012; Stolzenberg et al., 2013; Spohn, 2009; Sutton, 2013; Ulmer, 2012; Wooldredge et al., 2015). The generally higher odds of guilty pleas, convictions, and imprisonment for pretrial detainees implies that detention is more consequential for indigent defendants. Demographic subgroups falling disproportionately below the poverty line, particularly young Black men, might therefore face higher odds of pretrial detention and the corresponding cumulative disadvantages.

Differential Exposure to the Impacts of Pretrial Detention

As previously discussed, there is ample room for discretion in pretrial release decisions. Suspects may be treated differently at this stage of case processing based on their race/ethnicity, sex, and/or age. Various perspectives have been presented to explain why we might expect demographic disparities in pretrial release/detention.

Racial Disparities in Bond Amounts and Pretrial Detention

Whether examining racial or gender disparities at pretrial release, scholars have highlighted the potential applicability of a focal concerns framework. In their discussion of disparate sentencing practices, Steffensmeier and colleagues (1998) argued that judges have three "focal concerns" when determining the type and length of a sentence for a convicted defendant. First, they consider the blameworthiness of the defendant and the overall level of harm inflicted on the victim and society. Second, judges are concerned with protecting the community from any future harm by the individual. Finally, they are concerned with the practical implications of incarceration for the individual (e.g., physical or mental well-being), his or her dependents and the costs of caring for them, and the available bed space for incarceration. These practical concerns have also been raised in previous studies of imprisonment (e.g., Daly, 1987; Freiburger, 2010; Kruttschnitt & McCarthy, 1985; Kruttschnitt, 1984; Steffensmeier, 1980). From a focal concerns perspective, suspects who are charged with committing more serious offenses, who inflict more harm on their victims, who have a prior criminal record, and/or whose detention would not generate undue "practical" concerns are more likely to be imprisoned because they are perceived as a greater risk to society and can be detained without unanticipated costs to the system and to the suspect's family. The focal concerns perspective was subsequently applied to an understanding of pretrial release decisions and outcomes because all of these ideas are potentially applicable to a magistrate's decisions regarding bond amounts and the denial of bond altogether (Demuth, 2003; Demuth & Steffensmeier, 2004; Wooldredge et al., 2015).

Racial threat theory (Blalock, 1967; Blumer, 1955) provides another perspective for understanding possible racial disparities in pretrial dispositions. Blalock (1967) argued that Whites may perceive a threat to their political, social, and economic power when the proportion of a minority population increases within an urban area. To control the perceived "threat" to the status quo posed by growing numbers of minorities, those who control government and crime control will use the criminal justice system to keep minorities at bay, presumably through harsher treatment that reduces their freedom to compete (Stolzenberg et al., 2004). This perspective suggests that Blacks will be treated more harshly, even at the stage of pretrial release, if they are perceived to pose a threat to Whites. In his review of 30 studies of bond amounts and pretrial release, Free (2004) concluded that racial disparities were more likely to be found in jurisdictions with Black populations greater than 10 percent. Wooldredge et al. (2015) also found support for racial threat in their analysis of roughly 3,000 felony suspects in a large northern jurisdiction with a population consisting of one-third Black residents.

Several studies have investigated the treatment of minorities at the initial appearance.[2] This focus has been driven primarily by a concern that racial disparities in pretrial detention can further disadvantage minority defendants both in the criminal justice system (at later stages of case processing) as well as in their communities (Ulmer & Johnson, 2004). The findings have been mixed, however. While several authors did not find a suspect's race to impact the likelihood of obtaining pretrial detention when the legal factors of offense seriousness and prior record were controlled (Albonetti, 1989; Frazier, Bock, & Henretta, 1980; Holmes, Daudistel, & Farrell, 1987; Holmes, Hosch, Daudistel, Perez, & Graves, 1996; Nagel, 1983; Petee, 1994; Stryker, Nagel, & Hagan, 1983), others concluded that minorities were treated more harshly than Whites even when taking these legal factors into consideration (Ayres & Waldfogel, 1994; Chiricos & Bales, 1991; Demuth, 2003; Demuth & Steffensmeier, 2004; Katz & Spohn, 1995; Kutateladze et al., 2014; LaFree, 1985a; Lizotte, 1978; Patterson & Lynch, 1991; Richey-Mann, 1993; Spohn, 2009; Sutton, 2013; Wooldredge et al., 2015). Regarding a suspect's ethnicity, a national study conducted by Cohen and Reaves (2007) revealed that Latinos were less likely than non-Latinos to be released prior to trial (cf. Maxwell & Davis, 1999).

While prior research highlights the main effects of a suspect's race/ethnicity and sex on type of release, bond amounts, and the odds of pretrial detention, many scholars argue that it is important to examine how demographic attributes may also interact with each other to influence pretrial decisions and outcomes (Katz & Spohn, 1995). Without consideration of these interaction effects, no racial disparities may appear when in fact there is disparate treatment for certain demographic subgroups of minorities (Zatz, 1985). For example, in citing the focal concerns perspective, Katz and Spohn (1995) argued that Black males may be perceived to be more blameworthy and dangerous than White males, generating significantly lower odds of pretrial release for Black males.

Aside from possible race × sex interaction effects on pretrial decisions, others have also explored possible race × age interactions. Grounded again in the focal concerns perspective, young men in general, and young, Black men specifically, may be perceived by judges as more blameworthy or a greater risk to the community (Steffensmeier et al., 1998), and may face higher bond amounts and higher odds of detention relative to other similarly situated race × age groups (Demuth, 2003; Wooldredge et al., 2015; for a general review of related research, see Johnson, Ulmer, & Kramer, 2008; Ulmer, 2012).

Gender Disparities in Treatment at Pretrial

The focal concerns of an individual's blameworthiness, community protection, and practical implications of incarcerating convicted individuals might also be relevant for understanding the generally more lenient treatment of females at pretrial release. In the sentencing literature it has been argued that females are perceived by judges as more willing to participate in treatment programs (Meyer & Jesilow, 1997), as less dangerous or at lower risk for recidivating (Hessick, 2010), and/or as less blameworthy if their criminality was encouraged or driven by male partners or an addiction to drugs or alcohol (Demuth & Steffensmeier, 2004; Hessick, 2010). Judges are also less inclined to incarcerate women with dependent children because the children might otherwise be placed in the state foster care system if relatives are unable or unwilling to provide proper care (Koons-Witt, 2002). Considerations of dependent children could also work against female suspects, however, if judges are concerned that a mother's criminality will jeopardize a child's well-being (Freiburger, 2010; Griffin & Wooldredge, 2006). Again, these ideas might also apply to pretrial decision-making and whether magistrates typically make it easier for women to obtain pretrial release relative to men.

The chivalry/paternalism thesis is also relevant to pretrial decisions if male judges associate certain female suspects with their own daughters (Bishop & Frazier, 1984; Visher, 1983), making it more difficult for them to treat females as harshly as they would males appearing before them (for applications of this idea to sentencing decisions, see Bishop & Frazier, 1984; Farnsworth & Teske, 1995; Griffin & Wooldredge, 2006; Visher, 1983). This "protection" is more likely to be directed toward females who are perceived as docile and too fragile to face a lengthy period of incarceration. Females who adhere to the traditional gender roles of housewife or mother are likely to be treated more leniently by the court.

Consistent with these ideas, empirical studies have also produced evidence of gender disparities in pretrial decisions and outcomes. When held in jail prior to trial, women are incarcerated for significantly shorter periods of time (Steury & Frank, 1990). Regarding bond amounts, female suspects are often assigned lower amounts relative to males (Demuth & Steffensmeier, 2004; Goulette et al., 2015; Kruttschnitt, 1984, Turner & Johnson, 2006). Women are also more likely than men to be granted nonfinancial release options (Steury & Frank, 1990) or to be released on their own recognizance (Demuth & Steffensmeier, 2004), which also contributes to their lower odds of pretrial detention.

The interest of male judges to protect female suspects may not apply to all women, however (Agozino, 1997; Belknap, 2007; Chesney-Lind & Pasko, 2004; Chigwada-Bailey, 1997; Crawford, 2000; Franklin & Fearn, 2008; Martin & Stimpson, 1997/1998; Visher, 1983). According to gender conflict theorists, there is strong evidence to suggest that females are still considered "less valuable" than men. In comparison to males, females still report unequal pay for their work, they are less visible in positions of economic and political power, and they are still victimized at the hands of men

(Franklin & Fearn, 2008). These inequities enable men in authoritative positions to use their power to control women and keep them in a subservient status. Within the criminal justice system, men can use the law to punish women who threaten the social order or their power. This perspective leads to a prediction that women could actually be treated *more* harshly than men, but this scenario would depend on the type of offense charged, based on how men define a "threatening" female. As such, women charged with violent crimes might be treated more harshly than other groups of women (Franklin & Fearn, 2008). Scholars have called this the "evil woman" thesis (Chesney-Lind, 1977; Kruttschnitt, 1984; Visher, 1983).

The "evil woman" thesis also predicts that minority females will be treated more harshly than other females (Visher, 1983). While White women may generally be perceived by men as docile and in need of protection (Bickle & Peterson, 1991), especially if they prescribe to the roles of wife and mother or engage in the more typical "female offenses" (e.g., minor property crimes) (Belknap, 2001; Bickle & Peterson, 1991; Crew, 1991; Daly, 1987; Kaukinen, 1995; Young, 1986), Black females may be perceived by judges as more independent and less worthy of protection when they assume the role of raising children on their own (Belknap, 2007; Black, 1980). In combination with the stereotype of Black females as more crime-prone, loud, and forceful (Collins, 2004; Miller, 2008; Moore & Hagedorn, 1996; Sinden, 1981), the "evil woman" thesis suggests that Black females will be treated more harshly at pretrial release in comparison to White females. Support for this argument was found by Demuth and Steffensmeier (2004), who found that Black females had the highest odds of being detained before trial, followed by Hispanic females and then White females.

In their analysis of pretrial release decisions and outcomes for a sample of over 3,000 felony suspects in a large northern jurisdiction, Goulette et al. (2015) found mixed support for the "evil woman" thesis and gender conflict theory. While Black females were assigned significantly higher bond amounts in comparison to White females, lending support to the thesis, both Black and White females had the same likelihood of obtaining pretrial release. Lending support to gender conflict theory, women charged with injuring a victim during the commission of the offense were assigned significantly higher bond amounts relative to men although they had lower odds of remaining in pretrial detention (Goulette et al., 2015). These findings suggest that bond amounts in this particular court may be used to punish "violent" female suspects more severely than similarly situated men, perhaps because they are perceived as less likely to conform to traditional gender roles (Franklin & Fearn, 2008).

Other Influences on Pretrial Detention

In addition to demographic effects on pretrial release decisions and outcomes, prior literature suggests that type of attorney can impact the likelihood of pretrial release. While suspects who have the means to do so may hire a private attorney to represent them in their criminal cases, it is estimated that 80 percent of felony suspects are indigent and must have defense counsel provided for them. Indigent suspects may be assigned counsel through one of three types of programs. First, an indigent suspect may be represented by assigned counsel where local courts create a list of private attorneys who are available for appointment as needed (Cohen, 2014). Second, a suspect may be represented by a contract attorney who has a financial agreement with the government to provide their services for a specific period of time (Davies & Worden, 2009; Spangenderg & Beeman, 1995). Finally, indigent suspects may use the services of a public defender. Public defenders are full-time employees of a public or private non-profit organization or are direct employees of the government to offer indigent defense (Cohen, 2014). Public defender offices do not exist in rural counties and are typically found only in more urban counties with the demand for such services.

Scholars often contend that suspects who are able to retain private counsel are more likely to post bond and secure pretrial release than suspects who are assigned counsel or use a public defender

(Katz & Spohn, 1995; Rodriguez et al., 2006; Wooldredge et al., 2015). While public defenders must deal with heavy caseloads and may not have the time to provide their clients with adequate time and attention (Williams, 2013), proponents of the public defender system argue that public defenders are more experienced and skilled than assigned or contract attorneys (Cohen, 2014). Unlike other defense attorneys, public defenders may have a better professional relationship with the judges and prosecutors they are the most likely to interact with on a regular basis, potentially giving them the upper hand in negotiating more favorable outcomes for their clients in guilty plea agreements (Flemming, Nardulli, & Eisenstein, 1992; Hartley, Miller, & Spohn, 2010; Heumann, 1978).

The empirical literature on the performance of defense attorneys during pretrial proceedings has provided mixed findings based on attorney type. While private attorneys have been found to negotiate lower bond amounts for their clients in comparison to public defenders (Farrel & Swigert, 1978) and are more successful at securing pretrial release (Holmes et al., 1996; Turner & Johnson, 2006; Williams, 2013), Hartley et al. (2010) concluded that type of attorney did not significantly impact the likelihood of a suspect being released on his/her own recognizance. Turner and Johnson (2006) found that public defenders obtained smaller bond amounts for their clients during one particular year in Lancaster County, Nebraska, but this finding did not hold true the following year. Since minority suspects are overrepresented in the class of indigent defendants (Appleman, 2012) and are less likely to retain private counsel (Stolzenberg et al., 2013), they may experience increased disadvantages at the initial appearance and thereafter relative to Whites.

The Contribution of Pretrial Detention to Cumulative Disadvantage

In recent years, some scholars have investigated whether particular groups of suspects are more likely to experience cumulative disadvantage across the court system, with pretrial detention leading to harsher outcomes at later points and culminating in significantly higher odds of imprisonment and longer prison sentences (Baumer, 2013; Bushway & Forst, 2013; Goulette et al., 2015; Kutateladze et al., 2014; Rehavi & Starr, 2012; Stolzenberg et al., 2013; Spohn, 2009; Sutton, 2013; Ulmer, 2012; Wooldredge et al., 2015). In turn, those individuals who are sentenced to prison are likely to face additional barriers related to successful reintegration back into the community after release. For example, they are likely to face challenges in obtaining employment and, in turn, adequate financial support for themselves and their families (Bushway & Sweeten, 2007).

While cumulative disadvantages in case processing can be faced by any defendant regardless of race or gender, scholars contend that minorities and males may be more likely to experience cumulative disadvantages if they are unable to obtain pretrial release (Baumer, 2013; Bushway & Forst, 2013; Goulette et al., 2015; Kutateladze et al., 2014; Rehavi & Starr, 2012; Stolzenberg et al., 2013; Spohn, 2009; Sutton, 2013; Ulmer, 2012; Wooldredge et al., 2015). Spohn (2009) investigated the effects of pretrial release on sentencing outcomes for individuals convicted of drug crimes in three U.S. District Courts over a three-year period. She found that pretrial detention resulted in harsher sentences for males but not for females. Goulette and colleagues (2015) observed that *both* men and women who were unable to obtain pretrial release had a significantly higher likelihood of being sentenced to prison, but pretrial detention did not impact the length of imprisonment.

In analyzing data from New York County, Kutateladze and colleagues (2014) found that Blacks and Latinos experienced greater disadvantages throughout the court system with a greater percentage of Black defendants experiencing pretrial detention and being sent to prison relative to Whites. While Latinos were also more likely to experience pretrial detention than Whites, the odds of both groups receiving a prison sentence were not significantly different when controlling for other covariates of imprisonment. Wooldredge et al. (2015) estimated multilevel path models to investigate the differential treatment of race groups in a northern urban court. The authors found that young, Black men had the highest odds of experiencing cumulative disadvantages relative to any

Other Unanticipated Consequences of Pretrial Detention and Implications for Life Outside the Criminal Justice System

There is growing concern that pretrial detention has become even more punitive over time (Appleman, 2012), especially when considering the unanticipated consequences of pretrial detention. First, while prisons house convicted individuals, jails house persons who have been convicted as well as those who have yet to be processed. In some jurisdictions, suspects awaiting trial can be housed with dangerous or violent individuals, putting them at risk of being physically and emotionally abused by others (Appleman, 2012; Weiser, 2009). For example, several individuals housed in the jail at Rikers Island in New York sued officials, claiming that they were attacked and beaten while guards did nothing. In some instances, these individuals claimed that the guards ordered these attacks to occur (Weiser, 2009). Other lawsuits were filed against two Rikers' guards who allegedly recruited and trained incarcerated teens to restrain others with the intended goal of maintaining order within the unit for the guards (Eligon, 2009).

Concerns over the conditions of a suspect's confinement are further exacerbated when jails become crowded (operating well over intended capacities) to the point where facilities are no longer able to accommodate the number of individuals housed within. Petteruti and Walsh (2008) described how the Los Angeles County jail became crowded to the point where incarcerated individuals were forced to sleep on the floor. As these facilities acquire more individuals, the infrastructure and amenities can deteriorate to the point where concerns associated with violating incarcerated individuals' constitutional rights against cruel and unusual punishment are often cited. For example, because the Central Detention Facility in Washington, D.C. was so crowded during the mid-2000s, individuals lived without running water in their cells. Many of the showers located in the facility did not operate, and there were complaints made about animal feces found within the facility (Petteruti & Walsh, 2008). Such issues can put the health and safety of both incarcerated individuals *and* staff in jeopardy (Appleman, 2012).

Pretrial detention can also negatively impact the health and overall well-being of detainees who suffer from physical or mental health issues. Since nearly 70 percent of individuals housed in jail are in need of seeing a health care professional at the time of arrest (Minton, 2013), this population is at a high risk of spreading and transmitting diseases while incarcerated (see Chapter 6). Crowded facilities further increase this risk, especially when the population is constantly changing (Appleman, 2012; Petteruti & Walsh, 2008). Contagious diseases such as human immunodeficiency virus (HIV), tuberculosis, hepatitis, and bacterial infections, including methicillin-resistant staphylococcus aureus (MRSA), are all found in jail populations at a much higher rate than in the general population (Petteruti & Walsh, 2008; Talvi, 2007). With nearly 40 percent of individuals in jail having reported suffering from a chronic medical condition (Minton, 2013), these individuals are also more susceptible to experiencing complications related to their medical condition while incarcerated. The leading causes of death for persons in jail are heart disease, cancer, liver disease, and respiratory diseases (Noonan, 2010). These consequences may be magnified by the often inadequate equipment and limited numbers of jail staff capable of diagnosing or treating more serious health problems. These risky situations also exist for pretrial detainees even if they are in jail for relatively short periods of time (Petteruti & Walsh, 2008).

There are also concerns with the mental health of pretrial detainees, since it is estimated that nearly 75 percent of those in jail suffer from both mental health and co-occurring substance abuse problems (Minton, 2013). Jail facilities are often inundated with these individuals since many of the larger mental health facilities have closed (Petteruti & Walsh, 2008). Individuals suffering from schizophrenia, bipolar disorder, anxiety, or depression are often arrested and booked into a local detention facility because there is no other place for them. This can create problems not only for these individuals but also for other incarcerated individuals and jail staff. If mental health issues go undiagnosed or staff are unable to manage erratic behavior, then others are at higher risk of violent victimization. A short period of confinement can also traumatize individuals suffering from undiagnosed depression, thereby increasing the odds of self-inflicted injuries (Gilmore & Guerra, 2010). Attempted suicides are quite common in jails (Petteruti & Walsh, 2008). Research has also revealed that depressed individuals are more likely to act in ways that lead officers to use coercive force against them (Couturier, Maue, & McVey, 2005), potentially adding to the trauma they have already experienced during confinement.

The Arrestee Drug Abuse Monitoring Program (ADAM II) was resurrected by the Office of National Drug Control Policy (ONDCP) in 2007 to interview volunteer male arrestees and collect urine samples from them at 10 sites (reduced to five sites in 2012). In addition to measuring drug use among booked arrestees, the ADAM II data can track usage patterns over time in these specific U.S. counties. While usage patterns have varied across the research sites, 70 percent of arrestees have tested positive for at least one drug at the time of arrest in Chicago, Minneapolis, New York, Portland, and Sacramento (ONDCP, 2012). Marijuana was the most widely used drug in most of the sites, followed by cocaine and methamphetamine. Opiate use has increased since 2007 among male arrestees at some of the sites (ONDCP, 2012).

Individuals who are taken into custody while under the influence of drugs or alcohol can create problems for jail staff and others because they sometimes engage in risky behaviors that they would not engage in otherwise (Tibbetts, 2014). These individuals pose additional risks to others if they suffer from a communicable disease such as hepatitis or HIV. Intravenous drug users are at an increased risk of contracting such diseases if they use unclean needles or engage in unprotected sex (Kremling & Adams, 2014). Research suggests that Blacks and Hispanics are more likely to report drug dependency relative to Whites (Galea & Rudenstein, 2005), with minority females often exhibiting the most chronic health problems (Nolen-Hoeksema, 2004). According to the Centers for Disease Control (2008), Black females are 15 times more likely to be infected by HIV than White females and 4 times more likely to become infected by the virus than Hispanic women. There are few options available to jail staff for treating drug addiction among detainees since drug treatment programs are virtually non-existent in local detention facilities (Dolovich, 2009).

Pretrial detention can also result in steep fees and serious consequences for indigent suspects who cannot afford these fees. In Florida and Michigan, for example, detainees are required to pay daily supervision fees as well as additional fees for medical or dental services, regardless of whether they have the ability to pay (Diller, 2010). Suspects who acquire debt while in pretrial detention run the risk of being assessed late fees and of being jailed for their inability to pay, even when found not guilty of the original charge(s) that led them to be detained in the first place (Appleman, 2012). Still, other jurisdictions require pretrial detainees to pay a fee to meet and consult with the local public defender (ACLU, 2010). These required fees can overwhelm indigent detainees who are already incapable of posting bond, and they may feel compelled to waive their right to counsel simply because they cannot afford the necessary fees to meet with the public defender (Appleman, 2012). Since minority suspects are more likely to be indigent and unable to afford retained counsel (Wooldredge et al., 2015), these individuals may be placed at a greater disadvantage when taking their case to trial or considering possible plea agreements. Not invoking their right to counsel could expose indigent suspects to harsher case outcomes as well as other (corresponding) negative consequences (e.g., loss of employment and greater financial hardships for dependents).

These immediate negative consequences of pretrial detention might lead some suspects to plead guilty rather than opt for trial or to accept the first plea agreement with which they are presented rather than wait for a "better" offer. Aside from the direct consequences of conviction, including having to endure the corresponding punishment, pleading guilty will expose the individual to additional collateral consequences (Budeiri, 1981; Rabinowitz, 2010; Roberts, 2009; Murray, 2015; Sacks & Ackerman, 2012). These consequences involve restrictions on personal freedoms beyond those imposed by the criminal courts ("civil penalties") that can continue to impact a defendant long after his or her sentence has been served (Bender, 2012; Pinard, 2006; Pinard, 2010). Collateral consequences can limit offenders' civil rights (Pinard, 2006; Travis & Petersilia, 2001), parental rights (Dalley, 2000; Dodge & Pogrebin, 2001; Olivares, Burton, & Cullen, 1996), and spousal rights (Buckler & Travis, 2003; Burton et al., 1987). Convicted felons may be prohibited from serving on a jury, voting in general elections, and holding public office (Burton et al., 1987). Offenders' future employment options can also be severely limited because they are often considered ineligible for professional licensures. Or, felony convictions may result in individuals being removed from civil service or becoming disqualified from public employment (Freisthler & Godsey, 2005; Pager, 2003; Tewksbury, 2005). Suspects who plead guilty to felony charges may have further difficulty finding employment if potential employers use background checks or require applicants to disclose their criminal records (Blumstein & Nakamura, 2009; Bushway, Nieuwbeerta, & Blockland, 2011; Kurlychek, Brame, & Bushway, 2006, 2007; Soothill & Francis, 2009; see Chapter 5). Individuals who are convicted of a felony offense also may be eligible for harsher treatment in future criminal cases due to sentencing enhancements. Suspects who plead guilty to a sex crime are likely to be required to register as a sex offender so that residents can be notified (Roberts, 2009; see Chapter 11). Failure to register with local authorities could result in additional charges and further imprisonment for the individual convicted of a sex offense (Bender, 2012). Individuals who have a felony record also may be restricted from holding a driver's license (Pinard, 2006) or possessing a firearm (Goulette, Reitler, Flesher, Frank, & Travis, 2014). Finally, noncitizens who are convicted of a felony offense face possible deportation, impacting not only them but their immediate families (Bender, 2012; Roberts, 2009; see Chapter 13).

While pretrial detainees may be assessed fees for medical and dental services or the services of the local public defender's office, their financial outlook may worsen further after a felony conviction. Individuals with prior felony convictions may be prohibited from applying for welfare benefits or government housing (Murray, 2015; Roberts, 2009). Also, individuals who are convicted of drug offenses are ineligible from applying for student loans (Murray, 2015).

Persons convicted of committing a felony offense may also struggle to find viable housing. Under state laws, landlords are allowed to evict individuals who have been suspected or convicted of certain crimes (Gaines, 2014; see Chapters 3 & 10). Individuals who are convicted of a sex crime and who appear on the sex offender registry can have an exceptionally hard time finding housing since they cannot live close to certain public areas (Bender, 2012). They can be prohibited from living with friends or family who reside within these restricted zones (Murray, 2015).

Pretrial detainees who waive their right to defense counsel, or who must rely on the services of a public defender, may not be adequately informed of these collateral consequences since they are often not discussed in court (Ewald & Smith, 2008). While criminal justice practitioners, including prosecuting and defense attorneys, judges, and supervisory probation and parole officers in Ohio perceived many of the identified collateral consequences to impact only a small percentage of individuals with prior felony convictions (Goulette et al., 2014), scholars continue to argue that these restrictions and barriers should be made known to suspects who are contemplating a plea agreement (Bender, 2012; Murray, 2015). The U.S. Supreme Court in *Padilla v. Kentucky* (2010) argued that suspects facing deportation as a result of a felony conviction should be informed of such a consequence before accepting a plea agreement. However, whether indigent defendants who waive their right to counsel are informed of these potential consequences remains to be seen (*Padilla v. Kentucky*, 2010).

Pretrial detention can also have far-reaching consequences for the children of detainees (see Chapter 8 for a discussion related to paternal incarceration). While judges may be concerned with detaining a mother of dependent children, a mother's criminal behavior may be deemed too dangerous for the well-being of her children and the judge may feel that there is no choice but to hold her until final disposition. Once a child's mother is taken into custody, her children may be placed in the state's foster care system (Petteruti & Walsh, 2008), isolating them further from other family members and friends. This disruption can lead some children to develop psychological problems (Lee, Blitz, & Srnka, 2015; Smith & Palmieri, 2007) or to exhibit aggressive or attention-seeking behaviors (Dubowitz et al., 1994). The children of detained female suspects may be placed in the care of a relative, which is more often the case among African American mothers relative to White mothers (Burton, 1992; Cox, 2002; Heywood, 1999; Population Reference Bureau, 2011). While there is evidence to suggest that children who are placed in the care of a relative may exhibit fewer behavioral problems and have healthier experiences than juveniles who are placed in traditional foster care (Winokur, Holtan, & Batchelder, 2014), other research contends that these living situations are not without problems. Such problems can include caregiver distress leading to inconsistent parenting practices (Rodgers-Farmer, 1999; Smith et al., 2008), poor adjustment of the children (Dolbin-MacNab & Keiley, 2006; Dunifon, 2013; Hayslip & Kaminski, 2005; Kelley et al., 2011; Shelton & Harold, 2008; Smith et al., 2008), higher risk of children developing emotional problems (Neely-Barnes, Graff, & Washington, 2010), difficulties with peers (Smith et al., 2008), and poorer physical and emotional well-being later in life (Carpenter & Clyman, 2004).

Pretrial detention can lead to several burdens for family members to overcome, especially since pretrial detainees are no longer able to financially contribute to the household. If they were employed before being booked into the county jail, many of them are likely to lose their jobs even if they are detained for only a short period of time (Wiseman, 2014). Job loss can hinder an individual's ability to pay supervision fees incurred in detention while also creating economic hardships for family members during their absence. Spouses of pretrial detainees may struggle to pay the bills and are more likely to fall below the poverty line (Dolovich, 2009; Pogrebin, Dodge, & Katsampes, 2001; Sullivan, 2010). These financial burdens may continue even after the individual is released from detention because of the stigma associated with being arrested and being held in pretrial detention which, in turn, can reduce job opportunities (Wiseman, 2014).

Yet another "consequence" of pretrial detention is related to the criminal justice system itself as opposed to the individual detainee. Considering the focal concern of available resources for housing detainees, the associated costs can be quite heavy (Henrichson, Rinaldi, & Delaney, 2015). These costs vary considerably across jurisdictions, where providing for an individual in pretrial detention ranges from $51.33 per day in Guadalupe County, Texas, up to $571.27 per day in New York City (Henrichson et al., 2015). Recent estimates suggest that pretrial detention costs anywhere from $84–$124 million annually (Wiseman, 2014). With 85 percent of jail costs being paid by municipal governments, this can result in local jurisdictions having to scale back on other budgetary considerations. While Henrichson et al. (2015) suggest that the only real solution to cutting the budget is by reducing the size of a jail population, many jurisdictions are investigating whether it may be necessary to design and construct new facilities to accommodate the ever-growing pretrial detention population (Wiseman, 2014). In short, the potentially negative consequences of pretrial detention for both detainees and local economies may only worsen in the foreseeable future.

Considerations for Empirical Studies of the Collateral Consequences of Pretrial Detention

Research on disparities in pretrial decisions and outcomes continues to grow in light of the virtual absence of research on the collateral consequences of pretrial detention. This is an important omission given the potential consequences of pretrial detention for *any* detainee, as described in this chapter, and especially because these consequences are necessarily more likely for the demographic subgroups of suspects with the highest odds of pretrial detention (i.e., young minority men). The ability to identify the collateral consequences of pretrial detention and to assess their impact on suspects is critical for developing a more comprehensive understanding of how minorities and the poor are further disadvantaged within and by the U.S. criminal justice system.

The "collateral consequences" of a decision or behavior technically involves any unintended or unanticipated effects. As such, in this chapter we have discussed two relatively broad groups of collateral consequences for pretrial detainees including those within versus outside the criminal justice system, and those from either group are worthy to pursue as outcome measures in empirical studies of the topic. The first group of consequences from within the system involves the disadvantages at subsequent decision points that culminate to generate harsher case outcomes for defendants. Consistent with our earlier discussion, research on the "cumulative disadvantages" of pretrial detention might focus on whether guilty pleas, trial convictions, and prison sentences are more common among detainees versus similarly situated defendants released prior to trial. Also relevant are the magnitude of charge and/or sentence reductions accompanying guilty pleas, if detainees are at a disadvantage in plea negotiations (also previously discussed). The ability to also estimate whether these disadvantages accrue disproportionately for minorities in general and/or for young minority men in particular will provide enormous insight into racial disparities in treatment that have previously gone unrecognized.

The second group of collateral consequences falling outside the criminal justice system, which is probably the more popular focus of discussions on the subject, includes the social, economic, and psychological impacts of pretrial detention on incarcerated individuals and their families. In this chapter we focused on the physical and mental health of detainees, particularly those with drug addictions or preexisting illnesses (e.g., HIV), economic hardships due to jail fees and possible job loss while incarcerated, the impact of these economic hardships on dependent family members, subsequent barriers to employment due to the stigma of incarceration, the emotional effects on dependent children (particularly those of incarcerated mothers), and the other consequences owing to the higher odds of conviction and a prison sentence for pretrial detainees (infringements on welfare benefits, government or other housing, voting, professional licensures, jury duty, holding public office, employment as a civil servant, student loans, driver's license, residency of immigrants, parental rights, and spousal rights). Comparisons of these experiences between those detained versus released prior to trial would be useful not only from a "justice" perspective but also from a cost/benefit perspective due to the resulting economic burdens placed on local and state governments.

Analyses of cumulative disadvantages within a system may be more feasible at this point in time compared to analyses of collateral consequences outside the system because the former can be conducted with electronic data archived by most urban courts whereas the latter would require access to other public records and/or survey data. The availability of electronic data bases capturing all arrested suspects and their movement through a court system has grown dramatically over the last decade, and we assume these data files are now common in all metropolitan statistical areas across the U.S. Even so, they are likely to vary considerably in the comprehensiveness of information, not just in terms of missing data (pieces of information) but also the number of data fields provided. Cities comparable in size (e.g., Columbus, Ohio, and Cincinnati, Ohio) can differ in the information available to researchers for not only creating the required measures for a statistical analysis (case dispositions and outcomes) but also for creating the covariates necessary for matching detainees to those released prior to trial (or, at a minimum, for the necessary statistical controls in a multivariate analysis). It is preferred that related studies include more than one geographic area (Sudman, 1976), but a multi-jurisdiction project can limit available measures when, for example, one jurisdiction records specific bond amounts whereas another jurisdiction does not.

Analyses of the second group of collateral consequences will be more challenging given the need to obtain both court data and personal data on the experiences of both pretrial detainees and those released prior to trial *after* their files have been closed. Overcoming problems with locating these individuals, who can be highly mobile even within the same metro area, and gaining their cooperation to participate in this type of study will be challenging. Nonetheless, in the absence of any information to date, quantitative studies of very small samples in conjunction with case studies of a handful of individuals will provide useful information to guide future research not only in terms of how to frame predictions but also in terms of identifying practical constraints in related research and suggestions for facilitating "successful" projects. In his practical guide to sampling, Seymour Sudman (1976) discussed how "good" a sample needs to be in light of existing information on a topic.

Conclusion

In this chapter we highlighted the importance of pretrial release decisions and outcomes for shaping the subsequent experiences of criminal suspects (throughout case processing as well as after release) and their families. While most suspects are assigned bond at the initial appearance, indigent suspects face difficulties posting even small bond amounts. Research suggests that males and minorities are less likely to obtain pretrial release than Whites or females, placing the first two groups at greater risks of being charged supervision fees while in detention and experiencing further trauma if they suffer from mental illness, drug or alcohol addiction, and/or other chronic health problems. Failure to obtain pretrial release might also lead some defendants to accept less desirable guilty plea agreements in order to get out of jail. For defendants who opt for trial, pretrial detention may contribute to a judge's and/or jury's stereotypes of certain defendants as more blameworthy and greater threats to the community, possibly increasing the odds of conviction and imprisonment and, in turn, limiting their future employment opportunities, housing options, and the ability to financially support any dependents. Growing pretrial detention populations also contribute to the financial burdens of local governments. With these collateral consequences in mind, we made some suggestions for future research in order to better understand the impacts of pretrial detention on offenders, their families, and the communities in which they reside.

Notes

1 For examinations of gender disparities in sentencing see Albonetti, 1997; Bickle & Peterson, 1991; Blackwell, Holleran, & Finn, 2008; Crawford, 2000; Daly, 1994; Doerner & Demuth, 2010; Doerner & Demuth, 2014; Engen & Steen, 2000; Griffin & Wooldredge, 2006; Griswold, 1987; Jeffries, Fletcher, & Newbold, 2003; Johnston, Kennedy, & Shuman, 1987; Koons-Witt, 2002; Kramer & Ulmer, 1996, 2002; Moore & Miethe, 1986; Mustard, 2001; Nagel, 1990; Nagel & Johnson, 1994; Rodriguez, Curry, & Lee, 2006; Scott, 2010; Spohn & Holleran, 2000; Steffensmeier, Kramer, & Streifel, 1993; Steffensmeier, Ulmer, & Kramer, 1998; Ulmer, Light, & Kramer, 2011.
2 For example, see Albonetti, 1989; Ayres & Waldfogel, 1994; Chiricos & Bales, 1991; Demuth, 2003; Demuth & Steffensmeier, 2004; Frazier, Bock, & Henretta, 1980; Holmes, Daudistel, & Farrell, 1987; Holmes et al.,1996; Katz & Spohn, 1995; Kutateladze et al., 2014; LaFree, 1985b; Lizotte, 1978; Nagel, 1983; Patterson & Lynch, 1991; Richey-Mann, 1993; Spohn, 2009; Stryker, Nagel, & Hagan, 1983; Sutton, 2013; Wooldredge et al., 2015.

References

American Civil Liberties Union. (2010). In for a penny: The rise of America's new debtor prisons. Retrieved from www.aclu.org/report/penny-rise-americas-new-debtors-prisons

Agozino, B. (1997). *Black women and the criminal justice system: Towards the decolonization of victimization.* Aldershot, UK: Ashgate.

Albonetti, C. (1987). Prosecutorial discretion: The effects of uncertainty. *Law & Society Review, 21,* 291–313.

Albonetti, C. (1989). Bail and judicial discretion in the District of Columbia. *Sociology and Social Research, 74,* 40–47.

Albonetti, C. (1991). An integration of theories to explain judicial discretion. *Social Problems, 38,* 247–266.

Albonetti, C. A. (1997). Sentencing under the federal sentencing guidelines: Effects of defendant characteristics, guilty pleas, and departures on sentence outcomes for drug offenses, 1991–1992. *Law & Society Review, 31,* 789–822.

Appleman, L. I. (2012). Justice in the Shadowlands: Pretrial detention, punishment", & the sixth amendment. *Wash & Lee Law Review, 96,* 1297–1369.

Ares, C., Rankin, A., & Sturz, H. (1963). The Manhattan bail project: An interim report on the use of pre-trial parole. *New York University Law Review, 38,* 67–95.

Ayres, I., & Waldfogel, J. (1994). A market test for race discrimination in bail setting. *Stanford Law Review, 46,* 987–1047.

The Bail Reform Act of 1984, 18 U.S.C. §§ 3141–3150, 3156 53.

Baumer, E. (2013). Reassessing and redirecting research on race and Sentencing. *Justice Quarterly, 30,* 231–261.

Belknap, J. (2001). *Invisible woman: Gender, crime, and justice.* Belmont, CA: Wadsworth.

Belknap, J. (2007). *The invisible woman: Gender, crime, and justice* (3rd ed.). Belmont, CA: Wadsworth/Thompson.

Bender, P. (2012). Exposing the hidden penalties of pleading guilty: A revision of the collateral consequences rule. *George Mason Law Review, 19,* 291–318.

Bickle G. S., & Peterson, R. D. (1991). The impact of gender-based family roles on criminal sentencing. *Social Problems, 38,* 372–389.

Bishop, D. M., & Frazier, C. E. (1984). The effects of gender on charge reduction. *Sociological Quarterly, 25,* 358–396.

Black, D. (1980). Dispute settlement by the police. In D. Black (Ed.), *The manners and customs of the police* (pp. 109–192). New York, NY: Academic Press.

Blackwell, B. S., Holleran, D., & Finn, M. A. (2008). The Impact of the Pennsylvania sentencing guidelines on sex differences in sentencing. *Journal of Contemporary Criminal Justice, 24,* 399–418.

Blalock, H. M. (1967). *Toward a theory of minority-group relations.* New York, NY: Wiley.

Blumer, H. (1955). Reflections on theory of race relations. In A. Lind (Ed.), *Race Relations in World Perspective* (pp. 3–21). Honolulu: University of Hawaii Press.

Blumstein, A., & Nakamura, K. (2009). Redemption in the presence of widespread criminal background checks. *Criminology, 47,* 327–359.

Buckler, K. G., & Travis, L. F. (2003). Reanalyzing the prevalence and social context of collateral consequence statutes. *Journal of Criminal Justice, 31,* 435–453.

Budeiri, P. (1981). Collateral consequences of guilty pleas in the Federal criminal justice system. *Harvard Civil Rights-Civil Liberties Law Review, 16,* 157.

Burton, V. S., Cullen, F. T., & Travis, L. F. (1987). The collateral consequences of a felony conviction: A national study of state statutes. *Federal Probation, 51,* 52–60.

Burton, L. M. (1992). Black grandparents rearing children of drug addicted parents: Stressors, outcomes, and social service needs. *The Gerontologist, 32,* 744–751.

Bushway, S. D., Nieuwbeerta, P., & Blockland, A. (2011). The predictive value of criminal background checks: Do age and criminal history affect time to redemption? *Criminology, 49,* 27–60.

Bushway, Shawn & Forst, Brian. (2013). Studying discretion in the processes that generate criminal justice sanctions. *Justice Quarterly, 30,* 199–222.

Bushway, S., & Sweeten, G. (2007). Abolish lifetime bans for ex-felons. *Criminology and Public Policy, 6,* 697–706.

Carpenter, S. C., & Clyman, R. B. (2004). The long term emotional and physical wellbeing of women who have lived in kinship care. *Children and Youth Services Review, 26,* 673–686.

Centers for Disease Control and Prevention. (2008). MMWR analysis provides new details on HIV incidence in U.S. populations. Retrieved from www.cdc.gov/nchhstp/newsroom/docs/CDC_Incidence_MMWR.pdf

Chesney-Lind, M. (1977). Judicial paternalism and the female status offender: Training women to know their place. *Crime & Delinquency, 23,* 121–130.

Chesney-Lind, M., & Pasko, L. (2004). Girls' troubles and "female delinquency". In M. Chesney-Lind & L. Pasko. *The female offender: Girls, women, and crime,* 2nd edition. Thousand Oaks/London/New Delhi: Sage Publications. pp. 9–30.

Chigwada-Bailey, R. (1997). Black women's experiences of the criminal justice system. London: Waterside.

Chiricos, T., & Bales, W. (1991). Unemployment and punishment: An empirical assessment. *Criminology, 29,* 701–724.

Clark, J., & Henry, D. (1997). The pretrial release decision. *Judicature, 81,* 76–81.

Cohen, T. H. (2014). Who is better at defending criminals? Does type of defense attorney matter in terms of producing favorable case outcomes. *Criminal Justice Policy Review, 25*(1), 29–58.

Cohen, T. H., & Reaves, B. A. (2007). *Pretrial release of felony defendants in state courts: State court processing statistics, 1990–2004.* Washington, DC: Bureau of Justice Statistics.

Collins, P. H. (2004). *Black sexual politics: African Americans, gender, and the new racism.* New York, NY: Routledge.

Couturier, L., Maue, F., & McVey, C. (2005). Releasing inmates with mental illness and co-occurring disorders into the community. *Corrections Today, 67*(2), 82–85.

Cox, C. B. (2002). Empowering African American custodial grandparents. *Social Work, 47*(1), 45–54.

Crawford, C. (2000). Gender, race, and habitual offender sentencing in Florida. *Criminology, 38,* 263–280.

Crew, B. K. (1991). Sex differences in criminal sentencing: Chivalry or patriarchy? *Justice Quarterly, 8,* 59–83.

Dalley, L. P. (2000). Imprisoned mothers and their children: Their often conflicting legal rights. *Hamline Journal of Public Law and Policy, 22,* 1–44.

Daly, K. (1987). Structure and practice of familial-based justice in a criminal court. *Law & Society Review, 21,* 267–290.

Daly, K. (1994). Gender and punishment disparity. In G. S. Bridges & M. A. Meyers (Eds.), *Inequality, crime, & social control.* Boulder, CO: Westview Press.

Davies, A. L. B., & Worden, A. P. (2009). State politics and the right to counsel: A comparative analysis. *Law & Society Review, 43,* 187–219.

Demuth, St. (2003). Racial and ethnic differences in pretrial release decisions and outcomes: A comparison of Hispanic, Black, and White felony arrestees. *Criminology, 41,* 873–907.

Demuth, S., & Steffensmeier, D. (2004). The impact of gender and race/ethnicity in the pretrial release process. *Social Problems, 51,* 222–242.

Diller, R. (2010). The hidden cost of Florida's criminal justice fees. Research report prepared for the Brennan Center for justice at the New York University Law School.

Doerner, J., & Demuth, S. (2010). The independent and joint effects of race/ethnicity, gender, and age on sentencing outcomes in U.S. federal courts. *Justice Quarterly, 27,* 1–27.

Doerner, J. K., & Demuth, S. (2014). Gender and sentencing in the federal courts: Are women treated more leniently? *Criminal Justice Policy Review, 25*(2), 242–269.

Dodge, M., & Pogrebin, M. R. (2001). Collateral costs of imprisonment for women: Complications of reintegration. *The Prison Journal, 81,* 42–54.

Dolbin-MacNab, M. L., & Keiley, M. K. (2006). A systematic examination of grandparents' emotional closeness with their custodial grandchildren. *Research in Human Development, 3,* 59–71.

Dolovich, S. (2009). Foreword: Incarceration American-style, *Harvard Law & Policy Review, 3,* 236–259.

Dubowitz, H., Feigelman, S., Harrington, D., Starr Jr., R., Zuravin, S., & Sawyer, R. (1994). Children in kinship care: How do they fare? *Children and Youth Services Review, 16,* 85–106.

Dunifon, R. (2013). The influence of grandparents on the lives of children and adolescents. *Child Development Perspectives, 7*(1), 55–60.

Eligon, J. (2009, January 23). Correction officers accused of letting inmates run Rikers Island Jail. *The New York Times,* p. A20.

Engen, R. L., & Steen, S. (2000). The power to punish: Discretion and sentencing reform in the war on drugs. *American Journal of Sociology, 105,* 1357–1395.

Ewald, A. C., & Smith, M. (2008). Collateral consequences of criminal conviction in American courts: A view from the bench. *Justice System Journal, 29,* 145–167.

Farnsworth, M., & Teske, R. H. C. (1995). Gender differences in felony court processing: Three hypotheses of disparity, *Women and Criminal Justice, 62,* 23–44.

Farrell, R., & Swigert, V. (1978). Prior offense record as a self-fulfilling prophecy. *Law & Society Review, 12,* 437–453.

Flemming, R., Nardulli, P., & Eisenstein, J. (1992). *The craft of justice: Politics and work in criminal court communities.* Philadelphia, PA: Pennsylvania University Press.

Foote, C. (1954). Compelling appearance in court: Administration of bail in Philadelphia. *University of Pennsylvania Law Review, 102,* 1031–1079.

Franklin, C. A., & Fearn, N. E. (2008). Gender, race, and formal court decision-making outcomes: Chivalry/paternalism, conflict theory or gender conflict? *Journal of Criminal Justice, 36,* 279–290.

Frazier, C., Bock, W., & Henretta, J. (1980). Pretrial release and bail decisions: The effects of legal, community, and personal variables. *Criminology, 18,* 162–181.

Free, M. D. (2004). Bail and pretrial release decisions: An assessment of the racial threat perspective. *Journal of Ethnicity in Criminal Justice, 2*(4), 23–44.

Freiburger, T. L. (2010). The effects of gender, family status, and race on sentencing decisions. *Behavioral Sciences and the Law, 28*, 378–395.

Freisthler, M., & Godsey, M. A. (2005). Going home to stay: A review of collateral consequences of conviction, post-incarceration employment, and recidivism in Ohio. *Toledo Law Review, 36*, 525–544.

Gaines, L. K. (2014). Policing the drug problem. In L. K. Gaines & J. Kremlings (Eds.), Drugs, crime, & justice: Contemporary perspectives (3rd ed., pp. 42–59). Illinois: Waveland Press, Inc.

Galea, S., & Rudenstein, S. (2005). Challenges in understanding disparities in drug use and its consequences. *Journal of Urban Health: Bulletin of the New York Academy of Medicine, 82*, 5–12.

Gilmore, M., & Guerra, M. K. (2010). Crisis care services for counties: Preventing individuals with mental illnesses for entering local corrections systems. Report from the Community Services Division of the County Services Department. Retrieved from www.uwgb.edu/bhtp/tools/Crisis_Care_in_CJ.pdf

Griffin, T., & Wooldredge, J. (2006). Sex-based disparities in felony dispositions before versus after sentencing reform in Ohio. *Criminology, 44*, 893–923.

Griswold, D. B. (1987). Deviation from sentencing guidelines: The issue of unwarranted disparity. *Journal of Criminal Justice, 15*, 317–329.

Goldkamp, J. (1979). *Two Classes of Accused*. Cambridge, MA: Ballinger Press.

Gottfredson, M., & Gottfredson, D. (1988). *Decisionmaking in criminal justice: Towards the Rational exercise of discretion*. New York, NY: Plenum.

Goulette, N., Reitler, A., Flesher, W., Frank, J., & Travis, L. (2014). Criminal justice practitioners' perceptions of collateral consequences of criminal conviction on offenders. *Criminal Justice Review, 39*(3), 290–304.

Goulette, N., Wooldredge, J., Frank, J., Travis, L. (2015). From initial appearance to sentencing: Do female defendants experience disparate treatment? *Journal of Criminal Justice, 43*, 406–417.

Hartley, R., Miller, H., & Spohn, C. (2010). Do you get what you pay for? Type of counsel and its effect on criminal court outcomes. *Journal of Criminal Justice, 38*, 1063–1070.

Hawkins, D. (1981). Causal attribution and punishment for crime. *Deviant Behavior, 2*, 207–230.

Hayslip, B., & Kaminski, P. (2005). Grandparents raising their grandchildren: A review of the literature and suggestions for practice. *The Gerontologist, 45*(2), 262–269.

Henichson, C., Rinaldi, J., & Delaney, R. (2015, May). *The price of jails: Measuring the taxpayer cost of local incarceration*. New York, NY: Vera Institute, Center on Sentencing and Corrections.

Hessick, C. B. (2010). Race and gender as explicit sentencing factors. *The Journal of Gender, Race, and Justice, 14*(1), 127–142.

Heumann, M. (1978). *Plea bargaining: The experiences of prosecutors, judges, and defense attorneys*. Chicago, IL: University of Chicago Press.

Heywood, E. M. (1999). Custodial grandparents and their grandchildren. *The Family Journal: Counseling and Therapy for Couples and Families, 7*, 367–372.

Holmes, M., Daudistel, H., & Farrell, R. (1987). Determinants of charge reductions and final dispositions in cases of burglary and robbery. *Journal of Research in Crime and Delinquency, 24*, 233–254.

Holmes, M., Hosch, H., Daudistel, H., Perez, D., & Graves, J. (1996). Ethnicity, legal resources, and felony dispositions in two southwestern jurisdictions. *Justice Quarterly, 13*, 11–30.

Human Rights Watch. (2010). The price of freedom: Bail and pretrial detention of non-felony low-income defendants in New York City 2. Retrieved from www.hrw.org/sites/default/files/reports/us1210webwcover_0.pdf

Jeffries, S., Fletcher, G., & Newbold, G. (2003). Pathways to sex-based differentiation in criminal court sentencing. *Criminology, 41*, 329–353.

Johnson, B. D., Ulmer, J. T., & Kramer, J. H. (2008). The social context of guidelines circumvention: The case of federal district courts. *Criminology, 46*(3), 737–783.

Johnston, J. B., Kennedy, T. D., & Shuman, I. G. (1987). Gender differences in the sentencing of felony offenders. *Federal Probation, 51*, 49–55.

Katz, C., & Spohn, C. (1995). The effect of race and gender on bail outcomes: Test of an interactive model. *American Journal of Criminal Justice, 19*, 161–184.

Kaukinen, C. E. (1995). Women lawbreakers constructed in terms of traditional definitions of feminity: The sentencing of women in conflict with the law (Unpublished master's thesis). University of Windsor, Ontario, Canada.

Kelley, S. J., Whitley, D. M., & Campos, P. E. (2011). Behavior problems in children raised by grandmothers: The role of caregiver distress, family resources, and the home environment. *Children and Youth Services, 33*, 2138–2145.

Kellough, G., & Wortley, S. (2002). Remand for plea: Bail decisions and plea bargaining as commensurate conditions. *British Journal of Criminology, 42*, 186–210.

Koons-Witt, B. A. (2002). The effect of gender on the decision to incarcerate before and after the introduction of sentencing guidelines. *Criminology, 40*(2), 297–327.

Kramer, J. H., & Ulmer, J. T. (1996). Sentencing disparity and departure from guidelines. *Justice Quarterly, 13*, 81–105.

Kramer, J., H., & Ulmer, J. T. (2002). Downward departures for serious violent offenders: Local court "corrections" to Pennsylvania's sentencing guidelines. *Criminology, 40*(4), 897–932.

Kremling, J., & Adams, C. (2014). Minorities and drugs. In L. K. Gaines & J. Kremlings (Eds.), *Drugs, crime, & justice: Contemporary perspectives* (3rd ed., pp. 465–494). Illinois: Waveland Press, Inc.

Kruttschnitt, C. (1984). Sex and criminal court dispositions: The unresolved controversy. *Journal of Research in Crime and Delinquency, 21*, 213–232.

Kruttschnitt, C., & McCarthy, D. (1985). Familial social control and pretrial sanctions: Does sex really matter? *The Journal of Criminal Law and Criminology, 76*, 151–175.

Kurlychek, M. C., Brame, R., & Bushway, S. D. (2006). Scarlet letters and recidivism: Does an old criminal record predict future offending? *Criminology and Public Policy, 5*, 483–504.

Kurlychek, M. C., Brame, R., & Bushway, S. D. (2007). Enduring risk? Old criminal records and predictions of future criminal involvement. *Crime and Delinquency, 53*, 64–83.

Kutateladze, B., Andiloro, N., Johnson, B., & Spohn, C. (2014). Cumulative disadvantage: Examining racial and ethnic disparity in prosecution and sentencing. *Criminology, 52*, 514–551.

LaFree, G. (1985a). Official reactions to Hispanic defendants in the southwest. *Journal of Research in Crime and Delinquency, 22*, 213–237.

LaFree, G. (1985b). Adversarial and non-adversarial justice: A comparison of guilty pleas and trials. *Criminology, 23*, 289–312.

Lee, Y., Blitz, L. V., Srnka, M. (2015). Trauma and resiliency in grandparent-headed multigenerational families. *Families in Society: The Journal of Contemporary Social Services, 96*(2), 116–124.

Lizotte, A. (1978). Extralegal factors in Chicago's criminal courts: Testing the conflict model of criminal justice. *Social Problems, 25*, 564–580.

Manns, J. (2005). Liberty takings: A framework for compensating pretrial detainees. *Cardozo Law Review, 26*, 1947.

Martin, M., & Stimpson, M. (1997/1998). Women, race and sentencing in Oklahoma: A preliminary analysis. *Journal of the Oklahoma Criminal Justice Research Consortium, 4.*

Maxwell, S., & Davis, J. (1999). The salience of race and gender in pretrial release decisions: A comparison across multiple jurisdictions. *Criminal Justice Policy Review, 10*, 491–501.

McCoy, C. (2007). Caleb was right: Pretrial decisions determine mostly everything. *Berkeley Journal of Criminal Law, 12*, 135–149.

Meyer J., & Jesilow P. (1997). *"Doing justice" in the people's court: Sentencing by municipal court judges.* Albany, NY: State University of New York Press.

Miller, J. (2008). Violence against urban African American girls. *Journal of Contemporary Criminal Justice, 24*, 148–162.

Minton, T. D. (2013). *Jail inmates at midyear 2012—Statistical Tables.* Washington, DC: Bureau of Justice Statistics.

Moore, C. A., & Miethe, T. D. (1986). Regulated and unregulated sentencing decisions: An analysis of first-year practices under Minnesota's felony sentencing guidelines. *Law & Society Review, 20*, 253–277.

Moore, J. W., & Hagedorn, J. M. (1996). What happens to girls in the gang? In C. R. Huff (Ed.), *Gangs in America* (2nd ed., pp 205–220). Thousand Oaks, CA: SAGE Publications.

Murray, B. M. (2015). Beyond the right to counsel: Increasing notice of collateral consequences. University of Richmond Law Review, 49, 101–153.

Mustard, D. B. (2001). Racial, ethnic, and gender disparities in sentencing: Evidence from the U.S. federal courts. *Journal of Law and Economics, 44*, 285–314.

Nagel, I. (1983). The legal/extra-legal controversy: Judicial decisions in pretrial release. *Law & Society Review, 17*, 481–515.

Nagel, I., & Johnson, B. (1994). The role of gender in a structured sentencing system: Equal treatment, policy choices, and the sentencing of female offenders under the United States sentencing guidelines. *Journal of Criminal Law and Criminology, 85*, 181–221.

Nagel, I. H. (1990). Structuring sentencing discretion: The new federal sentencing guidelines. *The Journal of Criminal Law & Criminology, 80*, 883–943.

Neely-Barnes, S. L., Graff, J. C., & Washington, G. (2010). The health-related quality of life of custodial grandparents. *Health & Social Work, 35*, 87–97.

Nolen-Hoeksema, S. (2004). Gender differences in risk factors and consequences for alcohol use and problems. *Clinical psychological review, 24*, 981–1010.

Noonan, M. (2010). *Mortality in local jails, 2000–2006*. Washington, DC: U.S. Department of Justice, Bureau of Justice Statistics.

Office of National Drug Control Policy. (2012). *ADAM II: 2011 Annual report*. Washington, DC: Author. Retrieved from http://abtassociates.com/reports/2012/arrestee-drug-abuse-monitoring-program-ii-(adam-ii.aspx)

Olivares, K. M., Burton, V. S., & Cullen, F. T. (1996). The collateral consequences of a felony conviction: A national study of state legal codes 10 years later. *Federal Probation, 60*, 10–17.

Padilla v. Kentucky, 559 U.S. 356 (2010).

Pager, D. (2003). The mark of a criminal record. *American Journal of Sociology, 108*, 937–975.

Patterson, E. B., & Lynch, M. (1991). Bias in formalized bail procedures. In M. Lynch & E. B. Patterson (Eds.), *Race and criminal justice*. New York, NY: Harrow and Heston.

Petee, T. (1994). Recommended for release on recognizance: Factors affecting pretrial release recommendations. *The Journal of Social Psychology, 134*, 375–382.

Petteruti, A., & Walsh, N. (2008). Jailing communities: The impact of jail expansion and effective public safety strategies. Justice Policy Institute Report.

Pinard, M. (2006). An integrated perspective on the collateral consequences of criminal convictions and reentry issues faced by formerly incarcerated individuals. *Boston University Law Review, 86*, 623–690.

Pinard, M. (2010). Reflections and perspectives on reentry and collateral consequences. *Journal of Criminal Law and Criminology, 100*, 1213–1224.

Pogrebin, M., Dodge, M., & Katsampes, P. (2001). Collateral costs of short-term jail incarceration: The long-term social and economic disruptions. *Corrections Management Quarterly, 5*(4), 64–69.

Population Reference Bureau. (December 2011). *Today's research on aging: Program and policy implications*. Retrieved June 16, 2015, from www.prb.org/pdf11/TodaysResearchAging23.pdf

Rabinowitz, M. (2010). *Holding cells: Understanding the collateral consequences of pretrial detention. Unpublished dissertation*. Evanston, IL: Northwestern University.

Rehavi, M. M., & Starr, S. (2012). Racial disparity in federal criminal charging and its sentencing consequences. *Journal of Public Economics, 122*(6), 1320–1354.

Reitler, A., Sullivan, C., & Frank, J. (2013). The effects of legal and extralegal factors on detention decision in US District Courts. *Justice Quarterly, 30*, 340–368.

Richey-Mann, Coramae. (1993). *Unequal Justice: A Question of Color*. Bloomington, IN: Indiana University Press.

Roberts, J. (2009). Ignorance is effectively bliss: Collateral consequences, silence, and misinformation in the guilty-plea process. *Iowa Law Review, 95*, 119.

Rodgers-Farmer, A. Y. (1999). Parenting stress, depression, and parenting in grandmothers raising their grandchildren. *Children and Youth Services Review, 21*(5), 377–388.

Rodriguez, S. F., Curry, T. R., & Lee, G. (2006). Gender differences in criminal sentencing: Do effects vary across violent, property, and drug offenses? *Social Science Quarterly, 87*, 318–339.

Sacks, M, & Ackerman, A. R. (2012). Pretrial detention and guilty pleas: If they can't afford bail they must be guilty. *Criminal Justice Studies, 25*(3), 265–278.

Scott, R. (2010). The effects of *Booker* on inter-judge sentencing disparity. *Federal Sentencing Reporter, 22*, 14–108.

Shelton, K. H., & Harold, G. T. (2008). Interparental conflict, negative parenting, and children's adjustment: Bridging links between parents' depression and children's psychological distress. *Journal of Psychology, 22*(5), 712.

Sinden, P. (1981). Offender gender and perceptions of crime seriousness. *Sociological Spectrum, 1*, 39–52.

Smith, G. C., & Palmieri, P. A. (2007). Risk of psychological difficulties among children raised by custodial grandparents. *Psychiatric Services, 58*(10), 1303–1310.

Smith, G. C., Palmieri, P. A., Hancock, G. R., & Richardson, R. A. (2008). Custodial grandmothers' psychological distress, dysfunctional parenting, and grandchildren's adjustment. *International Journal on Aging and Human Development, 67*(4), 327–357.

Soothill, K., & Francis, B. (2009). When do ex-offenders become like non-offenders? *Howard Journal of Criminal Justice, 48*, 373–387.

Spangenderg, R., & Beeman, M. (1995). Indigent defense systems in the United States. *Law and Contemporary Problems, 58*, 31–50.

Spohn, C., & Holleran, D. (2000). The imprisonment penalty paid by young, unemployed Black and Hispanic male offenders. *Criminology, 38*, 281–306.

Spohn, C. (2009). Race, sex, and pretrial detention in federal court: Indirect effects and cumulative disadvantage. *Kansas Law Review, 57*, 879–901.

Steffensmeier, D. (1980). Assessing the impact of the women's movement on sex-based differences in the handling of adult criminal defendants. *Crime and Delinquency, 23*, 344–356.

15 Collateral Effects of Pretrial Detention

Steffensmeier, D., Kramer, J., & Streifel, C. (1993). Gender and imprisonment decisions. *Criminology, 31*(3), 411–446.

Steffensmeier, D., Ulmer, J., & Kramer, J. (1998). The interaction of race, gender, and age in criminal sentencing: The punishment cost of being young, Black, and male. *Criminology, 36(4)*, 763–797.

Steury, E. H., & Frank, N. (1990). Gender bias and pretrial release: More pieces of the puzzle. *Journal of Criminal Justice, 18*, 417–432.

Stolzenber, L., D'Alessio, S. J., & Eitle, D. (2004). A multilevel test of racial threat theory. *Criminology, 42*(3), 673–698.

Stolzenberg, Lisa, D'Alessio, Stewart, & Eitle, David. (2013). Race and cumulative discrimination in the prosecution of criminal defendants. *Race and Justice, 3*, 1–25.

Stryker, R., Nagel, I., & Hagan, J. (1983). Methodological issues in court research: Pretrial release decisions for federal defendants. *Sociological Methods and Research, 11*, 469–500.

Sudman, S. (1976). *Applied Sampling.* New York, NY: Academic Press.

Sullivan, L. (2010, January 22). Bail burden keeps U.S. jails stuffed with inmates. NPR. Retrieved from www.npr.org/2010/01/21/122725771/Bail-Burden-Keeps-U-S-Jails-Stuffed-With-Inmates

Sutton, John. (2013). Structural bias in the sentencing of felony defendants. *Social Science Research, 42*, 1207–1221.

Talvi, S. J. A. (2007, December 4). Deadly staph infection "superbug" has a dangerous foothold in U.S. jails. Retrieved from www.alternet.org/story/69576

Tewksbury, R. (2005). Collateral consequences of sex offender registration. *Journal of Contemporary Criminal Justice, 21*, 67–81.

Tibbetts, S. G. (2014). The influence of drugs on brain activity and resulting criminality. In L. K. Gaines & J. Kremlings (Eds.), *Drugs, crime, & justice: Contemporary perspectives* (3rd ed., pp. 42–59). Illinois: Waveland Press, Inc.

Travis, J., & Petersilia, J. (2001). Reentry reconsidered: A new look at an old question. *Crime and Delinquency, 47*, 291–313.

Turner, K. B., & Johnson, J. B. (2006). The effect of gender on the judicial pretrial decision of bail amount set. *Federal Probation, 70(1)*, 56–62.

Ulmer, Jeffery. (2012). Recent developments and new directions in sentencing research. *Justice Quarterly, 29*, 1–40.

Ulmer, J. T., & Johnson, B. (2004). Sentencing in context: A multilevel analysis. *Criminology, 42*, 137–177.

Ulmer, J., Light, J., & Kramer, J. (2011). The 'liberation' of federal judges' discretion in the wake of the *Booker/Fanfan* decision: Is there increased divergence between the courts? *Justice Quarterly, 28*, 800–837.

Visher, C. A. (1983). Gender, police arrest decisions, and notions of chivalry. *Criminology, 21*, 5–28.

Wald, P. (1964). Pre-trial detention and ultimate freedom: A statistical study. *New York University Law Review, 39*, 631–655.

Weiser, B. (2009, February 5). Lawsuits suggest pattern of Rikers guards looking other way. *The New York Times*, p. A21.

Williams, M. R. (2013). The effectiveness of public defenders in four Florida counties. *Journal of Criminal Justice, 41*, 205–212.

Winokur, M., Holtan, A., & Batchelder, K. E. (2014). Kinship care for the safety, permanency, and well-being of children removed from the home for maltreatment. *Cochrane Database of Systematic Reviews, 1*, 1–242.

Wiseman, S. R. (2014). Pretrial detention and the right to be monitored. *The Yale Law Journal, 123*, 1344–1404.

Wooldredge, J., Frank, J., Goulette, N., & Travis, L. (2015). Is the impact of cumulative disadvantage on sentencing greater for black defendants? *Criminology and Public Policy, 14*, 187–223.

Young, V. D. (1986). Gender expectations and their impact on Black female offenders and victims. *Justice Quarterly, 3*, 305–327.

Zatz, M. S., & Hagan, J. (1985). Crime, time, and Punishment: An exploration of selection bias in sentencing research. *Journal of Quantitative Criminology, 1*(1), 103–126.

16

THE IMPACT OF RESTRICTIVE HOUSING ON INMATE BEHAVIOR

A Systematic Review of the Evidence

Ryan M. Labrecque and Paula Smith

Introduction

Restrictive housing (RH)—often referred to as solitary confinement—is one of the most severe punishments that justice officials can impose upon inmates in the modern correctional era. Although corrections officials and researchers often refer to RH by a variety of names, prior scholarship suggests there are three sub-types, including *disciplinary segregation* (i.e., punishment for serious misconduct), *protective custody* (i.e., protection of vulnerable inmates), and *administrative segregation* (i.e., isolation of disruptive or dangerous inmates; Mears, 2016). Regardless of terminology, this type of housing typically involves seclusion in a closed cell for 20 or more hours per day with little to no access to services, programming, privileges, or contact with other people (Gendreau & Labrecque, 2018).

Proponents often justify the use of RH on the premise that it deters violence and misbehavior within correctional institutions, and further reduces criminal behavior after release (see Mears & Castro, 2006). Its prevalence in North American correctional facilities indicates a high level of administrative support for RH. To illustrate, a recent Bureau of Justice Statistics report reveals nearly 20% of prison inmates and 18% of jail inmates in the U.S. spent time in RH during the previous year (Beck, 2015). Another report from the Office of the Correctional Investigator finds more than 24% of inmates in the Canadian federal prison system spent time in RH over the course of one year (Zinger, 2013).

Despite its widespread use, there are growing concerns about the collateral consequences of RH. Critics contend, for example, that its use violates inmates' constitutional rights, contributes to physical and psychological problems, and increases subsequent criminal behavior (e.g., Haney, 2003; Lovell, 2008). Although a full analysis of the many potential collateral consequences is beyond the scope of the current chapter, our focus here is on the relationship between RH and inmate behavior by systematically reviewing the available empirical literature. This work builds upon prior reviews (e.g., Gendreau & Goggin, In press; Steiner & Cain, 2016) in three important ways: (1) it includes a more extensive body of research; (2) it provides a more comprehensive analysis of the research findings separated by outcome type and methodological quality; and (3) it identifies gaps in knowledge and sets an agenda for future research in this area.

Assessing the Impact of Restrictive Housing

Despite the ongoing and frequently contentious debate regarding the use and effects of RH, the theoretical underpinnings of this correctional practice remain unclear and without agreement

(Mears, 2016). This is problematic because research shows that interventions are most effective when grounded in a well-supported theory (Rossi, Lipsey, & Freeman, 2004). Theories explain what a particular strategy seeks to achieve and provide a rationale for the expected pattern of results. In the absence of theoretical guidance, "there is little prospect that the program will be effective" (Rossi et al., 2004, p. 135). We begin with a brief review of three theoretical perspectives as a means to contextualize the potential impact this practice might have on inmate behavior (see also Gendreau & Goggin, In press; Morris, 2016; and Steiner & Cain, 2016).

The first perspective contends RH is necessary for ensuring safety, order, and control within the correctional institution and beyond. This position aligns with deterrence theory and rests on the assumption that the unpleasant nature of RH discourages future antisocial behavior. From this view, the existence of RH reminds inmates that noncompliance with institutional rules and expectations will result in their placement in this aversive environment (i.e., general deterrence). Further, due to the negative experiences in RH, individuals held in such settings will refrain from misbehavior out of a desire to remain in the general population (i.e., specific deterrence). As such, this perspective argues that RH operates as a punisher by decreasing subsequent criminal behavior.

The second perspective holds RH is criminogenic. This position aligns with several general criminological theories, including deprivation, social bonds, social learning, labeling, strain, and defiance. From this view, the harsh conditions and idleness of RH intensify the pains of imprisonment, which cause its inhabitants to adopt antisocial values as a coping response. Restrictive housing further weakens prosocial social bonds, decreases perceptions of fairness and respect, bestows a negative label, and provides few if any opportunities for rehabilitation. Accordingly, this perspective insists RH has the unintended consequence of increasing criminal behavior.

The third perspective suggests RH has little effect on inmate behavior. This position is consistent with the importation and behavioral deep freeze theories, which describe institutional adjustment as an extension of one's previously held values and motivations. From this perspective, inmate behavior is determined by preexisting socialization factors (e.g., antisocial attitude, on-going community ties, post-prison expectations) that are carried into RH. Subsequently, this perspective maintains that RH has a null effect on criminal behavior.

It is important to acknowledge that it is also possible for two or more of these perspectives to be correct. For example, RH may differentially impact certain individuals, with some positively affected, others adversely affected, and yet others unaffected. The effect of RH might also be moderated by individual characteristics (e.g., age, gender, race, mental health status, risk for recidivism), the conditions of confinement in RH (e.g., physical structure, correctional climate, how inmates are treated by staff), or the nature of the placement (e.g., length of time in RH, reason for placement, opportunities to earn release). It is of significant scholarly and policy relevance to determine if, with whom, and under what conditions RH produces a positive, negative, or null effect (Frost & Monteiro, 2016). Such knowledge would be helpful to correctional authorities in devising the best policies for reducing criminal activity both in and out of prison. Likewise, there is a critical need to take stock of what is known about the effects of RH on inmate behavior.

Systematic Review of the Evidence

There exist few empirical investigations that directly assess any of the previous theoretical perspectives and even less research that examines if there are certain inmate characteristics that differentially influence the impact of RH on behavioral outcomes. In order to cumulate knowledge on the impact of RH, this study systematically reviews the existing evaluation literature. Scholarship in this area varies greatly on many dimensions that are important to understanding its effect, including the type of methodology used, the setting and sample characteristics included, and the types of RH and outcomes evaluated. In light of these considerations, we chose not to use meta-analytic techniques to summarize the literature. As an alternative, a systematic review provides the opportunity to discuss in greater detail the differences in the research design, methodological quality, and analytical strategy of the research in the current literature base. It also serves as a mechanism to identify gaps in knowledge and provide direction to researchers on areas in need of further empirical inquiry. Nonetheless, it is our contention that as more methodologically rigorous studies become available, a quantitative synthesis of the research is essential to generate mean effect size (ES) estimates and systematically explore the influence of moderators.

Research Design and Method

Literature Retrieval

The current investigation identifies relevant studies though several steps. This involves a keyword search using the terms "restrictive housing," "solitary confinement," "administrative segregation," "disciplinary segregation," and "supermax" in multiple computerized database systems, including the National Criminal Justice Reference Service, PsycINFO, Sociological Abstracts, and Google Scholar. This also includes a search of the indexes in the journals that frequently publish research on RH, such as *Criminology*, *Justice Quarterly*, and *The Prison Journal*. It further involves a search in the resource libraries of the National Institute of Justice and National Institute of Corrections and the annual conference programs of the American Society of Criminology and Academy of Criminal Justice Sciences for non-peer reviewed research. Finally, it includes a review of the reference lists from each of the identified studies to determine if there are other relevant works not discovered by the other means.

Eligibility Criteria

The inclusion criteria of this review require a primary study to involve a quantitative analysis of the effects of RH on any one of three categories of behavioral outcomes: *aggregate measures of institutional violence, individual measures of post-release recidivism*, or *individual measures of institutional adjustment*. This process excludes studies examining non-behavioral outcomes, such as physiological and psychological indices (for more information on medical and mental health outcomes, see Kapoor & Trestman, 2016; and Morgan et al., 2016). It also omits discussions of ethical and legal issues related to the use of RH (for more information on constitutionality concerns, see Cohen, 2016). We organize this evidence review by outcome type and describe the findings by methodological approach and scientific rigor. As discussed above, the operationalization of RH in the current investigation broadly includes placement for punitive, protective, or other management purposes. Wherever possible, this review makes distinctions between the type of RH evaluated and provides descriptions of the specific correctional system in which the study took place.

Results

This review identifies 37 empirical evaluations on the behavioral effects of RH. Among these studies, eight examine the impact of RH on aggregate measures of institutional violence, including indicators of inmate-on-inmate and inmate-on-staff violence (e.g., stabbings, homicides, assaults). Three of the institutional violence studies take place in a single state prison system and five occur in multiple states. Fifteen evaluations assess the influence of RH on post-release recidivism, including measures of revocation, re-arrest, re-conviction, and re-incarceration. Seven of the recidivism studies investigate the effects of RH generally, six focus on the impact of the supermax exclusively, and two involve the effects of disciplinary segregation. Eleven of the recidivism investigations occur within a single state system, one occurs in the U.S. federal system, and three take place in the Canadian federal system.

Sixteen evaluations examine the impact of RH on indicators of institutional adjustment.[1] Five of the institutional adjustment studies include measures of attitude or emotions related to criminal behavior, three involve administrative decisions to release inmates early, five involve measures of institutional misconduct, and three assess the influence of moderators on misbehavior in prison. Within these works, seven use a broad measure of RH, eight limit their investigation to disciplinary segregation, and one involves separate analyses for disciplinary and administrative segregation. Ten of the institutional adjustment studies take place in a single state prison system, one occurs in the U.S. federal system, four take place in the Canadian federal system, and one includes prisons from the U.S. and Canada.

In the current investigation, we use the Maryland Scientific Methods Scale to assess the methodological rigor of the research design in these RH evaluations (see Sherman et al., 1997). Accordingly, this review includes two "Level 1" studies (i.e., correlation); 15 "Level 2" studies (i.e., nonequivalent comparison group design, or a pre-post comparison without a comparison group); 11 "Level 3" studies (i.e., quasi-experimental design with the use of a regression technique to account for group differences, or a repeated measures design without a comparison group); and nine "Level 4" studies (i.e., quasi-experimental design with the use of a matching technique to account for group differences, or a repeated measures design with a comparison group). This review does not include any "Level 5" studies (i.e., randomized control trial). For the purposes of this review, we categorize Level 1 and Level 2 studies as "low quality," Level 3 studies as "medium quality," and Level 4 studies as "high quality."

From the 37 studies included in this systematic review, we find a total of 119 separate ESs, with 40 involving an institutional violence outcome, 39 involving a recidivism outcome, 31 involving an institutional adjustment outcome, and nine involving a moderator analysis between two different types of inmates who are both exposed to an RH condition. Our analysis focuses on two aspects of each ES: direction and statistical significance. More specifically, we code the direction of an ES as "negative" if the sign of the effect indicates an improvement on the variable of interest (e.g., reduces violence, recidivism, misconduct) and as "positive" if the sign of the effect indicates a detriment on the variable of interest (e.g., increases violence, recidivism, misconduct). We use $p < .05$ as our threshold for determining statistical significance.

Table 16.1 summarizes the ES information for the studies included in this review. As can be seen in the table, two-thirds of the ESs are positive. This suggests the majority of the empirical research finds the experience of RH to be iatrogenic toward inmate behavioral outcomes. The table also reveals, however, that only about one-third of these ESs reach statistical significance at the .05 level. Further, the percentage of statistically significant ESs drops appreciably when examined by methodological quality, with 50% of the low quality, 32% of medium quality, and 28% of high quality ESs reaching statistical significance.

Table 16.1 also separates these findings by outcome type. All three subcategories indicate a greater proportion of positive effects than negative effects. Recidivism outcomes report the highest level of detriment, with 85% of the ESs falling in the positive category. A general pattern also emerges within these subcategories with higher quality studies reporting fewer statistically significant findings. The one exception is with respect to the institutional adjustment outcomes, where medium quality studies possess fewer significant effects compared to high quality studies (18% vs. 33%). The relatively small number of studies and ESs included in both of these categories may have some bearing on these results. Next, we review this body of research by outcome type and methodological strategy (see also Appendix).

Table 16.1 Summary of Effect Size Estimates, by Outcome Type and Methodological Rigor

	# Studies	# Effect Sizes	% Neg.	% Pos.	% Sig.
All behavioral outcomes	33	110	34.0	66.0	36.1
Low quality	16	39	27.8	72.2	50.0
Medium quality	11	53	40.8	59.2	32.1
High quality	6	18	27.8	72.2	27.8
Inmate violence	8	40	47.2	52.8	44.4
Low quality	4	18	55.6	44.4	60.0
Medium quality	4	22	38.9	61.1	40.9
Recidivism	14	39	15.4	84.6	33.3
Low quality	7	10	0.0	100.0	40.0
Medium quality	3	14	14.3	85.7	35.7
High quality	4	15	26.7	73.3	26.7
Institutional adjustment	13	31	42.9	57.1	32.3
Low quality	7	11	0.0	100.0	54.6
Medium quality	4	17	64.7	35.3	17.7
High quality	2	3	33.3	66.7	33.3

Institutional Violence

Early research on the impact of RH examines the impact of policy changes (e.g., prison lock-down; construction of supermax prisons) on measures of institutional violence. For example, a study in California compares estimates of violence throughout the state prison system before and after the 1973 "lock-down" of the four highest security facilities (Bidna, 1975). This investigation reports an overall reduction in the rates of stabbings and assaults and an increase in the rate of stabbings within the higher security settings post-lock-down.

A similar investigation in Texas examines the trends in institutional violence before and after a massive lock-down in 1985 of the state's gang members (Ralph & Marquart, 1991). This research describes the decrease in the number of homicides following the lock-down—25 homicides in 1985, 5 in 1986, and 3 in 1987—as evidence of the success of this policy change. Further, a survey of 416 men incarcerated during this time indicates an increase in perceptions of safety in the general population in the aftermath of the lock-down (Crouch & Marquart, 1990). The conclusion from these works is that RH helps reduce violence and improve one's feelings of safety throughout the prison system. This management strategy also increases the number of people in RH and transfers violence to these higher security settings. One must interpret these findings cautiously as these investigations involve only two states and include a relatively short observation period before and after a major policy change.

Another investigation using national level prison data shows that the decrease in prison riots, homicides, assaults, escapes, disturbances, and arsons between the 1980s and early 2000s does not correlate with the changes in the use of RH during this time (Useem & Piehl, 2006). This study highlights that in 1982, there are 5.4 inmates per 1,000 in RH, and in 2011, there are 5.2 inmates per 1,000. The authors argue if RH is an effective deterrent of institutional violence, this reduction in use during this period should increase, not decrease, such violence. This suggests RH may not be responsible for improving prison order. As with the previous studies, the research design of this investigation remains speculative because it fails to consider historical threats to validity. This design cannot rule out the possibility that other policies and practices occurring in tandem with changes in the use of RH may influence these results.

Other studies employ more sophisticated research designs and statistical techniques to assess the effect of RH on measures of institutional violence. The findings from this group of works remain mixed. For example, a study using a multiple interrupted time series design to assess if the opening of a new supermax facility in three states (Arizona, Illinois, and Minnesota) led to different levels of violence in comparison to a state without a supermax prison (Utah) during the same time period (Briggs, Sundt, & Castellano, 2003). The investigators find the addition of a supermax prison had no effect on levels of inmate-on-inmate violence and a mixed effect on inmate-on-staff violence throughout the prison systems examined. These findings call into question the ability of RH to reduce institutional violence. There are, however, some concerns about the generalizability of these results as the study includes only four states.

Another analytic approach involves the use of multilevel structural equation modeling. For example, one study uses a nationally representative sample of adult men from state prisons to assess the effect of different administrative control strategies on inmate assaults (Huebner, 2003). This study finds the percent of the inmate population in RH is not related to the number of inmate-on-inmate or inmate-on-staff assaults. Another investigation examines the influence of different facility-level characteristics on inmate levels of violence across state-operated prisons in the U.S. (Steiner, 2009). This study reports mixed effects of the proportion of inmates held in disciplinary segregation and protective custody on measures of violence. Finally, another study investigates the impact of different types of administrative controls on measures of inmate deviance for men and women in state-operated prisons (Wooldredge & Steiner, 2015). This study finds that the proportion of inmates held in RH has a positive relationship with both violent and non-violent misconduct offense levels; however, the magnitude of these relationships is considerably weaker when the authors control for the population composition.

Post-Release Recidivism

Research on post-release recidivism suggests inmates who experience RH in custody are more likely to recidivate than those who do not spend time in this type of placement. For example, a study in Connecticut finds 92% of those placed in RH during their commitment were re-arrested within three years compared to 66% of those with no such experience in custody (LPRIC, 2001). Another study in Colorado reveals 64% of inmates who experienced RH in custody were re-incarcerated within three years of release (O'Keefe, 2005), which is higher than the average state recidivism rate of 50% for all inmates (Rosten, 2004). Similarly, a California study indicates nearly 70% of those paroled who spent time in RH during their commitment were re-incarcerated within three years compared to 65% of those with no RH experience (Seale et al., 2011).

Support for higher rates of recidivism among RH inmates is not limited to research conducted in state correctional systems or the U.S. For example, a study in the U.S. federal prison system finds that of the inmates released from the Alcatraz Federal Penitentiary (i.e., RH group), 50% were re-incarcerated during follow-up compared to 37% of a random sample of inmates released from the Leavenworth Federal Penitentiary (i.e., non-RH comparison group; Ward & Werlich, 2003). Further, three studies in the Canadian federal prison system also indicate higher recidivism rates among inmates exposed to RH.

The first study reports 62% of the inmates who experienced RH in custody were re-incarcerated for a new offense compared to 38% of a random sample of non-RH inmates from the general prison population (Motiuk & Blanchette, 2001). The second study reveals that placement in involuntary RH is positively associated with re-incarceration for a new criminal offense within two years of release from prison (Smith, 2006). The third study finds 59% of the women who experienced RH in custody had their post-release supervision revoked compared to only 29% of the women who did not experience RH (Thompson & Rubenfeld, 2013). This study further indicates that RH has a more deleterious effect on post-release supervision revocations of non-Aboriginal compared to Aboriginal women.

Although it may be tempting to conclude from such research that RH has a criminogenic effect, these studies involve nonequivalent comparison groups. Correctional administrators place inmates in RH for chronic or serious misbehavior, or when administrators feel it is unsafe to manage them in the general population (Metcalf et al., 2013). Inmates in RH thus tend to possess more extensive criminal histories and other criminogenic risk factors than the inmates in the general population (Labrecque, 2018). It is therefore not surprising that direct comparisons between these two groups find RH inmates to have higher recidivism rates. Nonetheless, it remains possible that the experience of RH may increase one's propensity toward post-release recidivism. This causal determination requires empirical research that can account for these underlying group differences. Failure to control for these confounding variables may inadvertently lead to the interpretation of the cause of RH as its effect.

One way researchers attempt to account for potential confounders is to employ multivariate regression techniques, including logistic and linear regression. A study in a Northeastern state prison system uses regression analyses and finds that among a sample of men released from custody who experienced placement in a supermax unit during their commitment, the length of time in RH is not statistically associated with re-incarceration or length of time until re-incarceration during an approximately five-year follow-up period (Pizarro, Zgoba, & Haugebrook, 2014). This study further shows that direct release from RH to the community is also not statistically related to the two types of recidivism examined.

Other studies attempt to address the issue of group selection bias by using more advanced statistical matching techniques (e.g., frequency matching, propensity score matching) to construct a control group of non-RH inmates who are similar to the RH inmates on a multitude of criminogenic factors (e.g., offender demographics, criminal history). The matching process helps account for the potential influence of the included covariates on the outcome of interest. This type of research primarily investigates the effect of long-term RH (i.e., supermax) on post-release outcomes and suggests that this experience has a weak to null effect on recidivism.

A study in Washington matches a sample of inmates released from custody who spent at least 12 weeks in supermax confinement during their commitment to a sample of inmates released during the same time who did not experience RH during their prison term (Lovell, Johnson, & Cain, 2007). Although the RH group has more new felony convictions after three-years from release than the non-RH group (53% vs. 46%), this difference is not statistically significant. The study further reports that length of time spent in RH does not make a significant independent contribution to felony recidivism beyond that of the control variables. This investigation does, however, find that inmates released directly from RH to the community have a higher recidivism rate than those returned to the general population at least three months before being released to the community (69% vs. 46%, respectively). It is worth noting that the direct release inmates are also younger and have more extensive criminal histories in comparison to the gradual release group; and when these two groups are matched on age and criminal history, the difference in outcome is no longer statistically significant.

Another evaluation in Washington reports that spending 90 days or more in supermax during one's sentence leads to a 9% increase in new felony convictions among inmates without a serious mental illness ($p < .05$) and a 4% decrease among inmates with a serious mental illness ($p > .05$; Lovell & Johnson, 2004). This study also reveals that this differential influence applies to new-person offense outcomes, where the negative relationship among the non-mentally ill is statistically significant at the .01 level, but the association among those with a serious mental illness is not statistically significant.

A study in Florida uses propensity score matching to match a sample of men released from prison who served 90 or more days in supermax confinement to a control group of inmates released during this time period who did not experience RH, but were similar to the supermax group on 13 demographic, criminal history, and institutional behavior variables (Mears & Bales, 2009). This investigation reports no significant difference in the number of three-year post-release new felony convictions between the RH and non-RH matched groups; however, it finds RH inmates are more likely to receive a new conviction for a violent offense than non-RH inmates (24% vs. 21%, respectively). This study further reveals that duration spent in RH and timing of release from RH (i.e., direct or later release) does not have any influence on any of the recidivism outcomes examined.

Finally, an investigation in Ohio employs propensity score matching to match a sample of men released from custody who served any amount of time in supermax confinement during their sentence to a sample of non-RH inmates also released during the same time periods who are similar on 16 demographic, social, and criminal history variables (Butler, Steiner, Makarios, & Travis, 2017). Although the findings indicate RH inmates are more likely than matched non-RH inmates to be arrested within one-year post-release for a new felony offense (25% vs. 16%) and to be returned to prison within seven-years post-release (67% vs. 56%), these differences are not statistically significant.

In sum, the available regression-based and matching literature indicates that the experience of supermax, the length of time spent in supermax, and the timing of release from supermax are *not* statistically associated with post-release recidivism measures in two-thirds of the effect sizes in this study. One should not interpret this as evidence that supermax necessarily has no effect on recidivism. For one, this research includes only five studies from four state jurisdictions. Second, the relatively small sample sizes in three of these four matching investigations likely influence the non-significance in the findings. Finally, the matching studies generally report higher recidivism rates among the inmates from the supermax group in comparison to the inmates from the matched control group, regardless of how the outcome variable is operationalized (e.g., arrest, conviction, incarceration). Although this seems to indicate that supermax may produce slight criminogenic effects, one should also interpret this conclusion with caution, as these studies match the RH and non-RH groups primarily on demographic and criminal history indicators. As such, these works fail to account for other potential factors that may influence placement in RH, such as institutional behavior, prior segregation experience, and mental health status, which raise questions about the comparability of the two groups and the validity of the findings.

The research on supermax prisons may also not generalize to other variants of RH confinement, such as when it is used for punitive, protective, or other administrative purposes. Two recent investigations tackle this question by assessing the impact of disciplinary segregation on recidivism outcomes. The first study takes place in Ohio and involves a random sample of men and women released from state custody (Butler et al., 2014). Approximately half of the inmates in this study experienced a stay in disciplinary segregation at some point during their commitment and were more likely to be arrested for a new felony within one year of release compared to the non-RH group (26% vs. 22%, respectively). A multivariate logistic regression analysis further reveals that RH placement is associated with a 40% increase in the odds of a new felony re-arrest.

The second study in Minnesota includes men and women released from the state's custody (Clark & Duwe, 2016). Approximately one-third of these inmates spent time in RH for disciplinary purposes. The investigation uses event history analysis and finds that direct release from RH to the community does not have a significant effect on post-release supervision revocations, new arrests, or new convictions. This study also shows the proportion of one's sentence spent in RH is statistically related to supervision revocations but not arrests and convictions. These findings fall in line with the supermax evaluations described above, but work in this area is far from definitive.

Finally, this recidivism research focuses primarily on the general effect of RH and much less on the differential impact this setting has among various subpopulations of offenders. One exception involves an investigation that separates its findings by inmate age group. This study uses longitudinal survey and administrative data from adolescents who were adjudicated of a criminal offense and finds that inmates who experience RH as a juvenile (ages 14 to 17) have nearly identical counts of arrest as those who experience RH as an adult (ages 18 to 26; Clark & Pyrooz, 2016). Continued research on moderators will be invaluable for i·lentifying if there are certain people who may be especially susceptible to that iatrogenic effects of RH.

Institutional Adjustment

ATTITUDINAL/EMOTIONAL OUTCOMES

There are several ways to assess institutional adjustment, one of which includes indicators of antisocial attitude and negative emotions, such as anger and hostility. The RH research using cross-sectional designs is mixed, with some findings suggesting a null effect and others indicating iatrogenic effects. A study in three prisons in the U.S. and Canada compares the psychological reactions to the experience of confinement between men and women with experience in RH to those with no experience (Suedfeld, Ramirez, Deaton, & Baker-Brown, 1982). In two of the institutions, the investigators find no statistically significant difference between groups on a hostility scale measure, and in the other facility the RH inmates report higher scores than the non-RH control group.

Another study in a federal prison in Kentucky compares levels of psychological distress between men in three types of housing, general population (i.e., least restrictive), administrative segregation, and disciplinary segregation (i.e., most restrictive; Miller & Young, 1997). This study reveals inmates in more restrictive settings report higher levels of hostility. Finally, an investigation in a single state prison system examines inmate attitudes and orientation (Wolff, Morgan, & Shi, 2013). This evaluation includes multilevel modeling and finds that the number of days spent in RH has a significant, positive, and weak effect on criminal sentiments, aggression, and self-control among men, and finds no statistically significant difference among women.

This cross-sectional research is informative; however, it only provides information on inmates at one point in time. In response, more recent research undertakes longitudinal investigations that assess individuals at multiple points in time. This strategy allows researchers to speak more directly about the causal effects of RH and provides the opportunity to compare rates of change between the RH and non-RH groups.

An investigation in three Canadian prisons compares the psychological effects of inmates in RH to a random set of inmates from the general population at three time points: baseline, 30 days later, and 60 days later (Zinger, Wichmann, & Andrews, 2001). Although the RH group reports higher levels of anger across all three assessment periods than the non-RH control group, both groups show a reduction in aggression score after 60 days. Another longitudinal study in Colorado involves three conditions: RH, general population, and a psychiatric facility (O'Keefe, Klebe, Stucker, Sturm, & Leggett, 2010). The study assesses for differences in psychological symptoms between the RH inmates in comparison to the control groups during regular interviews for one year. This investigation reveals that among mentally ill inmates, RH did not statistically influence scores on a composite anger-hostility scale; however, this experience led to a significant increase in anger-hostility among non–mentally ill inmates.

DISCRETIONARY RELEASE OUTCOMES

Another indicator of institutional adjustment involves the administrative decision to release an inmate early from custody (e.g., parole). Correctional authorities use discretion in this process based

16 Restrictive Housing and Inmate Behavior

in part on their perception of how successful they believe the inmate will be in the community. Three investigations in Canada find that inmates who experience RH are less likely to be granted discretionary release than those who do not (Motiuk & Blanchette, 2001; Thompson & Rubenfeld, 2013; Wichmann & Nafekh, 2001). These results should be interpreted cautiously as misbehavior in prison often justifies placement in RH, and the parole board often relies on institutional behavior as a basis for making release decisions. Nonetheless it remains possible that if RH increases one's antisocial behavior in prison, or the perception that one will not be successful if released to the community, this experience may negatively impact an inmate's probability for early release.

INSTITUTIONAL MISCONDUCT OUTCOMES

More recently, RH research involves evaluations on measures of institutional misconduct, the majority of which involves short-term disciplinary segregation and finds that the setting produces a null effect. A study in Oregon uses multivariate linear regression analyses controlling for other known correlates of misbehavior and reveals that the experience of disciplinary segregation is not a statistically significant predictor of the total rule violations (Lucas & Jones, 2017). Another study in Ohio uses pooled time series analysis and finds that the experience of disciplinary segregation, and the number of days spent in disciplinary segregation, during a three-month time wave does not have any statistically significant effect on the prevalence or incidence of violent, nonviolent, or drug infractions during the subsequent three-month time wave (Labrecque, 2015). Another investigation in Ohio using logistic regression reveals that the length of time spent in disciplinary segregation has no statistically significant effect on subsequent institutional misconduct among gang and non–gang affiliated inmates (Motz, Labrecque, & Smith, 2017).

A study in Texas uses propensity score matching to test the effect of disciplinary segregation as a response to an initial act of violence on subsequent violent behavior in custody (Morris, 2016). This study reveals no statistically significant group differences on either the occurrence or timing of subsequent violent infractions. Another study in Texas compares the total counts of punishment (i.e., reprimand, cell restriction, loss of privileges) before placement in disciplinary segregation to those incurred upon release and finds no evidence of a deterrent effect (Medrano, Ozkan, & Morris, 2017).

In sum, the available regression-based and matching literature indicates that the experience of short-term disciplinary segregation is *not* statistically associated with subsequent institutional misconduct in more than 90% of the ESs in this study. While informative, one should interpret these findings cautiously as the research base includes only five studies from three state jurisdictions.

MODERATOR ANALYSES

Some recent research examines whether disciplinary segregation has a differential impact on institutional misconduct based on inmate gender, race, and mental health status. This research primarily uses propensity score matching techniques with data from Ohio (see Labrecque, 2015). In general, this work concludes that disciplinary segregation has a relatively similar effect on behavioral outcomes across these dimensions, with some noteworthy exceptions. For example, men appear to have lower rates of violent misconduct, similar rates of non-violent misconduct, and higher rates of drug misconduct compared to women (Labrecque, Smith, & Gendreau, 2015). White inmates also appear to have similar rates of violent misconduct and higher rates of non-violent misconduct compared to non-white inmates (Labrecque, 2016). Finally, inmates with a record of a serious mental health condition appear to have similar rates of violent misconduct and lower rates of non-violent and drug misconduct compared to those without evidence of such disorders (Smith, Labrecque, & Gendreau, 2015).

Discussion

Restrictive housing remains a highly controversial correctional practice. Its proponents contend it is an effective deterrent, which dissuades inmates from criminal activity. There are growing concerns, however, by many human rights activists, scholars, and correctional authorities that RH has many damaging collateral consequences, including increasing criminal behavior. Despite its widespread use in North American prisons, there is a notable lack of empirical research on its impact on behavioral outcomes (Labrecque & Smith, 2013). In response, several criminal justice organizations and correctional scholars urge researchers to increase empirical investigations of RH (see Garcia, 2016). This chapter contributes to our current understanding by systematically reviewing the empirical literature on the behavioral effects of RH.

The results of this investigation reveal that contrary to what the deterrence position holds, RH does not appear to be an effective means of reducing criminal behavior. Indeed, only one-third of the ESs included in this review indicate an improvement on these behavioral indicators. Although the finding that the direction of the ESs is overwhelmingly positive may seemingly provide support for the criminogenic perspective, one should keep in mind that only one-third of the total ES estimates are statistically significant at the .05 level. Further, estimates from the high-quality studies, which more effectively account for confounding variables than low quality studies, report approximately half the amount of statistically significant findings as the low-quality studies. Although we did not quantitatively analyze the strength of the ESs in this investigation, our subjective interpretation from this review is that most of the effects—and particularly those from higher quality studies—suggest that RH is associated with a null to weak effect on behavioral measures. As this literature base continues to expand, we encourage scholars to meta-analyze this research in order to help determine with more precision the magnitude of the impact of RH on criminal behavioral outcomes.

This review also highlights the need for more research to assess if RH affects certain subgroups of inmates differently. It is possible that some types of inmates are more vulnerable to suffering from the adverse effects of this experience (e.g., young, women, mentally ill). This investigation uncovers only nine ESs from four unpublished works on this topic. Therefore, we are unable to say much from an empirical standpoint about the influence of individual moderators on these outcomes. The research base is also devoid of empirical analyses that assess for the influence of key situational factors, such as prison management strategies and institutional culture, which may also moderate the effects of RH (see Gendreau & Labrecque, 2018). It is important that future research accounts for these theoretically relevant constructs.

In addition to its lack of impact on subsequent inmate behavior, there are many other factors that corrections officials must consider in choosing whether or not to use RH. For example, even if RH prevents institutional misconducts by temporarily incapacitating certain inmates, it may do so at a cost. These potential collateral consequences should not be understated, and they might include such unintended outcomes as reduced access to medical, mental health, and other treatment services. Furthermore, RH might cause deleterious effects on inmates by blocking opportunities for social interaction, recreation, and family visitation; increasing anger, frustration, and risk for self-harm; causing or exacerbating physical and psychological problems; and imposing a negative label. Moreover, applied researchers observe that RH tends to be over-used in facilities with greater capacity within these types of units (Shames, Wilcox, & Subramanian, 2015). The absence of clear criteria for measuring client progress creates a problem in many institutions where inmates are held without a specific case management plan for transitioning back into general population. This does not make sense given the finite resources available in the criminal justice system and especially in light of the fact that RH is one of the most expensive ways to house inmates. We contend, therefore, that decisions to use RH should not rest solely on its ability to influence behavior but must also consider the many potential collateral consequences this setting may produce. To the extent that RH does negatively impact these outcomes, its use remains questionable on ethical, practical, and legal grounds.

In closing, this systematic review of the empirical literature finds limited evidence to suggest that RH is effective in improving inmate behavior, which makes its continued use, especially at its current levels, a tough correctional policy to defend. Recently, several jurisdictions undertook policy initiatives to improve living conditions, preclude certain inmates, reduce the time spent, and increase the availability of services in RH settings (see Smith, 2016). Moving forward, correctional authorities and researchers should prioritize the further development, implementation, and evaluation of these reformation strategies. These efforts hold great promise not only for improving the management of inmates in custody, but also for making prisons and communities safer environments.

Appendix

Summary of Aggregate Institutional Violence Outcomes

Authors	Design	Setting	Sample	Independent Variable	Dependent Variable	Effect/Sig.
Bidna (1975)	Pre-post	California state prison system	Prison population	1973 lock-down of four prisons	Total stabbings	Neg./★
					Fatal stabbings	Neg./ns
					Staff assaults	Neg./ns
					Stabbings in GP	Neg./★
					Stabbings in RH	Pos./★
Crouch & Marquart (1990)	Pre-post	Texas state prison system	Prison population	1985 lock-down of gang members	Homicides	Neg./nr
					Perceptions of safety	Neg./nr
Ralph and Marquart (1991)	Pre-post	Texas state prison system	888 gang members	1985 lock-down of gang members	Homicides	Neg./nr
					Assaults	Neg./nr
					Weapons assaults	Neg./nr
					Sexual assaults	Neg./nr
Useem and Piehl (2006)	Correlational	U.S. prison system	Prison population	Trend in the use of RH between 1980s and 2003	Riots	Pos./nr
					Inmate homicides	Pos./nr
					Staff homicides	Pos./nr
					Inmate assaults	Pos./nr
					Staff assaults	Pos./nr
					Escapes	Pos./nr
					Disturbances and arsons	Pos./nr
Briggs et al. (2003)	Repeated measures	Arizona, Illinois, Minnesota, and Utah state prison systems	Prison population	Construction of supermax in three states	Inmate assaults (Arizona)	nr/ns
					Inmate assaults (Illinois)	nr/ns
					Inmate assaults (Minnesota)	nr/ns
					Staff assaults (Arizona)	Neg./★
					Staff assaults (Illinois)	Pos./★
					Staff assaults (Minnesota)	nr/ns
Huebner (2003)	Regression	U.S. state prison system	4,168 men from 185 prisons	% of inmate pop. in RH	Inmate assaults	Neg./ns
					Inmate assaults	Pos./ns

Steiner (2009)	Regression	U.S. state prison system	512 men's prisons across 45 states	% of inmate pop. in RH (DS)	Inmate assaults (1995)	Pos./ns
					Inmate assaults (2000)	Neg./★
					Inmate assaults (2000)	Neg./ns
					Collective violence (1995)	Pos./ns
					Collective violence (2000)	Neg./★
					Collective violence (2000)	Neg./★
				% of inmate pop. in RH (PC)	Inmate assaults (1995)	Pos./ns
					Inmate assaults (2000)	Pos./★
					Inmate assaults (2000)	Pos./★
					Collective violence (1995)	Neg./ns
					Collective violence (2000)	Pos./ns
					Collective violence (2000)	Pos./ns
Wooldredge and Steiner (2015)	Regression	U.S. state prison system	247 prisons across 40 states	% of inmate pop. in RH	Assaults	Pos./★
					Nonviolent misconducts	Pos./★

Note: RH = restrictive housing. GP = general population. Pos. = positive effect. Neg. = negative effect. ★ = $p < .05$. ns = not significant ($p > .05$). nr = not reported.

Summary of Recidivism Outcomes

Authors	Design	Setting	Treatment	Control	Dependent Variable	Effect/Sig.
LPRIC (2001)	NECG	Connecticut state prison system	Any RH	No RH	Re-arrest	Pos./nr
O'Keefe (2005)	NECG	Colorado state prison system	Any RH	No RH	Re-incarceration	Pos./nr
Seale et al. (2011)	NECG	California state prison system	Any RH	No RH	Re-incarceration	Pos./nr
Ward and Werlich (2003)	NECG	U.S federal prison system	RH (Alcatraz)	No RH (Leavenworth)	Re-incarceration	Pos./nr
Motiuk and Blanchette (2001)	NECG	Canadian federal prison system	Any RH	No RH	Re-incarceration	Pos./★
					Re-incarceration (new offense)	Pos./★
Smith (2006)	Correlational	Canadian federal prison system	Any RH	No RH	Re-incarceration	Pos./★
					Revocation	Pos./★
Thompson and Rubenfeld (2013)	NECG	Canadian federal prison System	Any RH (Aboriginal women)	No RH (Aboriginal women)	Revocation	Pos./★
			Any RH (non- Aboriginal women)	No RH (non- Aboriginal women)	Revocation	Pos./★
Pizarro et al. (2014)	Regression	Northeastern state prison system	*Months in RH (supermax)*		Re-incarceration	Neg./ns
					Months until re-incarceration	Pos./ns
			Direct release from RH (supermax)		Re-incarceration	Pos./ns
					Months until re-incarceration	Pos./ns
Lovell et al. (2007)	Matching	Washington state prison system	≥ 90 days in RH (supermax)	No RH (supermax)	New felony	Pos./ns
			Direct release from RH (supermax)	Later release from RH (supermax)	New felony	Pos./★
Lovell and Johnson (2004)	Matching	Washington state prison system	≥ 90 days in RH (MI in supermax)	No RH (MI in supermax)	New felony	Neg./ns
			≥ 90 days in RH (NMI in supermax)	No RH (NMI in supermax)	New felony	Pos./★
			≥ 90 days in RH (MI in supermax)	No RH (MI in supermax)	New felony (person offense)	Neg./ns
			≥ 90 days in RH (NMI in supermax)	No RH (NMI in supermax)	New felony (person offense)	Pos./★

Study	Method	Sample	RH variable	No RH group	Outcome	Result
Mears and Bales (2009)	Matching	Florida state prison system	≥ 90 days in RH (supermax)	No RH (supermax)	New felony	Pos./ns
					New felony (violent offense)	Pos./★
					New felony (property offense)	Pos./ns
					New felony (drug offense)	Neg./ns
					New felony (other offense)	Neg./ns
Butler et al. (2017)	Matching	Ohio state prison system	Any RH (supermax)	No RH (supermax)	Re-arrest	Pos./ns
					Re-arrest (felony offense)	Pos./ns
					Re-incarceration	Pos./ns
					Re-incarceration (new offense)	Pos./ns
Butler et al. (2014)	Regression	Ohio state prison system	*Any RH (DS)*		Re-arrest	Pos./★
					Re-arrest (felony)	Pos./★
			Days in RH (DS)		Re-arrest	Pos./★
					Re-arrest (felony)	Pos./★
Clark and Duwe (2016)	Regression	Minnesota state prison system	*Direct release from RH (DS)*		Revocation	Pos./ns
					Re-arrest	Neg./ns
					New felony	Pos./ns
			Proportion of sentence in RH (DS)		Revocation	Pos./★
					Re-arrest	Pos./ns
					New felony	Pos./ns
Moderator analyses						
Clark and Pyrooz (2016)	NECG	Adjudicated delinquents in Philadelphia and Phoenix	Any RH (juvenile)	No RH (adult)	Number of new arrests	Neg./ns

Note: NECG = nonequivalent comparison group. RH = restrictive housing. *Italics* = RH variable used in regression analyses. DS = disciplinary segregation. PC = protective custody. MI = mentally ill. NMI = non-mentally ill. Pos. = positive effect. Neg. = negative effect. ★ = $p < .05$. ns = not significant ($p > .05$). nr = not reported.

Summary of Institutional Adjustment Outcomes

Authors	Design	Setting	Treatment	Control	Dependent variable	Effect/Sig.
Attitudinal/emotional outcomes						
Suedfeld et al. (1982)	NECG	3 prisons in U.S. and Canada	Any RH	No RH	MAACL–hostility (Inst. A)	nr/ns
					MAACL–hostility (Inst. B)	nr/ns
					MAACL–hostility (Inst. C)	Pos./★
Miller and Young (1997)	NECG	Kentucky federal prison	Any RH (AS)	No RH	BSI–hostility	Pos./★
			Any RH (DS)	No RH	BSI–hostility	Pos./★
Wolff et al. (2013)	Regression	A state prison system	*Days in RH (men)*		CSS-M	Pos./★
					BPAQ-SF	Pos./★
			Days in RH (women)		CSS-M	Neg./ns
					BPAQ-SF	Neg./ns
Zinger et al. (2001)	NECG	3 Canadian federal prisons	Any RH	No RH	AQ	nr/ns
O'Keefe et al. (2010)	Repeated measures with control group	Colorado state prison system	One year in RH (NMI)	No RH (NMI)	Hostility-Anger Control	Pos./★
			One year in RH (MI)	No RH (MI)	Hostility-Anger Control	Pos./ns
Discretionary release outcomes						
Wichmann and Nafekh (2001)	NECG	Canadian federal prison system	Any RH	No RH	Discretionary release	Pos./ns
Motiuk and Blanchette (2001)	NECG	Canadian federal prison system	Any RH	No RH	Discretionary release	Pos./★
Thompson and Rubenfeld (2013)	NECG	Canadian federal prison system	Any RH (Aboriginal women)	No RH (Aboriginal women)	Discretionary release	Pos./★
			Any RH (non-Aboriginal women)	No RH (non-Aboriginal women)	Discretionary release	Pos./★
Institutional misconduct outcomes						
Lucas and Jones (2017)	Regression	Oregon state prison system	*Days in RH (DS)*		Total rules violations	Neg./ns

Study	Analysis	Prison system	RH variable	Comparison	Outcome	Result
Labrecque (2015)	Repeated measures	Ohio state prison system	*Any RH (DS)*		Violent misconduct	Neg./ns
					Nonviolent misconduct	Neg./ns
					Drug misconduct	Pos./ns
			Days in RH (DS)		Violent misconduct	Neg./ns
					Nonviolent misconduct	Neg./ns
					Drug misconduct	Pos./ns
Morris (2016)	Matching	Texas state prison system	*Any RH (violent inmate in DS)*	No RH (violent inmates)	Violent misconduct	Neg./ns
Medrano et al. (2017)	Pre–post	Texas state prison system	*Any RH (capital inmates in DS)*		Total punishments	Pos./nr
Motz et al. (2017)	Regression	Ohio state prison system	*Days in RH (gang-affiliated in DS)*		Violent misconduct	Neg./ns
					Nonviolent misconduct	Neg./★
					Drug misconduct	Neg./ns
			Days in RH (non gang-affiliated in DS)		Violent misconduct	Pos./ns
					Nonviolent misconduct	Neg./ns
					Drug misconduct	Pos./ns
Moderator analyses						
Labrecque et al. (2015)	Matching	Ohio state prison system	*Any RH (women in DS)*	Any RH (men in DS)	Violent misconduct	Pos./★
					Nonviolent misconduct	Neg./ns
					Drug misconduct	Neg./★
Labrecque (2016)	Matching	Ohio state prison system	*Any RH (non-white in DS)*	Any RH (white in DS)	Violent misconduct	Pos./ns
Smith et al. (2015)	Matching	Ohio state prison system	*Any RH (MI in DS)*	Any RH (NMI in DS)	Nonviolent misconduct	Neg./★
					Violent misconduct	Pos./ns
					Nonviolent misconduct	Neg./★
					Drug misconduct	Neg./★

Note: NECG = nonequivalent comparison group. RH = restrictive housing. *Italics* = RH variable used in regression analyses. DS = disciplinary segregation. AS = administrative segregation. MI = mentally ill. NMI = non-mentally ill. Pos. = positive effect. Neg. = negative effect. ★ = $p < .05$. ns = not significant ($p > .05$). nr = not reported.

Note

1 The investigations by Motiuk and Blanchette (2001) and Thompson and Rubenfeld (2013) include measures of post-release recidivism and institutional adjustment.

References

Beck, A. (2015). *Use of restrictive housing in U.S. prisons and jails, 2011–12.* Washington, DC: U.S. Department of Justice.

Bidna, H. (1975). Effects of increased security on prison violence. *Journal of Criminal Justice, 3*(1), 33–46.

Briggs, C., Sundt, J., & Castellano, T. (2003). The effect of supermaximum security prisons on aggregate levels of institutional violence. *Criminology, 41*(4), 1341–1376.

Butler, H., Steiner, B., Makarios, M., & Travis, L. (2014). Assessing the effect of exposure to disciplinary segregation on offenders' odds of recidivism. Presented at the Annual Meeting of the Academy of Criminal Justice Sciences in Philadelphia, PA.

Butler, H., Steiner, B., Makarios, M., & Travis, L. (2017). Assessing the effects of exposure to supermax confinement on offender post-release behaviors. *The Prison Journal, 97*(3) 275–295.

Clark, K., & Pyrooz, D. (2016). Restricting more than housing: The effects of restrictive housing on recidivism among juveniles. Presented at the Annual Meeting of the American Society of Criminology in New Orleans, LA.

Clark, V., & Duwe, G. (2016). From solitary to the streets: The effect of restrictive housing on recidivism. Presented at the Annual Meeting of the American Society of Criminology in New Orleans, LA.

Cohen, F. (2016). Restricted housing and legal issues. In *Restrictive housing in the U.S.: Issues, challenges, and future directions.* Washington, DC: National Institute of Justice.

Crouch, B., & Marquart, J. (1990). Resolving the paradox of reform: Litigation, prisoner violence, and perceptions of risk. *Justice Quarterly, 7*(1), 103–123.

Frost, N., & Monteiro, C. (2016). Administrative segregation in U.S. prisons. In *Restrictive housing in the U.S.: Issues, challenges, and future directions.* Washington, DC: National Institute of Justice.

Garcia, M. (ed.). (2016). *Restrictive housing in the U.S.: Issues, challenges, and future directions.* Washington, DC: National Institute of Justice.

Gendreau, P., & Goggin, C. (In press). Solitary confinement and punishment: Effects on misconducts and punishment. In D. L. Polascheck, A. Day, & C. R. Hollin (Eds.), *The handbook of psychology and corrections.* Hoboken, NJ: John Wiley and Sons.

Gendreau, P., & Labrecque, R. (2018). The effects of administrative segregation: A lesson in knowledge cumulation. In J. Wooldredge & P. Smith (Eds.), *Oxford handbook on prisons and imprisonment.* Oxford: Oxford University Press.

Haney, C. (2003). Mental health issues in long-term solitary and "supermax" confinement. *Crime & Delinquency, 49*(1), 124–156.

Huebner, B. (2003). Administrative determinants of inmate violence: A multilevel analysis. *Journal of Criminal Justice, 31*(2), 107–117.

Kapoor, R., & Trestman, R. (2016). Mental health effects of restrictive housing. In *Restrictive housing in the U.S.: Issues, challenges, and future directions.* Washington, DC: National Institute of Justice.

Labrecque, R. (2015). *The effect of solitary confinement on institutional misconduct: A longitudinal evaluation.* Washington, DC: U.S. Department of Justice.

Labrecque, R. (2016). Assessing for racial disparity in the use and effects of disciplinary segregation: A propensity score matching analysis. Presented at the Annual Meeting of the American Society of Criminology in New Orleans, LA.

Labrecque, R. (2018). Special or segregated housing units. In K. D. Dodson (Ed.), *Handbook of offenders with special needs.* New York, NY: Routledge.

Labrecque, R., & Smith, P. (2013). Advancing the study of solitary confinement. In J. Fuhrman & S. Baier (Eds.), *Prisons and prison systems: Practices, types, and challenges* (pp. 57–70). Hauppauge, NY: Nova Science Publishers.

Labrecque, R., Smith, P., & Gendreau, P. (2015). Gender-based differences in the effects of solitary confinement on institutional behavior. Presented at the Annual Meeting of the American Society of Criminology in Washington, DC.

Legislative Program Review and Investigations Committee. (2001). *Recidivism in Connecticut.* Hartford, CT: Office of Policy and Management.

Lovell, D. (2008). Patterns of disturbed behavior in a supermax prison. *Criminal Justice and Behavior, 35*(8), 985–1004.

16 Restrictive Housing and Inmate Behavior

Lovell, D., & Johnson L. (2004). *Felony and violent recidivism among supermax prison inmates in Washington state: A pilot study*. Seattle, WA: University of Washington.

Lovell, D., Johnson, L., & Cain, K (2007). Recidivism of supermax prisoners in Washington state. *Crime and Delinquency, 53*(4), 633–656.

Lucas, J., & Jones, M. (2017). An analysis of the deterrent effects of disciplinary segregation on institutional rule violation rates. *Criminal Justice Policy Review*. Advance on-line publication.

Mears, D. (2016). Critical research gaps in understanding the effects of prolonged time in restrictive housing on inmates and the institutional environment. In *Restrictive housing in the U.S.: Issues, challenges, and future directions*. Washington, DC: National Institute of Justice.

Mears, D., & Bales, W. (2009). Supermax incarceration and recidivism. *Criminology, 47*(4), 1131–1166.

Mears, D., & Castro, J. (2006). Wardens' views on the wisdom of supermax prisons. *Crime and Delinquency, 52*(3), 398–431.

Medrano, J., Ozkan, T., & Morris, R. (2017). Solitary confinement exposure and capital inmate misconduct. *American Journal of Criminal Justice. 42*(4), 863–882.

Metcalf, H., Morgan, J., Oliker-Friedland, S., Resnik, J., Spiegel, J., Tae, H., Work, A., & Holbrook, B. (2013). *Administrative segregation, degrees of isolation, and incarceration: A national overview of state and federal correctional policies*. New Haven, CT: Liman Public Interest Program.

Miller, H., & Young, G. (1997). Prison segregation: Administrative detention remedy or mental health problem? *Criminal Behaviour and Mental Health, 7*, 85–94.

Morgan, R., Gendreau, P., Smith, P., Gray, A., Labrecque, R., MacLean, N., Van Horn, S., Bolanos, A., Batastini, A., & Mills, J. (2016). Quantitative synthesis of the effects of administrative segregation on inmates' well-being. *Psychology, Public Policy, and Law, 22*(4), 439–461.

Morris, R. (2016). Exploring the effect of exposure to short-term solitary confinement among violent prison inmates. *Journal of Quantitative Criminology, 32*(1), 1–22.

Motiuk, L., & Blanchette, K. (2001). Characteristics of administratively segregated offenders in federal corrections. *Canadian Journal of Criminology, 43*(1), 131–143.

Motz, R., Labrecque, R., & Smith, P. (2017). The effect of gang affiliation on post-solitary confinement institutional misconduct. Presented at the Annual Meeting of the Academy of Criminal Justice Sciences in Kansas City, MO.

O'Keefe, M. (2005). *Analysis of Colorado's administrative segregation*. Colorado Springs, CO: Colorado Department of Corrections.

O'Keefe, M., Klebe, K., Stucker, A., Sturm, K., & Leggett, W. (2010). *One year longitudinal study of the psychological effects of administrative segregation*. Colorado Springs, CO: Colorado Department of Corrections.

Pizarro, J., Zgoba, K., & Haugebrook, S. (2014). Supermax and recidivism: An examination of the recidivism covariates among a sample of supermax ex-inmates. *The Prison Journal, 94*(2), 180–197.

Ralph, P., & Marquart, J. (1991). Gang violence in Texas prisons. *The Prison Journal, 71*(2), 38–49.

Rossi, P., Lipsey, M., & Freeman, H. (2004). *Evaluation: A systemic approach* (7th ed.). Thousand Oaks, CA: SAGE Publications.

Rosten, K. (2004). *Statistical report: Fiscal year 2003*. Colorado Springs, CO: Colorado Department of Corrections.

Seale, L., Atkinson, J., Grealish, B., Fitzgerald, T., Grassel, K., & Viscuso, B. (2011). *California Department of Corrections and Rehabilitation: 2011 adult institutions outcome evaluation report*. Sacramento, CA: Office of Research, Research and Evaluation Branch.

Shames, A., Wilcox, J., & Subramanian, R. (2015). *Solitary confinement: Common misconceptions and emerging safe alternatives*. New York, NY: VERA Institute of Justice.

Sherman, L., Gottfredson, D., MacKenzie, D., Eck, J., Reuter, P., & Bushway, S. (1997). *Preventing crime: What works, what doesn't, what's promising*. Washington, DC: National Institute of Justice.

Smith, P. (2016). Toward an understanding of "what works" in segregation: Implementing correctional programming and reentry-focused services in restrictive housing units. In *Restrictive housing in the U.S.: Issues, challenges, and future directions*. Washington, DC: National Institute of Justice.

Smith, P. (2006). *The effects of incarceration on recidivism: A longitudinal examination of program participation and institutional adjustment in federally sentenced adult male offenders* (Unpublished PhD dissertation). University of New Brunswick, Canada.

Smith, P., Labrecque, R., & Gendreau, P. (2015). An evaluation of the impact of solitary confinement on offenders with mental illness. Presented at the Annual Meeting of the International Academy of Law and Mental Health in Vienna, Austria.

Steiner, B. (2009). Assessing static and dynamic influences on inmate violence levels. *Crime and Delinquency, 55*(1), 134–161.

Steiner, B., & Cain, C. (2016). The relationship between inmate misconduct, institutional violence, and administrative segregation: A systematic review of the evidence. In *Restrictive housing in the U.S.: Issues, challenges, and future directions*. Washington, DC: National Institute of Justice.

Suedfeld, P., Ramirez, C., Deaton, J., & Baker-Brown, G. (1982). Reactions and attributes of prisoners in solitary confinement. *Criminal Justice and Behavior, 9*(3), 303–340.

Thompson, J., & Rubenfeld, S. (2013). *A profile of women in segregation*. Ottawa, ON: Correctional Service of Canada.

Useem, B., & Piehl, A. (2006). Prison buildup and disorder. *Punishment and Society, 8*(1), 87–115.

Ward, D., & Werlich, T. (2003). Alcatraz and Marion. *Punishment and Society, 5*(1), 53–75.

Wichmann, C., & Nafekh, M. (2001). Moderating segregation as a means to reintegration. *Forum on Corrections Research, 13*, 31–33.

Wolff, N., Morgan, R., & Shi, J. (2013). Comparative analysis of attitudes and emotions among inmates: Does mental illness matter? *Criminal Justice and Behavior, 40*(10), 1092–1108.

Wooldredge, J., & Steiner, B. (2015). A macro-level perspective on prison inmate deviance. *Punishment and Society, 17*(2), 230–257.

Zinger, I. (2013). Segregation in Canadian federal corrections: A prison Ombudsman's perspective. Presented at the International Conference on Human Rights and Solitary Confinement in Winnipeg, Manitoba, Canada.

Zinger, I., Wichmann, C., & Andrews, D. (2001). The psychological effects of 60 days in administrative segregation. *Canadian Journal of Criminology, 43*(1), 47–83.

17

THE IMPACTS OF PRIVATIZATION IN CORRECTIONS

The State of Evidence and Recommendations for Moving Forward

Andrea Montes Lindsey and Daniel P. Mears

Introduction

In recent years, policy makers have increasingly debated the privatization of correctional sanctions and services and, at the same time, scholars increasingly have undertaken studies to understand its uses and effects (see, e.g., Armstrong & MacKenzie, 2003; Bales, Bedard, Quinn, Ensley, & Holley, 2005; Duwe & Clark, 2013; Feeley, 2002; Gaes, Camp, Nelson, & Saylor, 2004; Makarios & Maahs, 2012; Office of the Inspector General, 2016; Porter, 2017; Spivak & Sharp, 2008; Stillman, 2014; Yates, 2016). Interest in corrections privatization heightened in 2016 when the United States Department of Justice announced that it would not renew, or would limit to the extent possible, contracts with private prison operators (Yates, 2016; see also Office of the Inspector General, 2016). Interest arose yet again in 2017 when the new attorney general announced that the Department of Justice would return to their previous policy and contract with private prison operators when needed (Sessions, 2017).

The 2016 decision broke from a longstanding reliance on private companies and individuals to implement aspects of corrections. In America, this reliance traces back to the 1700s, when colonists could purchase the labor of transported felons (Butler, 1896; Ekirch, 1985a, 1985b; Morgan, 1987). The aspects of corrections that are privatized have changed over time. However, government reliance on privatization has remained a constant—indeed, privatization pervades all aspects of contemporary corrections. In addition, and despite the fact that many media and scholarly accounts equate privatization with private prisons, it actually encompasses far more. It includes fine collection, court operations, community-based treatments and services, probation and parole supervision, and the operation of juvenile facilities and jails (Ericson, McMahon, & Evans, 1987; Feeley, 2002; Lindsey, Mears, & Cochran, 2016; Roberts & Powers, 1985).

The federal government's 2017 revocation of the private prison moratorium highlights the existence of an ongoing debate about the use of private companies to implement corrections. As the era of mass incarceration took hold (Clear & Frost, 2013; Mears & Cochran, 2015), policy makers increasingly advocated for the use of private prisons and extolled the virtues of privatization more generally (Anderson, Davoli, & Moriarity, 1985). They argued that privatization ensures the efficient use of taxpayer dollars and does so without jeopardizing service quality or the achievement of relevant outcomes (Crants, 1991; Logan, 1988, 1990; Moore, 1998; Segal & Moore, 2002). Opponents countered that privatizing corrections creates a situation in which companies profit from punishment, seek to expand the web of social control, and mistreat or underserve correctional populations (American Civil Liberties Union, 2011; Anderson, 2009; Bauer, 2016; Logan, 1988, 1990; Stillman, 2014). As we discuss below, however, neither of these arguments rests on a strong empirical foundation. To date, there exists no systematic, credible empirical evidence to suggest that private corrections or public corrections, as compared to each other, operates more effectively and at less cost or does so in a comparable or more ethical manner (Kish & Lipton, 2013; Lindsey et al., 2016; Mehigan & Rowe, 2007; Roberts & Powers, 1985; Schneider, 1999).

The goals of this chapter are to argue just that—namely, privatization debates rely on weak empirical evidence—and that, at the same time, many opportunities exist for advancing scholarship and policy and practice on private corrections. We first discuss the history and prevalence of private corrections and the role of privatization internationally. Second, we present a conceptual framework for examining private corrections; we use this framework to assess the state of evidence on how private corrections compares to public corrections. Third, we discuss the salience of the concept of collateral consequences to the privatization debate. Finally, we identify ten recommendations that span three domains—research, theory, and policy and practice—for advancing scholarship and improving corrections.

Background

History and Prevalence of Private Corrections

Private corrections has existed in America since the 1700s. An early form of privatization included the receipt of individuals who were convicted of a crime and transported by European governments (Butler, 1896; Ekirch, 1985a, 1985b; Morgan, 1987). After America gained its independence, state governments continued to rely on private individuals and organizations to implement different aspects of corrections. Houses of refuge, which, in the 1800s, confined youth involved in the juvenile justice system, are one such example. Austin Reed provided an evocative account of such housing. In the mid-1800s, he was indentured by his mother to a farmer for setting fire to the farmer's home. Reed, who was Black (the farmer was White), was 10 years old at the time. The court sentenced him to ten years at a house of refuge, where manual labor constituted a central part of the daily routine (Reed, 2016). His experience was typical—houses of refuge had leeway to contract out to private citizens the labor of youth under their supervision (Bernard & Kurlychek, 2010; Frey, 1981; Teeters, 1960).

Other examples illustrate that privatization historically was (and remains) a core feature of corrections. In the mid-1800s, a Boston business owner partnered with local courts to provide community-based supervision for individuals convicted of a crime and considered by the courts as lower-risk, a practice that laid the groundwork for modern-day probation (Petersilia, 1997; Sieh, 1993). Around the same time, San Quentin Prison opened under the management of several businessmen (Lamott, 1961; McAfee, 1990). And, as yet another example, after the Civil War, former slaves were frequently placed under correctional supervision and, as punishment, "leased" to private citizens, many of whom were former slave owners (Adamson, 1983; Taylor, 1942; Zimmerman, 1949).

In the 1900s, the private sector continued implementing aspects of corrections. For example, private entities ran industrial schools for youth involved in the juvenile justice system (Fox, 1970), supervised youth placed on probation (Flexner & Baldwin, 1914; Schultz, 1973), and operated juvenile facilities (Bureau of Justice Statistics, 1989). In addition, the labor of people in prison was sold to local governments and companies (Jackson, 1927; Mullen, Chabotar, & Carrow, 1985; Schaller, 1982). In the 1980s, the contracting out of jail and prison operations became more common (Hanson, 1991; McDonald, 1992, 1994). By 2015, private prisons housed 126,272 individuals (Carson & Anderson,

2016). In contemporary America, however, privatization extends well beyond the operation of residential facilities, jails, and prisons. It also includes private contracts for a wide range of other corrections activities, including fine collection, court operations, community-based services, and probation and parole supervision (Ericson et al., 1987; Feeley, 2002; Lindsey et al., 2016).

Private Corrections Is Not Just an American Phenomenon

Private corrections companies operate through similar contracts in other countries. For example, the United Kingdom's first private prison opened in 1991, just a few years after the opening of the first private prison in contemporary America (Liebling & Ludlow, 2016). In fact, private prisons exist in at least ten countries other than the United States (Mason, 2013). Although the United States houses more people in private prisons than any other country, other countries, such as Australia and the United Kingdom, house larger proportions of their incarcerated population in private prisons (Harding, 2001). Private companies also implement other correctional sanctions and services. For example, England outsources their electronic monitoring supervision, and Sweden purchases electronic monitoring technology and equipment from the private sector (Whitfield, 2001). Accordingly, discussions about private corrections are not unique to the United States and have implications worldwide.

The State of Evidence

Contentious debates about the merits and impacts of private corrections have accompanied its long history (see Anderson et al., 1985; Feeley, 2014; Levinson, 1985; Logan, 1988, 1990; Mehigan & Rowe, 2007). These debates stem largely from ideological and philosophical differences about government's role and effectiveness and they typically focus on prisons. However, privatization, as emphasized above, encompasses many other activities. Accordingly, our focus here considers the privatization of all aspects of corrections, not just prisons. In so doing, we draw on Lindsey et al.'s (2016) conceptual framework for assessing the state of evidence of private corrections. They argued:

> Privatization in the correctional system can include aspects of any of the following: fine collection, court operations, community-based services and treatment, probation and parole supervision, and the operations of residential facilities, jails, and prisons. The dimensions relevant for informing the privatization debate include the following: (1) the extent of need; (2) the amount and quality of services; (3) impacts on outcomes, both intended and unintended; (4) cost-efficiency; (5) development of innovative solutions; (6) impacts on social control; and (7) ethical considerations.
>
> (Lindsey et al., 2016, p. 312)

In what follows, we describe this framework, which highlights the range of dimensions relevant for adjudicating privatization's merits and impacts relative to those of public corrections, and we use it to summarize the state of evidence on private corrections.

Dimension 1. Extent of Need

The *extent of need* for public corrections and private corrections, respectively, represents a key aspect of the privatization debate. In determining need, two related questions must be answered: First, does a correctional problem exist and, second, if so, will public corrections or private corrections address that problem more effectively, efficiently, and ethically? To discern the extent of need of any type of corrections, whether public or private, decisionmakers must consider all potential solutions or "counterfactual conditions" (Lindsey et al., 2016, p. 314). For example, when courts face difficulty collecting fines, this problem may undermine efforts to reimburse the courts, pay restitution to victims, and create a specific or general deterrent effect. The question, then, is how to proceed. Courts could contract with a private fine collector to address the need. However, an empirical assessment of the problem and potential solutions—of which privatization is but one—might find that the simplest, most efficient approach is to invest in an online payment system that allows individuals to more easily pay their fines.

Jurisdictions, however, typically do not consider a wide range of alternatives or undertake assessments that compare the relative effectiveness and efficiency of various approaches. Instead, they continue with "business as usual" practices or they assume that these or alternative practices no longer are viable and so contract with a private vendor on the assumption or hope that doing so will result in greater cost-efficiency. To determine the conditions under which privatization, or any public corrections effort, is needed, a robust research literature on correctional privatization must exist. There is, however, no such literature. More precisely, there exists no systematic credible research that sheds light on the extent of need to privatize any aspect of corrections. Indeed, there is little systematic empirical evidence about the need for most aspects of corrections, public or private (Mears, 2010).

Dimension 2. Amount and Quality of Services

The private corrections debate requires systematic documentation of another consideration—the extent to which a given privatization effort provides the *amount and quality of services* that it is supposed to provide. It is not enough that a service costs less. There must be a provision of services commensurate with what public corrections would offer. Put differently, policy makers and the public expect that privatization results in an "all else equal" situation in which the only difference from public corrections is cost. They expect, more specifically, that less is paid *for the same amount and quality of services*. If this *ceteris paribus* condition fails to be met, the public pays less than it would for public corrections but it also receives less.

The importance of this *ceteris paribus* condition cannot be understated. To illustrate, consider court-mandated mental health treatment. How many sessions and at what frequency does a public mental health professional provide counseling sessions? How well are the sessions run? If counseling is privatized, are a comparable number of sessions afforded to individuals and to what extent is the quality of these sessions comparable to what individuals receive when they see public mental health professionals? If less is provided, then paying less does not demonstrate cost-efficiency. It simply means less was paid and less was provided.

Comparisons of public and private programs that do not provide the same service amount or quality ignore a critical aspect of what policy makers expect when they privatize corrections. We need, then, comparisons that assess not only cost but also the amount and quality of services that private contractors provide and how that compares to what public corrections agencies otherwise would have provided. Such comparisons are important for another reason. Without information about the comparability of services provided, valid assessments of effectiveness and cost-efficiency cannot be undertaken.

It is notable, then, that the literature on privatization effectiveness and cost-efficiency largely ignores service amount and quality. A number of empirical studies have compared the service quality of public and private juvenile facilities (e.g., Armstrong & MacKenzie, 2000, 2003; Levinson, 1985) and public and private prisons (e.g., Blakely & Bumphus, 2004; Burkhardt & Jones, 2016; Camp et al., 2002; Crewe, Liebling, & Hulley, 2015; Hulley, Liebling, & Crewe, 2011; Logan, 1992; Makarios & Maahs, 2012; Perrone & Pratt, 2003; Urban Institute, 1989; see also Gaes et al., 2004; Lundahl, Kunz, Brownwell, Harris, & Van Vleet, 2009). These studies provide insights into certain aspects of quality, such as overcrowding and incarcerated individuals' perceived respect from correctional officers. However, they do not compare service amount. Indeed, no systematic empirical research has been undertaken that compares the amount or quality of various types of privatization relative to their public corrections counterparts. By extension, it remains unknown to what extent privatization achieves what its proponents assume—the provision of comparable or better services and, at the same time, comparable or better outcomes at less cost.

Dimension 3. Impacts on Outcomes

Impacts on outcomes are a primary focus of the privatization debate. Credible comparisons of public and private corrections efforts must consider their respective impacts on both intended outcomes, such as decreased recidivism, and unintended outcomes, such as increased unemployment, increased drug use, and, more generally, potential collateral consequences. Such comparisons are necessary to shed light on whether private corrections achieves comparable or better outcomes and, in turn, whether privatization is more cost-efficient than public corrections.

This observation highlights a critical point—evaluating privatization impacts by focusing on a single outcome may generate invalid estimates of effectiveness. For example, a study may find that people released from private jails have a lower likelihood of recidivism. That finding alone appears to be a reason to consider privatization. However, a study that assesses other outcomes may find that people released from private jails are more likely to use drugs and experience unemployment—such findings would suggest that privatization is less effective overall. Even more, such studies do not assess outcomes for correctional systems or society more generally.

It is, therefore, striking that empirical studies to date have focused primarily on recidivism. For example, scholars have compared the recidivism of people incarcerated in public prisons and in private prisons (Bales et al., 2005; Duwe & Clark, 2013; Farabee & Knight, 2002; Lanza-Kaduce, Parker, & Thomas, 1999; Spivak & Sharp, 2008) and the recidivism of juveniles who were housed at public and private residential facilities (Bayer & Pozen, 2005). These studies have produced conflicting results. Thus, how privatization affects recidivism remains an empirical question. Several studies have examined privatization's impact on in-prison misconduct (Camp & Daggett, 2005; Farabee & Knight, 2002) and juvenile adjustment (Armstrong & MacKenzie, 2000); here, again, little consistent evidence of impacts exists. More relevant here, though, is that extant studies provide little to no systematic empirical basis for evaluating the overall effectiveness of private prisons and private residential facilities because all relevant outcomes are not included. The same observation holds even more so for other aspects of corrections that have gone largely unstudied.

The point, then, bears emphasis: without evaluations of the full range of outcomes relevant to any particular type of private corrections, there is no basis for claiming that privatization achieves comparable or better outcomes at less cost. As with service provision, the most that might be said is that a government agency may pay less than what it otherwise might have, but in so doing, it may well receive less and obtain worse outcomes.

Dimension 4. Cost-Efficiency

The privatization debate often centers on *cost-efficiency*. Can private organizations provide similar or better services and achieve comparable or better outcomes than public agencies and do so at less cost? Cost-efficiency analyses rely not only on the amount of money spent but also on the extent of need, service quality and amount, and impacts on outcomes. Without this additional information, the validity of a cost-efficiency analysis is undermined.

Several examples illustrate the point. Consider, first, the fact that if a particular service costs less in the private sector, that does not imply cost-efficiency. It does so only if comparable services were provided and comparable outcomes were achieved. Consider, second, the need for a jail. It may cost less to operate a private jail than to expand public jail capacity to hold more people. However, if no need for this extra capacity exists, then there is no cost-savings. A third example—it may cost less to operate a private juvenile facility, but if the facility provides fewer services and its youth are more likely to recidivate, it may be *less* cost-efficient than a public juvenile facility. Similarly, public and private substance abuse treatment may cost the same amount but if people who receive public treatment are more likely to abstain from future drug use and crime, then public treatment may be the more cost-efficient approach.

Of the conceptual framework's seven dimensions, cost-efficiency—especially cost-efficiency of private prisons—has garnered the most empirical attention (see, however, Pratt and Winston's [1999] study of the cost-efficiency of juvenile residential facilities). The body of literature on private prisons has produced conflicting results, with some studies finding that private prisons may be more efficient, others finding no difference, and still others finding that public prisons are more efficient (Lundahl et al., 2009; Perrone & Pratt, 2003; Pratt & Maahs, 1999). Although this work has advanced efforts to understand the potential benefits of privatization, several critical limitations attend to them. First, the studies' generalizability to other private prisons or to other types of privatization remains unknown. Second, most studies, including those examined in reviews (see, e.g., Pratt & Maahs, 1999), do not include all dimensions relevant to conducting a cost-efficiency analysis. They do not, for example, document that service amounts and quality are comparable or what the effects of privatization were across a range of outcomes. That is not due to a lack of effort; conducting research across such dimensions requires relevant data, and these frequently may not exist or be readily available.

Dimension 5. Innovative Solutions

Innovative solutions are new ways of addressing correctional issues. These solutions ideally improve business-as-usual services, outcomes, and cost-efficiency. A common argument in the privatization debate is that private entities have greater flexibility, which allows them to develop innovative solutions to correctional issues. However, the logic behind this claim is vague and refers generally to the idea that in an open marketplace businesses are induced to find creative ways to develop new products or to manufacture existing products less expensively. Whether that claim is true in corrections remains unevaluated. In addition, on the face of it, public corrections would appear to provide considerable leeway for innovation.

Regardless, the question remains: How can an impact on innovation be assessed? Comparisons of the innovativeness of public and private corrections are not simple. First, what constitutes innovation? Consider, for example, the use of video conferencing for visiting people in prison. This technology may enable visitation to occur more easily or in lieu of an in-prison visit (Santoro, 2009). Some observers might view this technology as innovative, others may not. If it does count as innovation, it is an innovation that could be developed by either sector.

Second, comparisons of innovative solutions also would entail assessing the effectiveness and efficiency of the new approach. This step is crucial. Presumably, some innovations are beneficial while others may be ineffective and inefficient and, possibly, even harmful. Consider again the use of video conferencing technology. Visitation through these means may be of low quality and in turn may contribute to a lower likelihood of future visits. However, it may instead increase the frequency of visits and the number of individuals who receive visits. It is only in the second scenario that policy makers would want to continue investing in this technology.

Such challenges make it difficult to provide an empirical assessment of whether privatization results in more innovation and, in turn, greater effectiveness and cost-efficiency. Indeed, to date, no research exists to suggest that public or private corrections innovates more, or less, than the other, or that public or private innovations are more likely to benefit, rather than harm, the people who are under correctional supervision, corrections systems, or the public.

Dimension 6. Impacts on Social Control

The privatization debate suggests that public corrections and private corrections differentially *impact social control*. Privatization critics argue that the private sector's potential for profit-making contributes to net-widening by incentivizing the endorsement of practices and policies that unnecessarily increase the number of people under correctional supervision (see Feeley, 2002). Such practices may include lobbying for the adoption of punitive policies or demanding contracts that extend months or years beyond the anticipated service need.

These arguments, however, do not consider that public corrections may contribute to unnecessary net-widening as well. A county, for example, may respond to a spike in delinquency by increasing the number of beds at their juvenile facility. When this temporary need subsides, those beds likely will continue to be used, but they may be occupied by youth who typically would not be appropriate candidates for incarceration. In such instances, it may be that privatization would provide the county with flexibility to temporarily contract for bedspace when needed and then to terminate contracts when the bedspace need no longer existed.

Arguments about how public corrections and private corrections, respectively, affect the amount and quality of social control are mostly speculative. There has been no body of credible empirical research that examines these arguments. A preliminary step towards doing so requires first determining when expansions of formal social control are necessary and, separately, when they are unnecessary. *Necessary* expansions are not the result of corrections, public or private, but instead are due to changes in need, including rising crime rates, limited capacity to punish, and policy shifts that call for an increase in one or more aspects of corrections. *Unnecessary* expansions are driven by something other than need. For example, they include situations in which a private contract is implemented not because of a needs evaluation but instead because additional funds are available and a policy maker or administrator assumes that more or different corrections is needed. Consider juvenile court diversion programs—these programs may emerge because someone thinks that they provide an effective alternative to traditional court sanctions. These programs, however, can result in net-widening: youth who previously would have received no sanction may be sent to diversion and, at the same time, there may be no change in the number of youth who receive other sanctions (Mears et al., 2016).

Dimension 7. Ethical Considerations

Not least, there are *ethical considerations* when deciding whether to privatize correctional services. Empirical comparisons of ethical considerations are challenging not only because of the difficulty in quantifying "ethics," but also because of disagreement about what constitutes an ethical concern. For some individuals, profit-making is not an ethical concern when systematic and credible empirical evidence finds that private companies provide higher quality services, more effectively achieve intended outcomes while avoiding adverse unintended outcomes, and cost less than public corrections. For others, however, profiting from the administration of punishment will always constitute an ethical concern.

An additional consideration is that debates about privatization typically ignore or set aside the ethical concerns that may arise with *public* corrections. For example, when private entities provide higher quality substance abuse treatment that reduces recidivism and drug use, it may be unethical *not* to use private treatment. In addition, public corrections officers often receive higher salaries than their private correctional officer counterparts (Blakely & Bumphus, 2004). One could argue that providing such benefits incentivizes what might be viewed as "punishment as a vocation" and raises ethical questions. Ideally, people would seek to work with incarcerated individuals out of a motivation to help, not to secure a higher salary or more benefits.

To date, there have been few attempts to compare the ethical concerns of public and private corrections. One exception is Reisig and Pratt's (2000) assessment of the "ethical dilemma" of privatizing prison operations (p. 211). Systematic comparisons across different aspects of public and private corrections, however, are still needed. Such comparisons could draw on interviews and surveys that focus on identifying citizens' ethical concerns with both public corrections and private corrections. A nationally representative survey may find that as a society there is less concern about public versus private and more concern about the provision of a particular level of service and treatment. Alternatively, it may find that the public believes it intolerable to contract out any aspect of corrections. Absent such assessments, the ethical considerations of public and private corrections cannot be grounded in empirical facts. Instead, they will flounder on what appear to be irresolvable ideological and philosophical differences.

State of Evidence Summary

The clear implication from the discussion to this point is that little is known about the privatization of corrections. Table 17.1, which presents Lindsey et al.'s (2016) conceptual framework that guided the discussion above, provides a visual summary. The table's matrix juxtaposes each of the different types of private corrections with each of the seven dimensions that were discussed. Several observations warrant emphasis.

First, the question marks highlight that although many empirical studies focus on private corrections, there is little systematic, rigorous empirical research across the different types of privatization and across each dimension. For example, many studies have focused on the cost-efficiency of public and private prisons. However, there exists no ongoing, systematic empirical comparison across jurisdictions and across different types of privatization. In short, there is little credible scientific basis for claiming that private corrections is needed or is implemented better than public corrections, that it is more effective or efficient than public corrections, or that it generates other benefits, such as greater innovation.

Table 17.1 Dimensions for Assessing Private Corrections

Types of Privatization	Dimensions of Privatization[1]						
	1. Extent of Need	*2. Amount/ Quality of Services*	*3. Impacts on Outcomes*	*4. Cost-Efficiency*	*5. Innovative Solutions*	*6. Impacts on Social Control*	*7. Ethical Considerations*
Fine Collection	?	?	?	?	?	?	?
Court Operations	?	?	?	?	?	?	?
Community-Based Services	?	?	?	?	?	?	?
Probation Supervision	?	?	?	?	?	?	?
Parole Supervision	?	?	?	?	?	?	?
Residential Facility Operations	?	?	?	?	?	?	?
Jail Operations	?	?	?	?	?	?	?
Prison Operations	?	?	?	?	?	?	?

1 Lindsey et al.'s (2016) conceptual framework described these dimensions as relevant for assessing the state of evidence on private corrections as compared to public corrections.

Second, by the same token, there exists little systematic empirical research for claiming that *public* corrections is better. Indeed, the effectiveness and efficiency of public corrections efforts remain largely unknown. How much more effective, for example, are public prisons, as tools of punishment, in comparison to private prisons or to public or private probation? By and large, there exists no research that answers such questions (see, generally, Lindsey et al., 2016; Mears & Barnes, 2010; Nagin, Cullen, & Jonson, 2009; Villettaz, Gilliéron, & Killias, 2014).

Third, when these two observations are juxtaposed against one another, a critical insight emerges: specifically, any assessment of privatization requires a simultaneous assessment of public corrections. Such assessments ideally would occur over time and across jurisdictions. The undertaking of them would illuminate whether privatization constitutes a more, or less, effective, efficient, and ethical approach to corrections when compared to public corrections, and, by contrast, when public corrections may be the better option. To illustrate, consider a situation in which, over time, private prisons become increasingly ineffective. If public prisons at the same time become increasingly more effective, greater investment in them and disinvestment from private prisons would make sense. The only way to identify this change and then to know how to proceed is to conduct ongoing evaluations that assess *both* public and private corrections efforts and to do so across all of the dimensions identified in Table 17.1.

Potential Collateral Consequences of Private Corrections and Public Corrections

The discussion to this point highlights that much of corrections—both public *and* private—occurs in the equivalent of a "black box," with little light shed on day-to-day operations or impacts (Mears, 2008, 2010). This black box makes it difficult to compare empirically the differences in effectiveness and efficiency between public and private corrections. In turn, that creates a situation in which jurisdictions have little credible scientific basis for choosing public or private corrections or knowing when to do so. It also means that privatization decisions necessarily flow from assumptions that accord with ideological or philosophical preferences.

There is, however, a related concern—scholarship on prisoner reentry in recent decades has highlighted the problem of collateral consequences (see Huebner & Frost, Introduction in this book). It has highlighted, for example, that greater reliance on punitive policies has contributed to a range of adverse effects, such as unemployment, homelessness, and disenfranchisement of minorities through voting restriction laws that target individuals convicted of felonies (Harris et al., 2017; Travis, 2005; see also, in this volume, Apel & Ramakers, Chapter 5; Kirk, Chapter 3). This reliance also has had adverse consequences for children of prisoners, correctional institutions, and society more generally (Clear & Frost, 2013; Hagan & Dinovitzer, 1999; Huebner & Gustafson, 2007; Mears & Cochran, 2015; see also, in this volume, Northcutt Bohmert & Wakefield, Chapter 8; Cochran & Toman, Chapter 14).

An implication of this research is that policy assessments of corrections should identify and assess a broad range of effects, including the potential for collateral consequences, and not only recidivism or crime rates. By extension, such assessments should occur for both public and private corrections efforts. Little systematic empirical evidence documents the collateral consequences of private corrections. Some media accounts highlight the potential for graft or victimization of incarcerated individuals, but this potential exists as well in public corrections.

More generally, privatization may entail many of the collateral consequences that have been identified in accounts of the punitive turn in corrections. As conceptualized here and in Table 17.1, collateral consequences involve unintended harms and extend well beyond impacts on individuals convicted of a crime. Net-widening is one such example. To the extent that privatization efforts arise through political "backdoor" channels and culminate with expansion of corrections when such an expansion is unnecessary, society ultimately pays through higher taxes and missed opportunities to invest funds in ways that might more appreciably improve public safety and promote justice. Critics of privatization may claim that collateral consequences of privatization are minimal, just as opponents may claim that they are considerable. Resolution of such claims requires systematic empirical research of public and private corrections across the above-identified dimensions.

Ten Recommendations for Advancing Research, Theory, and Policy and Practice

The importance of privatization lies in its potential to create greater improvements or harms for correctional systems, people under correctional supervision, and the public. Its importance, too, is that it highlights the need for a greater understanding of all aspects of corrections, public and private. However, as we have argued, there exists little credible empirical research that identifies the conditions under which private corrections or public corrections is warranted. Accordingly, we identify ten recommendations, listed in Table 17.2, for advancing (1) research, (2) theory, and (3) policy and practice about corrections and, in particular, private corrections.

Domain 1. Research

Empirical research has yet to shed light on how public corrections and private corrections compare in their relative operations and effects. Without systematic, credible research, the conditions under which private corrections operates more effectively and efficiently than public corrections will remain unknown. Here, we identify four recommendations for advancing research on public and private corrections.

Recommendation 1. Use Consistent and Clear Definitions and Operationalizations of Privatization

Part of the confusion about how public corrections and private corrections differ in their operations and effects, respectively, stems from uncertainty about what constitutes "private corrections" and,

Table 17.2 Ten Recommendations for Advancing Private Corrections Research, Theory, and Policy and Practice

Domain 1. Research
1. Use consistent and clear definitions and operationalizations of privatization.
2. Collect data on all types of corrections across all 7 dimensions in Table 17.1 (need, service amount/quality, impacts, efficiency, innovation, social control, ethics).
3. Compare all aspects of public and private corrections across all 7 dimensions in Table 17.1 (need, service amount/quality, impacts, efficiency, innovation, social control, ethics).
4. Identify factors that may influence the effects and efficiency of public or private corrections.

Domain 2. Theory
5. Understand factors that contribute to support for or against private corrections.
6. Identify factors that influence the service quality, effectiveness, and cost-efficiency of public corrections and private corrections, respectively.

Domain 3. Policy and Practice
7. Require empirical monitoring of public and private corrections efforts.
8. Rely on empirical evaluations to identify impacts of public and private corrections.
9. Base decisions about using public or private corrections on empirical research.
10. Incentivize effective, efficient, and ethical corrections (whether public or private).

conversely, what constitutes "public corrections." To illustrate, imagine a juvenile placed on probation who is supervised by a public probation officer but who receives his or her court-mandated substance abuse treatment and mental health treatment from private providers. Here, it may be difficult to determine whether the youth is experiencing private or public probation. Or consider a prison where the state employs the warden and correctional officers, but where private companies provide the medical, educational, and substance abuse services. Is the prison public, private, or quasi-public or private? Consider yet another situation in which a private contractor hires former public probation officers. Here, the officers clearly work for a private company, but the skills they bring to their day-to-day performance emanate from their public corrections training and experiences. It is, again, not clear how exactly to classify this situation or to interpret the results of a study that assesses "private probation."

This uncertainty about what privatization means has contributed to diverse operationalizations of private corrections. For example, almost every study about the effects of private prison incarceration on recidivism measures privatization differently (e.g., one or more days in a private prison, more than half an incarceration term in a private prison, release from a private prison). This inconsistency makes it difficult to compare effects across studies.

We therefore recommend development and use of a clear and consistent definition and operationalization of privatization. The definition and measure should rely on up-to-date information about how governments and correctional systems define and use private corrections. For example, it would not make sense to define private probation as having no contact with a public agency if all people placed on probation are processed by public intake officers. Consistency in the operationalization of privatization in studies will result in opportunities for scholars to produce research that can better accumulate into a coherent body of knowledge about the effectiveness and efficiency of private corrections and public corrections, respectively.

Recommendation 2. Collect Data on All Types of Corrections Across All Seven Dimensions in Table 17.1 (i.e., Need, Service Amount/Quality, Impacts, Efficiency, Innovation, Social Control, Ethics)

Table 17.1 illustrates that privatization extends to all aspects of corrections. To date, however, empirical research on privatization has focused almost exclusively on prisons, and even for prisons, there exists no systematic empirical comparisons to public corrections. The studies that do exist focus primarily on cost-efficiency and, to a lesser extent, service quality and impacts. Almost no research exists across the other dimensions presented in Table 17.1.

These research gaps stem in part from the lack of relevant data. For some of the dimensions, such as innovative solutions and ethical considerations, almost no relevant data exist. For other dimensions, such as cost-efficiency and impacts, data exist but they are limited and tend to focus on a narrow range of outcomes and on particular time periods and jurisdictions. Such limitations impede scholars' ability to make valid comparisons between public and private corrections.

Accordingly, we recommend the collection of data for each type of corrections across all dimensions described in the conceptual framework. This effort may entail improving existing systems, such as ensuring consistent reporting of official data across jurisdictions. It also may include expanding what data corrections agencies collect. For example, agencies could augment their administrative records data with information from surveys of correctional staff, individuals under correctional supervision, and the public. Such data collection approaches would facilitate empirical comparisons of public and private corrections, inform theoretical discussions about the mechanisms that result in differential impacts, and place policy discussions on a more evidence-based platform. They are, too, in our view, feasible. And without the information, there is no way to evaluate whether private or public corrections is better than the other.

Recommendation 3. Compare All Aspects of Public and Private Corrections Across All Seven Dimensions in Table 17.1 (i.e., Need, Service Amount/Quality, Impacts, Efficiency, Innovation, Social Control, Ethics)

Some accounts suggest that private companies should not be held accountable for outcomes (e.g., Thomas, 2005). However, a typical argument for privatizing correctional services is that private companies will provide the same thing public corrections agencies provide but do so at a lower cost. This argument suggests that private companies should be accountable for, at a minimum, the same outcomes as their public agency counterparts. In addition, because the effectiveness and efficiency of public and private corrections can only be understood relative to each other, it is impossible to compare their impacts if they are not held to the same standards.

Accordingly, we recommend research that compares each aspect, or type, of public and private corrections across the seven dimensions in Table 17.1. Such assessments require identifying appropriate points of comparison and counterfactuals. For example, a comparison of public and private prisons requires that the prisons have comparable characteristics, such as housing similar populations. Or when assessing outcomes for individuals who received private supervision, the comparison group should be individuals who realistically could have received private supervision but did not. Studies that use inappropriate points of comparison will produce inaccurate and distorted estimates of the effectiveness and efficiency of private corrections.

Recommendation 4. Identify Factors That May Influence the Effects and Efficiency of Public or Private Corrections

A central goal of the privatization debate is to identify whether public or private corrections operates more effectively and cost-efficiently. It is unlikely, however, that one approach is *always* more effective or efficient. Instead, the effectiveness or efficiency of public corrections and private corrections, respectively, likely depends on a variety of factors. To illustrate, privatization may be more effective in rural areas as compared to urban areas because it allows small jurisdictions to partner with out-of-town service providers that can bring otherwise unavailable resources to their community. Private probation might be effective only for the lowest-risk individuals, perhaps due to the capacity of a particular private organization. Capacity in turn might be influenced by the availability of qualified applicants.

Some factors may influence the effectiveness of both public corrections and private corrections. Consider, for example, a downturn in the economy, which might increase the recidivism of publicly and privately supervised populations. Perhaps, however, a public corrections agency's performance can withstand economic changes better. Or consider another example—the perceived legitimacy of correctional officers may influence the behavior of incarcerated individuals, whether in public or private facilities. The perceived legitimacy of officers, however, may vary greatly depending on the particular public prison or private prison vendor. The factors that impede, amplify, or otherwise influence corrections may vary as well depending on the type of corrections under consideration. For example, factors that influence probation supervision, such as the professional demeanor of officers, may not matter for fine collection or food services.

There is, in short, a need for research that goes beyond one-time studies of particular privatization efforts and that identify the conditions under which private corrections—as well as public corrections—can be effective and cost-efficient. Such information can help adjudicate debates about privatization. More generally, it can guide efforts to improve the effectiveness of all corrections, whether public or private.

Domain 2. Theory

The theoretical logic by which private corrections provides a more effective and cost-efficient alternative to public corrections remains unclear. At the same time, a critical larger context is the debate about privatization and what influences it. Here, then, we identify two recommendations for advancing theoretical discussions of private corrections.

Recommendation 5. Understand Factors That Contribute to Support for or Against Private Corrections

The lack of systematically collected data and empirical analyses of public and private corrections has created a situation where decisions about whether to privatize correctional services hinge primarily on ideological and philosophical views. There remains, however, little understanding about what factors influence support for privatization. Identification of such factors may advance theoretical discussions about when and under what circumstances private companies should be used to implement correctional sanctions and services.

Political ideology clearly constitutes one potential divide that predicts support for private corrections. However, liberals and conservatives alike can and do support privatization. Other factors may also influence support. Past experiences with privatization may be relevant. The transparency of the privatization process also may be relevant. When the public perceives privatization efforts to be undertaken in an open and transparent manner, they may be more likely to support it. Support may be influenced, too, by views about profit. Some individuals may support privatization when it is undertaken by non-profit organizations and oppose it when it is undertaken by for-profit businesses. It is possible, too, that different social and demographic divides in support exist. Such possibilities only begin to scratch the surface and yet may contribute directly to views about and support for privatization.

For these reasons, we recommend research that examines factors that contribute to support for or against private corrections, with a focus on distinct groups, including the public, policy makers, and decisionmakers, as well individuals under correctional supervision. Such assessments may contribute to an improved understanding of the theoretical mechanisms that influence the adoption or implementation of privatization. It also may shed light on when private corrections has a higher chance of achieving important outcomes. For example, when public corrections' staff view private correctional officers as illegitimate, their resulting treatment of these officers may contribute to ineffective supervision of people incarcerated in a private prison.

Recommendation 6. Identify Factors That Influence the Service Quality, Effectiveness, and Cost-Efficiency of Public Corrections and Private Corrections, Respectively

Privatization proponents argue that privatizing correctional sanctions and services may contribute to higher quality services and more effective and efficient operations as compared to public corrections. This argument implies that public and private corrections are implemented differently, which in turn contributes to differences in service quality, effectiveness, and efficiency. However, the theoretical logic by which private corrections, or public corrections, might provide higher quality services and result in more effective or efficient corrections is far from clear. One such example can be found in discussions about efficiency. A common argument is that private corrections can be more efficient because private vendors operate with less bureaucracy and greater flexibility. However, no evidence exists to support such a claim.

We recommend identifying explicitly the theoretical mechanisms by which different aspects of public and private corrections may operate to impact a range of dimensions, including service quality, effectiveness, and efficiency. For example, if private fine collection efforts are more successful than public fine collection efforts, why? What unique aspects of private efforts would explain their greater success? Do private fine collectors also have low rates of probation violations? Identification of causal mechanisms will contribute to the development of theories that explain how privatization operates, including when it may result in better, worse, or comparable services, outcomes, or efficiency as compared to public corrections.

Domain 3. Policy and Practice

Policy makers have called for greater government accountability and reliance on evidence-based policy and practice. In this section, we identify four recommendations for advancing policies and practices to a more evidence-based, theoretically informed foundation.

Recommendation 7. Require Empirical Monitoring of Public and Private Corrections Efforts

Public corrections agencies typically use audits to monitor their private correctional contracts. Audits, however, serve to identify compliance with particular rules or contract requirements. They do not provide empirical evidence that a given corrections sanction or service is needed, well implemented, or effective (Mears, 2010). For example, just because a private prison passes an audit does not mean it provides the same amount and quality of supervision, protection, and services that a comparable public prison provides. Such assessments necessarily require systematic and ongoing research that monitors and examines both public and private corrections.

We recommend conducting continuous empirical evaluations to determine whether public corrections and private corrections are run effectively, efficiently, and ethically. Ongoing evaluations can help administrators identify and address problems as they arise and shift to private or public corrections as appropriate. In addition, they can help to minimize or avoid collateral consequences by ensuring that corrections efforts are carefully monitored, identifying potential harms and their causes, and using this information to guide corrective steps.

Recommendation 8. Rely on Empirical Evaluations to Identify Impacts of Public and Private Corrections

To date, only a handful of studies have compared the effectiveness of private and public corrections. In addition, existing studies are limited in three important ways. First, they examine a narrow set of outcomes, such as recidivism. This limited focus cannot be used as evidence that a particular service is more effective than another service. In fact, this service may result in a range of unintended outcomes or collateral consequences that outweigh identified benefits. Second, the studies focus on specific time points. One-time studies do not suffice for ensuring efficient use of resources. For example, one study might find that private prisons afford incarcerated individuals fewer opportunities for visitation as compared to what public prisons afford (Office of Program Policy Analysis and Government Accountability, 2007). This snapshot view, however, does not reflect the amount of visitation access that private prisons or public prisons provide over time. Third, they focus on particular jurisdictions and have not been systematically replicated across places. These jurisdictions may be unique in ways that make private corrections, or public corrections, more effective. For example, one state may require multiple on-site monitors for private prisons, which might create better implementation of these services and in turn greater effectiveness. The same procedures may not be in place in a neighboring state.

These limitations impede researchers' ability to compare the impacts of public and private corrections, but they also restrict cost-efficiency comparisons. Credible cost-efficiency analyses require information about impacts and their associated costs. For example, it may cost less to operate a private residential facility, but if the facility produces higher recidivism rates, cost-efficiency analyses should capture the costs associated with the higher rate of recidivism. Absent credible impact evaluations, cost-efficiency analyses cannot shed light on how the costs of public corrections and private corrections compare to each other.

We recommend, therefore, that federal, state, and local jurisdictions require ongoing data collection and analysis aimed at monitoring and assessing all critical operations and potential outcomes of all correctional efforts. This information will create opportunities for identifying the intended and unintended impacts of all aspects of public and private corrections and the conditions under which each type of corrections operates more effectively and efficiently.

Recommendation 9. Base Decisions About Using Public or Private Corrections on Empirical Research

Decisions about whether to privatize correctional services typically are made without empirical evidence. This situation has contributed to instances of "blanket" policy making, such as making an entire aspect of corrections (e.g., prisons, residential facilities) entirely public or private. For example, in Florida all juvenile residential facilities are operated by private contractors (Florida Department of Juvenile Justice, 2012), and in Maine all public defender services are provided by contracted attorneys (Langton & Farole, 2010).

It is unlikely, however, that public corrections, or private corrections, is *always* the more effective and efficient approach. It is more likely that under certain conditions public corrections is more effective and efficient and under other conditions private corrections is more effective and efficient. It also may be the case that the best approach encompasses a "blend" of public and private corrections that leverages each sector's strengths while at the same time minimizing their weaknesses (see, generally, Salamon, 2002, p. 14).

We recommend basing decisions about whether to use public or private corrections not solely on political ideology or philosophical views but on research that evaluates the dimensions highlighted in Table 17.1. This approach requires implementing the above recommendations and, in particular, investing in the infrastructure for undertaking ongoing data collection and analyses.

Recommendation 10. Incentivize Effective, Efficient, and Ethical Corrections (Whether Public or Private)

Corrections systems currently rely on audits and contractual requirements to motivate compliance. Such steps may (or may not) increase compliance with rules or regulations, but they likely do little to improve effectiveness and efficiency. Indeed, few incentives exist to motivate improved corrections. Correctional systems, however, could provide incentives for achieving intended outcomes and avoiding adverse unintended outcomes. For example, an agency could provide bonuses to (public or private) probation officers whose clients achieve job stability.

Such an idea has been proposed by a number of scholars. For example, Wright (2010) suggested the use of financial incentives to increase private prison adoption of evidence-based programs. More recently, Cullen, Jonson, and Mears (2017) argued for the use of accountability measures to incentivize improved correctional treatment: "Wardens, prison staff, probation and parole chiefs, and officers should all be judged on whether offenders who pass through their organizations return to crime" (p. 24). Incentives for effective, efficient, and ethical corrections may take the form of financial payments or bonuses. But contract renewals, or the continued use of public corrections, also could be tied to the achievement of particular outcomes and the avoidance of other outcomes.

There is, we believe, little risk, and much to gain, in exploring different strategies to incentivize improved corrections. We therefore recommend doing so to motivate effective, efficient, and ethical public and private corrections. Incentives, and the monitoring required to determine service quality and whether outcomes are met, can act as accountability mechanisms that may improve effectiveness and efficiency across all of corrections. This information also may result in empirically informed decisionmaking by providing policy makers with clear reasons for adopting or stopping the use of a particular service or policy.

Conclusion

The privatization of corrections may be a good idea. More likely, it is an approach that under certain conditions may be highly effective and under others may be ineffective and even harmful. One particular risk—what can be viewed as a collateral consequence—is net-widening and the attendant drain it creates on public coffers. This situation, however, aptly characterizes public corrections. It, too, can improve public safety, but it also holds the potential to waste taxpayer dollars and create collateral consequences that worsen rather than improve public safety and, more generally, society. There is, then, a need for research that identifies the conditions under which privatization is the best option. With such research, there exists the possibility of placing correctional policy on an evidence-based platform.

References

Adamson, C. R. (1983). Punishment after slavery: Southern state penal systems, 1865–1890. *Social Problems, 30*, 555–569.

American Civil Liberties Union. (2011). *Banking on bondage: Private prisons and mass incarceration.* New York, NY: American Civil Liberties Union.

Anderson, L. (2009). Kicking the national habit: The legal and policy arguments for abolishing private prison contracts. *Public Contract Law Journal, 39*, 113–139.

Anderson, P., Davoli, C. R., & Moriarity, L. J. (1985). Private corrections: Feast or fiasco? *The Prison Journal, 65*, 32–41.

Apel, R., & Ramakers, A. (2018). Impact of criminal punishment on employment. In N. A. Frost & B. M. Huebner (Eds.), *Handbook on the consequences of sentencing and punishment decisions.* New York, NY: Routledge.

Armstrong, G. S., & MacKenzie, D. L. (2000). *Private versus public sector operation: A comparison of the environmental quality in juvenile correctional facilities.* Washington, DC: Department of Justice.

Armstrong, G. S., & MacKenzie, D. L. (2003). Private versus public correctional facilities: Do differences in environmental quality exist? *Crime and Delinquency, 49*, 542–563.

Bales, W. D., Bedard, L. E., Quinn, S. T., Ensley, D. T., & Holley, G. P. (2005). Recidivism of public and private state prison inmates in Florida. *Criminology and Public Policy, 4*, 57–82.

Bauer, S. (2016, July/August). My four months as a private prison guard. *Mother Jones.*

Bayer, P., & Pozen, D. E. (2005). The effectiveness of juvenile correctional facilities: Public versus private management. *Journal of Law and Economics, 48*, 549–589.

Bernard, T. J., & Kurlychek, M. C. (2010). *The cycle of juvenile justice.* New York, NY: Oxford University Press.

Blakely, C. R., & Bumphus, V. W. (2004). Private and public sector prisons—A comparison of select characteristics. *Federal Probation, 68*, 27–31.

Bureau of Justice Statistics. (1989). *Children in custody, 1975–85: Census of public and private juvenile detention, correctional, and shelter facilities, 1975, 1977, 1979, 1983, and 1985.* Washington, DC: Bureau of Justice Statistics.

Burkhardt, B. C., & Jones, A. (2016). Judicial intervention into prisons: Comparing private and public prisons from 1990 to 2005. *Justice System Journal, 37*, 39–52.

Butler, J. D. (1896). British convicts shipped to American colonies. *The American Historical Review, 2*, 12–33.

Camp, S. D., & Daggett, D. M. (2005). *Quality of operations at private and public prisons: Using trends in inmate misconduct to compare prisons.* Washington, DC: Federal Bureau of Prisons.

Camp, S. D., Gaes, G. G., & Saylor, W. G. (2002). Quality of prison operations in the U.S. federal sector: A comparison with a private prison. *Punishment and Society, 4,* 27–53.

Carson, E. A., & Anderson, E. (2016). *Prisoners in 2015.* Washington, DC: Bureau of Justice Statistics.

Clear, T. R., & Frost, N. A. (2013). *The punishment imperative: The rise and failure of mass incarceration in America.* New York, NY: New York University Press.

Cochran, J., & Toman, E. L. (2018). Mass jail incarceration and its consequences. In N. A. Frost & B. M. Huebner (Eds.), *Handbook on the consequences of sentencing and punishment decisions.* New York, NY: Routledge.

Crants, D. R. (1991). Private prison management: A study in economic efficiency. *Journal of Contemporary Criminal Justice, 7,* 49–59.

Crewe, B., Liebling, A., & Hulley, S. (2015). Staff–prisoner relationships, staff professionalism, and the use of authority in public- and private-sector prisons. *Law and Social Inquiry, 40,* 309–344.

Cullen, F. T., Jonson, C. L., & Mears, D. P. (2017). Reinventing community corrections. *Crime and Justice.* doi:10.1086/688457.

Duwe, G., & Clark, V. (2013). The effects of private prison confinement on offender recidivism: Evidence from Minnesota. *Criminal Justice Review, 38,* 375–394.

Ekirch, A. R. (1985a). Bound for America: A profile of British convicts transported to colonies, 1781–1775. *The William and Mary Quarterly, 42,* 184–200.

Ekirch, A. R. (1985b). The transportation of Scottish criminals to America during the eighteenth century. *Journal of British Studies, 24,* 366–374.

Ericson, R. V., McMahon, M. W., & Evans, D. G. (1987). Punishing for profit: Reflections on the revival of privatization in corrections. *Canadian Journal of Criminology, 29,* 355–387.

Farabee, D., & Knight, K. (2002). *A comparison of public and private prisons in Florida: During- and post-prison performance indicators.* Los Angeles, CA: Query Research.

Feeley, M. M. (2002). Entrepreneurs of punishment: The legacy of privatization. *Punishment and Society, 4,* 321–344.

Feeley, M. M. (2014). The unconvincing case against private prisons. *Indiana Law Journal, 89,* 1401–1436.

Flexner, B., & Baldwin, R. N. (1914). *Juvenile courts and probation.* New York, NY: The Century Co.

Florida Department of Juvenile Justice. (2012). *DJJ transitions residential programs to private operation.* Tallahassee, FL: Department of Juvenile Justice.

Fox, S. J. (1970). Juvenile justice reform: An historical perspective. *Stanford Law Review, 22,* 1187–1239.

Frey, C. P. (1981). The house of refuge for colored children. *The Journal of Negro History, 66,* 10–25.

Gaes, G. G., Camp, S. D., Nelson, J. B., & Saylor, W. G. (2004). *Measuring prison performance: Government privatization and accountability.* Walnut Creek, CA: Rowman and Littlefield.

Hagan, J., & Dinovitzer, R. (1999). Collateral consequences of imprisonment for children, communities, and prisoners. *Crime and Justice, 26,* 121–162.

Hanson, L. S. C. (1991). The privatization of corrections movement: A decade of change. *Journal of Contemporary Criminal Justice, 7,* 1–20.

Harding, R. (2001). Private prisons. *Crime and Justice, 28,* 265–346.

Harris, A., Huebner, B., Martin, K., Pattillo, M., Pettit, B., Shannon, S., . . . Fernandes, A. (2017). *Monetary sanctions in the criminal justice system: A review of law and policy in California, Georgia, Illinois, Minnesota, Missouri, New York, North Carolina, Texas, and Washington.* Houston, TX: Laura and John Arnold Foundation.

Huebner, B. M., & Gustafson, R. (2007). The effect of maternal incarceration on adult offspring involvement in the criminal justice system. *Journal of Criminal Justice, 35,* 283–296.

Huebner, B. M., & Frost, N. A. (2018). The consequences of sentencing and punishment decisions. In N. A. Frost & B. M. Huebner (Eds.), *Handbook on the consequences of sentencing and punishment decisions.* New York, NY: Routledge.

Hulley, S., Liebling, A., & Crewe, B. (2011). Respect in prisons: Prisoners' experiences of respect in public and private sector prisons. *Criminology and Criminal Justice, 12,* 3–23.

Jackson, H. T. (1927). Prison labor. *Journal of the American Institute of Criminal Law and Criminology, 18,* 218–268.

Kirk, D. S. (2018). The collateral consequences of incarceration for housing. In N. A. Frost & B. M. Huebner (Eds.), *Handbook on the consequences of sentencing and punishment decisions.* New York, NY: Routledge.

Kish, R. J., & Lipton, A. F. (2013). Do private prisons really offer savings compared with their public counterparts? *Economic Affairs, 33,* 93–107.

Lamott, K. (1961). *Chronicles of San Quentin: The biography of a prison.* New York, NY: Van Rees Press.

Langton, L., & Farole, D. (2010). *State public defender programs, 2007.* Washington, DC: Bureau of Justice Statistics.

Lanza-Kaduce, L., Parker, K. F., & Thomas, C. W. (1999). A comparative recidivism analysis of releasees from private and public prisons. *Crime and Delinquency, 45,* 28–47.

Levinson, R. B. (1985). Okeechobee: An evaluation of privatization in corrections. *The Prison Journal, 65,* 75–94.

Liebling, A., & Ludlow, A. (2016). Privatising public prisons: Penality, law and practice. *Australian and New Zealand Journal of Criminology.* doi:10.1177/0004865816671380.

Lindsey, A. M., Mears, D. P., & Cochran, J. C. (2016). The privatization debate: A conceptual framework for improving (public and private) corrections. *Journal of Contemporary Criminal Justice, 32,* 308–327.

Logan, C. H. (1988). *Private prisons: Cons and pros.* Washington, DC: National Institute of Justice.

Logan, C. H. (1990). *Private prisons: Cons and pros.* New York, NY: Oxford University Press.

Logan, C. H. (1992). Well kept: Comparing quality of confinement in private and public prisons. *Journal of Criminal Law and Criminology, 83,* 577–613.

Lundahl, B., Kunz, C., Brownwell, C., Harris, N., & Van Vleet, R. (2009). Prison privatization: A meta-analysis of cost and quality of confinement indicators. *Research on Social Work Practice, 19,* 383–394.

Makarios, M. D., & Maahs, J. (2012). Is private time quality time? A national private-public comparison of prison quality. *The Prison Journal, 92,* 336–357.

Mason, C. (2013). *International growth trends in prison privatization.* Washington, DC: The Sentencing Project.

McAfee, W. M. (1990). San Quentin: The forgotten issue of California's political history in the 1850s. *Southern California Quarterly, 72,* 235–254.

McDonald, D. C. (1992). Private penal institutions. *Crime and Justice, 16,* 361–419.

McDonald, D. C. (1994). Public imprisonment by private means: The re-emergence of private prisons and jails in the United States, the United Kingdom, and Australia. *The British Journal of Criminology, 34,* 29–48.

Mears, D. P. (2008). Accountability, efficiency, and effectiveness in corrections: Shining a light on the black box of prison systems. *Criminology and Public Policy, 7,* 143–152.

Mears, D. P. (2010). *American criminal justice policy: An evaluation approach to increasing accountability and effectiveness.* New York, NY: Cambridge University Press.

Mears, D. P., & Barnes, J. C. (2010). Toward a systematic foundation for identifying evidence-based criminal justice sanctions and their relative effectiveness. *Journal of Criminal Justice, 38,* 702–810.

Mears, D. P., & Cochran, J. C. (2015). *Prisoner reentry in the era of mass incarceration.* Thousand Oaks, CA: SAGE Publications.

Mears, D. P., Kuch, J. J., Lindsey, A. M., Siennick, S. E., Pesta, G. B., Greenwald, M. A., & Blomberg, T. G. (2016). Juvenile court and contemporary diversion: Helpful, harmful, or both? *Criminology and Public Policy, 153,* 953–981.

Mehigan, J., & Rowe, A. (2007). Problematizing prison privatization: An overview of the debate. In Y. Jewkes (Ed.), *Handbook on prisons* (pp. 356–376). Portland, OR: Willan Publishing.

Moore, A. T. (1998). *Private prisons: Quality corrections at a lower cost.* Los Angeles, CA: Reason Public Policy Institute.

Morgan, K. (1987). English and American attitudes towards convict transportation 1718–1775. *History, 72,* 416–431.

Mullen, J., Chabotar, K. J., & Carrow, D. M. (1985). *The privatization of corrections.* Washington, DC: National Institute of Justice.

Nagin, D. S., Cullen, F. T., & Jonson, C. L. (2009). Imprisonment and reoffending. *Crime and Justice, 38,* 115–200.

Northcutt Bohmert, M., & Wakefield, S. (2018). Impacts of incarceration on children and families. In N. A. Frost & B. M. Huebner (Eds.), *Handbook on the consequences of sentencing and punishment decisions.* New York, NY: Routledge.

Office of the Inspector General. (2016). *Review of the Federal Bureau of Prisons' monitoring of contract prisons.* Washington, DC: Office of the Inspector General.

Office of Program Policy Analysis and Government Accountability. (2007). *Some inmate family visitation practices are not meeting the legislature's intent.* Tallahassee, FL: Office of Program Policy Analysis and Government Accountability.

Perrone, D., & Pratt. T. C. (2003). Comparing the quality of confinement and cost-effectiveness of public versus private prisons: What we know, why we do not know more, and where to go from here. *The Prison Journal, 83,* 301–322.

Petersilia, J. (1997). Probation in the United States. *Crime and Justice, 22,* 149–200.

Porter, E. (2017, January 11). Prisons for profit may cost society. *The New York Times,* p. B1.

Pratt, T. C., & Maahs, J. (1999). Are private prisons more cost-effective than public prisons? A meta-analysis of evaluation research studies. *Crime and Delinquency, 45,* 358–371.

Pratt, T. C., & Winston, M. R. (1999). The search for the frugal grail: An empirical assessment of the cost-effectiveness of public versus private correctional facilities. *Criminal Justice Policy Review, 10,* 447–471.

Reed, A. (2016). *The life and the adventures of a haunted convict*. New York, NY: Random House.

Reisig, M. D., & Pratt, T. C. (2000). The ethics of correctional privatization: A critical examination of the delegation of coercive authority. *The Prison Journal, 80*, 210–222.

Roberts, A. R., & Powers, G. T. (1985). The privatization of corrections: Methodological issues and dilemmas involved in evaluative research. *The Prison Journal, 65*, 95–107.

Salamon, L. M. (2002). The new governance and the tools of public action: An introduction. In L. M. Salamon (Ed.), *The tools of government: A guide to the new governance* (pp. 1–18). Oxford: Oxford University Press.

Santoro, S. (2009, February 21). Pinellas' mobile video visitation bus simplifies jail visits. *Tampa Bay Times*. Retrieved from www.tampabay.com/news/humaninterest/pinellas-mobile-video-visitation-bus-simplifies-jail-visits/977859

Schaller, J. (1982). Work and imprisonment: An overview of the changing roles of prison labor in American prisons. *The Prison Journal, 62*, 3–12.

Schneider, A. L. (1999). Public-private partnerships in the U.S. prison system. *The American Behavioral Scientist, 43*, 192–208.

Schultz, J. L. (1973). The cycle of juvenile court history. *Crime and Delinquency, 19*, 457–476.

Segal, G. F., & Moore, A. T. (2002). *Weighing the watchmen: Evaluating the costs and benefits of outsourcing correctional services*. Los Angeles, CA: Reason Public Policy Institute.

Sessions, J. B. (2017). *Rescission of memorandum on use of private prisons*. Washington, DC: Office of the Attorney General.

Sieh, E. W. (1993). From Augustus to progressives: A study of probation's formative years. *Federal Probation, 57*, 67–73.

Spivak, A. L., & Sharp, S. F. (2008). Inmate recidivism as a measure of private prison performance. *Crime and Delinquency, 54*, 482–508.

Stillman, S. (2014, June 23). Get Out Of Jail, Inc.: Does the alternative-to-incarceration industry profit from injustice? *The New Yorker*, 46–61.

Taylor, A. E. (1942). The origin and development of the convict lease system in Georgia. *The Georgia Historical Quarterly, 26*, 113–128.

Thomas, C. W. (2005). Recidivism of public and private state prison inmates in Florida: Issues and unanswered questions. *Criminology and Public Policy, 4*, 89–100.

Travis, J. (2005). *But they all come back: Facing the challenges of prisoner reentry*. Washington, DC: The Urban Institute.

Teeters, N. K. (1960). The early days of the Philadelphia house of refuge. *Pennsylvania History: A Journal of Mid-Atlantic Studies, 24*, 165–187.

Urban Institute. (1989). *Comparison of privately and publicly operated correctional facilities in Kentucky and Massachusetts*. Washington, DC: Urban Institute.

Villettaz, P., Gilliéron, G., & Killias, M. (2014). *The effects on re-offending of custodial vs. non-custodial sentences: An updated systematic review of the state of knowledge*. Stockholm: Swedish National Council for Crime Prevention.

Whitfield, D. (2001). *The magic bracelet: Technology and offender supervision*. Winchester: Waterside Press.

Wright, K. A. (2010). Strange bedfellows? Reaffirming rehabilitation and prison privatization. *Journal of Offender Rehabilitation, 49*, 74–90.

Yates, S. Q. (2016). *Reducing our use of private prisons*. Washington, DC: Office of the Deputy Attorney General.

Zimmerman, J. (1949). The convict lease system in Arkansas and the fight for abolition. *The Arkansas Historical Quarterly, 8*, 171–188.

PART V

Broad Implications

18

"RAISE THE AGE" LEGISLATION AS A PREVENTION APPROACH TO ADDRESS MASS INCARCERATION

Danielle Tolson Cooper and Jennifer L. Klein

While mass incarceration in the adult criminal justice system is a prominent and well-discussed collateral consequence of determinate sentencing and truth-in-sentencing policies across the United States (see Introduction), there are about 41,000 individuals under the age of 18 (referred to as youth) included in the count of more than 2 million individuals (accounting for both youths and adults) who are incarcerated in local, state, federal, and military facilities across all levels of confinement in the United States (e.g., detention centers, jails, and prisons; Wagner & Rabuy, 2017). Of the millions of individuals who are incarcerated, it is estimated that 34,000 are youth who are confined to a juvenile facility (Wagner & Rabuy, 2017). This includes 6,600 youth who are being held in a facility because they violated the terms of their probation (known as a technical violation), and an additional 600 or more youth are being held for violating laws that apply only to minors, such as curfew violations and incorrigibility (known as status offenses).

However, the count of 34,000 youth is limited to those who reside in juvenile facilities (Wagner & Rabuy, 2017). There are an additional 4,500 youth who are under supervision in an adult facility who are included among the millions who are incarcerated but not included in the tally of youth who are incarcerated. Not included in any part of these estimates are the nearly 20,000 youth who reside outside of their homes in other types of residential facilities (known as congregate care), where they are under the state's supervision but technically not categorized as incarcerated populations (Wagner & Rabuy, 2017).

In total, nearly 60,000 youth are estimated to currently be under state, or occasionally federal, supervision while living outside of their homes. Although these youth make up less than 1% of the total incarcerated population in the United States, it is likely that each adult who is incarcerated was once a youth that at some point in their life became justice-involved (Loeber & Farrington, 2012). Furthermore, many adults who are incarcerated are parents who have limited, if any, access to their own sons or daughters while they are incarcerated (see Chapter 8; Glaze & Maruschak, 2008; Western & Pettit, 2010; Wildeman, 2014). Since research suggests that about one in every three people in the United States have had an arrest before they reach 25 years of age (Brame, Turner, Paternoster, & Bushway, 2012), reducing negative experiences that lead to justice-involvement for those under 18 years old should be a main focus for those interested in reducing the collateral consequences of punishment, such as mass incarceration (Tremblay & Craig, 1995). Ideally, by addressing the needs of thousands of justice-involved youths and young adults with a trauma-informed justice system, those youthful offenders will be less likely to reoffend (Ko et al., 2008), which could subsequently reduce the number of adults incarcerated during their lifetime as well.

Early History of Juvenile Justice Reform in the U.S. (Pre-1990s)

For more than a century after the formation of the United States, children above the age of 7 were punished in the same system as adults when they committed offenses (Fox, 1969; Platt, 1977). Following the passage of the 1899 Illinois Juvenile Court Act, a wave of reform began that led to almost every state establishing their own juvenile court jurisdiction by the 1920s (Feld, 1990). The legal doctrine of *parens patriae* (meaning "parent of the country") became a part of the rationale for the rehabilitation orientation of the juvenile justice system (Tappan, 1949). Additionally, the lower and upper ages of inclusion for the juvenile justice system were clarified in legal statutes, along with the minimum age of criminal responsibility, which signifies an individual's eligibility to be criminally prosecuted in the adult criminal justice system (Schultz, 1973). At the time these laws were passed in the early 1900s, the age boundaries separating the handling of youths who commit offenses from adults who commit offenses were arbitrarily decided and over time the boundaries and protections associated with juvenile justice have continued to evolve (Cauffman, Donley, & Thomas, 2017; Farrington, Loeber, & Howell, 2017).

During the 1960s through the 1980s, several landmark court cases provided rulings that acknowledged constitutionally guaranteed procedural protections for juvenile offenders during court proceedings (Feld, 1990). First, the United States Supreme Court (referred to as the Court) ruled to provide due process for juveniles who were being waived to the adult court (*Kent v. United States*, 1966). Then, the Court asserted that youth under the age of 18 should be guaranteed the same rights in court as adults who are accused of committing a crime; this provided youth with the right to remain silent, the right to an attorney, the right to confront witnesses against you, and the right to advanced notice of charges (*In re Gault*, 1967). After the first two cases drastically changed the court procedures and due process rights for justice-involved youth, the Court continued to hear and decide cases, which further nuanced the boundaries and protections associated with juvenile justice (*Breed v. Jones*, 1975; *In re winship*, 1970; *McKeiver v. Pennsylvania*, 1971; *New Jersey v. TLO*, 1985; *Schall v. Martin*, 1984; *Swisher v. Brady*, 1978). Due to the rapid change in procedural rights for justice-involved youth, this period in history became known as the "due process revolution" (Feld & Bishop, 2010). While most of these cases dealt with juveniles who were at risk for receiving a severe punishment (e.g., loss of liberty), the influence of these cases has had lasting impacts on the justice processing of juveniles throughout the United States who have committed any type of offense (Feld, 1988).

During the same time that case law was being used to reshape procedures for justice-involved youth, Congress also implemented three age-specific laws that modified the rights and privileges of adults and children in the United States. First, Congress passed and ratified the 26th Amendment in 1971, which lowered the voting age in state and local elections from 21 to 18 years old, addressing criticisms that individuals could be drafted for military service at 18 years of age, yet in most states were prevented from voting in any election until 21 years of age (Karlan, 2002).

Next, Congress passed the Juvenile Justice and Delinquency Prevention Act (JJDPA) of 1974, which created federal involvement to justice reform for juvenile offenders at the state level by providing funding to states that agreed to provide several major protections for justice-involved youth (Raley & Dean, 1986). The JJDPA mandated "sight and sound" separation of offenders under the age of 18 from offenders over the age of 18. By the last reauthorization of the JJDPA in 2002, the policy additionally mandated the removal of juveniles from adult jails and called for each state to study the level of disproportionate minority contact (DMC; formerly, known as disproportionate minority confinement) of justice-involved youths.

Lastly, Congress passed the National Minimum Drinking Age Act in 1984, which encouraged states to pass legislation raising their age to purchase and possess alcohol from 18 to 21. This act was passed in an effort to decrease the number of alcohol-involved traffic fatalities that had been consistently increasing since WWII, when the drinking age was originally lowered to 18 years of age (Hingson, 2009).

"Get Tough" Movement and Juvenile Justice
Reform in the U.S. (1990–2005)

As social unrest and crime rates grew in the late 1980s and into the 1990s, arrests of youth, as well as the murders of youth, peaked—leading to the highest court processing rate of youth and the highest murder rate of youth in United States history (Baum, 2005; Sickmund, 2003). The increasing level of crime worried communities and resulted in politicians fearing that they were no longer dealing with wayward youth but instead that they were dealing with juvenile "super predators" (Bennett, DiIulio, & Walters, 1996; Gluck, 1997). The fear of the juvenile super predators came at a time when the public was consistently demonizing youth and the politicizing juvenile justice reform efforts (Merlo & Benekos, 2017). Due to the increased implementation of punitive policies, which were consistent with similar increases in the adult system, this period in history became known as the "get tough" movement.

By the mid-2000s, many states passed laws that made it easier for youth to be waived or transferred from the juvenile justice system into the adult justice system by increasing prosecutorial waiver and mandatory transfer laws, while decreasing judicial discretion (Brown, 2012). The states also made it easier to transfer youth through legislation that expanded the list of crimes that would be exclusively dealt with in the adult criminal justice system (Feld, 1993). With legal changes affecting the juvenile jurisdictions in each state, concerns arose about whether the functions of the juvenile justice system were separate enough from those of the adult criminal justice system, and discussions ensued about the total abolishment of the juvenile justice system in an effort to move forward with a single streamlined system for all offenders (Bishop, Lanza-Kaduce, & Frazier, 1998; Feld, 1997, 1999b).

Overall, the "get tough" movement reflected the fears of the public at the time, and the resulting political response was not well informed or grounded in research (Feld, 1999b). While policies were tough for juvenile offenders, they were even more stringent for adult offenders, which led to the mass incarceration of individuals in the United States through the use of determinate sentencing structures (see Chapter 1; Clear & Frost, 2015). In a recent report from the National Center of Juvenile Justice, Hockenberry and Puzzanchera (2017) estimated that the number of juvenile court-based delinquency cases was roughly 400,000 in 1960 (at the start of the "due process revolution"), and that number continued to rise until the late 1990s (during the "get tough" movement) when the number of juvenile court-based cases peaked at over 1,800,000 (Hockenberry & Puzzanchera, 2017). Not only did these "get tough" policies lead to more justice-involved youth that ever before, the number of youth growing up with justice-involved parents also soared (see Chapter 8; Wildeman, 2014).

Recent History of Juvenile Reform (2005 to Present)

In contrast to the punitive momentum of the "get tough" movement that continued into the mid-2000s, there have been indicators over the past decade signaling a legal shift back to the traditional philosophy of the juvenile justice system (Bernard & Kurlychek, 2010). In a landmark decision in 2005, the United States Supreme Court abolished the death penalty for those who eligible committed crimes as a juvenile, which was previously limited to those juveniles who were 16 or 17 years of age (*Roper v. Simmons*, 2005). The research on adolescent development used by the Supreme Court in their 2005 decision emphasized that juveniles who are justice-involved were different from adults who are justice-involved (Steinberg, 2013). Recent advances in neuroscience also substantiated that "although 16-year-olds may have cognitive ability similar to adults, their ability to avoid impulsive, short-term, peer influence decisions in highly emotional situations (the situations most youths find themselves in when making criminal decisions) remain significantly diminished until around age 25" (Cauffman et al., 2017, p. 73).

In 2010, the United States Supreme Court continued to apply this logic in stating that juveniles deserve to be treated differently from adults, when they ruled that the sentence of life without parole (LWOP) was unconstitutional for juvenile offenders who committed non-homicide offenses while under the age of 18 (*Graham v. Florida*, 2010). Again, in 2012, the Court reaffirmed the developmental differences between juvenile and adult offenders, when they ruled that the use of mandatory life without parole sentences for juvenile offenders was also unconstitutional (*Miller v. Alabama*, 2012). However, the *Miller* ruling was not applied retroactively. In 2016, the Court re-reviewed their ruling and applied their decision in *Miller* retrospectively to those juveniles who had been previously sentenced under mandatory life without parole policies (*Montgomery v. Louisiana*, 2016).

Based on these rulings, the United States Supreme Court has recognized biological and social research related to the inherent differences between juvenile and adult offenders, and it has subsequently altered the sentencing policies surrounding some of the most punitive criminal sanctions available, capital punishment and life without parole. In a similar parallel to the pre-2005 reform efforts for juvenile justice, these new changes in case law occurred while there were also changes in legislation affecting juvenile offenders. Since its original passage in 1974, and subsequent reauthorizations in 1992 and 2002, the Juvenile Justice and Delinquency Prevention Act (JJDPA) has continued to provide funding to states that comply with federal standards (Brown, 2012). These changes represent major juvenile justice reform. However, for youth who are justice-involved, there are still many questions and concerns about the best way to address their delinquent and criminal behaviors while acknowledging the potential for harm that comes with justice-involvement.

Collateral Consequences of Justice-Involvement for Youths

With each piece of juvenile justice reform that increased the likelihood of receiving a more severe punishment came the "adultification" of the juvenile justice system, which moved it away from some of its most key formative features: "individualization, rehabilitation, welfare, discretion, and informality" (Bolin & Applegate, 2016, p. 324; Feld, 1990). Empirical research on juveniles in the adult criminal justice system has predominately focused on juveniles who are transferred or waived from the juvenile court. However, the greater majority (up to 90%) of juveniles who end up in the adult criminal justice system are there because of state statutes that exclude them from the juvenile justice system based on their age at time of offense (Griffin, Addie, Adams, & Firestine, 2011).

In 2005, more than 6,000 cases were judicially waived, and since then, the substantive decrease in the number of waived cases (42% between 2005 and 2014) is largely due to the exemptions by age making waiver unnecessary (Hockenberry & Puzzanchera, 2017). Of those youth who were judicially waived in 2005, the largest percentage of cases were for crimes committed against a person (44%), then for property crimes (32%), and finally for drug and public order crimes (14% and 8%, respectively). Although records estimate 4,500 youth are currently under supervision in adult facilities (Wagner & Rabuy, 2017), the available statistics do not distinguish between youth who are transferred to the adult criminal justice system through prosecutorial waiver, judicial waiver, and legislative mandate. Therefore, it is not possible at this time to further nuance the role that transfer and waiver mechanisms have played in the number of youth incarcerated in adult correctional facilities.

As the number of youth in the adult criminal justice system continued to increase during the "get tough" movement, researchers documented many collateral consequences that accompany transferring youth to the adult justice system, specifically those who committed serious felony offenses

(Bishop, Frazier, Lanza-Kaduce, & Winner, 1996; Johnson, Lanza-Kaduce, & Woolard, 2011; Jordan, 2012; Lanza-Kaduce, Lane, Bishop, & Frazier, 2005). A systemic review of existing transfer studies conducted prior to 2003 found that transferring juveniles to the adult criminal justice system increased their likelihood of later engaging in violent behaviors as adults (McGowan et al., 2007). More recently, practitioners and scholars have shared research findings that support that youths who are transferred to adult criminal courts (a) have a lower likelihood of graduated sanctions being available in response to their delinquent or criminal behaviors; (b) have limited, if any, access to specialized rehabilitation and education programs available in the juvenile justice system; and (c) are at an increased risk of being victimized (by inmates and staff) and attempting suicide (Arya, 2007; Johnson et al., 2011; Slobogin, 2013; Taylor, 2015; Woolard, Odgers, Lanza-Kaduce, & Daglis, 2005).

Similar to the number of youth serving time in adult facilitates, in 2005 the largest percentage of cases involving youth in juvenile detention was for crimes committed against a person (31%). Unlike transferred youth, property crimes were not the second largest group; instead public order crimes ranked second, followed closely by property offenses, and then by drug crimes (30%, 29%, and 10%, respectively; Hockenberry & Puzzanchera, 2017). Of all the youth processed through juvenile court in 2005, about one-third, or 34%, were adjudicated delinquent or judicially waived to adult court. Although the greater majority (approximately 60%) of the cases resulted in probation as the most restrictive disposition, more than one-quarter, or 26%, of the cases resulted in out-of-home placement, which includes placement in juvenile facilities and in residential home placements (Hockenberry & Puzzanchera, 2017).

Despite the consequences of justice-involvement for youth, the juvenile justice system remains the ideal alternative to youth being prosecuted in the adult criminal justice system. In both situations, there are still associated collateral consequences to removing the youth from their homes, such as disruption of contact with social support systems and inconsistencies in educational opportunities. However, the juvenile justice system in most states is better suited to address those concerns.

Prevention as a Framework for Justice Reform Efforts

As different pieces of reform from the 1990s continued to shape the goals of the juvenile and adult criminal justice systems, researchers began to conceptualize frameworks that allow them to identify patterns and draw comparisons among key themes that predict successful prevention, specifically with interest in interventions for those exhibiting dysfunctional behaviors like delinquency and crime (Coie et al., 1993; Tremblay & Craig, 1995). "Crime prevention from a developmental perspective is largely based on the idea that criminal activity is determined by behavioral and attitudinal patterns that have been learned during an individual's development" (Tremblay & Craig, 1995, p. 151).

Researchers outlined several principles of prevention science over two decades ago, and they emphasized the need to identify causal relationships, target those at the highest risk of dysfunction, and use developmental research approaches to look across the life-course to better understand person and environment interactions (Coie et al., 1993). Since then, there has been a greater acceptance that youth are more susceptible to rehabilitation than adults, and more efforts have been made to address developmental risk and protective factors, such as "individual characteristics, family characteristics, and environmental characteristics," that predict engagement in delinquency and crime (Benekos & Merlo, 2016; Tremblay & Craig, 1995, p. 158)

At the primary level of prevention, the goal is to identify "conditions of the physical and social environment that provide opportunities for or precipitate criminal acts" (p. 290). Primary prevention occurs through educational campaigns announcing crimes and their sentences, environmental design that makes committing crimes harder, and other well-being programs that reduce exposure to environments that encourage delinquent and criminal activities (Brantingham & Faust, 1976).

At the secondary level of prevention, the goal is the "early identification of potential offenders" (p. 290). Secondary prevention occurs through programs that target neighborhoods where crime has already been prevalent, as well as techniques that identify individuals who might be at risk for engagement in delinquent and criminal behaviors, and screening their need to be referred to additional assessments or interventions (Brantingham & Faust, 1976).

At the tertiary level of prevention, the prevention effort is focused on "actual offenders and involves intervention in their lives in such a fashion that they will not commit further offenses" (p. 290). Tertiary prevention occurs through efforts to reform, rehabilitate, and incapacitate individuals who are already involved in delinquent and criminal activities, so that they do not continue or worsen their engagement (Brantingham & Faust, 1976).

As mentioned, one of the collateral consequences of the justice-involvement and punishment of millions of adults and thousands of youth is mass incarceration. However, by focusing on tertiary prevention efforts, reoffending by justice-involved youth can be reduced, and therefore, mass incarceration of youth (as well as adults in the long term) would be reduced as a result. To promote tertiary prevention as an approach to reduce mass incarceration, advocates for age-related and trauma-informed practices in juvenile justice policy have emphasized that raising the age for the juvenile jurisdiction will potentially reduce the likelihood that youthful offenders will cycle through the justice system multiple times (Benekos & Merlo, 2016; Loeber & Farrington, 2012).

The Growing Momentum of the Raise the Age (RTA) Movement

Each state has legislatively mandated the qualifying age limitations for who has the right to be treated as a juvenile and who is eligible to be punished as an adult (Zang, 2016). Currently, most states determine that youth who are under the age of 18 have consideration in the juvenile justice system. Most commonly, the "Raise the Age" (RTA) movement includes laws that raise the upper age of the juvenile jurisdiction to 16, 17, or 18, which is sometimes identified as the age of last inclusion, but other times they are identified as the age of first exclusion. Both terms (last inclusion and first exclusion) are similar but not synonymous and both are used to identify at what age a youth can no longer be processed in the juvenile court jurisdiction (for example, if 17 is the age of last inclusion, then 18 is the age of first exclusion). A few states, such as Connecticut, Massachusetts, Vermont, and Iowa, have also introduced legislation that proposed raising the age of inclusion in the juvenile justice system to include individuals as old as 20 or 24 years of age (Farrington, Loeber, & Howell, 2012; National Conference of State Legislatures, 2017). The RTA movement also includes another subset of laws that focuses on raising the lower age of the juvenile jurisdiction from 7, 10, or 12, which identifies the age beyond the defense of infancy, and the ability to be included in the juvenile court jurisdiction. These laws set the minimum age of criminal responsibility, which protect against inclusion in the adult court jurisdiction.

Overall, the RTA movement is a response to the problem of excluding juveniles from the juvenile justice system, "with the goal of making legal boundaries between adolescence and adulthood consistent with the available scientific evidence on maturity of judgment, culpability, and amenability to treatment" (Cauffman et al., 2017, p. 74). This emphasis on keeping juveniles in the juvenile jurisdiction is a prevention approach based on empirical research that suggests that youth who are kept in the juvenile justice system have an increased potential for receiving treatment and educational opportunities specific to their developmental needs (Slobogin, 2013). Specifically, it is expected that Raise the Age policies would reduce recidivism by increasing employability (see Chapter 5), facilitating healthier social and familial relationships (see Chapter 8), and improving access to services addressing youths' mental, emotional, and physical health (see Chapter 6; Cauffman et al., 2017).

Adolescent brain development research has been credited as the main argument for why researchers and policy makers are concerned about the inclusion of youths and young adults in the adult criminal justice system (Farrington et al., 2017). There is a growing body of research that suggests that young people's brains are developing well into their mid-20s, especially males (see review of brain research and links to justice-involvement in Bonnie & Scott, 2013). Research on adolescent brain development, which demonstrates the opportunity for rehabilitation of young people and highlights the need for interventions that decrease the likelihood for recidivism, has been pivotal to the Raise the Age Movement and other aspects of juvenile justice policy (Benekos & Merlo, 2016). The growing acknowledgment from practitioners and policy makers that youth are different, in many ways, from adults is evidenced in both the court cases and state legislation changes that have advocated for trauma-informed treatment of youth who are justice-involved. This highlights that the United States is experiencing the pendulum starting to swing back away from the punitive policies that were put in place in the late 1990s toward a renewed focus on rehabilitation for those under supervision within the juvenile justice system (Bernard & Kurlychek, 2010; Siennick, 2017).

A Decade of Policy Changes to the Juvenile and Adult Court Jurisdictions

At the beginning of 2007, over thirty states (as well as the District of Columbia) had already set the upper age of inclusion for their juvenile justice system at 17. At this point, however, some states continued to exclude 16-year-olds and 17-year-olds from the juvenile justice system. Specifically, three states (Connecticut, New York, and North Carolina) used 15 as the upper age of inclusion, and another ten states used 16 as the upper age of inclusion in the juvenile court jurisdiction. In less than a decade (from 2007 to 2017), the legal landscape for juveniles who were justice-involved in the United States had evolved substantially toward the use of rehabilitative treatment. Practitioners and policy makers worked together in addressing concerns regarding ways to reduce youths' exposure to trauma and other victimizations that would increase their risk for justice-involvement (Monahan, Steinberg, & Piquero, 2015). By 2015, the United States went from having thirteen states to nine remaining states that excluded 17-year-olds from their juvenile jurisdiction (Zang, 2016).

Even more recently, in 2016, Louisiana and South Carolina passed laws to raise their upper age of inclusion from 16 to 17. Finally, in 2017, after being the last two states for nearly a decade that excluded 16-year-olds from their juvenile jurisdiction, both New York and North Carolina passed laws to raise their upper age of inclusion from 15 to 17. As of the 2017 legislative season, the United States is on its way to having zero states that exclude 16-year-olds and only five states (Georgia, Michigan, Missouri, Texas, and Wisconsin) that still exclude all 17-year-olds in their state from being included in their juvenile jurisdiction. It will take several years for all of the recent polices to be implemented in their respective states.

With the successes that different states have experienced while raising the upper age of exclusion from the juvenile justice system to 16, 17, and 18, some states have already pushed onward to the next horizon of juvenile justice reform—Raise the Age 2.0, which focuses on the inclusion of young adults in the juvenile justice system or providing them similar protections that are received by those in the juvenile jurisdiction. As mentioned, legislators in Connecticut, Massachusetts, Vermont, and Iowa have publicly discussed and proposed legislation to raise the upper age of exclusion from the juvenile justice system to 21 years old, but these proposals have yet to be successfully passed into law anywhere in the United States (National Conference of State Legislatures, 2017).

By policy makers engaging with practitioners, researchers, and youth advocates in the RTA movement, it is more likely that legislation will pass that holds youths and young adults accountable for their actions and reduces the likelihood for future contact with the juvenile justice system (as well as future contact with the criminal justice system; Cauffman et al., 2017; Rossum, 2012; Siennick, 2017; Slobogin, 2013). With the goal of improving interventions available to youths and young adults who have offended in mind, the juvenile justice system's focus on diversion, inclusion of family and victims' voices, and the use of specialized professionals make it better suited to respond to offending by youths and young adults (A. A. Fagan, 2013; Taylor, 2015). Since 2005, a lot of progress has been made through the RTA movement to reduce the punitive practices that arose during the "get tough" movement of the 1990s; this progress can be seen through the decrease in the amount of juveniles entering into the system in comparison to pre-2005 numbers (Hockenberry & Puzzanchera, 2017).

Declining Delinquency Rates for Justice-Involved Youths

Although estimates have indicated that juvenile court caseloads went up 141% between 1960 and 2014, the 42% decrease in the number of delinquency cases processed by juvenile courts from 2005 to 2014 shows progress in reducing the punitive effects of policies passed during the "get tough" movement and a return to the original rehabilitative goals of the juvenile justice system (Hockenberry & Puzzanchera, 2017). It should be noted, however, that this reduction in juvenile caseload numbers is due, in part, to more youth being handled in the juvenile court jurisdiction due to exclusionary policies that limit what ages and what crimes can be considered in the juvenile jurisdiction.

In 2014, youth were most frequently being processed in court for committing property crimes (34%), followed by crimes against a person (27%), public order crimes (26%), and drug crimes (13%). To categorize these crime rates further, Hockenberry and Puzzanchera (2017) estimated that "of the 974,900 delinquency cases processed in 2014, 53% involved youth younger than 16, 28% involved females, and 43% involved White youth" (p. 9). When comparing the decrease in delinquency rates from 2005 to 2015 for male and female offenders (39% and 38%, respectively), the number of delinquency cases decreased at a similar rate across all offense types, with crime rates for bother genders being the lowest they had been since 2005 (Hockenberry & Puzzanchera, 2017).

When comparing rates across racial groups, delinquency case rates dropped for all racial groups from 2005 to 2014; however, in 2014 the delinquency case rate for Black juveniles remained 3 times higher than the rate for White, Hispanic, and American Indian youth (Hockenberry & Puzzanchera, 2017). Additionally, cases involving Black youth, in comparison to those involving White youth, were more likely to receive detention (25% vs. 18%), formal processing (62% vs. 52%), waiver (1% vs. 0.6%), and out-of-home placement (28% vs. 22%), but they were less likely to being adjudicated delinquent (50% vs. 54%) or be placed on probation (61% vs. 64%; Hockenberry & Puzzanchera, 2017). Feld (1999a) had previously raised concerns about the disproportionate impact of the reforms on Black youths, and nearly 20 years later, concerns about racial and ethnic disparity in the justice system still exist (Davis & Sorensen, 2013).

Recent Research on Raise the Age Policies

As the RTA movement has grown more popular among policy makers and practitioners throughout the United States, researchers have emphasized the importance of studying specific deterrence, which is focused on reducing recidivism (Cauffman et al., 2017; Fowler & Kurlychek, 2017; Gibson & Krohn, 2012). Over the past two decades, researchers conducted a few studies that have used different methodological and statistical approaches to create comparable groups of youth who have experienced juvenile court processing and youth who have received adult court processing. Altogether, the existing research on the effects juvenile versus adult court processing on recidivism reduction have been mixed, but there has also been no evidence of increases in reoffending due these policy changes that encourage juvenile court processing over adult court processing (Siennick, 2017).

In one of the earlier studies, a sample of 15- and 16-year-olds from New Jersey processed in the juvenile court was matched with a sample of 15- and 16-year-olds from New York processed in the adult court, and it was found that those who were processed in juvenile courts were less likely to be arrested and if they were arrested they experienced more time before their rearrests than did youth in the adult court (J. Fagan, 1996). Because this study used youth from two different state jurisdictions, it is unclear how different state policies and cultures influenced the outcomes.

To overcome this limitation, researchers began conducting research in a single jurisdiction and matched youth who were similarly situated but handled differently. Three different studies have been conducted using samples of youth from Florida (some youth who were handled by the juvenile court and matched using propensity score matching with youth that were handled by the adult court) and revealed similar findings as were found in the Fagan study; youth handled in the juvenile justice system had better recidivism outcomes than those processed in the adult court (Bishop et al., 1996; Johnson et al., 2011; Lanza-Kaduce et al., 2005). In the latter of the three studies, the researchers further concluded that it was access to graduated sanctions (e.g., layers of treatment options leading up to secure placement) as opposed to "leapfrogging" over treatment that made the difference for whether juvenile versus adult processing led to increased recidivism (Johnson et al., 2011). While these studies overcame the jurisdictional issue that was present in the Fagan study, they compared the outcomes of statistically generated matches and used a sample of youth, leading to concerns about sampling bias.

To overcome these criticisms from the studies conducted in Florida, researchers engaged in a study using a full population of youth, instead of a sampling, from a single jurisdiction. Most recently, a study was conducted on youth processed by courts in Connecticut, which raised the age in 2010 to allow for the inclusion of 16-year-olds in the juvenile justice system, and the findings continued to support that juvenile court processing was associated with lower recidivism in comparison to similar youth who were exposed to adult court processing (Fowler & Kurlychek, 2017). These researchers compared the entire population of 16-year-olds who had been arrested and processed in the juvenile courts in 2010 with those who had been processed in the adult courts in 2009, as well as created a subsample from both courts of individuals who had been convicted. The results of this natural experiment around policy change in Connecticut further supported the assertion that youth who are processed in juvenile court are less likely to reoffend than youth who are processed in adult courts.

In addition to the research on specific deterrence, there has also been a study looking at general deterrence, which is focused on reducing overall crime through criminal sanctioning and policy efforts (Loeffler & Chalfin, 2017). Instead of using individual level data, the researchers conducted their study using aggregate data from the National Incident-Based Reporting System (NIBRS), and their findings showed no difference in recidivism among those who were processed in the juvenile court versus those processed in the adult court. Although this research did not support the notion that juvenile court processing reduces recidivism, it also did not show any benefit to adult court processing or harm from juvenile court processing.

Next Steps for Research on the RTA Movement

In order to improve the research on the effects of the RTA movement, researchers have outlined research needs that must be addressed before an evaluation of Raise the Age can be completely implemented (Gibson & Krohn, 2012). For example, difficulties arise concerning the fact that when legislation is introduced and passed into law, it often takes multiple years before complete implementation occurs, which makes it difficult to isolate effects of the law in comparison to other influential factors. Specifically, this occurred when Connecticut passed the law in 2007 to raise the upper age of inclusion of their juvenile justice system to 18, but then waited three years to implement for 16-year-olds in 2010 and five years to implement for 17-year-olds in 2012. While the implementation over several years allowed for the state and its service providers to prepare for service delivery to 16-year-olds and adjust to their inclusion in the juvenile justice system before embracing 17-year-olds as a part of a phase-in process, it also raised practical questions about how this information was captured in the state's administrative (i.e., criminal history, court processing, and treatment) data and what is the best way to study the effects of the policy change (as seen in the use of NIBRS data for the analysis conducted on Connecticut's RTA legislation in Loeffler & Chalfin, 2017).

Conclusion and Implications

Researchers have estimated that older youth (15- to 17-year-olds) and young adults (18- to 25-year-olds) have the highest arrest rates for all offender populations involved in the criminal justice system (Farrington, 1986; Sampson & Laub, 1992; Sweeten, Piquero, & Steinberg, 2013). These findings are concerning as young people run the risk of developing into adult offenders post-release from juvenile justice supervision. These findings also emphasize that the criminal justice system is not an adequate solution for public safety or for rehabilitation and improvement of the young people currently under its supervision.

Using a tertiary prevention perspective provides a framework to understand the opportunity to help youthful offenders from becoming justice-involved again, later on as adults. The continued inclusion of youthful offenders in the juvenile justice system is supported by research that suggests that inclusion in the adult criminal justice system leads to issues for youthful offenders, such as an increased likelihood of sexual and physical victimization, as well as the increased likelihood of suicide due to social and physical isolation (Scott, Underwood, & Lamis, 2015). Unfortunately, when young people are in adult prisons, they experience reduced exposure to prosocial peers and increased exposure to older peers who have likely engaged in more serious offenses than what led them to be justice-involved. This is concerning also from a developmental crime prevention perspective, which suggests that the younger juveniles who are exposed to older, more criminal individuals have an increased likelihood of continued justice-involvement themselves (Tremblay & Craig, 1995).

For those concerned about public safety, Raise the Age legislation requires more attention from researchers, practitioners, and policy makers. Despite existing research acknowledging that young people have a strong potential for rehabilitation, it is important to acknowledge the expectations of society and of the victims in how crimes are handled and in how offenders are sentenced. Therefore, one of the biggest concerns for those focused on maintaining public safety with increasing inclusion in the juvenile justice system is the fact that the juvenile's criminal record could potentially be expunged, or at the very least sealed, as well as the court proceedings could be closed. Although there are mixed results about whether or not raising the age impacts the rates of juvenile offending overall, protection from the collateral consequences of the adult criminal justice system represent other desirable reasons to Raise the Age (Siennick, 2017).

As we move into the era of Raise the Age 2.0, where the goal is to raise the upper age of exclusion beyond 18, to 21 or higher, there are many areas that should be further explored. Researchers have called for the implementation of experimental courts, similar to drug courts or veteran courts, for young adults who are charged with criminal offenses (Farrington et al., 2012), which would prevent the state from making statewide changes to policy that have little evidence of effectiveness (Gibson & Krohn, 2012). Researchers have also called for the evaluation of polices currently implemented in other countries, especially given the prospect of cultural differences having an impact on the outcomes (Farrington et al., 2012). Researchers have also emphasized the unanswered question of reentry, particularly asking what special needs should be considered to assist those juveniles reentering communities after spending time in facilities away from home (Gibson & Krohn, 2012). Lastly, they have called for research focused on the public safety effects of Raise the Age policies, specifically those effecting schooling and labor markets (Loeffler & Chalfin, 2017).

This growth is a part of the cycle of juvenile justice reform (Bernard & Kurlychek, 2010), which swings back and forth from punitive to rehabilitative philosophies. As policy changes continue to unfold, questions about the differences between the juvenile and the adult criminal justice system will continue to arise. Researchers suggest that "such an emphasis on implementing age-specific policies irrespective of jurisdictional considerations echoes elements of past policy proposals to abolish the juvenile justice system altogether in favor of a system with age-appropriate policies and legal safeguards" (Loeffler & Chalfin, 2017, p. 65). In order to answer these questions, researchers will have to continue to improve risk and need assessments, potentially linking these assessments with trajectories of offending, as well as curate data sources that can be coupled with administrative data in order to capture a more comprehensive picture of the effect of legislation efforts informed by the RTA movement (Gibson & Krohn, 2012). With the changes that have occurred in the past decade alone, the future looks full of promise for reducing the effects of punishment through tertiary prevention.

References

Arya, N. (2007). *Jailing juveniles: The danger of incarcerating youth in adult jails in America.* Retrieved from https://ssrn-com.unh-proxy01.newhaven.edu/abstract=1697706

Baum, K. (2005). *Special report: Juvenile victimization and offending, 1993–2003.* Washington, DC. Retrieved from https://static.prisonpolicy.org/scans/bjs/jvo03.pdf

Benekos, P. J., & Merlo, A. V. (2016). A decade of change Roper v. Simmons, defending childhood, and juvenile justice policy. *criminal Justice Policy Review,* 0887403416648734

Bennett, W. J., DiIulio, J. J., & Walters, J. P. (1996). *Body count: Moral poverty—And how to Win America's War Against Crime and Drugs.* New York, NY: Simon & Schuster.

Bernard, T. J., & Kurlychek, M. C. (2010). *The cycle of juvenile justice.* Oxford: Oxford University Press.

Bishop, D., Frazier, C. E., Lanza-Kaduce, L., & Winner, L. (1996). The transfer of juveniles to criminal court: Does it make a difference? *Crime & Delinquency, 42*(2), 171–191. doi:10.1177/0011128796042002001

Bishop, D., Lanza-Kaduce, L., & Frazier, C. E. (1998). Juvenile justice under attack: An analysis of the causes and impact of recent reforms. *University of Florida Journal of Law & Public Policy, 10,* 129.

Bolin, R. M., & Applegate, B. K. (2016). Adultification in juvenile corrections: Examining the orientations of juvenile and adult probation and parole officers. *American Journal of Criminal Justice, 41*(2), 321–339. doi:10.1007/s12103-015-9298-2

Bonnie, R. J., & Scott, E. S. (2013). The teenage brain: Adolescent brain research and the law. *Current Directions in Psychological Science, 22*(2), 158–161. doi:10.1177/0963721412471678

Brame, R., Turner, M. G., Paternoster, R., & Bushway, S. D. (2012). Cumulative prevalence of arrest from ages 8 to 23 in a national sample. *Pediatrics, 129*(1), 21–27.

Brantingham, P. J., & Faust, F. L. (1976). A conceptual model of crime prevention. *Crime & Delinquency, 22*(3), 284–296. doi:10.1177/001112877602200302

Breed v. Jones, No. No. 73–1995, 421 519 (Supreme Court 1975).

Brown, S. A. (2012). *Trends in juvenile justice legislation: 2001–2011.* Denver, CO. Retrieved from www.ncsl.org/documents/cj/TrendsInJuvenileJustice.pdf

Cauffman, E., Donley, S., & Thomas, A. (2017). Raising the Age. *Criminology & Public Policy, 16*(1), 73–81.

Clear, T. R., & Frost, N. A. (2015). *The punishment imperative: The rise and failure of mass ncarceration in America.* New York, NY: New York University Press.

Coie, J. D., Watt, N. F., West, S. G., Hawkins, J. D., Asarnow, J. R., Markman, H. J., . . . Long, B. (1993). The science of prevention: A conceptual framework and some directions for a national research program. *American Psychologist, 48*(10), 1013–1022. doi:10.1037/0003–066X.48.10.1013

Davis, J., & Sorensen, J. R. (2013). Disproportionate minority confinement of juveniles: A national examination of black—White disparity in placements, 1997–2006. *Crime & Delinquency, 59*(1), 115–139. doi:10.1177/0011128709359653

Fagan, A. A. (2013). Family-focused interventions to prevent juvenile delinquency. *Criminology & Public Policy, 12*(4), 617–650. doi:10.1111/1745–9133.12029

Fagan, J. (1996). The comparative advantage of juvenile versus criminal court sanctions on recidivism among adolescent felony offenders*. *Law & Policy, 18*(1–2), 77–114. doi:10.1111/j.1467–9930.1996.tb00165.x

Farrington, D. P. (1986). Age and crime. *Crime and Justice, 7,* 189–250.

Farrington, D. P., Loeber, R., & Howell, J. C. (2012). Young adult offenders: The need for more effective legislative options and justice processing. *Criminology & Public Policy, 11*(4), 729–750. doi:10.1111/j.1745–9133.2012.00842.x

Farrington, D. P., Loeber, R., & Howell, J. C. (2017). Increasing the minimum age for adult court. *Criminology & Public Policy, 16*(1), 83–92.

Feld, B. (1988). The juvenile court meets the principle of the offense: Legislative changes in juvenile waiver statutes. *The Journal of Criminal Law and Criminology (1973–), 78*(3), 471–533. doi:10.2307/1143567

Feld, B. (1990). Transformation of the juvenile court. The. *Minn. L. Rev.*, 75, 691.

Feld, B. (1993). Criminalizing the American juvenile court. *Crime and Justice*, 197–280.

Feld, B. (1997). Abolish the juvenile court: Youthfulness, criminal responsibility, and sentencing policy. *Journal of Criminal Law & Criminology*, 88, 68.

Feld, B. (1999a). *Bad kids: Race and the transformation of the juvenile court*. Oxford: Oxford University Press.

Feld, B. (1999b). The honest politician's guide to juvenile justice in the twenty-first century. *Annals of the American Academy of Political and Social Science*, 564, 10–27.

Feld, B., & Bishop, D. (2010). Procedural rights in juvenile courts: Competence and consequences. In B. C. Feld & D. M. Bishop (Eds.), *Oxford Handbook on Juvenile Crime and Juvenile Justice*. Oxford: Oxford University Press. DOI: 10.1093/oxfordhb/9780195385106.013.0027. Retrieved from https://experts.umn.edu/en/publications/procedural-rights-in-juvenile-courts-competence-and-consequences-2

Fowler, E., & Kurlychek, M. C. (2017). Drawing the line: Empirical recidivism results from a natural experiment raising the age of criminal responsibility. *Youth Violence and Juvenile Justice*, 0(0), 1541204017708017. doi:10.1177/1541204017708017

Fox, S. J. (1969). Juvenile justice reform: An historical perspective. *Stanford Law Review*, 22, 1187.

Gibson, C. L., & Krohn, M. D. (2012). Raising the age. *Criminology & Public Policy*, 11(4), 759–768. doi:10.1111/j.1745–9133.2012.00851.x

Glaze, L., & Maruschak, L. (2008). *Parents in prison and their minor children*. Washington, DC. Retrieved from http://www.ohiofathers.org/Files/Admin/parents%20in%20prison%20and%20their%20children.pdf

Gluck, S. (1997). Wayward youth, super predator: An evolutionary tale of juvenile delinquency from the 1950s to the present. *Corrections Today*, 59(3), 63–66.

Graham v. Florida, No. 08–7412, 130 2011 (Supreme Court 2010).

Griffin, P., Addie, S., Adams, B., & Firestine, K. (2011). Trying juveniles as adults: An analysis of state transfer laws and reporting. Retrieved from www.ncjrs.gov/pdffiles1/ojjdp/232434.pdf

Hingson, R. W. (2009). The legal drinking age and underage drinking in the united states. *Archives of Pediatrics & Adolescent Medicine*, 163(7), 598–600. doi:10.1001/archpediatrics.2009.66

Hockenberry, S., & Puzzanchera, C. (2017). *Juvenile court statistics 2014*. Pittsburg, PA: The National Center for Juvenile Justice. Retrieved from https://www.ojjdp.gov/ojstatbb/njcda/pdf/jcs2014.pdf

In re Gault, 387 1 (Supreme Court 1967).

In re winship, 397 358 (Supreme Court 1970).

Johnson, K., Lanza-Kaduce, L., & Woolard, J. (2011). Disregarding graduated treatment: Why transfer aggravates recidivism. *Crime & Delinquency*, 57(5), 756–777. doi:10.1177/0011128708328867

Jordan, K. L. (2012). Juvenile transfer and recidivism: A propensity score matching approach. *Journal of Crime and Justice*, 35(1), 53–67. doi:10.1080/0735648X.2011.632133

Karlan, P. S. (2002). Ballots and bullets: The exceptional history of the right to vote. *University of Cincinnati Law Review*, 71, 1345.

Kent v. United States, 383 541 (Supreme Court 1966).

Ko, S. J., Ford, J. D., Kassam-Adams, N., Berkowitz, S. J., Wilson, C., Wong, M., . . . Layne, C. M. (2008). Creating trauma-informed systems: Child welfare, education, first responders, health care, juvenile justice. *Professional Psychology: Research and Practice*, 39(4), 396–404. doi:10.1037/0735–7028.39.4.396

Lanza-Kaduce, L., Lane, J., Bishop, D. M., & Frazier, C. E. (2005). Juvenile offenders and adult felony recidivism: The impact of transfer. *Journal of Crime and Justice*, 28(1), 59–77.

Loeber, R., & Farrington, D. P. (2012). *From juvenile delinquency to adult crime: Criminal careers, justice policy and prevention*. Oxford: Oxford University Press.

Loeffler, C. E., & Chalfin, A. (2017). Estimating the crime effects of raising the age of majority. *Criminology & Public Policy*, 16(1), 45–71.

McGowan, A., Hahn, R., Liberman, A., Crosby, A., Fullilove, M., Johnson, R., . . . Stone, G. (2007). Effects on violence of laws and policies facilitating the transfer of juveniles from the juvenile justice system to the adult justice system: A systematic review. *American Journal of Preventive Medicine*, 32(4, Supplement), 7–28. doi:http://dx.doi.org/10.1016/j.amepre.2006.12.003

McKeiver v. Pennsylvania, 403 528 (Supreme Court 1971).

Merlo, A. V., & Benekos, P. J. (2017). *Reaffirming juvenile justice: From gault to montgomery*. New York, NY: Taylor & Francis.

Miller v. Alabama, No. 10–9646, 132 2455 (Supreme Court 2012).

Monahan, K., Steinberg, L., & Piquero, A. R. (2015). Juvenile justice policy and practice: A developmental perspective. *Crime and Justice*, 44(1), 577–619.

Montgomery v. Louisiana, No. No. 14–280, 136 718 (Supreme Court 2016).

National Conference of State Legislatures. (2017). Juvenile justice bills tracking database. Retrieved from www.ncsl.org/research/civil-and-criminal-justice/ncsls-juvenile-justice-bill-tracking-database.aspx

New Jersey v. TLO, No. No. 83–712, 469 325 (Supreme Court 1985).

Platt, A. (1977). *The child savers: The invention of delinquency.* Chicago, IL: University of Chicago Press.

Raley, G. A., & Dean, J. E. (1986). The juvenile justice and delinquency prevention act: Federal leadership in state reform. *Law & Policy, 8*(4), 397–417. doi:10.1111/j.1467–9930.1986.tb00388.x

Roper v. Simmons, No. 03–633, 543 551 (Supreme Court 2005).

Rossum, R. A. (2012). Holding juveniles accountable: Reforming America's "juvenile Injustice System". *Pepperdine Law Review, 22*(3), 1.

Sampson, R. J., & Laub, J. H. (1992). Crime and deviance in the life course. *Annual Review of Sociology, 18*(ArticleType: research-article/Full publication date: 1992 / Copyright © 1992 Annual Reviews), 63–84.

Schall v. Martin, No. No. 82–1248, 467 253 (Supreme Court 1984).

Schultz, J. L. (1973). The cycle of juvenile court history. *Crime & Delinquency, 19*(4), 457–476. doi:10.1177/001112877301900402

Scott, M., Underwood, M., & Lamis, D. A. (2015). Suicide and related-behavior among youth involved in the juvenile justice system. *Child and Adolescent Social Work Journal, 32*(6), 517–527. doi:10.1007/s10560-015-0390-8

Sickmund, M. (2003). *National report series bulletin: Juveniles in court.* Washington, DC: Department of Justice or OJJDP. Retrieved from https://www.ncjrs.gov/pdffiles1/ojjdp/195420.pdf

Siennick, S. E. (2017). Drawing, and redrawing, the line between juvenile and adult court jurisdiction. *Criminology & Public Policy, 16*(1), 41–44.

Slobogin, C. (2013). Treating juveniles like juveniles: Getting rid of transfer and expanded adult court jurisdiction. *Texas Tech Law Review, 46*, 13–37.

Steinberg, L. (2013). The influence of neuroscience on US Supreme Court decisions about adolescents' criminal culpability. *Nature Reviews Neuroscience, 14*(7), 513–518.

Sweeten, G., Piquero, A., & Steinberg, L. (2013). Age and the explanation of crime, revisited. *Journal of Youth and Adolescence, 42*(6), 921–938. doi:10.1007/s10964-013-9926-4

Swisher v. Brady, No. No. 77–653, 438 204 (Supreme Court 1978).

Tappan, P. W. (1949). *Juvenile delinquency.* New York, NY: McGraw-Hill Companies.

Taylor, M. (2015). Juvenile transfers to adult court: An examination of the long-term outcomes of transferred and non-transferred juveniles. *Juvenile and Family Court Journal, 66*(4), 29–47. doi:10.1111/jfcj.12050

Tremblay, R. E., & Craig, W. M. (1995). Developmental crime prevention. *Crime and Justice, 19*, 151–236. doi:10.2307/1147597

Wagner, P., & Rabuy, B. (2017). *Mass incarceration: The whole pie 2017.* Retrieved from www.prisonpolicy.org/reports/pie2017.html

Western, B., & Pettit, B. (2010). *Collateral costs: incarceration's effect on economic mobility.* Washington, DC: Pew Charitable Trusts. Retrieved from http://www.pewtrusts.org/~/media/legacy/uploadedfiles/pcs_assets/2010/collateralcosts1pdf.pdf

Wildeman, C. (2014). Parental incarceration, child homelessness, and the invisible consequences of mass imprisonment. *The ANNALS of the American Academy of Political and Social Science, 651*(1), 74–96.

Woolard, J. L., Odgers, C., Lanza-Kaduce, L., & Daglis, H. (2005). Juveniles within adult correctional settings: Legal pathways and developmental considerations. *International Journal of Forensic Mental Health, 4*(1), 1–18. doi:10.1080/14999013.2005.10471209

Zang, A. (2016). *U.S. age boundaries of delinquency (JJGPS State Scan).* Pittsburg, PA: National Center for Juvenile Justice.

19
MASS INCARCERATION IN JAIL AND FAMILY VISITATION

Emma Conner

Introduction

As mass incarceration has exploded over the past 40 years, scholars have developed an ever-increasing body of research that seeks to uncover the experiences of individuals entangled in the criminal justice system, including the children and families of incarcerated individuals (Hagan & Dinovitzer, 1999; Patillo, Western, & Weiman, 2004; Christian, 2005; Comfort, 2002). Between 1991 and 2007, the number of parents in prison increased by 79% (Glaze & Maruschak, 2008). An estimated 2.7 million children were affected by parental incarcerated, accounting for 2.3% of the population under the age of 18 years old (Western, 2006). More than 5 million children have *ever* experienced parental incarceration, a statistic that likely underestimates the true population (Murphey & Cooper, 2015). As a result, a burgeoning body of literature has developed to consider the myriad ways parental incarceration impacts family outcomes including marriage (Wakefield & Wildeman, 2014), financial status (Geller, Garfinkel, & Western, 2011), children's academic performance (Murray, Loeber, & Pardini, 2012) and behavioral outcomes (Perry & Bright, 2012; Wildeman, 2010; Wakefield & Wildeman, 2014; Bloom & Steinhart, 1993), and intergenerational criminality and system–involvement (van de Rakt, Murray, & Nieuwbeerta, 2012; Huebner & Gustafson, 2007; Roettger & Swisher, 2011; Besemer et al., 2011; Murray & Farrington, 2008), amongst others.

Despite the scholarly attention to the phenomenon of mass incarceration and literature devoted to children of incarcerated parents, there remains a gap in the extant knowledge regarding key experiences of children and families affected by a major piece of the criminal justice apparatus: jails. The lack of research on jails is anomalous in itself, given the large role jails play in the function of the prison industrial complex (see Cochran & Toman, Chapter 14 in this volume), and more troubling because the unique correctional functions and attributes of jail have potential impacts for children and families that have yet to be identified and addressed. Preliminary research indicates that even short, low-level contact with the criminal justice system can create family turmoil (Comfort, 2016), but it is unknown how this compares to the collateral consequences of longer-term parental incarceration.

The extant literature on families of incarcerated individuals theorizes that maintaining connections during incarceration helps prisoner reentry by strengthening social bonds and social capital and reducing general strain (Bales & Mears, 2008; Cochran & Mears, 2013; Dyer, Pleck, & McBride, 2012). Likewise, for the family of incarcerated loved ones, maintaining bonds can reduce strain and help maintain attachment between parents and children (Snyder, Carlo, & Coats Mullins, 2002;

Pollock, 2003), though visitation itself can also increase strain, negative emotions, and trauma (Arditti, 2003; Arditti, 2012; Comfort, 2003). While factors such as distance and cost have been empirically established as a barrier to visitation (Braman, 2001; Christian, 2005), they are not systematically linked to jurisdiction, although state or county confinement may overlap with these barriers. Additionally, the emotional trauma of visitation for both family and the incarcerated individual is likely to vary by the nature of the relationship prior to arrest, criminal history, length of incarceration, and visitation setting. To the extent that these dimensions also vary by prison and jail, they merit systematical consideration by those who study visitation as a primary collateral consequence of jail incarceration.

In the following sections, I enjoin the literature on mass incarceration in jail with the burgeoning empirical literature on visiting and family processes during incarceration. In this overview, first I will discuss what makes the jail a unique carceral space worthy of further investigation. Then I will review the extant literature on the collateral consequences of incarceration for families and children, focusing specifically on visitation. Next, I will advance a research agenda that calls for an integration of these analytic areas, with specific attention given to the way in which mass incarceration in jail impacts visitation and connectedness for children and families. I will conclude with a consideration of current visitation policies and recommendations.

Mass Incarceration in Jail

In the United States, over 2.3 million people are held in confinement in state and federal prisons, local jails, juvenile facilities, and immigration detention centers (Wagner & Rabuy, 2017). Despite the massive role of jail in the overall growth and function of the criminal justice system (Subramanian, Henrichson, & Kang-Brown, 2015), scholarship on mass incarceration typically focuses on prisons, including the experience of individuals inside prison (Clemmer, 1940; Sykes, 1958; Jacobs, 1977; Rhodes, 2004); the reentry process from prison (Petersilia, 2003; Maruna, 2001 Visher & Travis, 2003); and collateral consequences of incarceration for employment opportunities (Pager, 2003; Geller et al., 2011; Western & Pettit, 2005), housing, (Geller & Curtis, 2011; Wildeman, 2014), mental and physical health (Haney, 2003; James & Glaze, 2006; Schnittker & John, 2007), and family outcomes (Braman, 2001; Comfort, 2002, Wakefield & Wildeman, 2014; Wildeman, Turney, & Yi, 2016). In comparison to this thorough literature, the information regarding the experiences of those facing jail is underdeveloped (see Cochran & Toman, Chapter 14 in this volume). Nevertheless, understanding what goes on in jails, and the lives of those impacted by jail, is important for their sheer size, with 3,163 local jails in the United States (Wagner & Rabuy, 2017). Additionally, compared to prison, jails serve multiple functions, including a stopping point on the way to prison, as well as a primary agency to manage local social problems, such as civilian drug use, interpersonal conflict, and violence (Simon, 2016).

Like the growth in prison incarceration, the proliferation of jails during the 1980s led to a current average daily population of 728,000 individuals in jails, up from 250,000 individuals in the 1980s (Minton & Zeng, 2016). Similarly, jail incarceration disproportionately affects people of color and women (Subramanian et al., 2015). Black individuals comprised approximately 35% of the jail population in 2014 but only 13% of the general population. While the nationwide jail incarceration rate for Latino individuals is 269 per 100,000 people, 3 times lower than Black people, it reaches 1,032 per 100,000 in Pennsylvania, 934 per 100,000 in New Mexico, and 917 per 100,000 in Massachusetts (Subramanian et al., 2015). Further, the number of women in jail has increased 14-fold since 1970, to nearly 110,000 nationwide (Swavola, Riley, & Subramanian, 2016).

Despite some significant similarities between prison and jail—hyperincarceration of people of color and more recently, women—the characteristics of jails diverge from prison in a number of important ways. While the average daily population of people in jail accounts for approximately 27% of those in confinement, (Carson & Anderson, 2016), this snapshot of jail incarceration does not include the enormous churn that includes the almost 12 million admissions to jail every year (Wagner & Rabuy, 2017). Thus, while the average daily population of prisons is higher than jails, jails admit and release far more people every year. Despite this quick turnover, the average length of stay increased 2.5 times between 1978 and 2014 from nine to 23 days (Subramanian, Delaney, Roberts, Fishman, & McGarry, 2015), essentially doubling the overall U.S. jail population. Notwithstanding this growth, we know little about its effects on those who cycle in and out of jail or their families.

The average length of stay obscures the fact that many localities are high above the average, such as Philadelphia (89 days; Subramanian, Henrichson, & Kang-Brown, 2015). And yet, the overall growth in jail incarceration is primarily driven from small and mid-sized counties. Just under half of all jail prisoners are held in small counties, and the fastest growth is in rural and suburban communities rather than urban areas since 1970 (Subramanian et al., 2015. Again, for both people of color and women, small counties are the main driver of this growth. Thus, a significant minority of individuals in jail remain for an extended period of time—weeks, months, or years—and drive up the average length of stay, but complicating the story, the majority of growth is due to rapid cycling of individuals through jails in smaller counties, rather than notorious super-jails.

Perhaps the most significant difference between prisons and jails is the diverse use of jails compared to prisons (Subramanian, Henrichson, & Kang-Brown, 2015). While individuals incarcerated in prison have been convicted of an offense and sentenced, those in jail are there for pretrial detention, low-level misdemeanors, violation or parole or probation, bed-rentals/state decarceration, and immigration detention (Bureau of Justice Statistics, 2017; Wagner & Rabuy, 2017). The growth in local jails is driven largely from the pretrial population, including individuals who are too poor to pay bail (Rabuy & Kopf, 2017). Approximately 60% to 70% of jail prisoners on any given day have not been convicted of any crime (Subramanian, Delaney, et al., 2015). Family dynamics may be different for these individuals than for an incarcerated parent in prison who has been sentenced to a determinate amount of time and convicted of an offense. The uncertainty of the future and the financial hardship of attorney fees, collect calls, and inmate needs may be an unrecognized burden that affects jail visitation (Arditti, 2003; Arditti, Lambert-Shute & Joest, 2003; Comfort, 2016).

Similar to pretrial detention, immigration detention keeps individuals in confinement with no end in sight. While 60% of the 380,000 to 442,000 people held in detention each year are in privately run facilities, many are detained in local jails (CIVIC, 2016). They are not guaranteed a right to visit family and are often more disconnected from their communities than other individuals in jail. Comparatively, even less is known regarding the demographics of these visitors and their added obstacles, such as the vulnerability associated with an undocumented status (Patler & Branic, 2017).

A final and increasingly popular trend in jail incarceration is bed-rental for state and federal agencies, particularly for the purpose of state decarceration. Up to 22% of those incarcerated in jail are being held for another agency. This practice is particularly common in rural areas, where state beds can be outsourced to local jails for profit (Subramanian, Delaney, et al., 2015). Approximately 45,000 individuals, or 6% of the jail population, is held on behalf of federal authorities such as the U.S. Marshals and U.S. Immigration and Customs Enforcement (Wagner & Rabuy, 2017). In 2011, the Supreme Court ordered California to reduce its prison overcrowding (Lofstrom & Raphael, 2016), and as a result, California has joined a group of approximately 20 other states that since the 1990s have contracted with local jails to house state prisoners for longer than a one-year sentence that would typically have been served in a state facility (Albert, 2010). While there are some seemingly obvious benefits for relocating individuals closer to home for longer sentences, these efforts have not been systematically evaluated. Prison policies, including visitation rules, can apply to a mostly uniform group, legally speaking, while jails must accommodate a heterogeneous group of individuals, including those who have not been convicted of a crime, or additionally face civil charges in the case of immigration detention (Cramer, Goff, Peterson, & Sandstrom, 2017; Boudin, Stutz, & Littman, 2013).

In the following section, I will review the literature on the collateral consequences of incarceration on children and families, with a particular eye towards the aforementioned circumstances of jail incarceration and visiting. In this section, I will present three recommendations for lines of inquiry regarding jail incarceration and family visitation.

Family Visitation and Jail

The effects of incarceration reach outward beyond the prisoner to families, particularly children. Nationally, it is estimated that over 1.1 million incarcerated men are fathers and 120,000 women are mothers of minor children (National Resource Center on Children & Families of the Incarcerated, 2014). In California alone, there are 503,000 children who have had a parent in prison, and 13% of Kentucky's children have experienced parental incarceration (Murphey & Cooper, 2015). Parental incarceration is a distinctly racialized experience, with Black and Latino children 2 to 7 times more likely than White children to experience it in their life (Annie E. Casey Foundation, 2016). While a substantial number of children experience the incarceration of parents in federal and state facilities, these numbers disclose little about the lives of children and parents under the control of local jail facilities.

Consequently, there is a sizable body of literature on family experience with incarceration generally, and the research suggests deleterious effects (see Northcutt Bohmert & Wakefield in Chapter 8 of this volume for an in-depth discussion). The literature on children's outcomes has established that children of incarcerated parents are less likely to reunite with their parent post-release and are economically worse off (Wakefield & Wildeman, 2014; Geller et al., 2011), notwithstanding prior poverty and substance abuse in many cases (Wakefield & Wildeman, 2014; Perry & Bright, 2012). A substantial body of literature on the long-term consequences of paternal incarceration establishes that children of incarcerated parents are more likely to exhibit problem behavior as children (Murray & Murray, 2010; Dallaire, Ciccone, & Wilson, 2010; Hagan & Dinovitzer, 1999), delinquency as adolescents, (Geller, 2013; Murray, Loeber, & Pardini, 2012), and are convicted of crimes as adults (Roettger et al., 2010, Roettger & Swisher, 2011; Foster & Hagan, 2007; Huebner & Gustafson, 2007). Additionally, evidence suggests that children of incarcerated parents exhibit more health problems and academic difficulties than their peers (Johnson & Easterling, 2012; Murray & Farrington, 2005; Murray et al., 2012; Wildeman, Wakefield, & Turney, 2013). Notably, the literature focuses on parental incarceration in general, both in jails and in prisons—or in prison only.

To the extent that outcomes associated with incarceration can be mitigated by a reinforced connection with the parent, visitation is viewed as vital for children to develop a secure attachment to their parent, see that their parent is physically unharmed, and spend quality time with him or her (Arditti, 2003; Murray & Murray, 2010; Dyer, Pleck, & McBride, 2012). Further, although prosocial ties with the children or other family prior to incarceration may not have been sufficient to prevent offending (Maruna, 2001; Cochran, 2014), maintaining ties to social networks outside of prison is considered helpful for a prisoner's success post-release (Petersilia, 2003). While these ties may contribute to the "pains of imprisonment" (Sykes, 1958) during incarceration, they may also reduce strain by alleviating feelings of isolation and help provide something to look forward to (Bales & Mears, 2008; Duwe & Clark, 2013). This, in turn, may reduce misconduct, violence, and misbehavior during incarceration (Siennick, Mears, & Bales, 2012; Cochran, 2012). Further, visits may strengthen social bonds so that social networks are stronger upon post-release. Prisoners who receive visits may be better suited to find housing, employment, and social support and have a smoother re-entry, with lower rates of recidivism (Cochran & Mears, 2013).

Though visitation to jail and prison are often studied together empirically, the lived experience is quite different. While prison visits are often "contact" and therefore allow parents and children to touch, jail visitation is usually in a booth or overcrowded row of telephones (Rabuy & Wagner,

2015). Additionally, visitation to prisons often lasts several hours, whereas jail visitation resembles an assembly line, with families visiting for 20 minutes through Plexiglas before the next family takes their place. Seated around a table, families in prison can buy food, talk, play games, and touch and kiss (Poehlmann, Dallaire, Loper, & Shear, 2010; Cramer et al., 2017; Boudin, Stutz, & Littman, 2013). Visitation in a prison visiting room much more closely resembles family life and intimate moments like sharing food, helping with homework, and engaging in play (Comfort, 2002). Some prisons have added play areas, including toys and games, so that parents and children can play together and children will be less frightened and intimated by the prison environment (Arditti, 2003; Arditti, Lambert-Shute, & Joest, 2003). While entry procedures to local jails may be slightly less invasive because of less security, the visiting is less intimate and may be more traumatic for children who can only see their parent through glass and cannot make contact (Cramer et al., 2017).

Although there is far less scholarly attention, both institutions are increasingly providing video visitation, at times without the opportunity for face-to-face visitation (Fulcher, 2013, Phillips, 2012). The implementation of video visitation varies slightly but includes visitation over a live video rather than face-to-face, with technology that is often expensive but poorly placed in each facility and outdated. "Prison Skype" is sometimes offered for free to encourage video visitation rather than in-person visits, but is often costly and can cost the visitor up to $1.50 a minute for a 20-minute virtual session (Rabuy & Wagner, 2015).

Despite these substantial differences in type of visitation, the conceptual framework of the proposed outcomes, benefits, and drawbacks of visitation are based upon studies of prison, with scant data from jail (Wildeman et al., 2016; Arditti, 2003; Arditti et al., 2003; Apel, 2016). The few studies of jail reveal the need to broaden the scope of the visitation literature to include a wider breadth of jail studies. Apel (2016) found that a median of one month in jail or prison predicted an immediate and persistent decrease in the likelihood of marriage. This finding, though based on prison and jail, indicates the effects of incarceration occur early on (Northcutt Bohmert & Wakefield, 2018). Arditti's (2003) study of 56 caregiver and child visitors to one jail revealed that after an average of 4.2 months of parental incarceration, a full two-thirds of caregivers reported they were much worse off financially. This change in financial circumstance pushed many families over the poverty line, due to a loss of income from the incarcerated parent, child support, attorney fees, collect calls from jail, and money for the parent's needs in jail. System-involved families may find it more difficult to withstand parental incarceration as an additional risk in an accumulation of disadvantages, in addition to existing economic insecurity, lack of opportunity, and structural inequality (Arditti, 2003; Dallaire, 2007; Johnson & Waldfogel, 2002).

Additionally, 55.6% of Arditti's sample reported frequently not wanting to visit, although 59.3% of the incarcerated parents nevertheless received weekly visits. Comparatively, 4.6% of parents in state prison and 5.9% of parents in federal facilities reported weekly visits, while 58.5% and 44.7% report no visits, respectively (Glaze & Maruschak, 2008). A likely factor contributing to the different rates in visitation is the distance between visitors and incarcerated parents. While mothers incarcerated in state prison are an average of 160 miles from home and fathers are an average of 100 miles (Travis, McBride, & Solomon, 2005), the parents in Arditti's (2003) sample were an average of 18.4 miles. The relatively shorter distance might help to mitigate the difficult feelings related to visitation, creating less of an overall sense of burden.

More than half of Arditti's sample reported that their visits went very badly, while only three participants reported the visits went very well. This statistic may indicate that the visiting conditions of most jails are exceptionally harmful. Many visitors reported a serious problem with visiting was the Plexiglas barrier and lack of contact (Arditti, 2003). This fundamental difference in visiting between most jails and prisons represents not only a physical condition of the room but an emotionally painful and traumatic condition of visitation that undermines the ability to connect and thrive (Cramer et al., 2017). This lack of contact, rude and demeaning behavior from staff, and lack of privacy during visitation reflect the experience of "secondary prisonization" described by Comfort (2003) in her study of women partners of men incarcerated at San Quentin State Prison.

On the other hand, Arditti found that 32% of her sample reported that the current period of incarceration solved a problem because it allowed the incarcerated parent to "straighten out" or become sober and learn a lesson from the experience. This feeling, although reported amongst families of parents incarcerated in state and federal facilities (Northcutt Bohmert & Wakefield, 2018), may be more salient for parents who cycle in and out of the criminal justice system frequently, violate parole or probation, or have acute mental health problems, issues endemic to jail (Subramanian, Delaney, et al., 2015).

While the studies cited above, as well as the Bureau of Justice Statistics census provide a foundational understanding of visitation to jail, they highlight several gaps to be filled. In the following section I will advance three basic lines of inquiry in order to more fully understand the consequences of parental incarceration of jail for family visitation. These research questions will inform empirical understanding, theory, and policy recommendations for parental visitation in jail.

Advancing a Research Agenda

Recommendation 1.1—Examine Which Parents Go to Jail and Why

The aforementioned studies indicate that there are differences in who goes to jail and the experience of visiting. The Bureau of Justice Statistics should expand its annual census of jail inmates in order to provide a nationally representative, large dataset for researchers and policy makers to utilize. Currently, the annual census of jail inmates collects data on population and capacity by jurisdiction, offense, race, and gender, most broadly. In contrast, the Survey of Inmates in State and Federal Correctional Facilities collects this data, plus information regarding the number of incarcerated parents and their children (Bureau of Justice Statistics, 2016). *Parents in Prison and Their Minor Children* (Glaze & Maruschak, 2008), based on information from the Survey of Inmates in State and Federal Correctional Facilities, covers demographic information, including how many mothers and fathers are incarcerated in state and federal facilities; the race of incarcerated parents and their children; the age of incarcerated parents and their children; the living arrangements prior to incarceration; the financial contribution of parents prior to incarceration; the commitment crime of parents; the current caregiver of the children; the access to classes and work assignments for parents; and most importantly, various measures of contact between incarcerated parents and children.

A counterpart is necessary for parents and children affected by jail. The annual census should also determine how many parents in jail have not been convicted of an offense; how many are serving a short-term sentence; how many have violated parole or probation; and how many are serving a state sentence. In short, an annual census will allow researchers and policy makers to determine the representativeness of pioneering qualitative work (Arditti, 2003; Arditti et al., 2003) and examine trends in inmate composition and sentencing changes (i.e., in pre-trial detention and bail) and associated changes in jail visiting. Do parents incarcerated in jail receive the same number of visits as parents in prison? Do parents who cycle in and out of jail frequently receive fewer visits? Do parents in jail have the same financial difficulties prior to and immediately after incarceration? Who takes care of their children after they are incarcerated? Does this vary depending on why the parent is incarcerated? How many families use video visitation? Do incarcerated parents do better post-release if they receive visits, even for a short period of time? With answers to these questions, it will be possible to more fully examine how the experience of visiting is impacted.

We also know little about the services provided to parents incarcerated in jail. A standardized, annual survey would greatly improve our knowledge and ability to develop policies surrounding what is needed in terms of parenting classes, substance abuse and mental health services, and employment and housing post-release. All of these services impact the ability for parents to effectively parent both in jail and after they are released (Mears & Cochran, 2014; Swavola et al., 2016). Moreover, the likelihood for caregivers and children to attempt to interact with incarcerated parents who are in need of assistance may depend on the ability for these parents to access services while incarcerated (Hairston, Rollin, & Jo, 2004; Bales & Mears, 2008). Therefore, it is essential to determine on a national level who receives what services in jail.

Recommendation 1.2—Examine the Differences in Logistical Obstacles of Family Visiting in Jail Compared to Prison

In addition to developing a fuller understanding of which parents are in jail and who their children and caregivers are, research is also needed to assess the experience of visitation in jail compared to prison. It is suggested that because jails are closer to home, it is better for families (Arditti, 2003; Bales & Mears, 2008; Christian, 2009; Hickert, Tahamont, & Bushway, 2017). Logistical barriers, such as cost, distance, and time, may be less burdensome when traveling to a local jail but still present a significant obstacle to visiting. Additionally, research suggests that visitation in jail is emotionally painful and traumatic, similar to visitation in prison (Arditti, 2003; Arditti et al., 2003; Cramer et al., 2017). Further study is required to assess the unique challenges of jail, particularly in relation to prison, before it is hailed as a better alternative for families.

One of the major obstacles to visitation is economic hardship. Families suffer the loss of income and in-kind support once their loved one is incarcerated (Glaze & Maruschak, 2008; Braman, 2001; Geller et al., 2011; Wacquant, 2009). Individuals with a criminal record face "negative credentialing" (Pager, 2003) that may permanently alter a family's economic chances post-release and exacerbate existing poverty. The individuals in jail who are too poor to pay bail are more likely to eventually be convicted of a crime, face a longer sentence, and therefore lose employment during incarceration in jail, not only prison (Rabuy & Kopf, 2017; Gupta, Hansman, & Frenchman, 2016; Sacks & Ackerman, 2014). Visiting a loved one may require the cost of taking time off work; public transportation or gas; and food before, during and after the visit, particularly if it is far away (Christian, 2005; Comfort, 2003). Video visitation can be expensive (Rabuy & Wagner, 2015), and families of incarcerated people are more likely to already face poverty and economic insecurity (Cramer et al., 2017). Additionally, they are the least likely to have access to a computer or device with a webcam and necessary bandwidth (Cramer et al., 2017). As Arditti found (2003), two-thirds of her sample felt an immediate economic hardship after their loved one was incarcerated in jail.

Thus, for the disproportionately poor and minority individuals who remain incarcerated in jail prior to conviction, jail is likely to constrain the ability for family to visit. In the case of a disposition that does not involve incarceration, the economic setbacks that occur during jail alone can have lasting effects for an individual and extend outward to the family and children in terms of housing, employment, and well-being (Schwartz-Soicher, Geller, & Garfinkel, 2011; Arditti, Smock, & Parkman, 2005; Christian, Mellow, & Thomas, 2006; Arditti, 2003; Johnson & Waldfogel, 2002; Northcutt Bohmert & Wakefield, 2018). Therefore, the issue of cost of visiting in jail versus prison merits further consideration. What is the average cost for a caregiver and child to visit a parent in prison compared to jail? How does this compare for a parent in jail who does not have a determinate sentence? Does the cost become prohibitive over time? How do families budget for in-person or video visits when both are available? Does this change once a parent is sentenced to a state or federal prison? All of these questions have implications for policy and the daily lives of incarcerated parents, their children, and their children's caregivers.

Relatedly, distance is frequently cited as a barrier to visitation (Christian, 2005; Bales & Mears, 2008; Poehlmann et al., 2010). However, there is little information on how distance actually affects a family's decision to visit a parent. Video visitation in some locations, such as Dallas County, requires families to travel to on-site terminals for a virtual visit (Rabuy & Wagner, 2015). Families in the many small and mid-sized counties that have experienced a surge in incarceration rates may find visiting a local jail is substantially easier than prison, though the majority of incarceration in jail still occurs in urban areas that may be difficult and lengthy to reach (Subramanian, Henrichson, & Kang-Brown, 2015). For example, families who visit urban super-jails like Rikers Island can spend several hours on public transportation from any of the boroughs in New York City or the surrounding metropolitan area. Additionally, in large states such as California, if an individual is arrested in Los Angeles County but resides in neighboring San Bernardino County, families could have to travel over 100 miles. Therefore, a local jail may be more convenient for some families but intractable for others. Does the distance to the jail deter families from visiting? Does it depend on whether the visit is contact, non-contact, or video? Does this depend on why the parent is in jail? Does it depend on how long he or she will be in jail? Does it depend on his or her history in jail? These questions are unanswered but likely influence a family's decision to visit, and grapple with the distance and related cost of visiting.

Recommendation 1.3—Examine the Experience of Family Visiting in Jail Compared to Prison

Most importantly, the emotional experience of visiting each location can vary significantly in several physical ways that impact the potential for families to reconnect and add to the logistical obstacles. Visitation provides one of the only opportunities for parents and children to mend broken connections and discuss the event or circumstances that led to incarceration (Arditti, 2005; Pierce, 2015; Mignon & Ransford, 2012; Comfort, 2002). Visitation may theoretically provide a space for families to maintain or strengthen social bonds and parents to strengthen social capital (Christian et al., 2006; Duwe & Clark, 2013). The conditions of jail visitation, as noted by Arditti (2003), are especially undesirable for fostering these interactions and relationships. Visitors to jail, like prison, submit to the rules of the institution, surveillance, loss of freedom, and "pains of imprisonment" (Sykes, 1958) when they visit, thus experiencing "secondary prisonization" (Comfort, 2003). Visitors are forced to submit to searches of their person and belongings, which can be frightening and traumatic to children (Arditti, 2003; Sturges, 2001; Hairston, 1991; Johnston, 1995). Additionally, these searches may appear arbitrary and change from visit to visit, treating visitors as though they are also prisoners, and reduce the quality of the visit according to visitors (Sturges, 2001; Pierce, 2015; Cramer et al., 2017). Visitation to both jails and prisons involve waiting rooms that are large and hectic with metal detectors, searches, and possibly waits of over an hour (Cramer et al., 2017; Arditti et al., 2003; Comfort, 2002; Comfort, 2003).

Although relatively little is known about how visitation in prison and jail works, a trending solution to the surfeit of visitors in over 500 local jails and state prisons has been to use video visitation (Rabuy & Wagner, 2015). Jails and prisons prefer video visitation because of the reported safety benefits, although there is little evidence to prove video visitation has reduced the entry of contraband into facilities that have replaced in-person visitation (Cramer et al., 2017, Fulcher, 2013). In addition to the financial burden of video visitation, families find it more alienating (Sturges & Al-Khattar, 2009). Frequent glitches and pixilation precludes eye contact and feelings of intimacy. It can be more difficult to conduct private visitations with loved ones, as incarcerated parents are often surrounded by other prisoners (Rabuy & Wagner, 2015). Although distance may be the most common factor prohibiting visitors from visiting state prisons, jails utilize video visitation more often than state facilities and are more likely to completely replace in-person visitation with video visitation (Cramer et al., 2017). In reference to the benefit of video visitation versus in-person visitation, Illinois Department of Corrections Spokesman Tom Shaer explained, "I can't imagine the scenario in which someone would travel to a prison and then wish to communicate through a video screen rather than see a prisoner face-to-face" (Rabuy & Wagner, 2015, p. 6). This attitude regarding video visitation signifies an understanding that it is unfair to travel a long distance and not see a family member. However, it ignores the frustration and ambiguous loss of families impacted by jail: living close by, but not being able to have in-person contact. In California, state lawmakers voted in 2017 to require all but eight California county jails to provide the space for in-person visitation in response to public protest after the elimination of face-to-face visitation in jails (Ulloa, 2017).

These variable conditions of visiting in jail and prison suggest that the goals of visitation—connection, stability, conflict resolution—are attainable to a varying degree, in part depending on whether a parent is incarcerated in a local or state setting. While an unknown number of families are unable to visit prison because of its distance, similarly, an unknown number of families choose not to visit jail because of the short length of visits and likely do not return because they find the visits awkward and distressing. For those who do visit, it seems exceedingly difficult to parent or maintain a connection with a growing child through glass for a short period of time. Similarly, further research is needed to evaluate the outcomes of extended use of video visitation. How do families account for the physical attributes of the visiting room in their decision to visit? Does the Plexiglas barrier or video screen in many jail visiting rooms deter caregivers and children from visiting parents? Does it deter parents from wanting to see their children? Do families weigh the privacy and contact of a jail visit with its relative ease in terms of distance and cost? Do families visit prison more often because most visits are contact, despite the distance and cost?

As mentioned previously, in 2011, California passed AB109, or public safety realignment, in order to address prison overcrowding. The resulting network of policies transferred the responsibility for non-violent, non-serious, and non-sexual offenders as well as parole violators to the county from the state (Lofstrom & Martin, 2015). As a result, there are currently almost 2,000 men and women serving more than five-year sentences in county jails that would have previously received day-long contact visits in prison but are now subject to the visitation policy of each individual jail (Lofstrom & Raphael, 2016). How does the visitation experience of these men and women compare with men and women in state prison in California with similar sentences and comparable histories? How do their families make decisions about whether or not to visit? If they have been incarcerated in jail previously, is visitation in jail different when their sentence is longer? How do individual jail policies, which are subject to local jurisdiction, compare to each other? California is a useful case study to examine the tension and similarity between the experience of visiting a parent in jail and prison.

Policy Recommendations

Given the scholarship on the complexity of visitation, I will now present three recommendations for policy based on what is presently known regarding visitation to jail and familial connectedness. Policy should focus on reducing obstacles for families, improving the visitation experience, and tailoring it to the jail setting as much as possible. In the section below, first, I will discuss the increased use of video visitation as a substitution for in-person visitation. Then, I will make recommendations for the processing or waiting room as an untapped area for potential to improve visitation between incarcerated parents and their children. Finally, I will discuss the potential to individualize jail visitation policies and parenting programs, given the local and autonomous nature of jails compared to prisons (Cochran & Toman, 2018).

First, video visitation is a useful tool for loved ones who are unable to visit a facility. Families are able to avoid the cost of travel and time off work, as well as any other expenses associated with the half-day or full-day journey to jails or prisons (Cramer et al., 2017). In order for video visitation to be a tool within reach for more families, it should be offered remotely for visitors and not in on-site terminals, as in locations such as Dallas County (Rabuy & Wagner, 2015). Otherwise, it is as burdensome, less fulfilling, and more distressing. Additionally, video visitation should be offered free-of-charge to incarcerated individuals and their families, who are often the least able to deal with the additional costs of video visitation and required technology (Cramer et al., 2017). In Racine County, Wisconsin, for example, the incarceration rate is 534.2 per 100,000 people (compared to the state average of 329.6 and the national average of 339.2), families can pay $29.95 for a 20-minute video visit if they have the Securus Video Visit application (Rabuy & Wagner, 2015). This practice is in contradiction to recommendations from the American Bar Association and American Correctional Association that incarcerated individuals have access to "family friendly communication policies" (Rabuy & Wagner, 2015, p. 22).

Second, the waiting area is rarely mentioned in policy discussions but is an unused area for improvement for family visitation (Arditti et al., 2003). Almost three-quarters of visitors to a jail in Virginia stated the wait to see their loved one was a slight to serious problem (Arditti, 2003), and one visitor expressed frustration at spending "more time waiting than the actual visit" (p. 123). This time could be used for formal or informal networking and programming for caregivers and children, including referrals to support groups and play areas for children. In addition to improving the conditions of the visit by making the waiting area "child friendly" with books and toys, providing such a section could help foster a sense of community and reduce the stigma and isolation associated with incarceration (Arditti, 2012; Bales & Mears, 2008). Waiting areas should also provide referrals to community resources and social support that are specific to each community. Because jails are run at the local level, it is possible to customize their referrals based on localized welfare policies and social and economic problems such as poverty and drug abuse (Cochran & Toman, 2018).

The local and diverse nature of jails leads to my final policy recommendation: to grow and individualize programs inside jail, particularly those aimed at family and reentry. Because jails are typically smaller and have budget and staffing limits, they may offer fewer programs than prisons (Subramanian, Delaney, et al., 2015). However, specific localities may find that they have a higher proportion of incarcerated parents and it is worthwhile to focus on parenting classes or interventions, particularly if these individuals have not yet been convicted of a crime and will remain incarcerated for an indeterminate amount of time. For example, Community Works, a non-profit in San Francisco, provides services to mothers in jail, including cognitive-behavioral parenting education classes and contact visits (Swavola et al., 2016). Additionally, the organization works at the local level with other agencies that often interact with the criminal justice system, such as child protective services, to increase the likelihood of family reunification post-release (Community Works, 2016). The Family Support Program in Allegheny County, Pennsylvania, provides on-site coached phone calls to provide conflict resolution in case a difficult situation arises during parent-child phone calls (Swavola et al., 2016). Although these programs have not been systematically evaluated, they point to the possibility for jails to enact more hands-on and tailored programs for parents.

Another way jails can tailor their programs to their population and local policies is to include programs for detained immigrants. Although the detained population has grown to 477,000 individuals (Wagner & Rabuy, 2017), few studies analyze the experience of detained immigrants and their families. Early results, though, indicate that family experiences replicate those of non-immigrant detainees (Patler & Branic, 2017). While these cases are handled differently in court, the ambiguous loss that children face—the uncertainty of their parent's future—parallels the experience of children in the criminal justice system (Johnson & Waldfogel, 2002; Arditti, 2012). Children whose parents are detained due to immigration charges would likely benefit from resources and services that demystify the ambiguity surrounding their parent's detainment. Programs such as Community Works that aid in emotional and logistic connection of families would be beneficial for families facing detention, particularly because immigration detention includes the added obstacle of documentation (Patler & Branic, 2017; Brayne, 2014). Services that focus on familial connection and reentry, with attention to cultural and language differences, would be a benefit in jails.

Conclusion

Mass incarceration has not ended, but since 2007, the overall incarceration rate has trended downward (Petersilia & Cullen, 2015). Every year since 2009, the combined prison and federal population declined. Despite political and media rhetoric that suggests a movement away from hyperincarceration, trends in jail incarceration suggest that mass incarceration is not coming to an end (Subramanian et al., 2015). Community corrections, including local jails, is considered by many to be more effective, more humane, and better for families and communities in the long-term (Beckett, Reosti, & Knaphus, 2016) by allowing low-level offenders to be close to home, while keeping serious offenders in prison, though the net effect may remain relatively unchanged.

Public discourse and legislation continues to support mass incarceration, albeit closer to home, which has a significant impact on families of incarcerated individuals. In general, policy makers and families both agree that it is preferable not to send incarcerated parents hundreds of miles away from their homes (Murphey & Cooper, 2015; Christian, 2009), but there must be a critical examination of the realities of visitation to both state and county jail to understand what the rise of local jail means for affected families. While the most obvious difference in visiting a loved one in prison versus jail is that jail is closer and usually more accessible, there are pros and cons of visiting each that are not entirely possible to quantify. Family visitation is an emotional experience that can be positive and negative, largely depending on the level of uncertainty related to the future (Arditti, 2003; Arditti, 2012; Nesmith & Ruhland, 2008), which in turn can be related to whether a parent is incarcerated in jail or prison. Visitation may therefore be imbued with a sense of ambiguity and anxiety that undermines its ability to be therapeutic. Visitation to jail is a double-edged sword in its ability to bring families closer but also create new obstacles and tensions. Given these significant potential impacts of visitation in jail, further research is necessary to inform better theory and policy.

References

Albert, B. (2010). *State prisoners in county jails.* Washington, DC: National Association of Counties.

Annie E. Casey Foundation. (2016). *A shared sentence: The devastating toll of parental incarceration on kids, families, and communities.* Baltimore, MD: Annie E. Casey Foundation.

Apel, R. (2016). The effects of jail and prison confinement on cohabitation and marriage. *The Annals of the American Academy of Political and Social Science, 665*(1), 103–126.

Arditti, J. A. (2003). Locked doors and glass walls: Family visiting at local jail. *Journal of Loss and Trauma, 8*(2), 115–138.

Arditti, J. A. (2005). Families and incarceration: An ecological approach. *Families in Society, 86,* 251–258.

Arditti, J. A. (2012). Child trauma within the context of parental incarceration: A family process perspective. *Journal of family Theory & Review, 4,* 181–219.

Arditti, J. A., Lambert-Shute, J., & Joest, K. (2003). Saturday morning at the jail: Implications of incarceration for families and children. *Family Relations, 52,* 195–204.

Arditti, J. A., Smock, S., & Parkman, T. (2005). "It's been hard to be a father": A qualitative exploration of incarcerated fatherhood. *Fathering, 3,* 267–283.

Bales, W. D., & Mears, D. P. (2008). Prisoner social ties and the transition to society: Does visitation reduce recidivism? *Journal of Research on Crime and Delinquency, 45*(3), 287–321.

Beckett, K., Reosti, A., & Knaphus, E. (2016). The end of an era? Understanding the contradictions of criminal justice reform. *The Annals of the American Academy of Political and Social Science, 664*(1), 238–259.

Besemer, S., van der Geest, V., Murray, J., Catrien, C. J. H., Bijleveld, & Farrington, D. P. (2011). The relationship between parental imprisonment and offspring offending in England and the Netherlands. *British Journal of Criminology, 51,* 413–437.

Bloom B., & Steinhart, D. (1993). *Why punish the children? A reappraisal of the children of Incarcerated mothers in America.* San Francisco: National Council on Crime and Delinquency.

Boudin, C., Stutz, T., & Littman, A. (2013). Prison visitation policies: A fifty-state survey. *Yale Law & Policy Review, 32,* 149–190.

Braman, D. (2001). *Doing time on the outside: Incarceration and family life in urban America.* Ann Arbor, MI: University of Michigan Press.

Brayne, S. (2014). Surveillance and system avoidance: Criminal justice contact and institutional attachment. *American Sociological Review, 79*(3), 367–391.

Bureau of Justice Statistics. (2008). *Survey of inmates in state and federal correctional facilities.* Retrieved from https://www.bjs.gov/index.cfm?ty=dcdetail&iid=275Bureau of Justice Statistics. (2017). *What is the difference between jails and prisons?* Retrieved from www.bjs.gov/index.cfm?ty=qa&iid=322

Carson, E. A., & Anderson, E. (2016). *Prisoners in 2015.* Washington, DC: Bureau of Justice Statistics.

Christian, J. (2005). Riding the bus: Barriers to prison visitation and family management strategies. *Journal of Contemporary Criminal Justice, 21*(1) 31–48.

Christian, J., Mellow, J., & Thomas, S. (2006). Social and economic implications of family connections to prisoners. *Journal of Criminal Justice, 34,* 443–452.

Christian, S. (2009). *Children of incarcerated parents.* Washington, DC: National Conference of State Legislatures.

Clemmer, D. (1940). *The prison community.* New York, NY: Holt, Rinehart, and Winston.

Cochran, J. C. (2012). The ties that bind or the ties that break: Examining the relationship between visitation and prisoner misconduct. *Journal of Criminal Justice, 40,* 433–440.

Cochran, J. C. (2014). Breaches in the wall: Imprisonment, social support, and recidivism. *Journal of Research in Crime and Delinquency, 51*(2), 200–229.

Cochran, J. C., & Mears, D. P. (2013). Social isolation and prisoner behavior: A conceptual framework for theorizing prison visitation and guiding and assessing research. *Journal of Criminal Justice, 41,* 252–261.

Cochran, J. C., & Toman, E. L. (2018). Mass jail incarceration and its consequences. In B. M. Huebner & N. A. Frost (Eds.), *The ASC division on corrections & sentencing volume 3 handbook on the consequences of sentencing & punishment decisions.* New York, NY: Routledge.

Comfort, M. (2002). Papa's house: The prison as domestic and social satellite. *Ethnography, 3*(4), 467–499.

Comfort, M. L. (2003). In the tube at San Quentin: The "secondary prisonization" of women visiting prisoners. *Journal of Contemporary Ethnography, 32*(1), 77–107.

Comfort, M. (2016). "A twenty-hour-a-day job": The impact of frequent low-level justice involvement on family-life. *The Annals of the American Academy of Political and Social Science, 665*(1), 63–79.

Community Initiatives for Visiting Immigrants in Confinement. (2016). *Information for families.* San Francisco, CA: CIVIC.

Community Works Project WHAT! (2016). *We're here and talking.* San Francisco, CA: Community Works.

Cramer, L., Goff, M., Peterson, B., & Sandstrom, H. (2017). *Parent-child visiting practices in prisons and jails.* Washington, DC: Urban Institute.

Dallaire, D. H. (2007). Incarcerated mothers and fathers: A comparison of risks for children and families. *Family Relations, 56,* 440–453.

Dallaire, D. H., Ciccone, A., & Wilson, L. (2010). Teacher's experiences with and expectations of children with incarcerated parents. *Journal of Applied Developmental Psychology, 31*(4), 281–290.

Duwe, G., & Clark, V. (2013). Blessed be the social tie that binds: The effects of prison visitation on offender recidivism. *Criminal Justice Policy Review, 24*(3), 271–296.

Dyer, W. J., Pleck, J. H., & McBride, B. A. (2012). Imprisoned fathers and their family relationships: A 40-year review from a multi-theory view. *Journal of Family Theory & Review, 4,* 20–47.

Foster, H., & Hagan, J. (2007). Incarceration and intergenerational social exclusion. *Social Problems, 54*(4), 399–433.

Foster, H., & Hagan, J. (2009). The mass incarceration of parents in America: Issues of race/ethnicity, collateral damage to children, and prisoner reentry. *Annals of the American Academy of Political and Social Science, 623,* 179–194.

Fulcher, P. A. (2013). The double-edged sword of prison video visitation: Claiming to keep families together while furthering the aims of the prison industrial complex, *Florida A&M Law Review, 9,* 83–112.

Geller, A. (2013). Paternal incarceration and father-child contact in fragile families. *Journal of Marriage and Family, 75,* 1288–1295.

Geller, A., & Curtis, M. A. (2011). A sort of homecoming: Incarceration and the housing security of urban men. *Social Science Research, 11,* 1196–1213.

Geller, A., Garfinkel, I., & Western, B. (2011). Paternal incarceration and support for children in fragile families. *Demography, 48* (1), 25–47.

Glaze, L. E., & Maruschak, E. (2008). *Parents in Prison and their Minor Children.* Washington, DC: Bureau of Justice Statistics Bulletin.

Gupta, A., Hansman, C., & Frenchman, E. (2016). The heavy costs of high bail: Evidence from judge randomization. *Journal of Legal Studies, 45,* 471–505.

Hagan, J., & Dinovitzer, R. (1999). Collateral consequences of imprisonment for children, communities, and prisoners. *Crime and Justice, 26,* 121–162.

Hairston, C. F. (1991). Mothers in jail: Parent-child separation and jail visitation. *Affilia, 6*(2), 9–27.

Hairston, C. F., Rollin, J., & Jo, H. (2004). *Family connections during imprisonment and prisoners' community reentry.* Chicago, IL: Jane Addams Center for Social Policy Research.

Haney, C. (2003). Mental health issues in long-term solitary and 'supermax' confinement. *Crime & Delinquency, 49*(1), 124–156.

Hickert, A., Tahamont, S., & Bushway, S. (2017). A tale of two margins: Exploring the probabilistic processes that generate prison visits in the first two years of incarceration. *Journal of Quantitative Criminology.* Advance online publication. doi:10.1007/s10940-017-9351-z

Huebner, B. M., & Gustafson, R. (2007). The effect of maternal incarceration on adult offspring involvement in the criminal justice system. *Journal of Criminal Justice, 35,* 283–296.

Jacobs, J. (1977). *The penitentiary in mass society.* Chicago, IL: University of Chicago Press.

James, D. J., & Glaze, L. E. (2006). *Mental health problems of prison and jail inmates.* Washington, DC: U.S. Department of Justice, Bureau of Justice Statistics.

Johnson, E. I., & Easterling, B. (2012). Understanding unique effects of parental incarceration on children: Challenges, progress, and recommendations. *Journal of Marriage and Family, 74,* 342–356.

Johnson, E. I., & Waldfogel, J. (2002). Parental incarceration: Recent trends and implications for child welfare. *Social Service Review, 76*(3), 460–479.

Johnston, D. (1995). Parent-child visits in jail. *Children's Environments, 12*(1), 25–38.

Lofstrom, M. & Martin, B. (2015). *Public safety realignment: Impacts so far.* San Francisco, CA: Public Policy Institute of California.

Lofstrom, M., & Raphael, S. (2016). Incarceration and crime. *The Annals of the American Academy of Political and Social Science, 664*(1), 196–220.

Maruna, S. (2001). *Making good: How ex-convicts reform and rebuild their lives.* Washington, DC: American Psychological Association.

Mears, D.P., & Cochran, J.C. (2014). *Prisoner reentry in the era of mass incarceration.* Thousand Oaks, CA: SAGE Publications.

Mignon, S. I., & Ransford, P. (2012). Mothers in prison: Maintaining connections with children. *Social Work in Public Health, 27*(1–2), 69–88.

Minton, T. D., & Zeng, Z. (2016). *Jail inmates in 2015.* Washington, DC: Bureau of Justice Statistics.

Murphey, D., & Cooper, P. M. (2015). *Parents behind bars: What happens to their children?* Bethesda, MD: Child Trends.

Murray, J., & Farrington, D. P. (2005). Parental imprisonment: Effects on boys' antisocial behaviour and delinquency through the life-course. *Journal of Child Pyschology and Psychiatry, 46*(12), 1269–1278.

Murray, J., & Farrington, D., P. (2008). The effects of parental imprisonment on children. *Crime and Justice, 37*(1), 133–206.

Murray, J., Loeber, R., & Pardini, D. (2012). Parental involvement in the criminal justice system and the development of youth theft, marijuana use, depression, and poor academic performance. *Criminology, 50*(1), 255–302.

Murray, J., & Murray, L. (2010). Parental incarceration, attachment and child psycho pathology. *Attachment & Human Development, 12*(4), 289–309.

National Resource Center on Children & Families of the Incarcerated. (2014). *Children and Families of the incarcerated fact sheet.* Camden, NJ.

Nesmith, A., & Ruhland, E. (2008). Children of incarcerated parents: Challenges and resiliency, in their own words. *Children and Youth Services Review, 30,* 1119–1130.

Northcutt Bohmert, M., & Wakefield, S. (2018). Impacts of incarceration on children and families. In B. M. Huebner & N. A. Frost (Eds.), *The ASC division on corrections & sentencing volume 3 handbook on the consequences of sentencing & punishment decisions.* New York, NY: Routledge.

Pager, D. (2003). The mark of a criminal record. *American Journal of Sociology, 108,* 937–975.

Patillo, M., Western, B., & Weiman, D. (2004). *Imprisoning America: The social effects of mass incarceration.* New York, NY: Russel Sage Foundation.

Patler, C., & Branic, N. (2017). Patterns of family visitation during immigration detention. *RSF: The Russell Sage Foundation Journal of the Social Sciences, 3*(4), 18–36.

Perry, A. R., & Bright, M. (2012). African American fathers and incarceration: Paternal involvement and child outcomes. *Social Work in Public Health, 27,* 187–203.

Petersilia, J. (2003). *When prisoners come home: Parole and prisoner reentry.* New York, NY: Oxford University Press.

Petersilia, J., & Cullen, F. T. (2015). Liberal but not stupid: Meeting the promise of downsizing prisons. *Stanford Journal of Criminal Law and Policy, 2*(1), 1–43.

Pierce, M. B. (2015). Male prisoner perceptions of the visitation experience: Suggestions on how prisons can promote prisoner-family relationships. *The Prison Journal, 95*(3), 370–396.

Phillips, S. D. (2012). *Video visits for children whose parents are incarcerated: In whose best Interest?* Washington, DC: The Sentencing Project.

Poehlmann, J., Dallaire, D., Loper, A. B., & Shear, L. D. (2010). Children's contact with their incarcerated parents: Research findings and recommendations. *American Psychologist, 65*(6), 575–598.

Pollock, J. M. (2003). Parenting programs in women's prisons. *Women & Criminal Justice, 14*(1), 131–154.

Rabuy, B., & Kopf, D. (2017). *Detaining the poor: How money bail perpetuates an endless cycle of poverty and jail time.* Northampton, MA: Prison Policy Initiative.

Rabuy, B., & Wagner, P. (2015). *Screening out family time: The for-profit video visitation industry in prisons and jails.* Northampton, MA: Prison Policy Initiative.

Rhodes, L. A. (2004). *Total confinement: Madness and reason in the maximum security prison.* Los Angeles, CA: University of California Press.

Roettger, M. E., & Swisher, R. (2011). Associations of fathers' history of incarceration with sons' delinquency and arrest among black, white, and Hispanic males in the United States. *Criminology, 49*(4), 1109–1147.

Roettger, M. E., Swisher, R. R., Kuhl, D. C., & Chavez, J. (2010). Paternal incarceration and trajectories of marijuana and other illegal drug use from adolescence into young adulthood: Evidence from longitudinal panels of males and females in the United States. *Addiction, 106*, 121–132.

Sacks, M., & Ackerman, A. R. (2014). Bail and sentencing: Does pretrial detention lead to harsher punishment? *Criminal Justice Policy Review, 25*(1), 59–77.

Schnittker, J., & John, A. (2007). Enduring stigma: The long-term effects of incarceration on health. *Journal of Health and Social Behavior, 48*(2), 115–130.

Schwartz-Soicher, O., Geller, A., & Garfinkel, I. (2011). The effect of parental incarceration on material hardship. *Social Service Review, (85)*3, 447–473.

Siennick, S. E., Mears, D. P., & Bales, W. D. (2012). Here and gone: Anticipation and separation effects of prison visits on inmate infractions. *Journal of Research in Crime and Delinquency, 50*(3), 417–444.

Simon, J. (2014). *Mass incarceration on trial: A remarkable court decision and the future of Prisons in America.* New York, NY: New Press.

Simon, J. (2016). The new goal. *The Annals of the American Academy of Political and Social Science, 664*(1), 280–301.

Snyder, Z. K., Carlo, T. A., & Coats Mullins, M. M. (2002). Parenting from prison. *Marriage & Family Review, 32*(3–4), 33–61.

Sturges, J. E. (2001). Visitation at county jails: Potential policy implications. *Criminal Justice Policy Review, 13*(1), 32–45.

Sturges, J. E., & Al-Khattar, A. M. (2009). Survey of jail visitors about visitation policies. *The Prison Journal, 89*(4), 482–496.

Subramanian, R., Delaney, R., Roberts, S., Fishman, N., & McGarry, P. (2015). *Incarceration's front door: The misuse of jails in America.* New York, NY: Vera Institute of Justice.

Subramanian, R., Henrichson, C., & Kang-Brown, J. (2015). *In our own backyard: Confronting growth and disparities in American jails.* New York, NY: Vera Institute of Justice.

Swavola, E., Riley, K., & Subramanian, R. (2016). *Overlooked: Women and jails in an era of reform.* New York, NY: Vera Institute of Justice.

Sykes, G. M. (1958). *The society of captives.* Princeton, NJ: Princeton University Press.

Travis, J., McBride, E. C., & Solomon, A. L. (2005). *Families left behind: The hidden costs of reentry.* Washington, DC: Urban Institute Justice Policy Center.

Ulloa, J. (2017). Lawmakers try again to sway Gov. Jerry Brown on more jail visits for families. Retrieved from latimes.com

Van de Rakt, M., Murray, J., & Nieuwbeerta, P. (2012). The long-term effects of parental imprisonment on criminal trajectories of children. *Journal of Research in Crime and Delinquency, 49*, 81–108.

Visher, C. A., & Travis, J. (2003). Transitions from prison to community: Understanding Individual pathways. *Annual Review of Sociology, 29*, 89–113.

Wacquant, L. (2009). *Punishing the poor: The neoliberal government of social insecurity.* Durham, NC: Duke University Press.

Wagner, P., & Rabuy, B. (2017). *Mass incarceration: The whole pie 2017.* Northampton, MA: Prison Policy Initiative.

Wakefield, S., & Wildeman, C., 2014. *Children of the prison boom: Mass incarceration and the future of American inequality.* New York, NY: Oxford University Press.

Western, B. (2006). *Punishment and inequality in America.* New York, NY: SAGE Publications.

Western, B., & Pettit, B. (2005). Black–white wage inequality, employment rates, and incarceration. *American Journal of Sociology, 111*(2), 553–578.

Wildeman, C. (2010). Parental incarceration and children's physically aggressive behaviors: Evidence from the fragile families and child wellbeing study. *Social Forces, 89*(1), 285–309.

Wildeman, C. (2014). Parental incarceration, child homelessness, and the invisible consequences of mass imprisonment. *The Annals of the American Academy of Political and Social Science, 651*(1), 74–96.

Wildeman, C., Turney, K., & Yi, Y. (2016). Paternal incarceration and family functioning: Variation across federal, state, and local facilities. *The Annals of the American Academy of Political and Social Science, 665*, 80–97.

Wildeman, C., Wakefield, S., & Turney, K. (2013). Misidentifying the effects of parental incarceration? A comment on Johnson and Easterling (2012). *Journal of Marriage and Family, 75*, 252–258.

20

THE HARDEST TIME

Gang Members in Total Institutions

David C. Pyrooz and Meghan M. Mitchell

In the free world, the members of gangs can walk to a convenience store, visit the local library, attend sporting events, or meet with friends at a park. They can even get in a car to drive several blocks over to attack the members of rival gangs. Even if gang members are on probation or parole, or subject to the conditions of a civil gang injunction, they still have what members of gangs in prison do not have: autonomy. Prisons are what Erving Goffman (1968) famously noted as *total* institutions. In addition to the severe restrictions on autonomy they impose, prisons also deprive inmates of social status, physical and emotional security, and heterosexual relationships. There is monolithic structuring of routines, limits on status attainment, constant worry about safety, and considerable restrictions to merely communicate with loved ones. Prisons dictate what inmates eat, what they read, where they walk, and with whom they live. Such distinctions seem rather obvious to penology scholars. However, these very features are believed to lead to stark differences in the form and function between street and prison gangs.

Just as differences exist between street and prison gangs, life in the gang is also different from life outside of a gang in prison. Hans Toch (2007) noted that there are "striking parallels" between the witches of yesteryear and the prison gang members of today. Both groups engage in "nefarious predations," are "inhospitable" to outsiders, their "stigmata" collated and due process "streamlined," and accusations against them made uncontestable (p. 275–281). Unlike witches, however, these differences are magnified because the actions and behaviors of gangs and gang members are well documented in prison—prison violence, uprisings, and disorder are linked to gangs (Reiter, 2016; Useem & Reisig, 1999), gang members engage in disproportionately high rates of misconduct (Gaes, Wallace, Gilman, Klein-Saffran, & Suppa, 2002), and contraband and protection markets are closely associated with gangs (Lessing, 2016; Skarbek, 2014). These are the very reasons that correctional officials rank gangs as a major issue facing contemporary prisons (Association of State Correctional Administrators, 2013), which is used to justify the need for different correction policies and practices for gang members. Well-known prison biographies (e.g., Jack Henry Abbott, Rene Enriquez) and classic criminological works (Sykes, 1958) emphasized the pains of imprisonment as "hard time" (Johnson, 1996). But as a consequence of correctional policy and practice, particularly for housing and programming, prison life for gang members may be the hard*est* time.

The purpose of this chapter is to document the collateral consequences of incarceration for gang members. In doing so, first, we review the evidence on the ways in which prison is believed to both create and moderate gangs and gang members. Second, we describe the differential treatment of gang members in prison, focusing on housing and programming. Notably, we present the results of a 2016 survey of state prison systems in the United States that provides an updated view of gang-related housing and programming policies and practices. In the final section, we outline the implications for policy and research with the goal of advancing the next generation of scholarship in this area. Our goals in this chapter are rather modest, directed toward understanding the ways in which prison maintains collateral consequences for housing and programming among gang members. For a broader overview of gangs and prisons, we would advise readers to consult the works of Gaston and Huebner (2015), Griffin, Pyrooz, and Decker (2013), Mitchell, Fahmy, Pyrooz, and Decker (2017), and Skarbek (2014).

Gangs on the Street, Gangs in Prison

The emergence of street gangs in U.S. cities has been documented extensively (see Adamson, 2000; Decker & Van Winkle, 1996; Howell, 2015; Thrasher, 1927). There is evidence that prison gangs have existed since the early 1950s, as reported in the works of Camp and Camp (1985), Irwin (1980), and Orlando-Morningstar (1997). While it is a matter of some debate (Smith, 2017), it is believed that the Gypsy Jokers, in the Washington state prison system, were the first prison gang. Other major prison gangs emerged shortly after in California prisons with the most well-known Latino gangs—the Mexican Mafia and La Nuestra Familia—forming in 1957 and 1965, respectively. The Mexican Mafia, or La Eme, developed out of a group of inmates who were street gang members from East Los Angeles for the purposes of protection, illicit activities, and power. When their predatory actions extended from whites and blacks to other Latinos, particularly Latinos from rural areas of northern California, it gave rise to La Nuestra Familia (Camp & Camp, 1985). As the rivalry between northern and southern California emerged along generational lines of Latinos, the remaining racial groups in California prisons soon began forming alliances; white inmates formed the Aryan Brotherhood in 1967, aligning with the southern Latinos, while black inmates formed the Black Guerilla Family in 1966, aligning with the northern Latinos. A key feature of these gangs is their intense focus on race and ethnicity as core qualities of membership and for the identification of rivalries. This remains largely true today. Indeed, these four gangs remain among the most dominant in California prisons.

It might be an overstatement to claim that the proliferation of gangs across U.S. prison systems is linked to California. However, many of the gangs that soon emerged in other prison systems took on California prison gangs' namesakes, partly due to imitation but also due to the migration of gang members. Indeed, in the 1970s gangs such as the Arizona Aryan Brotherhood and the Arizona Old Mexican Mafia emerged, along with the Aryan Brotherhood, Nuestra Familia, and Black Guerilla Family in Utah (Camp & Camp, 1985; Orlando-Morningstar, 1997). The Texas Syndicate, in fact, did not originate in Texas, but instead developed in the early 1970s in California among a small group of inmates from Texas who banded together for protection (Camp & Camp, 1985, p. 187). Upon returning to Texas, these inmates brought with them the Texas Syndicate into the prison system, which was free of gangs up until that point (Crouch & Marquart, 1989). After the *Ruiz* v. *Estelle* case rendered the mode of governance—building tenders, or inmates elites—in the Texas prisons unconstitutional, eight gangs emerged within three years of the 1983 consent decree, including groups with origins in the prison (e.g., Aryan Brotherhood and Texas Mafia) and groups with origins in the free world (e.g., Mexican Mafia, Hermanos de Pistoleros Latinos, and Crips) (Beaird, 1986; Crouch & Marquart, 1989; Ralph & Marquart, 1991).

Just as street gang members in Los Angeles contributed to the rise of prison gangs in California, the street gangs of Chicago also contributed to the rise of prison gangs in Illinois. The street gangs that emerged in the aftermath of activism in the 1960s were responsible for the bulk of gang activity in Illinois prisons, as documented excellently by Jacobs (1974). Gangs like the Disciples, El Rukns, Latin Kings, and Vice Lords were the most well known, and their presence is felt in several prison systems throughout the United States. These are groups that Jacobs described as having close linkages between the free world and prison.

Although street and prison gangs have some commonalities, stark differences still exist. Pyrooz, Decker, and Fleisher (2011), comparing street and prison gang members along demographic, criminal activity, organizational structure, and normative orientations, held that several features distinguished gangs in prison from gangs on the street. Prison gangs were more organized, exerted higher levels of control and discipline over their members, and engaged in a wider range of entrepreneurial activities than street gangs. Violence tended to be more instrumental than symbolic, behavior is more covert than overt, and allegiances to the gang are stronger rather than fleeting. What is perhaps among the most defining features of gangs in prison is race. In street gangs, neighborhood allegiances are typically the core organizing attribute. But in prison gangs, race generally trumps neighborhood alliances, and even rival street gangs will unite around race or ethnicity in prison (Goodman, 2008; Trulson, Marquart, & Kawucha, 2006). In general, gangs are believed to be different in prison—both in form and function—even if a gang is active in both prison and street settings.

Why might this be the case? It is necessary to take a step back to consider the broader theoretical context from which such observations may arise, which is, the deprivation and importation perspectives of inmate behavior and social organization. The deprivation perspective, closely associated with works of Clemmer (1940), Goffman (1968), and Sykes (1958), views outcomes such as inmate behavior and social organization as endogenous to the prison environment. The importation perspective, closely associated with the works of Irwin and Cressey (1962) and others (DeLisi, Trulson, Marquart, Drury, & Kosloski, 2011), rejects such a blank slatist view and instead holds that inmate behavior and social organization is exogenous of prisons. Rather, these important outcomes are a reflection of the biography, culture, and structures brought into prisons. Schwartz (1971) distinguished these two perspectives as falling into camps of "indigenous influences" and "cultural drift." As Kreager and colleagues (2016) pointed out, despite numerous tests of these perspectives, the research suffers from either (1) an overreliance on administrative data, which cannot tap the "cultural concepts at the heart" of these perspectives, or (2) case studies in a handful of prisons, which struggle to reach inferences and capture the hidden elements of social organization (e.g., structure and hierarchy).

Against this theoretical backdrop, we consider the implications of imprisonment for a range of observations related to gangs. There are at least four areas where deprivation and importation theories are relevant to gang-related activity in prison:

(1) explaining differences and similarities in the form and function of gangs in street and prison settings;
(2) understanding the collateral consequences of incarceration for gang membership and outcomes endogenous to gang membership;
(3) identifying the emergent properties of gangs, as well as the properties associated with continuity and change in gangs; and
(4) determining if the sources of gang violence in prison settings have their origins outside or inside of prison walls.

These broad areas of study consist of deep and complementary literatures when it comes to street gangs, but not prison gangs, unfortunately. These areas all require, at minimum, extensive observation or surveys, or at maximum, repeated observation or surveys, to be able to offer sound explanations as well as solutions. Indeed, there are very different policy prescriptions associated with the deprivation and importation perspectives, which is why these areas should occupy a position of primacy in institutional corrections research.

There are reasons to expect that prison may both create and moderate gang activity. Theoretically and empirically, we know far more about gang membership (area #2 above) than elsewhere, which is why we devote the remainder of this section to that end. This work aims to address the question: *do gang members go to prison or does prison create gang members?* A recent longitudinal study of serious offenders in Philadelphia and Phoenix addressed this question theoretically and empirically (Pyrooz, Gartner, & Smith, 2017). This study began by noting that gang members are disproportionately found in incarcerated settings more than street settings, by a factor of at least 25. Gang members are less than 1 percent of the general population of adults, yet constitute around 15 percent of the U.S. prison population. Prior research (e.g., Varano, Huebner, & Bynum, 2011; Winterdyk & Ruddell, 2010) has documented a mix of gang membership being imported into prisons as well as emerging in prison. Pyrooz and colleagues then situated these observations in what they broadly defined as effects endogenous to incarceration (i.e., origination model) or exogenous to incarceration (i.e., manifestation model), along with a blend of the two (i.e., intensification model). They noted that the link between incarceration and gang membership is "indisputable," but serious questions remain about the mechanisms underlying the relationship.

The *origination* model holds that prison is the driving force of gang membership for inmates. Consistent with the deprivation perspective, inmates seek out associations with gangs because of the pains of imprisonment, broadly construed. Gangs provide a mode of adaptation to the total institution. Where prisons lack status attainment, safety, governance, and resources, membership in a gang meets those needs. A pure version of this model views incarceration as the source of gang membership, as onset and continuity occur in prison and exit occurs post-prison. This is why rates of gang membership are extremely high in prison relative to the general population. Of course, this approach recognizes the existence of street gang members, but membership in gangs in prison is functionally different than the street.

The *manifestation* model views prison as irrelevant to gang membership. Consistent with the importation perspective, inmates bring with them into prison their biography, propensities, and culture, including gang membership. Variation in gang membership is explained not by the forces found inside prison, but those found outside of prison. Indeed, all inmates are subject to forms of deprivation, yet only some inmates are gang members. A pure version of this model holds that the parameters of gang membership—onset, continuity, and change—should occur in prison at a rate that is indistinguishable from outside of prison. Moreover, the reason rates of gang membership are elevated in prison is a product of the offenders the criminal justice system detects, arrests, prosecutes, and sentences, especially once accounting for factors that jointly predict incarceration and gang membership (e.g., age, socioeconomic status, etc.).

The *intensification* model blends these perspectives by recognizing (1) that gang members are indeed high-rate offenders who are likely to end up in prison, but (2) there are features of the prison environment that should influence continuity and change in gang membership. The organizational structure of gangs is expected to promote continuity in gang trajectories. The determinants of disengagement are also missing from prison settings, such as romantic relationships, employment, and prosocial alternatives to gangs. Prison system responses to gangs likely influence gang trajectories adversely. As we discuss in the next section, being classified as a gang member places restrictions on programming and can steer gang members toward restrictive housing arrangements.

Pyrooz and colleagues (2017) found mixed evidence in support of these perspectives by examining rates of gang membership—including joining and leaving—before, during, and after incarceration. Based on the results, they concluded there was "minimal evidence for the origination model, some evidence for the manifestation model, and considerable evidence for the intensification model" (p. 293–294). If the intensification model best represents the relationship between gang membership and incarceration, at least based on the available evidence, then it is necessary to understand how prisons contribute to prolonging gang careers. We are particularly interested in the role of correctional policies and practices, which is why we turn our attention to two of the most impactful aspects of incarceration: housing and programming.

Gang Members, Housing, and Programming

In this section we review what is known about gang members, housing, and programming in prison and extend the research by providing new findings based on a survey we administered to U.S. prison

20 The Hardest Time

systems in 2016. We secured completed surveys from 39 U.S. prison systems containing responses to questions pertaining to gangs, gang members, and housing. We highlight the results with respect to restrictive housing practices and gang-targeted programming.

Housing Gang Members

Winterdyk and Ruddell (2010) surveyed correctional officials from 37 prison systems about their strategies for managing gangs and security threat groups. A total of eight strategies were identified in the survey, ranging from restrictions on privileges (e.g., visits, program participation, commissary) to loss of good time and, most important to this book chapter, segregation or isolated housing. Most officials highly endorsed segregation with 75 percent viewing it as "very effective" and another 19 percent viewing it as "somewhat effective." None viewed restrictive housing as ineffective despite the controversy surrounding its use.

Reiter (2016) described in lurid detail the nature and historical development of restrictive housing practices in California, which disproportionately affected gang members. She noted that inmates were locked in dilapidated facilities housed in 6-by-8-foot cells, with limited access to basic amenities, such as hot water, exercise, and human contact, and restricted from work and educational opportunities. Notably, gang members were most harshly impacted due to their alleged associations based on tattoos, books, letters, or drawings. Once confirmed, gang members were placed *indeterminately* in a secure housing unit (SHU). These validations were subjected to a high degree of correctional staff discretion, and many are believed to be inaccurate. Typically, the only way out of SHUs was to snitch, parole, or die (Reiter, 2012). The one-way ticket to restrictive housing is what prompted the hunger strikes of 2011 and 2013, as well as the class-action lawsuit, *Ashker v. Governor of California*, which was settled in 2015. Part of the settlement involved reviewing all of the indeterminately placed inmates—over 95% of them qualified to leave a SHU, either through a step down program or by direct transfer to the general population.

Why would gang members in California, or any prison system, be placed in restrictive housing at disproportionately high rates? There are three primary types of restrictive housing: disciplinary, protective, and administrative (Labrecque & National Institute of Justice, 2016). Gang affiliates fit squarely into the logic and practice of each form. For *disciplinary* uses of restrictive housing, studies consistently reveal that gang affiliates are involved in higher rates of misconduct than are non-gang inmates (Gaes et al., 2002; Griffin & Hepburn, 2006; Huebner, 2003; Pyrooz, Turanovic, Decker, & Wu, 2016; Sheldon, 1991). Therefore, placing high-rate offenders in restrictive housing units is believed to reduce individual misconduct and institutional disorder in a manner that is consistent with deterrence, incapacitation, and normalization theories (Mears & Reisig, 2006; Mears & Watson, 2006). Since gang affiliates have long been considered the "bad apples" in prisons (e.g., DiIulio, 1987), they are placed squarely in the crosshairs of correctional policies as well as the most prominent theories of restrictive housing.

For *protective* uses of restrictive housing, there are scenarios where current and former gang members would require secure housing due to vulnerability to victimization. Gang affiliates may be housed in a prison where rival gangs outnumber them, so placement in restrictive housing prevents elevated tensions or even violence. Gang dropouts may have outstanding debts to the gang or have violated gang codes of conduct, particularly in the event that they have "debriefed" or informed correctional officials of gang practices (e.g., see Toch, 2007). There are also instances where gang affiliates bring personal conflicts with fellow or ally gangs and gang members from the street to the prison. In fact, it is not uncommon for gang members to request protective custody (Fong & Buentello, 1991) or to be placed in protective custody upon debriefing (Fischer, 2002).

For *administrative* uses of restrictive housing, which is the most controversial aspect of the restrictive housing/gang membership link, gang members are placed in restrictive housing not for misconduct or vulnerability to victimization, but for the threat or safety risk they pose to the prison staff, inmates, or the institution at large. This is controversial for at least three reasons. First, unlike restrictive housing for disciplinary and protective purposes, administrative segregation is based on the potential for problem behavior rather than having "earned" or "needed" restrictive housing. Second, placement into restrictive housing is usually indeterminate, that is, until the threat wanes. Because gang affiliation is the source of the threat, release to the prison's general population requires that gang members convince authorities that they are no longer affiliated with a gang (Burman, 2012; Tachiki, 1995). Third, the decision to place an inmate into restrictive housing is made administratively, which often entails wide discretion.

Based on the pathways from gang membership into restrictive housing, it would be expected that gang members are placed disproportionately in restrictive housing. There are several studies that offer evidence of this relationship. Beck's (2015) findings from the National Inmate Survey, 2011–12 show that there was more gang activity in facilities with higher concentrations of inmates with prolonged periods in restrictive housing. Labrecque's (2015b) meta-analysis included three studies that combined to reveal a modest to moderate relationship with restrictive housing. In a separate study, Labrecque (2015a) found that gang affiliation was related to any placement and prolonged placement in restrictive housing in Ohio. Pyrooz (2016), drawing on public reports of official records, reported that gang members in California and Texas were 71 and 16 times more likely to be housed in restrictive housing than non-gang members, respectively. Lastly, at the national level, Pyrooz and Mitchell (2018) found that gang members are overall 3 times more likely than non-gang members to be in restrictive housing, which was due primarily to administrative rather than disciplinary or protective purposes.

This leads us to present new evidence on the correctional policies and practices that contribute to the disproportionate placement of gang members in restrictive housing. It has been five years since research on these gang-targeted have been updated (Butler, Griffin, & Johnson, 2013; Jacobs & Lee, 2012), and much has changed in restrictive housing policy and practice in that time (Frost & Monteiro, 2016; Obama, 2016). Butler et al. reviewed the policies of 42 state prison systems in 2010 to determine the admission criteria for inmates to be eligible for "long-term administrative segregation" in supermax facilities or units. Affiliation with a gang or STG was an adequate reason for placement in supermax confinement in 14 of the 42 (34 percent) states. As part of their investigative reporting for *Mother Jones* magazine, Jones and Lee obtained information from 40 state agencies about their gang validation and segregation policies. They identified 13 states where there was a possibility that validation as a gang affiliate could result in placement in restrictive housing. There was 69% correspondence between the two works, which could be due to shifting policies and practices or the methods used to obtain the information. Altogether, these reports identified 21 prison systems that placed gang affiliates in restrictive housing based on their status as gang members rather than their behavior as inmates.

Table 20.1 contains the results of our survey, conducted in 2016. We note three things before we discuss the findings. First, findings from Butler et al. (2013) and Jacobs and Lee (2012) are included to give readers a sense of changes over the last five years. Second, 39 state prison systems completed a survey, but only 38 provided valid responses to questions one and two below, while 37 systems responded to question three. Third, we operationalize correctional policy and practice for segregating gang members along a continuum from status to behavior to highlight both the subtle and less than subtle pathways into restrictive housing, as follows:

(1) *Gang status only*—can a gang or STG member be placed in segregated housing based solely on their gang affiliation?

(2) *Gang status + risk*—can a gang or STG member be placed in segregated housing if they were deemed a security risk but have not engaged in behavioral misconduct?

20 The Hardest Time

(3) *Gang status + behavior*—can a gang or STG member be placed in segregated housing if they engage in any of the followed gang-related activities: recruitment, intimidation, or possession of gang paraphernalia?

The bottom rows of Table 20.1 provide aggregate information about restrictive housing and gang affiliation in U.S. state prison systems. Overall, we find that it is the exception to place gang affiliates in restrictive housing units based solely on their status as a gang affiliate, but the norm is to place gang affiliates in restrictive housing units based on unique gang-related behaviors. Indeed, 13 percent of prison systems (or a total of five) endorsed the former practice, but 95 percent (or a total of 35)

Table 20.1 Gang Affiliation as a Segregation Determinant by Multiple Operationalizations, 2010, 2012, and 2016

Authors:	Butler et al. (2013)	Jacobs & Lee (2012)	Pyrooz and Mitchell (present study)		
Data collection year:	2010	2012	2016		
Question content:	Membership in a gang or STG was included as admission criteria into long-term segregation	Membership in a gang or STG was a possible determinant of placement in segregation	Can a gang or STG member be placed in segregated housing based solely on their gang affiliation?	Can a gang or STG member be placed in segregated housing if they were deemed a security risk but haven't engaged in behavioral misconduct?	Can a gang or STG member be placed in segregated housing if engaged in gang recruitment or intimidation or gang paraphernalia?
Alabama	No	No	No	Yes	Yes
Alaska	No	No	—	—	—
Arizona	No	—	No	No	No
Arkansas	No	No	No	Yes	Yes
California	Yes	Yes	No	Yes	Yes
Colorado	Yes	No	No	No	Yes
Connecticut	Yes	—	Yes	Yes	Yes
Delaware	—	No	No	Yes	Yes
Florida	No	Yes	No	Yes	Yes
Georgia	No	—	—	—	—
Hawaii	—	Yes	No	Yes	Yes
Idaho	No	—	No	Yes	Yes
Illinois	Yes	—	No	Yes	Yes
Indiana	Yes	Yes	No	Yes	Yes
Iowa	—	No	Yes	Yes	Yes
Kansas	No	No	—	—	—
Kentucky	Yes	No	No	Yes	Yes
Louisiana	No	—	—	—	—
Maine	No	No	—	—	—
Maryland	—	No	No	Yes	No
Massachusetts	No	No	No	No	Yes
Michigan	No	—	—	—	—
Minnesota	No	No	No	Yes	Yes

(Continued)

Table 20.1 (Continued)

Authors:	Butler et al. (2013)	Jacobs & Lee (2012)	Pyrooz and Mitchell (present study)		
Data collection year:	2010	2012	2016		
Question content:	Membership in a gang or STG was included as admission criteria into long-term segregation	Membership in a gang or STG was a possible determinant of placement in segregation	Can a gang or STG member be placed in segregated housing based solely on their gang affiliation?	Can a gang or STG member be placed in segregated housing if they were deemed a security risk but haven't engaged in behavioral misconduct?	Can a gang or STG member be placed in segregated housing if engaged in gang recruitment or intimidation or gang paraphernalia?
Mississippi	Yes	No	No	Yes	Yes
Missouri	No	—	—	—	—
Montana	No	No	No	No	Yes
Nebraska	Yes	No	No	Yes	Yes
Nevada	No	—	No	No	Yes
New Hampshire	No	Yes	No	No	Yes
New Jersey	No	No	No	Yes	Yes
New Mexico	Yes	—	No	Yes	Yes
New York	No	Yes	—	—	—
North Carolina	No	No	No	No	Yes
North Dakota	—	No	No	No	Yes
Ohio	Yes	Yes	No	Yes	Yes
Oklahoma	No	No	—	—	—
Oregon	No	No	No	Yes	Yes
Pennsylvania	Yes	Yes	Yes	Yes	—
Rhode Island	No	No	No	Yes	Yes
South Carolina	No	Yes	No	Yes	Yes
South Dakota	No	No	No	No	Yes
Tennessee	Yes	Yes	—	—	—
Texas	—	Yes	Yes	Yes	Yes
Utah	—	No	—	—	—
Vermont	No	No	No	No	Yes
Virginia	No	No	—	—	—
Washington	Yes	No	Yes	Yes	Yes
West Virginia	Yes	Yes	No	Yes	Yes
Wisconsin	—	No	No	Yes	Yes
Wyoming	No	Yes	No	Yes	Yes
Valid N	42	40	38	38	37
Frequency "No"	28	27	33	10	2
Frequency "Yes"	14	13	5	28	35
Proportion "Yes"	33%	33%	13%	74%	95%

Note: Prison systems missing data are labeled "—"

20 The Hardest Time

endorsed the latter practice. These findings stand in contrast to the results reported by Butler et al. (2013) and Jacobs and Lee (2012), which raises the question: what, if anything, changed over the last five years?

Fourteen of the prison systems that were documented by either Butler et al. (2013) or Jacobs and Lee (2012) to rely on inmate gang status as a determinant of restrictive housing reported to us that they no longer follow this practice. High profile examples of this are found in states like California and Colorado, both of which underwent substantial changes in restrictive housing policy. California's shifts in policy were prompted by inmate uprisings brought about by presumed affiliates of gangs and litigated reform (Reiter, 2016), while Colorado's were generated by the execution of the prison system's executive director by a formerly segregated, gang-involved inmate and internal reform (see Lin, 2017; Prendergrast, 2014). But the overall change in restrictive housing practices for gang affiliates across U.S. prison systems is rather remarkable over such a short period of time. Indeed, prison systems are no longer relying on gang status as a marker to place inmates in restrictive housing.

While such shifts may appear at first glance to be a noble ending to a controversial practice, it still does not account for the fact that gang members are indeed overrepresented in restrictive housing. It would be premature to conclude that protective and disciplinary purposes were the primary explanation for the continued disproportionalities. One alternative method is to remove gang affiliates from the general population by deeming them as a security risk, which is what three-quarters of the prison systems identified as a reason for placing gang affiliates in restrictive housing. A second method is to criminalize the behaviors that are ancillary characteristics of gang affiliation, which nearly all prison systems identified as a reason for placing gang affiliates in restrictive housing. Whether "risk" and "behavior" are perfect substitutes for "status"-based pathways into restrictive housing is unclear and in need of further investigation.

Gang Members and Prison Programming

It is notable that Winterdyk and Ruddell's (2010) survey of prison administrators excluded programming from the study, instead focusing on strategies to manage, not rehabilitate, gang members. Perhaps it is a reflection of a leading position that gang members are largely irredeemable. Research, however, may suggest otherwise. Some have argued that assessing the criminogenic needs is warranted for effective programming and rehabilitation among gang members (Krienert & Fleisher, 2001; see also Davis & Flannery, 2001). Krienert and Fleisher studied 704 Nebraska inmates at an intake facility, of whom 12 percent were gang members, finding that gang members possessed greater social deficiencies than non-gang members, including lower educational levels, fewer employment opportunities, and a higher likelihood of drug use. The authors held that these deficiencies were great enough to warrant targeted programming for gang members, which in turn could help to increase prison safety and decrease recidivism rates.

Providing targeted programming for prison gang members is challenging for a number of reasons. Limited programming options exist in prisons generally, and the current programs typically are understaffed and only accessed by less than one-third of all prisoners (Crittenden & Koons-Witt, 2017; Petersilia, 2003; Phelps, 2011). Moreover, as previously mentioned, the risk for placement into restrictive housing for gang members is notably higher than that of the general population. Once in segregation, it is unclear how many inmates—regardless of gang status—access prison programming, and evaluations of these programs are virtually nonexistent (Smith, 2016, p. 344). Despite what we know about correctional programming in general, through numerous meta-analyses and systematic reviews (see Davidson, Gottschalk, Gensheimer, & Mayer, 1984; Garrett, 1985; Lipsey, 1992; Lösel & McGuire, 1995; Smith, Gendreau, & Swartz, 2009 for examples), these efforts may still fall short in meeting the different or more acute needs of prison gang members.

The evidence in support of effective interventions in the lives of gang members is mixed. Two studies, nonetheless, are relevant to consider the efficacy of programming for gang members. Boxer and colleagues (2015) evaluated whether gang members were just as likely to have their cases closed successfully as non-gang members in Multisystematic Therapy (MST), a multi-component program linking youth and their families to community-based resources. MST has been labeled an "effective" program according to crimesolutions.gov and a "model" program according to Blueprints for Healthy Youth Development. But in the case of Boxer and colleagues, the evidence was not positive. Based on sample of 168 youth split evenly by gang involvement, they found that the cases for 69 percent of gang-involved youth were closed successfully compared to 81 percent of non-gang-involved youth. As Boxer and colleagues noted, the "best practices" according to leading registries of program effectiveness may not work for gang members.

Di Placido and colleagues (2006) recognized the challenges associated with leading gang management strategies: transferring gang members to other prisons might result in new gang recruitment, isolation is costly and may paradoxically increase gang cohesiveness, and disassociation programs are perceived by gang members as risky (Fong & Vogel, 1995). Drawing on Andrews and Bonta's (2003) risk, need, and responsivity model, Di Placido and colleagues examined the impact of three cognitive-behavioral treatment programs—79 percent aggression-based, 14 percent psychiatric-based, and 8 percent sex offender—on institutional misconduct and post-release recidivism in Canada. A group of 160 prison inmates, split evenly across gang status and treatment status into four groups, were matched on age, sentence length, and convictions. The treated gang members were about 20 percent less likely to recidivate than untreated gang members and 6 percent less likely than non-gang members. The treated gang members were less likely to engage in major forms of institutional misconduct than the untreated gang members but not the untreated non-gang members. The authors argued that self-improvement programs, like cognitive-behavioral therapy, might be more palatable to gang-involved inmates than alternative programs that promote disassociation.

Despite Di Placido and colleagues' (2006) findings, it is important to recognize that the norms of gangs may present significant challenges to programming efforts. As Jacobs (2001, p. vi) noted, "Gang leaders are not likely to be pleased by subordinates shifting their allegiance to professional staff and pro-social goals." And gang members might also subvert the program altogether. Jacobs identified several issues that may emerge in classroom or program settings, such as: classes may become sites for gangs to meet and conduct gang business; teachers and staff may be intimidated by the presence of gang members; staff might become demoralized by the inability to effect change among gang members. Jacobs argued that the primary goal of policy should be clear: "We want to reduce the gang phenomenon as much as possible, which means reducing the size, power, and influence of gangs" (p. vi). One way to do that is to intervene to promote disengagement from gangs. What are prison systems doing to accomplish this goal?

Table 20.2 presents the results of our survey that asks prison systems to identify programs that are designed to facilitate leaving gangs. Out of the 38 valid responses, we can conclude that most prison systems do not have programs to intervene with gang members. Only 14 of the prison systems reported that these programs existed in their institutions. But out of these 14 prison systems, it would be a stretch to conclude that these are actual *programs* consisting of various types of treatment components designed to facilitate changes in gang-related behavior and identity. Instead, of the 16 programs listed (California and Texas each reported two), half were debriefing and renunciation. This is more reflective of a policy than a program.

Debriefing involves informing correctional officials about the inner workings of a gang, including naming members, identifying leadership and hierarchy, and reporting rules of the gang (e.g., see Reiter, 2016; Tachiki, 1995; Toch, 2007). While debriefing may result in changes such as reclassifying gang status and returning to general population housing, the onus is not so much on the debriefing policy to effect change as it is on the individual gang member to seek out the program. The practice

Table 20.2 Programs to Facilitate Disengagement From Gangs in State Prison Systems

	Survey Questions	
	Does your agency have a program for gang members that is designed to facilitate leaving their gang?	If "yes": Name of the program
Alabama	Yes	Renunciation
Alaska	—	
Arizona	Yes	Debriefing
Arkansas	No	
California	Yes	Debriefing Step down program
Colorado	No	
Connecticut	Yes	Security risk group program
Delaware	No	
Florida	Yes	Renunciation
Georgia	—	
Hawaii	No	
Idaho	Yes	Step down program
Illinois	Yes	Renunciation
Indiana	Yes	Debriefing
Iowa	No	
Kansas	—	
Kentucky	No	
Louisiana	—	
Maine	—	
Maryland	Yes	Renunciation
Massachusetts	No	
Michigan	—	
Minnesota	No	
Mississippi	Yes	Renunciation
Missouri	—	
Montana	No	
Nebraska	No	
Nevada	No	
New Hampshire	No	
New Jersey	No	
New Mexico	Yes	Restoration to population
New York	—	
North Carolina	Yes	STG Management Unit
North Dakota	No	
Ohio	No	
Oklahoma	—	
Oregon	No	
Pennsylvania	No	
Rhode Island	No	
South Carolina	No	
South Dakota	No	
Tennessee	—	
Texas	Yes	Gang Renouncement & Disassociation Administrative Segregation Diversion

(*Continued*)

David C. Pyrooz and Meghan M. Mitchell

Table 20.2 (Continued)

	Survey Questions	
	Does your agency have a program for gang members that is designed to facilitate leaving their gang?	If "yes": Name of the program
Utah	—	
Vermont	No	
Virginia	—	
Washington	No	
West Virginia	No	
Wisconsin	No	
Wyoming	Yes	Renunciation
Valid N	38	Renunciation/Debriefing: N=9
Frequency "No"	24	Segregation step down program: N=3
Frequency "Yes"	14	Gang-targeted program: N=4
Proportion "Yes"	37%	

Note: Prison systems missing data are labeled "—"

of debriefing is believed to be wrought with procedural error (Tachiki, 1995; Toch, 2007) and the consequences associated with debriefing are perceived to be substantial (Decker & Pyrooz, 2015; Hunt, Riegel, Morales, & Waldorf, 1993). Debriefing is a one-way street; once entered, inmates must be mentally and physically prepared because there is no returning to pre-debriefing states. Word spreads quickly in prisons, and debriefing is snitching in its worst form.

Other prison systems identified incentive- and cognitive-based programs that are designed to ease gang members away from restrictive housing ($n=7$). For example, California's step down program is designed to last 24 months. It consists of four steps (see California Department of Corrections and Rehabilitation, 2012; Pyrooz, 2016 for additional information), and the goal of the program is for offenders to earn enhanced privileges as they demonstrate their ability to coexist among others. At each step, the Institutional Classification Committee reviews the inmate's file for compliance to housing policies, obedience to directives, and hygiene and living condition upkeep. Programming, privileges, and services are provided prior to the final step where inmates are placed in general housing with continued monitoring of their behavior for a 12-month period, particularly with respect to continued or emerging gang ties.

Compared to the step down program in California, Texas's curriculum is more heavily centered on cognitive interventions and is delivered in nine months through their Gang Renouncement and Dissociation (GRAD) program (Texas Department of Criminal Justice, 2014). During the early phases, inmates are exposed to the programming and group recreation—which was prohibited in segregation—while single-celled. Programming intensifies as inmates are double-celled, often with a rival gang member. Inmates are given the opportunity to apply their skills in group programming while watching movies, role playing, and journaling. Finally, inmates are transferred to the general population and successful completion of the program involves a formal graduation ceremony where family and friends are welcome to attend. Texas also offers an Administrative Segregation Diversion (ASD). To our knowledge, this is the only program in the country available to gang-involved inmates at intake. When reincarcerated, previously confirmed STG members can go directly to segregation or participate in the diversion program. The programming courses are similar to GRAD.

Are these programs actually effective? Do inmates readily renounce their gang membership to get out of segregation? Unfortunately, these questions have not been addressed because these programs have not been subject to public evaluation. Descriptive statistics have been provided, however. For example, according to the most recent published data on the GRAD program, over 4,000 inmates have completed the program and only 19 have been re-confirmed as gang members (Burman, 2012). Moreover, the ASD has approximately a 50% participation rate and those refusing to participate do so for loyalty reasons. The STGMU in North Carolina, as well as the step down programs and debriefing/renunciation programs, have not been subject to scientific evaluation either. Therefore, any short- or long-term implications are unknown. Given the lack of evidence surrounding these programs, more research in this area is necessary to ensure that limited resources are deployed to effective interventions, particularly those that are targeted to gang members rather than the general prison population.

Policy and Research Implications

It remains an open question as to whether the prison experiences of gang members diverge in small or large ways from that of non-gang inmates. There are sound theoretical reasons to anticipate considerable social benefits of gang affiliation in prison. Why else would inmates retain street gang affiliations or assume prison gang affiliations when incarcerated? Whether those benefits are cancelled out by prison policy and practice is unclear. Is status, protection, and contraband worth *hard time*, that is, placement into solitary confinement and reduced access to already limited programming? Given the proliferation of gangs across prison systems since the 1980s, it appears that the answer to this question is "yes." It also appears that gang members are willing to tolerate the institutional consequences associated with membership and that gangs are resistant to the heavy-handed strategies devised by prison systems to combat the influence of gangs. What promotes gang membership in prison settings, as well as what discourages gang membership, is not clearly understood. The continued lack of knowledge on this topic means that correctional policy and practice remains underinformed, guided by guesswork and anecdote rather than sound research.

Which raises what is perhaps the most important question: what are the most effective responses to gangs in prison? To date, this question has few good answers. But it is indeed clear that restrictive housing is viewed as the leading strategy to manage gangs. This is why it is unsurprising that studies continue to reveal the overrepresentation of gang affiliates in restrictive housing. We have extended what is known on restrictive housing and gang affiliation in the United States by offering new evidence on gang-specific pathways into restrictive housing. It appears that prison systems are moving away from status-based pathways to restrictive housing for gang members. Only five states reported that such a practice remains in place today. This move away from these practices helps alleviate Tachiki's (1995) and Toch's (2007) primary concerns about the lack of due process for gang members. In theory, gang affiliates are no different from other inmates, as they have to earn or need their way into restrictive housing.

In practice, however, there appears to be a different story emerging. Near-perfect substitutes for gang status have appeared as alternative pathways into restrictive housing, including risk classification and the ancillary acts of gangs. It is unclear the extent to which gang affiliation factors into risk classification scores, which could, in turn, lead certain high-risk inmates to be placed in restrictive housing. The ancillary acts of gangs, like paramilitary exercises, written and verbal gang communication, and recruitment are not actions that are deemed misconduct *but for* the association with gangs. Religious groups in prison are permitted to engage in exercises, communicate with one another, and recruit new congregants. That is not the case for gang affiliates, which means that while status is no longer punished, status-analogous actions are punished nearly universally across prison systems. The implications of the phasing out of status-based pathways and phasing in of a greater reliance on gang status and behavior pathways are unclear. But shrewd observers of prison practices will likely seize on this policy sleight of hand, as rates of disproportionate restrictive housing for gang members will likely remain high.

While restrictive housing may be the first recourse to gangs in prison, alternative approaches are available that offer gang-targeted policies and programs to facilitate disengagement from gangs. Fong and Vogel (1995) were the first to recognize that gang membership in prison is not a life-long commitment; it was possible to leave a gang, but clearly the exit strategy was risky, as evidenced by their use of "defector" to describe the 48 ex-gang members in their study. While seven states offer actual programs, rather than policies, to facilitate gang exit, we remain in the dark with respect to the effectiveness of these programs. It is necessary to build a scientific knowledge base to evaluate the program processes and impacts. Burman's (2012) process evaluation in Texas uncovered a great deal about the GRAD program, but she was not granted the ability to conduct an impact evaluation, a notable omission. Based on the theoretical and empirical work in recent years on disengagement from gangs (Bubolz & Simi, 2015; Decker, Pyrooz, & Moule, 2014; Densley & Pyrooz, 2017; Flores, 2013; Maitra, McLean, & Holligan, 2017), we suspect that incentivizing exit alone via debriefing or step down will not produce success in disengagement in the absence of cognitive-based efforts. While push factors may be the prevailing motivation for leaving gangs behind bars, there are no complementary pull factors for gang members to latch onto. Gang leaving is a two-way street, consisting of the gang member, but also the stakeholders orbiting around him or her to accept or reject claims of exit (see Densley & Pyrooz, 2017). Nonetheless, it is important to remember that we lack a solid knowledge base on intervening in the lives of street gang members, where, due to the lack of evaluation, programs remain in a perpetual state of being considered "promising" (Roman, Decker, & Pyrooz, 2017).

Conclusion

The National Research Council (2014) identified a range of economic, physical and mental health, and social consequences associated with incarceration. And the labeling tradition in criminology has long held that formal social control can impose more harm than good. We have argued correctional responses to gangs in the form of policy and practice have led to collateral consequences of incarceration for gang members, particularly for housing and programming. In general, prison system responses to gangs have promoted management over rehabilitation. While prison is known as doing *hard time*, consistent with specific deterrence theory, these consequences are believed to render the prison experiences of gang members as the *hardest time*. Indeed, the placement of gang members in restrictive housing and the lack of meeting the programmatic needs of gang members has implications for institutional violence and disorder as well as prison reentry. Although this remains untested, one product of housing and programming policies and practices is that prison may have iatrogenic effects for gangs and their members—greater durability and organizational structure in gangs, prolonged involvement in gangs, and increased instrumental forms of gang violence. In effect, prisons may worsen gang activity altogether. The lack of research on gangs in prison leaves many of these conclusions, as well as policy implications, speculative at this time. The research on gangs in prison simply pales in comparison to what is known about gangs in street settings (see Pyrooz & Mitchell, 2015). As James Jacobs (2001, p. vi) lamented nearly two decades ago, "It is hard to understand why the prison gang phenomenon does not attract more attention from the media, scholars, and policy analysts." We, too, remain surprised by the gulf of research on gangs in prison. With the first contribution on gangs in the three volumes of the Division on Corrections and Sentencing's handbook series, we also hope to have identified critical policy, practice, and research issues to advance the next generation of scholarship in this area.

References

Adamson, C. (2000). Defensive localism in white and black: A comparative history of European-American and African-American youth gangs. *Ethnic and Racial Studies*, 23(2), 272–298.

Andrews, D. A., & Bonta, J. (2003). *The psychology of criminal conduct*. Cincinnati, OH: Anderson.

20 The Hardest Time

Association of State Correctional Administrators. (2013). *ASCA June 2013 current issues in corrections survey*. Hagerstown, MD. Retrieved from www.asca.net/system/assets/attachments/6468/ASCA%20June%202103%20 Current%20Issues%20in%20Corrections%20Surveyfin.pdf?1384359439

Beaird, L. H. (1986). Prison gangs: Texas. *Corrections Today*, 12–22.

Beck, A. J. (2015). *Use of restrictive housing in U.S. prisons and jails, 2011–12* (No. NCJ 249209). Washington, DC: Bureau of Justice Statistics. Retrieved from www.bjs.gov/content/pub/pdf/urhuspj1112.pdf

Boxer, P., Kubik, J., Ostermann, M., & Veysey, B. (2015). Gang involvement moderates the effectiveness of evidence-based intervention for justice-involved youth. *Children and Youth Services Review, 52*, 26–33.

Bubolz, B. F., & Simi, P. (2015). Disillusionment and change: A cognitive-emotional theory of gang exit. *Deviant Behavior, 36*(4), 330–345. Retrieved from https://doi.org/10.1080/01639625.2014.935655

Burman, M. L. (2012). *Resocializing and repairing homies within the Texas Prison System: A case study on security threat group management, administrative segregation, prison gang renunciation and safety for all*. Austin, TX: University of Texas at Austin.

Butler, H. D., Griffin, O. H., & Johnson, W. W. (2013). What makes you the "worst of the worst?" an examination of state policies defining supermaximum confinement. *Criminal Justice Policy Review, 24*(6), 676–694. Retrieved from https://doi.org/10.1177/0887403412465715

California Department of Corrections and Rehabilitation. (2012). *Security threat group prevention, identification and management strategy*. California Department of Corrections and Rehabilitation. Retrieved from https://assets. documentcloud.org/documents/452638/cdcr-reforms-7-0.pdf

Camp, G. M., & Camp, C. G. (1985). *Prison gangs their extent, nature, and impact on prisons*. U.S. Department of Justice. Retrieved from www.ncjrs.gov/pdffiles1/Digitization/99458NCJRS.pdf

Clemmer, D. (1940). *The prison community*. Boston, MA: The Christopher Publishing House.

Crittenden, C. A., & Koons-Witt, B. A. (2017). Gender and programming: A comparison of program availability and participation in US prisons. *International Journal of Offender Therapy and Comparative Criminology, 61*(6), 611–644.

Crouch, B. M., & Marquart, J. W. (1989). *An appeal to justice: Litigated reform of Texas prisons*. Austin, TX: University of Texas Press.

Davidson, W. S., Gottschalk, R., Gensheimer, L., & Mayer, J. (1984). *Interventions with juvenile delinquents: A meta-analysis of treatment efficacy*. Washington, DC: National Institute of Juvenile Justice and Delinquency Prevention.

Davis M.S., & Flannery, D. J. (2001) The institutional treatment of gang members. *Corrections Management Quarterly, 5*(1), 37–46.

Decker, S. H., & Pyrooz, D. C. (2015). The real gangbanging in prison. In J. Wooldredge & P. Smith (Eds.), *Oxford handbook on prisons and imprisonment*. New York, NY: Oxford University Press.

Decker, S. H., Pyrooz, D. C., & Moule, R. K. J. (2014). Disengagement from gangs as role transitions. *Journal of Research on Adolescence, 24*(2), 268–283.

Decker, S. H., & Van Winkle, B. (1996). *Life in the gang, family, friends, and violence*. New York, NY: Cambridge University Press.

DeLisi, M., Trulson, C. R., Marquart, J. W., Drury, A. J., & Kosloski, A. E. (2011). Inside the prison black box: Toward a life course importation model of inmate behavior. *International Journal of Offender Therapy and Comparative Criminology, 55*, 118–1207.

Densley, J. A., & Pyrooz, D. C. (2017). A signaling perspective on disengagement from gangs. *Justice Quarterly, 0*(0), 1–28. Retrieved from https://doi.org/10.1080/07418825.2017.1357743

Di Placido, C., Simon, T. L., Witte, T. D., Gu, D., & Wong, S. C. (2006). Treatment of gang members can reduce recidivism and institutional misconduct. *Law and Human Behavior, 30*(1), 93–114.

DiIulio, J. J. (1987). *Governing prisons*. New York, NY: Free Press.

Fischer, D. R. (2002). *Arizona department of corrections: Security threat group (STG) program evaluation* (Final Report). Washington, DC: National Institute of Justice, U.S. Department of Justice.

Flores, E. (2013). *God's gangs: Barrio ministry, masculinity, and gang recovery*. New York, NY: New York University Press.

Fong, R. S., & Buentello, S. (1991). The detection of prison gang development: An empirical assessment. *Federal Probation, 55*(1), 66–70.

Fong, R. S., & Vogel, R. E. (1995). Blood-in, blood-out: The rationale behind defecting from prison gangs. *Journal of Gang Research, 2*(4), 45–51.

Frost, N., & Monteiro, C. (2016). *Administrative Segregation in U.S. Prisons*. Washington, D.C: National Institute of Justice. Retrieved from www.ncjrs.gov/pdffiles1/nij/249749.pdf

Gaes, G. G., Wallace, S., Gilman, E., Klein-Saffran, J., & Suppa, S. (2002). The influence of prison gang affiliation on violence and other prison misconduct. *The Prison Journal, 82*(3), 359–385. Retrieved from https://doi. org/10.1177/003288550208200304

Garrett, C. J. (1985). Effects of residential treatment on adjudicated delinquents: A meta-analysis. *Journal of Research in Crime and Delinquency, 22*(4), 287–308.

Gaston, S., & Huebner, B. M. (2015). Gangs in correctional institutions. In S. H. Decker & D. C. Pyrooz (Eds.), *The Handbook of Gangs* (pp. 328–344). Chichester, West Sussex: John Wiley & Sons.

Goffman, E. (1968). *Asylums: Essays on the social situation of mental patients and other inmates.* New Brunswick, NJ: Aldine Transaction.

Goodman, P. (2008). It's just black, white or Hispanic: An observational study of racializing moves in California's segregated prison reception centers. *Law & Society Review, 42*(4), 735–770.

Griffin, M. L., & Hepburn, J. R. (2006). The effect of gang affiliation on violent misconduct among inmates during the early years of confinement. *Criminal Justice and Behavior, 33*(4), 419–466.

Griffin, M. L., Pyrooz, D. C., & Decker, S. H. (2013). Surviving and thriving: The growth, influence, and administrative control of prison gangs. In J. L. Wood & T. A. Gannon (Eds.), *Crime and crime reduction: The importance of group processes.* New York, NY: Routledge.

Huebner, B. M. (2003). Administrative determinants of inmate violence: A multilevel analysis. *Journal of Criminal Justice, 31*(2), 107–117. Retrieved from https://doi.org/10.1016/S0047-2352(02)00218-0

Hunt, G., Riegel, S., Morales, T., & Waldorf, D. (1993). Change in prison culture: Prison gangs and the case of the Pepsi generation. *Social Problems, 40*(3), 398–409.

Howell, K.B. (2015). Gang policing: The post stop-and-frisk justification for profile based policing. *University of Denver Criminal Law Review, 5*, 1–32.

Irwin, J. (1980). *Prisons in turmoil.* Boston, MA: Little, Brown and Company.

Irwin, J., & Cressey, D. R. (1962). Thieves, convicts and the inmate culture. *Social Problems, 10*(2), 142–155. Retrieved from https://doi.org/10.2307/799047

Jacobs, J. B. (1974). Street gangs behind bars. *Social Problems, 21*(3), 395–409.

Jacobs, J. B. (2001). Focusing on prison gangs. *Corrections Management Quarterly, 5*(1), vi–vii.

Jacobs, R., & Lee, J. (2012). Maps: Solitary confinement, state by state. Retrieved October 15, 2015, from www.motherjones.com/politics/2012/10/map-solitary-confinement-states

Johnson, R. (1996). *Hard time: Understanding and reforming the prison.* Belmont, CA: Wadsworth.

Kreager, D. A., Schaefer, D. R., Bouchard, M., Haynie, D. L., Wakefield, S., Young, J., & Zajac, G. (2016). Toward a criminology of inmate networks. *Justice Quarterly, 33*(6), 1000–1028. Retrieved from https://doi.org/10.1080/07418825.2015.1016090

Krienert, J.L., & Fleisher, M.S. (2001) Gang membership as a proxy for social deficiencies: A study of Nebraska inmates. *Corrections Management Quarterly, 5*(1), 47–58.

Labrecque, R. M. (2015a). *Effect of solitary confinement on institutional misconduct: A longitudinal evaluation.* University of Cincinnati, Cincinnati, OH. Retrieved from www.ncjrs.gov/App/Publications/abstract.aspx?ID=271153

Labrecque, R. M. (2015b, October). *Who ends up in administrative segregation? A meta-analytic review.* Presented at the National Institute of Justice Topical Working Group on the Use of Administrative Segregation in the United States, Arlington, VA.

Labrecque, R. M., & National Institute of Justice. (2016). The use of administrative segregation and its function in the institutional setting. In *Restrictive housing in the U.S.: Issues, challenges, and future directions* (pp. 49–84). Washington, DC: U.S. Department of Justice; Office of Justice Programs; National Institute of Justice.

Lessing, B. (2016). Inside out: The challenge of prison-based criminal organizations. *Brookings Institution, 1.* Retrieved from http://trafficlight.bitdefender.com/info?url=https%3A//www.brookings.edu/wp-content/uploads/2016/09/fp_20160927_prison_based_organizations.pdf&language=en_US

Lin, J. (2017). Program evaluation in the context of supervision regime change: Motivational interviewing in Colorado. *Justice Quarterly, 0*(0), 1–24. Retrieved from https://doi.org/10.1080/07418825.2017.1367027

Lipsey, M. W. (1992). Juvenile delinquency treatment: A meta-analytic inquiry into the variability of effects. In T. D. Cook, H. Cooper, D. S. Cordray, H. Hartmann, L. V. Hedges, R. J. Light, . . . F. Mosteller, *Meta-analysis for explanation: A casebook* (pp. 83–127). New York, NY: Russell Sage Foundation.

Lösel, F., & McGuire, J. (1995). The efficacy of correctional treatment: A review and synthesis of meta-evaluations. In *What works: Reducing reoffending* (pp. 79–111). Oxford: John Wiley & Sons.

Maitra, D., McLean, R., & Holligan, C. (2017). Voices of quiet desistance in UK prisons: Exploring emergence of new identities under desistance constraint. *The Howard Journal of Crime and Justice*, n/a–n/a. Retrieved from https://doi.org/10.1111/hojo.12213

Mears, D. P., & Reisig, M. D. (2006). The theory and practice of supermax prisons. *Punishment & Society, 8*(1), 33–57.

Mears, D. P., & Watson, J. (2006). Towards a fair and balanced assessment of supermax prisons. *Justice Quarterly, 23*(2), 232–270.

20 The Hardest Time

Mitchell, M. M., Fahmy, C., Pyrooz, D. C., & Decker, S. H. (2017). Criminal crews, codes, and contexts: Differences and similarities across the code of the street, convict code, street gangs, and prison gangs. *Deviant Behavior, 38*(10), 1197–1222. Retrieved from https://doi.org/10.1080/01639625.2016.1246028

Obama, B. (2016). Why we must rethink solitary confinement. *Washington Post.* Retrieved from www.washingtonpost.com/opinions/barack-obama-why-we-must-rethink-solitary-confinement/2016/01/25/29a361f2-c384-11e5-8965-0607e0e265ce_story.html

Orlando-Morningstar, D. (1997). Prison gangs. *Special Needs Offender Bulletin, 2,* 1–13.

Petersilia, J. (2003). *When prisoners come home: Parole and prisoner reentry.* New York, NY: Oxford University Press.

Phelps, M. S. (2011). Rehabilitation in the punitive era: The gap between rhetoric and reality in U.S. prison programs. *Law & Society Review, 45*(1), 33–68. Retrieved from https://doi.org/10.1111/j.1540-5893.2011.00427.x

Prendergast, A. (2014, August 21). After the Murder of Tom Clements, Can Colorado's Prison System Rehabilitate Itself? *Westword.* Retrieved from http://www.westword.com/news/after-the-murder-of-tom-clements-can-colorados-prison-system-rehabilitate-itself-5125050

Pyrooz, D. C. (2016). Gang affiliation and restrictive housing in U.S. prisons. In National Institute of Justice (Ed.), *Restrictive housing in the U.S. issues, challenges, and future directions* (pp. 117–164). Washington, DC: National Institute of Justice, U.S. Department of Justice.

Pyrooz, D. C., Decker, S. H., & Fleisher, M. S. (2011). From the street to the prison, from the prison to the street: Understanding and responding to prison gangs. *Journal of Aggression, Conflict and Peace Research, 3*(1), 12–24. Retrieved from https://doi.org/10.5042/jacpr.2011.0018

Pyrooz, D. C., Gartner, N., & Smith, M. M. (2017). Consequences of incarceration for gang membership: A longitudinal study of serious offenders in Philadelphia and Phoenix. *Criminology, 55*(3), 273–306.

Pyrooz, D. C., & Mitchell, M. M. (2015). Little gang research, big gang research. In *The Handbook of Gangs* (pp. 28–58). Chichester, West Sussex: Wiley-Blackwell.

Pyrooz, D. C., & Mitchell, M. M. (2018). *The disproportionate use of restrictive housing on gang affiliates in U.S. prisons: Findings from a national survey of prison systems* (Working paper).

Pyrooz, D. C., Turanovic, J. J., Decker, S. H., & Wu, J. (2016). Taking stock of the relationship between gang membership and offending: A meta-analysis. *Criminal Justice & Behavior, 43*(3), 365–397.

Ralph, P. H., & Marquart, J. W. (1991). Gang violence in Texas prisons. *The Prison Journal, 71*(2), 38–49.

Roman, C. G., Decker, S. H., & Pyrooz, D. C. (2017). Leveraging the pushes and pulls of gang disengagement to improve gang intervention: Findings from three multi-site studies and a review of relevant gang programs. Journal of Crime and Justice, 40(3), 316–336.

Reiter, K. A. (2012). Parole, snitch, or die: California's supermax prisons and prisoners, 1997–2007. *Punishment & Society, 14*(5), 530–563. Retrieved from https://doi.org/10.1177/1462474512464007

Reiter, K. A. (2016). *23/7: Pelican bay prison and the rise of long-term solitary.* New Haven, CT: Yale University Press.

Schwartz, B. (1971). Pre-institutional vs. situational influence in a correctional community. *The Journal of Criminal Law, Criminology, and Police Science, 62*(4), 532–542.

Sheldon, R. G. (1991). A comparison of gang members and non-gang members in a prison setting. *The Prison Journal, 71*(2), 50–60. Retrieved from https://doi.org/10.1177/003288559107100206

Skarbek, D. (2014). *The social order of the underworld: How prison gangs govern the American penal system.* New York, NY: Oxford University Press.

Smith, P. (2016). Toward an understanding of "what works" in segregation: Implementing correctional programming and re-entry-focused services in restrictive housing units. In National Institute of Justice (Ed.), *Restrictive housing in the U.S. issues, challenges, and future directions* (pp. 331–366). Washington, DC: National Institute of Justice, U.S. Department of Justice.

Smith, C. F. (2017). When is a prison gang not a prison gang: A focused review of prison gang literature. *Journal of Gang Research, 23*(2), 41–52.

Smith, P., Gendreau, P., & Swartz, K. (2009). Validating the principles of effective intervention: A systematic review of the contributions of meta-analysis in the field of corrections. *Victims & Offenders, 4*(2), 148–169. Retrieved from https://doi.org/10.1080/15564880802612581

Sykes, G. M. (1958). *The society of captives.* Princeton, NJ: Princeton University Press.

Tachiki, S. N. (1995). Indeterminate sentences in supermax prisons based upon alleged gang affiliations: A reexamination of procedural protection and a proposal for greater procedural requirements. *California Law Review, 83*(4), 1115–1149.

Texas Department of Criminal Justice. (2014). *Administrative segregation.* Huntsville, TX: Texas Department of Criminal Justice. Retrieved from https://assets.documentcloud.org/documents/2089812/texas-adseg-programming.pdf

Thrasher, F. M. (1927). *The gang: A study of 1,313 gangs in Chicago.* Chicago, IL: University of Chicago Press.

Toch, H. (2007). Sequestering gang members, burning witches, and subverting due process. *Criminal Justice and Behavior, 34*(2), 274–288. Retrieved from https://doi.org/10.1177/0093854806296663

Trulson, C. R., Marquart, J. W., & Kawucha, S. K. (2006). Gang suppression. *Corrections Today, 68*, 26–31.

Useem, B., & Reisig, M. D. (1999). Collective action in prisons: Protests, disturbances, and riots. *Criminology, 37*(4), 735–760. Retrieved from https://doi.org/10.1111/j.1745-9125.1999.tb00503.x

Varano, S. P., Huebner, B. M., & Bynum, T. S. (2011). Correlates and consequences of pre-incarceration gang involvement among incarcerated youthful felons. *Journal of Criminal Justice, 39*(1), 30–38.

Winterdyk, J., & Ruddell, R. (2010). Managing prison gangs: Results from a survey of U.S. prison systems. *Journal of Criminal Justice, 38*(4), 730–736. Retrieved from https://doi.org/10.1016/j.jcrimjus.2010.04.047

21
EXPORTATION HYPOTHESIS
Bringing Prison Violence Home to the Community

Don Hummer and Eileen M. Ahlin

Introduction

Non-institutional violence tends to cluster in certain neighborhoods (see Cantillon, Davidson, & Schweitzer, 2003; Kirk & Papachristos, 2011; Kubrin & Weitzer, 2003) and is particularly prevalent in those communities that are depleted of positive attributes such as collective efficacy (Sampson, Raudenbush, & Earls, 1997; Browning, 2002), human and financial capital (Burton & Jarrett, 2000; Ceballo, McLoyd, & Toyokawa, 2004; Jencks & Mayer, 1990; Wilson, 1987), and lack of capable informal and formal guardianship (Cohen & Felson, 1979; Hindelang, Gottfredson, & Garofalo, 1978). Institutional violence such as that occurring in our nation's prisons has its own causes and correlates including overcrowding (Wooldredge, Griffin, & Pratt, 2001; Wortley, 2002), interpersonal characteristics of victims and abusers (DeLisi, Berg, & Hochstetler, 2004; Huebner, 2003; Steiner & Wooldredge, 2008; Toch & Kupers, 2007), and management styles (Colvin, 1992; Huebner, 2003; Useem, 1985). Much scholarly research has been offered to explain why violence occurs independently in these two milieus, though less is known about bringing a culture of violence from prison back home to the community upon release.

Traditional theoretical offerings suggest that prison violence is due to importation of a culture of violence from the outside, deprivation of personal freedoms during imprisonment, or correctional officer responsiveness to incarcerated persons' behavior (Levan, 2013; Steiner et al., 2014). While these discussions are important for understanding the origins of prison violence and management strategies for addressing violence and disorder, focusing attention on the pre-prison and carceral experiences leaves a gaping hole in the theoretical puzzle. Primarily, the question that remains ill addressed is what happens when formerly incarcerated persons return to their communities? This is an important area of inquiry given the fact that the majority, upwards of 95% of persons incarcerated, will return home on parole or expiration of their sentence after serving time in jail or state or federal prisons (Hughes & Wilson, 2003; Jonson & Cullen, 2015). As we sit atop an apex of the United States' grand experiment with incarceration and contemplate how criminal justice will move forward as states begin to decarcerate and realign prison populations, we take this opportunity to flesh out a theoretical model of the collateral consequences of imprisonment as it relates to violence in the community. This exportation hypothesis considers the three main factors of prison violence, while extending theoretical application to the post-carceral period. This chapter first highlights the importance of importation, deprivation, and institutional control styles to the culture of prison violence. We then focus substantial discussion on the culture of prison violence itself before seguing into a discussion on how violence is exported from behind prison walls to the community. We conclude this chapter by offering a preliminary model of the exportation hypothesis to shed new light on the collateral consequence of exposure to prison violence for the community at-large.

Why Focus on Prison Violence?

The entries in this handbook approach the collateral consequences of punishment from myriad perspectives, and the enduring role prison violence has on the behavior of those incarcerated and on the communities to which they return are just two ways to examine the sustaining impact of criminal justice system processing. However, we believe that prison violence is one of the most damaging ways in which punishment through the criminal justice system transcends time and space to alter experiences for both persons incarcerated in prisons and people who have not been processed by the criminal justice system. The effects of prison violence do not begin or end during incarceration. Just as exposure to violence in the community can have long-range enduring negative consequences, it should be expected that exposure to violence while in prison could also have damaging effects on formerly incarcerated people when they return home. Further, it is expected that these adverse sequelae may transfer to the community and their inhabitants when formerly incarcerated persons bring their prison experiences back to neighborhoods, perpetuating the culture of violence. Before exploring the core of our exportation hypothesis, we briefly highlight the extant theories of prison violence to serve as a foundation for theoretical development.

Importation Theory

Importation theory suggests that prison violence is the direct result of the cycle of violence where incarcerated persons who engaged in or were exposed to community violence bring with them a culture of violence to the prison experience. Direct involvement in violent behavior is continued through an extension of similar behavior during incarceration (Irwin & Cressey, 1962), while exposure to violence in the community can independently influence violent behavior (Brady, Gorman-Smith, Henry, & Tolan, 2008; Flannery, Singer, & Wester, 2003; Spano, Rivera, & Bolland, 2006). Under this explanation, people incarcerated in prison bring the street code of violence (see Anderson, 1999; Mears, Stewart, Siennick, & Simons, 2013) with them to prison (see Steiner et al., 2014). Correctional facilities, because of stricter sentencing policies, have become repositories for large numbers of troubled individuals living in close proximity in less than desirable conditions (Mann & Hendrick, 2015). As such, prison becomes an extension of lifestyles forged by poorly managed mental health issues, a history of trauma and abuse, and corresponding anger management and impulse control deficiencies (Wolff & Shi, 2012). Importation theory suggests that people who are violent in prison were violent and/or antisocial before they were incarcerated and are simply continuing to use their learned or preferred means of interaction with others while housed in a correctional facility.

Deprivation Theory

Contrary to importation theory, deprivation theory purports that prison violence is the result of the conditions of confinement and that violence erupts during carceral stays because people incarcerated in prisons do not have access to creature comforts of home, such as access to privacy and ability to make choices; lack autonomy over their lives; and are without security (see Clemmer, 1940; Sykes, 1958). Prison life itself is believed to drive incarcerated persons to behave violently and respond to their confinement with aggression (Brosens, De Donder, Dury, & Verté, 2016; Camp, Gaes, Langan, & Saylor, 2003; Cunningham & Sorensen, 2007; DeLisi, Berg, & Hochstetler, 2004; Morris, Longmire, Buffington-Vollum, & Vollum, 2010; Wooldredge, 2003). The expanded use of imprisonment that began in the second half of the 20th century led to a decreased emphasis on addressing the issues prevalent within the offending population and bred an institutional environment that was a simmering cauldron that prison management and staff sought only to contain. These strategies aimed at housing an ever growing number of incarcerated persons and preventing as much disorder as possible, such as restrictions on movement and recreation options of people incarcerated in prisons, compounded already sub-standard environmental conditions (Alexander, 2012; Camp & Gaes, 2005; Camp et al., 2003). A contemporary view of deprivation theory is the application of strain theory. Personal adjustment to the carceral experience has been explored within the general strain theory framework, and scholars have identified the use of violence as an adaptation to the prison environment (see Blevins, Listwan, Cullen, & Jonson, 2010; Morris, Carriaga, Diamond, Piquero, & Piquero, 2012). Steiner, Ellison, Butler, and McCain's (2017) focus on in-prison victimization highlights the long-held scholarly emphasis on perpetrators rather than victims and exploring how the traditional theories of prison violence, including deprivation, may be applied to prison safety from the perspective of victims. They suggest that the relevance of deprivation theory as an explanation of prison violence may have reduced in salience after the prisoners' rights movements of the 1960s and as prison systems became less closed than in prior decades. However, with a burgeoning incarceration rate in the U.S. beginning in the 1970s and overcrowding in many of the nation's prisons the role of deprivation remains relevant to discussions on prison violence.

Institutional Control

Poor institutional control, or prison management, is the third mechanism underlying explanations of violence in prisons among incarcerated persons. McCorkle, Miethe, and Drass (1995) identify correctional officer style as an indicator of assaults among incarcerated persons as well as staff (see also Useem & Kimball, 1989). DiIulio (1987) approaches prison management from a multi-pronged perspective as it relates to both individual and collective institutional violence. He suggests that administrative details such as officer training, security of the facility, and staff turnover can result in violence prone situations. Prison violence research from Great Britain has shed light on an issue that is common across the globe regarding incarcerated people's perceptions of institutional control. When staff authority was defined as either "light" or "absent," incarcerated individuals became emboldened to organize and fill this control vacuum. Corresponding power struggles led to macro-level incidents of violence in British prisons in the early 1990s (see Crewe & Liebling, 2015; Crewe, Liebling, & Hulley, 2015). Similarly, in the United States the role of institutional control was elucidated by the effects of the New Mexico State Penitentiary prison riot in which 12 correctional officers were taken hostage, 33 people incarcerated were killed by fellow detainees, and hundreds of incarcerated individuals were sexually assaulted (Colvin, 1982; Serrill & Katel, 1980). Arguably the worst prison riot in American history, this 36-hour period of destruction, torture, and terror occurring in February 1980 resulted from organizational changes to the prison and the use of coercive management techniques. The results of the group-think mentality arising out of the overtaking of the New Mexico State Penitentiary by those incarcerated in the facility suggest that collective violence may be a more prolific result of institutional control gone awry than individual violence.

Institutional control in recent years has reflected an inmate-balance theoretical slant, and the height of prison riots experienced in the 1970s and early 1980s may have passed. Inmate-balance theory suggests that correctional officers tolerate minor infractions committed by persons incarcerated in prison as a way for them to assist correctional staff in maintaining order (Useem & Reisig, 1999). Moving from a state-centered approach to prison control (see Useem & Goldstone, 2002) and allowing incarcerated persons to have some control over their daily existence, the theory posits that people become more willing to adhere to the more serious rules of the institution. Useem and Goldstone (2002, p. 507) highlight several riots and disturbances in private prisons suggesting that inmate-balance is impractical in for-profit settings and even resulting in "mandate[s] to impose unusual disamenities on inmates."

Contrary to inmate-balance, solitary confinement is a form of institutional control whose benefits and disadvantages are frequently addressed in the scholarly literature. Isolating inmates is not a new phenomenon (Smith, 2006), though contemporary scholars and practitioners, and even former U.S. President Obama, have refocused attention on the appropriateness of the use of solitary confinement as a management technique to punish an act of violence engaged in during a period of incarceration. While additional research is certainly needed to determine the long-term effects of solitary confinement, particularly upon release, it has not been shown to influence future engagement in prison violence (see Morris, 2016).

The Culture of Prison Violence

The cycle of violence, where violence begets violence, and when victim becomes perpetrator, is well known in non-institutional settings (see Maxfield & Widom, 1996; Widom, 1989). This idiom is evident behind the closed doors of prisons, too. As Bowker (1980, p. 31) aptly states:

> All of the forms of prison victimization are related so that each becomes a causal factor in the other, forming an insane feedback system through which prison victimization rates are under constant pressure to increase. A similar feedback phenomenon occurs when prisoners feel constrained to take revenge for past victimization and to defend themselves in current victimizations. The interaction takes on the form of a macabre version of the game of musical chairs in which today's aggressor may become tomorrow's victim.

Importation, deprivation, and institutional control offer three theoretical explanations for why prison violence occurs, but how much violence is happening in our nation's institutions? Prison violence is understood to be ubiquitous and a given attribute of this particular total institution (see Gibbons & Katzenbach, 2006; Irwin, 1980; Johnson, 1987; Wooldredge, 1998) though reporting of general violence such as physical assault and robbery are accepted as underreported by incarcerated persons for fear of violating the inmate code (see McCorkle, 1993). Individuals incarcerated in Portugal highlight "staying out of trouble" as their main stressor during their time in prison and viewed adopting prison customs as a primary way to achieve this goal (Gonçalves et al., 2016). Physical victimization takes the form of inmate-on-inmate, staff-on-inmate, and inmate-on-staff with little substantive difference between reported prevalence rates of the various forms of violence (see Wolff, Blitz, Shi, Siegel, & Bachman, 2007). According to Bureau of Justice Statistics estimates, incarcerated persons are 18 to 27 times more likely to be assaulted than the general population (Catalano, 2005). Estimates of prison victimization range from 5.8% to 21% (James & Glaze, 2006; Lahm, 2009b; Wolff et al., 2007). Clearly violence is occurring in prison, though perhaps perceptions are not congruent with reality or reporting is substandard at best.

Two types of violence affecting people incarcerated that have been subject to more in-depth analysis are death—self-inflicted and felonious—and sexual assault.[1] In 2013, 11% of deaths among incarcerated persons were due to non-illness related causes such as suicide—the leading cause of death in jails since 2000 (Noonan, Rohloff, & Ginder, 2015). Suicides among jail inmates dropped precipitously from the mid-1980s before leveling off to a rate just above 40 per 100,000 inmates (Mumola, 2005). Homicides are rare in prison (see Reidy & Sorensen, 2017), though between 2000 and 2013, 302 jail inmates, 762 state inmates, and 116 federal inmates were victims of homicide while in custody (Noonan et al., 2015).[2] Without a deceased body to account for, data on sexual assaults are less reliable and self-report data are essential to quantify its occurrence. According to studies in response to the Prison Rape Elimination Act (PREA) of 2003, surveys of inmates utilizing national probability samples found that among adult inmates, sexual assault is more prevalent in state and federal prisons with 4% of inmates being the victim of such violence while 3.2% of adults in jail experience sexual victimization during their incarceration (Beck, 2014).

Violent victimization has serious repercussions beyond those associated with increased likelihood of becoming a violent perpetrator. Violence can be experienced directly as a victim or indirectly as a witness or hearing about someone else's victimization. The impact of exposure to prison violence on human suffering is tangible and may result in negative psychological sequelae (Haney, 2002) including thoughts of, or attempted, suicide (Liebling & Ludlow, 2016; Struckman-Johnson & Struckman-Johnson, 2002; Smith, Selwyn, Wolford-Clevenger, & Mandracchia, 2014) and may manifest as a need to respond to violent attacks with violence to fend off additional victimization (Steiner et al., 2017). Experiencing violence in prison can result in physical injuries (Ludwig, Cohen, Parsons, & Venters, 2012; Wolff & Shi, 2009a), post-traumatic stress and other psychological trauma (Wolff & Shi, 2009b; Jamieson & Grounds, 2013), as well as sexually transmitted disease (WHO/UNAIDS/UNODC, 2007). A systematic review of the literature on mental health during periods of incarceration by Walker, Illingworth, Canning, Garner, Woolley, Taylor, and Amos (2014) demonstrates a gap in the evidence and suggests that mental health in prison is subject to change and may improve over time. They call for longitudinal studies to track the mental health of those incarcerated. Such research would benefit by extending beyond periods of incarceration and tracking formerly incarcerated persons into the community to gauge change. There is also a need to establish causality between experiencing violence in prison and mental health. While Schnittker (2014) shows that mental health disorders are more disabling for formerly incarcerated persons compared to those who never experienced prison, the relationship between prison violence and mental health is not clear, and mental health disorders are higher among prisoners than the general population (Fazel, Hayes, Bartellas, Clerici, & Trestman, 2016). However, Jamieson and Grounds' work with previously incarcerated persons suggests that exposure to violence has lasting implications, even after release. They state that even among wrongfully convicted incarcerated persons "experiences of serious violence in prison, either as witnesses or victims, still troubled some of the men [after release], and were referred to as important turning points in the men's perception of themselves" (2013, p. 48).

There are myriad ways to help protect incarcerated persons against violence. At the structural level, improved facility security measures have contributed to a reduction in prison violence (Useem & Goldstone, 2002; Useem & Piehl, 2006), while people incarcerated in prison can protect themselves by remaining unaffiliated with a prison gang, which, though often viewed as a means of protection, is related to a higher probability of involvement in violent behavior (Gaes et al., 2002). Auty, Cope, and Liebling (2017) identify cognitive behavioral programs and social learning as the dominant approaches to addressing prison violence at the individual level. A more nuanced violence prevention program would have greater reach. A public health approach to violence prevention recognizes multiple sources of violence—such as the community, peers, and social context—and underscores a need for a multi-pronged method for prevention (see Centers for Disease Control and Prevention, 2016). In carceral settings, a public health approach would include identifying risk and protective factors of prison violence; screening for potential abusers and separating them from potential victims in housing situations; identifying and testing prevention strategies for reducing involvement in violence, exposure to violence, and addressing negative effects associated with experiencing violence; and developing best practices and ensuring their implementation and adoption across various carceral settings. Further, the prison context would need to be addressed. Haney (2013) reinforces the importance of viewing prison violence from a contextual milieu rather than focusing on psychological factors of persons incarcerated in prisons. Citing McElhaney and Effley (1999), Haney (2013, p. 83) states that "the recent trend towards community-based violence reduction programs is based implicitly on the new-found understanding that exclusively individual models of the causes of criminal behavior are not up to the task of effectively reducing it." This does not suggest that individual factors do not matter; rather the goal is to elevate context to equal importance in prevention efforts. Given the evidence suggesting the importance of context on inmate–on–inmate assault (Lahm, 2008), scholars and practitioners should pay at least equal attention to how context may influence exposure to violence in the prison setting. While context matters and serves as a buffer against exposure to community violence (see Antunes & Ahlin, 2017) there are still many unanswered questions about how the prison context may amplify exposure to violence perpetrated against others, and Morris and Worrall (2014) suggest that prison infrastructure is only associated with nonviolent inmate misconduct and not prison violence (for a discussion see Bottoms, 1999).

One promising avenue of inquiry that crosses both individual and structural characteristics is the concept of guardianship. According to routine activity theory (see Cohen & Felson, 1979), crime is more likely to occur when a lack of capable guardianship converges with motivated offenders and suitable targets. Motivated offenders are believed to be constant, while suitable targets in prison are ubiquitous. It is capable guardianship where prisons have the most leverage to effect change. For example, Teasdale, Daigle, Hawk, and Daquin (2016) suggest there is a lack of capable guardianship, either formal facility supervision or informal social controls from other inmates, to protect against sexual victimization in adult prisons. Capable guardianship could be introduced through increased monitoring and risk assessment at the individual level, while increased surveillance and reduction of hidden areas where assaults are more likely to take place can address the prison context.

Proactively addressing prison violence is not only important to provide security to correctional staff and persons incarcerated; it also provides an opportunity to reduce the ancillary effects of direct and vicarious victimization. The cycle of violence (Widom, 1989) extends beyond the family such that victims in custodial settings can become involved in violence while in custody (see DeLisi et al., 2010). Less is known about how the cycle of violence may extend beyond periods of confinement, though Dumond (1992) suggests that prison sexual assault survivors may be primed for violence when released from prison. However, other scholars refute the direct relationship between prison victimization and violence as a myth not adequately rooted in empirical evidence (see Lockwood, 1994).

There is empirical evidence to suggest that violence in the communities where many incarcerated persons resided before prison are prone to acceptance of a culture of violence as a way to navigate the streets, protect themselves, and maintain respect (see Anderson, 1999; Wacquant, 2001). Stowell and Byrne (2008) recognize that incarcerated persons' communities do influence prison culture, though they also challenge scholars to go beyond this simplified explanation of prison violence by considering how incarcerated people's acceptance and adherence to violence before incarceration is altered as a result of the prison experience (Gilligan, 1996) and then transferred back to the community and perhaps strengthened upon release (see Rose & Clear, 1998). Exposure to violence in the community has detrimental ramifications above and beyond the perpetuation of the cycle of violence where exposure to violence is related to engagement in violence (Brady et al., 2008; Flannery, Singer, & Wester, 2003; Gorman-Smith & Tolan, 1998; Spano, Rivera, & Bolland, 2006). More generally in the community, exposure to violence as a witness or hearing of someone else's victimization can lead to mental health issues (Fowler, Tompsett, Braciszewski, Jacques-Tiura, & Baltes, 2009; McGruder-Johnson, Davidson, Gleaves, Stock, & Finch, 2000; Zona & Milan, 2011) and internalizing disorders such as anxiety (Hurt, Malmud, Brodsky, & Giannetta, 2001) and depression (Fitzpatrick, Piko, Wright, & LaGory, 2005). Exposure to community violence is also an antecedent to externalizing behaviors such as aggression (Cooley-Quille, Turner, & Beidel, 1995) and can contribute to lower perceptions of control over one's environment (Farver, Ghosh, & Garcia, 2000). Scarpa, Haden, and Hurley (2006) identify the moderating effects of coping strategies on the relationship between exposure to community violence and aggressive behavior. Aggression and other anti-social coping mechanisms may be expressed as a response to experiences with violence in contexts over which someone has little control (see Shakoor & Chalmers, 1991) such as one prone to violence. This suggests the possibility of a reciprocal relationship as a negative environment may perpetuate a lack of perceived control (Lefcourt, 1982).

The combination of violence in carceral settings and community violence, whether perpetrated by formerly incarcerated persons or fellow neighborhood residents, is less explored in the scholarly literature. While there are ample data on recidivism amongst formerly incarcerated persons, the field has yet to fully examine the exportation of a culture of violence from the prison setting to the community. Exploration of such transference and acceptance of a violent culture from prison to the community may assist in our understanding of violence and incarceration as normative among residents of socially disorganized communities (Clear, 2009) and so-called million-dollar blocks where high concentrations of correctional populations resided before incarceration (NPR, 2012).

To understand whether the culture of prison violence and its effects extend beyond periods of incarceration, we need to link exposure to violence with involvement in violence through the lens of established theories of prison violence—importation, deprivation, and institutional control. In the next section, we propose a new theoretical model for examining exportation of violence from the prison experience. We outline how the culture of violence during periods of incarceration may diffuse beyond prison walls, negatively impacting the offender reentry experience, serve as a detriment to the safety of the community, and perhaps permeate the neighborhood culture by escalating acceptance of violence in the community.

Exportation Theory

Unlike the famed slogan of America's notorious "sin city," Las Vegas, Nevada, what happens in prison, doesn't stay in prison (see Stowell & Byrne, 2008). Because of the increased number of people who have experienced incarceration directly (see Cochran & Toman, Chapter 14), or as a result of a family member or friend being sent "up state,"[3] the happenings from behind prison walls creep out into society. Many aspects of incarcerated persons' lives are mundane and mirror the functions of a routinized city with set times for waking, meals, recreation, and lights out. But it is the ostensible truth that violence happens with less precision, though almost as frequently as much of the customary herding of people incarcerated in prison from one location to the next, and whose intensity is often exaggerated through the "carceral imaginary" (Griffiths, 2016, p. 1; see also Pickett, Mancini, Mears, & Gertz, 2015). Either through media, print, or experience, prison life including violence is increasingly palatable; though despite seeming acceptance of violence in prisons, citizens do not expect continued acceptance or involvement in violence among formerly incarcerated persons upon release. As increasing numbers of formerly incarcerated persons are released from jails and prisons, it is even more important to examine if reentrants can disengage from the culture of violence once out of prison. Even more detrimental to their prospects and the communities to which they return is what happens if they cannot leave their taste for prison violence behind. We suggest that the culture of prison violence is exported to communities when formerly incarcerated persons return home. Our exportation theoretical model (Figure 21.1) is a visual representation of how violence (in prison and in the community) may influence behavior among those incarcerated as well as persons in the community. First we discuss the components of the model, and then in the proceeding sections outline the extant work in each area (the letters given refer to the components in Figure 21.1).

To begin, the circles (*A: Exposure to community violence; B: Involvement in violent behaviors*) on the far left of the diagram represent the importation theoretical model of the culture of prison violence. As addressed above, a proclivity towards violence while incarcerated may stem from exposure to violence in the community prior to incarceration either by direct victimization or by hearing about or witnessing violent acts committed against others (vicarious victimization; see Daquin, Daigle, & Listwan, 2016). Importation is also influenced by incarcerated persons' prior negative life experiences and engagement in violence while on the streets. These two aspects of violence before incarceration

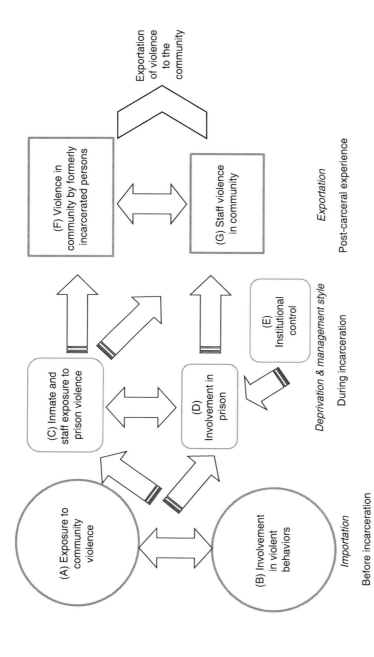

Figure 21.1 Exportation Theoretical Model

THEORETICAL MODEL:

A. Exposure to community violence leads to involvement in violent behaviors prior to incarceration (importation, cycle of violence)
B. Involvement in violent behaviors prior to prison leads to more exposure to violence (importation, cycle of violence)
C. Exposure to prison violence leads to involvement in prison violence (deprivation)
D. Involvement in violence in prison leads to more exposure to violence (deprivation)
E. Institutional control leads to involvement in prison violence (management style)
F. Exposure to and involvement in prison violence leads to formerly incarcerated persons' involvement in violence in the community (exportation)
G. Exposure to violence to and involvement in prison violence leads to staff violence in the community (exportation)

can influence each other, as exposure to community violence may increase involvement in violence while engaging in violence contributes to exposure to community violence for other inmates, staff, and visitors to the facility, and these background factors are also brought with inmates to the carceral experience influencing their behavior and that of others.

Towards the middle of the model are the two facets of the culture of prison violence that result from the prison experience—deprivation (*C: Inmate and staff exposure to prison violence; D: Involvement in prison violence*) and institutional management style (*E: Institutional control*). Similar to the importation section of our model, exposure to violence perpetrated by other incarcerated persons and violent behavior by those in prison themselves can increase violent behavior and exposure to violence. Someone who has a history of exposure to and involvement in violence prior to incarceration may be more likely to adopt the culture of prison violence while adding to the magnitude of their experience with violence. At the other end of the spectrum, persons new to the prison environment who have not previously served time, or perchance were not exposed to violence during their prior stints in prison, may be new to the culture of prison violence. The conditions of imprisonment are theorized to have an influence over behavior as it relates to violence.

Prison management is another theoretical argument underpinning prison violence. Institutional control practices and facility characteristics can either exacerbate or reduce involvement in violence among those in prison. Specifically, a review by Byrne and Hummer (2007) linked higher levels of prison violence and disorder with the following factors: prison crowding; staffing levels (and quality/experience); inadequate programming in prisons (access quality); ineffective classification/placement practices; a variety of poor management practices; inadequate facility design; situational contexts such as daily routines and prisoner autonomy; and institution-specific incarcerated persons' profiles, including the number of individuals who are violent or have a mental illness, median age, and racial/ethnic heterogeneity of the prison population (Levan, 2013; Steiner & Wooldredge, 2008, 2014). Wardens can outline the management difficulties associated with multi-level pressures within their individual facility and, externally, from the entirety of the system itself. For instance, a facility may implement a strategy to reduce violence between gang-affiliated inmates, however if the department of corrections in that specific state does not consider gang affiliation when assigning incarcerated people to facilities, the warden's efforts may be for naught. Institutional response to violence can have effects as damaging as exposure to violent incidents themselves. All too frequently, administrative response to violence equates to isolation of the offending person(s) from the rest of the facility's population. The psychological impact of long-term solitary confinement has been established in the empirical literature (see Campbell, 2016; Hagan et al., 2017; Labrecque & Smith, Chapter 16), however as a short-term solution, it remains a commonplace tactic in prisons nationwide (Garcia et al., 2016) and in other countries throughout the world such as Norway (see Ahalt & Williams, 2016), China, Brazil, England, Mexico, Poland, Kenya, and Germany (Weil, Gotshal, & Manges, 2016).

Formerly incarcerated persons released from prison return to communities, and the context of their destination is essential in determining success (see Kirk, 2009; Kirk, Chapter 3; Mears, Wang, Hay, & Bales, 2008). Those who reside in communities with ample resources are less likely to recidivate (see Kubrin & Stewart, 2006) and may be better positioned to relinquishing the culture of prison violence, whereas those who reside in disadvantaged violent neighborhoods may be more apt to use the inmate code on the outside. Using violence as a response to confrontations and situations in the community could be expected after a period of experiential learning from living in a culture permeated by the use of violence by incarcerated persons as well as by severe institutional control responses to prison violence that are incompatible with conflict resolution tactics in everyday society (Dawes, 1993; Reisig, 1998). Even using transitional placement prior to full release back to their community (such as residential community corrections centers) does not necessarily give formerly incarcerated persons time to shed the mind-set of prison life. Recent assessments of the institutional culture of these facilities demonstrate many of the same dilemmas that are commonplace in prisons exist also in transitional facilities, such as residential community corrections centers (Alladin & Hummer, Forthcoming; Cantora, Mellow, & Schlager, 2014; Gunter, Philibert, & Hollenbeck, 2009). It seems, then, that irrespective of the formerly incarcerated person's final stop on the path back to residence in the community, they overwhelmingly are reentering from an atmosphere of tension, harsh discipline, and the threat or perpetration of violence.

Taking Violence Home

The final section of the model presented in Figure 21.1 shows the exportation of violence after having direct and/or vicarious experiences with prison (*F: Violence in the community by formerly incarcerated persons*). For formerly incarcerated people, the process of reentry has been described as a "rite of passage" (Maruna, 2011). The normalization of the prison experience in some communities suggests that many, if not all, are expected to spend time in prison (see Anderson, 1999; Hirschfield & Piquero, 2010). In his thorough examination of prisoner reentry, Travis (2005) delved into the processes by which reentrants develop a new identity by adapting to their surroundings and engaging with others. Maruna (2001) suggests that some formerly incarcerated persons utilize a "redemption script" to rewrite their past experiences. This involves the process of "making good" that involves self-reconstruction through (1) establishment of core beliefs that characterize one's true self, (2) optimistic perception of personal control over one's destiny, and (3) desire to be productive and give something back to society. Such work requires more "self-reconstruction than amputation" (Maruna, 2001, p. 87). Depending on the length of incarceration and adoption and adherence to the culture of prison violence, the process of self-reconstruction may differ across formerly incarcerated persons. There has been great focus on attempts to "go straight" or leave a criminal past behind (see Maruna, 2001, 2004; Maruna & Roy, 2007; Ward, 2002; Ward, Mann, & Gannon, 2007) with an emphasis on rational choice or positive decision-making (Paternoster & Pogarsky, 2009). Collectively these works suggest that formerly incarcerated persons primarily seek to "do good" and embrace a law-abiding way of life. Scholars do not negate the possibility that at least some reentrants will not proactively seek a crime-free life, though this focus on "making good" does not address in-depth the barriers facing prosocial reentry as they relate to experiencing violence over three phases: pre-incarceration, imprisonment, and reentry. There is some scholarly attention paid to the baggage reentrants bring home associated with engagement in and exposure to violence, and in a systematic review Goff, Rose, Rose, and Purves (2007) identified a need for services addressing post-traumatic stress disorder among formerly incarcerated persons. We suggest that prison violence is a collateral consequence to the imprisonment experience and that it is possible some reentrants take the code of prison violence home to the community. This transference of violence from institution to neighborhood could be a collateral consequence that transcends from formerly incarcerated persons to others who may or may not have been involved in the criminal justice system, either introducing an added layer of exposure to violence or reinforcing violence as an acceptable response to situations. While incarcerated, those in prison often come to understand violence as an appropriate method for dealing with prison conditions and handling confrontations with peers and correctional staff (Byrne & Hummer, 2007; Lindegaard & Gear, 2014; Reid & Listwan, 2015). In certain communities, it may reinforce what is already an established pattern of violence and acceptance of violent behaviors as a means to address conflict among residents of a certain age (see Anderson, 1999; Stewart & Simons, 2010), which also can increase risk of victimization (Stewart. Schreck, & Simons, 2006).

Addressing violence as a collateral consequence to incarceration is essential for multiple reasons. One concern is the continued repercussions of violence upon release. Scholars note that misconduct among incarcerated persons, particularly behavior involving violence, is positively associated with recidivism (Cochran, Mears, Bales, & Stewart, 2014; Hill, 1985; Huebner, Varano, & Bynum, 2007; Lattimore, Visher, & Linster, 1995; O'Leary & Glaser, 1972). We propose that such exposure to

21 Exportation Hypothesis

violence or engagement in violent behavior may decrease reentrants' ability to return to society in a prosocial manner. The cycle of violence, whether introduced before incarceration or established during a stint in prison, may continue when the formerly incarcerated person hits the streets. Even if the individual does not engage in violence, the stories about his or her time in prison and the violence that occurred behind closed doors are often parlayed to friends, family members, and other (particularly younger) community residents, acting as a bypass for the inmate code of violence (see Conner, Chapter 19, for a discussion on family reunification).

Impact of Prison Violence on Staff

Correctional staff also have direct experiences with exposure to prison violence that can contribute to exportation of prison culture (*G: Staff violence in the community*). Empirical assessments of job satisfaction and stress are numerous for justice system actors. The notion that correctional facilities are stressful working environments has been established empirically (e.g., Kinman, Clements, & Hart, 2017; Lambert et al., 2009), yet the evidence does not demonstrate widespread violent victimization of staff. Lahm (2009a) highlights a 27% increase in inmate-on-staff assaults across three states between 1995 and 2000 after a decline from the height of prison violence in the 1980s. Sorenson, Cunningham, Vigen, and Wood's (2011) review of staff assaults in one state correctional system demonstrated a rate of victimization far below that of inmate-on-inmate assaults. Those incidents that resulted in serious injury to the employee were even less common. The victimization literature itself indicates that being specifically targeted for assault is not a prerequisite for the impacts of victimization to become manifest, rather repeated exposure to, and witnessing of, violent assaultive behavior against others can lead to long-term negative outcomes such as anxiety, depression, post-traumatic stress disorder, and health-related concerns (Boudoukha, Altintas, Rusinek, Fantini-Hauwel, & Hautekeete, 2013; Listwan, Daigle, Hartman, & Guastaferro, 2014; Stoyanova & Harizanova, 2016). The effects of a violent and stressful atmosphere are not salient just at the individual level of the employees themselves. Stress among correctional workers has been shown to lead to high levels of absenteeism, burnout, and turnover (Allisey, Noblet, Lamontagne, & Houdmont, 2014; Finney, Stergiopoulos, Hensel, Bonato, & Dewa, 2013; Schaufeli & Peeters, 2000), which in a cyclical pattern leaves institutions with an ongoing management issue of having to continually integrate new employees into the organizational culture, leading to a higher likelihood of institutional violence due to an inability to appropriately secure the facility (see Finn, 1998; Stohr, Self, & Lovrich, 1992).

Correctional workers, both new to the field and veteran, are susceptible to behaviors associated with recurring exposure to stress such as substance abuse, marriage/family problems, and anger/impulse control, behaviors that have been well-documented among police officers and correctional staff (e.g., Anshel & Brinthaupt, 2014; Can & Hendy, 2014; Gould, Watson, Price, & Valliant, 2013; Keinan & Malach-Pines, 2007)—particularly African-American women (Britton, 2003). Although it is difficult to isolate precisely which aspects of working in corrections form the primary stressors for a given employee, it is exposure to violence and the threat of danger that have been shown to be significant contributing factors (e.g., Goffman, 1961; Botha & Pienaar, 2006). Hours spent in an environment where the threat of violence is continual puts the employee in a state of agitation that does not dissipate once the individual leaves the facility. The role places correctional officers in a precarious position; they are responsible for responding to administrative orders while also maintaining supervision over incarcerated persons who they deal with on a basis more regularly than those officially meting out directives (see Pollock, 2013). The type of violence perpetrated by incarcerated persons has been shown to vary by gender, with women having less violent criminal histories prior to incarceration but greater emotion accompanying the violence they perpetrate during confinement (Britton, 2003). Correctional officer protection from prison violence is also gendered. Britton (2003, p. 141) states that "male inmates give [women correctional officers] more respect and (for good or ill) protection from violence." This suggests a nuanced perspective taking account of multiple ascribed characteristics may be necessary.

Routine stressors and pressures of daily life are exacerbated by exposure to violence, and those around the corrections worker (e.g., family, friends, acquaintances) are impacted by the culture of the correctional facility, even if they have never entered the institution itself (Lambert, Hogan, & Barton, 2004). Just as prison can change persons who are incarcerated, working in carceral settings can alter a person (Crawley & Crawley, 2012). There is evidence of "spill-over effects" where suspicion and expectation of obedience become occupational hazards in correctional officers' personal lives (see Crawley, 2002, 2004). Correctional officers are 39% more likely to commit suicide than persons employed in other professions (Stack & Tsoudis, 1997), they experience substantially higher levels of organization stress compared to law enforcement (Summerlin, Oehme, Stern, & Valentine, 2010), and report that as many as 30% of their coworkers engage in interpersonal violence while 11% self-reported being violent with an intimate partner (Valentine, Oehme, & Martin, 2012). This literature suggests that the cycle of violence is reasonably expected to perpetuate in situations where it has established a hold over prison staff, thereby extending into the community.

Normalization of Violence

The exportation hypothesis is the culmination of the three major theoretical perspectives of prison violence and extends these theories to the community context. As discussed in this chapter, there is evidence to suggest that each of these theories is a valid explanation of prison violence and a culture of violence in carceral settings. Deprivation theory and management explanations of prison violence and culture are clear manifestations of the prison environment and how actors manage their time in the prison setting. Analogously, importation theory may be simply a reflection of continued acceptance and adherence to a culture of violence in the prison setting (see Byrne & Taxman, 2006; Irwin & Cressey, 1962), while a theory of exportation suggests that those in prison contribute to violence in communities by bringing the prison culture home upon release.

Our exportation hypothesis integrates these mainstay explanations of prison violence and suggests that either as a whole or in part, their experiences may contribute to violence in the community. The expectation that reentrants will embrace, or at least accept, some normalization of violence has more of a direct linkage in the continuation of the cycle of violence beyond prison walls. People incarcerated in prisons, whether violent or not before or during confinement, are exposed at the very least indirectly to the ubiquitous nature and ongoing threat of prison violence. The literature on direct violent victimizations and ancillary experiences with violence suggest both can lead to negative consequences including the use of violence and other detrimental sequelae that may increase victimization risk. Further, such exposure to violence may normalize the behavior, even if it is not accepted, internalized, or acted upon. Witnessing, hearing about, or being on the receiving end of violence by others in the community may not garner a second glance or intervention by those exposed to high levels of institutional violence as it likely would among individuals who are not desensitized to such acts. Work by Sharkey (2006) posits that youth in violent areas are more adept at navigating the streets and protecting themselves to avoid dangerous situations; they have been acculturated to understand violence as a normal part of life and have learned how to adapt. Similarly, according to Taylor and Shumaker (1990) residents in violent communities may not believe their neighborhood is dangerous while outside observers may feel threatened and unable to manage the environment. This may lead to incongruent perceptions—ones that are dependent on the observer and their experiences with violence and a manifestation of the normalization of violence. Increased exposure to violence can lead to victimization through a reduction in capable guardians (Ahlin & Antunes, 2017) while personal actions also play a role in risk (see Gibson, Morris, & Beaver, 2009; Melde & Esbensen, 2011). Management of the environment and effective coping strategies can buffer the negative effects of exposure to violence (Scarpa, Haden, & Hurley, 2006) while adopting an internal locus of control over the environment could reduce engagement in violence (see Ahlin, 2014).

Beyond the culture of prison violence being transferred to the community by formerly incarcerated persons, we offer an additional pathway for the exportation of violence, and potential contributor to the normalization of violence, through staff experiences within the carceral setting. Correctional officers are on the front lines and are routinely exposed to, and at times must engage in, violence during the course of their duties. This commonly occurring part of the job can reduce the shock and abhorrence often equated with violent behaviors among those who are not overexposed to such acts. There is more research substantiating the negative effects of working in a high stress and volatile environment such as prison, though we would be remiss if we did not contemplate that even small short-term encounters such as those experienced by visitors or prison volunteers might not transfer into at least a superficial understanding of violence as normal in such a setting. Various media forms such as books, newspapers, television, and the internet continually make this information available to the general public, though it remains distanced from first-hand accounts and experiences. We do not suggest this type of exportation of violence is novel to the prison setting—it likely occurs in many other milieus where persons not involved in the criminal justice system come into contact with perpetrators or victims of violence such as police, social workers, and military personnel. However, what is unique in the prison setting is the interaction of persons who have not been processed by the criminal justice system with a violent environment as a result of the exponential increase in the use of prison as a sentencing option. Should there be a relationship between the normalization of violence and exportation of the prison culture by persons in contact with people incarcerated in prisons, there are clear policy implications that would reduce its occurrence.

Conclusion

Over 640,000 individuals were released from state and federal prisons in the U.S. in 2015. It is further estimated that around 9 million people are released from jails per annum, if those who are simply processed into the system are included in the count. The extent of violence in correctional facilities has been effectively documented in the empirical literature, and while we cannot state with certainty that each incarcerated person directly experienced violence (as a perpetrator or victim) or was exposed vicariously to violence, it is reasonable to infer that many previously incarcerated adults who are released each year back into communities may have been detrimentally impacted by institutional violence. Research detailing whether and how the reach of prison violence extends beyond custodial settings and is exported to the community remains elusive and could substantially contribute to scholarly discussions on institutional and community violence. Policies supporting justice realignment and reductions in prison populations provide the impetus to examine both direct involvement in and exposure to prison violence as we begin to shed light on the collateral consequences of sentencing and punishment decisions (see Huebner & Frost, Introduction).

It is also important to note that people who were previously incarcerated do not reintegrate back into society in a uniform geographic manner. Certain communities receive a disproportionate amount of releasees per annum. For example, in Pennsylvania, an overwhelming majority of the over 40,000 state department of corrections inmates released between 2007 and 2011 listed their official residence as in an urban area after leaving prison, regardless of where they had been residing prior to incarceration (see Zajac, Hutchison, & Meyer, 2014). Drilling down further, just a few dozen census tracts in the cities of Philadelphia, Pittsburgh, Erie, Allentown, and Harrisburg receive a large share of PADOC releasees. These communities are most at risk for the exportation of negative elements of institutional culture, particularly given that these communities are also characterized by lower levels of collective efficacy.

Correctional systems, along with other entities with vested interests and the ability to impact social policy, must recognize the process by which institutional violence is brought back to neighborhoods through cultural diffusion and its ramifications. Discussions of successful reintegration tend to focus, rightly so, on opportunities for formerly incarcerated persons and access to services (e.g., James, 2015; Hipp, Petersilia, & Turner, 2010; Mellow & Greifinger, 2007). However there is a growing recognition that long-term exposure to prison culture not only inhibits the formerly incarcerated person's probability of individual success (Visher & Travis, 2003), but also further deteriorates the community by transmitting attitudes and behaviors common to the institution back to these neighborhoods if they are unable to free themselves from their "prisonization" experiences (see Clemmer, 1940), particularly in communities characterized by high rates of incarceration and low social and financial capital (see Clear, 2009; Remster Villanova & Warner, Chapter 4). In this sense, the deleterious effects of victimization and witnessing the violent actions of others incarcerated are repeated outside prison walls, and children in these communities (particularly those with incarcerated family members, see Northcutt Bohmert & Wakefield, Chapter 8) are disproportionately impacted. The cyclical nature of violence, perpetuated disproportionately by younger community members, is certainly compounded by those elements of prison culture carried back by formerly incarcerated persons. Such acclimation to the prison culture, whether through full participation or mere acceptance while doing one's "bid," could lead to some need for resocialization upon release (see Zingraff, 1975). Some of this cultural appropriation is evidenced by persons adopting popular trends such as wearing loose-fitting pants low and prison-style tattooing[4] that can readily be seen adorning those who have never spent time in a correctional facility. However, it is those elements of the institutional culture that are *not* visible that are most insidious—the use of violence to resolve disputes, a lack of empathy, and the view of relations with others as a predator-prey dyad. It stands to reason these attitudes predated institutional cultural diffusion in certain neighborhoods, but they are reinforced and further expanded with every person returning from a stint of incarceration. Further, everyone impacted by the prison system may be at risk of desensitization to violence as well as the negative repercussions such exposure can have on behavior, mental health, and the community at-large. The collateral consequences of incarceration extend well beyond the period of detention and could have unintended ramifications for those who are in the thick of the culture of prison violence and perhaps in the margins of this aspect of society.

This is an important issue for future research, and our preliminary exportation hypothesis requires additional unpacking, development, and eventual testing. Further work is required to establish theoretical mechanisms for the transference of prison culture to the community. Should such mechanisms be identified, practical implications such as identification of persons at risk for transferring violent attitudes and behaviors from the carceral setting to the community could be adopted to allow parole and probation agents to provide additional support services to mitigate tendencies toward violence. International work by Singh, Bjorkly, and Fazel (2016) provides an interdisciplinary repository of instruments and practices to aid the development of violence risk assessments for persons formerly incarcerated prior to their release that could guide the development of risk assessments. To develop a full picture of the exportation hypothesis, additional studies will be needed that address the perspective of formerly incarcerated persons, institutional staff, and community members.

Notes

1 Physical assaults are also prevalent in the jail and prison setting, though enumeration of the problem due to underreporting by inmates and staff can be difficult (for a review see Byrne & Hummer, 2008) due to the pervasive institutional culture that supports underreporting (see Bottoms, 1999).

2 Intentional or involuntary manslaughter.

3 In Pennsylvania, persons incarcerated often refer to being sent to prison as being sent "up state." This geographic location is accurate for many incarcerated people as the majority of prisons are located north of the two main epi-centers that the majority of state prisoners call home—Philadelphia and Pittsburgh.

4 According to a study by Rozycki Lozano et al. (2011), prison-style tattoos among inmates lead to stronger adherence to a criminal lifestyle compared to other forms of tattoos among incarcerated persons and college students.

References

Ahalt, C., & Williams, B. (2016). Reforming solitary-confinement policy—Heeding a Presidential call to action. *New England Journal of Medicine, 374*, 1704–1706.

Ahlin, E. M. (2014). Locus of control redux: Adolescents' choice to refrain from violence. *Journal of Interpersonal Violence, 29*, 2695–2717.

Ahlin, E. M., & Antunes, M. J. L. (2017). Levels of guardianship in protecting youth against exposure to violence in the community. *Youth Violence and Juvenile Justice, 15*, 62–83.

Allisey, A. F., Noblet, A. J., Lamontagne, A. D., & Houdmont, J. (2014). Testing a model of officer intentions to quit: The mediating effects of job stress and job satisfaction. *Criminal Justice and Behavior, 41*, 751–771.

Antunes, M. J. L., & Ahlin, E. M. (2017). Youth exposure to violence in the community: Towards a theoretical framework for explaining risk and protective factors. *Aggression and Violent Behavior, 34*, 166–177.

Alexander, M. (2012). *The new Jim Crow: Mass incarceration in the age of colorblindness.* New York, NY: The New Press.

Alladin, T., & Hummer, D. (Forthcoming). The relationship between individual characteristics, quality of confinement and recidivism by offenders released from privately- and publically-managed residential community corrections facilities. *The Prison Journal.*

Anderson, E. (1999). *Code of the street.* New York, NY: Norton.

Anshel, M. H., & Brinthaupt, T. M. (2014). An exploratory study on the effect of an approach-avoidance coping program on perceived stress and physical energy among police officers. *Psychology, 5*, 676–687.

Auty, K. M., Cope, A., & Liebling, A. (2017). Psychoeducational programs for reducing prison violence: A systematic review. *Aggression and Violent Behavior, 33*, 126–143.

Beck, A. J. (2014). *PREA data collection activities, 2014.* Washington, DC: U.S. Department of Justice, Office of Justice Programs, Bureau of Justice Statistics.

Blevins, K. R., Listwan, S. J., Cullen, F. T., & Jonson, C. L. (2010). A general strain theory of prison violence and misconduct: An integrated model of inmate behavior. *Journal of Contemporary Criminal Justice, 26*, 148–166.

Botha, C., & Pienaar, J. (2006). South African correctional official occupational stress: The role of psychological strengths. *Journal of Criminal Justice, 34*, 73–84.

Bottoms, A. E. (1999). Interpersonal violence and social order in prisons. In M. Tonry & J. Petersilia, (Eds.), *Prisons* (pp. 205–282). Chicago, IL: University of Chicago Press.

Boudoukha, A. H., Altintas, E., Rusinek, S., Fantini-Hauwel, C., & Hautekeete, M. (2013). Inmates-to-staff assaults, PTSD and burnout: Profiles of risk and vulnerability. *Journal of Interpersonal Violence, 28*, 2332–2350.

Bowker, L. (1980). *Prison victimization.* New York, NY: Elsevier North Holland.

Brady, S. S., Gorman-Smith, D., Henry, D. B., & Tolan, P. H. (2008). Adaptive coping reduces the impact of community violence exposure on violent behavior among African American and Latino male adolescents. *Journal of Abnormal Child Psychology, 36*, 105–115.

Britton, D. M. (2003). *At work in the iron cage: The prison as gendered organization.* New York, NY: New York University Press.

Brosens, D., De Donder, L., Dury, S., & Verté, D. (2016). Participation in prison activities: An analysis of the determinants of participation. *European Journal on Criminal Policy and Research, 22*, 669–687.

Browning, C. R. (2002). The span of collective efficacy: Extending social disorganization theory to partner violence. *Journal of Marriage and Family, 64*, 833–850.

Burton, L., & Jarrett, R. (2000). In the mix, yet on the margins: The place of families in urban neighborhood and child development research. *Journal of Marriage and the Family, 62*, 1114–1135.

Byrne, J. M., & Hummer, D. (2007). Myths and realities of prison violence: A review of the evidence. *Victims & Offenders, 2*, 77–90.

Byrne, J. M., & Hummer, D. (2008). The nature and extent of prison violence. In J. M. Byrne, D. Hummer, & F. S. Taxman (Eds.), *The culture of prison violence* (pp. 12–26). New York, NY: Pearson.

Byrne, J. M., & Taxman, F. S. (2006). Crime control strategies and community change. *Federal Probation, 70*, 3–12.

Camp, S. D., & Gaes, G. G. (2005). Criminogenic effects of the prison environment on inmate behavior: Some experimental evidence. *Crime and Delinquency, 51*, 425–442.

Camp, S. D., Gaes, G. G., Langan, N. P., & Saylor, W. G. (2003). The influence of prisons on inmate misconduct: A multilevel investigation. *Justice Quarterly, 20*, 501–533.

Campbell, M. (2016). Vulnerable and inadequately protected: Solitary confinement, individuals with Mental Illness, and the laws that fail to protect. *Hofstra Law Review, 45*, 263–298.

Can, S. H., & Hendy, H. M. (2014). Police stressors, negative outcomes associated with them and coping mechanisms that may reduce these associations. *The Police Journal, 87*, 167–177.

Cantillon, D., Davidson, W. S., & Schweitzer, J. H. (2003). Measuring community social organization: Sense of community as a mediator in social disorganization theory. *Journal of Criminal Justice, 31*, 321–339.

Catalano, S. (2005). *Criminal victimization, 2004*. Washington, DC: Department of Justice. U.S. Bureau of Justice Statistics.

Cantora, A., Mellow, J., & Schlager, M. D. (2014). What about nonprogrammatic factors? Women's perceptions of staff and resident relationships in a community corrections setting. *Journal of Offender Rehabilitation, 53*, 35–56.

Ceballo, R., McLoyd, V. C., & Toyokawa, T. (2004). The Influence of neighborhood quality on adolescents' educational values and school effort. *Journal of Adolescent Research, 19*, 698–715.

Centers for Disease Control and Prevention. (2016). *The public health approach to violence prevention*. Retrieved from www.cdc.gov/violenceprevention/overview/publichealthapproach.html

Clear, T. R. (2009). *Imprisoning communities: How mass incarceration makes disadvantaged neighborhoods worse*. New York, NY: Oxford University Press.

Clemmer, D. (1940). *The prison community*. New York, NY: Rinehart & Company.

Cochran, J. C., Mears, D. P., Bales, W. D., & Stewart, E. A. (2014). Does inmate behavior affect post-release offending? Investigating the misconduct-recidivism relationship among youth and adults. *Justice Quarterly, 31*, 1044–1073.

Cohen, L. E., & Felson, M. (1979). Social change and crime rate trends: A routing activity approach. *American Sociological Review, 44*, 588–608.

Colvin, M. (1982). The 1980 New Mexico prison riot. *Social Problems, 29*, 449–463.

Colvin, M. (1992). *The penitentiary in crisis: From accommodation to riot in New Mexico*. Albany, NY: SUNY Press.

Cooley-Quille, M. R., Turner, S. M., & Beidel, D. C. (1995). Emotional impact of children's exposure to community violence: A preliminary study. *Journal of the American Academy of Child and Adolescent Psychiatry, 34*, 1362–1368.

Crawley, E. (2002). Bringing it all back home? The impact of prison officers' work on their families. *Probation Journal, 49*, 277–286.

Crawley, E. (2004). Doing prison work: The public and private lives of prison officers. New York, NY: Willan Publishing.

Crawley, E., & Crawley, P. (2012). Understanding prison officers: Culture, cohesion and conflicts. In J. Bennett, B. Crewe, & A. Wahidin (Eds.), *Understanding prison staff* (pp. 134–152). New York, NY: Willan Publishing.

Crewe, B., & Liebling, A. (2015). Staff culture, authority, and prison violence. *Prison Service Journal, 221*, 9–14.

Crewe, B., Liebling, A., & Hulley, S. (2015). Staff-prisoner relationships, staff professionalism, and the use of authority in public-and private-sector prisons. *Law and Social Inquiry, 40*, 309–344.

Cunningham, M. D., & Sorensen, J. R. (2007). Predictive factors for violent misconduct in close custody. *The Prison Journal, 87*, 241–253.

Daquin, J. C., Daigle, L. E., & Listwan, S. J. (2016). Vicarious victimization in prison: Examining the effects of witnessing victimization while incarcerated on offender reentry. *Criminal Justice and Behavior, 43*, 1018–1033.

Dawes, J. (1993). Managing serious violent offenders in south Australian prisons: Control, consensus, or responsibility. In S. Gerull & W. Lucas (Eds.), *Conference proceeding 19: Serious violent offenders: Sentencing, psychiatry, and law reform* (pp. 143–157). Canberra, Australia: Australian Institute of Criminology.

DeLisi, M., Berg, M. T., & Hochstetler, A. (2004). Gang members, career criminals and prison violence: Further specification of the importation model of prisoner behavior. *Criminal Justice Studies, 17*, 369–383.

DeLisi, M., Drury, A. J., Kosloski, A. E., Caudill, J. W., Conis, P. J., Anderson, C. A., Vaughn, M. G., & Beaver, K. M. (2010). The cycle of violence behind bars: Traumatization and institutional misconduct among juvenile delinquents in confinement. *Youth Violence and Juvenile Justice, 8*, 107–121.

DiIulio, J. J., Jr. (1987). *Governing prisons*. New York, NY: Free Press.

Dumond, R. W. (1992). The sexual assault of male inmates in incarcerated settings. *International Journal of the Sociology of Law, 20*, 135–157.

Farver, J. M., Ghosh, C., & Garcia, C. (2000). Children's perceptions of their neighborhoods. *Journal of Applied Developmental Psychology, 21*, 139–163.

Fazel, S., Hayes, A. J., Bartellas, K., Clerici, M., & Trestman, R. (2016). Mental health of prisoners: Prevalence, adverse outcomes, and interventions. *The Lancet Psychiatry, 3*, 871–881.

Finn, P. (1998). Correctional officer stress: A cause for concern and additional help. *Federal Probation, 62*, 65–74.

Finney, C., Stergiopoulos, E., Hensel, J., Bonato, S., & Dewa, C. S. (2013). Organizational stressors associated with job stress and burnout in correctional officers: A systematic review. *BMC Public Health, 13*, 82.

Fitzpatrick, K. M., Piko, B. F., Wright, D. R., & LaGory, M. (2005). Depressive symptomatology, exposure to violence, and the role of social capital among African American adolescents. *American Journal of Orthopsychiatry*, *75*, 262–274.

Flannery, D. J., Singer, M. I., & Wester, K. L. (2003). Violence, coping and mental health in a community sample of adolescents. *Violence and Victims*, *18*, 403–418.

Fowler, P. J., Tompsett, C. J., Braciszewski, J. M., Jacques-Tiura, A. J., & Baltes, B. B. (2009). Community violence: A meta-analysis on the effect of exposure and mental health outcomes of children and adolescents. *Development and Psychopathology*, *21*, 227–259.

Gaes, G. G., Wallace, S., Gilman, E., Klein-Saffran, J., & Suppa, S. (2002). The influence of prison gang affiliation on violence and other prison misconduct. *The Prison Journal*, *82*, 359–385.

Garcia, M., Cain, C. M., Cohen, F., Foster, H., Frost, N. A., Kapoor, R., . . . & Trestman, R. L. (2016). Restrictive housing in the US: Issues, challenges, and future directions. Washington, DC: U.S. Department of Justice.

Gibbons, J. J., Katzenbach, N. de D. (2006). Confronting confinement: A report of the Commission on Safety and Abuse in America's prisons. New York, NY: Vera Institute.

Gibson, C. L., Morris, S. Z., & Beaver, K. M. (2009). Secondary exposure to violence during childhood and adolescence: Does neighborhood context matter? *Justice Quarterly*, *26*, 30–57.

Gilligan, J. (1996). *Violence: Reflections on a national epidemic*. New York, NY: Random House.

Goff, A., Rose, E., Rose, S., & Purves, D. (2007). Does PTSD occur in sentenced prison populations? A systematic literature review. *Criminal Behaviour and Mental Health*, *17*, 152–162.

Goffman, E. (1961). Asylums: Essays on the social situation of mental patients and other inmates. New York, NY: Anchor Books.

Gonçalves, L., Gonçalves, R., Martins, C., Braga, T., Ferreira, C., Lindegaard, M. R., & Dirkzwager, A. (2016). Prisoners' coping strategies in Portugal. In C. Reeves (Ed.), *Experiencing imprisonment: Research on the experience of living and working in carceral institutions* (pp. 192–218). New York, NY: Routledge.

Gorman-Smith, D., & Tolan, P. H. (1998). The role of exposure to community violence and developmental problems among inner-city youth. *Developmental Psychopathology*, *10*, 101–116.

Gould, D. D., Watson, S. L., Price, S. R., & Valliant, P. M. (2013). The relationship between burnout and coping in adult and young offender center correctional officers: An exploratory investigation. *Psychological Services*, *10*, 37–47.

Griffiths, A. (2016). *Carceral fantasies: Cinema and prison in early twentieth-century America*. New York, NY: Columbia University Press.

Gunter, T. D., Philibert, R., & Hollenbeck, N. (2009). Medical and psychiatric problems among men and women in a community corrections residential setting. *Behavioral Sciences & the Law*, *27*, 695–711.

Hagan, B. O., Wang, E. A., Aminawung, J. A., Albizu-Garcia, C. E., Zaller, N., Nyamu, S., Shavit, S., Deluca, J., & Fox, A. D. (2017, in press). History of solitary confinement is associated with post-traumatic stress disorder symptoms among individuals recently released from prison. *Journal of Urban Health*, 1–8. doi:10.1007/s11524-017-0138-1

Haney, C. (2002). *The psychological impact of incarceration: Implications for post-prison adjustment*. Presented at the From Prisons to Home conference, National Institutes of Health, Washington, DC, January 30–31.

Haney, C. (2013). The contextual revolution in psychology and the question of prison effects. In A. Liebling & S. Maruna (Eds.), *The effects of imprisonment* (pp. 66–93). New York, NY: Routledge.

Hill, G. (1985). Predicting recidivism using institutional measures. In D. P. Farrington & T. Roger (Eds.), *Prediction in criminology* (pp. 96–118). Albany, NY: State University of New York Press.

Hindelang, M., Gottfredson, M. R., & Garofalo, J. (1978). *Victims of personal crime: An empirical foundation for a theory of personal victimization*. Cambridge, MA: Ballinger.

Hipp, J. R., Petersilia, J., & Turner, S. (2010). Parolee recidivism in California: The effect of neighborhood context and social service agency characteristics. *Criminology*, *48*, 947–979.

Hirschfield, P. J., & Piquero, A. R. (2010). Normalization and legitimation: Modeling stigmatizing attitudes toward ex-offenders. *Criminology*, *48*, 27–55.

Huebner, B. M. (2003). Administrative determinants of inmate violence: A multilevel analysis. *Journal of Criminal Justice*, *31*, 107–117.

Huebner, B. M., Varano, S. P., & Bynum, T. S. (2007). Gangs, guns, and drugs: Recidivism among serious, young offenders. *Criminology and Public Policy*, *6*, 187–222.

Hughes, T. A., & Wilson, D. J. (2003). *Reentry trends in the United States*. Washington, DC: U.S. Department of Justice, Bureau of Justice Statistics.

Hurt, H., Malmud, E., Brodsky, N. L., & Giannetta, J. (2001). Exposure to violence: Psychological and academic correlates in child witnesses. *Archives of Pediatric and Adolescent Medicine*, *155*, 1351–1356.

Irwin, J. (1980). *Prisons in turmoil*. Boston: Little, Brown and Company.

Irwin, J., & Cressey, D. R. (1962). Thieves, convicts and the inmate culture. *Social Problems, 10,* 142–155.

James, D., & Glaze, L. (2006). *Mental health problems of prisoners and jail inmates.* Washington, DC: Bureau of Justice Statistics.

James, N. (2015). *Offender reentry: Correctional statistics, reintegration into the community, and recidivism.* Washington, DC: Congressional Research Service.

Jamieson, R., & Grounds, A. (2013). Release and adjustment: Perspectives from studies of wrongly convicted and politically motivated prisoners. In A. Liebling & S. Maruna (Eds.), *The effects of imprisonment* (pp. 33–65). New York, NY: Routledge.

Jencks, C., & Mayer, S. E. (1990). The social consequences of growing up in a poor neighborhood. In L. E. Lynn & M. G. H. McGeary (Eds.), *Inner-city in the United States* (pp. 86–111). Washington, DC: National Academy Press.

Johnson, R. (1987). *Hard time: Understanding and reforming the prison.* Monterey, CA: Brooks/Cole.

Jonson, C. L., & Cullen, F. T. (2015). Prisoner reentry programs. *Crime and Justice, 44,* 517–575.

Keinan, G., & Malach-Pines, A. (2007). Stress and burnout among prison personnel: Sources, outcomes, and intervention strategies. *Criminal Justice and Behavior, 34,* 380–398.

Kinman, G., Clements, A. J., & Hart, J. (2017). Working conditions, work—life conflict, and well-being in UK prison officers: The role of affective rumination and detachment. *Criminal Justice and Behavior, 44,* 226–239.

Kirk, D. S. (2009). A natural experiment on residential change and recidivism: Lessons from Hurricane Katrina. *American Sociological Review, 74,* 484–505.

Kirk, D. S., & Papachristos, A. V. (2011). Cultural mechanisms and the persistence of neighborhood violence. *American Journal of Sociology, 116,* 1190–1233.

Kubrin, C. E., & Stewart, E. A. (2006). Predicting who reoffends: The neglected role of neighborhood context in recidivism studies. *Criminology, 44,* 165–197.

Kubrin, C. E., & Weitzer, R. (2003). New directions in social disorganization theory. *Journal of Research in Crime and Delinquency, 40,* 374–402.

Lahm, K. F. (2008). Inmate-on-inmate assault: A multilevel examination of prison violence. *Criminal Justice and Behavior, 35,* 120–137.

Lahm, K. F. (2009a). Inmate assaults on prison staff: A multilevel examination of an overlooked form of prison violence. *The Prison Journal, 89,* 131–150.

Lahm, K. F. (2009b). Physical and property victimization behind bars: A multilevel examination. *International Journal of Offender Therapy and Comparative Criminology, 53,* 348–365.

Lambert, E. G., Hogan, N. L., & Barton, S. M. (2004). The nature of work-family conflict among correctional staff: An exploratory examination. *Criminal Justice Review, 29,* 145–172.

Lambert, E. G., Hogan, N. L., Moore, B., Tucker, K., Jenkins, M., Stevenson, M., & Jiang, S. (2009). The impact of the work environment on prison staff: The issue of consideration, structure, job variety, and training. *American Journal of Criminal Justice, 34,* 166–180.

Lattimore, P. K., Visher, C. A., & Linster, R. L. (1995). Predicting rearrest for violence among serious youthful offenders. *Journal of Research in Crime and Delinquency, 32,* 54–83.

Lefcourt, H. M. (1982). *Locus of control: Current trends in theory and research* (2nd ed.). Hillsdale, NJ: Lawrence Erlbaum.

Levan, K. (2013). *Prison violence: Causes, consequences and solutions.* New York, NY: Routledge.

Liebling, A., & Ludlow, A. (2016). Suicide, distress and the quality of prison life. In Y. Jewkes, J. Bennett, & B. Crew (Eds.), *Handbook on Prisons* (2nd ed., pp. 224–245). New York, NY: Routledge.

Lindegaard, M. R., & Gear, S. (2014). Violence makes safe in South African prisons: Prison gangs, violent acts, and victimization among inmates. *Focaal—Journal of Global and Historical Anthropology, 68,* 35–54.

Listwan, S. J., Daigle, L. E., Hartman, J. L., & Guastaferro, W. P. (2014). Poly-victimization risk in prison: The influence of individual and institutional factors. *Journal of Interpersonal Violence, 29,* 2458–2481.

Lockwood, D. (1994). Issues in prison sexual violence, In M. C. Braswell, R. H. Montgomery, Jr., & L. X. Lombardo (Eds.), *Prison Violence in America* (2nd ed., pp. 97–102). Cincinnati, OH: Anderson Publishing.

Ludwig, A., Cohen, L., Parsons, A., & Venters, H. (2012). Injury surveillance in New York City jails. *American Journal of Public Health, 102,* 1108–1111.

Mann, R., & Hendrick, J. (2015). Editorial comment (Special edition, Reducing Prison Violence). *Prison Service Journal, 221,* 2–3.

Maruna, S. (2001). *Making good: How ex-convicts reform and rebuild their lives.* Washington, DC: American Psychological Association.

Maruna, S. (2004). Desistance from crime and explanatory style: A new direction in the psychology of reform. *Journal of Contemporary Criminal Justice, 20,* 184–200.

Maruna, S. (2011). Reentry as a rite of passage. *Punishment & Society, 13,* 3–28.

21 Exportation Hypothesis

Maruna, S., & Roy, K. (2007). Amputation or reconstruction? Notes on the concept of "knifing off" and desistance from crime. *Journal of Contemporary Criminal Justice, 23*, 104–124.

Maxfield, M. G., & Widom, C. S. (1996). The cycle of violence: Revisited 6 years later. *Archives of Pediatrics & Adolescent Medicine, 150*, 390–395.

McCorkle, R. C. (1993). Fear of victimization and symptoms of psychopathology among prison inmates. *Journal of Offender Rehabilitation, 19*, 27–41.

McCorkle, R. C., Miethe, T. D., & Drass, K. A. (1995). The roots of prison violence: A test of the deprivation, management, and "not-so-total" institution models. *Crime & Delinquency, 41*, 317–331.

McElhaney, S. J., & Effley, K. M. (1999). Community-based approaches to violence prevention, In T.P. Gullotta & S. J. McElhaney (Eds.), *Violence in homes and communities: Prevention, intervention, and treatment* (Vol. 11, pp. 1-38). London, UK: Sage.

McGruder-Johnson, A. K., Davidson, E. S., Gleaves, D. H., Stock, W., & Finch, J. F. (2000). Interpersonal violence and posttraumatic symptomology: The effects of ethnicity, gender, and exposure to violent events. *Journal of Interpersonal Violence, 15*, 205–221.

Mears, D. P., Stewart, E. A., Siennick, S. E., & Simons, R. L. (2013). The code of the street and inmate violence: Investigating the salience of imported belief systems. *Criminology, 51*, 695–728.

Mears, D. P., Wang, X., Hay, C., & Bales, W. D. (2008). Social ecology and recidivism: Implications for prisoner reentry. *Criminology, 46*, 301–339.

Melde, C., & Esbensen, F.A. (2011). Gang membership as a turning point in the life course. *Criminology, 49*, 513–552.

Mellow, J., & Greifinger, R. B. (2007). Successful reentry: The perspective of private correctional health care providers. *Journal of Urban Health, 84*, 85–98.

Morris, R. G. (2016). Exploring the effect of exposure to short-term solitary confinement among violent prison inmates. *Journal of Quantitative Criminology, 32*, 1–22.

Morris, R. G., Carriaga, M. L., Diamond, B., Piquero, N. L., & Piquero, A. R. (2012). Does prison strain lead to prison misbehavior? An application of general strain theory to inmate misconduct. *Journal of Criminal Justice, 40*, 194–201.

Morris, R. G., Longmire, D. R., Buffington-Vollum, J., & Vollum, S. (2010). Differential parole eligibility and institutional misconduct among capital inmates. *Criminal Justice and Behavior, 37*, 417–438.

Morris, R. G., & Worrall, J. L. (2014). Prison architecture and inmate misconduct: A multilevel assessment. *Crime & Delinquency, 60*, 1083–1109

Mumola, C. J. (2005). *Suicide and homicide in state prisons and local jails: Special report.* Washington, DC: Office of Justice Programs, Bureau of Justice Statistics.

Noonan, M., Rohloff, H., & Ginder, S. (2015). *Mortality in local jails and state prisons, 2000–2013—Statistical tables.* Washington, DC: U.S. Department of Justice, Office of Justice Programs, Bureau of Justice Statistics.

NPR. (2012). 'Million-dollar blocks' map incarcerations costs. Retrieved from www.npr.org/2012/10/02/162149431/million-dollar-blocks-map-incarcerations-costs

O'Leary, V., & Glaser, D. (1972). The assessment of risk in parole decision making. In J. West Donald (Ed.), *The future of parole* (pp. 135–198). London, UK: Duckworth.

Paternoster, R., & Pogarsky, G. (2009). Rational choice, agency and thoughtfully reflective decision making: The short and long-term consequences of making good choices. *Journal of Quantitative Criminology, 25*, 103–127.

Pickett, J. T., Mancini, C., Mears, D. P., & Gertz, M. (2015). Public (mis) understanding of crime policy: The effects of criminal justice experience and media reliance. *Criminal Justice Policy Review, 26*, 500–522.

Pollock, J. M. (2013). *Prisons and prison life: Costs and consequences.* New York, NY: Oxford University Press.

Reid, S. E., & Listwan, S. J. (2015). Managing the threat of violence: Coping strategies among juvenile inmates. *Journal of Interpersonal Violence*, Online First. doi:10.1177/0886260515615143

Reidy, T. J., & Sorensen, J. R. (2017). Prison homicides: A multidimensional comparison of perpetrators and victims. *Journal of Forensic Psychology Research and Practice, 17*, 99–116.

Reisig, M. D. (1998). Rates of disorder in higher-custody state prisons: A comparative analysis of managerial practices. *Crime and Delinquency, 44*, 229–244.

Rose, D. R., & Clear, T. R. (1998). Incarceration, social capital, and crime: Implications for social disorganization theory. *Criminology, 36*, 441–480.

Rozycki Lozano, A. T., Morgan, R. D., Murray, D. D., & Varghese, F. (2011). Prison tattoos as a reflection of the criminal lifestyle. *International Journal of Offender Therapy and Comparative Criminology, 55*, 509–529.

Sampson, R. J., Raudenbush, S. W., & Earls, F. (1997). Neighborhoods and violent crime: A multilevel study of collective efficacy. *Science, 277*, 918–924.

Scarpa, A., Haden, S. C., & Hurley, J. (2006). Community violence victimization and symptoms of posttraumatic stress disorder: The moderating effects of coping and social support. *Journal of Interpersonal Violence, 21*, 446-469.

Schaufeli, W. B., & Peeters, M. C. W. (2000). *International Journal of Stress Management, 7*, 19–48.

Schnittker, J. (2014). The psychological dimensions and the social consequences of incarceration. *The ANNALS of the American Academy of Political and Social Science, 651*, 122–138.

Serrill, M. S., & Katel, P. (1980). New Mexico: The anatomy of a riot. *Corrections Magazine 6*, 6–24.

Shakoor, B. H., & Chalmers, D. (1991). Co-victimization of African-American children who witness violence: Effects on cognitive, emotional, and behavioral development. *Journal of the National Medical Association, 83*, 233–238.

Sharkey, P. T. (2006). Navigating dangerous streets: The sources and consequences of street efficacy. *American Sociological Review, 71*, 826–846.

Singh, J. P., Bjørkly, S., & Fazel, S. (Eds.). (2016). *International perspectives on violence risk assessment*. Oxford: Oxford University Press.

Smith, P. N., Selwyn, C. N., Wolford-Clevenger, C., & Mandracchia, J. T. (2014). Psychopathic personality traits, suicide ideation, and suicide attempts in male prison inmates. *Criminal Justice and Behavior, 41*, 364–379.

Smith, P. S. (2006). The effects of solitary confinement on prison inmates: A brief history and review of the literature. *Crime and Justice, 34*, 441–528.

Sorenson, J., Cunningham, M. D., Vigen, M. P., & Woods, S. O. (2011). Serious assaults on prison staff: A descriptive analysis. *Journal of Criminal Justice, 39*, 143–150.

Spano, R., Rivera, C., & Bolland, J. (2006). The impact of timing of exposure to violence on violent behavior in a high poverty sample of inner city African American youth. *Journal of Youth and Adolescence, 35*, 681–692.

Stack, S. J., & Tsoudis, O. (1997). Suicide risk among correctional officers: A logistic regression analysis. *Archives of Suicide Research, 3*, 183–186.

Steiner, B., Butler, H. D., & Ellison, J. M. (2014). Causes and correlates of prison inmate misconduct: A systematic review of the evidence. *Journal of Criminal Justice, 42*, 462–470.

Steiner, B., Ellison, J. M., Butler, H. D., & Cain, C. M. (2017). The impact of inmate and prison characteristics on prisoner victimization. *Trauma, Violence, & Abuse, 18*, 17–36.

Steiner, B., & Wooldredge, J. D. (2008). Inmate versus environmental effects on prison rule violations. *Criminal Justice and Behavior, 35*, 438–456.

Steiner, B., & Wooldredge, J. D. (2014). Sex differences in the predictors of prisoner misconduct. *Criminal Justice and Behavior, 41*, 433–452

Stewart, E. A., Schreck, C. J., & Simons, R. L. (2006). "I ain't gonna let no one disrespect me" Does the code of the street reduce or increase violent victimization among African American adolescents? *Journal of Research in Crime and Delinquency, 43*, 427–458.

Stewart, E. A., & Simons, R. L. (2010). Race, code of the street, and violent delinquency: A multilevel investigation of neighborhood street culture and individual norms of violence. *Criminology, 48*, 569–605.

Stohr, M. K., Self, R. L., & Lovrich, N. P. (1992). Staff turnover in new generation jails: An investigation of its causes and prevention. *Journal of Criminal Justice, 20*, 455–478.

Stowell, J. I., & Byrne, J. M. (2008). Does what happens in prison stay in prison? Examining the reciprocal relationship between community and prison culture. In J. M. Byrne, D. Hummer, & F. S. Taxman (Eds.), *The Culture of Prison Violence* (pp. 27–39). New York, NY: Pearson.

Stoyanova, R. G., & Harizanova, S. N. (2016). Assessment of the personal losses suffered by correctional officers due to burnout syndrome. *The International Journal of Occupational and Environmental Medicine, 7*, 33–41.

Struckman-Johnson, C., & Struckman-Johnson, D. (2002). Sexual coercion reported by women in three Midwestern prisons. *The Journal of Sex Research, 39*, 217–227.

Summerlin, Z., Oehme, K., Stern, N., & Valentine, C. (2010). Disparate levels of stress in police and correctional officers: Preliminary evidence from a pilot study on domestic violence. *Journal of Human Behavior in the Social Environment, 20*, 762–777.

Sykes, G. M. (1958). *The society of captives: A study of a maximum security prison*. Princeton, NJ: Princeton University Press.

Taylor, R. B., & Shumaker, S. A. (1990). Local crime as a natural hazard: Implications for understanding the relationship between disorder and fear of crime. *American Journal of Community Psychology, 18*, 619–641.

Teasdale, B., Daigle, L. E., Hawk, S. R., & Daquin, J. C. (2016). Violent victimization in the prison context an examination of the gendered contexts of prison. *International Journal of Offender Therapy and Comparative Criminology, 60*, 995–1015.

Toch, H., & Kupers, T. A. (2007). Violence in prisons, revisited. *Journal of Offender Rehabilitation, 45*, 1–28.

Travis, J. (2005). *But they all come back: Facing the challenges of prisoner reentry*. Washington, DC: The Urban Institute.

Useem, B. (1985). Disorganization and the New Mexico prison riot of 1980. *American Sociological Review, 50*, 677–688.

Useem, B., & Goldstone, J. A. (2002). Forging social order and its breakdown: Riot and reform in US prisons. *American Sociological Review, 67*, 499–525.

Useem, B., & Kimball, P. (1989). *States of siege: U.S. prison riots, 1971-1986*. Oxford: Oxford University Press.

Useem, B., & Piehl, A. M. (2006). Prison buildup and disorder. *Punishment and Society, 8*, 87–115.

Useem, B., & Reisig, M. D. (1999). Collective action in prisons: Protests, disturbances, and riots. *Criminology, 37*, 735–760.

Valentine, C., Oehme, K., & Martin, A. (2012). Correctional officers and domestic violence: Experiences and attitudes. *Journal of Family Violence, 27*, 531–545.

Visher, C. A., & Travis, J. (2003). Transitions from prison to community: Understanding individual pathways. *Annual Review of Sociology, 29*, 89–113.

Wacquant, L. (2001). Deadly symbiosis: When ghetto and prison meet and mesh. *Punishment & Society, 3*, 95–133.

Walker, J., Illingworth, C., Canning, A., Garner, E., Woolley, J., Taylor, P., & Amos, T. (2014). Changes in mental state associated with prison environments: A systematic review. *Acta Psychiatrica Scandinavica, 129*, 427–436.

Ward, T. (2002). Good lives and the rehabilitation of offenders: Promises and problems. *Aggression and Violent Behavior, 7*, 513–528.

Ward, T., Mann, R. E., & Gannon, T. A. (2007). The good lives model of offender rehabilitation: Clinical implications. *Aggression and Violent Behavior, 12*, 87–107.

Weil, Gotshal & Manges, LLP. (2016). *Seeing into solitary: A review of the laws and policies of certain nations regarding solitary confinement of detainees*. Cyrus R. Vance Center For International Justice, and Anti-Torture Initiative, Center for Human Rights & Humanitarian Law at American University Washington College of Law.

WHO/UNAIDS/UNODC. (2007). Effectiveness of interventions to manage HIV in prisons e provision of condoms and other measures to decrease sexual transmission. Retrieved from www.who.int/hiv/idu/Prisons_condoms.pdf

Widom, C. S. (1989). The cycle of violence. *Science, 244*, 160–166.

Wilson, W. J. (1987). *The truly disadvantaged*. Chicago, IL: University of Chicago Press.

Wolff, N., Blitz, C. L., Shi, J., Siegel, J., & Bachman, R. (2007). Physical violence inside prisons: Rates of victimization. *Criminal Justice and Behavior, 34*, 588–599.

Wolff, N., & Shi, J. (2009a). Contextualization of physical and sexual assault in male prisons: Incidents and their aftermath. *Journal of Correctional Health Care, 15*, 58–77.

Wolff, N., & Shi, J. (2009b). Feelings of safety inside prisons among male inmates with different victimization experiences. *Violence & Victims, 24*, 800–816.

Wolff, N., & Shi, J. (2012). Childhood and adult trauma experiences of incarcerated persons and their relationship to adult behavioral health problems and treatment. *International Journal of Environmental Research and Public Health, 9*, 1908–1926.

Wooldredge, J. D. (1998). Inmate lifestyles and opportunities for victimization. *Journal of Research in Crime and Delinquency, 35*, 480–502.

Wooldredge, J. D. (2003). Keeping pace with evolving prison populations for effective management. *Criminology and Public Policy, 2*, 253–258.

Wooldredge, J., Griffin, T., & Pratt, T. (2001). Considering hierarchical models for research on prisoner behavior: Predicting misconduct with multilevel data. *Justice Quarterly, 18*, 203–231.

Wortley, R. (2002). *Situational prison control: Crime prevention in correctional institutions*. Cambridge: Cambridge University Press.

Zajac, G., Hutchison, R., & Meyer, C. A. (2014). *An examination of rural prisoner reentry challenges*. The Center for Rural Pennsylvania, Pennsylvania General Assembly: Harrisburg, PA.

Zingraff, M. T. (1975). Prisonization as an inhibitor of effective resocialization. *Criminology, 13*, 366–388.

Zona, K., & Milan, S. (2011). Gender differences in the longitudinal impact of exposure to violence on mental health in urban youth. *Journal of Youth and Adolescence, 40*, 1674–1690.

INDEX

Page numbers in *italics* indicate figures and those in **bold** indicate tables on the corresponding pages.

Aaltonen, M. 93
Abramson, L.Y. 130
Academy of Criminal Justice Sciences 292
acute stressor 108
Adam Walsh Act (AWA) 188, 195, 197
administrative segregation 292
Administrative Segregation Diversion (ASD) 372
admissions and continued occupancy policies (ACOPs) 56
adolescent brain development research 338–339
Adoption and Safe Families Act (ASFA) 166, 232
adult criminal behavior 152
adult criminal justice system 337
adult employment trajectories 93
advocacy-related activities 133
affective disturbance 125
African Americans 16; bond amount disparities for 274–275; children 143; disproportionate collateral sanctions effects on 44–45; health at reentry of 113; living in disadvantaged neighborhoods 72; mortality rate in prisons 109–110; parolees 61; residential instability, post-prison 60; systemic oppression of 17; War on Drugs and 177, 179
age-graded theory of crime 208
age-specific laws 334
"Aggravated Felonies" designation 225–226
aggression 125
aggressive law enforcement tactics 13
Albright, S. 96
Alexander, M. 17, 44, 176
Alien and Sedition Acts 223
Alien Enemies Act 223
All of Us or None 134
American Bar Association (ABA) 34, 53, 184, 213
American federalism 13

American jail confinement 92
American Journal of Public Health 257
American Law Institute 184
American Psychiatric Association 123
American Society of Criminology 292
Andersen, S. H. 93
Andersen, T. S. 135
Anderson, R. E. 124
Andrews, D. A. 370
anger 125
anomie 40
"anti-crime" law and order ethos 26
anti-crime rhetoric 18, 22
Anti-Drug Abuse Acts (ADAA) 35, 56, 178, 225
anti-immigration policies 27
antisocial personality disorder 145, 148
Antiterrorism and Effective Death Penalty Act (AEDPA) 226
anxiety 151; and panic attacks 125
Apel, R. 89–90, 258
Arditti, J. A. 258
Arizona Aryan Brotherhood 362
Arizona Old Mexican Mafia 362
Armstrong and freeman 194
Arrestee Drug Abuse Monitoring Program (ADAM II) 279
Arrigo, B. A. 125
Aryan Brotherhood (1967) 362
audits, experimental 95–96
Austin, J. 127
Aviram, H. 17

Bail Reform Act of 1984 272
banishment and transportation 222–223
"ban-the-box" initiatives 59, 215

Index

Barker, V. 22
barriers to education 209–210, 213
barriers to employment 180, 257, 277, 282
barriers to housing 53–58
Barrios, L. 235
Barton, W. H. 86
battered women 162–163
Beckett, K. 16
bed quota mandates 235
"bed rentals" 246
Bensel, T. 190, 191
Berg, M. T. 165, 167
Bernstein, N. 123, 128, 130
Bersot, H. Y. 125
Best, B. L. 128
Binswanger, I. A. 111
Black Guerilla Family (1966) 362
Blackstone, William 204
Blalock, H. M. 274
blanket housing bans 56
Blueprints for Healthy Youth Development 370
Bodkin, M. 131
bond amounts, disparities in 274–275
Bonikowski, B. 95
Bonta, J. 370
Bourdieu, P. 21
Boxer, P. 370
Bradley, K. H. 69, 164
brain development and age 213
Braithwaite, J. 136
Braithwaite, V. 136
"brand of inferiority" 212
Breed v. Jones (1975) 334
Brennan, T. 162
British Alien Act of 1793 223
"broken windows" policing 24
Brotherton, D. C. 235
Brown, J. D. 132
Brown, S. 97
Bucklen, K. B. 129
Bugajewitz v. Adams (1913) 224
Burchfield, K. B. 191
Bureau of Justice Statistics 351
Burgess-Proctor, A. 153
Bush, George W. 183
Button, D. M. 194

Cahill, S. P. 124
Cain, K. C. 125
California Public Safety Realignment Act 63
Cambridge Study of Delinquent Development 86, 148
Camp, C. G. 362
Camp, G. M. 362
Campbell, M. 4, 17, 22
Carson, E. A. 128
Castro, B. 232–233
Center for Community Alternatives 209

Center for Sex Offender Management (CSOM) 188
Center on Budget and Policy Priorities 55
Centers for Disease Control and Prevention (CDC) 113
Certificate of Qualification for Employment (CQE), Ohio 135
certificate of rehabilitation 135
Chamberlain, A. W. 73
children and families, impacts of incarceration on: conclusions on 155–156; emerging trends and 153–155; introduction to 143–144; parental incarceration 144–153; promising reforms and policies and 155; *see also* family visitation
child welfare system 147
Chinese Exclusion Act 223
chivalry/paternalism thesis 275
Cho, R. M. 152, 153
Christie, Chris 181
chronic physical health conditions 107, 110, 125
Cincinnati Metropolitan Housing Authority v. Browning 179
Circles of Support and Accountability (COSA) 192–193, 198
civil penalties 176, 183, 280
Civil Rights era 14, 16–17
Clark, K. 128
Clear, T. 17, 73, 78, 233
Cleary, H. 196
Clifasefi, S. L. 59
Clinton, B. 15, 60, 178
Cobbina, J. E. 165, 167
Code of Federal Regulations (CFR) 178
coercive mobility 78
cognitive behavioral therapy (CBT) 192, 194
cognitive dysfunction 125
Cohen, T. H. 272
collateral consequences 85, 161, 282; of conviction 53; of conviction and incarceration of women 163–167; defined 32; deportation 182–183, 221–236; of drug conviction 175–185; for housing 53–58, 175–185; of incarceration 33; poor health 111–112; of pretrial detention 261–263; of privatization of corrections 319–320; public assistance 180–181; of punishment 4, 32–33; restrictions on individuals 77; of sex offense conviction 188–199
collateral sanctions 46; collateral consequences of punishment and 32–33; common types of 34–37; concentrated disadvantage 43–45; conclusions on 45–47; criminal records and background checks 34–35; empirical findings 42–43; employment 36; of felony convictions 33–34; financial legal obligations 34; firearm restrictions 36; labeling/shaming/identity 39–40; life course perspective 41–42; opportunity/routine activities 38; predicted effects on recidivism by theoretical perspectives **37**; public assistance 35–36; rational choice/deterrence 38; recidivism 37; sex offender laws 37; social

401

bonds 41; social disorganization 40–41; strain 40; theoretical predictions **37**, 37–42; types of 34; voter disenfranchisement 36–37
Collins, S. E. 59
Comfort, M. 143
communities, effects of deportation on 232–233
community-based reentry program 211
community supervision 122
Community Works 355
confidentiality 207; in the early juvenile court 204–205; erosion of 205–207; record 207–208; restricted use 215; return to 213–214
consequences of punishment decisions 4
constitutional rights 278
contract attorney 276
control-focused legislation 188
Cook County, Illinois 87
Coronary Artery Risk Development in Young Adults study 115
Correctional Offender Management Profiling for Alternative Sanctions (COMPAS) 123
cost-burdened households 54
cost-efficiency analyses, privatization 315–316
county-level prison commitments 25
court-ordered treatment 169
Coutin, S. B. 227–228
Cressey, D. R. 363
Crime and Criminal Procedure Codes 34
Crime and the Community 205
Crimes Against Children and Sexually Violent Offender Registration Act 188
crimes involving moral turpitude (CIMT) 224
"criminal aliens" 224
criminal background checks 55, 57
criminal convictions 76, 89, 129; and deportations 229; records 34
criminalization and punishment 4, 14
criminal justice system 4, 14, 24, 33, 56, 77, 274; barriers 56–57; pretrial detention 278–281; psychological effects of contact with 122–136; *see also* punishment
criminal records 34, 208; and background checks 34–35; and databases mark 35; in employment decisions 210; erosion of confidentiality of 205–207; expungement of 57–58; juvenile (*see* juvenile records)
criminal self-concept 39
Criminology, Justice Quarterly, and *The Prison Journal* 292
Culhane, D. P. 61, 74
cultural drift 363
cumulative disadvantage 273, 277–278
Current Population Survey (CPS) 98
Curtis, M. A. 60, 61, 73, 74

Dailey, L. 127
Daly, K. 162
Danesh, J. 107
data infrastructure 64–65
day labor 92

Decker, S. H. 95, 363
delinquency, youth: maternal incarceration and 152; paternal incarceration and 150; rates of 340
DeMaris, A. 168
DeMichele, M. 194
Denq, F. 96
Department of Housing and Urban Development v. Rucker 179
Department of Justice's Civil Rights Division 24
deportation 182–183; after drug conviction 182–183; buildup toward stricter laws on 224–225; children and families, impact on 232; criminal convictions 221; data challenges 233–234; detention and 222, 233–234; effects of immigration enforcement and 229–231; emerging field of 227–229; first laws on 223; immigration enforcement policies, effects of 229–231; impact on children and families 232; impact on communities 232–233; introduction to 221–222; laws 222–224; national security and 225; nexus between criminal justice system and 225–227; non-citizens 221–222; origins of 222–224; research on 234–235; statistics on 221–222; studies on 227–229
depression 106, 110, 124; chronic 125
Desmond, M. 164
destigmatization 133
detained defendants 273
detainers 229
detention *see* deportation; pretrial detention
Diagnostic and Statistical Manual of Mental Disorders (DSM-5) 123
Di Placido, C. 370
disciplinary segregation 292
disclosure of court records 206
discretionary eviction 77
discrimination against individuals 54
disengagement 370, **371–372**
dis-integrative shaming 39
disproportionate minority confinement 334
distributional heterogeneity 99
diversionary programs 216
"doubling up" 73
Drakulich, K. M. 73
dramatization of evil 205, 215
drug court programming 24
drug offense convictions 35, 87, 175–177, 182; conclusions on 183–185; deportation and 182–183; diversion for low-level 24; by females 162; housing and 177–179; public assistance and 180–181; registries for 181–182
Dudeck, M. 124
Due Process Movement 206
"due process revolution" 334, 335
Dundes, I. 97

Easterling, B. 145, 147
economic insecurity: maternal incarceration and 151; paternal incarceration and 149; women and 164; *see also* employment; homelessness

Index

education: consequences of visible juvenile record on 207–210; post-secondary 209–210; primary and secondary 208–209

educational attainment: maternal incarceration and 152; paternal incarceration and 150

educational campaigns 337–338

Ehrlichman, J. 177

Eighth Amendment 63, 272

Ekiu v. United States (1892) 224

electoral power, decline of 25

electronic monitoring (EM) 194

emotional breakdowns 125

empirical criminology 65

employers 94–95; experimental audits and correspondence studies 95–96; willingness to hire 96–97

employment 36, 210–211; after incarceration 85, 257; consequences of visible juvenile record on 210–211; of convicted sex offenders 190–191; of women after incarceration 163–164

employment sanctions 44

employment-to-population ratios 233

episodic homelessness 75

erosion of confidentiality of criminal records 205–207

European legal systems 92–94

evidence-based practices 16

"evil woman" thesis 276

"excessive bail" 272

"ex-con" status 130, 216

ex-drug offenders 35

ex-offenders 34, 216

exportation hypothesis 379–380; culture of prison violence 382–385; deprivation theory 380–381; importation theory 380; institutional control 381–382; prison violence 380

exportation theory 385–388, *386*; normalization of violence 390–391; prison violence on staff 389–390

expungement of criminal records 57–58, 214

extrajudicial punishments 33

facially-neutral policy 55

Fair Housing Act 55, 58, 179

family attachments and stability 212

family friendly communication policies 355

family relationships and dissolution: with maternal incarceration 151–152; with paternal incarceration 149–150

family reunification programs 56

family separation fear 231

family visitation: advancing a research agenda on 351–354; conclusions on 356; emotional trauma of 347; introduction to 346–347; mass incarceration in jail and 347–349; obstacles of 352–353; parental 351–352; research on 349–351

Fang, X. 151

Farrall, S. 130

Farrington, D. P. 147, 148

Fazel, S. 107

federal activism 15; explanations for move toward more 16–17

federal funding 22

federal law and policy: evidence-based practices in 16; explanations 16–17; federal parole 15; legal and policy developments 15–16; sentencing reforms 15–16

felons 33–34, 70, 182; post-conviction location of 34; post-employment problems of 44

felony convictions, collateral sanctions of 43

female offenders *see* women, conviction and imprisonment of

financial legal obligations consequences 34

Finn, R. H. 96

firearm restrictions 33, 36, 43

First Amendment 206

Fleisher, M. S. 363

Fleury-Steiner, B. 123

Fong Yue Ting v. United States (1893) 223

Fontaine, P. A. 96

food stamps 54

Fortune Society 134

Foster, H. 154

Fourteenth Amendment 33

Fox, K. J. 193

Fragile Families and Child Wellbeing Study (FFCWS) 60, 73, 76, 90, 114, 150, 153

fragile freedom 128

Freeman, R. B. 89

Frost, Natasha 17, 125

Galgano, S. W. 95

Galvan v. Press (1954) 223

gang members 361–362; conclusions on 374; housing and programming for 364–373, **367–368**, **371–372**; policy and research implications for 373–374; on the street and in prisons 362–364

gang-related activity in prison 363, 367, 370

Garfinkel, H. 151

Garland, D. 16

Garretson, H. J. 135

Gaston, S. 148

Gatti, U. 123

Geier, T. J. 124

Geller, A. 60, 61, 73, 74, 90, 147

gender disparities in treatment at pretrial detention 275–276

gender-responsive programming 167–168, 193–194

General Education Diploma (GED) 163

General Strain Theory (GST) 40

Get Tough movement 206–207, 210, 335

Gies, S. 194

Giguere, R. 97

Giordano, P. C. 145, 152, 154

global positioning system (GPS) tracking 92, 192–193, 194

Goffman, A. 128

Goffman, E. 107, 132, 205, 361

Gonnerman, J. 122
Good Lives Model (GLM) 192, 198
Goodman, P. 17
Gorski, T. T. 124
Gottfredson, D. C. 86
Gottschalk, M. 21
Goulette, N. 276
"governing through crime" 16
government-funded housing assistance 53
Gowan, T. 74–75, 76
Graffam, J. 97
Graham v. Florida (2010) 336
Gramm, P. 38
Grassian, S. 125
Grogger, J. 87
Grounds, A. T. 124–125
Gunnison, E. 136

Hackett, S. 196
Hagan, J. 154
Hagan, J. M. 232–233
Hamilton, Z. K. 69
Haney, C. 123, 127
Harding, D. 58, 64–65, 75, 166
Harisiades v. Shaughnessy (1952) 223
Harmed-and-Harming behavior 162
Harper, J. 163
harsher punishments 13, 25
Haslewood-Pócsik, I. 97
health, incarceration and 105–106; mental health 107–108; pathways linking incarceration 108; physical health 106–107; spillover effects 108–109; theories of 112–114
health, reentry and 109, 114–115; collateral consequences of poor health 111–112; family, friends, and networks 112; neighborhoods 112; overview 109–110
health outcomes: of maternal incarceration 151; of paternal incarceration 148
healthy prisoner hypothesis 108
heart disease 106, 110
Heath, N. 124
Hedberg, E. 95
Helfgott, J. 76, 136
helplessness 125
Henrichson, C. 281
hepatitis B virus (HBV) 106
hepatitis C virus (HCV) 106
Herbert, C. 58, 77, 79, 166
Herman, J. 124
Hern, A. L. 189, 190
heterogeneity in jail incarceration: administrative styles and strategies 251; context influences jail populations and experiences 254; experiences 251–252; influence for jail populations 252; in jail experiences 251; jail inmates 249; local nature 251; misconduct and victimization 249; recidivism

251; social order 252; turnover rate 252; types of experiences 252–254; visitation rates in jails 253
Hinton, E. 17
Hipp, J. R. 62, 72, 77
Hirschi's social bond theory 41
Hispanic women 162
HIV/AIDS 106, 151
Holmes, M. D. 128
Holtfreter, K. 164
Holzer, H. J. 59
Homeland Security, Department of (DHS) 228
homelessness 61, 69–70, 74–76, 149; chronic 75; episodic 75; mechanisms of 76–78; parental incarceration and child 149; transitional 75; *see also* residential insecurities and neighborhood quality
hopelessness 125
House Bill 1510 59
housing 211–212; and assessing risk to property and other residents 58–59; barriers and opportunities in the UK 57–58; barriers to 53–58; collateral consequences of incarceration for 53–65, 177–179, 189–190; consequences of visible juvenile record on 211–212; continuum of 73; data infrastructure and 64–65; future research on 78–79; of gang members 364–369, **367–368**; homelessness and (*see* homelessness); market dynamics in 54; neighborhood attainment and 61; policy implications of findings on 79–80; residential instability and insecurity of 60; restrictions on 177; selection bias in 63–64; sex offender registration and notification and 62–63, 189–190; stigma and discrimination 54–55; subsidized 53–58, 177, 211; women's reentry and 164–165; *see also* public housing; restrictive housing (RH)
housing, barriers to 53; criminal justice barriers 56–57; housing market dynamics 54; lack of income and employment 54; opportunities in the UK 57–58; public housing and housing vouchers 55–56; stigma and discrimination 54–55
Housing and Urban Development, Department of (HUD) 56
"housing first" approaches 80
housing of gang members 365–369; gang affiliation and 366, **367–368**, 369; "long-term administrative segregation" 366; restrictive housing policy 369; restrictive housing types 365; secure housing unit (SHU) 365; security risk 369; segregation 365; "status"-based pathways 369
Housing Voucher Program 80
Huebner, B. 62, 89, 165, 167
Human Rights Watch (HRW) 24, 182
Hunter, B. 132
Hurricane Katrina 56, 57
hyperincarceration 347–348
hypersensitivity 125
hypertension 106, 110

Index

identity theory *see* labeling/shaming/identity theories

Illegal Immigration Reform and Immigrant Responsibility Act of 1996 (IIRIRA) 226–227

immigration: crime and 228; detention and 229, 348; policies against 27; *see also* deportation

Immigration Act of 1952 224–225

Immigration and Customs Enforcement (ICE) 221, 232

Immigration and Naturalization Act 223, 224

immigration detainers 225

immigration enforcement 228; policies and deportation 229–231; practices 231

imprisonment *see* incarceration

impulse control 125

incarcerated individuals *see* prisoners

incarceration 15, 99; Ds of 123; instrumental variables in 88; pains of 122–129; of parents 346; rates of 19, **19**, **20**; reentry and health after 105–115; residential insecurities and neighborhood quality following 69–80; *see also* mass incarceration, prison

incarceration, consequences of 122–123; negative collateral 33; post-prison supervision 128–129; posttraumatic stress disorder (PTSD) 123–125; prison doesn't stay in prison 127–128; solitary confinement 125; trauma and victimization 125–127

incarceration, employment prospects after 85; administrative research on 87–88; conclusions on 97–99; cross-national research 92–94; employers and 94–97; introduction to 85; non-representative research on 86–87; reentry research 91–92; research on 85–94; review of research findings on 85–94; survey research 88–91

incarceration, health effects of 105–106; mental 107–108; pathways linking mental and physical 108; physical 106–107; physical health 106–107; spillover 108–109

incarceration, maternal 76, 151; delinquency and 152; economic insecurity and 151; educational attainment and 152; family relationships and dissolution with 151–152; health outcomes of 151; *versus* paternal 152–153

incarceration, paternal: delinquency and 150; economic insecurity and 149; educational attainment and 150; family relationships and dissolution with 149–150; health outcomes of 148

incarceration-employment relationship 85–86, 87, 90, 91, 93, 94, 98, 99

incarceration impacts on children and families: conclusions on 155–156; emerging trends and 153–155; introduction to 143–144; parental 144–153; promising reforms and policies and 155

incarceration-reentry-health link 107

incentive- and cognitive-based programs 372

individualized bail determination 272

"individuals with criminal records" 215–216

inequalities and mass jail incarceration: in communities and society 259; experiences

260–261; gender-focused research 261; heterogeneity 260; jail reentry 261

infectious diseases 108

informal punishments 32

in-person visitation 353

in-prison programming 88, 93

In re Gault 206

In re winship (1970) 334

institutional adjustment, restrictive housing (RH): attitudinal/emotional outcomes 298; discretionary release outcomes 298–299; institutional misconduct outcomes 299; moderator analyses 299

Institutional Classification Committee reviews 372

institutional violence, restrictive housing (RH) 294–295

instrumental variables 88

intensification model 364; gang membership 364

intermediate sanction residences 77

Inventory of Collateral Consequences of Conviction 34

invisible punishments 33; *see also* collateral sanctions

Irwin, J. 127, 131, 245, 362, 363

Jacobs, James 207, 362, 370

jail incarceration 99, 347–349; conceptual framework for advancing theory and research on effects and consequences of 249–261, **250**; conclusions on 261–263; consequences for individuals, families and communities 256–259; court-designated sanction 247; criminal justice system 249; effectiveness as correctional sanction 254–256; employment opportunities after 347; family visitation (*see* family visitation); future theory and research on 249, **250**; heterogeneity in 249–254; individuals, families and communities, collateral consequences 256–259; inequality and 259–261; introduction to 245–246, *248*; longitudinal trends in *248*; for low-grade felony crimes 247; obstacles to visitation for 352–353; parent visits 351–352; as part of the criminal justice system 249; policy recommendations 354–355; privatization of (*see* private corrections); scholarship on 347; in United States over time *248*; visiting experience 353–354

Janetta, J. 62, 72

Johnson, E. I. 145, 147

Johnson, L. C. 125

judicial discretion 272

Judicial Recommendations Against Deportation (JRAD) 224, 226

Jung, H. 87

jurisdiction 314; juvenile 339; records 282

justice-involved women, collateral consequences for: gender-responsive programming 167–168; specialty courts 169; wrap-around services 168–169

justice-involvement for youths 336–337; delinquency rates and 340

JustLeadershipUSA (JLUSA) 134
juvenile court movement 204
Juvenile Justice and Delinquency Prevention Act
    (JJDPA) 334, 336
juvenile justice system 216, 339; adjudications in 213;
    adultification 336; policy changes to 339–340;
    reforms 334–335; registries 195–196; *see also*
    "Raise the Age" movement
Juvenile Law Center 214
juvenile offenders, growth in 206–207
juvenile records: basis for confidentiality in early
    juvenile court and 204–205; conclusions on
    216; confidentiality 214; consequences of visible
    207–212; erosion of confidentiality of 205–207;
    information 208–209; other impacts of visible 212;
    removing the stigma of 213–216
juvenile sex offender registries 195–196
juvenile super predators 207, 335

Kachnowski, G. 61
Kashy, D. A. 167
Katz, C. 275
Kleindienst v. Mandel (1972) 223
Kling, J. R. 87
Kohler-Hausmann, I. 26, 27
Kreager, D. A. 363
Kunst, M. 128
Kutateladze, B. 277

labeling/shaming/identity theories 39–40, 41, 45–46,
    132
labeling theory *see* labeling/shaming/identity
    theories
labor force participation 94, 233
Labrecque, R. M. 366
Landerso, R. 94
Laub, J. H. 86
La Vigne, N. 61, 150
"law and order" movement 17, 19, 24
Law Enforcement Assistance Administration (LEAA)
    14–15, 17, 22
Leasure, P. 135
LeBel, T. P. 129, 131–134
Lee, K. 61
Lee, R. D. 151
Legal Action Center 34
legal bystanders 143
legal debt 34
legal financial obligations (LFOs) 34, 41
Lemert, E. 205
Lens, M. C. 92
Lerman, A. E. 123
Levenson, J. S. 189, 190
Leyro, S. P. 233
Liem, M. 128
life course approach 154
life course perspective 41–42
lifetime bans on voting 39

lifetime criminal records 39
lifetime registration requirement 211
life without parole (LWOP) 336
Lindsey, A. M. 313
Link, B. G. 113
linking prisoners 110
Li Sing v. United States (1901) 223, 224
Listwan, S. J. 126
local law and policy: explanations 24–27; legal and
    policy developments 22–24
Loeffler, C. 87
Longazel, J. 123
"long-term administrative segregation" 366
Lösel, F. 192
Lott, J. R., Jr. 87
Lovell, D. 125
low-income minority communities 23, 24
low-level drug offenders 16, 20
Lukies, J. 97
Luo, F. 151
Lutze, F. E. 69
Lynch, M. 21
Lynch, S. 124
"lynchpin" holding reentry 79
Lyons, C. J. 87

Mack, J. 204–205
Mallik-Kane, K. 110, 111
Malone, D. K. 59
Mamalian, G. 61
mandatory sentencing laws 23
manifestation model, gang membership 364
Martin, G. 134
Maruna, S. 132–133, 135
Maryland Scientific Methods Scale 293
mass criminalization 34
mass incarceration, critiques of 17
mass incarceration, prison 14, 25, 85, 177; fiscal
    consequences 14; fiscal costs 13; rise of 13; social
    and political costs 14; trends 1
Massoglia, M. 106, 108
mass probation 18
mass punishment, growth in 4
maternal incarceration 76, 151; delinquency 152;
    economic insecurity 151; educational attainment
    152; family relationships and dissolution 151–152;
    health outcomes 151; *versus* paternal 152–153
Matsueda, R. L. 86
Mauer, M. 163
McCorkle, R. 123
McElrath, S. 145, 154
McKeiver v. Pennsylvania (1971) 334
McPherson, K. S. 125
mean effect size (ES) 292
Mears, D. P. 154
mental health: incarceration and 107–108, 257;
    problems 110
Metraux, S. 61, 74

Index

Michigan Study of Life After Prison 64
Midlife in the United States (MIDUS) study 115
Miller, Lisa 25
Miller v. Alabama (2010) 336
Mingus, W. 191
Minton, T. D. 252
misconduct offense levels 295
mobility, residential 61, 70–71, 79, 167
Model Penal Code 184
Monteiro, C. 125
Morash, M. 164, 167
Morenoff, J. 58, 166
Mother Jones magazine 366
Muftic, L. R. 146, 152
multijurisdiction project 282
Multisystematic Therapy (MST) 370
Mumola, C. 109
Munn, M. 127–128, 129, 131
Murakawa, Naomi 17
Murray, J. 147, 148
mutual-help group member 132

Nagin, D. 86, 259
Najdowski, C. J. 196
National Comorbidity Survey Replication (NCS-R) 124
National Criminal Justice Reference Service 292
National Fugitive Operations Program 227
National Inmate Survey 366
National Institute of Corrections 168
National Longitudinal Survey of Adolescent Health 64, 90, 114–115
National Longitudinal Survey of Youth 1997 (NLSY97) 71, 88–89, 211, 258
National Minimum Drinking Age Act 334
National Research Council 64, 374
national security and deportation 225
National Supported Work Demonstration 86
National Survey of American Life 124
National Survey of Children's Health 115
"negative credentialing" 352
neighborhoods: attainment 61; context of 72–73; future research on 76–79; health at reentry and 112; homelessness in 74–76; mechanisms of residential insecurity in 76–78; policy implications of conditions in 79–80; residential insecurities and quality of 69–70, 73–74; residential mobility 70–72
Nelson, B. 125
neoliberalism 16–17
Netherlands, the 92–94
net-widening 319–320
New Jersey v. TLO (1985) 334
New York City Housing Authority 56
New York State judicial committee 214
Nixon, R. 177
non-criminal disruptive behavior 77
non-criminal justice policy 34

non-homicide offenses 336
non-infectious diseases 106
non-violent felony offenders 254
Nordic countries, crime in 64, 94
normlessness 40
Northcutt Bohmert, M. 154, 168, 193
"nothing works" mentality 16

Obama, B. 15–16, 182
offender-funded models 24
offender registries 181
offense-specific restrictions 80
Office of National Drug Control Policy (ONDCP) 279
Omnibus Crime Bill (1994) 14, 15, 22
Omnibus Crime Bill and Safe Streets Act of 1968 14
omniopticism 129
"One Strike and You're Out" legislation 15
opportunity/routine activities 38, 45
origination model, gang membership 364
Orlando-Morninstar, D. 362
Ortiz, N. 95
out-of-prison ties 115

Padilla v. Kentucky 182–183
Page, J. 17, 21
Pager, D. 44, 95
"pains of imprisonment" 349, 361
Pains of Mass Imprisonment, The 123
paired-tester study 54
Pam Lychner Act (1996) 188
parental detention and deportation 232
parental incarceration 144–153; causal effects, research and identification 145–146; emerging trends in 153–155; maternal 151–153; paternal 149–150; promising reforms and policies in 155; reforms and policies 155; trends in 153–155; types of 146–147
parent legal vulnerability 231
parole 34, 61, 128; electronic tracking during 92; proportions 24; violations of 23–24, 60
paternal incarceration 349; delinquency 150; economic insecurity 149; educational attainment 150; family relationships and dissolution 149–150; health outcomes 148
Patriot Act 227
Payne, B. K. 194
Peabody Picture Vocabulary Test (PPVT) 153
peer pressure 133
permanent outcasts 136
Personal Responsibility and Work Opportunity Reconciliation Act of 1996 34, 230
Pettit, B. 87, 258
Phelan, J. 113
Phelps, M. 17, 18, 27, 169
Phillips, S. D. 149
physical health after incarceration 106–107
Pinard, M. 45

Index

plea bargaining 235
Pleggenkuhle, B. 80, 167
"plenary power doctrine" 223, 224
Pogrebin, M. 258
policy interest 206
policy-making processes 21, 22
political "backdoor" channels 319–320
political executives 16
politicization of crime 19, 23
"poor houses" 74
Porporino, F. J. 127
post-conviction exclusions 175
post-conviction mandates 221
Post Incarceration Syndrome (PICS) 124, 136
post-jail reintegration 258
post-prison employment 44, 87, 91
post-prison housing/Restrictive Housing (RH) 79;
    in custody 295–296; logistic and linear regression
    296; subpopulations of offenders 297–298;
    supermax prisons 297; time spent 296–297
post-prison mobility 71
post-prison neighborhoods 61, 72
post-prison supervision 128–129
post-prison surveillance 18
post-release recidivism 93, 115, 370
post-secondary education 209–210
posttraumatic stress disorder (PTSD) 33, 122,
    123–125, 136, 151
potential offenders identification 338
pre-prison neighborhoods 71, 72
Prescott, J. J. 62
presentence investigation (PSI) 87
pretrial detention 63, 79, 348; collateral consequences
    of 271–283; conclusions on 283; criminal justice
    system 278–281; cumulative disadvantage and
    277–278; differential exposure to the impacts of
    273–278; empirical studies of 281–283; gender
    disparities in treatment at 275–276; influences
    on 276–277; introduction to 271; pretrial
    "experience" and possible impacts on case
    outcomes 272–273; racial disparities in 274–275;
    unanticipated consequences of 278–281
Prewitt, K. 64
Pridemore, W. A. 108
primary and secondary education 208–209
prison biographies 361
prisoners 85–86; administrative research 87–88;
    cross-national research 92–94; health of returning
    114–115; mental health of 107–108; non-
    representative research 86–87; physical health of
    106–107; reentry research 91–92, 114–115; social
    organization and 363; survey research 88–91
prison-focused response to crime 21
prison gangs 362–364
Prison Inmate Network Study (PINS) 115
prison mask 123, 127, 128
prison programming and gang members:
    Administrative Segregation Diversion (ASD)

372; Blueprints for Healthy Youth Development
370; disengagement 370, **371–372**; Gang
Renouncement and Dissociation (GRAD)
program 372–373; incentive- and cognitive-
based programs 372; Institutional Classification
Committee reviews 372; institutional misconduct
370; Multisystematic Therapy (MST) 370;
post-release recidivism 370; reclassifying gang
status 370–371
prisons: expansion in spending on 20; policies 348;
    privatization of (*see* private corrections); "revolving
    doors" of 23–24
"Prison Skype" 350
private attorneys 276
private corrections: aspects of 321; background
    on 312–313; decisions regarding 325; effective
    and cost-efficient 322; empirical evaluations
    324–325; empirical monitoring 324; history
    and prevalence 312–313; incentives 325–326;
    introduction to 311–312; operationalizations
    320–321; potential collateral consequences
    of 319–320; prison moratorium 311; quality
    services 323–324; state of evidence 313–319,
    318; support factor 323
proactive stigma management strategies 132–135
probation: modern-day 312; and parole reports 87;
    systems for parole and 18
professional licensures 39, 280
programming for gang members 364–373, **367–368**,
    371–372
Prohibition 14
project-based rental assistance 55
prosecutorial power 15, 22–23; expansion of 26;
    informal nature of 25; "snitching" and 26
pro-social bonds 41
pro-social conformists 40
pro-social identities 42
pro-social opportunities 42
psychological distress 33
psychological effects of contact with the criminal
    justice system: conclusion on 136; directions
    for future research and policy on 135–136;
    introduction to 122; pains of imprisonment
    and 122–129; pains of post-prison supervision
    and 128–129; perceptions of and responses to
    stigma 129–135; posttraumatic stress disorder
    123–125; solitary confinement 125; trauma and
    victimization 126–127
psychological effects of stigma 130
PsycINFO 292
public assistance 35–36, 39, 180–181; after drug
    convictions 180–181; bans on 33
public defenders 276–277
public housing 55; banning of offenders for 15;
    housing vouchers for 55–56
public housing authorities (PHAs) 35, 55, 212
public safety 207; and mass incarceration 259;
    realignment 354

punishment: collateral consequences of 4, 32–33; federal law and policy on 14–17; future research on 27–28; historical trends in 13–14; local law and policy on 22–27; state law and policy on 18–22; *see also* criminal justice system
"punishment imperative" 17
"Punishment Without End, The" 208
Pyrooz, D. C. 363, 364, 366

racial and class inequalities 14
racial disparities 44, 60, 210, 274; in bond amounts and pretrial detention 274–275; employment 210; in housing 72; in imprisonment 25
racial threat theory 274
racism and collateral sanctions 44
rage 125
"Raise the Age" movement 338–339, 341–342; early history of juvenile reform and 335–336; "get tough" movement 335; implications 342–343; justice-involved youths, delinquency rates 340; justice-involvement for youths 336–337; justice reform efforts, prevention 337–338; juvenile and adult court jurisdictions, policy changes to 339–340; Juvenile Justice Reform in U.S. 334–335; "Raise the Age" (RTA) movement 338–339, 341–342; research on policies 340–341
Ramakers, A. 93
rational choice/deterrence theories 38, 45
reactive and protective stigma management strategies 130–132
Reagan, R. 15, 18
Reaves, B. A. 272
recidivism 40, 42, 43, 111, 114, 257, 292–293; collateral sanctions and 37; health and 111–112, 114; jail effect on 255; residential instability and 60; restrictive housing and 292–293, **294**, 295–298, **304–305**; theoretical perspectives of 34–37
reclassification of gang status 370–371
"redeemed" for employment 211
redemption rituals 39
redemption script 388
Reed, A. 312
re-enfranchisement of voting rights 40
reentry and health 109; collateral consequences of poor health 111–112; family, friends, and networks effects on 112; neighborhoods 112; overview 109–110
reentry experiences of jail inmates 255–256
Reentry Housing Pilot Program (RHPP) 80
registries: drug offender 181–182; sex offender 15, 39, 62–63, 195–197
rehabilitation 17, 204–205, 257; in jail 255–256; rehabilitative values and ideologies in 16
Reich, S. E. 97
re-integrative shaming 39
Reisig, M. D. 164
Reiter, K. A. 365
Remster, B. 76

residential insecurities and neighborhood quality 69–70, 73–74; future research 76–79; homelessness 74–76; mechanisms 76–78; neighborhood context 72–73; policy implications 79–80; residential mobility 70–72
residential instability 60; and housing insecurity 60
residential mobility 70–71, 79, 167
restricted use of juvenile records 215
restrictive housing (RH) 292; aggregate institutional violence outcomes **302–303**; criminal behavior and 300; criminogenic 291; discussion on 300–301; effect size estimates, by outcome type and methodological rigor **294**; eligibility criteria 292; evidence, systematic review of 291–292; impact of 290–291; inmate behavior 291; institutional adjustment outcomes 293, 298–299, **306–307**; institutional violence 294–295; introduction to 290; literature retrieval 292; multilevel structural equation modeling 295; operationalization of 292; post-release recidivism 295–298; recidivism outcomes 292–293, **294**, **304–305**; research design and method 292; safety, order and control 291; *see also* housing
Returning Home project 71, 91
returning prisoners, health of 114–115
RH *see* restrictive housing (RH)
Roadblock to Reentry Report Cards 34
Robbers, M. L. 190
Rockefeller Drug Laws 19, 20
Rockoff, J. E. 62
Rodriguez, N. 232–233
Rose, D. R. 73, 233
Rosenheck, R. A. 59
Rosky, J. W. 69
Rossi, P. H. 60
Ruddell, R. 365, 369
Rydberg, J. 128

Safe Streets Act (1968) 14
Sample, L. L. 190, 191
Sampson, R. J. 86, 145
Sargent Shriver National Center on Poverty Law 56
Schall v. Martin (1984) 334
Schappell, A. 126
Schmucker, M. 192
Schneider, D. 90
Schnittker, J. 124, 136
Schoenfeld, Heather 17
school-to-prison pipeline 32, 208
Schwartz, B. 363
sealing of records 214
"secondary prisonization" 351, 353
Second Chance Act 183
Section 8 housing 55–56, 177, 211
Secure Communities 227
Sedlak, A. J. 125
Sekol, L. 148
selection bias 63–64

self-fulfilling prophecy 205
self-incrimination 206
self-inflicted and felonious violence 382
self-reported delinquency 145, 148
Seligman, M. E. 130
Sentencing Project, 2014 36, 37, 45
sentencing reforms 15–16
Serious and Violent Offender Reentry Initiative (SVORI) 115, 127
sex offender laws 37
sex offender registries 15, 39, 62–63, 195; juvenile 195–196; in other countries 197
sex offender registry and notification (SORN) policies 37, 40, 45
sex offender-specific collateral sanctions 43
sex offense convictions 188–189; collateral consequences 189; conclusions on 197–199; employment and economy consequences of 190–191; gender responsive programming 193–194; housing consequences of 189–190; introduction to 188–189; juvenile registries 195–196; new directions for research and policy on 192–197; registries in other countries 197; sex offender registry policy 195; stigma and social relationships 191; technology and monitoring 194–195; treatment and supervision strategies 192–193; tribal registries 196
sexual assaults 18, 382
sexually transmitted diseases 106, 112
shaming theory *see* labeling/shaming/identity theories
Shinkfield, A. J. 97
short-lived relationships 164
SHU syndrome 125
Siennick, S. E. 154
Simon, D. A. 23
Simon, J. 16, 26
small-cell problems 146
Smith, S. W. 167
SNAP food stamps 35
"snitching" 26
social and economic inequalities 246
social bonds 41
social control theory 41
social disorganization 37, 40–41
social disorganization model 233
social disorganization theory 228
social exclusion of children 154
social inequality 21
social stigma 208
Society of Captives, The 122–123
socioeconomic status (SES) 113
Sociological Abstracts 292
Solid Start program 80
solitary confinement 122, 125, 292
specialty courts for women 169
Spelman, W. 259
Spencer, J. 97

Spohn, C. 95, 275
staff violence in the community 389
state decarceration 348
state law and policy: explanations 21–22; legal and policy developments 18–21
state lawmakers 13, 19
state-level collateral sanctions 45
state-level developments 21
state-level political actors 18
state of evidence, privatization: amount and quality of services 314–315; in correctional system 313; cost-efficiency 315–316; dimensions for assessing **318**; ethical considerations 317–318; extent of need 313–314; impacts on outcomes 315; innovative solutions 316; policy makers and 314–315; social control, impacts on 317
state policy choice *vs.* constitutional protection 206
Steffensmeier, D. 274
Stevenson, M. C. 196
stigma 205; of juvenile records, removing 213–216; perceptions of and responses to 129–130; proactive management strategies for 132–135; reactive and protective management strategies for 130–132
stigma and discrimination 54–55
stigmatization of prison 108
"stop snitching" campaign 26
strain theories 40
street gangs 362–364
street-level bureaucrats 47
street women 162
stress and deportation 231
"stress of transition" 77
stress process theory 113–114
stress-related illnesses 106
structural inequalities 14
Stuntz, W. J. 25–26
subsidized housing 53–58, 177, 211
Sudman, S. 283
Sugie, N. F. 92
supermax prisons 294–295; solitary confinement in 125
Supplemental Nutrition Assistance Program (SNAP) 33, 176
Supplemental Security Income (SSI) 54
Survey of Income and Program Participation (SIPP) 90
Survey of Youth in Residential Placement (SYRP) 126
suspension from school 209
Sweeten, G. 89–90
Swisher v. Brady (1978) 334
Sykes, B. L. 90
Sykes, G. M. 122

Tannenbaum, F. 205
Teasdale, J. D. 130
technical violation 128
technology, monitoring 194–195

teenage pregnancy 112
Temporary Assistance for Needy Families (TANF)
33, 35, 38, 54, 165, 230–231; after drug
convictions 176, 180–181
Tewksbury, R. 194
Texas Department of Housing & Community Affairs v.
The Inclusive Communities Project, Inc. 55
Texas prosecutors' association 22
"third mile" forms of activism 133
"Three Strikes" law 20
Toch, H. 361
Tonry, M. 23, 25
tough-on-crime laws 18, 24, 38
Transitional Aid Research Project 86
transitional homelessness 75
trauma and victimization 122, 123, 125–127
trauma-informed justice system 333
trauma-informed treatment of youth 339
trauma-related arousal 123
Travis, J. 153
treatment and supervision strategies, sex offense
192–193
tribal registries 196
Tromanhauser, E. 130
Trump, D. 16, 182
truth-in-sentencing laws 15, 22, 23
Tsai, J. 59
tuberculosis infection 106
Turner, S. 62, 72, 77, 194
Turner v. Williams (1904) 224
Turney, K. 90, 150, 151, 153

Uggen, C. 78, 145, 154
UK Rehabilitation of Offenders Act (1974) 57
unemployment and crime 211
Uniform Law Commission 184
unintended consequences 46
United Kingdom, housing barriers and opportunities
in the 57–58
United States ex rel. Bilokumsky v. Tod (1923) 223
United States Sentencing Commission (USSC) 228
Urban Institute Report 153

Van der Geest, V. R. 93
Vaughn, P. 4
Verbruggen, J. 93
Verma, A. 25
video visitation 350, 352, 354
violent victimization 363, 383
Visher, C. 110, 111
visitation *see* family visitation
voter disenfranchisement 33, 36–37, 42–43

Wacquant, L. 16, 21
Wahl, O. F. 134
Waldfogel, J. 86, 87
Wallace, D. 110
warlike anticrime mentality 24
Warner, C. 60
War on Drugs 16, 177, 179, 182
War on Terror 207
Weems v. United States 183
Welfare Act 230
Western, B. 60, 95, 258
Wheelock, D. 78
white parolees 61, 72
Whittle, T. 4
Wildeman, C. 76, 145, 150, 151, 153, 258
Winnick, T. A. 131
Winterdyk, J. 365, 369
Witness to Innocence 134
Wodahl, E. J. 128
Wolff, N. 126
women: burden of incarcerated family members on
109; living in poverty 164; pathways into crime
and 162–163; pretrial detention of 275; recidivism
among 111–112; specialty courts for 169
women, conviction and imprisonment of 161–162,
165, 276; child and family responsibilities 166;
collateral consequences of 163–167; disadvantaged
neighborhood contexts 166–167; finding
employment 163–164; gender-responsive
programming 167–168; introduction to 161–162;
mental health and 107; pathways into crime
162–163; securing housing after 164–165; social
services, obtaining 165–166; specialty courts 169;
wrap-around services 168–169
Women's Offender Case Management Model
(WOCMM) 168
Women's Prison Association (WPA) 134
Wong, T. K. 233
Wooldredge, J. 274, 277
wrap-around services 168–169

Yearbook on Immigration Statistics 229, 234
"Youthful Offender Seal" 214

Zadvydas v. Davis (2001) 223
Zajac, C. 129
Zakonaite v. Wolf (1912) 223
Zamble, E. 127
Zeng, Z. 252
zero tolerance policies 32
Zgoba, K. M. 62
Zweig, J. M. 127